# Extraordinary Projects for Ordinary People

# Extraordinary Projects for Ordinary People

**Do It Yourself Ideas From the People Who Actually Do Them**

Edited by Noah Weinstein

Skyhorse Publishing

Skyhorse Publishing books may be purchased in bulk at special discounts for sales promotion, corporate gifts, fund-raising, or educational purposes. Special editions can also be created to specifications. For details, contact the Special Sales Department, Skyhorse Publishing, 307 West 36th Street, 11th Floor, New York, NY 10018 or info@skyhorsepublishing.com.

Skyhorse® and Skyhorse Publishing® are registered trademarks of Skyhorse Publishing, Inc.®, a Delaware corporation.

Visit our website at www.skyhorsepublishing.com.

10 9 8 7 6 5 4 3 2

Library of Congress Cataloging-in-Publication Data is available on request.

ISBN: 978-1-62087-057-0

Printed in China

**Disclaimer:**
This book is intended to offer general guidance. It is sold with the understanding that every effort was made to provide the most current and accurate information. However, errors and omissions are still possible. Any use or misuse of the information contained herein is solely the responsibility of the user, and the author and publisher make no warrantees or claims as to the truth or validity of the information. The author and publisher shall have neither liability nor responsibility to any person or entity with respect to any loss or damage caused, or alleged to have been caused, directly or indirectly, by the information contained in this book. Furthermore, this book is not intended to give professional dietary, technical, or medical advice. Please refer to and follow any local laws when using any of the information contained herein, and act responsibly and safely at all times.

# Introduction

Armed with a creative idea, an openness to learn a new skill, a bit of how-to instruction and a sense of adventure, virtually anyone can make something extraordinary. *Extraordinary Projects for Ordinary People* contains over 150 projects authored by crafters, builders, makers and hobbyists who have a strong desire to share their knowledge and creativity. Showcasing breakthrough and innovative ways of repurposing, reusing, and reinventing not only what we make, but how we make it, this book is a collection of creative projects unlike any other. Each project contains multiple images with step-by-step instructions to help you follow along in recreating one of these extraordinary works, or to inspire you to make and share something amazing of your own.

All of the projects in this book are from Instructables.com. Instructables is the most popular project-sharing community on the Internet, and part of the Autodesk family of creative communities. Since August 2005, Instructables has provided easy publishing tools to enable passionate, creative people to share their most innovative projects, recipes, skills, and ideas. Instructables has over 70,000 projects covering all subjects, including crafts, art, electronics, kids, home improvement, pets, outdoors, reuse, bikes, cars, robotics, food, decorating, woodworking, costuming, games, and life in general.

-Noah Weinstein

# HOME IMPROVEMENT

# TECH

# RIDE

# ROBOTS

# CLOCKS

# COMPUTER

# ART

# GREEN

# SCIENCE

# TOOLS

# FOOD

# FURNISH

# PHOTOGRAPHY

# CRAFTS

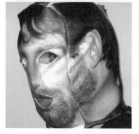

# COSTUMES

# GAMES

# FUN

# SOUND

# Editor's Note

The wonderful thing about Instructables is that they come in all shapes and sizes. Some users include hundreds of high-quality pictures and detailed instructions with their projects; others take the minimalist approach and aim to inspire similar ideas rather than to facilitate carbon copies. One of the biggest questions we faced when putting this book together was: How do we convey the sheer volume of ideas in the finite space of a book?

As a result, if you're already familiar with some of the projects in this book, you'll notice that only select photos made the jump from the computer screen to the printed page. Similarly, when dealing with extensive electronic coding or complex science, we've suggested that anyone ready to start a project like that visit the Instructables' online page, where you often find lots more images, links, multimedia attachments, and downloadable material to help you. This way, anyone who is fascinated by the idea of convering a car to run on trash can take a look here at the basic steps to get from start to finish. Everything else is just a mouse click away.

* Special thanks to Instructables Interactive Designer Gary Lu for the Instructables Robot illustrations!

# home improvement

The brick construction centric category of home improvement is sometimes overlooked when it comes to making something extraordinary. Too often people think that in order to make something amazing, in or out of your home, you have to spend a lot of money, live in a big mansion, or turn your pool into a giant saltwater aquarium for tropical fish, (Hey, wait a minute, that last example might not be a bad idea!) Too often people think that walls should be straight, doors can only be opened with handles, and that floors are something that have to be purchased at big box stores.

Not only do the projects included in this chapter create something fun and unique out of the places that we live, but they also show how it's possible to rethink discrete parts of the home that builders often take for granted as having to be done a certain way. Questioning and reinventing these conventions advances not only the spaces where makers live, but also lead the way in customized DIY home improvement for us all.

# Making a Motorized Secret Entrance

By flaming_pele!
(http://www.instructables.com/id/Making-a-Motorized-Secret-Entrance/)

If you're decorating along the lines of a haunted house or a superhero lair, a secret entrance is just the thing to get Halloween guests into your home. In our case, we threw a Superhero costume party and wanted to build a motorized, moving wall activated by a statue—a nod to the Batman series of the 60s.

Goals:
- Surprise guests with an apparently closed room as they walk in
- Give them a riddle to figure out how to open the hidden door/wall
- Keep the area this occupies to a functional minimum so it doesn't take up too much actual entertaining space

## Step 1: Planning the layout

We have a tiled area at our front door that defined a natural boundary for our fake room. The area is large enough for 2-3 guests to comfortably walk in and move around, and small enough that it doesn't occupy too much of the (real) room.

We decided that walking in from the front door, into a tiny room with only walls, wouldn't seem very plausible. To help sell the illusion, we hung a door in front of you as you walk in, but boarded it up, so the room appeared as a small vestibule that was no longer passable. We left the knob off this door, just to keep guests from trying to go through it (despite the boards). Which leads me to a point about safety . . .

## Step 2: Framing and safety

It's important to realize that guests may push on any wall, looking for a way in, and you don't want anything collapsing. Sometimes Halloween props can be flimsy and just for looks; this isn't one of those times. So I took care to build a sturdy structure framed mostly with 2x4s. Given our particular geometry and materials used, we got away with only anchoring one top corner to the actual wall with a single screw.

For the section of the wall that makes up the secret door, we used lighter materials so the job of moving it would be easier on the motor. It consists of just one 2x4 on the edge where it hinges, a 1x3 across the top, a 1x4 across the bottom, and a lightweight 2x3 steel stud on the side that moves. Since this section was light, just two hinges were used to connect it to the other framing.

There's about an inch gap at the top and bottom of the framing of this section, so there's plenty of clearance to move. The gaps would be covered once the "walls" were added.

## Step 3: Walling it in

The walls and a false ceiling were added with panels of pink insulation foamboard. It's lightweight, easy to cut, hang, and paint, plus easy to re-use for a different project later. Two-inch masking tape works great to cover seams and screws—in spooky lighting it disappears nicely.

You could do any faux paint finish inside—we just painted everything white to blend with our existing doors and (real) walls.

## Step 4: Adding the wheel and motor

A small 12 volt motor was used to motorize the door. The motor came with a gearbox with an output (free) speed of around 60-90 rpm. A motor that's nicely geared down is what's needed here—for one, you don't want the door moving too fast, and the gearing lets you use a pretty small motor. Once everything is hooked up, it takes the motor about 6-7 seconds to open the door. The slow speed helps give the illusion that the wall is very heavy, plus it's safe in case anyone is standing too close on the other side.

The wheel is a hard rubber wheelchair wheel salvaged from some past robotics projects.

The wheel and motor were mounted so the wheel extends below and supports the bottom of the door framing.

## Step 5: Electrical work

The motor is powered by a typical 120vac-12vdc adapter. I mounted a double pole, double throw (DPDT) switch outside of the fake room to operate the door in either direction.

To open the door from inside the room, two limit switches were mounted just under the base of a statue. The switches are wired as "normally closed." When the statue is resting on the switches, they are open, and they become closed when the statue is tilted. Two switches (rather than one) were used because it was an easy way to tie into the existing circuit with the DPDT switch.

## Step 6: Finishing touches

Some final details really help to pull everything together. Also, the surprise of the wall opening is heightened if the lighting/decor is different on either side of the room. Inside, we added some webbing and LED candles for a run-down, creepy atmosphere. Outside, we had hung different colored lighting and decorations.

We marked the swing of the door with an arc of gaffers tape on the floor. This would keep our guests aware of not standing too close as more people come in.

The final touch was a small riddle inside to give guests a clue of how to enter.

3

# How to Build an Earthbag Dome

By Owen Geiger
(http://www.instructables.com/id/How-to-Build-an-Earthbag-Dome/)

PHOTOS: Meemee Kanyarath

Note: If you're new to earthbag building, first read the introductory Step-by-Step Earthbag Building Instructable and How to Build an Earthbag Roundhouse. Also, my new Earthbag Building Guide and Earthbag Building DVD are now available.

We built this earthbag dome at our home in Thailand for *Mother Earth News Magazine* in 2007.

This multi-purpose dome can serve as a storage shed or cool pantry above ground, or as a rootcellar or storm shelter below ground. No building permit is typically needed, because it is below the minimum size required by building codes, is not inhabited,a and is not attached to a residence.

The key concept that makes earthbag domes work is corbelling. This means each course (each row) of bags is inset slightly from the course below. Corbelled domes made of adobe and stone have been built for thousands of years. The concept has been applied to earthbags in the last few decades.

### Basic project information:

18' exterior diameter; 8' interior diameter; 11' exterior diameter, 50 sq. ft. interior floor space; total cost of materials: $300, which is about $6/square foot.

### Tools:

- Tamper(s)
- round nose shovel(s)
- grape hoe or grub hoe (digging tool)
- 13" x 16" sheetmetal slider
- Knife
- hammer
- 2' level
- 2" x 4" x 10' leveling board
- tape measure
- fencing pliers
- handsaw
- trowel
- garden hose with spray nozzle
- 6' or 8' stepladder

The following instructions assume you have cleared and leveled the site, removed topsoil, positioned fill soil around the building site to minimize work, dug a trench to stable subsoil, put about 12" of gravel in the trench, and added two stakes with string lines: a center stake with string line to measure the radius, and a stake in front of the door to measure the dome curvature. Bags or tubes can be used.

## Step 1: Dome plans

Let's briefly take a look at the plans so you'll better understand the building process. The first drawing is the floorplan that shows the dimensions for the dome base and the angled buttresses in front. The buttresses provide reinforcing on both sides of the door and also act as retaining walls to hold back the earth. Make a rubble trench under the buttresses the same as the dome, and interlock (overlap) each course where the dome and buttresses intersect.

The second drawing is the dome section that shows key vertical dimensions, earthbag foundation, door and arch. Note the wood stake in front of the door. The string line on this stake guides the curvature of the dome (112" radius in this case). This dimension remains constant. Put the stake off to one side of the doorway so you're not tripping on it during construction.

## Step 2: Earthbag foundation

Use the same earthbag foundation building technique described in previous instructables. This includes poly bags, double-bagged

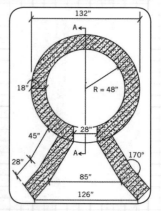

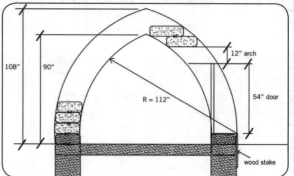

for strength, filled with gravel to prevent wicking moisture into upper courses. The bags sit directly on the rubble trench. Build the buttresses at the same time, in the same way. After the two gravel bag courses are finished, add soil around the sides of the dome and tamp solid to prevent the bags from moving.

## Step 3: Measure the radius

Use the string line on the center stake to measure the radius. Move the string to make sure each bag is the same distance from the center point. This creates a perfect circle. Repeat this step for every course except the very highest ones. By that point, the circles become so small that you can just eyeball them. Note: the string line on the center stake is lengthened to measure each course. Just make sure it remains a constant length for each entire course. (You could use temporary knots or pinch the string between your fingers.)

## Step 4: Level each course

Check each course for level after tamping. For small domes like this one, a straight 2x4 works great. Put the level on the 2x4 and gradually move it around over the center stake to check each bag. We fill each bag with the same number of buckets so the walls are almost self-leveling. Also, we're careful to use the same technique for each bag.

## Step 5: Moisten the soil

You're almost ready to start laying soil-filled earthbags. The soil in the earthbags needs to be slightly moist – just enough to pack densely into the bags. Use a garden hose to mist the soil. Test the moisture content by making a ball in your hand. If it looks wet or if water oozes out of the bags, then there's too much water. You'll soon recognize the proper moisture content. Also, a note how the soil in the photo on the top right has been distributed around the dome to minimize labor. Each bucket load is only moved a few steps. The reddish soil is called road base. It's the same material used to build roads in many parts of the world and is ideal for earthbag.

## Step 6: First course of soil-filled earthbags

Now that you're above the level where moisture can cause problems, you can start filling bags with soil. We use

2-gallon buckets to fill bags. The easiest way to fill buckets is with a sturdy hoe that's made for digging. We use a grape hoe to pull the soil into the buckets. And with just a flick of the tool, the bucket is pulled upright.

## Step 7: Tamping

Tamp each course solid, starting with the high spots. Keep the tamper moving so you don't create low spots. The first pass doesn't require much force. After you've gone around once, you can start tamping more vigorously. Final tamping is usually done with more force. You'll hear a change in pitch as the earthbags become solid.

## Step 8: Door anchors

There are various ways of attaching door and window bucks. On this dome we made six anchors with small pieces of steel welded together in a T-shape. Drill holes in the anchors and pin to the earthbags as shown with 1/4" steel rod. Distribute the anchors, three per side, so there are two near the bottom, two in the center and two near the top of the arched door opening. A steel door buck was welded to these anchors after the dome was built.

## Step 9: Barbed wire

Remember to always use 4-point barbed wire between courses. We used one strand on this dome due to its small size. Use two strands of barbed wire between every course for domes larger than this one.

5

## Step 10: Angle ends of bags toward the center

On straight earthbag walls, you can just butt the bags against each other. But for roundhouses and domes, you need to align the bag ends to the center point so the bags sit tightly against each other. Hit the bottom of each bag with a board until it aligns with the center of the dome. From above, bag joints look like mitered joints. Repeat this process throughout the dome. At the top, the process becomes more pronounced as the radius decreases.

## Step 11: Build the arch

You need a way to support the bags as you build the arch over the door. You could build an elaborate wood and plywood form. This might be worthwhile if you're building lots of arches the same size. But this dome has just one arch, so we lashed two used tires together for the form. Build some supports on each side of the door opening to hold the tires at the correct height. Add some horizontal blocking to hold everything together, but leave enough space in the middle to squeeze through and for the string line that will determine your dome curvature. Note: You could temporarily fill the space with adobes, bricks, etc. and remove them later, but then you lose access to the dome and can't use the string line.

It looks really complicated to build an arch, but it's not.

Make tapered earthbags about 12" high. Make sure you use the right soil mix that will withstand high pressure. Compact the bags from the sides and top as much as possible. The taper aligns with the center point of your form (the center of the tires in this case). You could use a string line for this or just eyeball it like I did.

## Step 12: Build the eyebrow

It's a good idea to include a protected overhang above entry doors to protect the door and shelter people going in and out. This eyebrow or overhang is made with hardwood table legs embedded between bags. Then short pieces of insect resistant eucalyptus wood were nailed to the table legs and covered with 6 mil plastic sheeting. The wood was varnished with polyurethane for greater durability. (The table legs were varnished in advance.)

## Step 13: Buttresses

Continue building the buttress at the same time as the dome. The bags and barbed wire interlock at every course. We added a few 1/2" pieces of rebar for added strength where it seemed it would do the most good: down through the top of the bags to help preventing overturning and where the buttresses connect to the dome. The buttresses are stepped to match the slope of the earth. The steps make it easy to climb on the dome. The lower part makes a nice bench.

## Step 14: Upper courses of earthbags

Continue the same process of laying and tamping bags. The corbel (overhang between courses) will increase the higher you go. Use the string lines at every course to arrive at the desired shape. Make sure each bag is angled toward the center point and tightly butted to the next bag. (This is what makes the dome really strong.)

Don't step on the inner edge of the corbel or the bag could tilt loose. Be extra careful working higher on the dome. You'll be working around barbed wire, tools laying on the wall, etc. Watch your step. Don't get in a rush. Take lots of breaks and drink plenty of water.

## Step 15: Living roof

The easiest method of finishing the dome is plaster. We live in a rainy climate where a plastered dome might leak. Plus, we wanted a beautiful plant covered dome in our backyard. Living roofs require a lot of regular maintenance just like gardening, so think long and hard before going this route. Without regular watering, weeding, and fertilizer, the living roof will turn into a giant weed patch, die, or maybe even erode away. We've worked hard to establish really healthy grass, as you can see in the photo.

The main steps for the living roof include adding two or three layers of 6 mil plastic sheeting ("black poly"). I put one layer directly against the dome and back side of the buttresses. Then I backfilled with earth (more road base) about half way up and added another layer of plastic. I added a third layer of plastic on the top of the dome where the risk of water penetration is greatest. Work carefully and try not to puncture the plastic. Gradually add soil on top of the plastic starting at the bottom and working up. Compact it slightly as you go. I used field dirt – soil from rice fields—for this step. It has enough clay to stay in place, but still enables grass to grow. Add drought resistant sod once the dome is covered in a layer of soil. Some pieces of sod require bamboo pins to keep from slipping. Time the project so the sod gets started during the rainy season. We have a lawn sprinkler on top of the dome and water it whenever it gets dry.

## Step 16: Plastering

The outside (front area only) is plastered with cement plaster with yellow iron oxide pigment. All edges are rounded slightly to soften the look. Plaster mesh isn't typically needed on earthbags, but we used plastic plaster mesh in this application due to the buttresses being exposed to the elements. Plastic mesh won't rust. We never plastered the inside since our dome is used as a tool shed. This allows people to come and see how the dome was built.

## Step 17: Conclusion

Domes are the strongest form in nature and easily support enormous forces. We added about 20 truckloads of soil on the dome without it moving one bit. I'm confident another 100 truck loads could be put directly on top and it wouldn't make any difference, because the dome is all in compression, and tamped earth (road base in our case) can support very high loads. So if you want to build underground, domes are a good way to go–that or round-houses. Both gain their strength from the circle; forces (loads) are transferred directly to the ground. There are no components to fail as in post and beam or wood frame walls.

Domes have lots of other advantages. They create the most floor space for a given length of wall. There are no wasted corners. The feeling inside is magical. Those who live in domes (and roundhouses) most likely never live in boxes again. Wind flows around domes and does not build up pressure against them. You can build domes without wood. You can build domes with minimal tools and materials–no nails, no wood, no plywood, no shingles. This makes domes a good candidate for those who lack carpentry skills and for emergency shelters for disaster areas and war refugees. Give people some rice or grain bags and a little training and soon they can build their own sturdy, safe shelters.

# Automated Pop-up Kitchen Spice Rack

By Troy (Firgelli Automations)
(http://www.instructables.com/id/Kitchen-Auto-mation-pop-up-spice-rack-or-wine-rack/)

This is a simple kitchen automation project. A Firgelli Automation FA-400-12-18" stroke linear actuator was used to pop up this spice rack. Of course the top would typically be the granite square that was cut out originally, and the spice rack could be a coffee machine, microwave, TV, wine rack or anything else you wish to hide in your kitchen. The actuator sits pointing upwards and as you can see the middle of the spice rack has a sort of hollow column, this is where the other end of the actuator fits inside. It's not required, however, if you use the Firgelli Automations column lift, which is a ready to go remote control lift mechanism.

## Step 1: Kitchen granite top

This customer wanted to have the spice rack lift up from the Kitchen island. First thing they did was cut a square hole in the granite top, the granite maker can do that for you. Typically you would use another square piece to fill the hole so that when the rack drops, the granite becomes flush with the top lid to look like a single piece of granite

## Step 2: Make a spice rack

The spice rack needs to have a hollow center so that the actuator shaft goes through the center and lifts the top, the bottom of the actuator is attached as shown below. The height is adjusted by propping up the base so that the limits of the actuator are such that when the actuator retracts and shuts off, the spice rack is fully closed.

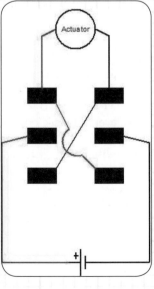

## Step 3: Controls

To make it go up and down, you need a 12vdc power source and a DPDT switch all available from Firgelli Auto. The actuators are all 2 wire and the power source is too.

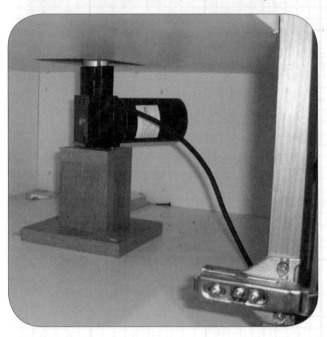

# How to Build an Octagonal Deck

By David Grice (cobourgdave)
(http://www.instructables.com/id/How-to-Build-an-Octagonal-Deck/)

This is a 12 foot deck I built in 2005. It has gone through 6 Canadian winters and one restain of the deck surface. This instructable will cover each step with pictures and the Bill of Materials. The costs shown are from 2005, with the total about $1500 Canadian, not counting tax, the cost of the tent, or maintenance.

## Step 1: Materials required

Tools required are:

- Hammer
- 4 ft Level
- Clam shell shovel or post hole auger
- Powered hand drill (I used a 1/2" hammer drill.)
- Hand Circular saw (Mine is a 7-1/4.")
- Shovel
- Wheelbarrow
- String
- Chalk

| A | B | C | D | E | F |
|---|---|---|---|---|---|
| item | count | unit cost | total | | Note: sales tax not included |
| premix cement | 17 | $3.98 | $67.66 | | |
| sona tube 10"x8' | 1 | $10.97 | $10.97 | | |
| sona tube 6"x4' | 8 | $3.92 | $31.36 | | |
| sona tube saddles | 8 | $2.94 | $23.52 | | |
| bolt washer nut | 2 | $3.54 | $7.08 | | |
| | | | | | |
| lumber | | | | | |
| 2x8x14' pressure treated lumber | 14 | $18.32 | $256.48 | | joists |
| 2x8x8' pressure treated lumber | 24 | 9.98 | 239.52 | | joists |
| 4x4x8 press treated lumber | 2 | $9.97 | $19.94 | | posts |
| 1.25x6x8 cedar decking | 51 | 11.79 | $601.29 | | decking |
| | | | | | |
| Miscellaneous | | | | | |
| screws | 13 | $6.99 | $90.87 | | deck screws by pound |
| 4" bolt, wshr, nut | 8 | $0.74 | $5.92 | | |
| 4" washer | 1 | 1.49 | 1.49 | | |
| joist hangers | 26 | 0.76 | 19.76 | | |
| wall anchors | 7 | $2.50 | $17.50 | | |
| cabot deck coating | 1 | 39.97 | 39.97 | | |
| washers | 1 | 9.98 | 9.98 | | end of deck planks |
| glue | 2 | $4.31 | $8.62 | | glue cedar inserts |
| totals | | | $1,451.93 | | |

## Step 2: Chalk out the deck

This is a 12 ft diameter cantelevered deck, with poured concrete piers. The structure that follows assumes you will want to attach the deck to the house. Find a spot 6 feet from the edge of your house (plus an allowance for a ledger board) more or less centered on the house entrance. Mark this spot as the central support column of the deck. Drive a peg. Attach your string to this peg and, draw a chalk circle with a radius of 6 feet and a second circle of 4 feet. Start marking the position of each of the 8 support posts. String a line to the right edge of your door and driving a peg at the intersection of this line and the 4 foot circle. Carefully rotate the string 45 degrees counter-clockwise. Strike this second chalk line and hope the subtended angle covers the door entrance. If it does, drive a peg at the 4 foot intersect. If it doesn't, fiddle with these two lines so that the 45 degree arc is centered on the door frame. After these first 2 pegs are in, progess around the circle until all post holes are pegged.

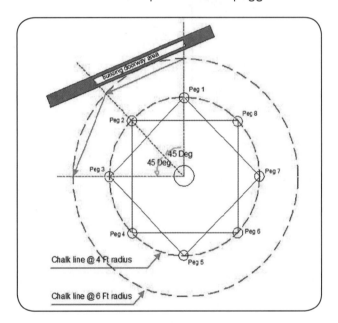

## Step 3: The center post

At the center post peg, dig a hole to below frost level. In my county, that means a minimum of 42 inches. Use a length of 10 inch Sona tube in this hole. Before pouring the concrete, mark the height of the pour by marking the periphery of the Sona tube at a point a joist width and a deck plank thickness, below the level of your house doorway. Cut the Sona tube at this height, mix the concrete and pour to the top. Imbed a 4 inch carriage bolt in the center. I used a 3/4 inch bolt. I didn't use rebar but, you may wish to.

Now dig a hole for each of the 8 outer posts using a 6 inch Sona tube, below frost level and about 3 inches above ground.

Now don't pour until you review the next step, which will instruct you to imbed saddles in the 8 posts.

## Step 4: Aligning the post saddles

Refer to the diagram in step 2. When imbedding the saddles in the outer 8 post pours, imbed the saddles in post 1 and post 3 to align with the rectangle shown in Step 2. Continue next with post 5 and 7 following the same rectangle. I call these the ODD numbered posts. The EVEN numbered posts are poured and the saddles aligned again using step 3 as a guide. Align post 2 and post 8 saddles, followed by post 4 and post 6.

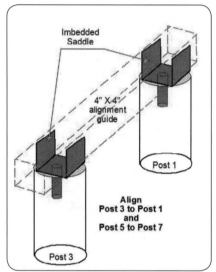

## Step 5: Starting deck foundation

With the concrete firm, use 3 inch deck or brass screws to fasten a pressure treated 4"x4" upright in each of the 8 saddles. These uprights are marked and cut so that the top of each is level with the center post. Screw pressure treated planks to the uprights to form a rectangle flush with the top of each upright.

## Step 6: Finish deck foundation

As in Step 5 the ODD numbered posts are framed to create a rectangle that intersects the rectangle of the EVEN posts. Follow the image, screw the pressure treated lumber in place, and then double up the rectangles. What we have now is an 8 pointed polygon which is the deck foundation. Each point or vertex of the polygon will support a deck joist. (If you start the rectangle with the ODD numbered posts, it doesn't matter, as long as you end up with the 8 pointed polygon.)

## Step 7: Deck joist

There are 8 main deck joists, each crossing a vertices and resting on the center post, giving us a 2 foot cantilever to the deck. Each joist is 6 feet long and sits at angle of 45 degrees from adjacent vertices.

Note that the joists pushed together at the center post and, as shown in the next step, four of the joists have been cut at a 45 degree angle to assure a tight fit. The joists will eventually be held down with the bolt in the center post.

## Step 8: Detail of joists on center post

This is a detail to show the joists mounted on the center post. They should be pushed together as we proceed.

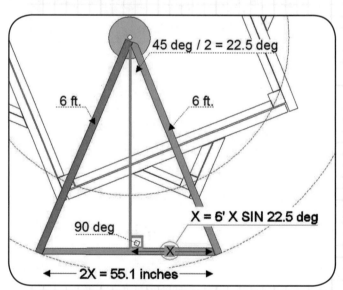

## Step 9: Some arithmetic

The circumference of the deck is formed by the end joists. This picture gives some detail about the calculation of the length of each end joist. Frankly, my advice is to cut one end of the end joist at 22.5 degrees; measure twice, then cut the second end at 22.5 degrees! The real secret here is to keep the subtended angle at 45 degrees. This calculation is based on a zero width line; at the very least the results are out by the joist thickness. How many planks have you ever seen that have exactly the same thickness? Take the calculation as an approximation only.

## Step 10: End joists all in place

At this point, joists have been installed. Look carefully and you see the joist ends on the center post are still floating free. You can now rotate the deck joisting to adjust the deck orientation to the house entrance. When are satisfied that the orientation is okay screw each main joist to the corresponding vertices. At this point, I sloped the ground under the deck and covered with several inches of gravel.

## Step 11: Connecting to the house

I used 2 ledger boards here to accommodate two vent pipes and to assure that I had an attachment surface beyond the entrance lintel.

Notice I have installed the first couple of CROSS joisting. There are a lot to come.

Last, this is a good time to bolt down the center post end of the joists.

## Step 12: Clamping the main joists to the center post

The 4 inch Carriage bolt imbedded in the center post is clearly too short to extend to the top of the joists, so I up-ended a second bolt and connected both bolts together, giving me a way to clamp the joists down. Of course I started by screwing a second nut and a large diameter washer to that second bolt, beforehand. This is a temporary solution, which we will alter when finishing the decking.

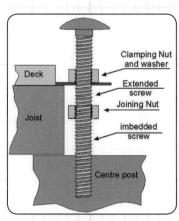

## Step 13: The Cross joists

The Cross joists are perpendicular to the end joists and are set at 16 inch centers. Notice that the joists are clamped at the center. This matrix of joists, end joists and cross joints is extremely strong. Can you see the last one I was about to install, which ends the task of installing the joists for the deck? All joists are secured with deck screws.

## Step 14: Installing the cedar deck

Start at the outer edge of the deck and work inwardly to the center. The first row of decking overhangs the end joists by 1-1/2 inches.

Each piece of deck planking is fastened between adjacent main joists. Use deck screws, alternately driving the screws either to the front edge or bottom edge of the plank in a zig zag pattern. DO NOT screw down the ends of the planking at this time keep the joints tight. Proceed around the periphery, with no spacing between planks. From time to time you will have to rip a board to keep the progression even. Keep the scrap, it will fit an inner circle.

## Step 15: The Center post clamping bolt

As you get closer to the center of the deck, you will need to insert some scrap joisting to provide a surface to mount the decking. Additionally, since the deck planking is firmly holding the joisting together, we have the opportunity to modify the center post clamping screw to assure that the final pieces of decking can be fastened in the center without interference.

## Step 16: Clamping bolt clearance

To get the clamping screw and nut below the bottom of the deck surface, we need to chisel out the edges of the main joists around the clamping screw and nut to accomodate the big washer. In fact, at this point I installed a second smaller washer between the clamping nut and the original large washer to reinforce the larger washer. Follow the image here and cut deep enough to accomodate screw and washer(s) and wide enough to JUST accept the largest washer. Mark the excess bolt length above the clamping nut, disassemble the nut and washer structure, and then hacksaw the bolt to length. You will probably have to try this a couple of times to get it right.

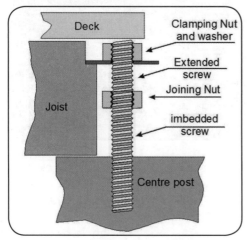

## Step 17: One of several mods

The connection of the Octagon deck to the house required a small alteration in the plan. Keep the octagon shape, but check the space between the wall and the deck and make it obvious. Here is the framing between the deck and house.

## Step 18: Between house and deck

Here is the decking between the octagon and the house wall.

## Step 19: Decking complete . . . sort of.

The deck looks great but my skills with the saw left rather wavy lines along the planking over the main joists. So my answer was to cover the joints with an inlay of cedar decking. Two reasons for this:
- Wavy lines
- Inlays clearly define the triangular segments of the octagon

## Step 20: Second mod.. inlays

To do the inlay:
- Rip a 6 foot piece of cedar decking about 3/8 inches thick.
- Use the 7-1/4 inch saw to cut the channel straddling the saw joints along the main joists to about 1/4 inch depth.
- Fasten all joints in the channel with a deck screw and washer
- Use contractors glue (waterproof) to glue the ripped strips into the channel.
- Use a hand plane to bring the level of the inlay to the deck surface. Sanding takes too much time.

## Step 21: The power saw as a router

Using the ripped piece of decking previously mentioned, straddle the saw joint with the cedar strip so that it is centered above the joint. Draw a line along the right edge of the strip. See red dotted line in the diagram.

Measure your power saw edge guide. What is the measurement to the saw tooth closest to the edge guide? It should typically be about 1-1/4 inch. See yellow rectangle in the diagram.

Use a piece of scrap wood no thicker than 1/4 inch and tack the scrap wood onto the deck to the right of the drawn line a distance equal to the measurement of the guide to saw blade and parallel to that line. See the brown rectangle in the diagram.

Make a cut from the vertice of the joint to the center of the deck. That's 1/8." Put the cedar strip between the scrap wood guide and the saw. Make another cut. That's a total of 1/2" channel. You got it! Proceed until you get close to the line on the left of the saw joint. Insert the strip, or make another cut. BE CAREFULL. MEASURE TWICE, CUT ONCE. PLEASE TRY ON A SCRAP OF WOOD BEFORE DOING THIS! When finished, clean out the uncut pieces with a wood chisel.

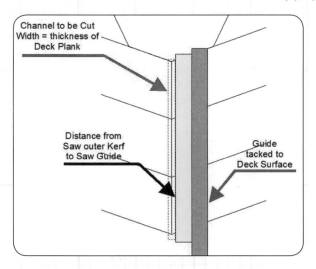

## Step 22: Inlays completed

It doesn't require a genius to see the improvement of the design with the inlays. The lines at the main joists are dead straight; the triangular features of the octagon pop right out.

Be sure to review this whole procedure. You don't want to glue a strip down before screwing the joints down. In this picture (aside from my wife's geraniums) notice that I had not decided how to finish the center. I eventually decided on a one-piece cedar octagon.

## Step 23: The tent mod

In our county, a hard roof on a gazebo or any deck changes all the rules. The setbacks for a deck move from 4 feet to 23 feet the minute your designs include a hard roof. The result is that I had to design for a tent roof. This design started with the intention of cedar rails and a semi-permanant roof.

As it happens, my wife found a really great buy on an octagonal garden tent (about $575 Cdn.) The problem was that the outfit selling the tent had little or no documentation and were not sure of the size. They guessed 14 feet. Does that mean 7 foot edge to edge or 7 foot radius? We bought it and found that the radius is about 13 feet 6 inches. They must include the diameter of the support poles in the 14 feet. Regardless, here is where the last design mod is described.

I couldn't increase the current radius, but I could put in extensions to the vertices to support the tent poles. Each post support is constructed of 4 pieces of wood. Two sides at 8 inches, cutting both ends at 22.5 degrees, and two center pieces at 4," again with 22.5 degree cut both ends. Assemble as shown here, glue and screw and mount at each vertice below deck level. Fasten deck planks following the pattern of the deck with a 1-1/2 inch overhang.

## Step 24: The end

That's it guys. I am not going to talk about the stairs, we all have been there.

This is my first instructable and it has been interesting. A couple of things:

- I sanded and refinished the deck in 2009. I probably will do it again in the future.
- The idea to push the deck planks tight together came from my local lumber yard person who noted that shrinkage will occur regardless, but less with cedar than PT. His opinion has been confirmed since very little shrinkage has ocurred. My pressure treated fence-planks have shrunk about 1/2 inch in width in the last 6 years.
- The deck has been very sturdy, even with a full band with instruments playing on it—no shaking or bouncing.

# Air-Powered Star Trek Style Door

By uiproductions
(http://www.instructables.com/id/Air-Powered-Star-Trek-Style-Door/)

I always wanted a piece of Star Trek and the Disney Monorail in my house, and one thing they have in common is that they both have automatic sliding doors. It would be the perfect, most geek-ified entryway for my bedroom.

Edit: Not every detail is included in this Instructable. I did the best I could using pictures I had taken 4 years ago. There are some more details on my blog if you would like to read more: http://uiproductions.blogspot.com.

To be acceptable as a permanent renovation to our house, I knew the door had to have a normal appearance, as well as be practical and maintenance free. To reduce the number of moving parts (and maybe for a little coolness factor), I decided to make the door air-powered. The air would be supplied by a small compressor and storage tank located in the attic. In order to open and close from the inside and out, the door needed a little bit of brainpower. I decided to use a small PIC microcontroller, my platform of choice still to this day. Arduino didn't exist back then.

With a rough plan in my head, I drew a quick CAD model of the door and the brackets that would connect the pistons to the door halves. I was ready to start purchasing parts.

## Step 1: Buy parts/tear out wall

Here are some of the parts I used:

- Craftsman 1 Gallon Air Compressor/Tank
- 32" wide, solid wood door from Home Depot (to be cut in half)
- Pocket Door Track from McMaster.com
- Two 16" stroke, 3/4" bore pneumatic pistons from McMaster.com
- A 5-way, 12V solenoid-operated valve from McMaster.com
- Various pneumatic hose, fittings, a regulator, push-on hose connectors, two valves for air supply and purge

Your parts will vary depending on your door size, your wall configuration, etc.

Start tearing out your wall with a hammer, crowbar, or any other destructive tools you can find laying around. This is the fun part of the project!

## Step 2: Install the track, hang the doors, and patch up one wall.

I proceeded to cut the solid wood door in half with a circular saw, sanding the edges when done. I considered using bi-fold doors which are already the right size, but they didn't give the appearance of a normal door when joined together.

With all of the interfering studs removed from the wall, I held the rear drywall in place with 3/4" thick wood boards, which would still leave room for the door to travel through the wall. I added a new 2x4 stud on one side to support the pocket door track, and installed the track and a door half using the included hardware. You can see below how the one half will slide into the wall cavity.

Some strips of drywall, mud, and trim take care of the hallway with no problems.

## Step 3: Fabricate door bracket/install pistons

Next I had to fabricate a bracket to connect the pistons above the door to the actual door. I welded up a bracket out of some steel flat bar from Home Depot and attached it to the back of the door with a spacer block. I could have really used some more advanced tools at this point, but I had to work with what I had at the time. You can fabricate this bracket from sheet metal, steel bar, wood, or whatever you can find.

With the two brackets fabricated and installed, I mounted the two 16" pistons above the door, side by side. Air supplied to the back of the pistons would open the doors, and air supplied to the front of the pistons would close the doors, as seen below. I rigged up the valve temporarily to test everything out.

## Step 4: Electronics

For the electronics, a simple on/off switch would have worked. But I wanted to get a little fancier and control the timing of the doors opening and closing. I made the circuitry from components that are readily available at Radio Shack and Sparkfun.com. The circuitry just waits for the button to be pushed then switches the air valve on so the door will open. After a few seconds, the valve switches back off and the door closes.

I mounted a DIP socket, a relay, and a few other components on a Radio Shack perf board, and placed the whole thing inside a plastic junction box. I also wired in two AC power switches, one supplying AC power to the wall adapter for the circuitry, and the other supplying power to the compressor in the attic. I wanted the whole system to be enabled and disabled from this "control panel," including the air supply.

## Step 5: Test it out/patch up the wall

After countless cycles of testing and tweaking the door operation with the wall open for a month or two, I finally felt comfortable closing up the wall.

From there it was just a matter of painting the wall, and it was back to looking stock. I purchased a blank white wall plate from Home Depot. I drilled it out for an illuminated pushbutton and a 3-position keyswitch, both of which I bought from McMaster. I also purchased a plastic hatch door from McMaster for the control box. Lastly, I added an air conditioning vent above the door. This lets the air venting noises be heard, and it also provides me access to the valve and pistons should anything go wrong.

After you've tested the door and patched up the wall, that's about it!

# Make a Hardwood Floor that Looks 3D from Your OWN Trees

By Richard Lange (Vyger)
(http://www.instructables.com/id/Make-a-Hard-wood-Floor-that-looks-3D-from-your-OWN-/)

I have cut a lot of logs over the years and I have always been impressed at how beautiful some of the wood looks inside. I always wondered if there wasn't something I could do with it besides burn it for firewood. But how can you make anything from trees without the large scale professional tools and a mill? I discovered there is a way, but I warn you it's not an easy project.

Cutting up logs and turning them into 2 inch diamonds, yep a crazy idea. That's what I am going to show you how to do in this instructable.

## Step 1: The chainsaw

For this job you have to start with a chainsaw.

One thing about chain saws to remember—the bigger they are, the more tired you get using them. You can cut all day with a medium size one and not feel like your arms are going to fall off. So unless you have really large logs and can afford an expensive saw, a medium 16 or 18 inch one will work great.

I have 2 kinds of logs for this project, big ones and really big ones. Logs under 3 inches in diameter won't really work for getting finished dimensions of 2 inches. Anything over 4 or 5 inches will work pretty good for this, but the way you cut the medium logs and the really big logs is different. Big logs can be cut into slabs. Since my finished size is going to be 2 inches I try and cut the slabs in 3 inch thick pieces. Small logs you can cut into two. The size you need to cut them to depends on how large a piece your band saw can handle.

A key to cutting straight is to have a sharp chain and a good bar. If some of the teeth on your chain are dull on one side, it will cause your saw to cut in an arc, which means you're cutting firewood and not wood for the floor.

Cutting in the snow has its benefits. You can use the snow to brace the logs to keep them where you want them. And if you cut all the way through the log and into the snow, it doesn't dull your chain.

A Y or fork or branching produces some of the more interesting grain patterns. Cut it straight through the center to make it manageable for your band saw. Don't try and cut from the top down straight through. The saw will wander all over. Start by cutting a line all the way down where you want your cut to go. That gives you a guide of sorts. Often when you cut like this the saw will cut out stringy wood. This is because you are cutting with the grain and rather than producing little flakes, it scrapes out long strips. Much like a hand plan does. It can clog your saw so if it gets jammed up stop, so and clear it out. If you get too much of this shredded wood jammed around the saw sprocket, it can cause your chain to fly off.

## Step 2: Cutting slabs and blocks

Start by measuring where you are going to make your cuts. You can just guess, but in my experience you often will guess wrong. It's easier to use a tape measure.

My finished size is going to be 2 inches so I am making 3 inch cuts. That sounds like a lot of waste and actually it is, but any chain saw is going to take out a pretty wide cut because the bar is not narrow. In addition, the cut is not going to be completely straight up and down. Even the best chain saw moves around while it's cutting and takes out extra wood. Finally, this slab is going to have to be processed further. It needs to be run through a planer in order to make the cut sides parallel so you will lose wood there too.

Start the cuts across the top following the lines you made. After getting these started, and I usually cut them as deep as the bar is, angle the saw down and cut lines down the front. These serve as guides so you can stay on a parallel cut.

Rock the saw between the cuts across the top and the cuts on the front. This allows you to keep both lines straight as you work down through the wood. You might notice that my trunk is sitting on top of another piece. This gives me clearance to cut the front lines. Often you will find your saw at about a 45 degree angle, cutting both top and front at the same time. Take your time and let the saw do the work.

Cut all the way down, but don't cut a piece off until you have all the slots cut almost all the way. This gives you the weight of the whole log as a stabilizer until you get them all cut. Having another log underneath also prevents you from cutting into the ground and dulling your saw when you get to that last little bit. After you get through these, you are ready to take them inside for the next step.

## Step 3: Logs are imperfect but there are ways to work around it

A lot of times logs will rot from the center outward. In these the core is not going to be any good. When you run across these try to cut the good wood on either side of the bad part. How can you tell if it's bad? Looking at the end you will see that the core wood is different, soft and spongy looking. It also doesn't leave sharp lines when cut, kind of like cutting warm butter.

**Wet verses dry:**

This is a good place to talk about wet wood verses dry wood. You can't use wet wood for your floor; it has to dry out first, but wet wood cuts easier than dry wood (usually). An exception here is really wet wood that is frozen solid; that's like cutting rock. But dry wood is stable and it's usually done cracking and warping. You can cut a parallel slab of wet wood, leave it sit for the summer to dry out and find that its warped into a U while drying. I prefer to let the wood dry for several years before I do anything with it. When the bark peels off of it and leaves just the bare wood then it's close to being ready. Of course you take a chance of it rotting in the meantime, but at least you can work with it without it changing shape and shrinking, which is what wet wood will do. This means you have to plan way ahead or find trees that are already dead and dried.

## Step 4: A finer cut

Now that you have your slabs and dissected logs done ,you can move indoors and work with power tools. Smaller logs can go directly to the band saw. Why not go straight to a table saw? Table saws are great tools but they have their drawbacks. The maximum height of the cut of the blade of my old Craftsman table saw with its 10 inch blade is 2 1/2 inches. Also table saws can't handle any kind of twisting or rocking of the cutting stock. If the material does anything except move in a straight line, it will usually bind up the blade. The blade has no flex to it. On the other hand, band saw blades are just fine with the wood moving a little, and they can usually handle much thicker wood. My band saw is one of the smaller ones.

This saw cuts wood almost up to 5 inches thick so I cut all my logs to be just under that. This saw comes with a 3/8 inch blade, but its worthless for cutting anything thick like these logs. You need to get a full 1/2 inch blade for it. Actually, several blades. I found that dry, rock hard ash wood dulls the teeth on these pretty fast.

The main goal with the band saw is to cut logs down into blocks that are small enough to fit on the table saw.

## Step 5: Planing slabs

The reason you have to plane these slabs is so they can run flat on the table saw and not bind up the blade. I tried cutting both planed ones and unplaned ones. The planed ones were much easier to work with. The unplaned ones rocked around on the high spots and were very difficult to move through the saw blade without binding it up. Also, when the two sides of the slab are not parallel and it's too thick a piece to cut all the way through, you cannot flip it over and cut it through from the other side. The saw blade is pointing in a different direction because the surfaces are not parallel and the two cuts won't match up. So, it's a little extra work to plane them, but it saves later on.

Raise the plane above the work piece and slowly lower it down as you run pieces through it. I usually work only one piece at a time rather than trying to run multiple pieces through one after the other. Be very careful doing this. If you go too fast the planer blades can impact on a high point and can actually break. You want it to shave the high points down gradually. It might take a lot of passes to accomplish this. After you get a flat side, turn the slab over about every 2 or 3 passes so you shave down both sides evenly. Keep going until the chain saw marks are mostly gone. If your slab is too wide to fit your planer, you might have to cut it in two with the chain saw.

Planing produces a lot of saw dust and chips. I bagged up a lot of mine and gave it to a friend who used it as bedding for his dog. It is soft and warm and smells great (depending on the kind of wood). And when it gets dirty, you can dump it in the garden to use for compost.

## Step 6: Finally, the table saw

Once you get blocks small enough for your table saw, you begin to get results that look more like lumbar and less like logs.

To cut the slabs, you might need to free cut them through the middle. If the slabs don't have flat edges, you can't run them along the rip fence. You need to get a flat face to glide along the rip fence. If the slabs are too thick for your saw blade to cut clear through, you can flip them over and cut them again from the backside. Another option is to run them on your band saw. The band naturally follows the partial cut and glides right through.

After you get a stack of rough cut sticks, you are ready to move on to the final cut. The reason for making a rough cut first is to make certain you get the right size. You can't uncut a piece of wood, so even though it seems like a waste of wood, you need to do a rough cut before you move on to the final cut. The rough cut size I am working with is 1 1/4 inch by 2 1/4 inch. The intended finished size is 1 inch by 2 inches.

I found it a good idea to let the rough cut pieces "rest" for several days. A few weeks would be even better. If they still have moisture in them it lets them dry out more. In addition, if they are going to do any warping or cracking now is the best time for it before you start finished cutting. An even bigger problem is shrinking. As

wood looses moisture, it shrinks. If it shrinks below your target dimensions, you will not be able to use it.

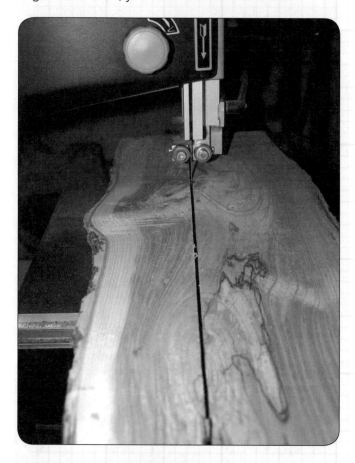

## Step 7: Making the final cuts

To do the finished cuts, I used a fine tooth saw blade. The blade I have been using up until now is a 40 tooth general purpose blade. Now I am moving to an 80 tooth blade. The larger number of teeth make a smoother, finer cut. This is where we need to get exact so precision becomes the priority.

To measure for these cuts, do not go by the markings on the rip fence guide. Those were fine for the rough cuts but not for this. Measure from the edge of the saw tooth to the rip fence. Actually put the measure under the tooth so you can see it line up. Don't use a tape measure; its not accurate enough for this. Use a good ruler that is accurate.

I made 4 cuts on each stick. I cut them first to 1 1/8 and 2 1/8. This way I cut every side of the stick with the fine tooth blade. This blade actually puts a little shine on the wood after it cuts because of the fineness of the blade.

## Step 8: Sanding

You need to decide which side is going to be the top for each stick. Then each top needs to be sanded. You do this now because it's a lot easier to sand a stick than it is to sand a little rhombus piece. You could wait and sand them after they are in place in the floor (and you may need to do that anyway), but it's easier for now to take out any flaws and saw marks while you have a chance.

A stationary belt sander would be nice to have for this job, but I don't have one. What I do have, however, works just as good. It's a Craftsman 3 inch belt sander and I got the stand to go with it when I bought it long ago. The stand turns it into a stationary sanding machine. Bolt it down to a portable work bench and you are all set for mass production.

I started with a 50 grit fast cutting paper and ran everything through to take out the flaws. I followed it up with a fine 80 grit, which didn't leave behind any sand marks.

Just a suggestion: By now you should have invested in some dust masks—this is a good place to use them.

## Step 9: Spline

Rather than just gluing my pieces together in a flat butt joint, I decided to use a spline to join them. I could have used the traditional tongue and groove method but that would have involved a lot more cutting and I would have lost even more wood. A spline can work just as well, if not better than most other methods for joining surfaces.

A spline is a small flat piece of wood that fits into a slot in order to help hold jointed pieces together.

One of the advantages of using this method is that the spline will help with any cracks in the wood like you see in the pictures. The spline together with the glue will reinforce the piece at the same time that it holds it together.

I needed to switch saw blades for this. I used my 60 tooth Craftsman blade. The teeth on this blade are narrower so the slot that it cuts is smaller. I have a lot of thin plywood pieces called door skins that fit perfectly in this slot so I don't need to cut any wood specially to use for the spline.

Set your blade height to what you plan to use. I cut mine 1/2 inch deep. Cut the slots on both sides. I ran all my pieces twice to make sure the slots were clean. Cut them with the face towards the rip fence. By doing this, you make sure that all the tops of the boards will line up level with each other even if a piece's thickness is a little off.

Cutting these now is a lot easier than after the rhombus's are cut. You will still have to cut a slot into each side of those but you will already have half of it done by cutting these now.

You might notice that I put a finish on these pieces. Normally you would wait until after the floor is in place to put a finish on them, but because I was planning on taking pictures of the pieces and showing the possible designs I put a couple of coats of finish on them after I sanded them.

## Step 10: The last step, make a jig and cut the rhombus

A cutting jig is a saw accessory that helps you make complicated cuts that turn out the same every time. To cut the angles for the rhombus, you need to make a jig. It's not hard to do if you follow the steps.

First you need a piece of wood (or plastic) that will fit into the miter guide slot in the saw table. This stick has to fit tight to keep the jig from moving anywhere except back and forth but be lose enough to slide freely in the slot. Next, find a big enough piece of plywood to fit the saw table and cut at least 2 sides square. The square corner will be at your lower right hand position. Set your rip fence for 2 inches—the final dimension of your pieces and use your ruler to measure it. Then slide your plywood up the rip fence and make a cut in it about half way down. Stop and turn off your saw but don't move the plywood. Now with the plywood still in place and not having moved, screw the plywood to the stick in the miter guide slot. This fastens and locks your jig in place square with your blade. It should now be able to slide back and forth along the rip fence, but not bind with it or the saw blade.

Now you need a good protractor or angle guide. Move the rip fence over out of the way and put the protractor on the saw blade. You need to measure and set your angle with the blade, not the edge of the jig. It's the blade that counts. The angle you are setting is 60 degrees. Be exact. Mark your board as to where this angle is. Then take a straight piece of wood and place it along the line and check it again with the protractor. When you get it dead on, then screw it down to the board. This is the guide for cutting all your sticks. You may have to (very likely) adjust this angle to get it correct. I was 1/2 a degree off in my initial setting and my rhombus pieces would not fit together correctly. This is a very exact angle, it needs to be as close to 60 degrees as possible. You can adjust the angle of the guide stick by loosening the screws, all but the one nearest the blade, and pivoting it on that screw. Once you get it right, don't ever move it.

Make a push stick with the front cut to the same angle as your rhombus pieces and make it as thick as they are. A rejected stick from your cutting makes a perfect push stick. Screw a piece of wood to the top so it reaches over your cut piece. The idea is that once you cut off that little diamond it's going to vibrate from the saw blade running. If it turns even a little bit sideways and a tooth of that blade catches it, it will launch straight back at you. Your push stick keeps it straight against the rip fence and allows you to push it on past the blade and the top prevents it from popping up out of your slot.

I added a bumper board to the front once I had tried the jig out and had it all correct. The bumper actually works really good. You hold the stick to be cut against your guide with your left hand, hold your push stick in your right and then just push the whole thing into the saw blade with your hip. After a very short time you develop a rhythm and it's almost like a machine cutting. All your little rhombus pieces slide out the back and make a nice pile.

You will have short pieces left over from your sticks that you can't hold to your guide with your fingers because the pieces are too short. Save them and cut them at the end using a clamp to hold them to the guide. You won't waste them, they can be cut, but don't try and do it by hand that close to the blade.

## Step 11: The results

Finally, from a tree to a rhombus. Now sit down at your table or on your floor and start playing with your pieces. Put three different colored pieces together and look at it for a moment and you will see a box. It can either be a solid box with the outside corner towards you or it can be an open box with only the 2 back sides on it. Your eyes might flip back and forth between the two. Since we live in a 3D world our brain is used to seeing in 3D and when it sees something like this it tries to interpret it as such.

Now make 3 boxes and push them together, add 3 rhombus to the blank edges and you are once again back to a 6 sided figure. But now it looks like 3 boxes inside of another corner of a bigger box, or does it? Take six pieces of all the same color and make a star out of them. It's the same pieces, just a different arrangement and it looks completely different, until you notice that it actually has boxes in it like the other one. The more you play the more fun it gets. The patterns that emerge are amazing and your eyes keep trying to make sense of it.

Getting this far, to the finished floor pieces, is as far as this instructable is going to go. Actually installing the floor will be another instructable in itself. (Rhombus part 2 ?) I need to make a bunch more batches of Rhombus's until I have enough.

You can make these pieces out of conventional wood stocks. Left over scraps would work perfectly. I started out with logs because I wanted to do something with my own wood. That is optional. You will need to make a cutting jig though even if you use different wood.

Have fun with it.

# tech

Ever since primitive humans started shaping sticks and stones into tools for food foraging, technology has been an integral part of the human experience. As humanity evolved, our technology has evolved with us, gaining momentum with each additional innovation. Technological innovation is now progressing at such a staggering exponential rate that it is hard to keep up with it—which is just how it should be!

The projects that follow are prime examples of people's desire to ever innovate. Whether creating something practical like a low-cost eye-tracking device for ALS patients, or something more whimsical like a clap-off bra, the projects that follow are not only advancing technological innovation, but are providing cutting edge technology to regular people.

# Cloning Sheep

## By Plusea
(http://www.instructables.com/id/Cloning-Sheep/)

This Instructable describes how to clone a willing sheep. First of all you need a volunteer sheep with good intentions, who will not mind to be cloned and reproduced multiple times. In the case of the sheep that I chose to clone, he had a secret plan for world domination.

Sheep cloning project website: http://www.plusea.at/?p=508

## Step 1: Materials and Tools
- 1 Sheep volunteer
- 3D scanner
- 3D printer
- Mold casting material
- Plaster, gypsum or other casting materials
- Casting equipment: mold release spray, cups, sticks, newspaper . . . .
- Good intentions

## Step 2: 3D Scan
Get your sheep subject to sit still while you 3D scan them. Sheep tend to get super excited to representations of themselves and are easily distracted.

Once you have a clean 3D scan, you still might need to clean up the data, close all the holes and prepare it for printing.

## Step 3: 3D Print
From your 3D scan you can now print out the first replication of your sheep. You will need to keep your original sheep close at hand though, to make sure the 3D print bears a close resemblance.

After 3D printing the first sheep clone must undergo a horrible etching bath to remove support material. Be nice to them and reward them for undergoing this process. It is not fun.

And, as the original, also its clones are fascinated by representations of the self and are easily distracted by them.

## Step 4: Mold Making
3D printing is not a cheap process, so in order to make multiples of your 3D printed clone sheep it is best to make a mold from it so that you can cast multiples.

Build a rig from legos and submerge half of the clone sheep in liquid polyurethane, which becomes rubbery when cured. Once one half is ready apply Vaseline to the surface and fill up the other half. This way the two halves do not stick together and you can open up the mold to safely remove clone sheep.

## Step 5: Casting
To make replicas of sheep you need to prepare the mold for casting. Make the hole in the mold (the result of how you mounted your sheep when casting the mold) cylindrical so that the casting material will flow in nicely and that it is big enough for air-bubbles to escape.

Use mold release to ensure your casting materials will not stick to the mold. Use rubber bands to hold the two mold halves together.

Prepare your casting materials. Pour into mold. Let Cure. Remove.

The clones of your clone resemble your clone much more than your first cone resembles the original. This can lead to tensions and might require some effort on your behalf in making them all feel comfortable around each other.

## Step 6: Mass-cloning
Now you're all set to replicate your sheep as many times as you want. The casting process does not always run smoothly so do not worry if a few of your clones turn out different (missing parts of the body, or miss-aligned mold halves . . . ) you should still love them and count them to your army of sheep.

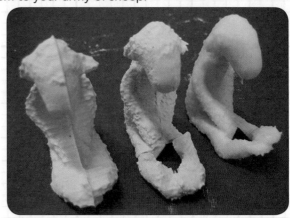

# The Droidalyzer—An Open Source, Bluetooth Alcohol Detector Accessory for Android Phones

By Al Linke (alinke)

(http://www.instructables.com/id/The-Android-Breathalyzer/)

The Droidalyzer is an open source, Bluetooth alcohol detector accessory for Android Phones. Pair the Bluetooth enabled Droidalyzer to your Android phone and then use it to detect your alcohol level.

The Droidalyzer is not a professional Breathalyzer and is for entertainment purposes (i.e., fun). It does not output a blood alcohol content (BAC) reading and rather plays different audio responses relative to alcohol levels with four character voices to choose from. After each alcohol reading, you're prompted with various options such as calling a preset designated driver, calling a taxi, finding nearby friends and places (via Facebook integration), and even a random drunk dial option if you're feeling adventurous.

### Hardware features

- Small form factor, easily fits in your pocket
- Doubles as a phone charger with the included re-chargeable battery (use a standard USB charger)
- Mouth piece not required to keep things sanitary when sharing the alcohol detector among friends

### Android app features

- Four selectable characters (old english gentleman, pirate, spooky, and mean guy) who speak the alcohol detection results in their own personality
- Verbal alcohol detection responses can also be person-

alized using Text to Speech
- Support for English, French, Spanish, and Simplified Chinese
- Pre-store designated driver and taxi phone numbers
- Simulation mode that allows you to try the app without the hardware

This is the DIY version if you want to build your own from scratch. A productized version is available at http://droidalyzer.com.

### Materials:

- Altoids Tin—$2
- IOIO Board—$50
- Seeed Lipo Rider—$10
- Seeed Grove Alcohol Sensor—$8
- LIPO Battery—$6
- Bluetooth Dongle—$5
- On/Off Switch—$1
- Another IOIO board or a PIC3KIT programmer (required if using Bluetooth to upgrade the IOIO firmware to Bluetooth compatible)
- Android Phone—2.3.3 or above if using Bluetooth. Android 1.6 and above will also work but you'll need to connect the Droidalyzer to your phone with a USB cable as opposed to using Bluetooth.

The key component of this project is the IOIO board (pronounced yoyo) which enables an Android phone to receive data from external sensors (an alcohol sensor in this case). There are a few other methods to interface Android to external sensors including new hardware and an API from Google called ADK but IOIO in my opinion is the most mature and the easiest way to go. Plus this project needs to communicate over Bluetooth as opposed to a hardwired USB cable, which ADK does not support. Ytai Ben-Tsvi, the guy who runs IOIO, has things well documented at IOIO Wiki as well as an active support community for questions and was kind enough to allow us to use IOIO in this project.

(http://www.youtube.com/watch?v=Iaaznp5IcQ8&feature=player_embedded)

A little more nitty gritty detail on how it works

(http://www.youtube.com/watch?v=q2Reqfw44pY&feature=player_embedded)

## Step 1: Preparing the components

First thing you'll need to do is upgrade your IOIO to be Bluetooth ready.

If you're using an Altoids tin for the enclosure, you'll need to de-solder the connectors on the Seeed Grove alochol sensor and Seeed LIPO rider as there won't be enough room with the connectors to mount everything inside the tin.

## Step 2: Schematic

Pin 40 gets the analog output of the alcohol sensor.

Heating up the alcohol sensor takes up battery life. So to conserve the battery, the app will only turn on/heat

tech

up the alcohol sensor when it is needed. When pin 1 is LOW, power goes to heat up the alcohol sensor. When pin 1 is HIGH, power is turned off to the alcohol sensor.

The Seeed LiPO Rider takes the 3.3V out from the LiPO battery and outputs the 5VDC that the IOIO needs to run. Plug any standard USB charger into the mini USB port on the Seeed LiPO Rider to charge the battery.

## Step 3: Assembly

Wire up everything per the schematic and be sure to leave enough length in the wires such that you can mount all the components in the Altoids tin. Like any project, do a test with your Android phone before final mounting to ensure everything is working as it should. The pictures illustrate the assembly positioning of the components.

## Step 4: The Droidalyzer Android app

The Droidalyzer Android app is available on the Android Market from the link and QR code below. The app has a simulation mode so even if you don't have the Droidalyzer hardware, you can still install the app (it's free) and play around to see the functionality knowing of course it won't detect any actual alcohol without the Droidalyzer hardware. You can also see how it works from the screen grabs below.

App Link from Android Market (Free) (https://play. google.com/store/apps/details?id=talkingbreathalyzer. main.source)

Once you've got the app, pair the Droidalyzer to your Android phone. This pairing will only work on Android phones 2.3.3 and above, the bluetooth pairing code is: 4545 and the Droidalyzer will show up as "IOIO" in Bluetooth settings. If you've got a phone below Android 2.3.3 but above 1.6, then you can still do the project but not over Bluetooth and instead will need to use a USB cable to connect the Breathalyzer to the phone. If using a USB cable, then you'll also need to turn on USB debugging. From your phone, go to Settings —> Applications —> Development —> USB debugging (ensure the box is checked).

Note also that not all Android phones support IOIO, a list of supported Android phones can be found here: (https://groups.google.com/forum/#!topic/ioio-users/pW0wlUQnlUl)

After you've got the Droidalyzer paired or USB connected, then launch the app and if all goes well, the top of the screen will read "Breathalyzer Status: Connected."

Note that the Droidalyzer is not a professional breathalyzer and is for entertainment purposes only (i.e., fun) and by no means should be used to determine whether or not one should drive after consuming alcohol. It does not output BAC but rather outputs 4 levels of alcohol consumption: No Alcohol Detected, Almost Sober, Tipsy, and Drunk.

# Candied LEDs

By Emily Daniels (emdaniels)
(http://www.instructables.com/id/Candied-LEDs/)

A fun experiment combining simple electronics and common food stuffs. You'll need:

- 4 cups of sugar
- 2 cups of water
- Wire
- electrical tape
- assorted LEDs
- paper cups
- wax paper
- stove
- medium sized pot

## Step 1: Preparing the sugar syrup

Boil the 2 cups of water in the medium sized pot, adding the sugar 1 cup at a time and waiting for it to dissolve. It's important to keep stirring the pot and not to let the sugar cook too much or it will burn.

## Step 2: Wrapping the LEDs

Take the LEDs, wire and electrical tape and wrap the wire around the leads, securing them with the tape. Wet the heads of the LEDs slightly and roll them in sugar to coat them and provide a base for the crystals to grow.

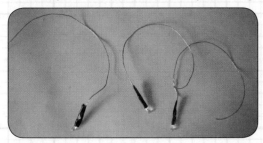

## Step 3: Pouring the syrup

After turning the sugar syrup off wait 5-10 minutes for it to cool, then pour it into either glass jars or paper cups. My first attempt was with glass jars but I found the crystallization took too long so I transferred the mixture to individual paper cups and that made it much easier. Wrap the ends of the wire around a pencil and lower it into the cups, adjusting the wire wraps to the height of the sugar line so that the head of the LED is totally immersed in the sugar.

## Step 4: Unwrapping the crystals

Set aside in a cool place away from direct light and wait 1-4 weeks, depending on how large you want the crystals to be. Peel off the paper cup from the sugar crystal and carefully break off the unconnected crystals from the main crystal formation around the head. Running it under warm water helps.

## Step 5: Dry and test

Set on a sheet of wax paper and allow to dry for a day or so. After completely dry, test with a 3V coin cell battery. You'll notice that the sugar helps diffuse and extend the luminosity of the LED to a much larger area.

## Step 6: Play!

I'd advise you not to eat this experiment. LEDs are small enough to be accidentally swallowed so use caution if you do this experiment with kids. Have fun!

My obsession with LEDs has led me to this. Aurora 9x18 is a thing of beauty (if I can say so myself)—162 RGB-LEDs in a circular configuration. The color of each circle is controlled by a microcontroller using a twisted form of PWM.

The microcontroller (PIC24F08KA101) only has one PWM module, yet Aurora is capable of 27 (9xR,G,B) independent brightness control. This Instructable reveals the inner-working of Aurora 9x18 through the building process.

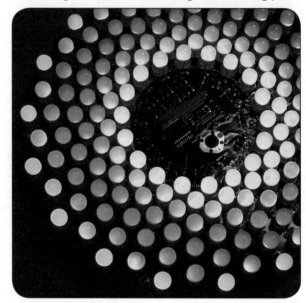

## Step 1: Concept

A RGB LED is nothing more than a LED that actually encases 3 small LEDs of primary colors inside. RGB LEDs can create wide range of colors by combining 3 primary colors—Red, Green, and Blue. By changing the ratio between the 3 colors, you get many in-between colors. RGB LEDs are often called full-color LEDs.

Most of the brightness controlling circuit utilizes the method called PWM. Many of microcontrollers today have a PWM controller or more built in; however there are usually less than 4 or 5 of them in a controller. So if I were to control 9 LEDs, I would need to use multiple controllers or external circuits. If those 9 LEDs were RGB LEDs, then there would be 27 PWM controllers needed.

I've gone through a few approaches—multiple microcontrollers working together in various configurations—and some are complex and exotic. I was trying to solve more than just the number of LEDs that I can control—I wanted to make the fades in/out of brightness as smooth

as possible. Turned out, 8 to 10 bit PWM resolution that most PIC microcontrollers provide was not good enough to create smooth transition in the darker/dimmer part of the brightness change. When the brightness is low, the transitions look more like steps than fading. Due to human eye's non-linear or exponential response to light, intensity necessitates gamma correction of the brightness change curve, which requires at least 12 bits of PWM resolution to give smooth fades (in my conclusion).

If I simply design a circuit where each LED is controlled by it's own PWM controller having 12 bit or more resolution, I'd have to use a speciality LED controller IC. While this solves the problem, the added cost and size to the final product did not appeal to me. (Those LED controller IC are not very small or cheap.)

So I came up with an idea of combining PWM with multiplex drive. I further broke up each PWM cycle into multiple pulses, so that multiple LEDs were lit multiple times within one PWM cycle. (Kind of a hybrid between PWM and PDM, I guess.) This way, the average output of LEDs are a sum of the many pulses within the short period. So combining more than one PWM pulses increases effective PWM resolution.

This technique also helpes reduce the perceived flicker of the light out of LEDs. Aurora 9x18's LED refresh rate is about 246 Hz, but LEDs blink a lot more often. This creates the illusion of a much higher refresh rate.

R/G/B buses go up momentarily, taking turns. These pulses control the actual duration that LEDs light up. Each common lead of the LEDs controls whether that LED will light during the period that R/G/B buses increase. The actual timing that LEDs light up are marked with the color.

The condition here is:
- LED 1 is on level 1 red (the lowest brightness)
- LED 2 is on level 2 green
- LED 3 is on level 3 blue
- LED 4 is on level 3 yellow (red + green)
- LED 5 is on level 3 purple (red + blue)
- LED 6 is on level 3 turquoise (green + blue)
- LED 7 is on level 255 (maximum brightness) white

\* time scale is about 8.1 ms for the entire width of the chart.

Hope this explains the way Aurora controls the brightness/colors of LEDs.

**References:**
- (http://en.wikipedia.org/wiki/Pulse-width_modulation)
- (http://en.wikipedia.org/wiki/Pulse-density_modulation)

## Step 2: Circuit

Aurora 9x18 has 18 RGB LEDs in each of 9 circles, a total of 162 LEDs. Each circle of LEDs are connected in parallel, so there are 9 LED circuits (x3 because they are RGB) to control.

I chose PIC24F08KA101 as the controller. It needed to be powerful enough (16 bit), and requires minimal external parts (no crystal needed to run at the max speed of 32 MHz) to save space.

The circuit itself is quite simple. The microcontroller is connected to a joystick-like switch (5 switches in it) and there are 3 MOSFETs and 12 BJTs controlling the current that goes into LEDs. There's a 3.3V linear voltage regulator to supply for the PIC as well. (The LED circuit is driven by 5V power.)

If you look at this circuit you might realize that it's just like 9x3 matrix circuit, but instead 3 rows are replaced with 3 primary colors of RGB LEDs. So now you know that RGB channels are multiplexed—in other words those 3 colors turn on one by one, not together at the same time. In general I don't like multiplexing, but I needed to compromise in favor for the simplicity and physical space.

Given that this microcontroller only has one PWM module (to control the brightness of LEDs), I had to come up with a way of extending that PWM signal into 3. I'm doing that with a simple "AND" logic utilizing the lower part of the R/G/B bus driving circuit. In short, R-BUS only turns on when PWM signal is high and R-DRV signal is low. For G-BUS, PWM -> high and G-DRV -> low, and so on. This circuit works remarkably well, saving my precious space on the board and a few dimes.

I'm using MOSFET on the high-side switch simply because BJTs that I can find in the small package do not handle the current drawn by 162 LEDs in parallel (about 3 A peak!). This MOSFET (DMP3098L) has a remarkable current handling capability. Highly recommended.

Low-side (column, or each LED) driver/switch circuit is very straight forward. NPN BJT is a common emitter configuration.

There are 1k Ohm resistors connected to the output of each driver. Those resistors help the transistors turn off quicker when there are no LEDs conducting (transistors turn off quicker when there is current going through drain or collector). Those transistors are switching at the timing in the order of nanoseconds, so turn on/off speed becomes critical.

In a nutshell, those resistors allow PWM to run at a higher speed (less visible flicker).

**References:**
- (http://ww1.microchip.com/downloads/en/DeviceDoc/PIC24F16KA102_Family_datasheet_39927b.pdf)
- (http://ww1.microchip.com/downloads/en/DeviceDoc/PIC24F16KA102_Family_datasheet_39927b.pdf)

## Step 3: PCB

I wanted to make this object as small as possible, so designing the PCB took some work. In reality, I went back and forth between the circuit design and PCB design, trying to reduce part count to the minimum.

I had the PCB fabricated by DorkbotPDX. They have a community based PCB program (kind of like BatchPCB) that I like. As you can see, the boards are beautifully manufactured (in the USA). The solder mask is dark purple.

**Links**
- http://dorkbotpdx.org/wiki/pcb_order

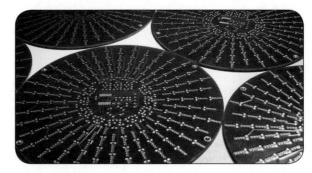

## Step 4: Parts

Here are the list of parts, or BOM. You can download a BOM file that can be uploaded to Digi-Key for quick ordering.
- 162x 150Ohm (0603)
- 9x 220 Ohm (0603)
- 13x 1k Ohm (0603)
- 3x 470 Ohm (0603)
- 1x 10k Ohm (0603)
- 2x 10uF (0603)
- 1x 1uF (0603)
- 1x AP7333-33 or AP7313-33
- 3x DMP3098L
- 12x MMBT2222A
- 1x PIC24F08KA101
- 1x 4-way Stick Switch (Panasonic EVQQ7)
- 162x 5mm Tricolor LED (common-cathode)—AliExpress.com
- 1x 5V regulated power supply or 4 NiMH batteries and case

I source LEDs directly from China via AliExpress. Takes a few days for delivery, but the prices are great. Other parts are available at Digi-Key.

You can substitute transistors if you have something compatible. BJTs can be substituted by a number of others; finding substitutes for the MOSFET might not be easy, however.

## Step 5: Tools and supplies
- Magnifier visor or other visual aid device
- Solder paste in syringe
- Tweezers
- Electric hot plate
- Soldering iron
- Solder (Flux core. Go for the highest quality solder you can afford.)
- Wire cutter (I recommend this one.)

- Microchip PIC programmer (supports PIC24F08KA and capable of In-circuit programming through a standard 6-pin ICSP connector) and a computer

## Step 6: Assembly

Due to the high number of part count (371 parts), and tight and unusual placements, the assembly requires excellent soldering skills and takes quite an effort.

As most of the parts are SMD (surface mount device), I use the "paste, place and grill" method. If you have built a few things with SMD, you would know what I mean. There are many ways to solder SMD parts, and you are free to go with any method that you are comfortable with. I will show how I've done this one.

Count and prepare all SMD parts for the placement. I recommend prepping the SMD parts, so that they are ready to be placed on the PCB as soon as you dispensed the solder paste on it.

## Step 7: Assembly 2—Dispense solder paste on PCB

I wanted to use stencil for this step, but unfortunately due to the PCB layout I could not have made the stencil (low cost stencils cannot contain non 90 degree angle parts). So I manually dispense microscopic dubs of solder paste using a syringe. This is a tortuous process.

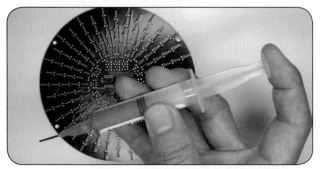

## Step 8: Assembly 3—Place SMD parts on PCB

After the mind-numbing process of dispensing solder paste, you get to pick and place the SMD parts. Due to the overwhelming number of parts, you need to proceed with a plan. Please follow the part placement guide that I prepared. This PCB does not have markings for parts (for a cosmetic reason), you will have to rely on the placement guide for correct placement.

I recommend following the order listed, starting from the center and moving outwards. Also be mindful of electrostatic charge. Use anti-static desk mat if you have one. Or place aluminum foil under the PCB like I do.

Pay extra attention to the orientation of the switch. With this switch placed in a wrong orientation, you can't even program the microcontroller. Then you will need hot air reworking equipment to remove the switch. (Yes, I made that mistake once and had to purchase a hot air tool . . . ) This one is more obvious, but make sure that the PIC is in the correct orientation as well.

P.S. careful not to over caffeinate yourself when you

work on SMD placement. You fingers will shake, and make the placement difficult.

## Step 9: Assembly 4—Grill

I then place the PCB on a hot plate. (Yes, the one from the kitchen.) I'm using an old and retired one. So long as it heats up hot enough, it will get the job done—I think. A laser thermometer is a must, unless you've done this a million times so you know the temperature setting by heart.

After carefully placing the PCB (not to disturb the SMD parts on it) on the hot plate (I use the center part, because the temperature seems to be more stable there), turn on the power. I'd turn the temperature control to the highest, then watch the actual temperature of the hot plate around the PCB. Then turn down the dial when the temperature hits close to 160 degrees C (yes, I use Celsius here). Then try keeping the temperature around the same for a minute or two. Then finally turn up the dial again to let the temperature hit over 200 degrees. At this point, you'll see the solder melt and maybe a little smoke coming off the solder paste.

As soon as you can see all the solder paste melted, turn of the hot plate. Some people keep the PCB on the hot plate to cool down, but I get too nervous so I take it off. However, be careful not to cool the PCB down too quickly. (Do not place it on a cold surface.) Use tweezers to handle the PCB of course.

After the PCB has cooled down enough to touch, it's time for inspection. I wear a magnifier visor to examine all the details. Unless you are super good (or maybe I'm not good enough), there will be a few things to fix. SSOP (PIC24F) legs are close together, so check carefully for bridging. I always have to use solder wick to un-bridge them.)

## Step 10: Assembly 5—Electronic check & Programming

Before moving on further, take out your multi-tester and check the Ohm reading of the power connector and ICP connector pads. Make sure there are no shorts.

Then fire up your PC, launch Microchip IDE and program the PIC microcontroller on the PCB with the HEX file provided. You need to connect a 5V regulated power supply—I use a straight 2 pin header to supply the 5V to the PCB (be mindful of the polarity—round pad is positive and square pad is negative), and a 5 pin header to connect (square pad marks the MCLR pin) the programmer. Mine is ICD 2, but any compatible programmer should work.

If your programmer is an older one like mine, you need to make sure that the programming voltage for high voltage programming mode is below 9V. Microchip suggest using high-speed shunt regulator on MCLR pin to clip the voltage—I found this overkill—I just put a 7.5 V zener diode between MCLR and GND. It works! Just use the PCB pads as though they are the female connector. Give a bit of tension sideways to make sure the electrical connection is stable.

If all is well, you'll see the IDE reporting successful programming. If not, go back to more inspection.

## Step 11: Assembly 6—Testing the LEDs

Since there are some percentage of defects in any parts and it sucks to find out that the LED you just soldered onto the PCB was defective, I'd test all 162 LEDs before soldering onto the PCB.

Since testing RGB-LED with a multi-tester is tedious, and there are no RGB-LED tester commercially available, I have a home made a RGB-LED tester.

It's a simple rig with an 8 bit microcontroller (PIC16F627) I just had laying around. It takes 5 minutes to put together, and I promise that I will put another Instructable on it.

Desoldering and removing through-hole parts from PCB is a pain and sometimes damages the PCB. Testing the LEDs is totally worth the time.

## Step 12: Assembly 7—Soldering LEDs

You are almost there! As an added assurance, do a quick test. Stick 9 LEDs into the holes—make sure that the orientation is correct, and push in tight. Put them into two straight lines. Then connect the power. If you see the color fading, you really are almost there.

Now try keeping your head cool and carry on with the assembly. Now remove the 9 LEDs that you tested with.

You need to cut the leads of LEDs before you insert into the PCB, like the picture shown.

Then insert the LEDs starting from the inner-most circle. Flip over and solder. Then connect the power and check if all LEDs are working. Repeat until you solder all of the LEDs.

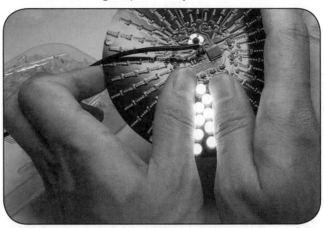

## Step 13: Assembly 8—Power Supply

I use 2 pin Molex connector to connect the power supply. The supply needs to be 5V regulated type with at least 1A capacity. You can remove the plug from the AC adapter and attach an Molex plug like I did, or solder the leads from the power supply directly to the PCB.

You can also use NiMH batteries to power Aurora 9x18. 4 NiMH batteries connected in series provide just about 5V, perfect power supply for most circuits that call for regulated 5V power. 4 AA NiMH can power Aurora 9x18 for hours.

## Step 14: Enjoy!

I hope you enjoy the beautiful and hypnotic color patterns as much as I do. I have 5 well tweaked parameters in current firmware to choose from. The up/down of the switch changes the pattern, while left/right changes the speed. Push of the switch pauses/un-pauses the move. Hold down the switch for two seconds turns the lights off.

There might be more functions added to the firmware, as there is a plenty of room left on the programming memory.

The 5 pin header contains two pins that can be used as analog inputs—so there are possibilities of adding interactivity based on analog input, such as sound. Hackers are invited.

# Interactive LED Table

## By Deadly Computer
### (http://www.instructables.com/id/Interactive-LED-table/)

Here is a guided instructable on how to make your own Interactive LED table using one of the kits from Evil Mad Sciencitst (http://www.evilmadscientist.com/article.php/tablekits).

## Step 1: Choose your size, and design a table

Evil Mad Scientist offers 2 sizes for their table, a 6 panel kit and an 8 panel kit. Both of them can be configured in 3 different ways, so before you can start designing your table, you should choose which size you want to buy. I chose the 6 panel kit, and this instructable will focus on that size. If you choose the 8 panel kit, you can still use this guide, just remember to change the measurements to your own. Next make a rough sketch of how you want your table to look. If you are good with Google Sketchup, I suggest you use that to get some nice 3-D views of it.

## Step 2: Buy the lumber

After you've made your design, and measured out all the materials you need, time to take a trip (or two as in most cases with DIY stuff) to Home Depot/Lowes to get the wood. I choose regular 1x4 pieces of pine for the legs, and 1x3 pieces for the tray to hold the LEDs.

## Step 3: Put the legs together

Lay out the wood on the floor (or table), and make the marks for cuts. Cut them (use a miter saw—much, much more accurate then by hand), be sure to choose the nicer side of the wood for the top* (if you're staining it, if painting, it doesn't matter). I'm doubling up the wood so that it looks better, that requires lots of cuts, and screws. Pre-drill the holes, and counter-sink the screws so that you don't see them.

## Step 4: Fill in the holes

After the legs are built, you should fill in the cracks and screw holes with wood filler. I also ran a router with a 1/4 inch half circle bit around the edges to smooth them off, and make them look nicer. Then sand it, and repeat it until it is smooth enough for you (it is after all, your table).

## Step 5: Stain & polyurethane (or paint) the legs

I chose Minwax Cherry 235 for the stain color, and Minwax Polyurethane for the finish on my table, you can choose whatever you want. I also put 3 coats of stain, and 2 coats of polyurethane on them so that it would look good.

## Step 6: Build the tray to hold the LEDs

The tray is a very important part of the build process.

The LEDs and circuit board must be rigidly attached to something, and that's where the tray comes in. You can make the tray any size you want (as long as it's bigger than the minimum size your boards can fit in). Mine is 46x31 inches.

I decided to use a 1/8in piece of MDF in a tray of 1x3 pine. 1/2 inch from the bottom of the 1x3's we made a 1/8 diameter groove to slide the MDF in.

Originally, I wanted to have the ends connected via tongue and groove notches and glue, but we didn't have the correct tools (even though we tried our best to make them), so I just opted to screw the ends together, it works just the same, and looks just as good (most people will be looking at the top anyway!)

## Step 7: Cross braces

Without them, the table will just fall apart (well, not really, but they add a lot of stability). Put both sets of legs on top of each other, and tray on top of that, take the wood you're using for the cross brace, and measure it out, mark it, and cut (it helps to have 2 or more people for this part).

Sand the edges to make it a little nicer-looking and you're done.

## Step 8: Get the kit parts together

Now comes the most exciting part, making the individual boards that contain the LEDs, and all that fun stuff. All this stuff is included in the kit from Evil Mad Scientist, depending on the size of the kit, and other options (PCB color, LED color(s), your items may differ). It will help to get a good soldering iron, and some replacement tips. As for the 1lb of solder, it's the smallest size they sold online, and no, I did not use all of it.

## Step 9: Solder lots of LEDs, and resistors in

The kits come with very detailed instructions on how to put in the resistors, capacitors, LEDs, and microchips. It's a very simple, if not long process.

The most time consuming process is matching the LEDs. That took me about an hour per board. But after some communication with the guys over at EMS, I learned that I was just being way too OCD about it, and really should only take a minute or two per set. (That should be reflected in the newest instructions sent with the kits I've been told).

## Step 10: Repeat step 9 five (or seven) more times

Repeat step 9 five more times if you have the 6 panel kit, or seven more times if the 8 panel kit. You definitely want to test each panel as you finish them, this way you can be sure they all work. Here is a video of the 5 panels connected together:

(http://www.youtube.com/watch?v=Wp5STHMym4E &feature=player_embedded)

## Step 11: Attach legs to the tray

This is where I made a slight modification to my table design. Originally, I had the legs bolted to the outside of the tray, but after getting the opinions of my friends, I found out that that isn't exactly the best looking solution.

Finally, I decided that because there was 2.25 extra inches on the inside of the tray, I would cut one part of the legs off, to insert behind it.

## Step 12: Put the PCBs into the tray

Take apart the tested panels, and begin positioning them inside the tray. (Note, they should only be able to fit one way if you made the tray the correct size.)

Be sure to decide where you want the switch, and power plug to be located, so you can drill an access hole for those before you install that board.

The PDBs come with 3/4 long 6-32 standoffs to give clearance. The 3/4 inches wasn't enough to get over the bolts for the legs, so we used 1.5 inch screws with nuts keeping them from moving down.

(Note: The closer you get to the sensors, the brighter the effect is, so that's another advantage to moving them up a further 3/4 of an inch.)

## Step 13: Put the glass on

We put 1/4 inch wide black speaker gasket around the top of the try to prevent the glass from slipping around. It gives the table a nice finished look, I think.

## Step 14: You're done, time to play!

That's it, you're finished!

After all that hard work, you should have a very nice, very fun, very awesome interactive LED table.

Total cost for this table: around $650, the most expensive part being the kit from EMS. Considering you can buy pre-made tables for up to $2200, I'd say it's totally worth doing it yourself!

## Digital Window Sticker (Arduino Controlled)

By Andrew L. Sandoval (als_liahona)
(http://www.instructables.com/id/Digital-
Window-Sticker-Arduino-Controlled/)

A bumper-sticker sized L.E.D. matrix that displays images in sequence from an SD card, to produce an animated sign or "window sticker." Arduino controlled! Also includes Windows, Mac, and Linux code for converting .xbm image files into Digital Window Sticker files. Perfect for a shop or home window, or a fun desktop sign!

### Step 1: Parts list

Digital Window Sticker Parts List

- 1 Arduino Compatible Bare Bones Board KIT (BBBKit), ask for the LM7805 regulator!, $15.00
- 1 USB BUB Board, optional, see notes . . . ,$12.00
- 2 2416 Dot Matrix Display DE-DP016, now available in Green: DE-DP017, see not, $11.64 (23.28)
- 1 Radio Shack Printed Circuit Board 276-170, see PCB note below, $2.99
- 1 Radio Shack 8x6x3 Project Enclosure 270-1809, $6.99
- 1 74HC4050 Hex NON-Inverting Buffer *, $0.09
- 1 16-pin DIP Socket, $0.75
- 1 LM3940 3.3v Regulator, $1.75
- 1 .47uF Tantalum Capacitor, $0.32
- 1 33uF Tantalum Capacitor *, $0.19
- 1 33uF Electrolytic Capacitor *, $0.11
- 1 1x20 Female .100" header receptacle, see header receptacle note below, $0.75
- 1 2x8 Shrouded Box Header, $0.49
- 1 Breakout Board for SD-MMC Card, see SD-MMC Card note below, $17.95
- 8 4-40 3/4" machine screws with 2 nuts each, $3.98
- 1 Low Capacity SD Card (e.g. 512 MB)
- 1 9-volt power source
- Solder and 22-gauge wire of various colors

NOTE: The BBB Kit is an Arduino clone produced by moderndevice.com. At $15.00 for a complete Arduino kit, it is one of the least expensive options. I could have cut a few dollars off of the cost by using an alternate Arduino

board and a separate supply list for each Arduino component, but the convenience of a single supplier for the Arduino portion of this project was worth the $3 to $5 I may have saved. You should be able to make this project with any Arduino.

The USB BUB Board plugs into the BBB (Arduino). It has the FTDI USB to serial converter needed to program your BBB Arduino. If you have already have an ICSP programmer, or an Arduino with a ZIF socket for programming the Atmega 328p, it is not necessary to purchase the USB BUB, though it is useful if debugging the microcontroller code, through the Arduino IDE's Serial Port Monitor.

**PCBs**

If you wish to follow the step-by-step instructions I am providing you will need the Radio Shack printed circuit board, and you will need to trim the ends of it to fit properly in the enclosure. This also means you need a right-angle connector on the 2x8 Shrouded Box Header (that the ribbon cable from the displays plugs into). The right-angle connector is required so that the pins can be bent to bridge the breadboard gap on the Radio Shack PCB.

**Jameco***

Each of the items listed above with an asterisk(*) can be purchased from Jameco, but require a minimum order of 10, so if calculating the cost keep this in mind. (It is always good to have extra parts!)

**Header Receptacle**

The BBB has 18-pins for the power-supply and Arduino pins to plug into a breadboard. Use the 20-pin header receptacle to plug the BBB into your printed circuit board as shown in the following instructions, with the following variations:

- I did not have a 20-pin header receptacle, but I did have 2 8-pin receptacles. This will work fine. It is a tight fit to get them to align properly, but it works. You'll notice that 2 of the BBB pins are left unconnected.
- If you use the 20-pin header receptacle, 2-pins will remain unconnected. Mark your board so that when you plug-in the BBB you know where it goes.
- You could also forgo the breadboard pins on the BBB, and the socket on the secondary PCB, and simply run wires directly to the needed locations. This may provide some flexibility with enclosures.

The 2x8 Shrouded header box is for plugging in the ribbon cable from the display matrices. As mentioned above under PCBs, the right-angle version is needed if you have a gap like that on the Radio Shack PCB. You could possibly use the same board and cut copper traces to make a straight header box work properly. I purchased my header box from a local supplier (M.C. Howards Electronics in Austin, TX), but they only had a few and I've not seen any more in subsequent trips.

**SD-MMC Card**

Wow, this is an over-priced component if there ever was one. It works great! In fact, don't bother with any of the Arduino SD card Shields.

Finally, use a variety of wires when wiring the PCB. It

will make it easier to trace connections. As you will see, I used red, black, green, yellow, and white. I wish I had more colors.

Regarding the 9-volt power supply: A 9 volt battery will work, but you will have strange problems when it begins to diminish. Once the battery voltage (when tested on a meter) drops below 7 volts your display may light up fine, but there will be insufficient current to power the Arduino and the behavior is somewhat unpredictable. A 9 volt wall-wart works great, and the LM7805 on the BBB should be able to handle a 12-volt input, like that from an auto-adapter.

**Tools**

I used the following tools to complete this project:
- A quality, variable wattage soldering iron
- Wire cutters
- Wire strippers
- A multimeter (helpful for testing)
- A large solder-less breadboard, for testing—you may not need this
- A Dremel, with cutting wheels and drill bits (for making openings in the enclosure case)
- A variable speed drill and various drill bits

  ***Software***
- Arduino IDE 0017
- My micro controller code (see Step 3)
- GIMP image editor, or another editor capable of producing .xbm files
- My xbmtodws code, to create image files for the SD card from .xbm files

## Step 2: Assemble the BBB Arduino and USB BUB

Follow the instructions provided by Modern Device to assemble the BBB Arduino. Instructions: (http://moderndevice.com/Docs/BBB_RevE_Instructions03.pdf).

When assembling the BBB, remember to use an LM7805 voltage regulator in place of the L4931CZ50LDO. The smaller voltage regulator might work

just fine, but we are pulling quite a bit of current to power up to 768 L.E.D.s. The optional inductor is not needed for this project. You can follow the instructions on creating a solder bridge if you'd prefer to save the inductor, or if you'd rather not deal with the surface mount component. Nevertheless, it is not difficult to solder and I used it on my board.

If you also purchased the USB-BUB follow the assembly instructions to complete it. Instructions: (http://moderndevice.com/Docs/BUB_instructions.02.pdf)

When assembling the USB-BUB, I selected Configuration 2, though in practice I only ever use Configuration 1 (no jumper).

## Step 3: Program your Arduino
### BBB jumpers

Set the USB|EXT jumper on your BBB to the USB side so that we can program it using the USB-BUB without supplying an external power-supply. (Or, supply a 9 volt power supply on the D.C. input jack and keep the jumper on the EXT side.) When this step is completed you want to move the jumper back to the EXT side!

The other jumper with +5v|EXT|+V should be on the +5v side always.

### FAT16 library installation

Next, download the FAT16 library and the Digital-WindowSticker.pde file below. The FAT16 library needs to be unzipped/untared into the hardware/libraries directory where your Arduino IDE is located. On my Windows system, I keep the current version of the Arduino IDE in c:\temp\arduino-0017\. Once the FAT16 library is in place there should be a set of files in [c:\temp\arduino-0017\\hardware\libraries\Fat16\. The FAT16 library is also available here: http://code.google.com/p/fat16lib/. It is written by Bill Grieman. A copy of this library that is known to work with the Digital Window Sticker is available in the files below (Fat16.tar.gz or Fat16.zip).

### Arduino IDE

Start the Arduino IDE.

Open the DigitalWindowSticker.pde file using the IDE. There are two ways you can do this:
- Download and open the file in a text editor, copy the contents to the clipboard, paste the contents into a new sketch in the Arduino IDE, and then save the sketch as DigitalWindowSticker
- Download the DigitalWindowSticker.zip or DigitalWindowSticker.tar.gz file and extract the files to the directory containing your sketches. Then open the Digital-WindowSticker sketch in the Arduino IDE.

Next, compile the sketch. If there are any errors, make sure you are using version 0017 of the Arduino IDE, with the Atmega328 board selected (Arduino Duemilanove or Nano w/Atmega328). Also make sure you've properly unpacked the FAT16 library, into the hardware/libraries directory, where other Arduino libraries reside.

### Program the Arduino

Plug-in the USB-BUB, and wait for the drivers to be

installed, or coach your system into loading the drivers. In the Arduino IDE, a new COM port should show up under Tools|Serial Port. Select the new port for the USB-BUB.

Plug the USB-BUB into the BBB as shown in the photo in Step 2, and Upload the compiled code from the Arduino IDE.

### Prepare for External Power Source

Now that the Arduino is programmed, move the BBB jumper back to the EXT side (not the USB side) so that it will be powered by the external 9 volt source.

## Step 4: Assemble the SD-MMC Card Breakout Board

Simply solder a set of header pins to the SD-MMC card breakout board.

### Alternatives

- Uses wires to connect the SD-MMC card breakout board directly to the printed circuit board in the next step. Doing so will give you flexibility with where the SD card socket is located in your enclosure.
- Solder a bare SD card socket to your selected printed circuit board as part of the next step.

### Notes:

Only the following pins are used:

- CS (for SPI access to the SD Card)
- DI (data input for SPI access to the SD Card)
- VCC is the 3.3v power source for the card
- GND is the common ground
- DO is the data output, which can be connected directly to pin 12 of the Arduino
- WP is used to detect a missing card. This will be connected to pin 2 of the Arduino
- COM needs to be connected to GND

## Step 5: Build the circuit

Use the schematic below as a reference as you build the circuit. An Eagle schematic file is attached as well as a the image file Schematic.png. Use the photos below for hints. Remember that if you find it more convenient, you can use any of the gates on the 74HC4050. Just reference the datasheet.

### About the circuit

The 74HC4050 is used to convert 5-volt signals sent from the Arduino to the 3.3 volts required by the SD card. There are 6 buffers on the 74HC4050, only three are used by this circuit. All inputs come from the Arduino, and the outputs go to the SD card. The forth SPI connection runs directly from DO on the SD card to Arduino digital pin 12. (The Arduino can read the lower voltage signals just fine.)

Some Arduino projects that use SD cards use a resistor network to drop the 5-volt signal to 3.3 volts. For me this didn't work well. I found one SD card that worked and several that did not. As soon as I hooked up the 74HC4050 all of my SD cards worked.

The SD card has an SPI mode. We connect it to the Arduino SPI pins 10, 11, 12, and 13 through the 74HC4050.

The LM3940IT is a "1A Low Dropout Regulator for 5v to 3.3v Conversion." It takes the 5-volt input from the BBB Arduino board and produces a steady 3.3v that powers both the 74HC4050 and the SD card. Before starting I recommend marking the input pin on the LM3940 to distinguish it from the output pin while building the circuit. The ground pin is in the middle.

The other "component" on the board is the shrouded box header used to connect the LED Display Matrices to the Arduino. The 5-volt power from the BBB Arduino needs to be connected to the displays and to the input on the LM3940. As you will see below, we use the power rail on the circuit board to carry ground on one side, and 3.3 volts on the other. We will directly connect the BBB's 5 volt pin to the LM3940 and the shrouded box header for the LED displays.

### Prepration

Start by laying out the components on the circuit

board. If you intend to use the enclosure I've used, in the way I've used it, try to follow the layout in the photos below. It doesn't have to be exact as long as all of the right connections are made, and nothing is connected that shouldn't be. Be careful in planning where the DC jack and the header pins for the USB-BUB on the BBB, as well as the SD card socket will be physically located. This will be important when you place it in the case. If you use the same holes in the PCB that I used, you can get the same match, but beware that it took a fair amount of grinding and cutting to get it to work with the plastic enclosure. Again, it works great, but clearly demonstrates that I am new to the Dremel.

After placing the parts on the printed circuit board, use a thin point Sharpie to mark the pin numbers/labels for the BBB connection and the pin numbers for the shrouded box header. If you don't know where pin 1 is on the box header, attach a ribbon cable into the box header and a solid wire into the other end of the ribbon cable where the red wire lines up and use your meter to test for continuity. You may also want to plug the ribbon cable into the LED display and check continuity between what you think is pin 1 on the box header, and what you think is pin 2, pin 15, and pin 16. Then mark it on the PCB. On top of the LED display are the pins from the shrouded box header soldered to it, one on each side. This makes it very easy to match up your box header pins to those on the display.

## Solder the Components

Once you have things laid out on the board and have marked pin numbers it is time to solder each of the main components. I recommend the following order: The 16-pin DIP socket for the 74HC4050, the LM3940IT, the capacitors need for the 3.3 volt regulator (see next section below), the SD card breakout board, the shrouded box header, and then the header pin receptacles for connecting the BBB

## 3.3 Volt Regulator Capacitors

I elected to keep the capacitors for the 3.3 volt regulator as near as possible to the LM3940. I use two 33&micro;F capacitors between the ground pin and the output pin. One is tantalum capacitor, the other is electrolytic. To save cost, the tantalum capacitor does not require a high voltage rating. 6-volts is just under twice what should ever come out of the regulator and should suffice. REMEMBER that both the electrolytic and the tantalum capacitors are polarized! The long pin needs go into a pad connected to the output of the LM3940, and the short pin into a pad connected to the ground (middle pin) of the LM3940. The leads are small enough that you can fit both in a single hole for each pin.

A .47µF tantalum capacitor goes between the ground pin (middle pin) on the LM3940 and its input pin. This capacitor is also polarized. Be sure the short pin goes into a pad connected to ground and the long pin into a pad connected to the +5v input pin.

The voltage regulator part of the circuit is now ready to be tied to power rails.

## Placing the wires

Now comes the tedious part: running all of the wires. The more colors of wire you have the easier this will be. Try to keep the wires as direct and short as possible, and flat against the board to avoid clutter and enhance visual traceability.

## Power rails

Start by wiring all of the power connections. I selected the rail behind the LM3940 for the 3.3-volt power line, and the rail on the other side of the board as ground. Run one wire from the output pin of the LM3940 to the rail behind it. Run another wire from the ground pin (middle pin) to the rail on the opposite side of the board.

Next connect the +5v input of the LM3940 to a pad connected to pin 12, 14, or 16 of the box header, and from another pad connected to that line of the box header, run a wire to the +5v line that will come from the BBB Arduino. Pin 16 on the box header is used for +5v in the photos below. This will complete the voltage regulator portion of the circuit.

Now connect a black wire from pin 11, 13, or 15 of the box header to the ground rail. Also connect the ground pin from the BBB to the ground rail. Pin 15 of the box header is used for GND in the photos below. This will complete the power connections for the LED displays and the sources from the BBB circuit.

Connect pin 15 of the box header to the COM pin on the SD-MMC card breakout board, and then connect the COM pin of the breakout board to pin 8 on the 16-pin DIP socket. Also connect the GND pin of the SD-MMC card breakout board to the COM pin of the breakout board. All connections to ground should now be complete.

To complete the power rails, connect pin 1 of the 16-pin DIP for the 74HC4050 to the 3.3 volt power rail. Also connect the Vcc pin of the SD-MMC breakout board to the 3.3 volt power rail.

## Wire-up the LED displays to the Arduino

Connect the following box header pins to Arduino (BBB) pins:

- Pin 2 of the box header (CS2) to Digital Pin 5 on the Arduino BBB receptacle
- Pin 1 of the box header (CS1) to Digital Pin 4 on the Arduino BBB receptacle
- Pin 5 of the box header (WR) to Digital Pin 6 on the Arduino BBB receptacle
- Pin 7 of the box header (DATA) to Digital Pin 7 on the Arduino BBB receptacle

The photos below show each connection.

## Wire-up the SD-MMC card to the 74HC4050 and the Arduino

First the easy one . . . Connect the DO pin of the SD-MMC breakout board to Digital Pin 12 on the Arduino.

Next connect Pin 7 of the 16-pin DIP for the 74HC4050 (3A) to Digital Pin 13 on the Arduino BBB receptacle. Then connect pin 6 of the 74HC4050 (3Y) to the CLK pin on the SD-MMC card.

Now connect Pin 9 of the 16-pin DIP for the 74HC4050

(4A) to Digital Pin 11 on the Arduino BBB receptacle. Then connect pin 10 of the 74HC4050 (4Y) to the DI pin on the SD-MMC card.

Finally, connect Pin 11 of the 16-pin DIP for the 74HC4050 (5A) to Digital Pin 10 on the Arduino BBB receptacle. Then connect pin 12 of the 74HC4050 (5Y) to the CS pin on the SD-MMC card.

Don't forget to insert the 74HC4050 into the DIP socket as shown in the photo below.

This completes the wiring needed to read files from the SD Card.

**Hookup the card detect**

In order to be able to tell if a card is present in the SD socket, connect the CD pin on the SD-MMC breakout board to Arduino Digital Pin 2.

**Connect the BBB to the header receptacle**

To finish the circuit connect the BBB to the header receptacle. Be sure to align the pins so that they match the labels on our circuit board! After the enclosure is properly prepared we will connect the ribbon cable from the LED displays, completing the circuit!

## Step 6: The enclosure

As mentioned previously, I am not overly talented with a Dremel. I urge you to post suggestions on better ways of modifying the enclosure to hold the circuit. Nevertheless, this is what I did:

**Hack the board**

Start by scoring each end of the Radio Shack Printed Circuit Board (well away from any copper traces), and use a pair of pliers to break away the unneeded side. When you are done, the board should fit lengthwise against the 6-inch side of the enclosure.

**Preping the LED matrix displays**

Each of the Display boards has a DIP-switch that controls whether or not the board responds to CS1, CS2, CS3, or CS4. Make sure the board on the left side of the display (when it is facing outwards) has CS1 turned on, and all other switches off. Make sure the right-board has CS2 turned on, with all other switches turned off.

**Hack the enclosure – lid**

The lid of the enclosure is used to hold the LED displays together. To do this, you need to cut a hole in the lid exactly the length and width of the two displays together. I cut up a cardboard box exactly the size of the two LED displays, not counting the circuit board they are mounted to, or the other components on the board —

just the size of the LED cubes. I then placed this on the inside of the lid and taped it in place with masking tape. I used a box knife to repeatedly score the lid along the sides of the cardboard until the cutout was complete. A little bit of follow-up shaving with the box knife provided a nice firm fit for the LED displays, with the rest of the board behind the plastic.

Next I put the LED displays in place and used a drill with a tiny bit (3/64) to drill holes through each of the screw holes on the display boards. (4 per board, 8 total.)

I placed a 4-40 3/4" machine screw in each hole from the top of the lid. On the inside I secured each screw with a 4-40 nut. On the top screws I placed a second nut to provide a buffer equivalent in height to the transistors on the boards.

With this in place, each display was back into the lid, with the screws going through the screw holes, and another nut added to hold the boards in place.

**Hack the enclosure – inside**

Now use some ingenious method (I used masking tape to mark approximate areas) to make slots on the side of the enclosure where the following items can be accessed:

- The SD card socket
- The DC power jack on the BBB
- The USB-BUB pins for connecting the serial monitor to the BBB (for debugging, reprogramming, and simply because they need to protrude if the SD card is going to be accessible, due to my lack of engineering that part in advance)

To do this, I used a Dremel with a cutting wheel. The resulting slots are much larger than necessary, and not super straight. I polished it a bit. I also used a grinding wheel to remove some of the plastic inside the box so that the DC jack on the BBB board is flush against the outside edge of the enclosure. I found that my DC input jack wouldn't go in far enough otherwise. NOTE: The cutting wheel on the Dremel cuts, but it also melts the plastic.

I then placed the boards inside the bottom of the enclosure, aligned the DC jack and the SD card socket just where I thought they'd be sufficiently accessible, and then used a hot glue gun to glue the board to the bottom of the enclosure. I also added some hot glue around the DC jack to keep pressure off of the header receptacle when inserting the jack. I placed a small amount of hot glue on the bottom of the PCB before placing it in the enclosure and quickly set it in place. I then lined the entire edge of the PCB with hot glue, again, to keep it firmly in place when plugging in the DC jack or SD cards.

**Attach the cable and lid**

We can now finally attach the ribbon cables that came with the display board. The short cable should connect the two display boards to each other. The longer cable can go into the other header box on either board. (The bus is shared!) The other end of the longer cable should be plugged into the header box on our printed circuit board. Make sure you orient the cable correctly so the notch aligns.

Attach the lid to the enclosure and tighten the 4 corner screws. The Digital Window Sticker is now complete. If you remove the SD card and power the unit with a 9-volt DC supply through the BBB's DC jack, you should see a message on the display telling you to insert an SD card.

If you don't see the message it is time to pull out your multimeter and verify there are no shorts and that each connection is wired correctly according to the schematic.

Congratulations on your new Digital Window Sticker. In the next step you'll see how to place images on the SD card.

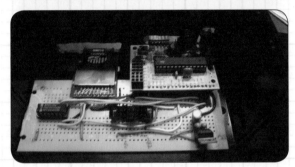

## Step 7: Creating and displaying images

This circuit reads files from the SD card and displays them on the LED display. In order to accomplish this the following must be understood:

- Your SD card must be formatted with a FAT16 file system. This is the default for most older cards, and cards less than 2 GB.
- FAT16 limits the number of files in the root directory to 512. The micro controller is only programmed to read files from the root directory.
- Files are read from 0.dws to 511.dws, sequentially.
- When the micro controller reaches a file it can't read (say 10.dws after reading 9.dws) it will restart at 0.dws.
- .dws files are bitmap files with the bits ordered in rows. The first eight bits fills the first row of LEDs on the left-hand side of the display. 16-bits are required for one full row, and there are 48 rows. (24-per display board.)
- To create a .dws file, start with an XBM (x-bitmap) file and use my command-line program xbmtodws to convert the file.

The best cross-platform tool I've found for creating .xbm files in GIMP. .xbm files are bitmap files that run from left to right. Each byte represents eight black or white pixels. The images below show how to create a Digital Window Sticker template in GIMP, and how to save files as .xbm files.

### Conversion

After creating the .xbm files you want to display, run them through xbmtodws. Full source code is attached for xbmtodws. It compiles on Windows with Visual Studio 2005, on Mac OS X with g++, and on Linux with g++. There is a build-linux.sh for examples of how to compile on linux, and a build-macos.sh that shows how to build on Mac.

xbmtodws requires Boost 1.40.0 header files. It uses Boost Spirit to parse the .xbm files, and Boost dynamic_ bitset to simplify changing the bits from left-to-right, to top-to-bottom.

Pre-compiled versions of xbmtodws are included in the attached files (xbmtodws-1.0.zip and xbmtodws-1.0.tar. gz). The Linux version is in xbmtodws\xbmtodws\linux. The Mac version is in xbmtodws\xbmtodws\macosx. The Windows (32-bit) version is in xbmtodws\release.

xbmtodws creates a 100-byte .dws file from each 16-by-48 pixel .xbm file. 96-bytes are pixel data, and 4 bytes contain time to display the image in milliseconds.

### Converting a file called fred.xbm

Windows: xbmtodws.exe fred.xbm

Linux/Mac: xbmtodws fred.xbm

By default the image will be displayed for 1 second (1000 milliseconds). To change the display time use the -delay nnnMilliseconds command-line argument. For example, to show the image for 10 seconds use: xbmtodws.exe fred.xbm -delay 10000.

xbmtodws will create a new file called fred.dws. To display this file, copy it to the root directory of the SD card and give it a numeric name with the .dws suffix (e.g. 0.dws). Remember that if you leave a gap in the numbers, say you have files 0.dws, 1.dws, and 3.dws, only files 0 and 1 will display. An error will be detected reading 2.dws and the microcontroller will start again at 0.dws.

Another option is to invert the image. Use the -inverse flag to invert the image when the .dws file is created.

### Animations

It is possible to create animations like those shown in the video on the Intro screen, by creating a sequence of images with small movements between frames and a short delay.

You now have complete instructions to create your own Digital Window Sticker. Please post feedback showing how you use your Digital Window Sticker!

# Clap-Off Bra

## By Randy Sarafan (randofo)
### (http://www.instructables.com/id/Clap-Off-Bra/)

The first time I read about Syrian Lingerie (http://news.bbc.co.uk/2/hi/7786564.stm) I was quite moved. In the West, we often think of Arab cultures as sexually repressed societies, when—in fact—it turns out that they are clearly leaps and bounds ahead of us in advancements in lingerie technology. Those of us in Western cultures have a thing or two to learn from the Syrians about gaudy electronic lingerie.

Henceforth, it became my mission to fast-forward lingerie technology in the West. I figured the first step in this critical mission was to replicate some of the advancements made in Syria. The article of lingerie that resonated most with my inner sensibilities was the clap-off bra. I immediately resolved to make my own clap-off bra as a springboard into Western lingerie innovation.

On a quiet morning, two years ago, I first set out to make a clap off bra in order introduce it to a much more conservative Western audience. After a long arduous process, I am finally proud present to you a reliably working prototype.

As Seen on Kathie Lee on the *Today Show* and Hoda on the *Tonight Show* (27 minutes in).

## Step 1: How NOT to make a clap-off bra.

Before I make anything, I always look for existing devices that already exist that I can model my project after. I knew clap-off bras clearly already existed somewhere (Syria). So, I looked all over the internet for a clap-off bra so I could see how the Syrians made it work. Despite hours of searching, I couldn't find a single instance of one that wasn't poorly 'shopped in 4chan.

This lack of reference annoyed me, but by no means stopped me from my pursuit. My first thought was to use a solenoid. This failed. It got too hot. I immediately wrote off all electromagnetic solutions as potential burn hazards. In retrospect, this was a horrible mistake.

My second thought was to build a tiny spring-loaded quick release mechanism. Of course, making a spring-loaded quick release mechanism is a lot easier to speculate about than actually build. This too ended in disaster. I took some time off from the project.

I then partnered with occasional collaborator Noah Weinstein. We discussed various possibilities for opening the bra and finally decided upon exploding the bra off. Unsurprising, the initial test demonstrated that an exploding button in the front of a bra was going to end in disaster. Yet, this did give us another idea.

We finally decided that we were going to get a large metal button, coat it in nitrocellulose and create a brief incendiary event that would burn the thread away. Hence, when the thread burns away, the button would fall off and the bra would open. Fortunately for whatever poor girl who was going to have to wear this, that approach did not work either. No matter what thread we used, we could never get it to fully incinerate and release the button. This disheartened us and the project was laid to rest yet again.

A year or so passed and I decided to try an idea that Noah and I discussed in passing, but never executed. The fourth iteration involved pulling the pin out of the center of a hinge, such that by removing the pin, the bra would separate. We initially didn't want to do this because it would involve using a large motor attached to the bra and this didn't seem very "classy." Nonetheless, I figured I would give it a go.

I went out and bought the smallest servo motor I could find and on the first attempt to pull out the pin with the motor, I tore the gears apart and the weak little servo was destroyed. As it turns out, pulling out a pin that runs vertically using lateral force is nearly impossible. Once again, I found myself in overly-complicated mechanical quick release territory. I consulted "ridiculous clothing" expert Rachel McConnell and she surveyed the situation and surmised that my current approach was pretty hopeless. Normally I would just ignore the project for a few more months, but I was hell bent on just finishing the darned thing.

In talking to Rachel about my long list of failures, I recounted the one idea someone suggested to me early on that I had yet to try. Basically, this involved using a small electromagnet and a strong rare earth magnet and polarizing the electromagnet in such a way that it repels the rare earth magnet. Rachel supposed this would work and I supposed I would give it a try.

So, I went to Radioshack to get some magnet wire to wind an electromagnet. They didn't have any. I went to another they didn't have any either. I went to a third, and they too didn't have any. I headed back and had a moment of inspiration. An electromagnet is basically a coil with some metal in the middle. I just needed to find something with a coil. I tore apart my work station looking for a decent-sized coil of any sort, but to no avail. I finally turned to my office-mate—and all-around good guy—Paul Jehlen, and said to him, "Hey, you wouldn't happen to have any solenoids or big relays or anything with a coil in it?" He produced a defective 5V DPDT relay. This was perfect as it is essentially just an electromagnet that controls a switch.

I carefully cut open the DPDT relay, and exposed the coil. I stuck a rare earth magnet to the end and then powered it up and tried to repel it. This didn't work. The magnet was too strong and it would just reposition itself.

Out of sheer curiosity I checked to see how strong the magnet was with a screwdriver that I had lying around. To my amazement, the electromagnet had a fair amount of pull and was able to lift the screwdriver at 5V. I got to thinking, "I wonder what would happen if I gave the 5V coil a full 9V?" So, I did just this and discovered that the coil didn't heat up as much as I had expected it to and the magnet got significantly stronger. It was now apparent to me that the simple electromagnet inside of a relay powered at 9V was going to get the job done.

Now that we know a bunch of ways not to make one, it is time to actually go ahead and get the job done.

## Step 2: Go get stuff

**You will need:**
- A front opening strapless under-wire bra
- Black fabric
- Small nut and bolt
- (x2) Prototype circuit boards
- An Arduino (w/ATMEGA168 DIP chip)
- 28 pin socket
- (x2) 22pF capacitors
- (x2) 0.1uF capacitors
- 10uF Capacitor
- 16mhz crystal
- 1K resistor
- 10K resistor
- 100K resistor
- 2N3904 NPN transistor
- 7805 voltage regulator
- 5V SPST relay
- 5V DPDT relay
- An electret microphone
- 9V battery connector
- A spare USB cable
- 1" shrink tube
- Threadlocker
- A small grommet
- Elastic band

- Double stick tape
- Quick-setting epoxy
- Ribbons and frills
- Sewing stuff
- Soldering stuffTools of various sorts

## Step 3: Remove the clasp

Cut the clasp off of the bra using cutting pliers (or similar).

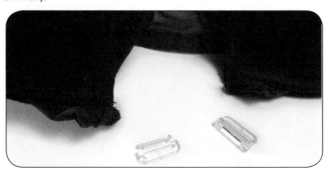

## Step 4: Prepare the electromagnet

Carefully break open the casing for the relay to expose the electromagnet. To avoid damaging the coil, you should start cracking open the case on the side with the switch contact pins. It is okay if the contacts get destroyed, but if you break the coil, then you will need to get a new relay.

## Step 5: Prepare the perf board

Put your relay into the center of one of the prototype circuit boards and make cut marks around the outline of the relay. These will be used in a moment.

## Step 6: Chomp!

Cut your two prototype circuit boards down to size. To do this I use a paper cutter (or what I like to call a "chomper"). If you don't have a paper cutter, you can also cut them using scissors with slightly less precise results.

One board should have a 1/4" trimmed off of each long end, such that you are left with a long strip.

The other board should be cut to a small square using the markings you made in the last step.

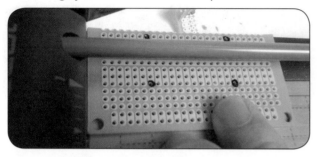

## Step 7: Solder the circuit

Put together the circuit using the 28 pin socket in place of the ATMEGA168 chip (for the time being).

Also, don't worry about the electromagnet and electret mic (for now)

## Step 8: 4-wire cable

Take your USB cable and cut off each end such that you are left with a section of cable roughly 6" to 8" long.

## Step 9: Grommet

Cut a small bow-tie shaped section of fabric that will fold over one of the existing sections of fabric in the front of the bra (the part the clamp was attached to).

In the center of this bow-tie cut a small opening and fasten a grommet.

## Step 10: Screw it

Insert the bolt through the grommet from the back towards the front. Fasten it with a nut.

## Step 11: Sew

Fold the bow-tie over the fabric section in the front of the bra that used to hold one side of the clasp. Sew the fabric down to the bra over the existing fabric. I double-backed the stitch for extra strength.

## Step 12: Cut

Make sure that the nut and bolt are fastened tight. Using a hacksaw or rotary tool, cut the bolt flush with the nut.

## Step 13: Lock it

Twist off the nut and apply threadlocker to the threading of the bolt. Twist the nut firmly back on.

## Step 14: Attach the cable

Peel back the jacket of the USB cable to expose 4-colored wires.

Attach these wires to the circuit board as follow:
- Green—2N3904 transistor ground
- White—Junction of 0.1uF and 10K resistor
- Red—SPST 5V relay switch
- Black—Circuit ground

## Step 15: Program it

Visit this Instructable's project page to download the code for your Arduino board.

## Step 16: Transfer

Transfer the ATMEGA168 chip from the Arduino board to the socket on the circuit board.

## Step 17: Solder the small board

Solder the electromagnet and electret microphone to the smaller circuit board.

## Step 18: Epoxy

Remove 2"–3" of jacket from the free end of USB cable. Epoxy the colored wires the small circuit board, such that you still have some wiggle room to work with (i.e. strip and solder) the wires.

## Step 19: Solder it up

Solder the wires to the circuit board as follows:

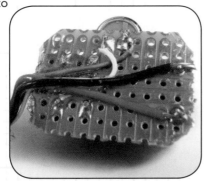

- White—Microphone signal
- Green—Microphone ground
- Red—Electromagnet coil
- Black—Electromagnet coil

## Step 20: Sew it down

Sew down the small electromagnet board to the fabric in the front of the bra to which the clasp used to attach (and the one not with a nut and bolt attached, obviously).

## Step 21: Insulate

Lay down a strip of fabric beneath the long circuit board such that it protrudes 1" past the board on each end. Slide the 1" diameter shrink tubing over the fabric and circuit board. Quickly heat the shrink tubing with a heat gun just long enough for it to tighten around the board.

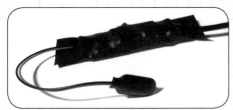

## Step 22: Sew it up

Sew the USB cable along the underside of the bra until you reach the end of the cup. Repeat this stitch a few times so it is nice and strong and then stop sewing.

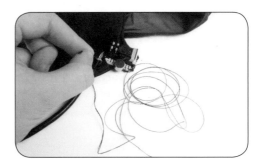

## Step 23: Attach the Circuit

Sew the circuit board to the top of the back strap of the bra. Attaching it to just the top avoids bunching.

## Step 24: Attach the battery

Sew your elastic straps perpendicular to the bra strap at the top and bottom (such that it will hold the battery). When you are done, slide the 9V battery under the straps.

## Step 25: Make a bow

Take your ribbon and make a bow large enough to hide the electromagnet in the front of the bra. If, like me, you don't know how to make a bow, find someone like Scoochmaroo (who "loves making bows more than anything else") to do it for you.

## Step 26: Attach the bow

Attach the bow to the top of the electromagnet by using strong permanent double-sided tape or hot glue.

## Step 27: Clasp on. Clap Off.

Plug in the battery. Put the bra on as per normal using the electromagnetic clasp. When you are ready for it to come off, simply clap twice.

If you want to be "modest" about it, you can make your own LED Heart Pasties (http://www.instructables.com/id/LED-Heart-Pasties/)

A super-special thanks to Danica Uskert for helping demonstrate the bra.

## Turn Signal Bike Jacket

### By leahbuechley
(http://www.instructables.com/id/turn-signal-biking-jacket/)

This tutorial will show you how to build a jacket with turn signals that will let people know where you're headed when you're on your bike. We'll use conductive thread and sewable electronics so your jacket will be soft and wearable and washable when you're done. Enjoy!

## Step 1: Supplies

Get your supplies. You need:
- LilyPad Arduino main board
- FTDI connector
- mini USB cable
- LilyPad power supply
- 16 LilyPad LEDs
- 2 push button switches

- a spool of 4-ply conductive thread
- a digital multimeter with a beeping continuity tester. This is the one I have (http://www.radioshack.com/product/index.jsp?productId=2103175&cp=&sr=1&origkw=multimeter&kw=multimeter&parentPage=search)
- a garment or a piece of fabric to work on
- a needle or two, a fabric marker or piece of chalk, puffy fabric paint, a bottle of fabric glue, and a ruler (Available at your local fabric shop or Joann Stores.)
- a pair of scissors
- double sided tape (optional)
- a sewing machine (optional)

disclosure: I designed the LilyPad, so I'll make some $ if you buy one.

## Step 2: Design

**Plan the aesthetic and electrical layout of your piece**

Decide where each component is going to go and figure out how you will sew them together with as few thread crossings as possible. Make a sketch of your design that you can refer to as you work. The photos below show the sketches for my jacket. Stitching for power (+) is shown in red, ground (-) in black, LEDs in green, and switch inputs in purple.

**Important note about the power supply**

As you design, plan to keep your power supply and LilyPad main board close to each other. If they are too far apart, you are likely to have problems with your LilyPad resetting or just not working at all.

Why? Conductive thread has non-trivial resistance. (The 4-ply silver-coated thread from SparkFun that comes with the LilyPad starter kit has about 14 ohms/foot.) Depending on what modules you're using in your construction, your LilyPad can draw up to 50 milliamps (mA) of current, or .05 Amps. Ohm's law says that the voltage drop across a conductive material—the amount of voltage

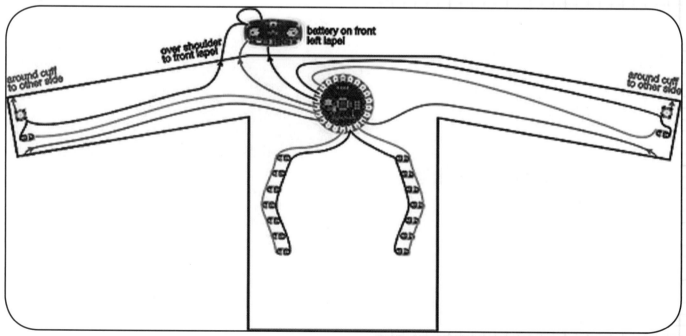

over shoulder to front lapel

battery on front left lapel

around cuff to other side

around cuff to other side

that you lose as electricity moves through the material—is equal to the resistance of the conductive material times the amount of current that is flowing through it.

For example, if your LilyPad is a foot away from the power supply, the total resistance of the conductive material that attaches your LilyPad to your power supply is about 28 ohms. (14 Ohms in the conductive thread that leads from the negative terminal of the power supply to the negative petal on the LilyPad and 14 Ohms in the conductive thread that ties the positive terminals together). This means we can expect a drop of 1.4 Volts (28 Ohms * .05 Amps.) This means that while 5 Volts is coming out of the power supply, the LilyPad will only be getting 3.6 Volts (5 Volts—1.4 Volts). Once the voltage at the LilyPad drops below about 3.3 Volts, it will reset. The resistance of the traces from + on the power supply to + on the LilyPad and—on the power supply to—on the LilyPad should be at most 10 Ohms. Plan the distance accordingly.

If all of this was confusing, don't worry! Just keep the LilyPad and power supply close to each other in your design.

**Transfer the sketch to your garment**

Use chalk or some other non-permanent marker to transfer your design to the garment. If you want, use a ruler to make sure everything is straight and symmetrical.

Use double sided tape to temporarily attach LIlyPad pieces to your garment. This will give you a good sense of what your final piece will look like. It will also keep everything in place and, as long as the tape sticks, make your sewing easier.

## Step 3: Sew your power supply and LilyPad to your jacket

**First, trim the leads off of the back of the power supply**

Get out your LilyPad power supply piece and trim the metal parts that are sticking out the back of it. Small clippers like the ones shown in the photo work well, but you can also use scissors.

**Stabilize your battery on the fabri**

Generally, you want to do everything you can to keep the power supply from moving around on the fabric. I recommend gluing or sewing the battery down before starting on the rest of the project. You may also want to glue or sew something underneath the power supply to help prevent it from pulling on the fabric and bouncing around as you move.

If you are working on a thin or stretch piece of fabric—first of all, reconsider this choice! It's much easier to work on a heavy piece of non-stretchy fabric. If you are determined to forge ahead with a delicate fabric, choose the location for your power supply wisely. It's the heaviest electronic module, so put it somewhere where it will not distort the fabric too badly. Definitely glue or sew something underneath the power supply

**Sew the + petal of the power supply down to your garment.**

If you are new to sewing, check out this great introduction before you start for info on how to thread a needle, tie knots and make stitches (http://www.instructables.com/id/How-to-Sew./). Cut a 3-4 foot length of conductive thread. Thread your needle, pulling enough of the thread through the needle that it will not fall out easily. Tie a knot at the end of the longer length of thread. Do not cut the thread too close to the knot or it will quickly unravel.

Coming from the back of the fabric to the front, poke the needle into the fabric right next to the + petal on the power supply and then, from the front of the fabric, pull it through. The knot at the end of the thread will keep the thread from pulling out of the fabric. Now make a stitch going into the hole in the hole in the + petal on the power supply. Do this several more times, looping around from the back of the fabric to the front, going through the + petal each time.

Pay special attention to this stitching. It is the most important connection that you'll sew in your project. You want to make sure you get excellent contact between the petals on the power supply and your conductive thread. Go through the hole several times (at least 5) with your stitching. Keep sewing until you can't get your needle through anymore. Do not cut your thread, just proceed to the next step.

**Sew from the battery to the LilyPad**

Once you've sewn the + petal of the battery down, make small neat stitches to the + petal of your LilyPad. I used a jacket with a fleece lining and stitched only through the inner fleece lining so that no stitches were visible on the outside of the jacket.

**Sew the + petal of your LilyPad down, finishing the connection.**

When you reach the LilyPad, sew the + petal down to the fabric with the conductive thread. Just like you were with the battery petal, you want to be extra careful to get a robust connection here. This stitching is making the electrical connection between your power supply and LilyPad.

When you are done with this attachment, sew away from the LilyPad about an inch along your stitching, tie a knot, and cut your thread about an inch away from the knot so that your knot won't come untied.

**Put fabric glue on each of your knots to keep them from unraveling**

Once the glue dries, trim the thread close to each knot.

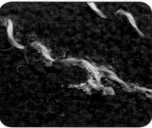

## Step 4: Test your stitching
**Measure the resistance of your stitching**

Get out your multimeter and put it on the resistance measuring setting. Measure from power supply + to LilyPad + and power supply – to LilyPad –. If the resistance of either of these traces is greater than 10 ohms, reinforce your stitching with more conductive thread. If you're not sure how to measure resistance, check out this tutorial (http://www.ladyada.net/learn/multimeter/resistance.html).

Put a AAA battery into the power supply and flip the power supply switch to the on position. The red light on the power supply should turn on. If it doesn't and you're sure you flipped the switch, quickly remove the battery and check for a short between your + and – stitches. (Most likely there is a piece of thread that's touching both the – and + stitching somewhere.) You can test for a short between + and – by using the beeping continuity tester on your multimeter. See this tutorial for information on how to use the continuity tester (http://www.ladyada.net/learn/multimeter/continuity.html).

Also check the resistance between the + and – stitching. If the resistance is less than 10K Ohms or so, you've got a mini-short (probably a fine conductive thread hair that is touching both + and –) that you need to find and correct.

If the power supply does turn on, look at your LilyPad. It should blink quickly each time you press its switch. Once these connections are working properly, turn off the power supply and remove the battery.

**Insulate your power and ground stitching**

So, your jacket is now full of uninsulated conductive stitches. This is fine when a body is inside of it. A body will prevent sewn traces from contacting each other. But when the jacket is off of a person and you bend or fold it, traces will touch each other and short out. To fix this problem, cover your traces with puffy fabric paint (or another insulator like a satin stitch in regular thread). But, you don't want to cover traces until you're sure that everything works! So, use good judgment in when to coat traces.

## Step 5: Sew on your turn signal LEDs
**Sew in your left and right signals**

Using the same techniques you used to sew the

power supply to the LilyPad, attach all of the + petals of the lights for the left turn signal together and to a petal on the LilyPad (petal 9 for me) and all of the + petals for the right signal together and to another LilyPad petal (11 for me). Attach all of the – petals of the lights together and then to either the – petal on the LilyPad or another LilyPad petal (petal 10 for me). Refer back to my design sketches if any of this is confusing.

Remember to seal each of your knots with fabric glue to keep them from unraveling. Be careful to avoid shorts; don't let one sewn trace touch another. In this case, the – traces for the LEDs are all connected, but you want to make sure that the + traces for the left and right signals do not touch the – trace or each other.

**Test your turn signals**

Load a program onto your LilyPad that blinks each turn signal to make sure all of your sewing is correct.

Here's my test program:

```
int ledPin = 13; // the LED on the
LilyPad
int leftSignal = 9; // my left turn
signal is attached to petal 9
int rightSignal = 11; // my right turn
signal is attached to petal 11
int signalLow = 10; // the—sides of my
signals are attached to petal 10
  void setup()
  {
  pinMode(ledPin, OUTPUT); // sets the
ledPin to be an output
  pinMode(leftSignal, OUTPUT); // sets
the leftSignal petal to be an output
  pinMode(rightSignal, OUTPUT); // sets
the rightSignal petal to be an output
pinMode(signalLow, OUTPUT); // sets the
signalLow petal to be an output
digitalWrite(signalLow, LOW); // sets the
signalLOW petal to LOW (-)
  }
  void loop() // run over and over again
  { d
  elay(1000); // wait for 1 second
  digitalWrite(leftSignal, LOW); // turn
the left signal off
  delay(1000); // wait for 1 second
  digitalWrite(rightSignal, HIGH); //
turn the right signal on
  delay(1000); // wait for 1 second
  digitalWrite(rightSignal, LOW); // turn
the right signal off
  delay(1000); // wait for 1 second
  }
```

If your turn signals don't work, use your multimeter (and the instructions from the last step) to test for shorts or bad connections and make sure that your program matches your physical layout.

tech

**Insulate your turn signal stitches**

Cover your traces with puffy fabric paint. Remember, you don't want to cover traces until you're sure that everything works! Use good judgment in deciding when to coat traces.

## Step 6: Sew in your control switches

**Place your switches**

Find a spot for your switches where they'll be easy to press when you're riding your bike. I mounted mine on the underside of my wrists. I found a good spot by trying out different places.

Once you've found a good position, push the legs of the switch through the fabric and bend them over on the inside of the fabric.

**Sew in your switches**

Sew your switches into the garment. Sew 1 leg to the switch input petal on the LilyPad and another leg, one that is diagonally across from the first, to ground or another LilyPad petal. I used petal 6 for the switch input on the left side and petal 12 for switch input on the right side. I used – for the – connection on the left side, but petal 4 for the – connection on the right side. Refer back to my design drawings if any of this is confusing.

When you're done sewing, go back and reinforce the switch connections with glue. You don't want your switches to fall out of their stitching.

## Step 7: Sew in your indicator LEDs

**Sew a single LED onto the sleeve of each arm**

These will give you essential feedback about which turn signal is on. They'll flash to tell you what the back of your jacket is doing, so make sure they're in a visible spot. Sew the + petals of each LED to a LilyPad petal and the – petals of each LED to the – side of the switch (the – trace you sewed in the last step). I used petal 5 for the LED +

on the left side and petal 3 for the LED + on the right side. Again, refer back to my design drawings if any of this is confusing.

As always, remember to glue and trim knots and be careful not to create any shorts.

Once you sew both wrist LEDs, you're done with the sewing phase of the project! Now, on to programming . . .

## Step 8: Program your jacket

**Decide on the behavior you want**

I wanted the left switch to turn on the left turn signal for 15 seconds or so, and the right switch to do the same thing for the right signal. Pressing a switch when the corresponding turn signal is on should turn the signal off. Pressing both switches at the same time should put the jacket into nighttime flashing mode. The wrist mounted LEDs should provide feedback about the current state of the jacket. Please visit this instructables page for more information.

**Program your jacket**

To program your garment, copy and paste my code into an Arduino window and load it onto the LilyPad. You may have to make some small adjustments first depending on where you attached lights and switches. Play with delays to customize your blinking patterns. Follow my LilyPad introduction instructions if you need more information on how to program the LilyPad or how to make sense of my code.

**Plug your battery back in and see if it works and . . . go biking!**

**Insulate the rest of your traces**

Cover the rest of your traces with puffy fabric paint. Again, don't coat anything until you're sure it works.

**About washing**

Your creation is washable. Remove the battery and wash the garment by hand with a gentle detergent.

Note: silver coated threads will corrode over time and their resistance will gradually increase with washing and wear. To limit the effects of corrosion, insulate and protect your traces with puffy fabric paint or some other insulator. You can also revive exposed corroded traces with silver polish. Try this on a non-visible area first to see what it does to your fabric!

## HDDJ: Turning an Old Hard Disk Drive into a Rotary Input Device

By nvillar

(http://www.instructables.com/id/HDDJ-Turning-an-old-hard-disk-drive-into-a-rotary/)

A couple of years ago we built a fun system that would allow DJs to mix music tracks in interesting ways. Our design called for an input device that would allow the DJ to quickly seek through a track and find a specific playback position, and we wanted to be able to do this by spinning a rotary control with a flick of the wrist—much like turntable DJs can spin the record back and forth to do the same.

We found that we had only limited choices for building our device: we first tried to use rotary encoders, but it is not easy to find a cheap encoder that spins smoothly and freely. Another alternative was to buy some audio equipment (like turntables) that spin well and feel good to use—but this seemed both expensive and wasteful for our purposes. Then, while looking for inspiration amongst assorted junk in the lab, we came upon a broken hard disk drive with its case open. We admired the quality of the bearings in the motor that drives the disk plates, enjoyed the fact that even a soft flick would get it spinning for a long time, and wondered whether we could sample an output from it when it was spun by hand, in much the same way that an electric motor, when turned, acts as a dynamo and outputs a voltage.

The answer is yes—and it's a very simple process to turn a hard disk into a rotary input device that has some unique properties. All you'll need is an old hard disk drive, a few op amps, resistors and a programmable microcontroller of some kind.

In this Instructable we'll show the basic principles behind this hack, then provide the schematics and firmware for the HDDJ device that we used in our project, and which includes a few extra buttons, lights and a motorized slider for good measure.

### Step 1: Crack open a hard disk drive

Old, unwanted or broken hard disk drives (HDDs) are usually free and easy to get hold of. They come in all shapes and sizes, but the most common are the 3.5" HDDs that are used inside desktop PCs. We experimented with a number of different 3.5" HDD models, and found that most are suitable for our purposes (and would guess that smaller, laptop-sized disks would work just as well). The largest variation lies in how easy it is to open the case of some compared to others. Seagate HDDs, which often use plain Phillips screws in the casing, are our favorite.

The first step is to open the drive by removing all the screws that hold the case closed. Often these are torx screws, and you'll need an appropriate screw driver. Sometimes a screw will be hidden behind a label—so if you have trouble opening the case after all the screws seemed to have been removed, poke at the labels to find the culprit. If there is a label saying "Warranty Void if Removed," then, for sure, remove it.

Open the case, and reveal the disk platters in all their untouched glory. Never again will they be so free of fingerprints.

Remove the actuator that holds the read-write head, which stops the platters from spinning around freely. It's up to you how much more you want/need to remove (rule of thumb: anything sharp should go). The only thing that you need to keep attached are the frame, platters and spindle motor.

Thanks to Wikipedia for the "Anatomy of a Hard Disk Drive" image.

### Step 2: Solder wires to the spindle motor contacts

Turn the HDD over, with the exposed platters facing down. Some older HDDs will have four wires coming out of the back of the spindle motor, in which case you can skip this step. Most, however, have an orangey-transparent flat-flex cable. In this case, what we are looking for are four exposed contacts at the back of the motor that we can solder some wires to.

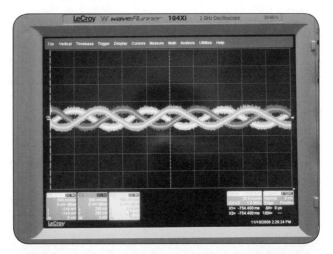

## Step 3: Probing the motor output

This is not really a necessary step, but more an illustration of what exactly we are trying to do.

If you have access to an oscilloscope with multiple inputs, connect three of them to three of the wires soldered to the spindle motor contacts in the previous step (it doesn't matter which three). Connect the probes' ground clips to the fourth wire, then set the platter spinning.

The scope images below show the three waveforms that are generated when the HDD platter is spun by hand (the scale is set to 500mV per division in the vertical axis, and 20ms per division in the horizontal axis). Three perfect phase-shifted sinusoidal waveforms!

As the platter gradually slows down, the waveforms decrease in both... as the platter gradually slows down: they all decrease in both frequency and amplitude by the same amount.

These waveforms carry a lot of information, not only how fast the platter is spinning, but also in which direction it is spinning (clockwise, or anti-clockwise). More on this later.

The raw signals, as generated by spinning the motor by hand, are simply too subtle to be sampled directly by a microcontroller, so the next step is to amplify them into useful levels.

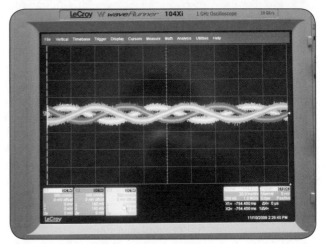

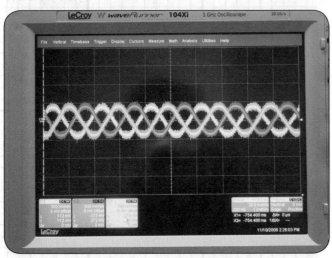

## Step 4: Amplifying the output

Now you have signals coming from your HDD's spindle motor, it's time to amplify them, and in the process convert them to square waves that can be fed into a microcontroller.

The amplification can be done with a simple comparator circuit. Each comparator (the triangles in the schematic) has two inputs (+ and -) and one output. When the voltage on the (+) input is less than the voltage on the (-) input the output will be pulled down to the negative supply voltage, otherwise it will be pulled to the positive supply voltage or, depending on the model of comparator, float at high impedance (in which case a pull up resistor is required).

We have wired an LM324D opamp to function as a comparator The LM324D includes 4 comparator modules in a single package, which is perfect because in our case we need three (the 4th is not shown in the schematic).

One of the lines from the HDD is used as a reference, and is connected to the (-) inputs of all the comparators. The other three lines are connected to each of comparators (+) inputs. Also important, are the power supply pins of the comparators. The negative supply is connected to ground, while the positive supply is connected to Vcc (in our case +5V).

When the voltage of a signal pin from the HDD is greater than the reference the comparator output will be

+5V, otherwise it will be ground. The outputs of this circuit (second image) can now be connected directly to the input pins of the microcontroller.

## Step 5: Measuring direction and velocity of spin

In this step we take the outputs from the amplifier circuit in step 4 and input it to a microcontroller to convert them to something a bit more useful.

The images below show the output from the amplifier circuit as the HDD platter is spinning at various decaying velocities. As the velocity decreases the period of the wave increases. The first two images below show the platter turning in different directions. If we look at the order in which the rising edges of the waves occur we see that in the first image (spinning clockwise) it's Yellow Blue Pink, whereas in the second (spinning anticlockwise) its Yellow Pink Blue.

The code for the microcontroller watches the inputs from amplifier for a rising edge. It also keeps track of which inputs the last two rising edges occurred on (we'll call the inputs Y, P and B). If we detect a rising edge on input Y, and the previous rising edge was on P and before that B, we know that the platter is spinning clockwise, same for P, B, Y and B, Y, P. Conversely if we detect a rising edge on Y, and the previous two rising edges were on B and P respectively, we know the direction is anticlockwise, and same for B, P, Y and P, Y, B. Any other combinations are regarded as noise and ignored.

In our implementation we use a PIC microcontroller. The inputs from the amplifier are connected to the interrupt pins of the microcontroller; these generate an interrupt on the rising edge of the input. Our code then looks at which input generated the interrupt and which inputs generated the last two interrupts. If a clockwise spin is detected a '>' character is output to the PC, if an anti-clockwise spin is detected a '<' is output.

Because the frequency of the interrupts depends directly on the frequency of the waves, which is proportional to the speed of the platter the computer software can work out the velocity of the platter from the frequency at which it receives '<' or '>' characters.

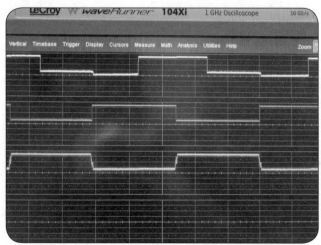

## Step 6: Schematics and firmware for the HDDJ device

For our original DJing project we equipped the hard disk drive with eight additional buttons, six LEDs and a motorized fader to make the HDDJ device. We designed a custom circuit board and wrote some firmware that allowed us to connect all these controls (plus the input from the HDD platter) to a PC via USB. Here you can download the files needed to recreate this design in EAGLE format, plus the firmware that needs to run on the PIC microcontroller (youll need a suitable PIC programmer to do this).

How to test the HDDJ device

1. Install the driver provided in the ZIP file.

2. Plug in the HDDJ to a USB port of your computer (it will mount as a virtual serial connection, and assign it a COM port).

3. Use a terminal program (like Putty) to connect to the COM port, at 115200bps, 8 data bits, no parity bit, and one stop bit.

4. Try spinning the HDDJ platter: you should see a stream of '<' characters appear as it spins counter-clockwise, and '>' characters as it spins clockwise. The frequency of characters will depend on the velocity of spin.

5. Moving the fader will output the character 'f' followed by a number between 0 and 100. To control the position of the fader type the character m into the terminal window, followed by a number between 0 and 100, and then hit return.

6. Pressing the buttons will output the character 'b' followed by a number between 0 and 8. To turn the LEDs on and off type the character l into the terminal window, followed by a number between 0 and 6, and then hit return.

For our project we wrote a bit of software that communicated with the HDDJ via the USB serial line using this protocol. It would be a relatively small (but useful) step to adapt it to, for example, translate the control sequences MIDI messages, which would let you use the HDDJ with generic music or VJ'ing software out of the box.

# 1300 Lumen Bike Light
## By Kyle Lammie (brainiac27)
(http://www.instructables.com/id/1300-Lumen-Bike-Light/)

Let me start with this: I love biking at night. Everything from the empty streets to the cool air keep me biking into the night. But my quick setup of a LED flashlight pipe-clamped to my stem was not cutting it. I needed more power. I needed a true headlight.

And so was born my second LED lighting project. It totaled about $150 after several trips to the hardware store and a custom water bottle battery pack. 1300 lumens is about the total output of the LED star, the actual output through the lens will be about 10% lower. It is still comparable to both of my car's headlights combined and, even when under-driven, is plenty bright for any biking needs.

Fun Feature—The b2flex board is capable of flashing the LED in a strobe pattern at full strength with an effect similar to a police dazzler. NOT recommended for biking. Blinding muggers and spontaneous rave parties, maybe.

### Parts List
- CREE XPG R5 3-up star
- 3-up Carlco Optics
- Arctic Alumina Adhesive (Note: Needs to be the ADHESIVE)
- CPU Heatsink I choose this on based on size and a radial design for looks, Personal Choice.
- B2Flex LED driver To save money one could use a buckpuck from LEDSupply, I wanted the extra features.
- Project Box
- 2.5mm Jack
- 2.5mm Plug (I reused some broken headset cords)
- Off-mom-on button: Any will work as long as you can easily push it.
- Any 3mm or 5mm LED, low power.
- Handlebar Mount Be sure to measure your own handlebars to get the right size.
- Lexan—At least 3x3 Square, any thickness
- 1 inch PVC slip plug
- Aluminum bar -at least 1" wide, 1/8" thick
- Various Hardware
- 4 10-36 thread 1 1/2" machine screws with fitting locknuts and washers
- 4 small machine screws, max 3/8" long
- A 1 1/2" x 1/4" machine bolt, hex head with matching nut

### Battery Pack
- 1x Female Tamiya Connector
- 1x Male Tamiya Connector
- 14.4v Battery Pack The size is only dependent on budget.
- NiMH Charger
- Double-Conductor Cable: I used a old lamp cord
- Cheap Water Bottle- Bigger than battery pack
- Optional—3" heatshrink

The battery pack is only NiMH due to the cost of starting a lithium setup from scratch. If you have a 4-cell charger, a lithium pack would be the cheaper (and lighter) route.

## Step 1: The driver enclosure

The driver, the b2flex driver, really is a cool little bit of engineering. Sporting a micro controller, the driver has several sets of configurations for applications like automotive, cycling, camping, and general use. I am in no way affiliated with TaskLED, the driver is just a huge step above the standard buck constant current drivers. But with the added features comes added complexity which I've addressed to varying extents.

First, the mounting holes for the board and holes for wires were drilled out. I then used machine screws and nuts to clamp the board down. Nylon screws and nuts should have been used but it is what I had on hand. No matter what method you use, be careful on how tight you secure the board. The Inductor on the back is brittle and cracked when I tightened down on it.

The interface holes include LED power, the 2.5mm jack, status LED, and battery connection. Sizes will of course vary depending on what cabling and status LED you use. An 1/8" drill will get you pretty far though. To keep wires short, I soldered connecting wires after the board and components were mounted.

To follow my order, install both the 2.5mm jack and the status LEDs without the board installed. Hotglue works for the LED and the jack should be panel mount i.e. clamp right to the enclosure. I had to use a scrap jack and JB weld it in.

Next begin to install the battery connector and the LED leads. For all board soldering, a flux pen is essential. Use a pencil tip iron and carefully begin to add the connections to the board. Connections should be labeled and easy to figure out; consult the b2flex manual if you are confused.

A final bit of hot glue for the battery and LED leads for strain relief finishes the enclosure. Two holes in the corners opposite the closure screws will be used to mount the enclosure to the heatsink.

## Step 2: The heatsink and LED assembly

Because of the LED exceeding 10W, a major heatsink is used to keep the LED as cool as possible. A radial CPU heatsink was used for its cost and attractive look. I wanted to keep a radial style to the whole light and this one fit the bill perfectly. Any CPU heatsink should be enough but even mine became toasty after a while.

First, the heatsink went through some prep work. The thermal paste was scrapped off and cleaned with rubbing alcohol. I decided to go a step further and polish the part of the heatsink I will mount the LED to. While there are arguments for and against polishing (aka lapping) I felt the finish was terrible on the heatsink and some time spent with 400 and 800 grit sandpaper yielded a better surface. Using the "wrong" side of the heatsink didn't help the finish either.

Carefully solder on the LED leads from the driver enclosure. Higher temps can be used, the star will try to dissipate the heat quickly and possible damage the LEDs. Don't get frustrated and let the star cool off between joints.

Clean both the top of the heatsink and the bottom of the LED star with rubbing alcohol. Then mix together a small amount of the thermal adhesive. Apply a small amount to the center of the heatsink and press the LED

star in place, trying to center the best you can. The lens should then follow shortly after, pushing down as far as possible. Some sort of clamping method must then be used such as weights. While a junk bin is one option, it is best to look for books or some other weight that is less . . . volatile. Consult the Alumina adhesive manual for detailed (and slightly snarky) instructions.

At this time, use the excess thermal adhesive you just mixed to attach a piece of scrap aluminum to the gold square on the b2flex board as a heatsink. To create a larger mass, cut a square with a small tab on one side and fold the tab over onto the face of the square. This impromptu heatsink is necessary to drive the led at the full 1500ma for any length of time. Place a small dab of the adhesive on the gold square and press the tab of the heatsink onto this. Because a heatsink this size is a little more than needed, a stable connection is all that is necessary. Don't worry about clamping too much. Just make sure the heatsink is not touching any exposed contacts of the driver board.

After an hour, the weights can be removed and tested with a voltage source between 14 and 25v. Don't worry, the light should be dim unless you have already messed with the current set point. Default is 350ma, severely under-driving the LED star. This will be greatly remedied after construction.

## Step 3: The battery

As I said before, a lithium setup would be much better for this application. But without the money for specialty chargers, I really had no choice but to use NiMH. If you have a lithium setup already, the b2flex driver features voltage warning and cut-off set points to protect lithium packs. If interested, consult the b2flex manual.

The battery I used was a Tenergy 14.4v NiMH battery. The closer the battery is to the drive voltage of the LED star + 1.7v, the more efficient the driver will be. No guideline is given by TaskLED for 3 LEDs, so assume more than a 1.7v margin. In picking your own battery, just stay away from NiCd batteries. They are not suited vary well for this project.

First, I enclosed the battery in 3" heatshrink. This is optional and slightly over-kill, I just had the heatshrink left over from a laptop battery project. Other coverings include glass-reinforced tape and even duct tape if you do not care to get this battery back. Wire was then added to the existing leads to extend it, I added about 4 feet of scrap lamp cord that I marked the ground conductor on.

The enclosure was made of a cheap sports bottle from my local bike store. A constriction in the middle was cut out leaving the body and top. Foam padding was cut and inserted around and at the bottom of the bottle and the battery was fitted inside. The tip of the bottle was drilled out and the cord was fed through. A knot in the cord adds strain relief and silicone was added to provide some water-resistance. The top and bottom were simply glued together with silicone, pop-rivets or some mechanical fastener would be much safer.

Last, the male connector was soldered to the end of the lamp cord, completing the battery pack.

## Step 4: The mount

Aluminum bar stock was used to make a simple bracket to which the heatsink and driver enclosure is mounted to. The stock is 1"x1/8" aluminum, available from Lowes. My first attempt at measuring, cutting, and bending resulted in far too small of dimensions. Your results may vary but I ended up bending and cutting as I went, starting from the center and working out. Cut a 12" section to start out with and mark the center. I then centered the driver enclosure an this, angling it diagonal to the bar (see the photo). The mounting holes drilled earlier were then transferred to the bar stock and drilled.

Follow the diagram to mark and make the bends. Think ahead and keep in mind the layout of your vise, make sure you can clamp where you need to for each bend. To make a bend, clamp the bar stock firmly in a vice so that the bend point is where the top of the vice jaws meet the bar stock. Then hammer the bar stock in the direction of the bend until a tight, 90 degree angle bend is formed. Repeat for all bends.

Unless you are some blacksmithing wizard, the sides will not end up exactly where you want. As long as the driver fits and the ends make a gap around 3/4" of an inch, the bracket will do. Trim the end so that they match up and are about 5/8" long. Next drill the 1/4" hole on each end for the mounting bolt

Now to mount the driver to the heatsink. Pass 2 small machine bolts and washers (i believe 10-36 and 1 1/2" long, cut to size) between the heatsink's fins on opposite sides into the holes drilled in the bracket. Put the driver in place and pass the threads through the mounting holes drilled in the enclosure. Using locking nuts, tighten the bolts until everything is snug. Replace the cover on the enclosure.

## Step 5: LED enclosure

As this light will be used on a bicycle in adverse conditions, a cover for the LEDs and lens is recommended. A 3/4" PVC pipe cap fits the LED star and lens nicely. A small machine lathe would clean up this step considerably but if that applies to you, you most likely would know how to adapt the instructions yourself.

Drill a 3/4" hole in the center of the cap and sand the fitting until the total depth is the same as the height of the lens and LED star. Next, cut a small notch in the bottom with a knife to fit the leads to the LED star. Do a test fit and sand to make sure the whole thing fits.

Next, place a small square of lexan over the fitting and drill 4 small holes, screwing in small machine screws as you go. Try for a square arrangement if possible and measure it out if it concerns you enough. Once finished, sand down the lexan to fit the profile of the fitting. Remove the lexan plate and add a very small bead of clear silicone around the edge of the fitting. Screw the plate back on, taking care to incrementally tighten the screws so that the silicon spreads evenly around the fitting. Remove any excess and place over the LED lens. I later clamped this cover to the heatsink using the same bolt and washer method used for mounting the heatsink to the bracket.

## Step 6: The remote

The remote is still the weak point of this build only because of money constraints. Pressure-activated switches are used on laser sights for firearms and would work perfectly with a 2.5mm plug soldered on the end. Else, any momentary switch will do as long as you can comfortable mount it and use it. I hid the small switch I ended up using under the rubber hood on my brake/shifter. Firm pressure to the area activates the switch fairly reliably without too much change to my grip on the handlebars.

Of course this step can be skipped by mounting a switch to the enclosure and cutting out the 2.5mm jack. If that works for your riding style (maybe mountain bikes) I would recommend skipping the external remote.

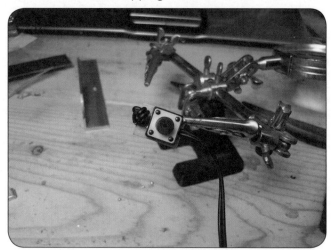

## Step 7: Mounting it to the bike and setting the B2flex

To mount the light assembly to your bike, first clear a small place on your handlebars for the universal clamp. Then screw down and tighten the clamp until very snug. A turn or two of electrical tape on the handlebar can increase friction a bit more if it is a problem. Feed the 1/4" bolt through the top of the bracket, a washer, the universal mount, another washer, and then the bottom of the bracket. Tighten the nut until the light becomes difficult to swivel. A locknut can be used if you do not plan on taking the light on and off. I later made a hand-held

mount for the light so I stuck with a standard nut.

Programming the b2flex is pretty simple so long as you have a reliable remote. My setup ended up with the following:

- Power-On Disabled
- 1500ma Drive current
- UIB2 with Trimode
- L1 at 500ma
- L2 at 1200ma
- L3 at 1500ma

I really recommend you to read through the manual and pick out your own settings. There is a huge amount of flexibility to fit whatever needs you have.

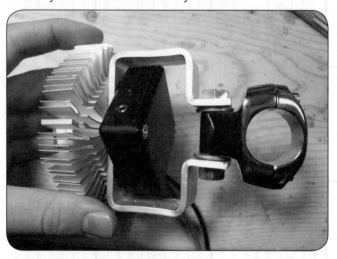

## Step 8: The conclusion

So that is my 1300 lumen bike light. There are many things you can do to make it you own and even better. Most of all, it desperately needs a cutoff shield so you are not blinding car drivers. But beyond that, enjoy your LED bike light much brighter and cheaper than most bike-specific lights. If replaceable lenses are important, the LED cover could easily function as a lens holder as long as no adhesive is allowed to fill the alignment holes in the LED star.

Have fun, be safe, and enjoy the night.

# The EyeWriter 2.0
## By thesystemis
### (http://www.instructables.com/id/The-EyeWriter-20/)

The EyeWriter is a low-cost eye-tracking apparatus + custom software that allows graffiti writers and artists with paralysis resulting from Amyotrophic Lateral Sclerosis to draw using only their eyes.

The original design, as shown here, featured a pair of glasses as the basis for the eyewriter design: (http://player.vimeo.com/video/6376466)

Since that first video, we've been hacking on and developing the project, and we have a new design, which we've called "eyewriter 2.0" which improves the accuracy of the device, and allow for people whose heads are moving slightly to also use an eye tracker. The original eyewriter, designed for a paralyzed Graffiti artist TEMPT1, is designed to be worn on a completely motionless head. The 2.0 design, which uses a camera and LED system mounted away from the head, can be used by people whose heads are moving slightly, such as MS patients, and people who wear glasses, etc.

This eyewriter system is cheap, and completely open source. At the moment, it costs about $200 in parts. Traditional commercial eye trackers costs between $9000-$20,000, so this is a magnitude of order cheaper, and is designed to help anyone who wants or needs an eyetracker.

We've been showing off and demoing the 2.0 device — Check out the eyewriter 2.0 in action — we even hooked it up to a robotic arm, to draw the artwork people make with their eyes:

(http://www.switched.com/2010/12/13/eyewriter-teams-up-with-robotagger-to-print-kids-ocular-artwork/print/)

(The 2.0 device was designed with help and input from Takayuki Ito, Kyle McDonald, Golan Levin and students of the eyewriter collab at Parsons MFADT. Thanks also to the Studio for Creative Inquiry/CMU for hosting a session for development)

## Step 1: Overview

The basic idea approach is that we'll be doing a few things. First, we'll be making LED illuminators for the sides of the screen and the center. Second, we'll be hacking the PS3 eye camera to get the vertical sync (when the frame of video is being taken) and to make it sensative to IR. Third, we'll be programming and building the arduino/cirucit to control the blinking. Finally, we'll setup the base for the system and go through the basics of the software.

From a technical perspective, the 2.0 system works by strobing 3 IR illuminators every frame. On even frames, it uses the center illuminator (located around the camera lens) and on odd frames it uses the 2 side illuminators. On even frames, the pupil appears bright, since the IR light is actually bouncing off the back of your eye, like red eye effect. On odd frames, your pupil appears dark. The difference between the two allows us to isolate and track the pupil in realtime. Additionally, the glints (reflections of the IR illuminators) of the dark frame are tracked, and these, plus the info on the pupil, is calibrated to screen position using a least squares fitting process for an equation that provides a mapping of glint/pupil position to screen position.

## Step 2: Parts list

There are a fair number of parts required to make this device. For a complete listing, please visit this Instructable's project site.

## Step 3: Software—openFrameworks & EyeWriter

The Eyewriter 2.0 requires a few pieces of software for building and running. In this step we will explain how to download and install an IDE, openFrameworks, and the eyeWriter software.

### A. Integrated Development Environment (IDE)

- An integrated development environment (IDE) is a software application that provides comprehensive facilities to computer programmers for software development.
- Download and install an Integrated Development Environment (IDE) to run openFrameworks if necessary.

53

http://www.openframeworks.cc/setup

**B. openFrameworks**

- Openframeworks is a c++ library designed to assist the creative process by providing a simple and intuitive framework for experimentation.
- Download and install openFrameworks if necessary. http://www.openframeworks.cc/download

**C. EyeWriter GitHub**

- GitHub is a web-based hosting service for projects that use the Git revision control system. It is a platform that allows people to exchange and share code.
- Visit the EyeWriter source page on GitHub: http://github.com/eyewriter/eyewriter/tree/remoteEyetracker
- Click Download Source on the top right menu.
- Choose ZIP format.
- After download is complete, unzip the file and place the "eyewriter-xxxxxxx" folder into openFrameworks "apps" folder.
- Open the "apps/eyewriter-xxxxxxx/eyeWriterTracker/RemoteEyeTracker.xcodeproj" file to test that all installations are working correctly. The source code should load in your IDE software.
- Please be sure you're compiling for your current Operating System (the eyewriter software was originally compiled for OSX 10.5 so you might need to change compiling from 'base SDK' to 'OSX 10.6')
- Build and Run the source code. The Tracking screen should load in video demo mode.

## Step 4: Software—camera & Arduino

We will also need to install two additional pieces of hardware. Macam will allow our PS3 eye camera to talk to our computer and the Arduino software will permit our physical hardware to communicate with our software.

**Installing PS Eye drivers**

*For Mac:*

- Macam is a driver for USB webcams on Mac OS X. It allows hundreds of USB webcams to be used by many Mac OS X video-aware applications. Since we are using a PS3 camera, this software will allow our computers to recognize the hardware.
- Download the Macam driver from SourceForge. http://sourceforge.net/projects/webcam-osx/files/cvs-build/2009-09-25/macam-cvs-build-2009-09-25.zip/download
- After download is complete, unzip the file and place the macam.component file into your hard drives / Library/Quicktime/ folder.

*For PC:*

- download the CL-Eye-Driver:http://codelaboratories.com/downloads/

**Arduino**

- Arduino is a tool for the design and development of embedded computer systems, consisting of a simple open hardware design for a single-board microcontroller, with embedded I/O support and a standard programming language
- Download and install the Arduino software. http://arduino.cc/en/Main/Software
- Follow the Getting Started tips if you're unfamiliar with the Arduino environment. http://arduino.cc/en/Guide/HomePage

## Step 5: Load Arduino sketch

In this step you will have to load the Arduino sketch for the PS eye camera to work.

**A. Arduino Sketch (Only for PS Eye)**

- Load the Arduino EyeWriter sketch "apps/eyewriter-xxxxxxx/eyeWriterTracker/StrobeEye/StrobeEye.pde" in the Arduino IDE software. This needs to be done in order that the eyewritter software can recognize the hardware.
- With your Arduino board connected, upload the sketch to your board. Follow the Getting Started tips if you're unfamiliar with the Arduino environment. http://arduino.cc/en/Guide/HomePage

## Step 6: Hardware: power adapter

**Power Adapter**

In this step you will cut the wire of a power adapter to power your breadboard

- Clip off the connector jack of your 7.5 Volt Power Adapter. See image here (http://eyewriter.org/images/data/EW-2_0-manual_grafx/poweradapeter-cable.jpg)
- Use a Voltmeter to determine the positive and negative wires in the adapters exposed cord.
- Using a short strip of red and black wire, solder the red wire to the adapters positive wire, and solder the black wire to the adapters negative wire.
- Tape the exposed wires separately to keep positive and negative apart, then tape both together to ensure no wire is exposed.

## Step 7: Hardware: infrared LED's

**IR LED's**

- Gather 8 Infrared (IR) Light-Emitting Diodes (LED) and a small round Printed Circuit Board (PCB).

- To build LED arrays on the PCBs you'll need to know the positive and negative ends of each LED. Generally speaking the longer leg of the LED is the anode (positive), and the shorter leg is the cathode (negative). See image here (http://eyewriter.org/images/data/EW-2_0-manual_grafx/led-anode-scheme.jpg). On most LEDs, there will also be a flat spot on the cathodes side of the lens. From overhead, take note of which direction the wire bond points relative to positive and negative.

- Setup a circuit of 4 LEDs in series, in parallel with another set of 4 LEDs in series. See image here (http://eyewriter.org/images/data/EW-2_0-manual_grafx/led-glint-front.jpg). Clip the legs of the LEDs and solder them together. See image here (http://eyewriter.org/images/data/EW-2_0-manual_grafx/led-glint-back.jpg).

- After soldering the LED legs together to form the circuit, solder about 2 feet (60 centimeters) of the red and green intercom wire to the LED circuits positive and negative ends. See image here (http://eyewriter.org/images/data/EW-2_0-manual_grafx/led-glint-cable.jpg)

- To test the LED PCB panel, build the circuit below. Look carefully to see if your IR LEDs are glowing a faint red. See image here (http://eyewriter.org/images/data/EW-2_0-manual_grafx/ledRing-test.jpg)

- After confirming your IR LEDs are working, cover the back of the LED PCB panel with hot glue to keep all connections in place.

- Repeat steps 1–5 above to create another LED PCB panel.

- Using a larger round PCB, carefully drill press a hole into the center of the board. See image here (http://eyewriter.org/images/data/EW-2_0-manual_grafx/led-ring-drill.jpg)

- On the outer rim of the PCB, build a circuit of 4 parallel sets of 4 LEDs in series. The placement of the LEDs should allow the PS Eye camera to fit through snugly, without the camera blocking the LEDs. See image here (http://eyewriter.org/images/data/EW-2_0-manual_grafx/led-ring-back.jpg)

- After soldering the LED legs together to form the circuit, solder wiring to connect all 4 positive ends together and all 4 negative ends together, putting all 4 LED sets in parallel. See image here (http://eyewriter.org/images/data/EW-2_0-manual_grafx/led-ring-show-lens.jpg)

- Solder about 2 feet (60 centimeters) of the red and green intercom wire to the LED circuits positive and negative ends.

- To test the larger LED PCB panel, build the circuit below. Look carefully to see if your IR LEDs are glowing a faint red. See schematic here (http://eyewriter.org/images/data/EW-2_0-manual_grafx/ledRing-test.jpg)

- After confirming your IR LEDs are working, cover the back of the LED PCB panel with hot glue to keep all connections in place.

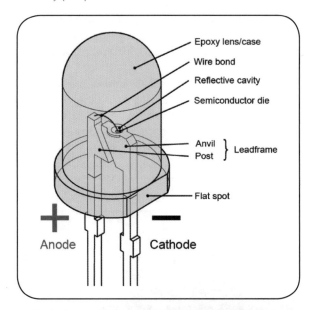

## Step 8: Hacking the PS Eye camera— preparing

In this step we will talk about how to take apart a PS Eye camera. This is necessary for you to be able to replace the lens on the camera, insert a infrared filter and wire the v-sync.

- Get a PlayStation (PS) Eye camera. Use at your own risk because the camera will undergo modifications voiding its warranty.

- Pry the four plastic screw caps off the back of the casing. See image here (http://eyewriter.org/images/data/EW-2_0-manual_grafx/psEye_screwLids.jpg)

- Unscrew the four screws underneath where the screw caps were. Keep these screws because you will need some later.

- With all four screws removed, pry off the back half of the casing. A flathead screwdriver and hammer, or a pair of pointed pliers should work. It requires significant force so be very careful not to damage anything inside or hurt yourself. See image here (http://eyewriter.org/images/data/EW-2_0-manual_grafx/psEye_openbox.jpg)

- Pull the cord aside and unscrew the two bottom screws beside the plastic holder. Keep these screws also. See image here (http://eyewriter.org/images/data/EW-2_0-manual_grafx/psEye-standScrews.jpg)

- Remove the stand piece.

- Unscrew the five screws around the board (two screws on the side, three screws on top). Keep these screws also. See image here (http://eyewriter.org/images/data/EW-2_0-manual_grafx/psEye-backScrews.jpg)

- With all five screws removed, lift the board out of the front casing.
- There are four microphones across the top of the board. Using wire cutters, clip off the microphones because they won't be used. See image here (http://eyewriter.org/images/data/EW-2_0-manual_grafx/psEye-cutmics.jpg)
- Now the PS Eye board is prepared for wiring. The next steps will connect wiring to the Vertical Synchronization (V-Sync) and Ground joints on the PS Eye board.

## Step 9: Hacking the PS Eye camera—VSync

In this step we will go through getting the v-sync off the camera. The v-sync is an electrical signal that comes from the camera which communicates the camera's refresh rate. Getting the camera's v-sync is crucial for this application to work because it is the only way we can match the camera's refresh rate to our infrared LED's.

- Locate the Ground joint on your PS Eye board. Some PS Eye models have 5 joints near the lens mount (left image below), while some have 4 joints (right image below). If your model has 5 joints, the Ground joint is

at the end closest to the lens mount. If your model has 4 joints, the Ground joint is also at the end closest to the lens mount, and twice as wide as the other joints. See image here (http://eyewriter.org/images/data/EW-2_0-manual_grafx/psEye-findVSync.jpg)

- Cut about 2 feet (60 centimeters) of your 4-color intercom wire, and split the red and green from the black and white.
- Split the red and green wire about 2 inches (5 centimeters) from one end, and strip off a small section of insulation at the end of the green wire. The green wire will be soldered to the PS Eyes Ground joint.
- Clip the PS Eye board and green wire to a stand, and prepare to solder the green wire tip to the Ground joint. Use a piece of thick paper or cardboard in between the clips teeth to prevent scrapes on the board. See image here (http://eyewriter.org/images/data/EW-2_0-manual_grafx/psEye-solderGround.jpg)
- Solder the green wire to the PS Eyes Ground joint.
- Locate the V-Sync via on the board. Its the via circled in the image below. See image here (http://eyewriter.org/images/data/EW-2_0-manual_grafx/psEye-spot-VSync.jpg). Attention: for more recent models of the PSEye camera (identified by the golden rim around the board) the VSync hotspot can be found on the front of the PCB, directly above the R19 resistor. See image here (http://eyewriter.org/images/data/EW-2_0-manual_grafx/newPSEye-hack-r19_manual.jpg). Very REcently a newer model was also introduced in the market (v9.2) see how to identify it in this image (http://eyewriter.org/images/data/EW-2_0-manual_grafx/psEye-v92.jpg) and how to find the vSync spot in this image (http://eyewriter.org/images/data/EW-2_0-manual_grafx/psEye-v92_solderPoint.jpg).
- Using a sharp knife, carefully pivot the knife tip on the via, and scrape off enough insulation coating to expose the metal contact below. See image here (http://eyewriter.org/images/data/EW-2_0-manual_grafx/psEye-cleanVSync.jpg).
- The red wire needs to connect to the exposed V-Sync via, but the wire is too thick to be soldered neatly to the small via, so a 30 gauge wire will be used in between. Strip the ends of a 2 piece of 30 gauge wire.
- Shorten the red wire, then solder one end of the 30 gauge wire to the end of the red wire. See image here (http://eyewriter.org/images/data/EW-2_0-manual_grafx/psEye-vSyncCabling.jpg)
- Before soldering the 30 gauge wire to V-Sync, a test should be performed to ensure all connections are correct. Build the circuit below. When the 30 gauge wire contacts the V-Sync via, the LED on the breadboard should flicker rapidly. see schematic here (http://eyewriter.org/images/data/EW-2_0-manual_grafx/psEye-vSyncCircuitTest.jpg).
- Using thin 0.022 inch (0.56 millimeters) solder, carefully solder the 30 gauge wire to the exposed V-Sync via. To confirm, ensure the LED on the breadboard is flickering.

## Step 10: Hacking the PS Eye camera – finishing

In this step we will talk about how to put your camera back into one piece.

- Unscrew the 2 screws holding the lens in place. Be careful not to break the fragile V-Sync connection. Detach the lens and keep both screws.
- Measure the square opening of the new lens mount. Cut a square from the filter sheet that is minutely smaller, and place it into the lens mount opening.
- With the filter in place, screw in the new lens mount. This will require some force, and one screw will go in at an angle because the new lens mount is a little too big for the board.
- Screw the new lens into the new lens mount on the board.
- Use hot glue to cover and secure the V-Sync connection.

## Step 11: Full circuit

In this step we will show how to put together the circuit on the breadboard. This is the initial step to getting your Arduino to work with the eyeWriter software.

- Build the circuit in the schematic below. (see schematic)
- After assembling the full circuit, the EyeWriter code is ready for live camera input. To switch from video demo mode to live camera mode, open the "apps/eyewriter-xxxxxxx/eyeWriterTracker/bin/data/Settings/inputSettings.xml," and edit the mode tag from 1 to 0.
- Open the "apps/eyewriter-xxxxxxx/eyeWriterTracker/RemoteEyeTracker.xcodeprof" file, and Build and Run the source code. The Tracking screen should load with

input from the PS Eye camera.

## Step 12: Building a wood base

In this step we talk about building a portable wood base. It is interesting to build this so that your system can have a stable infrastructure to rest on. This makes it easier to test, calibrate, and work with the eyeWriter.

**List of materials/parts needed for the base**

- 2* 5/16 wood rods—approx. 20 inches long (A)
- 2* 5/16 wood rods—approx. 1 1/2 inch long (D)
- 1* 20 x 4 x 1/2 inch wood piece (B)
- 3* 3 x 1 3/4 x 1 3/4 inch wood pieces (C)
- drill bit with approx. diameter of the wood rods

### Step 1:

Align the 2 pieces (C) with the third piece (C) as shown in the picture, clamp them together and drill through them at approx. 3/4inch close to the edge.

### Step 2:

Using the two pieces (C) that have the same holes aligned, place each of them on the edges of the piece (B), clamp the aligned (see picture for example) and drill a hole through them till about 1 1/2 inch deep on the (B) piece.

Use the short wood rods and put them throught the holes in the piece (B) edges and through each of the pieces (C).

### Step 3:

Drill a hole with enough diameter for the tripod head mount screw.

### Step 4:

With the bottom bar (B) and edge pieces (C) assembled, insert the rods (A) through the holes aligning them with the bottom bar length.

## Step 13: Using EyeWriter software—setup & tracking screen

In this step we will take you around the eyeWriter software so that you can set it up.

- Focus your camera by selecting Focus Screen on the first tab of the Computer Vision (CV) panel on the right. Rotate the lens of your camera until both video feeds look sharp, then deselect Focus Screen to return to the Tracking screen.
- Select load video settings on the first tab of the right panel.

**For PS3 Eye Camera:**

Ideally you want a bright, balanced image with minimal noise. An example image is shown below. Under the Webcam tab, slide the Gain and Shutter settings back and forth until the video looks ideal.

Under the Compression tab, if you're using a faster computer set your Frames per second (Fps) to 30. If you're using a slower computer set your Fps to 15.

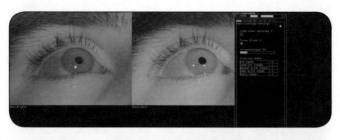

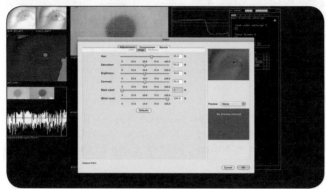

## Step 14: Using EyeWriter software—calibration screen

In this step we will go through the calibration setup.

- Press spacebar for instructions, then spacebar again to start. Look at the red dots as they appear.
- At the end of the calibration, the blue lines show any calibration inaccuracies. If there are any long blue lines, reset the calibration and press spacebar to start again.

## Step 15: Using EyeWriter Software—Catch Me

- Stare at the Catch Me box. As you stare, the box's color will turn green.
- When the box is fully green, it is caught and will appear somewhere else. Keep catching the boxes to test your eye-tracking calibration.

## Step 16: Using EyeWriter software—drawing

**Letter drawing**

- Drawing mode starts paused by default. Before you start drawing, you can toggle the background grid on or off. The background grid can be toggled at any time by pausing.
- To start drawing, switch to recording mode by staring at the paused button. As you stare, the button will turn green and switch to recording.
- Drawing works with vector points. Stare at a place on the canvas for about a second to make a point. Your green eye-tracking circle needs to stay very still to make a point.
- As you add points, they will stay connected by a stroke. You can create shapes and letters with these strokes. To make a new line, stare at the next stroke button.
- To change what you are drawing, you can undo point which removes the last point drawn, or undo stroke

which removes the entire last stroke drawn.

- To save the current shape or letter and move on to the next one, stare at next letter. Your recently drawn letter will appear at the top of the screen, and you have a new blank canvas to draw a new letter on.
- When you are finished drawing shapes and letters, stare at NEXT MODE to move on to Positioning mode.

**Positioning**

- By default, all your letters are selected and ready for positioning. You can select individual letters by staring at Select Letter.
- Select Rotate allows you to rotate your selection right (clockwise) and left (counter-clockwise).
- Select Shift allows you to move your selection up, down, left and right.
- Select Zoom allows you to zoom out and zoom in which shrinks and enlarges your selection.
- Auto Place will place your letters side by side in the order you drew them.
- When you are finished positioning your shapes and letters, stare at NEXT MODE to move on to Effects mode.

## Step 17: Using EyeWriter software—typing

- Stare at whichever key you wish to press. As you stare, the keys color will turn green then flash blue.
- When the key flashes blue, it has been pressed. You can see what youve typed at the top of the screen.
- To speak the words typed, press the SPEAK key on the bottom left of the screen. On the middle right of the screen, SPEAK WORDS OFF/ON toggles the option to speak words automatically after they are typed and a space is entered.
- Note the CAPS OFF/ON key on the bottom right of the screen. This toggles caps lock on and off, and is required to use the alternate characters on the number keys (! @ # $ % etc).

## Step 18: Using EyeWriter software—Pong

- The goal is to block the ball from passing your paddle at the bottom of the screen.
- The paddle will slide aligned with the x-position of your gaze. So you can stare at the moving ball and the paddle will slide horizontally in tandem.

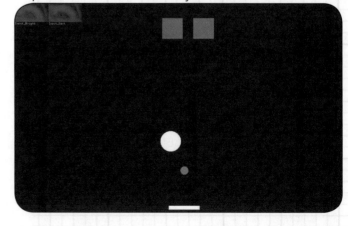

There's something uniquely satisfying about working on a project that can take you somewhere you've never been. There's also something wonderful about working on simple mechanical machines, where all the moving parts are right there for you to see. Projects in the "ride" chapter have both of these qualities.

People are constantly reinventing the way in which they get from place to place. While there's no need per se to change the way your bicycle looks, or fundamentally alter the way it's ridden, for some reason, people do. What we ride and how we ride it speaks loudly about who we are. We applaud this expressive voice, and for years, Instructables has been steadily stockpiling some of the greatest examples. We're excited to share the following extraordinary things—far beyond the bicycle—that you can ride and hopefully inspire you to create something of your own for the open road, steep hill, or drainage ditch.

## Side by Side Bicycle

By Carlos Gonzalez (carlitos)
(http://www.instructables.com/id/Side-by-Side-
Bicycle/)

The Side by Side bicycle, also known as a "sociable," or more recently as a buddy bike, appears to date back to 1896. Unlike a tandem, where the riders are in line to one another, here the riders are side by side. To build one, you start with a regular bike and make 3 modifications: pedals, seats, and handle bars. To accommodate riders of different weight, my idea was to slide the seats left/right such that the heavier rider sits closer to the frame. This adjustment is limited however since the farther the seats are extended in either direction, the more uncomfortable the pedaling becomes. Perhaps you will not need this feature. To reduce interference between the riders, the seats can be staggered as described and illustrated in this patent issued in 1979. This reference notes the use of a chain for the steering mechanism but I believe it's easier to build a linkage tie rod.

Riding side by side is so much fun and exciting! The Side by Side is safer than my "Antique Bicycle," although it too requires skill which is quickly attained through practice and teamwork.

### Step 1: Bill of materials

Here's what you will need to build the sociable bicycle:

- A bicycle
- A welder
- Extra set of bike pedals/cranks
- Extra bike seat
- Tubing
- 2 heim joints to make a steering tie rod

### Step 2: Pedals

When pushing off, each rider will have their foot resting on the pedal closest to the frame in the bottom most position (left side rider—right foot; right side rider—left foot). So cut off the left side crank and weld it back on so as to form a U. Now remove each pedal and in its place, weld a 6" long by 3/4" wide steel rod. I initially had welded a 1/2" rod to the original bolt from the pedal but was not strong enough as it twisted some while pedaling. You then make a custom pedal that will fit the 3/4" rod.

Simply use 5" of tubing that will slip over the rod and weld two 3/8" bent rods as in the picture.

With the custom-made pedal in place, weld at 90 degrees an extended crank and pedal. To make this extension, you will need to weld a rod to an extra crank to achieve the required double length—about 13 inches. You will not want to place too much of your weight on the outside pedal so use the inside pedal for pushing off and when stopping.

### Step 3: Seats

To the seat post, weld a tube to form a T. Using a tube that will slide inside the tube just welded, cut it to the length you want the seats apart from each other. Slide it in and now weld 2 short new seat posts at each end to accept the 2 seats. You can make both posts adjustable or just one as I did since the original seat post can also be adjusted. Drill a hole across both tubes, insert a bolt and tighten with a nut. If weight combination of the riders does not work well, remove the bolt and slightly slide the inside tube with the seats to adjust. Drill across the inside tube starting from the holes already drilled on the outside tube and reinsert the bolt.

## Step 4: Handlebars and steering

Only the left side driver will steer the bike so the left side handle bar will have a steering linkage. Weld tubing as shown to the left side of the head post tube. I used another bike's bottom bracket to make the steering mechanism. I welded a heim joint to the underside as well as another heim joint where the original handlebar used to be. I then connected the 2 heim joints with a tube acting as a linkage to make the steering possible. You will want to trim down the length of your handle bar so it does not interfere with the other rider. You could instead use a tie rod or perhaps sprocket and chain for the steering mechanism. Install the gear and brake controls onto this handle bar. Now weld a fixed handle bar for the right side driver and you are ready to ride! Since all that welding requires removing of paint to expose the steel, you will want to prime and paint at this time.

## Step 5: Riding

As the driver, place your right foot on the inside pedal (closest to the frame) at the bottom most position. Left foot on the ground. Hold the handle bars firmly while the passenger sits on the seat and puts both feet on the pedals. At this point, three feet are on pedals and the driver's left foot is acting as the "kickstand."

You then push off while releasing the brakes. I find a few pushes helps to get enough momentum for balancing.

Get seated and start pedaling while the passenger begins to help with the pedaling. The bike will lean slightly to one side when there is a difference in the riders' weights but this is normal as it helps in maintaining good balance. Once stopped, both riders should place the outside foot on the ground. Now enjoy an exciting ride in the park with someone special while socializing all the way. Oh what fun it is to ride side by side!

## Step 6: Riding solo

Riding solo on the Side by Side is surprisingly easy once you get past the fear of riding while the bike leans to one side. You can hold on to a pole as you mount it to get an idea for how far the leaning needs to be to stay balanced.

To start, keep your weight on the right foot/inside pedal while leaning the bike away from you and maintaining a straight and firm hold of the handle bars. You then push off with the left foot.

If you do not lean enough, you will begin turning left and sitting then is not possible. Since you will need to sit before you can pedal, the lean with some forward momentum is critical.

I find I can readily make sharp left turns and go around in circles without any leaning whatsoever.

Turning right is more challenging since you will need to lean the bike more as you steer slightly right.

Also, you do not want to turn right too sharply, especially while you have your outside left pedal down, since too much leaning will cause the outside right pedal on the right side to hit the ground.

Turning right is done slowly.

With a little practice, I find I can go in a straight line or go around in circles in either direction.

# 10 HP Hovercraft

By Roland E. MacDonald (mickydee)
(http://www.instructables.com/id/10-HP-Hover-craft/)

I was looking for a project that my grandson and I could build together. We decided on a hovercraft after watching a TV special. Knowing absolutely nothing about hovercraft we researched the web on the subject and found the Universal Hovercraft website to be the best source.

We had an old 10 HP Briggs horizontal shaft electric start engine from an old riding mower that looked like it would fit the bill. We bought the plans for their UH10F craft. We liked it because it only uses one motor. Most hovercraft use a separate motor for lift and thrust. This one directs approximately 1/3 of the thrust air to provide both lift and inflating the skirt. Most of the materials could be found at the local builders supply.

The only parts we needed to buy from Universal Hovercraft were the plans, propeller, propeller hub, and the skirt material. Although it busted our $500 budget we decided to purchase their materials kit which included all the epoxy, fiberglass, screws, and glue. The skirt is the heart of this thing and we didn't want to save penny's on something this critical. It was a fun project for the both of us. It would be a great father and son project.

## Step 1: Tools and materials list

Tools required:

- Table saw to cut 4 X 8 Foam and plywood
- Keyhole saw or saws all to cut openings for air ducts
- Scroll saw for plywood duct and body peices
- Shop vac for vacuum blanket
- Two to four saw horses
- Several plastic squeegees
- Basic hand tools

Materials list:

*From Home Depot, cost is about $80*
For the hull

- 1 sheet 1" white Styrofoam
- 4 sheets 2" blue construction foam 4 x 8
- 4 sheets 1 /8" plywood (doesn't have to be marine)
- 2 12' lengths 1 x 2 lumber (pine is fine)

*Hardware kit from Universal Hovercraft, $349*
This kit contains every little thing you will need to complete this project, including:

- plans
- fiberglass
- skirt
- glue
- skrit screws
- epoxy
- a 24' steering cable

*Drive Kit from Universal Hovercraft, $159*
Includes:

- propeller
- hub
- bushings

*Miscellaneous, $20*

- Small roll plastic sheeting 2 to 4 mills
- Paint

The total cost of the project was around $600 plus the cost of a new or used motor.

## Step 2: Building the hull

Cut the 2" foam to make a 5' x 10' rectangle. This dimension will provide a floatation of 600 lbs. If you need to support more weight double up on the foam. It won't weight much more. Skin the top side with the 1/8" plywood. Cut and glue the plywood strips to the foam, and then glue the 1 x 2 strips to the plywood. With a scroll saw cut the two holes for the lift, and skirt air. Glue a 6" wide piece of plywood across the hull where you will install the motor support post.

## Step 3: Vacuum bagging

The underside of the hull must be waterproof. The entire underside is covered with fiberglass cloth and epoxy. This can get a little messy if you are not careful. It is important to get all the air bubbles out before it dries. A simple vacuum blanket pulls everything down tight. Don't let this scare you; it is really quite easy. First cover the freshly epoxied fiberglass with a layer of thin plastic sheet. Then cover the sheet with a blanket.

This way the blanket won't stick to the fiberglass. Cover the blanket with a larger piece of plastic sheeting and tape it down to the floor all around the edges Make a small slit in the plastic and plug in the vacuum hose from your shop vac. Turn it on and watch the vacuum pull it down to the floor. If it won't pull a vacuum check for leaks in the tape. I ran the vacuum for about two hours and did a great job. When you take it apart the plastic will pull of easily as it will not stick to the fiberglass

## Step 4: Underside of the hull is now complete

This is what the underside of the hull should look like.

## Step 5: Making the duct

The duct is made from less dense 1" white Styrofoam. The plans show you how to lay out a curving arc that will wrap around the plywood plugs in the middle. Start by screwing together the two plywood discs to spacers the width of the duct. Wrap thee discs with a band of 1/8" plywood. After you cut the ducts to the proper shape (arc) Cut kerfs 3/4" deep all around the inside of the ducts so they will bend around the form easily. Be sure and maintain the exact centers of the discs. Later you will drill them out to the size of your motors crankshaft. Don't separate the duct from the form at this time. When it gets to be time to locate the duct to the hull these holes will let you mount the duct perfectly in line with your engine shaft. The plans go into great detail on this step and we didn't have any problems with it.

## Step 6: Making the motor support post

Cut a 2 x 4 piece of pine to the length specified in the plans and put it in the hole cut into the hull (center line of craft). Use plenty of epoxy for this. Cut a base plate from 3/4" plywood for mounting the engine. Fit rear legs from pine and drill and screw braces everywhere you can. This will keep vibration to a minimum I used gorilla glue in every joint. I put epoxy lay ups all around the post for added strength.

## Step 7: Mounting the duct

Temporarily mount the motor in place and drill the plywood disc to the size of your crank shaft. Set the duct in place and align it up with the motor crank. Use shims to assure good alignment. When you are satisfied that it looks straight anchor the duct in place with spray can expanding foam. Put it on heavy as it can be shaped or removed easily with a knife or file. When it hardens you should have a rigid mounted duct that is aligned with the motor crank shaft lined up with the center of the duct. At this time you can remove the plywood discs from the duct by removing the screws that hold the spacers. It should pop right out.

## Step 8: The propeller

You can buy the prop two ways, either finished or unfinished. You can save a lot of money by finishing your prop yourself.

First slide the prop onto the crank without the hub to see if it fits inside the duct without binding. A duct is most efficient when the prop fits closely inside the duct. Be very careful when removing tip material, it's easy to cutoff but hard to put back. Once you have the tip clearance set you can begin to sand the blades with a power sander and finish by hand. Once you get it smooth you MUST balance it to avoid vibration.

Hang the prop on a rod held in a vise to see which blade is heavier than the other. Don't short cut by shortening the tips. Just keep sanding the blades. Most props are pretty close when they arrive so it is not an undaunted task. Once it is balanced give it a couple coats of paint to preserve it. It's a good idea to paint a white band at the tips for safety's sake. By now the foam is hard so you can cut the bottom of the duct with a sabre saw to conform with the openings in the hull for lift air. Now is a good time to trial fit the prop and hub to the motor to make sure it runs true inside the duct. The motor should be bolted down securely. Turn the prop over slowly by hand. Check for at least 1/8" clearance all around. You can adjust by putting small shims under the motor mounts if needed.

## Step 9: Build the air chamber

The purpose of the air chamber is to divide the air flow between lift and thrust. The picture doesn't show it in its proper place. We just needed a flat area to glue and fiberglass it together. It is made from 1/8" plywood.

## Step 10: Install the air chamber

Slide the three sided chamber in place and glue or fiberglass in place. I prefer to use fiberglass whenever possible. When the bond is set install the top of the box. You will probably have to put a weight on the rear to hold it tightly to the bottom frame. When it is dry fiber glass the edges and you are done with the air box.

## Step 11: The rudders

The rudders are cut from 1" foam. Drill holes in the top and bottom to fit dowel pins. Glue the dowel pin in the bottom. The top pin just drops in to allow for removal of the rudder. I used a belt sander to fashion an airfoil to make them lighter and more aerodynamic. Don't make them too thin. Cover the rudders with one layer of fiberglass to give them strength. Glue small drilled blocks at the top of the duct, and the air chamber to receive the dowel pins. Connect the two rudders together at the bottom dowel pin with a short length of aluminum or wood stock. This is where the steering cables are attached. Run the cables through the air box and route them through eyelets to the control stick. Don't terminate them yet until you build the body. We used a 2' long piece of 1" PVC for a control stick.

## Step 12: Make it look good with a body

Start by laying out the basic shape with a marking pen and screwing 3/4" stock to the line. The 1/8" plywood bends easily to conform to the shape. Next clamp and glue the 3/4" stringers to the top. Fit a 2 x 4 between the sides to form a dash board. This is a good time to attach the throttle cable to either the dash or the side strips. Later on we put a lanyard connected to the kill switch in the dash. This is a requirement if you want to run it in any sanctioned races. Cover the top with a plywood sheet and fit some scrap foam to form the nose piece. Run the steering cables through the sides and attach them to the stick. Make a little seat that feels comfortable. We padded ours with some foam and scrap vinyl. Paint the whole craft with a couple coats of any paint you may have laying around. We chose white because it stays cool even in direct sunlight. A little trim color makes it unique to you and really makes it stand out. Now that it is painted is a good time to add a screen to stop wayward hands and arms from getting into the prop area. That could ruin a good day. We had some left over wire fencing and fashioned a guard from that. We also added four lifting handles in the corners to aid in lifting it on and off a trailer.

## Step 13: The skirt

I am sorry that I didn't take pictures of the skirt installation but the plans go into great detail on this step. I put the craft up on horses to make it easy to get at the inside attachment. The key to a good skirt is in the corners. They are over lapped and glued with the special glue tat is supplied by Universal Hovercraft. The skirt is held in place by 200 stainless screws and washers. The only tricky part is the screws around the rear of the air box. The skirt is very rugged and we have not had any trouble with it.

## Step 14: The big day: the test drive

The first thing we did was to drag it outside and start it up to check on how it hovered. The skirt filled up with air at a little more than idle and we could push it around easily. We gave it more throttle and it began to move forward. My grandson got in first and drove it all around the back yard. It seemed to respond good to steering control but we learned that it tends to side slip if you are going too fast when you go into the turn. Next I got in and also had good results. Time for the water tests. We took the hovercraft to my best friend's house, he lives on a 1000 acre lake and has a small beach to launch from. The craft floats well on its own and with a person that weighs 200 lbs. I elected to be the test pilot and put on a life jacket for safety. Starting the engine brought it up to a nice hover. Increasing the throttle a bit started the craft moving forward and away from the beach. More throttle and it began to move forward more briskly. It seemed to handle really good at full throttle until I tried my first turn. To my surprise I started to go sidewise and then backwards. With a little experience I learned to lean my body into the turns and reduce throttle slightly and was able to negotiate the turns much better. I don't know how fast I was going because I don't have a speed indicator, but I left a pretty good wake. Leaning forward seemed to increase the speed. When my grandson took his turn he seemed to go a little faster than me and he was riding more level than I was. I think maybe the seat should be a little more forward. We really had a blast and 8 or 10 people of all sizes and weights tried it out. The heaviest guy weighed around 300 lbs. Although it floated well, he could not get the performance that we could. Under 225 lbs. was OK.

We played for 2 hours and burned two tanks of gas and didn't have any problems. All in all it was a great test day. This craft is fun, easy to drive, and proved to be very safe. Our youngest pilot was 10 or 12 years old. My only other comment would be to install a quieter exhaust as the neighbors were not impressed with the noise. It attracted a lot of attention as many people had never seen a hovercraft before.

# Gravity Bike

### By Harlan Whitman
#### (http://www.instructables.com/id/Gravity-Bike/)

Howdy, We are S. I. N. Cycles builders of gravity fueled machines. This is our most recent build, hope you enjoy! Just want to add that if you are interested in some of our other machines check out http://sincycles.blogspot.com/.

A Gravity Bike? It is what it sounds like, a bicycle that goes downhill and otherwise has not much use. These machines are a joy to ride. They are almost soothing; just the sound of the wind and road. Speed varies depending on the hill. We regularly get up to 50mph but speeds up to and beyond 80mph can be accomplished. While the speeds may be questionably legal, these machines are legal on all public roads where bicycles are allowed.

If you ever care to race in an organized race, conforming to the IGSA standards might be a good idea. We build loosely around these rules and have not found the need or desire to go outside of those bounds. The rulebook can be found at http://www.igsaworldcup.com/rulebooks/2009_igsa_rulebook_final.pdf.

## The basic standards are:

- Wheel size—51cm/20" max
- Bike weight—34kg/75lbs max
- Axle to axle length—127cm/50" max
- Many more rules can be found in the rule book. But where we race, none apply.

## Tools needed or have access to:

- Welder
- Metal cutting tools of some kind—angle grinder and cut off wheels, metal band saw, hacksaw, hole saw
- Assortment of wrenches
- Drill press
- Vise
- The more the merrier!

## Materials

We dig through metal scrap bins for most of our metal material and then let the material inspire.

- We did buy 8ft of .75" x 1.5" x .125" mild steel for this project.
- Paint
- Rim Brakes
- Brake Levers
- Brake cable/housing
- L200 foam
- Wheel cover

- x2 20 inch wheels
- Old BMX bike to pluck any tidbits from
- Shaft collars
- Lead

We truly hope you enjoy this inside look!
—S. I. N. (Sir Isaac Newton) Cycles

## Step 1: Prototype

This is a critical step to create a comfortable ride. Everyone has their own body length and preference of how something should feel. So play around. We joke sometimes saying every bike is our prototype for the next bike we build.

As you can see in the photo our prototype is super high tech utilizing a chunk of wood, rope, zipties, a fork, and some wheels. It was just together enough that we could carefully straddle it and envision where the handle bars, kneelers, and rear pegs might be. Cardboard boxes, milk crates, and other random items come in handy at this stage.

Be sure to take more measurements than you think you need. Also plenty of photos sure don't hurt. Documentation is a wonderful thing.

Sometimes we will draw over the photo to play with the overall aesthetics and frame layout. It is cheaper to learn things on paper than steel.

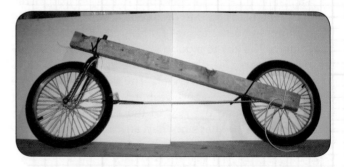

## Step 2: Get jiggy!

Great thing about gravity bike frames are the minimalistic needs. The front and rear axle must be aligned and the head tube needs to be true. Aside from those two things the rest of the frame design is up to where you want your body on the bike.

Our jig is made from mild steel .5" x 1.5" x .125 wall thickness and 1.5" square for the uprights because its what we had laying around. Drill holes in the jig at the distance in which you want your axle length to be. Ours is at 48 inches. We then used old 3/8" axles from BMX wheels and mounted those into the holes. These axles will be used to mount the fork and rear dropouts during the frame build and welding.

## Step 3: Frame

The materials for the frame are all over the place. We had an old donor bike that we salvaged parts from: the head tube, rear drop outs seat stay, and fork. We salvaged the old seat stay mainly for the v-brake tabs already on the frame. The two top tubes and lower tube are mild steel .75" x 1.5" x .125wall. The down tube and seat tube are cro-moly 1.5" diameter .125 wall thickness. The two top tubes are a straight shot from the head tube to the rear dropout. The down tube was bent on a hydraulic tubing bender. Many custom metal fab shops and railing shops will have a machine that can do this for very reasonable rates. The down tube was bent in this shape purely for aesthetic reasons. There are endless ways to get from the head tube to the rear dropout, be inventive and have fun.

We don't really do mechanical drawings before the build, so for us it's a lot of holding up in place and marking with sharpies. After the material is marked we use a hole saw to cope the tubing for a nice clean fit. When using hole saws make sure your materials is fixed firmly. The hole saw is aggressive and can grab the material sending it for a loop. A round hand file or drum sander is a great tool to finalize any copes that are not snugging up how you'd like. Remember it's much easier to take away more material then to add it.

The head tube angle or rake is set at 23 degrees which we have found to be a good middle ground for long straights and tight switchbacks.

Keeping your rear end off the tire is important. For this we took a piece of scrap tubing for the kneelers and welded it between the two top tubes to act as a rear fender.

This is the time to consider how you are mounting your seat. Ours has two small metal tabs that screw through into the seat.

This frame was TIG welded, but it could have been MIG welded. Just be sure and follow all safety procedures whilst welding.

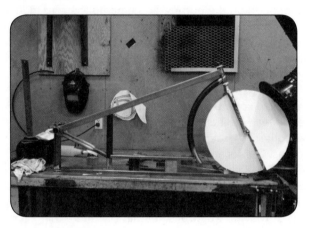

## Step 4: Kneeler

The kneeler is an area that takes a lot if not most of the weight from the rider. Material for this was found in scrap bins. We found 2"x2" box tubing scrap and cut triangle segments off of either side to get the structure seen in the photo. Then 4" x 4" x 3/8" thick steel plate and welded them to the box tubing. We strongly recommend not using pegs or round tubing for kneelers, your shin bones will agree. The idea is to have a wide surface area to distribute the energy from bumps.

Minicel L200 also known as Y20 was used for the kneeler padding. This foam is resilient and has excellent shock absorption abilities. A generous two inch thick piece was used to eliminate the chance of ever feeling any hard shock through the knee or shin. Other foams that would work well would be neoprene or sleeping pad material. Minicel can be purchased at http://www.foam-bymail.com/Minicel.html.

## Step 5: Ballast

Weight, it's your friend in this sport. Where the weight is located is also important. Pushing as much weight as possible below the axle height will give you a much more maneuverable bike. So what you can do is drill a hole in the frame and fill parts of it full of lead or concrete. Some builders will bolt on lifting weights this is nice because you can easily move the weight on the bike and or increase decrease the amount.

What we have done here is taken two steel hemispheres drilled a half inch hole in the center of both hemispheres. In one hemisphere we welded a piece of 1/2" all thread through the sphere. Leave a few inches on the inside and enough on the outside of the hemisphere to mount it to the frame. Then weld the two hemispheres together. Next, ground off excess weld to create a smooth looking sphere. A tube was welded to the sphere for a "wick" to be added later making a classy looking little bomb.

Now for the awesome nasty dangerous part. Filling the hollow sphere full of heavy stuff. Using a gas forge we melted lead pellets and then poured the melted lead into the sphere. A funnel is of great assistance during this process. Ours is an Ace model for about three dollars. This created a 25lb ballast. There was still room for more weight so we drilled a hole in the bottom tube of the frame and filled that full also. Do not try to cool these parts down with water. Just let them do there thing. It may take an hour or more. If you do not have a gas forge at your disposal an oxy/acetylene torch or MAPP Gas torch will also get the job done. If you go down this road please where a proper respirator and do it outside if possible.

The excess all thread that was left protruding from the sphere was enough to safely mount it in a vise for the pouring of lead. After the lead has cooled we drilled a half inch hole in the frame and mounted the ball. You can bolt the weight on using a nylock. We chose to cut the all thread down until only .125" was protruding out of the frame, and then welded it on.

## Step 6: Handlebars

This bike's handlebars are mounted directly to the front fork.

First, weld mounting points onto the fork. Welded just a few inches down from the fork crown are .875" tubes .25" wall thickness 2" long. The handle bars consist of .875" tube .125" wall. Many brake levers are designed for this size tubing. Cut two six inch pieces and two seven inch pieces.

To make the bars totally adjustable we used two piece clamp on shaft collars with a .875" bore. First take the shaft collars and weld them together into sets of two. To make sure the shaft collars are aligned with each other bolt them onto .875" tube butted firmly together. After you have four sets of dual shaft collars weld them onto the ends of the six inch and seven inch tubes. You can now position the bars to whatever suits you best.

Another option is to use a BMX handle bar stem and invert some standard BMX bars.

Shaft collars can be purchased sometimes at your local hardware store. If not, go to those who have it all: www.mcmaster.com.

## Step 7: Paint

At this point all metal fab that needs to be done is completed. Prep the frame by sanding the entire surface with 100 grit sandpaper. This is a good time to give the frame a full once over to check for any sharp areas. Think what might be sharp wrecking at 45mph. Baby proof it, make it soft like butter. Then to take care of all your greasy paw prints with some kind of surface cleaner. We prefer acetone, remember your protection. At this point you can tape off any areas where you don't want paint, like the head tube where the bearings go and on the kneeler plates where you will be gluing to. After everything is nice and clean give it a coat of primer and then top coat. After letting the topcoat kickoff you can tape off any areas for creating two tone effects. For this build tape off the frame around the bomb area. Then give that bomb a nice flat black coat. At this time we also installed the "wick" resin coated rope with some two part epoxy.

You can use fancy two part paint or rattle can, just be sure to follow the instructions. For this project we had to run some heaters to get the room up to an acceptable temp. Good practice to spray towards the end of a day forcing you to leave it over night before handling it.

## Step 8: Seat

For this bike the seat is more for when you're slowing to a stop or just sitting around before you bomb. The geometry of this frame puts most of your weight on the kneelers. This allows you to throw the bike around underneath you, so we wanted a low profile seat.

Start with a piece of half inch plywood. Lay the plywood on the frame and then trace from underneath to get the width of the seat. Then sketch out on the plywood the rest of the shape. Use a band saw or scroll saw to cut out your shape.

For seats we again like to use the Minicel L200. It's not the must squishy thing under you bum but it is tough and dampens vibrations and impacts well enough. One of the coolest things about this foam is how you can sculpt it. It cuts with a bandsaw with ease. You can use a hacksaw or hand saw also. Once you get the general shape blocked out you can use a coarse grit sandpaper to shape it further. It has a low moisture absorption rate so leaving it raw is always an option.

Once you have your desired shape you can wrap it in fabric or leather. Oregon Leather Supply has amazing scrap barrels with plenty of pieces that are big enough for a seat. We chose a piece of red leather. Ideally we like to use barge glue for this, but we where fresh out. Super 77 spray adhesive saved the day. First apply a layer to the foam and plywood and bond those two together. Then you can attack with the leather. Apply a layer over all of the foam, and then over a smaller section of the leather to get it started. Then as you start wrapping spray the inside of the leather pull and press down. Starting with your biggest flat surface and then working out from there tends to be the best option. It's a tedious procedure and in our shop we find cursing sometimes helps.

This frame has mounting holes preplanned for this seat. Although on other builds we have glued the seat straight to the steel with good results.

Other foams such as upholstery foam will work it's just not our preference. If you do happen to use upholstery foam, know that electric carving knives from the kitchen work wonders.

## Step 9: Wheels

No need to spend a whole lot of money here. This build is using two no big name loose ball bearing hub wheel sets. We rebuild our hubs cleaning out all the old crud and replace the old grease with a good quality lube. We are kind of low tech and just use regular white lithium grease and then blast a little Remington Teflon gun oil in there before sealing it all up. A clean proper adjusted looseball hub is a beautiful thing. Adjusting loose ball bearing hubs is no big deal if you've made it this far in the build you can do it. If you feel you need assistance most cycle shops will walk you through it.

Tubes are something that should be purchased fresh we recommend anything that claims to be heavy duty or extra tough. For this build we used Kenda Heavy Duty 2.25mm wall thickness. Average tubes are around .09mm thick less than half the thickness.

Tires that do not have dry rot cracks or threads showing will work. We recommend something with maximum rubber contact almost slicks. Animal ASM and Animal GLH are tried and true high PSI and awesome micro tread design gives great traction in many conditions. Higher PSI allows for low rolling resistance. You can always let a little air out if you're running a more technical course or rain.

Rear wheel covers are getting somewhat hard to come across nowadays keep your eyes open on eBay or Craigslist and you'll find a set sooner or later. These may have some aerodynamic benefit, but more importantly they keep your feet out of the rear spokes.

Alright now bolt those buggers on!

## Step 11: Best Part

When you build something with wheels you get to ride it. Really is an amazingly rewarding experience. BUT, let's be realistic, in the haze of that final assembly something might have been over looked. Roll around the drive way and make sure the brakes work and the wheels are on right side up and all of that good stuff. Now get your wrenches out and double check everything. OK now we are ready for a small test hill to see how it feels after you feel comfortable step it up. Have fun tell others what they are missing and get a group together. Remember to ride within your limits, and maybe push them every so often...

## Step 10: Final assembly

This is where you install the front fork with fresh grease and double check the nuts. Install brakes and brake cables leaving plenty of cable slack around the head tube that the cables will not pull tight when you turn the handlebars. Brake levers and grips. A neat trick to getting your grips on easily is to use hair spray. Just blast a bit down inside your grips and then quickly slide them on to the handle bar. You can also use a high pressure air nozzle ballooning the grip as you glide it on.

Applying the foam to the kneelers. You'll want to use a good strong water resistant glue. We recommend barge glue. It is very tenacious. Just apply a good even layer to the steel and to the foam. Let it sit for a few minutes. Then carefully align the foam and drop it on applying a decent amount of force. When the two coated surfaces touch each other, that's it, no shifting it around. Like I said tenacious.

You can use zip ties to lash down any loose items such a cable housing. Be sure and not cinch down to hard on zip ties over cable housing it can pinch the cable applying undesired cable drag.

# Drainage Luge

### By pbshoe
(http://www.instructables.com/id/Drainage-Luge/)

Have you ever seen those cement drainage pipes down hillsides? I see them wherever I go. They're meant to help water flow down hillsides without eroding the land. To me, they've always looked like a roller coaster ride.

So we decided to turn the drainage pipes into a ride, a sport if you will: DRAINAGE LUGE.

## Step 1: Get the parts

In order to build a board, you have to know a bit about the drainage pipes. The key facts are the following:
- Top width: 33 inches
- Height: 20 inches deep

We ended up going to a store and picking up two crummy skateboards for $8 a piece and taking them apart.

Parts list:
- Four skateboard trucks with bearings and wheels
- 16—2 inch 10/24 bolts, washers and lock nuts
- 3/4 inch plywood, 28 inches wide x 36 to 48 inches long (depending on how long you want the board)
- Wood glue
- Four C clamps (Size? as long as they open up enough for 2 inches)
- 3/4 inch plywood strips, 28 inches wide, 4 inches long
- Sandpaper or electric sander
- Drill (bits: 10/24 and1/2 inch)
- Two pieces of rope, roughly 8 inches each, thickness of 1/2 inch

## Step 2: Affix the reinforcements

Determine where you are going to put the trucks, length-wise, on the larger board. Cover the bottom of the strips with enough wood glue to affix, then attach the

clamps. Wait for the recommended period then move onto the next step. I recommend keeping the trucks towards each end of the board, but not at the very end. We've left roughly 4 inches on each end.

## Step 3: Prepping the board

It isn't necessary to add padding, fancy graphics or paint to these boards (but you can if you want to). But I think would behoove you to at least get the sharp edges-sanded off.

## Step 4: Install the trucks

Depending on the width of your board, you want to make sure that the outside wheels are roughly 30 inches apart. Measure twice for each truck that you install. Ensure that they are roughly 30 inches from outer wheel to outer wheel, but also make sure that they are the proper distance from the front of the board.

Once you are certain of your measurements and truck placements, it is time to do the marking of the drill locations. Use a pencil to mark in each truck hole, and remove the truck. Do this for each truck.

Use your drill to slowly drill through each whole. When finished with each truck, insert each bolt (from the bottom (or top of the board) so that the nuts are placed on the truck-side of the board. Once each bolt is on, ensure that the truck fits properly.

Once all trucks holes are drilled, add truck, bolts, washers and lock nuts and tighten.

## Step 5: Handholds

As an afterthought, we added some rope handholds to help with staying on the board, and to aid in steering.

At roughly the middle of the board, we drilled 1/2 inch holes, four inches apart on either side of the board, at roughly 2 inches from the edge. We then fed in the rope and knotted each end.

## Step 6: Test ride!

Now for the fun part. Riding the board.

Go to the top of the hillside, put on your boots, helmet and gloves, put the board in the pipe, mount and give yourself a few luge-like pushes. Before you know it, you will achieve incredible speeds.

To stop, use your feet to stop Fred Flintstone style on the dirt. Good luck, and practice safe drainage luge!

# Popsicle Stick Longboard Deck

## By Nathan Snip (nsnip)
(http://www.instructables.com/id/Popsicle-Stick-Longboard-Deck/)

I have wanted to make a longboard deck for some time, however I was having trouble finding cheap veneers. I started thinking about using popsicle sticks to construct my own veneers instead. Popsicle sticks are made from baltic birch, which is used to make wooden aircraft so I thought it might work for a longboard as well. Here's what I did.

## Step 1: Shaping the template

I figured out the shape I wanted and scaled it so I could use 5 sheets of 8 1/2 x 11" paper as a template. I just taped the sheets together, cut it out, and stood beside it to make sure it felt right.

## Step 2: Building the mold

I built a mold out of foam core or "Ready Board" which I bought at the dollar store. I cut out multiples with the curve I wanted with a scroll saw, these became the ribs of my mold. I scored the foam core with a razor blade so that the sheet could curve with the ribs. I marked out rib points with pencil and then I hot glued the ribs to the scored sheet.

To keep the popsicle sticks from sticking to the mold I covered the gluing surface with some glossy "marbled" vinyl I got at the dollar store.

The curved tail section of the mold was built up of more pieces of foam core.

## Step 3: Gluing the first layer

I purchased my glue and popsicle sticks. I used 2 bottles of Titebond III glue which I found at Lee Valley Tools. The popsicle sticks I purchased at the dollar store, they came in packages of 150 and were conveniently paper

taped in stacks of 50. I figured I needed about 1500 sticks for the board but I had a lot of rejects. I would say about a third of a package was unusable, because some of the sticks were warped or cracked.

I cut the round ends of the sticks off with a band saw.

I worked outward from the center of the mold gluing a row at a time. It was slow going; I figure I spent about 6-8 hours per layer.

## Step 4: Steam bending for the tail 1

For the popsicle sticks to have a smooth curve into the tail of the longboard I needed to steam bend them.

For the first layer I left the tail until last. I dry fitted pieces and numbered them. I boiled water in a sauce pan and put a colander between the pan and it's lid. This would allow the steam to fill a chamber and transfer heat to the popsicle sticks so they could be bent.

They didn't need much time—about 45 seconds to a minute in the steam was long enough to bend them. I had a few sticks break and had to replace them. After gluing the bent sticks in place I used a bag of sand on top of an extra piece of vinyl to help keep them in place while they dried.

For subsequent layers I would bend the tail pieces as I glued each individual line which worked much better.

## Step 5: Steam bending for the second layer

For the second layer the popsicle sticks would be glued perpendicular to the first layer to add strength like plywood. This is called cross grain. Since the mold bends in that direction, I needed to give the popsicle sticks for this layer a bend.

I built a jig that I could put a bunch of sticks into and steam at the same time. I placed the jig upside down above a large saucepan and covered some of the gaps with a rag. When steaming wood you want the steam to move around the wood. A steam chamber with a few holes in it is a good thing. The sticks only needed to be exposed to the steam

for 45 seconds to a minute. Once they had cooled I popped them out and added another bunch.

I covered the first layer with wax paper so that the next layer wouldn't stick to it. I marked the center line with a push pin and started gluing my second layer.

## Step 6: Steam bending for the tail 2

For the next layer I glued as before except I did the tail pieces row by row. This worked much better, allowing me to work diagonally out from the tail pieces. I used a rasp to even out the ends of the popsicle sticks and some sand paper glued to a board to straighten the edges and to thin thicker sticks.

After each layer I sanded the high spots down and sawed off the excess at the tail.

## Step 7: Gluing the layers and vacuum pressing

I made five layers total: three lengthwise layers and two cross grain layers. I stacked them in an alternating pattern so that the bottom, middle, and top layers went lengthwise.

I used a palm sander to even out each layer. I peeled off the wax paper and sanded the undersides of each layer.

I reinforced the mold with some side pieces. Next was a dry fit. Using a push pin as my center line, I marked each layer with pencil so I knew where to place them when gluing and to see if they would fit in my vacuum bag.

I bought some vacuum bags meant for shrinking clothing for storage. Each package has small bags for shirts and large bags for dresses. The large bag was just too small for my mold so I had to cut off a 2 inch piece before I did the final glue up.

I applied a liberal amount of glue and used a brush to evenly smear the glue across the top of each layer top and also to the bottom of the next layer and stacked them in place on the mold.

I sealed the bag and vacuumed out the air. Once again I used my trusty sand bag to apply extra pressure to the tail.

## Step 8: Cutting out the shape

I left the mold in the vacuum over night. After removing it from the vacuum I notice a couple of raised places which I would have to inject with glue after cutting the board out and sanding.

I used a jig saw to cut out the shape and used a belt sander to smooth the edges. Next was the palm sander to smooth and remove extra glue from the top and bottom. I used a damp cloth to clean off any fine saw dust that was left on the board.

## Step 9: Preparing for hardware

I added holes for the skateboard trucks with a drill press.

I bought trucks, wheels, bearings, grip tape, nuts, and bolts at a local skate shop. I decided a cool blue that reminded me of popsicles was a good color choice for the wheels.

## Step 10: Finishing

There was some more sanding needed on some spots on the top which were raised and needed to be injected with extra glue. After that I sealed the board with a few coats of shellac and applied some surf inspired grip tape lines. The grip tape is self adhesive and can be purchased at almost any skateboarding shop.

Overall there are much easier and faster ways to build a longboard deck, but I wanted to try using popsicle sticks just to see if it was possible.

# Pencil Bike

By ellenhereandthere
(http://www.instructables.com/id/Pencil-Bike/)

What could be more practical than a bicycle that doubles as a pencil? It is surprisingly easy to make this fun and functional "riding implement" out of an old kid's bike and a 4" x 4" wooden beam.

## Step 1: Start design on the CAD system

See Woodenbikes' genius "CAD" instructions (http://www.instructables.com/id/Office-Chair-Bike/step1/Design-your-bike-using-a-CAD-system-Cardboard-Aid/) to create a cardboard cutout of your body, so you can figure out proper positioning of wheels/seat/handlebars/etc. As he says, "Using a sophisticated 2D CAD system (Cardboard Aided Design) life size cutout of your foot/leg thigh/back and arm, pivoting on brads at the joints, you can design the bike on the ground to explore sizing and clearance issues. My CAD system sometimes has a Gooey interface if I spill something on it while designing. More seriously, like other CAD systems it has a GUI (Graspable User interface).

Make a cardboard cutout of your lower leg (with foot and pedal), thigh, torso, and straight arm (to a distance 2" back from your wrist). Use it to look for good riding position and clearances for knees to bars, heels to wheels etc. Use the CAD system to layout the riding position, cranks, wheels etc with attention for locating your hands, shoulder, seat-back angle, butt, knees and feet.

For detailed instruction on 12 Steps to designing a sweet handling recumbent, visit Bikesmith Design at http://bikesmithdesign.com/Design/12Steps.html.

## Step 2: Basic parts (A kid bike and some 4x4 lumber)

This is the 4x4 beam and the kid bike we used. The kid bike has 16" wheels and a coaster (back pedal) brake for simplicity.

## Step 3: Disassemble donor bike and start the design layout

Disassemble the donor bike paying attention to how the wheels attach to the frame, how the stem attaches to the steerer tube (in the fork), and how the pedals detach from the cranks (They unscrew in the direction they would unscrew if you were pedaling forward and they "locked up." (e.g. Rt foot pedal unscrews normally, and Left foot pedal unscrews strangely). Remove the bottom bracket[1] lock ring (also reverse threaded) and remove the BB cone and ball bearing race (the set of metal balls held together by a clip). Keep all these crank and BB parts together in a box since you will reassemble and disassemble them several times as the project progresses.

## Step 4: Mark and drill the headset holes

With the head angle figured out to give proper trail (the link is to a description of bike steering geometry and "trail" http://www.instructables.com/id/Mountain-Bike-Scooter/#step1), mark the headset (HS) center point on the top of the beam and use a carpenters square to mark

---

1 The bottom bracket (BB) is the main crank axle bearing

the position out to the side and to mark it at the head angle to indicate where the bottom HS hole will be centered on the underside of the beam.

Use a hole saw (cylindrical toothed drill bit) to drill the larger outer hole first that will support the outermost diameter of the HS cup. Drill it to a depth you want to set the cup, preferably just deep enough to surround all of the cup. (If you drill too deep and mount the cups too close together there is excessive leverage of the steerer tube on the two cups.) Repeat for the top HS cup.

Use a smaller diameter hole saw that matches the extended cylinder of the HS (where it was pressed in the metal bike's head tube) to drill the next hole deep enough to allow the HS cup to be pressed firmly into the beam. Repeat for the top HS cup.

Now drill the approximately 1 1/8" steerer tube hole in from the top and in from the bottom until the holes meet in the middle of the beam. It's OK if they don't align perfectly. You can use a rasp to smooth the transition between them. Gently use a chisel to chisel out the remaining cylinders of wood left between the cylindrical holes cut by the hole saws. Be careful to leave a smooth floor of wood to support the flared out floor of the bearing cups.

Now the bearing cups should be able to be fit in the holes and be seated on wood (not floating).

## Step 5: Mark and drill the crank bearing (BB) holes

We drew pencil lines to mark the center point locations for both sides of the BB holes.

Drill the largest diameter holes first (while you have good solid wood to hold the hole saw's stabilizing center bit). First drill all the holes and then come back to chisel wood out of the cylindrical cuts of the hole-sawed holes. (This leaves maximum wood to support the drilling operation.)

Use a hole saw selected to match the outer cylinder diameter of the bearing cup for a fairly tight fit. On the bike's right side (where the chain ring will be) drill/saw only as deep as needed to set the bearing cup in up to its protruding lip. Stopping at that level maximizes the supporting wood left in place as a "floor" to the hole. That floor helps support the cup.

From the left side of the bike Drill/saw the large hole to a depth that would have the bearing cups' outer protruding lips about 2 7/8" apart. That will about match the donor bike's original BB width (cup face to cup face). e.g. our inset depth was 5/8" below the surface (3 1/2" inch "4x4" minus 2 7/8"). This means the left cup would be about 5/8" inset into the 3.5" thick wood. Or you could slice about 5/8" off of the left face of the beam (so it's 2 7/8" wide) and mount the cup in to its lip depth just like the right side. We chose not to slice, but to drill deeper to preserve structural and artistic integrity (this time).

Drill 3 holes a little bigger than the BB axle (about 5/8") to form a slot in a direction that will accommodate threading the crank through the slot.

## Step 6: Shaping the 4x4 into a hexagonal pencil

We let the top and bottom planes of the 4x4 remain intact (but narrowed) and cut slanted strips off the two side faces of the 4x4 with a table saw to make a hexagon cross section. In the area where the BB and head-set[2] would be drilled through the wood, we left the 4x4 uncut to leave maximum wood for support of the holes and bearing cups. A draw knife is a fun way to shape the transition and to shape the point.

## Step 7: Cut the rear triangle off the donor bike

We actually did wear eye protection while building the bike. I (WB) have had a piece of rusty steel cut out of my cornea by an eye surgeon after my ophthalmologist looked at it, got very quiet, and had to leave the room. I can still use that eye for eyeballing measurements, but everything is off about 1/4 of an inch. So always, eat your veggies and wear your goggles.

## Step 8: Sanded Primed, and Painted

2 Head-set is the main steering bearing in a bike frame that connects the fork to the rest of the frame. The Head-set has bearing cups and cones that thread onto the fork's steerer tube.

75

## Step 9: Cut the stem and weld an extension between the pieces

The handlebar stem is cut carefully with a Sawzall ("cut carefully with a Sawzall" is an oxymoron, but we do the best we can) in a plane that anticipates the welding of a piece of square steel tubing in between the two offset pieces of the cut stem creating a very tall stem. (It has to be tall for knee clearance under the handlebars while pedaling.) Use the CAD system with the knee up to see how high the bars have to be to clear the knee.

## Step 10: Attach rear triangle to 4x4

There are different ways to do this. After much hemming and hawing, with considerable chin scratching we welded a piece of steel to the cut ends of the seat stays and then drilled holes through the steel and attached it to the beam with stout wood screws. We drilled holes through the remaining half of the BB shell and screwed it to the 4x4 with stout wood screws also.

## Step 11: Assembled with the seat attached

The seat is made from a chair back.

## Step 12: Admire your bike

## Step 13: Make the eraser

4 inch diameter aluminum flex duct is used to connect some used polyethylene packing foam to the pencil

wood, mimicking the band that is used to do the same on regular pencils. The foam was easy to cut into an eraser shape and was painted eraser pink. It has a great texture.

## Step 14: Ready for test riding

Ellen assembled the long chain out of regular bike chains following this handy instructable about using a chain tool (http://www.instructables.com/id/Using-a-Bike-Chain-Tool). After the chain was attached, it was tightened by simply positioning a chain tension roller wheel from a ten speed derailleur somewhere along the beam where it would both lift the chain above the front wheel and snug up all the slack in the chain.

## Step 15: Pencil bike in action

## Step 16: Future Bikes?

So many ideas. So little storage space.

Hopefully you will be inspired to make your own fun bikes!

Happy Trails!

# Tall Amphibious Couchbike

By Nic Welbourn (aka Limp Jimmy)

(nicos)

(http://www.instructables.com/id/Tall-Amphib-ious-Couchbike/)

That's right, tall, amphibious, and with a couch. Why? That's a good question...

The whole notion of an amphibious tall couch trike is the beer-induced brain child of a Rat Patrol member. I am simply the conduit between a fantastically absurd idea which should never have been done, and something that now exists and is actually practical to use in the real world... But it all started with beer.

More about the bike at http://www.rat-patrol.org/RPOz/FArt/mitzie.html, beer being essential at every step of the conception, design and building phases.

## Step 1: Beer

First we sat down and thought about the ergonomics of our world-beating Steer-by-beer concept—would it be easy enough to ride, steer AND drink beer at the same time. Some things are more important than others. A few beers later and we were satisfied it could be done.

Fortunately, I had picked up an old bunk bed frame the week before and it seemed to be about the right size and shape.

## Step 2: More beer

It had to be a tallbike so that the eye level of the pilots would be well above that of all but the tallest pedestrians (good for concerts and the like)...

Also, the couch had to be easy to remove for parties (4 bolts) and the like... good idea! Steer-by-beer was totally going to work!

Now we set about setting the pedal distance before making final decisions about the dimensions of the chassis.

## Step 3: Beer chassis

A bit of welding, 10 beers later we had a deal.

## Step 4: Floatation and beer

Floatation was quite an issue. It had to float yes, and while it would be OK if things dropped off here and there, it HAD to be UNSINKABLE. You know what they say about the dangers of mixing beer and water...

I figured (hoped) about 300 liters would be fine. I cut the bottom out of the plastic barrels, scuffed the joining surface, then after they had been sitting in hot sun for a while, a few of us smashed them together using epoxy resin and a huge piece of wood. Of course, beer played it's part too.

All of a sudden, the whole structure was totally rigid—wow, it worked really well!! Next we drilled a 10cm diameter hole in the side of the barrels, close to the end. So now we had bulkheads, which were filled with expanding polyurethane foam. Bomber.

Next, I used angle iron to make the float base, which had nylon strapping going through lugs to attach the floats. So far so very good.

## Step 5: Floatation, beer and propulsion

Seing as we were already building a tall trike with a serious inherent danger of off-camber cornering disaster, I thought it would also be great to have a reliable 360 degree-turning system, allowing it to (theoretically) spin on its own footprint in traffic.

The floatation frame attaches with only 4 bolts, the floats weigh about 80kg, so it needed to be able to just drop off when required.

So once the drive train was attached and working, we needed an aqua propulsion system—my idea was to use propellers, but that would have become caught in weeds and stuff, quite the hassle when all you want to do is drink a beer.

Fortunately I had outsourced the design, build and installation to some other Rat Patrollians... their idea was to use paddle wheels—it worked (slowly).

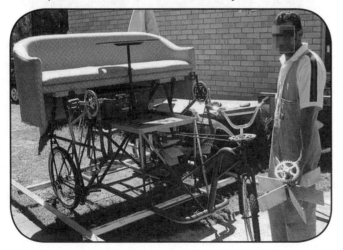

## Step 6: Testing (with beer)

Finally it was time to ride this thing into the water (dry photo showing floatation barrels prior to strapping)... I was only guessing the placement of the barrels and wondered about it's stability in the water.

Funny thing is... IT WORKED PERFECTLY THE FIRST TIME!!!!!!!!! Didn't expect that. Mmmmm, beer, the sweet taste of success!

## Step 7: Living the dream

OK, it probably has a top speed in the water of about 1 knot, but it's a STYLISH ride! The cops aren't sure how to take this one, it's a bike but it's much bigger than a car... or is it a boat? We are quietly confident that she is legal in this country.

Off we go the the Rat Patrol Oz 2007 FLOATilla (http://www.rat-patrol.org/RPOz/rides/FLOATilla2007.html)

That's 7 pretty easy steps on how to make a tall amphibious couchbike, right?

So, what's the next project...? Sleep.

# robots

While robots used to exist solely within the realm of science fiction, they are increasingly becoming a part of everyday life. Robots vacuum our floors, feed our cats, and even do our laundry. It used to take teams of engineers and scientists years of labor and toil in expensive research labs to build robots, but now you can build a robot in days from the comfort of your own home. This chapter puts a DIY robot within reach, even for the most inexperienced enthusiast. The inspirational projects that follow are proof that extraordinary robots can be built by ordinary people.

# Tree Climbing Robot

### By Ben Katz (Technochicken)
(http://www.instructables.com/id/Tree-Climbing-Robot/)

After I got comfortable programming and building with an Arduino, I decided to build a robot. I did not have any particular type in mind, so I wracked my brain (and the internet) for cool robot ideas. Eventually, somehow the idea popped into my head to build a robot that could climb trees. At first I dismissed the idea as beyond my skill level, but after further thought, and some time in Sketchup, I decided to take a shot at the challenge. This is the result of my efforts.

## Step 1: Design

I started out by creating a basic design in Sketchup. The robot was to consist of two segments, joined by a spine which could be extended or retracted. Each segment would have four legs with very sharp points as feet. To climb, the legs on the top segment would pinch together and the sharp feet would dig into the bark, securing the robot. Then the spine would be retracted, pulling up the bottom segment. The legs on the bottom segment would then grip the tree, and the top segment would release. Finally, the spine would extend, pushing the top segment upwards, and the process would repeat. The climbing sequence is somewhat similar to the way an inchworm climbs.

In my original design, all four legs in each segment were controlled by one highly geared down motor. I decided to ditch this idea for a few reasons. Firstly, I could not find the type of spur gear needed to mesh the legs together. Also, with all the legs linked together, the robot would have a hard time gripping uneven surfaces. Finally, I decided that the robot would be much easier to build if the motors drove the legs directly.

The other significant change I made from my original design was the way the spine worked. In my model, I used a rack and pinion type gearing system to extend and contract the spine. However, I could not find the necessary parts to build such a system, so I ended up using a threaded rod coupled to a motor to actuate the spine.

## Step 2: Tools and materials

**Microcontroller**
- Arduino Uno (any will work)

**Motor Controller**
- 3X L298HN—these can be gotten for free as samples from ST
- 2.5" x 3.125" Perf Board
- Terminal Strips
- 22AWG Solid core wire
- 3X Aluminum heatsinks (I cut in half an old northbridge heatsink)
- Thermal paste

**Power**
- 9V Battery (to power the Arduino)
- Approximately 12V LiPo or Li-ion battery (I modified a laptop battery, so I did not even need to buy a charger)
- 5V regulator (To regulate power to the motor controller logic circutry)
- 9V Battery clip
- Barrel connector (Must fit the Arduino power connector)

**Other Electronics**
- 4X 7 RPM Gear Motor (These power two legs each)
- 4X Thin linear trim pots (Rotation sensors for the legs)
- DPDT Toggle switch (Power switch)
- SPDT Slide switch (User input)
- 2X Mini Snap Action Switch (Limit switch)
- 3 10K resistors (Pull down)
- Headers
- Signal Wire (Old IDE cables work really well, and let you organize your wires easily)
- Heat Shrink Tubing

**Hardware**
- 12' 3/4" x 1/8" Aluminum Bar (These come in 6' lengths at my local hardware store)
- 6" x 3" acrylic sheet (Electronics are mounted to this)
- 6x Standoffs with screws
- 1' Threaded rod and corresponding 1/2" nut
- 2X 1' x 3/16" steel rod
- 1' x 3/16" I.D. Brass Tubing

- 4X 5mm Aluminum Universal Mounting Hub
- Pack of large T Pins
- 4X 3/32 screws (to mount the motors)
- An assortment of 4/40 screws and nuts
- Assorted hex screws and nuts
- 4X Bic pens (I used the plastic shafts to fix the pots on the legs in place)
- 4X Locknuts
- 5 Minute epoxy
- Sheet metal scraps (For spacing and mounting things. Bits of Meccano work well)
- Stick on Velcro (For holding on the batteries)
- Hard Drive reading head bearing
- 3/4" Plastic angle
- Electrical Tape
- Zip Ties

Tools

- Electric Drill/Drill press (As well as a lot of bits)
- Hacksaw
- Soldering Iron
- Pliers
- Allen wrench
- Assorted screwdrivers
- Wire Strippers
- C Clamp (These can be used to make nice 90 degree bends in the aluminum)
- Ruler
- Files

Nonessential

- Bench PSU
- Multimeter
- Breadboard

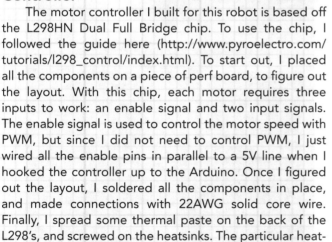

## Step 3: Motor Controller

The motor controller I built for this robot is based off the L298HN Dual Full Bridge chip. To use the chip, I followed the guide here (http://www.pyroelectro.com/ tutorials/l298_control/index.html). To start out, I placed all the components on a piece of perf board, to figure out the layout. With this chip, each motor requires three inputs to work: an enable signal and two input signals. The enable signal is used to control the motor speed with PWM, but since I did not need to control PWM, I just wired all the enable pins in parallel to a 5V line when I hooked the controller up to the Arduino. Once I figured out the layout, I soldered all the components in place, and made connections with 22AWG solid core wire. Finally, I spread some thermal paste on the back of the L298's, and screwed on the heatsinks. The particular heatsinks I used were made by cutting in half a northbridge heatsink from a computer motherboard, and drilling and tapping a hole for the screw. They are probably much larger than needed, but there is no harm in having over sized heatsinks. A higher resolution image of the labeled

board can be found here (http://imageshack.us/photo/ my-images/171/p6151152.jpg/).

When finished, this motor controller should be able to bidirectionally control 4 DC motors at up to 2A each (probably 2A continuously, because of the size of the heatsinks). As you may notice, this leaves me one motor short. My original design used a servo to actuate the spine, but I had to change my design to using a DC motor. To power it, I wired my third L298 chip to a molex connector (so I can disconnect the motor) and soldered on wires for all the connections. It does not look as pretty as my controller on a circuit board, but it works.

## Step 4: Power

The robot's power is supplied by two different sources. The Arduino and the motor controller logic circuitry are powered by a 9V battery, while the motors are powered by an approximately 12V Li-Ion battery pack.

I wanted to avoid having to buy an expensive LiPo/ Li-Ion battery pack and charger, so I searched through my piles of electronic junk for a device with an appropriate battery. I settled on the battery from a 12" iBook laptop. The battery was 10.8V and 50Wh, but it was a little large and heavy for my needs. To fix this, I tore it open and had a look at the internals. I found that the battery was comprised of six 3.7 volt cells. These cells were organized in pairs of two wired in paralleled. The three pairs were then wired in a series, making a total 11.1V. To shrink the pack but keep the voltage, I simply removed one cell from each pair. The final battery pack had only half the capacity and half the discharge rate of the original (now only 2C), but the full voltage. I then wrapped the cells together with electrical tape so they would hold their shape, and soldered a quick-disconnect connector to the battery leads.

## Step 5: Power, cont.

The Arduino and the logic circuitry for the motor controller are both powered by a 9V battery. While the Arduino can take 9V input, the logic circuitry requires 5V, so I wired a 5V regulator in paralleled to the 9V going to the Arduino. Now, why did I not just take advantage of the Arduino's internal 5V regulator? Well, basically I ran out of pins, and I did not want to overdraw the Arduino. In addition to the regulator, I soldered a barrel power connector to the 9V end of the circuit, to fit into the Arduino. Finally, I added a DPDT toggle switch to break the 12V battery circuit as well as the 9V battery circuit.

## Step 6: Legs

The legs are some of the most important parts of this robot, because their design determines whether or not the robot can grip onto trees. I decided to have four pairs of legs, each pair controlled by one motor.

To make the legs, I cut four 8.5" lengths of the aluminum bar. I marked the segments 2.5" from each end. At those marks, I bent the aluminum at a right angle, to make a "U" shape. If you do not have a bending brace (which I don't) you can get a clean bend by clamping the aluminum with a c-clamp right on the mark, and pushing the unclamped end against a solid surface, like a work bench.

## Step 7: Feet

To grip the tree, the robot has very sharp feet at the end of its legs (where else?). The feet are made from jumbo-sized T pins, which you can get at your local fabric store. To fasten them to the legs, I made some clamps out of aluminum. I cut 8 3/8" or so lengths of aluminum, and filed a thin groove lengthwise into each of them, for the pins to fit into. Then I drilled a pair of holes into the aluminum, and corresponding holes into the ends of the legs. The clamps were then bolted down to the legs, with the pins inserted in the grooves. I left about 3/8" of an inch of the pins extending from the legs, but the length can be adjusted by loosening the bolts.

## Step 8: Motor Hubs

The next step is to couple the legs to the motors. I found these handy 5mm mounting hubs, which were perfect for the job. I drilled four holes in a square on one side of each pair of legs, and screwed the hub to the legs with 4/40 screws. To fix the motors to the legs, you simply line up the flat side of the motor shaft with the screw in the hub, and tighten the screw.

## Step 9: Building the Frame

With the legs finished, the next step was to build a frame to hold the motors and legs together and in place. I started the frame by making a plate out of aluminum to hold the motors together. I drilled the plate to fit the screw holes of the motors and the gearbox shaft. The motors are held in place by 3/32 screws.

Next, I made a matching plate for the opposite side of the leg assembly. This plate holds the legs straight while they turn. I drilled holes through the legs, opposite to the motor hubs. Then I bolted the legs through the plate with washers and a locknut to hold them in place and let them spin freely on the bolt.

## Step 10: Frame, cont.

Next, I made a piece out of aluminum to fix the two opposite plate together. This piece sits between the pair of legs on each assembly, and is the primary structural support of each segment. As well as holding the robot together, it provides a place to mount the electronics and other components later on.

I bent the aluminum at right angles using a c-clamp, and drilled four holes in each end. I drilled matching holes in the motor plate and the opposite plate in each leg assembly, and then bolted everything together with 4/40 screws.

Once both segments of the robot were built and structurally sound, I could test their tree-gripping ability by hooking the motors up directly to a battery. Fortunately, they worked quite well, or I would have had nothing else to share.

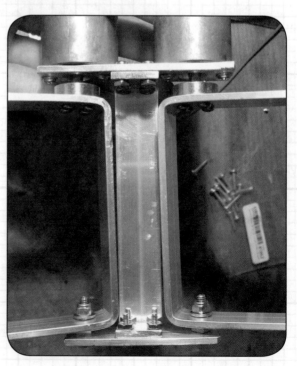

## Step 11: Electronics platform

To hold the electronics, I cut an approximately 6" x 3" piece of acrylic. I drilled six holes in it and screwed standoffs into the holes, to support the Arduino and the motor controller. Then I drilled four holes in the top of the leg assembly, and bolted the acrylic to the assembly, with spacers to lift it up above the motors. Finally, I screwed the Arduino and motor controller into the standoffs.

## Step 12: Rotation sensors

Rotation sensors are key to the operation of this robot. It has one rotation sensor per motor, so the robot knows the exact position of each leg at all times, allowing for precise control of the legs. For my rotation sensors, I used four very thin trimpots I had lying around. Pots are extremely easy to interface with the microcontroller, and are plenty precise for my purposes. They were not, however, very easy to interface with the hardware of my robot.

While designing and building the leg assemblies, I neglected to build in an easy way to connect the potentiometers to the legs. In the solution I came up with, one side of the pot is fixed to the inside of the leg by the protruding screw heads. The other side of the pot is fixed to the locknut on the end of the bolt that holds the leg in place. When the leg turns, the side of the pot fixed to the leg turns, while the side fixed to the locknut is held in place.

To interface the pots and the legs, I first sanded the plastic side of the pots flat. I took four squares of acrylic, approximately 3/4" on each side, and drilled four holes in each, corresponding to the four screw heads in each leg. Then I glued a potentiometer to the center of each acrylic square.

To fix the opposite side of the pots to the locknut I had to get even more creative. First, I glued metal standoffs scavenged from a PowerMac G5 case to the metal side of the pots. Then I glued the plastic shaft from a Bic pen to the metal side of the pots. The other ends of each pen were cut to fit within the metal legs. Then the pen shaft was forced over the square locknut and epoxied to it.

## Step 13: Backbone motor

To move up and down a tree, the robot extends and contracts by spinning a threaded rod that is fixed to the top segment. When the rod is spun clockwise the two segments are pulled together, and they are pushed apart when it spins counter clockwise. To spin the rod, I needed a relatively high-torque low-speed motor that would run at 12V, and I happened to find just such a motor in my box of parts. This particular motor came fitted with a brass gear. To assist with coupling the motor to the threaded shaft, I filed two sides of the gear flat.

To mount the motor to the robot, I bent a short length of aluminum to an "L" shape. I drilled a large hole out of the center of one of the faces (for the motor shaft and gear) and two small holes in both faces for bolting the motor to the metal and bolting the metal to the robot. I drilled corresponding holes into the back of one end of the segment of the robot without the electronics, so that the motor was positioned between the two legs.

## Step 14: Mounting the spine

There are a couple problems with getting a threaded spine to spin smoothly. First, it must be coupled to the motor well, and second it must have some sort of bearing fixed to it on which it can spin. One of the first things I found while trying to couple the motor shaft to the threaded rod was that the connection should be flexible for smooth operation. I made my coupling out of two segments of clear nylon tubing. A wider diameter segment fits tightly over the gear attached to the motor shaft, while a thinner segment fits into the larger tubing and tightly over the outside of the threaded shaft. The coupling is secured with a zip tie.

With only the coupling, the threaded shaft still cannot bear any load, because it would just pull off the motor. To support load, I made a bearing for the shaft out of an old hard drive read/write head bearing. I drilled out the center so that the threaded rod could pass through it. I then fed the rod through it, and fastened a nut on each side of the bearing, to hold the threaded rod in place. I then bolted the bearing down to the back of the robot's frame.

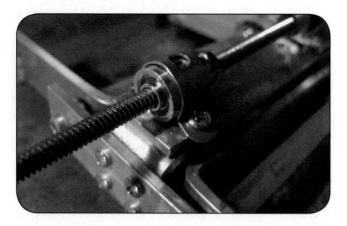

## Step 15: Mounting the spine, cont.

For the spine to work, it must pass through a nut that is fixed to the other segment of the robot. For ease of mounting, I used a large 1/2" long nut. To fix it to the segment of the robot, I cut two ~4" lengths of aluminum, drilled them to match the bolts that hold the acrylic piece, and mounted them through the screw holes, across the frame. These will later become supports for linear slides. I then drilled four more holes around the center of the back of the robot, with enough space between them for the nut to fit. I cut a piece of aluminum to run along the back of the robot, and drilled it to match the holes. I then placed the nut on the back of the robot, placed the bar of aluminum on top of it, and bolted through the bar, to sandwiched the nut between the two pieces of aluminum. Finally, I threaded the rod through the nut.

## Step 16: Linear slides

Without something holding the two segments of the robot in the same plane, the top segment would turn when the threaded rod turned, instead of moving up or down. To keep the two halves of the robot in the same plane, I built linear slides out of two steel rods and brass tubing.

First, I added a pair of aluminum bars to the segment of the robot without the electronics, to

match the pair on the other segment. To mount the steel rods and the brass tubing to these, I made a clamp system similar to the clamps holding the feet in place. To do this for the large diameter rods, I first clamped two 3/4" squares of aluminum together. I then drilled a 1/8" hole down the intersection of the squares, and then took them apart. I drilled two holes in each square, and corresponding holes in each supporting arm. Then I repeated the process four times. To get the slides perfectly parallel to the threaded rod, I had to bend up the supporting arms on the non-electronics segment of the robot.

## Step 17: Wiring the robot

The next step is to wire all the electrical components of the robot together. I started out by soldering long wires to the contacts on the motors. I twisted the wires together by chucking one end in an electric drill and holding the other end with pliers (a trick I learned from the Ben Heck show). Next, I wired together the pots on the legs. I did this using segments of ribbon cable from an old IDE cable. I wired the pots so that they all had a common ground and input voltage. The input voltage was connected to the +5V pin on the Arduino, and the four signal wires were soldered to headers and then connected to analog inputs A0—A3 on the Arduino.

Because this robot is autonomous, I needed a method for controlling the robot's actions so that I could get it to release from the tree. For this, I just used a simple slide switch connected to a digital input on the Arduino

Next, I wired the digital output pins on the Arduino to the inputs on the motor controller. First, I connected all the motor enabling pins on the motor controller to each other. The rest of the wiring went as follows:

- Enable Motors
- Motor 4 Input 2
- Motor 4 Input 1
- Motor 3 Input 2
- Motor 3 Input 1
- Control Switch empty
- Motor 2 Input 2
- Motor 2 Input 1
- Motor 1 Input 2
- Motor 1 Input 1
- Motor 5 Input 2
- Motor 5 Input 1

I then connected the motor's leads to the terminal strips on the motor controller, and connected the motor voltage terminal to the 12V battery pack, via a toggle switch. I connected the 5V regulator to the logic voltage terminal, via the same toggle switch.

I collected the umbilical cord of wires running between the two segments of the robot into a bundle, and fastened them together with zip ties and electrical tape, to keep them organized.

## Step 18: Limit switches

Because I used a regular DC motor instead of a servo or a stepper to spin the threaded rod that is the spine, the robot cannot know the degree of extension of the spine at all times. Therefore, limit switches must be used to prevent it from extending or contracting too much.

The spine has two limit switches. One is pressed in when the two segments of the robot are pulled close together, and the other becomes un-pressed when the threaded rod retracts past it. The latter is a switch like this (http://parts.digikey.com/1/parts/974782-switch-detect-lever-snapact-vert-zmcjf7l0t.html) glued parallel to the

robot

threaded rod, on the segment of the robot with the electronics. When the spine retracts, it pushes down the lever of the switch, and when it retracts, the switch opens.

The second limit switch is a push button switch that requires very little force to actuate. I mounted it on a strip of aluminum from the front of the electronics segment.

Both the switches are connected to the same 5V and ground lines as the potentiometers on the legs, and their signals go to inputs A4 and A5, which the Arduino is set to read as digital inputs rather than analog.

## Step 19: Battery holders

The last mechanical part of this project was to create a way to hold the batteries, while making sure that they are easy to remove for replacement or charging.

The perfect place for mounting the 9V battery was right above the Arduino, so I created a mounting system for it out of some scrap metal. A piece of metal (with an electrical tape insulated bottom) screws on above the Arduino through one of the standoffs. On top of the metal is a bit of stick-on velcro. A piece of metal bent into a "U" shape clips onto the 9V battery, and then sticks to the velcro above the Arduino board, holding the battery in place.

To hold the larger battery pack, I cut two brackets out of some soft plastic angle bar I had lying around. These brackets screw into the arms that hold the linear slides. The battery stays in mostly by friction, but a bit of velcro on one side helps to stop it from slipping out.

## Step 20: Programming

To climb up a tree, the robot goes through a simple series of motions. First, the top segment grips the tree and the bottom segment releases from the tree (if necessary). Then the spine contracts, pulling the bottom segment up towards the top segment. Next the bottom segment grips the tree, and afterwards the top segment releases from the tree. Finally, the spine extends, pushing the top segment upwards, and the cycle can start over again. For ease of programming, I wrote a function corresponding to each basic motion. These are as follows:

- closeTop
- closeBottom
- openTop
- openBottom
- Lift
- Push

By combining these functions in the proper order, the robot can be made to ascend or descend trees.

Opening the legs is very simple. The legs turn outwards from the tree until their rotation sensors reach a point set in the program. Then power is cut off to the motors. Closing the legs on the tree, however, is a little bit more complex. Since trees vary in diameter, the legs need to be able to grip a wide variety of diameters without reprogramming the robot for each size. To figure out when to cut off power to the motors, the controller first calculates the speed at which the legs are moving towards the tree. It does this by sampling the position of the legs' potentiometers every .05 seconds. It subtracts the previous value of the potentiometer from the current value to find the distance traveled by the legs over the time period. When the distance travels becomes close to zero (I used 1 in my program), it means that the legs have gripped into the tree and are beginning to slow down. Then the controller cuts of power to the motors, to prevent them from stalling out, or damaging themselves, the motor controller or the gearboxes.

The last piece to the programming puzzle is the method of controlling the robot's actions. If you look at the above movement cycle, you will notice that the robot is gripping the tree at all times. This makes it difficult to remove the robot, so I programmed the control switch to manually control the behavior of the robot. While the switch is off (circuit open), the robot keeps its legs open. Once the switch is turned on, the robot begins its climbing cycle. To remove the robot from the tree, the switch is turned back to the off position, and both sets of legs release.

# Groovin' Grover: A Microcontroller-Based Marionette

By talk2bruce
(http://www.instructables.com/id/
Groovin-Grover-A-Microcontroller-based-
Marionett)

Groovin' Grover is a marionette manipulated by four hobby servos and a Pololu Maestro microcontroller-based servo controller. You can control each of Grover's limbs independently and make him walk, wave, and most entertaining - make him dance. Groovin' Grover is easy to assemble and wire up. The Maestro Servo microcontroller is easy to program using free software from Pololu.

## Step 1: Parts List

You will need the following parts to assemble Groovin' Grover and his stage.

**Grover's Brawns and Brains:**

Four small inexpensive hobby servos like the TS-53 from Tower Hobbies.

One Pololu Micro Maestro 6-Channel USB Servo Controller available from Sparkfun and other internet sites.

One 6" Futaba J Plug or equivalent available from Tower Hobbies.

One 5 Volt Wall Wart (AC adapter). I had an extra one but you can find used ones at Thrift stores or new ones at electronics stores.

One 3 to 6 foot USB cable with a male USB mini-B connector and a male type A connector.

Two 1" pieces of Heat Shrink Tubing (alternatively, you can use electrical tape).

**Grover Himself:**

One 5 - 6" Grover finger puppet.

Four 1/4"-20 hex nuts (these will be used to add weight to Grover)

One small (1") safety pin (this will be use to help hold the weights inside Grover.)

**Grover's Stage:**

Two 8" x 12" x 1/4" pieces of plastic, wood, Masonite, or other firm non-conducting material. I used yellow plastic I had purchased for another project I never got around to build.

Four 12" 1/4"-20 threaded rods.

Sixteen 1/4"-20 hex nuts.

Four self adhesive rubber feet (medium size 1/4 to 1/2" in diameter, 1/2" tall).

Two and a half feet of self adhesive Velcro strips.

One 11 3/4" x 18 3/4" white cloth for the backdrop on the stage. I cut an old pillow case to make mine.

Two small plastic wire clamps (see photo below).

Two small machine screws and nuts for the wire clamps.

**Materials for Hanging Grover:**
- Clear Nylon Thread
- Sewing Needle
- Washer (1" outer diameter)
- Blue Painter's Tape.
- Four small paper clips.

**Software and Documentation:**

Pololu Maestro Servo Controller User's Guide: HTML version or PDF.version.

Maestro software and drivers are available at File Downloads section of the Micro Maestro Resources web page.

**Tools:**
- Soldering iron and solder
- Wire cutters / Wire Strippers
- Scissors
- Small wrench for use with the 1/4"-20 hex nuts
- Electric drill and 1/4" drill bit and drill bit to match machine screws for the wire clips
- Heat Gun for the heat shrink tubing
- Voltmeter
- Ruler

PC for developing and downloading programs to the microcontroller. The Pololu software currently only supports Windows and Linux.

## Step 2: Overview

Groovin' Grover is a microcontroller-based marionette. Each of Grover's limbs are controlled independently: he can be made to walk, wave, and of course, dance. Groovin' Grover is controlled by a Pololu Maestro 6-Channel Servo Controller. I chose this microcontroller because it is specially designed for controlling servos, is very easy to wire, has a simple programming language, has superb software for developing and debugging programs, and is inexpensive ~$20.

Mechanically, Grovin' Grover is based on a Grover finger puppet attached to four inexpensive hobby servos. The servos are attached to each of his limbs allowing for independent movement. I built a simple "stage" for holding Grover and the servos in place. I used Velcro to attach Grover and the servos to the stage so that the parts could be easily moved and adjusted for getting Grover into proper position. Painter's tape and paper clips are used to attach threads to the servo horns: the paper clips can be bent to get proper movement and the painter's tape is easily removed if threads ever need to be replaced.

The first figure below shows how Groovin' Grover is attached to the servos when he is in his initial position. Transparent nylon thread is used to attach his limbs to the servos. When rotated from the initial position, the servos pull up to raise his feet or hands and can be rotated back to the original position to lower his feet or hands. Programming is very simple: in the Maestro programming language the command "8000 1 servo" would cause servo 1 to rotate to the maximum position and raise his left hand. The command "4000 1 servo" would return servo 1 to the original position thus lowering his hand. If you put those commands in a loop with a small time delay after each servo command, Groovin' Grover would appear to be waving at you. The Popolu documentation for the microcontroller is well written and explains how to use the software and in detail how to program the microcontroller.

The second diagram shows Groovin' Grover and his stage. His stage is made of two platforms supported by threaded rods and hex nuts. Grover is suspended 4" from the upper platform: a piece of transparent nylon thread is threaded through the top of his head and attached to a washer. The washer is held in place on the upper platform using Velcro. Rubber feet are affixed to the bottom of the stage to prevent the washers from scratching the surface of where the stage is placed and to ensure that the stage doesn't rock back and forth when the servos are moving. A piece of white cloth hangs from the back of the stage as a backdrop. The backdrop is affixed to the bottom of the upper platform by Velcro. The backdrop hides power and USB cables and allows the transparent nylon thread to blend in with the background allowing Groovin' Grover to appear to float.

The third diagram shows the top of the upper platform where Groovin' Grover's electronics and servos are located. The PC-based program development and debugging software communicates with the microcontroller via the USB cable. Microcontroller power is supplied by the USB cable. The servos are powered by a 5 volt wall wart. The USB and power cables are held in place using plastic wire clamps: the wire clamps prevent the microcontroller from being accidentally pulled off the top of the platform. The microcontroller is affixed to the platform with a small piece of Velcro.

Each servo is attached to the microcontroller using standard connectors that come with the servos. Servo 0 controls the left foot; servo 1 controls the left hand; servo 2 controls the right hand; servo 3 controls the right foot. The servos need to be connected to the microcontroller exactly as shown in the diagram for Groovin' Grover to move properly. More information about the various connectors on the microcontroller can be found in the Pololu Maestro Servo Controller User's Guide.

Note: Throughout this instructable when Grover's limbs are described as left or right that is his left or right as he faces you.

The process for programming Groovin' Grover is simple. You launch the Maestro control center software and type your program into the "Script" window. You click "Apply Settings" to download the code to the microcontroller and then "Run Script". The control center includes features for debugging and manually moving servos as well as alternate way to develop scripts without using the programming language. I found the software to be very easy to use and the documentation to be well written.

## Groovin' Grover Placement

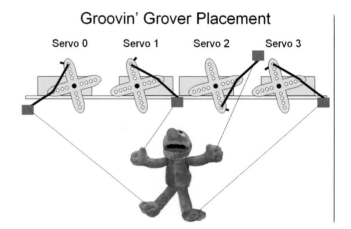

## Step 3: Construct Servo Power Supply

Groovin' Grover's microcontroller is powered via the USB cable but his servos require more power than a USB port can supply so in this step, a 5 volt wall wart (AC adapter) will be adapted to supply power to the servos. A typical wall wart is shown in the first photo.

Cut off the tip at the end of the wall wart's power cable as shown in the second photo. This tip will not be used and can be discarded or saved for a future instructable.

Pull the wires apart and strip off an 1/8" of insulation off the ends of the wires as shown in the third photo.

Making sure the stripped wires are not touching, plug in the wall wart and use a volt meter to test the polarity of the wires as shown in the fourth photo. If you are using an analog voltmeter, the needle on the meter should move to 5 volts as shown in the fifth photo or if you are using a digital voltmeter, the display should read +5 volts. If they don't reverse the test leads and try again. Make note of which wire is positive and which is negative.

Add two pieces of heat shrink tubing to the wires as shown in the sixth photo. The purpose of the heat shrink tubing will be to insulate the wires. If you don't have heat shrink tubing, you can wrap electrical tape around the connections after you finish the soldering step below.

Cut the Futaba J plug cable as shown in the seventh photo. Keep the end with the connector shown in this photo. Strip the red and black wires as shown.

Line up and solder the wires as shown in the eighth and ninth photos. Make sure to connect the red wire to the positive wire from the wall wart and the black wire to the negative wire from the wall wart. The white wire will be left unconnected.

Make sure the exposed connections are not touching, plug the wall wart in and using your voltmeter, verify that the red wire is positive and the black is negative. See tenth photo. Don't skip this step, if you have the polarity wrong you will likely damage the microcontroller and the servos.

Move the heat shrink tubing over the exposed connections as shown in the eleventh photo. Apply heat with a heat gun or soldering iron. The resulting shrunk tubing should look like the twelfth photo. If you are not using heat shrink tubing, you should wrap each of the exposed wires with electrical tape.

Cut the extra off the white wire, as shown in the last photo, and the servo power supply is now complete.

## Step 4: Prepare the Stage Platforms

Time to assemble the two platforms that will be used as Groovin' Grover's stage. The threaded rods will be used as support shafts for the two platforms. I used yellow plastic for the platforms as shown in the first photo. You can use wood, Masonite, plastic, or any other firm non-conducting material.

Mark the holes for the support shafts. The placement of the holes are not critical but I recommend making the holes 1/2" in the from the corners as marked in the second photo.

Drill the four holes using a 1/4" drill bit. I suggest clamping the two boards together and drilling them together to ensure the pieces fit well when assembled. The finished pieces are shown in the third photo.

Pick one of the platforms to be the upper platform and drill holes for the plastic wire clamps. These clamps will be used to hold the USB and power cables and prevent them from pulling the microcontroller off the platform. The holes should match the machine screws you selected to mount the holders. The holes should be drilled about 4" in the edges as depicted in the fourth photo.

Cut a 9 3/4" strip of Velcro and adhere it the front of the upper platform as shown in the fifth photo. This Velcro will be used to mount the servos. I used Velcro because it allows for the servos to be easily moved and adjusted after everything is assembled.

Flip over the upper platform and affix a 12" piece of Velcro along the backside as shown in the sixth photo. This strip of Velcro will be used to hold the cloth backdrop in place.

Take the lower platform and adhere the four rubber feet to the bottom as shown in the last photo.

## Step 5: Assemble the Stage

The stage consists of an upper and lower platform held together using supports shafts consisting of threaded rods and hex nuts. Each support shaft consists of one threaded rod and four hex nuts as shown in the first photo. The hex nuts on each end will hold the platforms in place.

Thread one hex nut onto the ends of each threaded rod as shown in the second, third, and fourth photos. The hex nuts should leave 1/2" of the rod exposed.

Insert each of the threaded rods into the lower platform and secure with hex nuts as shown in the fifth photo. Make sure that the hex nuts do not extend past the bottom of the the rubber feet. The rubber feet should be the only thing touching the surface where the stage is placed.

Place the upper platform onto the threaded rods as shown in the sixth photo.

Use four hex nuts to secure the upper platform as shown in the seventh photo.

The assembled stage is shown in the eighth photo.

## Step 6: Mount the Microcontroller

Velcro is used to mount the microcontroller to the top of the upper platform. The plastic wire clamps are used to hold the USB and power cables in place: the clamps will prevent the microcontroller from being accidentally pulled off the upper platform.

Attach a small piece of Velcro to the center of the top of the upper platform.

Attach the corresponding piece of Velcro to bottom of the microcontroller.

Affix the microcontroller to the upper platform using the Velcro.

Small plastic wire clamps and machine screws with nuts will be used the secure the USB and power cables to the upper platform.

Identify the mini-B connector on the USB connect: this connector will attach the to microcontroller.

Plug the USB cable into the microcontroller as shown in the sixth photo. Attach the servo power cable to the servo power pins on the microcontroller. Note the orientation of the white, red, and black wires. The white wire is unconnected. Please see the instructables page for this project to find more details on the microcontroller power connection.

Place a plastic wire clamp over each of the USB and the power cables and secure to the upper platform using the machine screws and nuts.

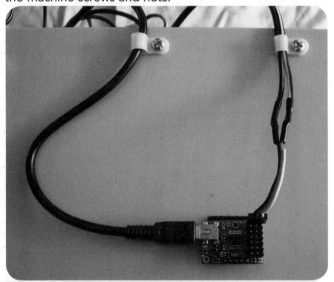

## Step 7: Mount the Servos

In this step the servos will be prepared for mounting on the top of the upper platform. Velcro is used to attach the servos to the platform. Velcro is used because it allows the servos to be easily repositioned after everything is assembled: this will allow you to make adjustments to how Groovin' Grover hangs.

Cut four pieces of Velcro the same width as the servos (approximately 1 1/2"). The orientation of the servos is important - note the positions of the servo horns in that photo.

Attach the Velcro to the servos as shown in the second photo. Use the corresponding piece of Velcro to what you put on the upper platform in step 4 "Prepare the Stage Platforms."

Mount the servos on the upper platform using the Velcro as depicted in the third and fourth diagrams and fifth and sixth photos. Note the position of the servo horns in the diagrams and photos. Proper placement is important to making Grover move correctly.

Connect the control wires from servo 0 as shown in seventh photo. Servo 0 is the leftmost servo as you face the stage. Note the orientation of white, red, and black wires.

Connect the control wires from servo 1 as shown in eighth photo. Servo 1 is the second from the left servo as you face the stage. Note the orientation of white, red, and black wires.

Connect the control wires from servo 2 as shown in ninth photo. Servo 2 is the second from the right servo as you face the stage. Note the orientation of white, red, and black wires.

Connect the control wires from servo 3 as shown in tenth photo. Servo 3 is the rightmost servo as you face the stage. Note the orientation of white, red, and black wires.

The eleventh photo shows the power cable and all four servo control wires attached.

If you have not yet installed the Maestro software for developing and downloading programs to the microcontroller, follow the instructions in the Maestro documentation to do so.

At this point you should connect the USB cable to the PC where you have the Maestro software installed and plug in the power supply for the servo. Launch the Maestro software. Go to the "Script" tab and enter the short program (the four servo commands) shown in the twelfth image below. Click "Apply Setting," then "Run Script." This will put the servos into proper position for attaching the the threads that connect Groovin' Grover's limbs to the servos.

Bend four small (1") paper clips as shown in the thirteenth photo. The threads controlling Groovin' Grover's limbs will be attached to these paperclips.

Attach the paper clips to the servo horns as shown in the last image below. The paper clips extend the range of motion provided by the servos.

### Paper Clip Placement

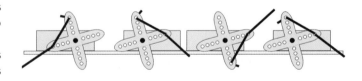

| Servo 0 | Servo 1 | Servo 2 | Servo 3 |

## Step 8: Prepare Grover

The Grover finger puppet needs to be prepared for hanging.

Cut approximately 6" of transparent nylon thread and using a needle, insert the thread through the top of Grover's head as shown in the third and fourth photos. Set Grover aside for the moment.

Cut a small piece of Velcro (set aside the matching piece of Velcro for use in a step below) to the size of the 1" outer diameter washer.

Tie the end of the thread from Grover's head to the washer. There should be about 4" to 5" of thread between his head and the washer.

Take the Velcro and stick it to the washer.

Take the matching half of Velcro and attach it to the front upper platform.

Using the Velcro'd washer, hang Grover.

The Grover finger puppet does not weigh enough for the limbs to move properly when pulled by the servos, so we need to add some weight to him. Stuff four 1/4"-20 hex nuts into the opening on Grover's bottom and use a safety pin to hold them in place. If you don't use a finger puppet, then you will need to cut the puppet open, insert the weights, and sew the puppet closed.

## Step 9: Hang Grover

It's now time to use the nylon thread to attach Grover to the servos. The goal is to hang Grover as shown in the first figure.

Starting with Grover's left leg, cut about 12" of the nylon thread. Lasso and tie one end of the thread around Grover's left ankle. Make sure the thread securely holds his angle and is not loose. Thread the other end to a needle and push it through the bottom of his foot and up through the top of foot.

Take the end of the thread, wrap it around of the end of paper clip attached to servo 0 and use a small piece of blue painter's tape to hold it in place as shown in the fifth photo. The best way to do this is to take the tape and fold it in half over the thread and paperclip. The thread should not have any slack in it and should be tight. Cut off the excess thread when you are satisfied with the placement.

Repeat the process for the right leg. This thread should be attached to servo 3.

Now lasso and tie a thread around Grover's left wrist. Using a needle, push the thread through the back of his thumb and out the front.

Attach the end of the thread to servo 1.

Repeat the process for attaching the thread to his right hand and to servo 2.

### Attaching Grover's Left Leg

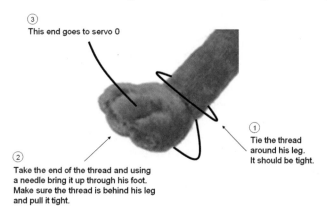

③
This end goes to servo 0

②
Take the end of the thread and using a needle bring it up through his foot. Make sure the thread is behind his leg and pull it tight.

①
Tie the thread around his leg. It should be tight.

## Step 10: Construct and Attach Backdrop

Time to make the backdrop for Groovin' Grover's stage. The backdrop will hide the power and USB cords and will make the transparent nylon threads attached to Grover difficult to see.

Cut a 11 3/4" x 18 3/4" piece of white cloth. I used an old pillow case.

Attach the matching piece of 12" Velcro that you attached to bottom the upper level of the stage in step 4 to the top of the cloth. Cut off any excess Velcro.

Using the Velcro, attach the backdrop to the bottom of the upper level of the stage.

## Step 11: Making Groovin' Grover Dance!

Time to program Groovin' Grover. Please see this instructables page for more information about programming.

Here's how the program works: the first 4 servo commands start the servos moving to put his hands and feet into their initial position. The first parameter of the servo command tells the servo what position to move to and the second parameter tells the microcontroller which servo should perform the action. The "moving_wait" subroutine is then called to wait until all the servos have reached their final position. Next, the "speed" command is used to set the servo to move slowly on the way up and a "servo" command is used to start the raising of the hand. "moving_wait" is called again to delay going to the next command until the hand is fully raised. The speed is set to be faster, the hand is lowered, and the program waits until the hand has finished moving. When "repeat" is reached, the program goes back to the command after "begin" and the hand is waved again and again.

There are interesting possibilities for extending this project. The microcontroller has additional capabilities for reading inputs from switches and can be used to turn other circuits on and off. One example would be to add a new capability to turn on music when Grover starts dancing and turn it off when he finishes.

# Build a Mobile Bar—BaR2D2

By James (Jamie) Price (jamiep)
(http://www.instructables.com/id/Build-A-Mobile-Bar-BaR2D2/)

BaR2D2 is a radio-controlled, mobile bar that features a motorized beer elevator, motorized ice/mixer drawer, six-bottle shot dispenser, and sound activated neon lighting. The robot is drivable so you can take the party on the road! It was created in my garage using standard hand/power tools and readily available parts and materials. The concept for BaR2D2 was born when a friend showed up to an event with a radio-controlled cooler. We joked about taking the idea to the next level and in the Spring of 2008, construction began.

Just a quick note about me—I am a regular DIYer and don't have any formal robotics, electronics, or mechanical training. I have picked up most of my skills from various hobbies and projects, as well as my father who is a skilled woodworker. If you have a basic knowledge of woodworking and working with low voltage power, then you can build a mobile bar! Enjoy!

## Step 1: Creating the framework

As far as tooling for this project, here is a pretty good idea of what you'll need:

- Drill Press
- Table Saw
- Router/table
- Hand Drill
- Screwdrivers
- Pliers
- Wire Strippers
- Soldering iron
- Voltmeter
- Various Clamps
- Vise
- Hammer
- Dremel Tool
- Utility Knife
- Heat gun (hairdryer will work)
- Welder
- Air Compressor
- Air Stapler/nailer
- Socket Set
- Belt Sander

First, purchase a sheet of 4ft x 8ft x 3/4 inch plywood. I used the flooring grade as it will be covered later.

Cut the sheet into 8 2ft x 2ft squares and mark their center points by drawing an X across the middle from the corners. Drill a 1/4 inch hole in the middle of them.

Using a router table, measure out 9 inches from the edge of the cutting bit and bolt your wood square loosely to it. Turn the router on and plunge it slowly upwards until it goes through the wood. Lock the router in place and proceed to rotate the squares until you complete the circle. Repeat eight times. This will give you 18 inch circles. Why 18 inches? I am using an off-the-shelf plastic dome that is that size. Specifically, it is a clear dome from Aspects used for bird feeders. This was purchased from a bird store for $35. The shot dispenser we are using is available on ebay new for $30.

Three of the circles will be cut into rings. To cut out the centers, I made a quick jig as pictured to be able to rotate the circles against it. Two of the finished rings should be 1.75 inches thick and one will be 1 inch thick.

Take one of the circles and setup the router to create a groove about 3/4 through the thickness for the dome to sit in.

## Step 2: Creating the vertical stringers and grooves

Next, I ripped the vertical stringers from poplar on the tablesaw. You will end up with six pieces that are 1 inch x 3/4 inch x 43 inches.

You will need a dado saw blade for the next steps. This tool allows you to stack blades and spacers to cut nice, clean grooves.

Cutting 3/4 inch grooves in the poplar vertical stringers and circles will make the bar fit together like a puzzle when assembled. Cut grooves at the end, then at ten inches down, then 20 inches, then 32 inches, and finally, the other end.

To cut the grooves in the circles, I stacked them, put a bolt in the middle to hold them together, then clamped them between two blocks and ran them through the dado blade as pictured. The six uprights will be spaced equally all the way around.

## Step 3: Assembling the main structure

Next, we will assemble our notched pieces with glue and screws. Use a hand drill to bore pilot holes in the pieces. Use a countersink bit on the vertical pieces to make the screws sit flush. Note: do not install the top ring for the dome yet as it gets installed later.

We used three of the vertical stringers to go the full length of the robot. The other three, we cut off and attached them from the table level to the bottom. Use a square to make sure everything is straight.

Note: You will have two rings left over at this point.

## Step 4: Priming and coating

Use wood filler to fill any voids or grain irregularities and sand the structure until it is smooth. Use a spray primer and sand/fill as needed.

The structure is now ready for coating. I used a black spray-on truck bed liner product. It will take six or more cans to get a good coat. This works best if your surface is sealed and smooth.

## Step 5: Building the drivetrain

I searched high and low for a good, reliable drivetrain solution and settled on an electric wheelchair due to the reliability. I combed Craigslist and scored a used one for $75. (These things cost upward of $1,000 if new!)

Strip the chair to its frame as it will most likely need to be repainted or thoroughly cleaned. My chair had an extra set of wheels out front that I stripped for aesthetic reasons. Make sure you keep all the wiring harnesses as we will reuse those! Plan on buying a new battery if the chair has been sitting. (These run about $75.) I purchased a 12 volt, 35 amp hour battery which is sufficient.

Once stripped, the frame needs to be degreased. I stripped and repainted the wheel rims at this point as well.

You will need three solid points to mount the main structure of the robot to the base. I used some parts off the discarded frame and had them welded to the front to make two of the mount points. You can see three 1/4 inch holes in the frame where the top of the bot will mount. At this point, test fit the battery and add any mounts or tiedowns necessary to keep it from moving around.

Once you have the frame reconfigured, repaint with a black semigloss spray. I used Krylon. The wheel covers on the back were also sprayed with the bedliner.

When dry, reassemble the frame and set aside.

Note: don't worry about trying to make the frame lighter. Any additional weight on the bottom only makes the robot more stable when moving.

## Step 6: Constructing the drawer

The motorized ice/mixer drawer goes in the bottom section of the robot keeping the center of gravity lower to the ground.

Purchase a set of 14 inch drawer slides and mount them to wood strips as pictured. We then use some 3/4 inch plywood to make a base that slides in and out. The drawer will be attached to that.

Use one of the rings we had set aside and cut two identical pieces from it to create the curved front of the drawer (20.5 inches of diameter). Use some of the vertical stringer scrap to make the vertical pieces. (face is 8.5 inches tall) Once the drawer face is done, use paper to create a template for the drawer bottom and cut that from 1/4 inch plywood. The sides and spacers can then be added. For the ice bin, I found a blue translucent one with a handle at the dollar store. It needs to be translucent for the light to illuminate the ice. The drawer body without the face is 14.5 inches wide.

Note: Continuously test fit the drawer. Spacer blocks were used to shim the drawer front to proper alignment level. The front will be sheeted with blue Sintra plastic in a later step.

To motorize the drawer, I purchased a 12 volt DC gear motor from a surplus store. 15 rpms gives the drawer a perfect speed when attached to a three-inch traction wheel. This wheel rides on the inside floor of the robot. I used screws and small springs to mount the motor. This allows you to adjust the tension and traction.

To control the elevator via the remote, I visited Team Delta and purchased a RCE220 rc switch. This allows the motor to operate in both directions, stop at limit switches, and be controlled from one button on the remote. Follow the instructions that came with the RCE220 to wire it.

I insulated the area below the ice bin with foil back bubble material. Simply make a paper template and then use that to cut the insulation. Use spray adhesive to attach it to the drawer.

To illuminate the ice, I installed two LED light pucks. I found a three-pack of these at the local drugstore.

The drawer gets trimmed a little later.

## Step 7: Making the beer elevator

The level above the mixer drawer houses the beer section. Beers rotate on a beer turntable and then an elevator brings them to the table level.

Since there wasn't a "beer elevator" at the store, I had to invent one. I bought a cordless caulk gun from Harbor Freight (http://www.harborfreight.com/) ($40) and disassembled it. This is basically a linear actuator that is extremely compact. This runs at 12 volts.

To control the elevator via the remote, I visited Team Delta (http://www.teamdelta.com/) and purchased a RCE220 RC switch. This allows the motor to operate in both directions, stop at limit switches, and be controlled from one button on the remote. Follow the instructions that came with the RCE220 to wire the elevator.

Using a hole saw, I drilled a 3.5 inch hole in the table top. This needs to be positioned so that the edge of the hole is just inside the ring on the table top. Directly under that hole, drill a 1.5 inch hole in the floor of the beer section. Using wood screws, mount the elevator to the underside of the beer level.

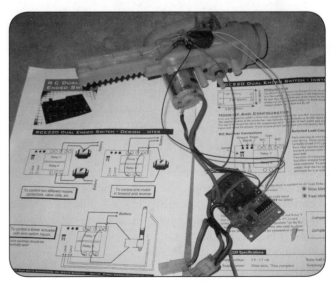

Next, cut two pieces of the Sintra about 18 inches and center mount them together. Draw your beer layout. Temporarily attach a paper template to the pieces and start drilling the large holes using a circle cutting bit on the drill press. Once you have the 15 holes drilled, you will mount the pieces on the router table and spin them to remove the unneeded parts. This will leave you with two beer guides. I later went back and drilled some holes for the sake of looks. I also drilled five equally spaced 1/4 inch holes that mount the pieces to the base.

For the base, I used the template to drill a hole about 1.5 inches around where each beer will sit. This allows the elevator to come up through the hole, but will not allow the beer to fall through it. I cut out the extra material between the hole and the edge with a table saw to allow extra clearance for the elevator.

The base also gets five holes for bolting the two beer guides to it. Use five 1/4 inch bolts about 5 inches long. These need to be countersunk under the base to allow it to spin. I centered and mounted a 6 inch lazy susan bearing (Home Depot) to the bottom of it.

To drive the turntable, I used one of the 12 volt, 15 rpm gear motors I earlier purchased from ebay. I used 2 inch x 2 inch steel angle to make a simple motor mount. I used a hole saw to cut out a 3 inch circle (wheel) that I epoxied to the motor shaft. Grip tape was applied for the outer tread. The motor was mounted under the floor of this level so that the wheel was allowed to protrude through a slot and contact the bottom of the turntable to rotate it.

A beer guardrail was also cut from 1/8 inch thick UHMW plastic. Mount this to the inside of the uprights to keep the beers snug.

## Step 8: Building the beer turntable

The beer turntable holds 15 beers and rotates them into position over the beer elevator for dispensing upon command from the remote control.

3/4 inch plywood is used for the base. Cut a 2 foot square, cut, and contact cement a piece of white 1/8 inch Sintra plastic to the top of it. Sintra is a brand name of expanded pvc sheet. This comes in 4 x 8 sheets in almost any color you could want and is usually about $30/sheet from any plastic supplier.

Using the earlier router table setup, mount the piece and cut it into a 16 inch circle.

## Step 9: Creating the mounting plate for the base

In the drivetrain step, we explained the need for three solid points to mount the robot body. This step explains how to make the male side. A plate was cut from 3/4 inch plywood at 45 degree angles on the tablesaw for a low profile (approximately 16 inches x 10 inches).

You will need to mark your three mount points from your drivetrain onto the plate and install 1/4 inch counter sunk bolts with nuts. The plate is then centered on the bottom of the robot body and attached with glue and screws from both sides for a solid mount.

We use split washers and wing nuts for quick assembly/disassembly. Holes were drilled to allow the wires for the battery and motors to pass through.

## Step 10: Adding the Electronics

The electronics for the mobile bar are fairly simple using off-the-shelf items. The entire robot runs off a 12 volt, 35 amp-hour SLA battery. The radio controller/receiver is a six channel Futaba model tuned for ground frequency use. This was purchased from The Robot MarketPlace.

A pair of Victor 883 Speed Controllers is used to control the drive motors on BaR2D2 and are set up for "tank-style" steering. Note: for ease of driving, we set the transmitter up to use one stick to control the drive (mixing function). Follow the instructions included with the speed controllers for installation and setup. These were mounted on a piece of Sintra.

I reused the wiring harnesses and plugs from the wheelchair to provide wiring from the battery, to a main switch and to the motors. This allows you to easily unplug everything for transport. The switches and wire were purchased at Radio Shack.

At this point, limit switches were on the beer turntable. They are wired in conjunction with the beer elevator and beer loading door so that: A) Anytime the elevator is up, the turntable can't spin, B) When the elevator goes back down, the turntable is allowed to rotate until the next beer hits a limit switch, C) The turntable and elevator

can't spin with the loading door open, D) A manual three-way switch allows for loading/off/dispensing of the beers. Zip-ties were used to secure the wiring.

## Step 11: Installing the plastic skin

The mobile bar is sheeted in 1/8 inch Sintra. Sintra is an expanded PVC plastic that comes in a rainbow of colors from any plastic supplier (usually in 4 x 8 sheets). The Sintra cuts like butter on the table saw (use a high tooth count blade for best results).

The easiest way to make the pieces is to first make a template from thin cardboard then cut the plastic piece. Make them a little oversized so you can make fine fitting adjustments.

The plastic is quite flexible and springy so ratchet straps were used to keep the larger pieces in place while they were attached. Drill pilot holes and attach the pieces with #6 wood screws.

The clear plastic that covers the beer level is 1/16 inch polycarbonate (also available from any plastic supplier). This was attached using an air stapler. Make sure you use a scrap and test the stapling pressure before you move on to your actual piece.

The table top was made using the router table setup just like the earlier bulkheads. Mount it using contact cement.

Make any cutouts where access points are needed (speed controllers, drawer, etc.).

## Step 12: Adding chrome trim

Adhesive backed chrome trim tape was used to finish the robot and give it some "bling." This comes in several thicknesses and colors from AutoZone.

Apply the trim per manufacturer instructions. A craft saw and miter block were used to make any angles that were needed. A Dremel tool also came in handy to fine sand some pieces.

A piece of plated gutter guard was used to cover the speed controllers then outlined with the chrome trim.

A chrome lid from an insulated travel mug was used to accent the opening of the beer dispenser (cut the center out of it and epoxy it on).

95

Center and mount the shot dispenser with wood screws. A template was drawn to aid in drilling equally spaced holes.

## Step 13: Installing the lighting

Two 15 inch neon rings were purchased from ebay. These come in many sizes and colors and are usually used for speaker installations. They operate via a 12 volt power transformer that has a built-in switch and sensitivity for pulsing to sound.

Mount the neon rings using the supplied hardware and instructions. Hide the wires using wire loom and run them through holes in the rings and serving level. Note: after mounting the lower neon ring, you would then attach the top wood ring to the structure and then mount the top neon ring.

The beers are illuminated by a camping light that has 60 white LED bulbs (ebay). This was attached with Velcro to the ceiling. For added brightness, a white Sintra circle was cut with the router and contact cemented to the ceiling of the beer area.

To enhance the lighting, a set of three blue LED pods (12 volt) were attached to the bottom of the robot body. These are commonly used to illuminate motorcycles and cast a soft blue glow under the robot. Note: these were not yet installed when the video was taken.

## Step 14: Finishing Touches

I ordered a set of LED flashing glasses available from ebay. These add a good deal of personality to BaR2D2.

A small ice scoop was purchased locally from a restaurant supply store.

A graphic designer buddy of mine drew up a great logo. This was taken to a sign shop that output/cut several logos in white adhesive-backed vinyl. Once applied, it looks like it rolled off a factory floor

We used some of the color inkjet iron-on transfers and made a few shirts to wear as well.

One item of note is the transport cradle. I used some 3/4 inch scrap plywood and traced an 18 inch circle on it

and cut it in half. Three threaded rods and nuts from Home Depot were used to attach them together. Foam pipe insulation provides a soft cradle for the robot to lie on. This cradle was necessary to get the bot into my SUV for transport.

## Step 15: Let's Party!

The radio-controlled portable bar (BaR2D2) made its debut at Dragon*con, the largest multi-media, popular culture convention focusing on science fiction and fantasy, gaming, comics, literature, art, music, and film in the US.

BaR2D2 was able to travel via street from hotel to hotel without issues. The large 12 volt, 35 amp-hour battery easily lasted eight hours before charging.

# Build an Autonomous Wall-E Robot

By DJ Sures (djsures)
(http://www.instructables.com/id/Build-an-auton-omous-Wall-E-Robot/)

Hi! After a kabillion requests, here you go! This robot is running the EZ-B available at http://www.ez-robot.com.

I started off with the toy titled "Interactive Wall-E." Available at Toys 'R' Us current price $34.99.

I am a robot hobbyist and have a lot of experience with the programming and design to give robots expression and life. The first bit advice I can lend is to be confident. Second advice is to be creative. Together, your mind will figure out the rest for you.

There are plenty of pieces available to you. My workshop is nothing special. I keep a supply of parts that are low cost. I usually collect items from disassembling other toys. Sadly, servos are the most expensive parts of the bunch.

For fasteners I use Zip Ties and an arrangement of small screws, bolts and nuts. All are available in cheap combo kits at your local hardware store.

To modify the casings, I use a speed adjustable dremel and sometimes my soldering iron to melt plastic. For dremeling, please keep a vacuum nearby. *Warning: For melting, keep a window open with a fan!!

Also, if you choose to melt plastic pieces, use a separate bit on your soldering iron. The plastic will burn to the tip and make soldering a pain in the butt!

Now for the programming part . . . This is actually very easy. I do my programming for my robots using the EZ-Robot Project and the EZ-B Robot Controller. It does not require any programming. You can just plug in your servo motors and control the robot from your PC. It also contains voice recognition and a bunch of other neat features. You can get it here: (http://www.ez-robot.com).

## Step 1: Parts

Okay hopefully you've created a nice work area. Someplace with a table/bench that you don't mind getting dirty/burning/scratching/etc. (i.e. don't use your dining room table!)

Here is a list of the parts I used:

- 1 EZ-B with SDK or EZ-Builder software (Available at http://www.ez-robot.com)
- 2 Parallex modified servos for the drivetrain (Available at:http://www.hvwtech.com/products_view. asp?ProductID=114)
- 1 GWS Standard servo for the head (Left and Right motion) (Available at: http://www.hvwtech.com/prod-ucts_view.asp?ProductID=878)
- 2 GWS Pico servos for the arms (Up and Down motion) (Available at: http://www.hvwtech.com/products_view. asp?ProductID=863)
- 1 GWS Micro servo for the head tilt (Available at: http://www.hvwtech.com/products_view. asp?ProductID=862)
- 2 Sharp Analog Distance Sensors (Available at: http://www.hvwtech.com/products_view.asp?ProductID=88)
- A collection of 3-Conductor Servo Cables (Available at: http://www.hvwtech.com/products_view. asp?ProductID=690)
- 1 Box of assorted small screws/bolts/nuts (Available at your local hardware store)
- 1 Hobby Hot Glue gun (Available at Walmart or hobby store)
- 1 bottle of Krazy glue, or any type of good strong plastic glue
- 1 Soldering Iron. I use an adjustable temp range soldering iron, which is costly but recommended. Sometimes you can come across these used in bargain classifieds or at electronic supply surplus shops.
- 1 Case of Jeweler Screw Drivers (Avaiable at Walmart or any hardware shop)

## Step 2: Take the toy apart

Using your screw driver set, you'll want to disassemble the entire toy. Keep track of how it came apart, because the goal is to re-assemble.

*Note: It is not necessary to take apart the Eye Encloser. The wires from the Eye Encloser can be connected to your micro.

## Step 3: Arms

You'll need to mount the servos onto the top part of the toy's case. This is going to be your first modification to the body. Hold the two midsized servos to where the original arm mechanism was and notice how to fit them.

The photo on this step shows a mounted servo, and the original mechanism. You'll of course want to have both servos mounted, one for each arm.

Use the dremel to cut away the plastic on the ends to fit the servos. Make sure you use a low speed on the dremel. Drill Style cutting bits work best.

I used the glue gun to create a nice tight fit for the servos.

I then melted two tiny holes in the plastic to fit small screws for additional support.

Mounting the arms to the servos is a little tricky. The servo packs come with a variety of bits and extensions. Be creative with those extensions. I took a 4 arm extension and trimmed it down to fit within the arm. No glue or screws were necessary.

Also, once you figured out how to mount the arm to the servo, make sure the servo and arm are both in the centered position. Because remember, the servo doesn't spin 360 degrees. It has a Start and Stop position! So for full movement, you're not going to want the arm mounted at bottom of the servo's positioning, or it will only be able to go up from that point.

## Step 4: Mounting the head/neck

The neck will mount to the GWS Standard servo. This will allow it to move left and right.

*Note: Like the arms, the servo needs to be centered.

I used a combination of the dremel and soldering iron to flatten the neck adapter. I then melted 3 small holes to fit screws onto the circular servo accessory.

To fit the servo and mounted head bracket, you'll need to dremel the hole larger. Also remove and break off any plastic pieces that prevent the servo from sitting flush against the plastic.

Recycling some of the Wall-E screws and mounting locations, you'll be able to mount the servo.

When I mounted the head to the neck bracket, I used a zip tie temporarily. I later replaced it with a bolt and nut.

## Step 5: Drivetrain—part 1

Now let's give Wall-E some wheels!

So the toy doesn't have any motors or drivetrain. It's a push toy. So you'll need to be very confident and creative here.

Twist and turn the wheels until the metal axel breaks loose. It's quite a struggle! I ended up using a dremel and cutting most of the pastic away that attached the axel to the wheels. You're going to want the inside of the wheels flat anyway, so don't worry.

Now we're going to simply pry out the center cap on the wheels. This will expose a philips head screw. Remove that screw and the wheels will come apart.

Using the 4 arm accessory of the Parallex Modified servos, melt corresponding holes into the inside of the wheels. Use small screws and attach the 4 arm accessory to wheel.

Trim off any part of the servo accessory that sticks out using the dremel. Do both sides the same. Look at the pics.

## Step 6: Drivetrain—Part 2

Okay now we're going to mount the drivetrain to the case. This is exciting becuase it's a lot of dremeling!

Take a good look at the pictures and see how much to cut away.

It's best to take this part slow. I use a marker to outline where to cut. I cut a little, then measure, cut a little, then measure, etc.

Once the servos fit flush and the mounting bracket fits to the case, then you must be close! Sweet!

To mount the servos, I first used a bead of hot glue gun to hold the servo in place. Glue guns are great because they'll provide a temporary mount, but not permanent by any means!

To securely mount the servos, I used zip ties! I used the nice fat zip tie, and a pair of pliers to tighten it up solid.

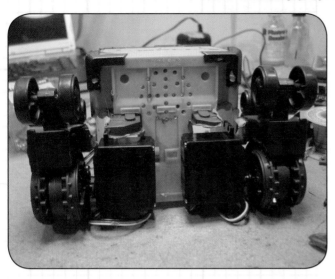

## Step 7: Distance Sensor and Assembly

I suppose you'll want your Wall-E to see. So did I!

So I used one of the sharp distance sensors mounted on his neck. I had to dremel a bit of the sensor housing to make it fit flush.

Maybe melt/drill a little hole through the top plastic of the box to push the wires through.

The wires that come with the sharp sensor are very small and easily break from fatigue. I replaced the wires with the Servo wire/plug combo that is listed in the parts.

I use those servo wire/plug combos for everything: LCD's, Speakers, LED's, etc.

Tuck all the wires through their holes when you assemble the unit.

## Step 8: Head Tilt

Nothing makes Wall-E come more alive than his eye tilting. It adds a lot of character to his personality.

The eyes of the toy are tiltable by hand, but not automated. I put a drop of Krazy Glue to hold both parts of the eyes together. That way, the servo moves both eyes. You may want to not Krazy Glue the eyes together for an even funnier expression.

I mounted the smallest servo of the parts list to the neck. Of course I used a yellow zip tie and some hot glue gun.

Then use a piece of hard wire from the servo arm to the head.

Also, the electrical wires from the servo are very short. I used the servo wire/plug combo to extend the wires. And covered up the solder joints with shrink wrap.

*NOTE: Do not attempt to move this tiny servo arm by hand! You will break the plastic gears inside. Trust me, I broke one by trying. If the piece isn't lined up, simply remove the arm and attach it in line. DO NOT TRY TO MOVE IT.

## Step 9: Circuit and Programming

This part isn't the most difficult because I am using the EZ-Robot project. It is a robot controller board that connects to your computer over Bluetooth. The robot board comes with software called EZ-Builder. The software allows you to control your robot without needing to program. You can also add a bunch of other features, including voice recognition.

## Step 10: Your Robot!

In autonomous mode, my Wall-E creates a 2 dimensional map of objects around him. This prevents him from getting stuck or backing into objects. The theory and logic behind this technique is difficult and the implementation can be very challenging.

In addition to his environmental awareness, his personality is also complex. His actions, movements and modes are not entirely random. He collects points and begins to favor successful actions. Much like you would expect a pet.

It's taken years of observing, programming and pulling my own hair to figure a lot of this out. Start slow, and be creative. Figure out ways to add personality quirks to your robots that bring them to life!

## Step 11: Battery . . . POWER!

Because my Wall-E does have 6 servos and a microcontroller, his power consumption is high.

Due to size constraints, I was limited to a small battery.

My choice was a 2000mha LION 7.4v cell. LION batteries don't like to be drained, so be prepared for a low life expectancy.

The 2000mhz battery gives my Wall-E about 60 minutes of life between charges.

You can purchase your battery at any Battery Depot or similar outlet.

## Step 12: Enjoy!

I hope you enjoy your new robot. For more information about my projects and robots, please feel free to visit my website at (http://www.dj-sures.com/robots).

# clocks

As hard as it is to change the way we think about the relentless passage of time, the projects in this chapter clocks have managed to do just that. There's actually a long-standing tradition of clock-hacking and reinventing on Instructables. The ubiquity and iconic status of the clock just begs reinvention. Additionally, the precision and attention to detail that working with clocks demands is significant, which means that at times, the bar is set pretty high. As a result, we've seen some absolutely amazing clock projects on the site.

While some makers choose to simply decorate clock faces, or adorn pre-existing clocks in some way, what sets the projects in this chapter apart is that these builders have found new ways to represent and visualize time, and in the case of the "Lunch Clock" specifically, to change the way time itself passes. Sound interesting? It is! These clock projects will change the way you think about time forever.

# The Wordclock Grew Up!

By Doug Jackson  (drj113)
(http://www.instructables.com/id/The-Word-clock-Grew-Up/)

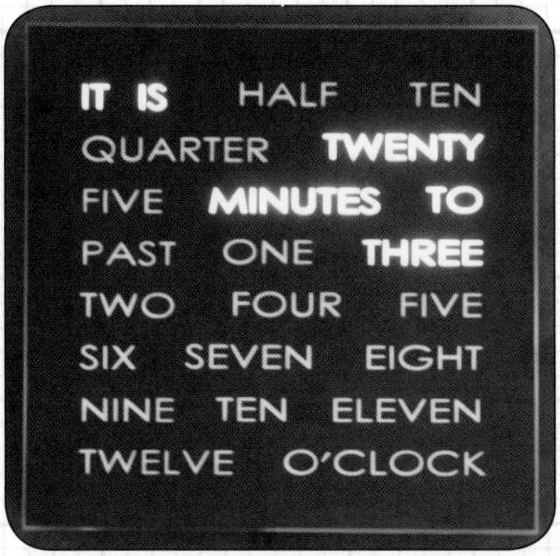

This clock uses an updated Arduino controller PCB. It has a DS1302 RTC onboard, to ensure that the timing is accurate, and an automatic dimming function kicks in between 7pm, and 7am, so you can still sleep if the clock is installed in your bedroom.

It is powered from a 12V DC, 400mA power supply. I have considered battery power, but LED clocks don't run for very long on batteries, so that is not an ecologically sensible idea. My old clocks used to run from an AC source, but I moved to DC when I implemented the RTC chip.

## Step 1: Parts list

Here is a parts list for the project:

Arduino compatable controller:
- Ardunio WordClock Controller PCB
- 10uF/25V electrolytic 1
- 18pF ceramic 2
- 100uF/25V electrolytic 1
- 0.1uF ceramic 2
- 270 Ohm 2
- 10k 1 (in the photo this looks like 10M)
- AtMega168 micro 1
- ULN2803A IC 3
- CD4094 IC 3
- DS1302 IC 1
- RED LED 1
- GREEN LED 1
- 1N4001 diode (or 1N4002, 1N4004 etc) 1
- 32768Khz Crystal 1
- 16 Mhz crystal 1

- 78L05 Regulator 1
- 2 Pin PCB screw connector 2
- 3 Pin PCB screw connector 1
- 5 pin 0.1 inch pin array 1
- 6 pin 0.1 inch pin array 1
- 26 pin 0.1 inch header 1
- Pushbutton 1
- 8 Pin IC Socket 1
- 14 pin IC Socket 2
- 16 Pin IC Socket 3
- 18 Pin IC Socket 3

LED display:
- White Strip LED kit (12V) 32 x 3 led segments (about 1.5m)
- 26 Way ribbon cable 1m
- 26 Way IDC ribbon connector 1

Enclosure:
- 3mm White Acrylic 264mm x 264mm
- 3mm Black Acrylic 270mm x 270mm x 1
- 3mm Black Acrylic 60mm x 264mm x 2
- 3mm Black Acrylic 60mm x 270mm x 1
- 3mm Black Acrylic 25mm x 264mm x 10
- 3mm Black Acrylic 20mm x 25mm x 8

Stencil:
- 300mm x 300mm vinyl stencil pre-cut
- 3mm Clear Acrylic 300mm x 300mm

Hardware:
- 2.1mm DC input socket (panel mount)
- 3mm x 6mm screw x 20
- 3mm x 10mm Hex standoff x 6
- Button PCB x 1
- Black push buttons (miniature) x 2
- 5 core IDC cable x 30cm

## Step 2: Creating the stencil

Start assembly by making the stencil. You can either get a stencil cut by a local sign writer to your own design, or use a pre-cut vinyl stencil from my web site.

I have always felt that the clock looks more majestic if there is a border around the letters (I normally use about a 30mm border), but you can use whatever size you would like.

Vinyl by itself is floppy, so it needs to be attached to a clear acrylic (Perspex) backing sheet to provide rigidity. Make sure that the acrylic sheet is the size you want the final clock to be.

Before you start, mix up a couple of drops of dish washing liquid with a cup of water, and load that into a spray bottle. We will use this to make applying the vinyl lots easier.

The vinyl stencil as supplied will typically be larger than required. This is so as to provide extra material for variations in face sizes. We need to cut the vinyl stencil to the final size of your acrylic sheet, allowing an extra 10mm allowance around the edges.

Lay the acrylic backing on top of the stencil, and mark out a cut line, then using a straight edge and a sharp hobby knife (or scalpel), cut the sheet to size.

Next, ensure that your working environment is clean–vacuum your table if necessary–or work inside the house, instead of the garage. Lock up your Golden Retriever dog and your cats. If you get small particles between the vinyl and the Perspex, you will have enormous trouble making the surface look flat.

Spend some time "weeding" the stencil, by removing the letters that you don't want there on the final stencil. The removed letters will provide space for the light to shine through. Once you have removed all of the letters (being careful to leave the centers of letters such as "A" and "P" behind), apply some masking tape along each row so that when we remove the backing sheet, the centers of the letters stay in the correct spot on the stencil.

Remove the protective cover from the clear Perspex, and lay the Perspex to one side, ready for covering.

Turn the vinyl sheet over so that the front is against your working surface, and remove the backing sheet from the vinyl stencil, being very careful to ensure that the vinyl does not stick to itself. Be very gentle so that you don't tear the vinyl.

Be gentle when you remove the backing to ensure that the bottoms of the letters are not stretched. You may find, for example, that the bottom of the letter R and W stays on the backing. Gently use a sharp instrument to detach them from the backing. This photo shows the base of an "R" character being loosened. The base of the "W" has to be loosened as well.

Spray the vinyl sheet with a liberal amount of the water/soap solution—don't panic—we will be squee-geeing this out later—it simply allows us heaps of extra time and movement to get the vinyl applied easily. In fact it makes application So easy.

DON'T DO THE APPLICATION DRY. Unless you are a professional sign writer. YOU WILL GO QUITE MAD.

Lie the Perspex on the top of the vinyl at an angle, starting with the bottom edge—carefully align the edge so that it is straight. Hold the top of the vinyl sheet taunt (you can have an assistant help you), then, and using a folding, or rolling motion lay the sheet on the vinyl. The folding or rolling motion will help to ensure so that most of the air and soapy water is expelled.

Turn the Perspex over and make sure that the alignment of the stencil is where you want it. Don't worry if the stencil is in the wrong spot, because you used water and soap (you did—didn't you?) you have tons of time to get it right. Then, using a squeegee, credit card, or your hand, gently flatten the stencil out to remove the excess water/soap mix. Use some paper towel to clean and dry the stencil as you expel liquid. As you expel the liquid, you will notice that the stencil locks onto the acrylic sheet. We want this gluing action to happen. Do not rub the front hard, as you will damage the surface.

Then remove each of the tape strips—one at a time. Again—be gentle—use a tissue to blot up the excess water/soap mix as you go. If you find that a letter is staying attached to the masking tape, simply use a sharp tool to detach it.

Once you have expelled all of the water/soap mix, and things are looking very flat, marvel at your work, and leave it to adhere for an hour or so.

Cut the vinyl sheet to the final size on the Perspex–I love the look of making the stencil 3–5mm smaller than the acrylic, allowing a small clear bit to frame the black vinyl. You may prefer to cut the vinyl even with the edge.

That completes the stencil assembly.

Enjoy looking at it, and then cover it with paper, attached with tape to ensure it doesn't get damaged and put it away somewhere safe where it won't get damaged.

## Step 3: Building the enclosure

## Step 4: Installing the strip LEDs

Next, we need to install the LEDs on the inside of the newly created light box enclosures.

There are two options at this stage—Either, you can use individual LEDs and resistors (which I feel is a little ugly, but it works), or you can use some of the "strip LEDs" that are used in modern kitchens for awesome lighting effects. I am focusing on installing strip LEDs, as they are so much simpler to install.

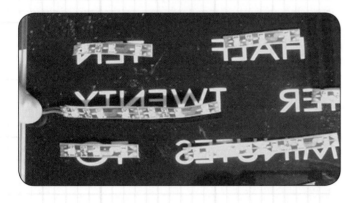

Strip lights are strips of flexible plastic PCB material that have groups of LEDs and resistors pre-installed. They are designed to run off 12V DC, and have an adhesive backing material attached, so installing them is as simple as removing the backing paper, and sticking them down. They can normally be cut into set of 3 LEDs, as individual light components. The photo on the shows a typical strip light. I used 2 x 1m Strip Lights for the project.

Start by cutting the Strip Light into the appropriate length sections for the words to be illuminated. In the case of my strip lights, there is a cut line every 3 LEDs, so I used 3 LEDs for the short words, and 6 LEDs for the longer words.

Once the individual words have been cut out from the strip lights use a small soldering iron to tin the ends—they are plastic coated, but should solder easily.

Next, remove the paper backing, exposing the sticky adhesive surface and attach the strips to the back of each small light chamber enclosure. Alignment is not incredibly critical, but try to get the strip centered along the word that

it is supposed to light up. Use the stencil as a guide to show you where to install the strips. Be careful when installing the strips to make sure that the + and – connections are uniform (i.e. all + up, or all + down)

Once the strips have been stuck down, use a small (3mm diameter) drill and drill a small hole beside the strip light for the cable to be wired through. Be careful to not drill a hole in the strip light material.

Next, hold the assembly up to a light, and mark the holes for the controller to be mounted—we use a light behind the assembly to make sure that the holes you will be drilling won't interfere with any of the strip lights.

Next, install 4 sets of short hex standoffs for the controller to be mounted on.

Continue assembly by soldering a wire between all of the + connections. Remember that the controller has a common + between all of the words—this is the wire we run next.

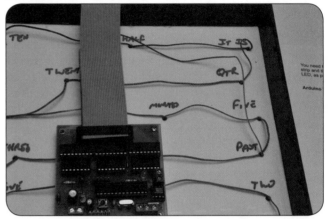

Now, strip the ends of the 26 way ribbon cable, and connect each lead to its respective word, as detailed in the manual for the controller board that you can get from here: http://www.dougswordclock.com/manuals/Arduino-Controller-v3-Assembly%20Manual.pdf. Be careful to allow extra slack on the end of the ribbon cable that has the connector, to allow it to plug into the controller board.

Once all of the strip lights have been installed and soldered, install the final baffles between the words using glue. Be careful to avoid dribbling glue everywhere!

## Step 5: Making the controller

Assembling the controller board is fairly simple.

Start by using Toner Transfer to etch a controller PCB—The layout for Toner Transfer is attached to this step as a PDF.

Then insert the 3 links on the component side of the PCB. Care must be taken to ensure that no solder bridges are produced during soldering, linking adjacent tracks on the PCB. I use of offcuts of component leads which have been bent using a pair of needle nose pliers for jumpers. There is no need to use insulated wire.

Continue assembly by inserting the IC Sockets, resistors, and 1N4004 diode. Be careful to with the orientation of the IC sockets. Pin one is indicated with a square pin on the PCB.

Then, insert and solder the rest of the resistors, capacitors, 78L05 voltage regulator and crystals in place. Again, be careful that the correct orientation is used for the electrolytic capacitors and diode. The following photo will help.

Continue assembly by installing the LEDs, 5 pin header, 6 pin header, 26 pin header and the 2 and 3 terminal connector blocks. The LEDs must be installed so that the short lead (cathode) is located at the bottom of the board (in the square hole)

Finally, insert the IC packages. Be very careful that the IC's are oriented so that pin one is in the correct location (matching the square hole on the PCB).

That completes assembly of the controller.

The build manual for the controller is at my web site www.dougswordclock.com

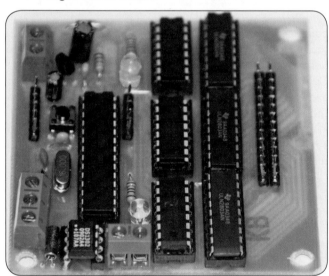

## Step 6: Programming the controller

If you have a kit from me, the AtMega168 chip will already be pre-programmed so you don't need to worry about this step.

Otherwise, if you have a new AtMega168, then you need to program it with the software to run the clock. There are two ways you can do this;

- Remove the AtMega168 from the controller board, and insert it into an Arduino and program it using the Arduino IDE and a USB cable, or
- Use a Sparkfun FTDI USB-232 cable, plugged into the 6 pin connector on the controller board. If you use the FTDI cable, then the WordClock controller looks like an Arduino board as far as the Arduino IDE software is concerned.

In any case, use the attached Arduino sketch to program the chip.

## Step 7: Final steps

The last steps we need to do are to finish the connections to the controller board, and plug it into the display cable.

Then we need to attach the stencil in a way that we can remove it if we need to, and to install some diffuser to the back of the stencil (I originally used tissue paper—now I use a sheet of oven baking paper). I used small blocks of Perspex glued to the stencil and attached with small screws through the side of the enclosure. Start by using masking tape to ensure that the edge of the enclosure is not glued to the stencil. Screw the four blocks onto the corners of the enclosure, apply some glue, and glue the enclosure to the stencil. Make sure that the enclosure is aligned so it is centralized on the stencil. The attached photos will help you make sense of this.

After that, we need to add a socket for the power cable, and mount the buttons to allow us to set the time.

Then, we need to install the back onto the enclosure—again, I used small blocks of Perspex and small screws, using the same technique that was used to glue the stencil.

That completes the clock—power it up, and you should see the display self test start up.

Set the time, and enjoy it.

# Lantern Clock

### By Jack Edjourian (hellboy)
### (http://www.instructables.com/id/Lantern-Clock/)

It's a beautiful Nixie Lantern clock, a little steam punk and a bit Victorian, made up of mostly of found components.

Parts list:

- Large slab of walnut 2" thick by 36" long and 12" wide
- Large slab of maple 1.5" thick by 30" long and 12" wide, both found on eBay
- 2" diameter clear acrylic tubing .125" wall about 12" long, any plastic store and eBay.
- An assortment of gears and gauge faces/bezels, knobs and metal bits,
- A nixie kit: I highly recommend a seller on eBay who goes under the name petes_kits (http://shop.ebay.com/petes_kits/m.html?_trksid=p4340.l2562). He has to my knowledge the only nixie prototypers board out there that gives the experimenter options of screw terminals, solder pads and designated nixie patterned mounts for leads, not to mention he always answers and is there to help you out.
- Some basic electronic skills
- A multimeter with a continuity function (prefer an audible function).
- 3 Blue leds
- A mill and lathe for custom parts, machining skills are very helpful
- Lots of brass and aluminum
- All sorts of hardware and locktite
- 12 conductor 28AWG ribbon cable
- 9VAC transformer, wall wart
- Assortment of gears, shafts and collars
- And finally...lots of imagination...

## Step 1: Finding the way

The first step was to gather all your resources and mix and match, try to figure what works and which direction you are willing to head in.

My original concept was to have each Nixie in its own chamber, but through trial Realized I did not want the clock to be lengthy.

After finding the diameter I was going to work in, I made sure the 2 Nixie tubes would fit side by side within the acrylic tube. This required a custom circuit board to be made to not only physically hold the nixies in place but to allow all the terminals to be easily soldered to. This also allowed me to place where I wanted the wires to terminate into the circuit board, out of site.

For the circuit board you will need:

- Copper clad single sided circuit board material
- Etching solution: http://www.allelectronics.com/make-a-store/item/ER-3/DRY-CONCENTRATED-ETCHANT/1.html
- Circuit board transfer http://www.allelectronics.com/make-a-store/item/TEK-5/TECHNIKS-PRESS-PEEL-PC-BOARD-KIT/1.html
- Etch cut drill mount

All materials were purchased from http://www.allelectronics.com/.

## Step 2: Direction found

The hub of the thinner gear was cross drilled and a steel shaft was inserted as the swing pivot. Same thing was done in the above attachment using an assortment of gears and spacers. A woven wire protective sheath was used to hide the 24 conductor ribbon wire harness.

The idea was to have the fixtures swing, have a friend who owns a yacht and the clock rocks perfectly with the motion of the ocean.

## Step 3: The wood

I found some great slabs of wood on eBay, bought some maple and walnut.

I planned on sandwiching the two contrasting colors of wood.

I rough cut the shapes I needed. Using a disc sander and a spindle sander I shaped the outside and inside curves.

I registered and drilled some through holes common to all the slabs. Inserting all thread rods, with washers and bolts allowed me to mechanically tighten and physically lock the slabs together so they can be mounted together into the mill and machined as one piece later to have the ability to disassemble and wire.

The components are temporarily mounted on pegs and posts and the clear coat process begins.

Make sure you are in a well ventilated space.

I brushed on 1-2 coats of clear catalyzed lacquer (cardinal), letting it all soak in. After it hardens, start the exhausting sanding process.

Be cautious not to use a heavy grit, the rule is not to sand through your clear coat layers; if you get to wood you have gone too far. Also be careful not to let clear drops harden, don't spray too heavy. To spray I used a cheap ($14) harbor freight HVLP spray gun, and it worked as well as one of my Binks guns.

I used 400–1500 grit through the sanding process. I later used automotive polishes of varying grits, hand and machine buffed parts.

2 coats brushed-sand-spray-sand-spray-sand-spray-sand-spray-sand-spray-polish buff.

Very time consuming took me days to complete but the more work you put into this step the better it looks in the end. Keep it up.

clocks

## Step 4: Electronics, buttons, and stuff

Using a 3mm led, each acrylic tube is edge lit, the fact the tube ends above the bottom of the bezel allows me to hide an LED here.

Painting edges white allows for a uniform bounce for the light.

Make sure to insulate the led conductors due to the brass gear that sits above it.

Getting things together, here you start sorting and testing all the leads coming to the electronics compartment, using spacers for the circuit board, mounting the switches.

## Step 5: Closing her up

The components are now together, using a multimeter check continuity from tube circuit board to wire end.

Circuit boards have a lot of traces in a small area. Each tube has 12 terminals. The old board I had from Pete required all 12 wires to connect to the board. His new prototype board has GREATLY simplified this; cathodes all tie in to the corresponding number cathode across the set of nixies for example cathode 1 tube 1 connects to cathode1 on tube 2 and so on, only the anodes (6 one per nixie) have to be connected one by one, not that hard at all.

Three pairs of wires power the blue LEDs used for tube illumination, since the clocks board has a power in range of 9VAC to 15VAC. I chose a 9VAC transformer, allowing me 3VAC per led, so I wired the LEDs in series and connected the two wires directly to the AC input jack. Since AC polarity isn't an issue at 60 cycles they illuminate the tubes perfectly.

Try and find an adapter with a 90 degree plug so you can drill and mount the power input plug facing down on the bottom cover plate.

The cover plated can be anything from plywood to fiberglass circuit board material, I chose the latter. Bear in mind the recess you milled this depth will be your material thickness for the cover plate.

## Step 6: Here it is...

Pete has included about 28 user settings, you can cycle through them using the adjust buttons, my favorites are the fading digits setting where all digits fade to the next instead of switching, the other is the slot machine function where user can set all digits to cycle every minute, hour, or 12 hours.

# Lunchtime Clock

## By Randy Sarafan (randofo)

(http://www.instructables.com/id/Lunchtime-
Clock/)

Have you ever wished lunchtime were longer, but didn't know where to find those few extra minutes? Well, wish no longer!

Thanks to great in advances in clock technology, I present to you a clock that speeds up 20% every day at 11:00 and slows down 20% every day at 11:48, giving you an extra twelve minutes of lunch to enjoy. Twelve minutes may not seem like a lot but, to put it into perspective, this is a full additional hour of lunchtime gained every week.

## Step 1: Go get stuff

You will need:
- (x1) Standard wall clock
- (x1) Adafruit DS1307 Real Time Clock Kit
- (x1) Arduino (w/ATMEGA168 DIP chip)
- (x1) Extra ATMEGA168 chip with Arduino bootloader installed (see last step)
- (x2) BC547 PNP transistors
- (x2) BC557 NPN transistors
- (x1) 28 pin socket
- (x2) 22pF capacitors
- (x1) 16mhz crystal
- (x1) 1K resistor
- (x1) 7805 regulator
- (x1) 4 pin socket
- (x1) 9V battery and connector

## Step 2: Remove the movement

Remove the clock movement from the clock body. This will require removing the front glass face from the clock as well as the clock's hands. Be gentle as not to break anything. You will have to reassemble everything later.

## Step 3: Hack the movement

The clock movement has a single coil stepper motor inside. The basic theory here is that we want to disconnect the coil from the clock's timing circuit and then attach wires to the coil so that we can control it ourselves.

So, knowing this, open up the clock movement and make careful mental note of where everything is (or take a picture).

Take apart the movement until the circuit board is free.

Locate the contacts on the circuit board where the motor is located. Notice these two contacts have traces that go off to the chip (hidden under the black blob). The idea is to use a razor blade or knife to scratch away at these traces until the connection with the chip is visibly broken.

For good measure, I also cut away the timing crystal, rendering the circuit more or less useless.

Lastly, I soldered about 6" of wire to each of the motor terminals.

When this was all done I put the whole thing back together. There wasn't a spot in the case where I could conveniently slip the wires through and I needed it to go properly back together, so I ended up cutting a small hole for the wires to pass through.

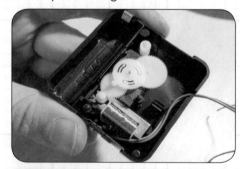

## Step 4: Reassemble the clock

Once your movement is good and hacked, but the clock back together.

Important: Make sure the hour, minute and second hand all line up at 12:00. I did not do this the first time around and quickly discovered that the clock would not display right unless all the hands were lined up.

## Step 5: RTC Kit

If you haven't done so already, but together your Adafruit DS1307 Real Time Clock Kit.

Here are some instructions for getting the job done: http://www.instructables.com/id/Assemble-an-Adafruit-DS1307-Real-Time-Clock-Kit/.

Also, while you are at it, set the time on the RTC board. So long as you don't take the battery out, you should only need to do this once (at least for the next 5 years or so until the battery dies). You can get in-depth instructions for setting the time on Ladyada's site (http://www.ladyada.net/learn/breakoutplus/ds1307rtc.html).

## Step 6: Build the circuit

The circuit is pretty simple. It is basically what the kids these days are calling a "hackduino," a socket for the RTC board and a crude H-bridge to control the motor.

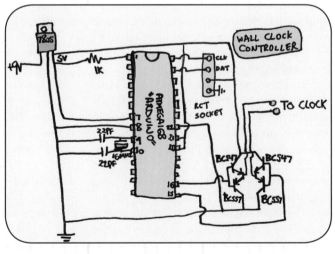

## Step 7: Program the chip

You will need to install the RTClib library for your code to work. Instructions to do this are on Ladyada's page (http://www.ladyada.net/learn/breakoutplus/ds1307rtc.html).

Download lunchtime_clock.zip, uncompress it, and then upload the lunchtime_clock.pde code onto your chip.

If you don't feel like downloading the file, here is the code:

## Step 8: Put it all together

Once programmed, transfer your ATMEGA168 chip from the Arduino to your circuit board.

Plug in your RTC board into the socket. Make sure the pins are lined up correctly before powering it up.

Attach your circuit board and battery to the back of the clock. In true last-minute DIY fashion, I used hot glue and gaffers tape to do this. Self-adhesive Velcro would be ideal.

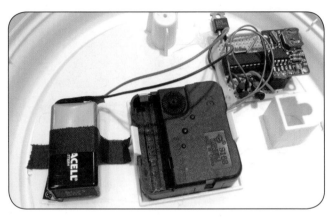

## Step 9: Synchronize the clocks

Put a new ATMEGA168 chip into the Arduino. Connect the Arduino once more to the RTC board.

Run the sample code from Ladyada's page (http://www.ladyada.net/learn/breakoutplus/ds1307rtc.html). Open the serial monitor. The time displayed here is the time you are going to want to sync your clock to.

I found it was easiest to set a third clock (my computer clock) to be perfectly in sync with the RTC board. Then, I powered down the Arduino, transferred the RTC board back to my circuit and set the Lunchtime Clock to a minute later than my computer time. At just the right moment, when the minute changed on my computer, I powered up the lunchtime clock to achieve synchronicity.

The lunchtime clock works extremely well and has thus far surpassed my expectations.

# Linear Clock

## By Sandy Noble (Euphy)
### (http://www.instructables.com/id/Linear-Clock/)

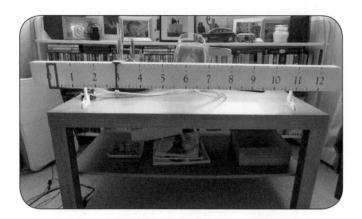

Round clocks are so 20th century! Here's something a bit more postmodern and obtuse.

I'll be showing you here another full design project, from idea to design to prototype. The object of our desire today is a linear clock, that is, one that has numerals arranged in a line rather than in a circle, and it'll fit very nicely into many homes and workplaces.

The actual build (starting at step 3) shows an easy to make version, that uses a set of simple parts, and this is my prototype clock. It's the clock I assembled as a proof of concept. It's simple enough that you can probably put it together in an evening if you have the right bits, and substantial and useful enough to be worth spending time on. It uses easy to find parts, doesn't destroy them in the process, and doesn't require anything that's special. It is also forgiving of sloppy production.

## Step 1: Design considerations and background

I like an analogue clock. For telling the time (I mean, as opposed to seeing how long to boil an egg) I think an analogue face more satisfyingly describes the nature of time. The experience of time is such an elastic and personal thing, and an analogue face is more open to interpretation.

There are almost always round, however, and for designers, the clock is usually a fairly abstract graphical exercise in styling. I have always been interested in different analogues for time, other than the round face with the sweeping pointers erupting from a central spindle. I like the idea that time can be measured with another kind of metamorphosis is appealing. Maybe an object will change shape over the course of a day, or a balloon will be against the ceiling in the morning and gradually sink throughout the day. Make it fall past a scale drawn on the wall and you have a rather elaborate clock. Do without the scale on the wall,

and the assembly still tells the time, but it is harder to be precise, and what metric exactly the device is showing becomes less obvious. Sand timers and water clocks are the most common non-conventional clocks. They suffer from a lack of precision in reading.

## Step 2: Development—how it's supposed to go

I gave myself a brief featuring the following MUSTs:
- Low power—ideally no trailing wires/battery.
- Cheap enough to fit into a mainstream boutique's retail price range.
- Same mechanism able to run horizontally or vertically.
- Silent when not moving.
- Lightweight—does not require special wall fixings.
- Aesthetically neutral—open to styling and colour/material choices.

I hummed and hawwed for so long, and eventually settled on a fairly simple mechanical design that uses a small solenoid as a latch to regulate the turning of a spring-loaded, snail-shaped cam. This would be the driving input to the gear train that moves the indicators.

The timing source itself was to be made from a quartz clock movement—the part that sends a pulse every second. There are lots of fancy-dan electronic solutions for this, with realtime clock ICs and radio clocks and things, but I went for a simple approach. This keeps initial costs down, and is much more within my own sphere of understanding.

## Step 3: The final design

The concept for this clock is that it uses the physical and graphical design vocabulary we instinctively understand and accept, but not in a configuration that we are familiar with. I hope to create an object that doesn't at first appear to be a clock, but could not conceivably be anything else. It has all the properties of a standard analogue timekeeper (hands, numerals), but it is distorted into a shape that is surprising. It begs a question ("what happens when the hands reach the end?") and answers it in a very satisfying way.

It also doesn't look odd. I'm looking to make it complement a mainstream contemporary home, so it uses the colors and materials that are found there. The shape is unusual though, and brings to mind the illuminated slot and roving indicator of a manual radio tuning dial. In its vertical form it makes me think of barometers or thermometers or other scientific equipment that makes it into the home.

Horizontally, it could stand alone hung on a wall, or more like, be used as a shelf or mantle-piece replacement. Turned vertically it is harder to place because we human beings are a lot less tuned to looking up and down than we are to looking from side to side. Vertically it needs a more sparse setting with a wall that's got a lot of vertical space available.

## Step 4: Prototype version—Introduction and parts list

However, on my way to a finished design on paper, I was also constructing a prototype using parts I already had, to help test some ideas.

The purpose of this prototype is to get something working as quickly as possible. Building the prototype will give me some good ideas about the complexity of the build and the length of time required. This in turn gives me some pointers about how many different versions I have time to test.

This is how I made my prototype, and the things you'll need to cobble this together. I used this set of pieces because it's what I came across first. Other kinds will certainly work too.

### Chassis

- I used foam core board (sometimes called kappaboard) to make my prototype. It's light, glues easily, and is stiff and strong. It's also easy to cut and not messy. Corrugated cardboard will also work handsomely.

### The running gear

- 2x Curtain rails—I got a PVC one from John Lewis' for &pound;7 ($11). You need two pieces, each as long as you want your clock to be. My prototype was 62.5cm long because I used a 125cm curtain rail sawn in two.
- 4x sewing machine bobbins for the driving wheels—plastic ones are easier to work with, and cheaper.
- 2x Pulleys for the non-driving end of the clock—I used these little pulley blocks I had, but sewing machine bobbins would be just as good probably.
- Thread that is thick enough to be controllable, some thin elastic cord, some bits of balsa sheet or other light, thin, strong sheet that will slide OK in the channel of the curtain rail.

### The brains

- Arduino with Adafruit Motorshield—This is definitely overkill, and I used this simply because I already had it and it works admirably. The stepping circuit on its own is not complicated and if you have an Arduino compatible board that isn't otherwise gainfully employed, then it's quite easy to whip up a circuit using L293 ICs on breadboard that will drive a couple of stepper motors. Look at Tom Igoe's stepper pages (http://www.tigoe.net/pcomp/code/circuits/motors/stepper-motors/) for circuits for driving steppers from an Arduino. However, what the Motorshield gives is a good quality library that allows you to turn the motors off entirely. The simpler circuit does not do this so easily.
- The logic/timing part of the code would be the same for all versions, but the interfacing code will be a little different.
- Any Arduino compatible board will work fine as far as I know.
- 2x Stepper motors. I tested this with some dead cheap little steppers that have almost no torque and only 20 steps per revolution. I paid next to nothing for them. I also made a version with some good quality NEMA17 steppers with 400 steps per revolution. I paid about

£14 for each of those and they weighed a pound each. I ended up using the cheap small steppers.
- In the Arduino code, modify the value "stepsPerRevolution" to reflect the kind of motor you have.
- You'll also need a 6-9v DC power supply to run your microprocessor (Arduino) when it's not tethered to the PC.

### Tools

- Knives mostly. Foamcore has a tendency to "crumb" if you don't have a really sharp knife, so use a fresh, long blade and always make sure the blade is moving through the foamcore using a sawing, or slicing action rather than cleaving or chopping.
- Adhesives—I've used anything I had around. Superglue, hot melt glue, contact adhesive and gummed brown paper tape.
- Soldering stuff, or screw terminals, and wire.

## Step 5: Prototype version—assemble the chassis

I'm making my clock face 10cm wide, so I've cut some panels of foamcore to size (100mm wide), and glued the curtain track onto them.

Stick the edges of the track onto the faces of the board for best results. Before glueing, make sure the tracks are straight, and bend them straight if they aren't. Also cut some rectangles to fit in between the rails, to help them stay straight and to allow you to put some clamps (i.e. elastic bands) around while the glue dries. Run your beads of glue along the card edges so as not to melt the foam too much.

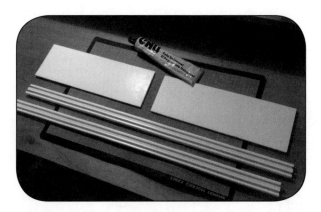

## Step 6: Prototype version—driving bobbins

Stick two of the sewing bobbins together (faces keyed with sandpaper and then superglued): In operation, one of these will wind thread up, the other will let it out. You might think that using just one bobbin, or a longer bobbin will work just as well, and you might be right. A problem will occur when the two lines become crossed over each other, however, and I wanted things to run as smoothly as possible.

Figure out a way to mount the bobbins directly to the shaft of your stepper. I was lucky because my stepper has a little brass collar that fits exactly into the bobbin, and centers it right away. I filled the core with hot melt glue and jammed it on. Epoxy putty would be a solution for a stronger bond. Remember to leave a little gap between the body of the motor and the bobbin so it turns freely—the thickness of a couple of sheets of paper would be enough, and you can draw a target on the paper to help center the bobbins.

Wind a piece of thread a fair bit longer than your clock onto each bobbin, in opposite directions; keep the ends safe with a bit of blu tack. You'll trim them to length later.

## Step 7: Prototype version—Mounting motors

Line up your bobbin stack against the end of your chassis—you should arrange it so that a piece of thread wound around the top bobbin will cleanly enter the slot in your curtain rail. It shouldn't touch the sides at all.

The thread will travel all the way down the slot, wrap around another idler wheel at the end, and then come back up and get wound onto the opposite side of the bobbin stack.

So make a bracket to hold the motors. Mine are small, and light, so are just friction-fit into two holes. This has the benefit of leaving a bit of wiggle room, but has the problem of being easily pulled out of position by other forces (i.e. dropping it on the floor). Use a knife with a long blade and a sawing action to cut intricate or internal shapes in foamcore board.

## Step 8: Prototype version—idlers

There needs to be an idler wheel (non-powered pulley wheel) on the other end of the clock. This should be positioned so that one side is ready to receive the thread from the center of the channel in the curtain rail. So the thread will exit the driving bobbin, travel directly

through the channel without touching the sides, and then cleanly wrap around the idler wheel.

The position of the return side of the thread isn't that important, except that it needs to have an unobstructed path through the whole length of the clock, and be able to cleanly wind around the take up bobbin. I had to cut a few sections of my internal supports out to clear the path.

The angle I have these little pulley sheaves at is nothing special. It might seem nice to have your thread loops travelling through both channels in the rail, one up and one down. Well, it would be nice, you're right, but it'll also be a pain, and there is no advantage gained.

## Step 9: Prototype clock—carriage and indicators

Make a little sled out of balsa wood with two legs, to slide along the curtain rail. Cut a notch in one of the legs to fasten the thread through, and that's that. I made mine actually in the rail itself, rather than trying to make it, and then fit it in. Though I admit I did slide it out once the glue had dried to butcher it to get the next step to work...

Eventually you'll cut a couple of bits of cardboard or something to use as the pointers.

Now, the next bit is good, but needs a bit of skill and judgment.

## Step 10: Prototype clock—threading!

The diameter of the driving bobbin changes depending on how much thread is on the bobbin—as more gets wound on then it gets thicker, and so the linear step size gets longer—that is, each step winds in more thread than the one before (because the thread is building up). In practice this means that the loop of thread gets slightly tighter as either one of the bobbins gets full.

To compensate for this variation (which is not big, but big enough to cause a problem), the two sides of the thread loop are joined by a piece of elastic. This puts enough tension on the thread to keep it in the groove while it's at its loosest, and has enough stretch to take the strain when it's tight.

- Make sure there is one full loops-worth of thread on each bobbin. That is, each bobbin should have enough thread to stretch from the bobbin, round the idler, then up to the other bobbin. Trim the thread so both sides are the same length.
- Wind half of the thread back onto the bobbin. Leave the ends stretched out through there normal route—the ends should meet at the idler.
- Hold both ends in pinched fingers and move them along the length of the clock, winding the thread on and off the power bobbins, feeling how much difference in tension there is between the extremes and the center of the travel. This will give you an idea of how tight your elastic can be. If there's hardly any difference (thin thread, or no overlap), then you don't need to leave much slack. If there's lots of difference (thick thread/cord, lots of overlap) then you'll need plenty of slack.
- Tie inch long loops in both ends of the thread. The two pieces of thread should no longer meet. Cut a piece of elastic long enough to bridge the gap between both loops and tie a knot in one end.
- Tie one end of the elastic to the thread coming up from the idler (from the takeup bobbin).
- Move the thread through the clock again to see where the loose loop of thread needs to be tied to the elastic. Tie a knot in the elastic, and then loop the thread onto it. I hedged my bets by making a couple of knots so I could try different tensions easily.
- The knot in the elastic should be enough of a kink to engage with the slot you cut in your little carriage. You could glue it if you wanted, but I found that once the knot was tucked into the channel, it stayed put anyway.

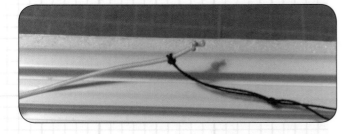

## Step 11: Prototype version—electronic bits

Arduino Duemilanove board and an Adafruit Motorshield. Usually it's not recommended to use the same power supply for the motors as for the Arduino, but in this case the motors are so weedy that they don't draw much power anyway, so I've just set the jumper on the motorshield to use the Arduino power supply.

It's straightforward. I made some extension cables with some 4-pin headers because the steppers I have happen to already have little connectors fitted, and the wires on them are tiny and fragile anyway.

I can't give a good introduction to steppers here (not just because I don't know much about it myself), but roughly put: Each stepper has two coils in it, and pulsing these two coils in a particular sequence and polarity (four steps) makes the rotor turn in a particular direction. The two coils are separate in a bipolar stepper like I'm using, so I have four wires coming out of the motor. (Actually I have five, because these are weird, but I just cut one of them.) The exact motors I have here are the very same kind described in outstanding detail in this brilliant instructable (http://www.instructables.com/id/Drive-a-Stepper-Motor-with-an-AVR-Microprocessor/).

Two of the wires will be connected to one of the coils, and the other two will be connected to the other coil. Use a multimeter to check for continuity to figure out which. Then connect one pair to output terminal 1 and 2 of one of the motorshield ports, and the other pair to 4 and 5. Unless you know the pinouts of your stepper, you might have got it right, or you might have the polarity of one of the coils switched.

To test the program without having to wait a minute between each physical tick, change the millisPerSecond value in the program to 200—this will run five times faster than usual. You can also change stepSize which will modify how many steps the motor takes per tick.

## Step 12: Prototype version—software

The software isn't complicated, but make sure you have the most recent version of Adafruit's own Motorshield driver (https://github.com/adafruit/Adafruit-Motor-Shield-library). There's a fix in it that is important for this code.

**The code**

There is an internal time representation, consisting of three ints: currentSeconds, currentMinutes and currentHours. This time is pre-set at start up and incremented while the program runs.

The main loop of the program makes a note of the start time, then continuously checks the current time to see if it's 1000 milliseconds later or not. If it is, then it increments the internal clock time (doTick()) and hits a procedure to change the position of the indicators on the clock (renderTime()).

The procedure doTick() deals with incrementing seconds into minutes, and minutes into hours, and resetting those values when necessary.

The procedure renderTime() deals with converting the time in H:M:S into positions on the clock face, or more correctly, positions of the stepper. The program has a concept of the current position of the indicators (preset on startup at 00:00—the far left position), and uses this initial start position to decide whether to move the stepper forwards or backwards.

Using the internal time keeping of the Arduino is fairly dodgy ground (see this instructable [http://www.instructa-bles.com/id/Arduino-Binary-Alarm-Clock/step4/Time-keeping/] for a good run down on why, and a possible solution). There's lots of ways round this if it's important: The main Arduino pages have a few ways to make it accurate, as well as stuff about using the Time library. I went for a more simple solution, given that it's a prototype (yes, that is my excuse for every time I make a hack).

I am using the AFMotor library for driving the steppers, because I am using the Adafruit motorshield. If you run the steppers through another circuit, you can probably use the regular Arduino stepper libraries with minimal code chopping. If you download the code, the file should be saved with a .pde on the end. Not sure how to change the filename on instructables! Code is available via http://www.instructables.com/id/Linear-Clock/step12/Proto-type-version-software/.

## Step 13: Prototype clock—Software adaptations

Your stepper motors will be different to mine. To adapt it to your particular stepper motor, you should:

**Change the statements that declare the motors**

```
AF_Stepper hourHand(20, 1); // hours
AF_Stepper minuteHand(20, 2); //
minutes
```

at the top, and change the 20 to however many steps your particular motors take to do a full revolution. 200 steps is popular (1.8 degrees per step). If you have no documentation about your stepper, then experimentation is the only way forward, I'm sure you can figure out a way of doing it.

**Change the stepsPerClock statement**

```
int stepsPerClock = 592;
```

This might be complicated, because it depends on the length of your clock, the number of steps per revolution of your motor and the diameter of your bobbins. There is a mathematical way of working it out, but I just measured how far 100 steps moved the carriage, then used that to calculate the total number of steps required to move the full length of the clock. Also remember that you need a bit of space for the carriage, so it doesn't fall out the end of the channel at either end.

**Change the current time**

The start time is hard-coded in this version. The next version will allow you to increment the time with some buttons attached to the Arduino.

```
int currentSeconds = 0;
int currentMinutes = 55;
int currentHours = 11;
```

means it's going to set itself to five-to-twelve once it's turned on. Again, there are smarter ways of doing this in the final version, but for this one, this is enough. I usually set it for a minute in the future, then upload to the Arduino and press reset when it's dead on. The pointers are a bit wobbly to notice a minute here or there anyway. You should manually rewind the indicators back to zero when you reset or turn it on.

**Change the speed of time!**

For testing purposes, I run it five times real-time by setting the line to

```
int const millisPerSecond = 200;
```

Real time is 1000 milliseconds per second, so change it to 1000 when you actually want to keep time with it!

## Step 14: Prototype clock—indicators and faces and finish

Test it by manually moving the carriages back to the start position (00:00) and then turning it on. If you are using the Arduino IDE, then you'll be able to see the internal time being counted out using the serial port monitor, and at the turn of the minutes and the hours, then the motors should run and your battle station should be fully operational!

Well, I know it won't be quite that easy, but that's the theory!

Print or draw a face, and stick a couple of lightweight cardstock pointers on, and hay presto! Make sure the hands aren't level, or they'll catch on each other as they pass.

At this point you can also tidy it all up and stick some extra bits on so it'll stand up on a surface or can be hung up. I'm sure it'd be easy enough to make up a case for it too, with the electronics tucked away inside.

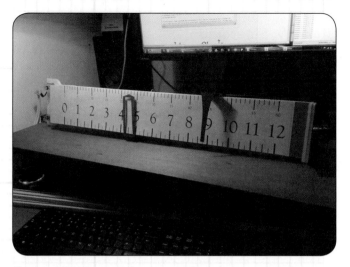

## Step 15: Towards a production model—reality check

My initial plans (sketched out in step 2) for the final production model are for a largely spring-driven machine, with a gear train to power both indicators from a single solenoid-actuated time source.

After building the prototype, I looked a bit askance at the extra complexity required by the production model, and decided that that particular battle was one for another day. I decided to make a more realistic prototype to test a few other mechanisms.

I sawed a 2-metre aluminum curtain rail into two pieces to use for this version. I figured the metal would be more stable, given the longer length. In practice, it didn't make a significant difference. The painted surface was smoother and harder, so there is less friction, but there are parts that are not painted, and the transition between the two zones is rough, and a right pain to try and file smooth. I'm not sure there's much benefit to using the metal, particularly if it's going to be enclosed anyway.

## Step 16: Refinement #1—bead chain loops

I used bead chain from some roller blinds—they are supplied with an endless loop that is a meter long—that is, there's two meters of cord, forming a loop that is a meter stretched out, perfect for my meter-long bits of curtain rail.

Thing is, the blinds only come with one sprocket, so I modeled another, and had a few 3D printed, along with a couple of brackets, and some little carriages to run in the slots of the rails. I used http://www.shapeways.com for my prints, but I've included the STLs online at (http://www.instructables.com/id/Linear-Clock/step16/Refinement-1-bead-chain-loops/) if you'd like them. In an earlier stage of the project I did make a couple of sprockets from balsa. They actually worked ok, but were predictably irregular.

Actually really pleased with this set up, they look great and were completely snag-free (hurray!). As I suspected though, they were too heavy for these little motors to move. With a more torquey motor these would be ideal, and I suspect I might end up using them. Certainly the neatest solution.

## Step 17: Refinement #2 thread and a friction drive

I reverted to using a loop of thread, along with my little steppers to get something working, though I tried a drive method using two meshing gears as a way of driving the thread, instead of the double bobbin. This nicely avoids the problem of the varying bobbin diameter (as the thread layers up).

As with the pulleys, the gears were bought from Rapid. The brass tubes were KandS Metals products, bought from the local hobby shop.

I added a couple of little plastic guides cut from sheet polystyrene to keep the thread in line with the gears.

All very nice, and did work, but unfortunately very touchy. Being friction-driven there's lots of room for slippage of the drive on the thread. There are too many variables that can change over the lifetime of the clock, even if it could be properly tuned to begin with. There are things I can do to improve that a little (use a grippier thread), but it'll never be quite good enough. I suspect any friction drive will have this same problem.

## Step 18: Refinement #3—The revenge of the double bobbin technique

So, the final iteration for this instructable is actually the closest design to the prototype. It uses the double bobbins, but positioned in a way to make the winding a little more even. And it is also pre-wound much more carefully so that one side fills at a more similar rate than the other empties.

It is still not as simple and as "closed-loop" as the bead chain system, but it is quiet and importantly, it works with these small steppers, which means it is light and cheap. Design is about compromise, and these iterations are the whole point of making prototypes. It is very rare indeed that designs drawn out on paper turn into perfect physical objects without a whole lot of shoehorning.

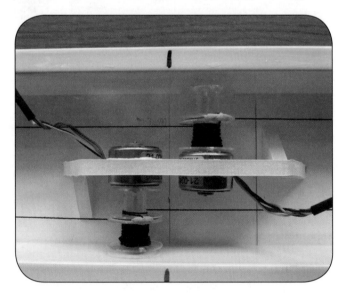

## Step 19: Finished article

Working in situ. I added some feet that are held in some general-purpose slots in the back of the clock. These slots could just as easily hold a piece of cord to hang the clock up. I'm not doing that bit yet because I think a case is more important.

## Step 20: Finessing

I added the finished touches to this version by mounting the electronics to the back of the clock. I strapped it to a bit of foamcore board and made some slots for that to go into on the back of the clock, in the same way as the legs are mounted. This leaves the power as the only wire hanging out of it, the rest securely mounted and tucked up and out of the way.

For this you'll need:
- A few inches of stripboard.
- Wire to make links.
- Headers to allow the pins on your motorshield to be plugged-into.
- 3x push-to-make switches and an LED (I used these right-angle tactile switches, and a sideways-looking LED because I knew this would be operated from the edge).

The code, available at (http://www.instructables.com/id/Linear-Clock/) has been modified so that the clock can be stopped and started with a button, and while it's stopped the time can be incremented manually with two extra buttons. This uses Alexander Brevig's Button library. This actually makes the clock usable in everyday life—you don't have to hook it up over USB to set the time! Still have to reset the time every time it loses power, but hey ho.

It's the little things like that, taking the rough edges off that transforms a prototype, and interesting or curious diversion, into a usable product.

The switches are connected to pin 2, pin 9 and pin 10, and the LED is on pin 13. Each switch simply connects that pin to ground. The pins have pull-up resistors already on them (built into the Arduino), so they will default to high (+5v) unless shorted to ground. The software looks out for a switch between low (button depressed) and high (button released). It does its thing when the button is released.

I think this is pretty neat.

## Step 21: Pointers

The carriages in the slide need to be able to hold the pointers at the right angle and distance from the face, and also need to hold the ends of the thread secure. I first used just blu-tack to stick the thread and the cardboard pointer to the carriage.

A problem with using a simple bent-card pointer is that it's very hard to keep it bent at the correct angle—it wants to unfold, and when it does it catches on the other pointer when they pass by each other.

I made some new pointers and super-glued some pieces of solid wire onto them, so they stuck out at right angles, like prongs. Then I secured them to the carriage by using a couple of pieces of the grippy plastic hooks from some command strip. This turned out to hold the thread and the wires pretty securely, and once in, I could lightly bend the wires to position the pointers almost perfectly.

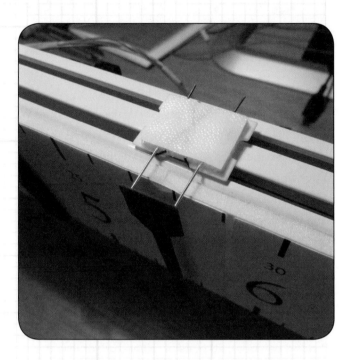

## Step 22: Appraisal and next steps!

In step 2 I drew up the list of demands as follows:

**Low power : ideally no trailing wires/battery**

Failed on this one. This current design uses an Arduino and stepper motors. The microprocessor on its own can run ok on batteries for a little while, but with the steppers, it's only going to be good for a week I guess. I am accepting this solution, however, because it occurred to me that wires don't necessarily have to be the black plastic hanging out of a wall wart. I anticipate a mains powered version of this clock in production would have a thin wire with a nice fiber woven sleeve, or a flat cable, like a speaker cable. Batteries is still the dream of course, but it's for a non microprocessor/stepper combination I think.

**Cheap enough to fit into a mainstream boutique's retail price range**

SUCCESS! I think anyway. In response to a reader's comment, I totted up the cost of a hypothetical version of this clock using a simplified electronic design (i.e., discrete driver circuit) and it came out at about $40. This could also be significantly reduced if parts were bought in bulk. The design isn't very complicated to build so labour wouldn't be too much. The case is not factored into that price however, and depending on fit and finish, it could conceivably be very expensive. Also packaging should be thought about.

Anyway, say $60 cost = $120 wholesale = $200+ retail. That's not too bad. If I sold just direct then I could keep costs down.

**Same mechanism able to run horizontally or vertically**

SUCCESS! This does not rely or use gravity in any stage, and the carriages and indicators are lightweight, so there is no impediment to running this clock in either orientation.

**Silent when not moving**

SUCCESS! The motors are completely powered down between movements so there should be no buzzing or humming that might otherwise get amplified by the case/wall. When it does move, it makes a noise from the carriages rattling in their grooves, but some patches of felt might help that.

**Lightweight—does not require special wall fixings**

SUCCESS! Actually shot myself in the foot a bit by upgrading to using aluminium rails for this version. It's heavier and doesn't really add anything. Even so, still not too heavy to hang on a normal picture hook. Of course a wooden case will change that, but even those need not be prohibitively strongly built. I am leaning more to recommending that this clock sits on a surface anyway (like on a mantlepiece or across the top of a bookshelf).

**Aesthetically neutral—open to styling and color/material choices**

SUCCESS. The reason I put this requirement in was so that I wouldn't produce some mechanism that was weird looking, or awkward to house. Basically insisting that the clock can be cased in whatever I like, rather than having to have a big hole in the top for a wheel to pop out, or a space below for a pendulum or something. I copped out a bit here by not having a case to show, but I think it's clear that any kind of case would fit fine around this mechanism.

I'm happy with it, and it's ticking away on my desk as we speak.

There are a few extra modifications that are required to make this a product:

**Changes:**

Use an endless loop of toothed/beaded chain instead of the double spools thread. This makes the diameter of the driving spool constant (the thread doesn't "layer") and have loose parts and tight parts. There is still slack to deal with, since the cord may stretch a little over its lifetime, but a much shorter spring or piece of elastic can deal with that.

- Use a discrete stepper driving circuit instead of the the Adafruit motorshield. The motorshield is very versatile, but overkill for what I need it for. I can probably make a more simple circuit using just the L293Ds and a couple of transistors, and that'll be a lot cheaper. Teamed with a less general-purpose version of the Arduino, this will save a whole lot of money.
- An indicator position detector at one end to allow it to self-calibrate on startup.
- A better time source. There's a hundred different ways of doing this, but it's likely to be the time keeping IC from a quartz clock.

# computer

The computer is the tireless workhorse of the digital age. Nameless and faceless, it sits inside its enclosure, processing countless zeroes and ones. It helps us do our work and keeps us entertained, even through the quiet late hours of the night when nearly everything else in the technological world has long been put to sleep. These amazing machines are too often trapped inside boring gray or black enclosures. Well, come on out computer! Behold the power of the following projects as the computer is catapulted out of its mundane housing, straight into a gray duct tape icosagon (20-sided polygon), 40 pints of mineral oil, or into the taxidermied carcass of a once living mouse!

We're not reinventing the computer so much as reinventing how we interact with it, bringing older and stranger machines along for the ride. For the poet in all of us, there's the currently trendy and yet timeless practice of tossing your conventional keyboard for the vastly preferred typewriter! What's that, the typewriter from your grandmother's basement doesn't have a USB cable? No problem—we've got step-by-step instructions to show you how you can convert mechanical typewriter keystrokes into fully functioning letters that will appear on your monitor.

# Vintage Radio Computer Tower

By Roy Guernsey (longwinters)
(http://www.instructables.com/id/Vintage-Radio-Computer-Tower/)

This was a fun project because it was quite easy, when the case was done, all you had to do was add the doo dads and you get a fun looking housing for your tower.

The work involved took about 40 hours, about 6 of wich were wasted on some stuff I decided to reject as unacceptable.

The Radio dial is a home construct I am trying to work to the goal of doing all my own construction of such things. Antique stores are usually expensive, and you can rarely find what you want to use.

The knife switch was a rare find in Alaska. It was not made by me.

If you had to buy all the wood and materials new without using scraps I would guess the cost to be $200.00

I think because I had so much of the stuff left over from furniture-making, my cost was about $30.00 give or take ten bucks.

## Step 1: The box construction

The only thing that is slightly unusual in my box construction is the curved front corner. I used a piece of 1 3/4 inch PVC as a corner.

I did this because I didn't want the case to be unnecessarily wide, and the hallow pipe allows the tower to slide right up close to the front without hitting a rounded corner piece.

I used hot glue to hold the corner in place, and I recommend you cut the pipe "oversize" to allow for your table saw blade thickness.

The sides of the box are thicker than the pipe which was handy, so I cut a rabbit down the edge to match the thickness of the pipe.

The top, bottom, and front are all Baltic birch plywood 9 ply. I made the sides overlap the top and bottom because I didn't want any seams to show when I skinned it up.

There is a rabbit on the front panel just like the side to accommodate the PVC 1/4 round.

A pin nailer held it together while the glue set.

## Step 2: The dial

I took a picture of a vintage radio dial, enlarged it, and printed it on plain old paper; I was trying to keep it simple.

I glued the picture of the dial to some corrugated card-board; huge mistake. MDF or anything else would have been better.

After my contact cement dried I cut out the lit part of the dial and used some of the same screen material I used on my web cam (from an air filter). I painted it red and glued the whole mess together with Hot Glue. I had some laminate film so I stuck it on the dial photo copy to give it a glossier look.

The brass frame was made of hobby store square tubing with round rod bent at 90 degrees to hold it together. The rod MUST be filed in the inside corner to make a snug fit (use a triangle shaped file). Then solder it from the back and buff.

## Step 3: Skinning it up

I wanted a vintage look and thought the round corner was critical to that appearance. I also knew the corner was tight and I did not want decorative edges or nails/screws to hold it down when it went around the corner and then stopped at the opening for access to the disc drive/USB ports, etc.

That edge would want to pop off if not done right, so I used steam and heat.

Don't fall for the temptation to cut your veneer way over size; it's quite difficult to trim the excess if it is over 1/4 inch.

I steamed and dried the corner about four times, before it wanted to keep the curve. The clamps hang off a piece of tape stuck to the veneer, not the wood it self, (that would crack it) The weight of the clamps was enough to make it curve when heat was applied.

At that point both sides were sprayed with 3M super 90 spray contact cement. No forgiveness it they touch out of alignment!

## Step 4: Clean it up

There it is, all covered up, ready for the base.

Do you see why I wanted a steamed curve now, because of that opening just after the corner?

I cut the hole out using a utility knife from the inside while the hole was on a solid surface so I would not rip the veneer.

The cleanup is done with a single cut file pushing inward only.

## Step 5: The base

This was a pain. I gave away my router table because it was inaccurate, I wished I had not right then. The easiest way to keep your router steady is to use a second piece of stock to let the non-cutting side of the router have a track to ride on.

I cut rabbits in the rounded pieces using my table saw. I just pushed the work against the fence as opposed to the table, and this made mounting the base very easy since I just used screws from inside with a little glue.

## Step 6: Face plate

I drew the design I wanted and cut it out using a jig saw. The inlays are from a router cut. After sanding the strip inlays flat I repeated the process with the 4 dots at their bottoms.

The process for making the various holes on the project is as follows. I wanted an exact fit for the fuse box, and the radio brass inlay.

I used a top follower bit and made a jig from scrap wood.

The fuse box width was copied by placing it between the blade and the fence. This made the wood I cut match

it's width perfectly. I suppose a good craftsman would just measure.

Now place that over the hole you have roughly cut and clean it up with your top follower bit and router.

## Step 7: Making it purdy

I like spray lacquer and use brushing thinned 50% sprayed through a primer gun (auto); the finish is world class. A good wiping stain is Masters gel style. Some steel wool will help to even it out before you spray the lacquer.

220 grit sand paper is good for veneer if used very sparingly.

Put your dials and gizmoes on and you're done. Wire up the LEDs, and shove your computer in there. This was a fun project.

Did anybody notice this baby has two 25 amp fuses and one 3" speaker? It's a power hog!

# Privacy Monitor Hacked from an Old LCD Monitor

By Toma Dimov (dimovi)
(http://www.instructables.com/id/Privacy-monitor-made-from-an-old-LCD-Monitor/)

Finally you can do something with that old LCD monitor you have in the garage.

You can turn it into a privacy monitor! It looks all white to everybody except you, because you are wearing "magic" glasses!

All you really have to have is a pair of old glasses, x-acto knife or a box cutter, and some solvent (paint thinner).

**Parts:**

- an LCD monitor of course
- single use 3D glasses from the movie theater (old sunglasses are just fine)
- paint thinner (or some other solvent such as toluene, turpentine, acetone, methyl acetate, ethyl acetate, etc.)
- box cutter (and CNC laser cutter, but that you don't really need, I'm sure x-acto knife and a steady hand would do just fine)
- screwdriver or drill
- paper towels
- superglue

## Step 1: Take the monitor apart

Find an old monitor that you are willing to sacrifice.

Take off the plastic frame by unscrewing all screws from the back.

## Step 2: Cut the polarized film

Most LCD monitors have two films on the glass—a polarized one to filter out the light you are not supposed to see, and a frosted anti-glare film. The anti-glare film we don't need, the polarized one we do—it is used for the glasses.

So, grab your cutting tool and cut the films along the edge. Don't be afraid to press; metal won't scratch the glass unless there is sand or other abrasives on it.

Then, start peeling. Make sure to save the polarized film; also remember the orientation.

## Step 3: Clean the film adhesive

After you remove the film, the glue will likely remain stuck to the glass, so here comes the messy part.

With some solvent, soften the glue and wipe it off with paper towels.

I started with OOPS, but that was not fast enough so I got some paint thinner.

I found out that if you cover the screen with paper towels and then soak them in paint thinner, you can let it sit longer and dissolve the adhesive without running and evaporating.

Scrape off the soft glue with a piece of plastic or wood.

Be careful not to get paint thinner on the plastic frame, because it will dissolve it.

## Step 4: Monitor—done

After cleaning the adhesive, assemble everything back the way it was. Before even making the glasses, you can test the monitor with the polarized film!

Notice how the upper left corner looks clear, because it has the anti-glare film removed. That is the part we are going to use to make the glasses.

Remember, this is a polarized film so the angle is critical. Back and front also matters.

If you don't have access to a CNC cutter or you don't want to wait for an online service, you can probably tape the old lenses on the film and then cut them out with an x-acto knife.

## Step 5: Pop the lenses out

For the glasses, I used single use 3D glasses from the movie theater, but you can use whatever you want.

Pop out the lenses or take the glasses apart if you can.

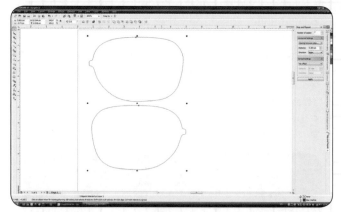

## Step 7: Reassemble glasses and enjoy!

Finally assemble the glasses and you are ready for some fun!

People might think you are crazy, staring at a blank white screen wearing sunglasses!

But I guess that makes it even more fun!

## Step 6: Scan, trace, cut

If you are going to use a CNC blade or laser cutter, scan and trace the parts.

You can find a local vinyl or laser cutting service, or you could send them to an online service like www.cutyourway.com.

I scanned the frames so I can use them as a reference for the lens orientation.

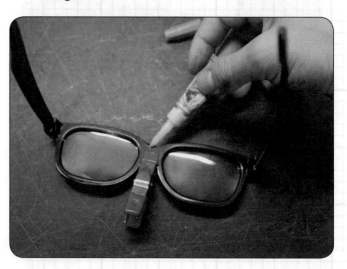

# How to Build Your Own USB Keylogger

By Andrea Gambi (Jamby)
(http://www.instructables.com/id/How-to-build-your-own-USB-Keylogger/)

Since I've searched a lot for a project like this, and I haven't found anything around the Web, I would like to share my experience of my personal USB Keylogger.

It's not really a pure "USB" Keylogger (because USB HID protocol is much more difficult than PS/2 protocol), but it adapts a USB Keyboard to PS/2 port, while (of course) recording the keys pressed.

In this way, even if it's discovered by anybody, it should be confused with a normal PS/2 Adapter.

It needs just a few components (SOIC PIC and EEPROM can be freely ordered as a sample from http://www.microchip.com/samples/)

- PIC 12F1822 (SOIC Version)
- EEPROM 24XX1025 (Any 1Mb version will be ok) (SOIC Version)
- 2 * 4k7 Resistor 1/8 W (Or any resistor of the same value as small as you can solder in the adaptor)
- Pickit 2/3 (For programming the picture and reading the EEPROM)
- An USB to PS/2 Adapter that can be opened.
- A GOOD solder and VERY GOOD soldering abilities.

Let's Start.

Some weeks ago, a friend of mine asked me to help him because his computer seemed blocked. Indeed, he couldn't even type his password to log in with his account.

I know that he is almost a novice and couldn't just change the keyboard instead of asking for my help. Anyway, I changed his keyboard, but I wanted to know why it wasn't working. I tried it on another computer without any result, except that the keyboard's LEDs blinked, so I wanted to go deeper. I took a Logic Analyzer and analyzed the PS/2 protocol. I discovered that the keyboard was switching off whenever the PC sent 0xFF (Reset) command. I solved it by simply replacing a capacitor that had blown up.

This is WHY I built it (for any similar case), I'm NOT responsible for ANY way you use this Keylogger.

Illegal is the WAY you use a Keylogger, not the Keylogger by itself.

I didn't want to make anything "immoral" or "illegal."

## Step 1: Circuit

The circuit is divided into two "zones":

One is the Adapter, which connects the GND and VCC pins of the PS/2 connector with their respective pins on the USB Connector and CLK and DAT pin to, respectively, D+ and D- pins.

The other zone is composed by the PIC and the EEPROM (and the I2C required pull-up resistors). The PIC takes care of detecting incoming Data from PS/2, decodes, and then writes it to the EEPROM.

## Step 2: Open up

Open up your USB to PS/2 Adapter.

It simply connects pins from USB female to the PS/2 male connector.

All the wires are glued together with some kind of silicone or something similar, so you have to carefully remove that with a diagonal pliers or anything similar.

You should remain with the separated Female USB and the Male PS/2 connector and the plastic holder.

## Step 3: Solder First "Zone"

This shouldn't be too hard, just join:

VCC -> VCC
GND-> GND
D+ -> CLK
D- -> DAT

See here for USB Pinout (http://pinouts.ru/Slots/USB_pinout.shtml).

See here for PS/2 Pinout (http://pinouts.ru/Inputs/PS2Mouse_pinout.shtml).

It will look like this:

## Step 4: Solder PIC and program it

You need to temporarily solder your PIC onto a small piece of surface-mount board so you can solder a wire to each pin, one by one.

No matter which way you have chosen, you need to be able to connect your PIC to Pickit 2 or any other PIC programmers that support PIC 12F1822.

I've written the code using PCW from CCS, so if you want to modify the code, feel free to modify or distribute it as you wish, just mention this guide if you want to redistribute it.

I've attached also the .hex if you want to simply copy what I've done (http://www.instructables.com/id/How-to-build-your-own-USB-Keylogger/step4/Solder-PIC-and-Program-It/).

I don't enter into the details of programming, because I expect that you already know how to do that.

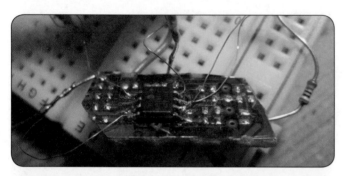

## Step 5: Solder PIC and EEPROM

Here's the bad step.

Here you need to take all your soldering abilities to correctly solder the PIC with the EEPROM and the two Pull-Up resistors.

It's REALLY not so easy, so, if you aren't an expert of soldering, I advise you to leave this project, or to ask a friend of yours to make that for you.

After some days of working, this is my result:

## Step 6: Read EEPROM after logged

After the soldering process and re-assembly your Keylogger, you should connect to the keyboard that you want to log and wait for the information, "legal" data, or anything you want to get from this Keylogger.

Then, unplug the Keylogger and re-plug in the keyboard.

Now, you have to read from the EEPROM, so, If you have also soldered the SDA and SCL pins to the two N/C pin of PS/2 (like it was on the circuit) you can now build a simple converter from PS/2 to the ICSP connector of your EEPROM-reader (in my case, Pickit 2).

See the documentation of your programmer to see exactly how to build it.

After read the EEPROM memory, you should save it to a file for better usage. You can do this with a simple Hex Viewer.

Remember that the data collected from PIC are pure "keyboard scancodes," so you need to convert to a readable version.

You can do this by hand, basing your conversion process to this link (http://www.beyondlogic.org/keyboard/keybrd.htm).

Another way is to use my homemade program, made to make this process easier.

I've attached it, but BE AWARE, IT'S AN ALPHA VERSION, it's FULL of bug and REALLY not optimized.

## Step 7: Conclusion

Here we are.

I don't know how many will have the bad idea of making this Keylogger, but, if you really want a homemade (and almost free) solution to log a keyboard, this is what you're searching for!

Feel free to comment and ask questions about this project.

# USB Typewriter

By Jack Zylkin (jackzylkin)
(http://www.instructables.com/id/
USB-Typewriter/)

There is something very magical about typing on those old-school manual typewriters. From the satisfying snap of the spring-loaded keys, to the gleam of the polished chrome accents, to the crisp marks on the printed page, typewriters make for a sublime writing experience. Now, the USB Typewriter lets you enjoy the magic of writing on a manual typewriter, without forfeiting the ability to use word-processing, email, web-browsing, or other modern desktop conveniences. Or, instead of using the typewriter as a computer keyboard, you can turn off your monitor altogether and type directly onto paper—while discretely saving a soft-copy for later use!

In this instructable, I'll help you bring your old type-writer back to life by converting it into a USB compatible keyboard for your PC, Mac, or tablet computer. The hack is intended as a full keyboard replacement, so you can get rid of that piece of disposable plastic you call a keyboard and use the desk space for a classic, functional work of art—A USB Typewriter!

## Step 1: Overview

Under the hood of almost every manual typewriter is a spring-loaded crossbar that runs underneath all the keys (see picture). Whenever a key is struck, part of that key pushes on the crossbar, and this causes the carriage to advance, the ink roll to move, and so on. We are going to repurpose this crossbar as a place to mount an array of metal contacts, which are attached to a long, narrow circuit board called the Sensor Board.

Take the time now to identify where the crossbar is on your typewriter—just look for a bar that swings up and down when you press a key.

## Step 2: How it works

You don't really need to know how this works to perform the mod, but since you are probably as geeky as I am about this sort of thing, read on:

**The Details:**

The USB Typewriter system consists of three main components: the Sensor Board, the USB Interface Board, and the Reed Switches.

- The Sensor Board is a long strip of flexible metal contacts that clip easily underneath the keys of the typewriter. Each contact is attached to a different pin on a chain of shift registers, which act like a fireman's "bucket brigade," passing a signal down the line from one pin to the next. When the signal being passed down the row of shift registers is intercepted by one of the keys, the microcontroller is alerted to a keypress.

- The USB Interface Board features an Atmega168P microcontroller (i.e. an Arduino chip), a USB socket, and some supporting components. By sending the CLK and SER signals, it controls the operation of the Sensor Board, and by monitoring the "chassis" signal, it can detect keypresses. The animation shows that the Interface Board can tell which key has been pressed, based on which pin of the sensor board was active when the chassis signal was detected. The interface board also controls the USB jack that connects to your computer.

- The Reed Switches: Because the Sensor Board only detects keys that strike the crossbar, several important keys go undetected. These include Shift, Space, and

Return. To deal with those keys, we use tiny switches that close when in the presence of a magnet.

The USB Typewriter is an open-source project! Although you don't need them to follow these instructions, you can find all of the Arduino microcontroller software HERE (http://www.instructables.com/id/USB-Typewriter/step2/HOW-IT-WORKS/).

## Step 3: Parts list

**Materials (included with the DIY Kit):**
- An assortment of small neodymium magnets
- Custom laser cut metal tabs ("feather contacts")
- Blank PCB circuit boards

**Electronics materials (included with the DIY Kit):**
- R1: 68 ohm resistor
- R2: 68 ohm resistor
- R3: 2.2 kohm resistor
- R4: 10 kohm resistor
- USB2: USB B type jack such as FCI 61729-0010BLF
- C1: 22pF capacitor
- C2: 22pF capacitor
- C3 22uF electrolytic capacitor
- Q1: 16MHz crystal oscillator
- C4: .01uF capacitor
- IC1: ATMEGA168, preloaded with USB Typewriter software
- S1 and S2: Omron B3F-1005 tactile switch
- D1 and D2: 3.6V Zener Diode (1N5227B)
- IC1...IC12: M74HC595B1R shift registers (QTY: 12)
- 3 or 4 reed switches to sense shift, space, return carriage, etc. (Meder PN# ORD211/10-15 AT)
- An Atmega168/328 microcontroller with Arduino bootloader and USB Typewriter software.

**Supplies (not included in kit):**
- A small roll of gaffer tape
- Stranded wire, preferably 24 AWG or 22 AWG
- Solder (lead free is the way to be)
- Superglue
- "Simple Green" or similar degreaser/cleaner (for de-gunking your typewriter keys)
- Can of compressed air (optional for cleaning your typewriter)

**Tools**
- Hot glue gun
- Wire strippers and clippers
- The usual assortment of tweezers, pliers, screwdrivers, and other hand tools for hackin'
- An old toothbrush (optional: for scrubbing gunky typewriter parts)
- Dremel rotary tool with a cutting disk, or, if you don't have a Dremel, some med-grit sandpaper.

## Step 4: File the keys

We need to scrape off the paint that is on the key-bars underneath the crossbar. This way, the key-bars can make electrical contact with the circuitry we will be attaching to the crossbar.

Using a folded-up wad of paper, prop the crossbar up and out of the way. Then, use a Dremel grinding tool to gently sand away the paint on the key-bars underneath, revealing the shiny metal. Be careful to avoid any springs that may be attached near the crossbar, because the Dremel will cut through them easily, and trust me—they are hard to replace! Use a metal file, sandpaper, or even a utility knife to scratch away the paint in areas near springs, or in any other hard-to-reach areas.

## Step 5: Tape the crossbar

We will be attaching electrical contacts to the crossbar, so it must first be insulated with gaffers tape or duct tape. I recommend using gaffer's tape, which is available at most photography stores, arts stores, hardware stores, or online. Make sure the crossbar is free of dirt and oil, which the tape will not stick to. If your tape is still not sticky enough, you can reinforce it with a few dabs of superglue.

## Step 6: Cut the sensor board

The sensor board included in the DIY Kit is longer than the crossbar on your typewriter. That is because it is designed to be cut to length. Using tin-snips, wire strippers, or scissors, and cut the sensor board so that it is the same length as the crossbar.

Unless they are very sharp, the scissors won't cut the board very easily, so go slow.

Important: Make sure you save the scrap you cut off—it will come in handy later!

## Step 7: Mark the contact locations

Place the blank sensor board onto the crossbar in the same position you intend to mount it. Then, use a Sharpie pen to mark off the approximate locations that the contacts need to be attached. One contact is needed for each key-bar that is underneath the crossbar. Do not worry if your marks are not very precise—the contacts are flexible and will eventually be bent into the correct position.

## Step 8: Populate the sensor board

Insert the 74HC595 Shift Registers into the sensor board and solder them in place.

Important: Make sure that the "Pin 1" markers on the chips are all facing towards the "top" of the board (see picture).

Also important: The leads of the Shift Registers will poke out of the other side of the board and form sharp spikes. These spikes are undesirable because they will poke through the gaffer tape insulation when you mount the sensor board to the crossbar. Use clippers to cut the spikes so they are flat instead of pointy—you don't need to cut them all the way off—just blunt them.

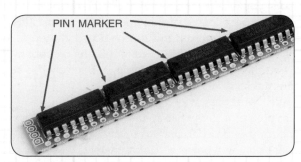

PIN1 MARKER

## Step 9: Attach flexible contacts

Into each of the solder holes you have marked on the sensor board in Sharpie pen, insert one flexible contact and solder it in place. If a mark falls between two holes, simply choose the hole that the mark is closest to.

If the board has been cut in such a way that some of the contacts are not connected to a shift register at all, you need only solder a jumper wire between these unconnected contacts and any of the unused pins on the rest of the Sensor Board.

Important: In 99% of the cases, you will want to attach the contacts so they stick out underneath the Sensor Board (i.e. on the opposite side from the chips). However if you have a Royal typewriter, you will want to go about things differently. Please read this note about Royal Typewriters before continuing (http://www.usbtypewriter.com/royal.html).

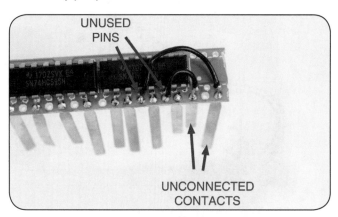

UNUSED PINS

UNCONNECTED CONTACTS

## Step 10: Assemble the interface board

The image below shows the location of all the components on the interface board. Note the orientation of the electrolytic capacitor—the grey stripe indicates the negative side. Also note the orientation of D1 and D2—the black stripe should point downwards. Finally, note the location of PIN 1 of the ATMEGA168 chip—the PIN 1 marker must be oriented towards the top of the board.

Also, don't get confused between C1, C2, and C4. C4 is marked "103" while C1 and C2 are marked "22J."

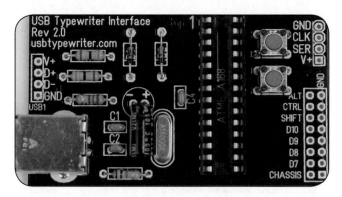

## Step 11: Test the interface board

Go to your computer and open up Notepad (on Windows) or TextEdit (on Mac). While holding down S1, plug in the USB Cable to the interface board. A message beginning "USB TYPEWRITER Rev 2.0" should appear on your screen! If not, review your connections and part orientations and try again.

You can repeat this process at various stages in the project to make sure everything is still working.

## Step 12: Connect the two boards

Using 4 equal lengths of stranded wire connect the sensor board to the interface board. But first, do a dry run (without soldering), loosely fitting the sensor board and interface board onto the typewriter to make sure that the wires are the correct length to reach from one board to the other. Make sure you leave some slack—it's better to have too much slack than too little!

After you make the connections, it's a good idea to test the electronics again (see Step 10).

computer

### Step 13: Pre-bend contacts

In the next step, the flexible contacts will be wrapped tightly around the crossbar. But to make that process easier, we will first pre-bend the contacts a little. Take a pack of Post-It Notes and tear off a chunk of notes that is the same thickness as the crossbar. Then, use the Post-It Notes as a template to fold the flexible contacts at a sharp 90 degree angle.

### Step 14: Attach sensor board to crossbar

This might be the trickiest part of the whole process. Carefully position the sensor board onto the crossbar, while slipping the contacts underneath it. Once you are happy with the way it is positioned, use small dabs of hot glue to keep the sensor board in place (see third picture above). Don't worry yet about positioning the contacts correctly.

### Step 15: Cut and bend contacts

The contacts are probably too long at this point. Cut them to a manageable length using clippers or small scissors, and then use tweezers to fold them down flat against the crossbar. Use the tweezers to coax each contact into position under the corresponding key-bar. The picture you see above shows a key being pressed and squarely hitting one of the contacts. You don't have to be super-precise—just make sure each contact is in the path of its corresponding key, and that none of the contacts are touching each other.

Also, make sure none of the contacts are touching any exposed metal, like springs, arms, or untaped parts of the crossbar. If any of the contacts won't stay in place, use a small amount of superglue to hold them down (Be careful with the superglue! Don't get it all over the contact!).

### Step 16: Prop the crossbar back

You are so close! Right now the contacts are successfully attached to the crossbar, but the problem is that many of them are probably too close to the keys. Ideally, each key should only touch its corresponding contact after it has been pressed more than halfway down. Therefore, we need to prop the crossbar back from the keys a little.

The method for propping the crossbar back is different for each typewriter. For example, if you look carefully you'll find that Remingtons all have adjustable tabs connected to either side of the crossbar that prop it back. Many Underwoods also have these tabs. Other Underwoods have a thin metal bar, perpendicular to the crossbar, which props it back. Smith Coronas have a hook that extends from the left side of the crossbar to the tension-adjustment spring. Regardless what kind of tab, hook, or bar your typewriter uses to prop back the crossbar, you will have to either a) bend it a little or b) add a shim. The best source of shim material is the plastic PCB scrap you cut away from the sensor board in Step 5. You ideally want to add about 1.5mm-2mm of separation between the keys and the crossbar, and luckily this scrap is 1.6mm thick.

**The quick and easy way**

If you are unsure what system your typewriter uses to prop back the crossbar, there is a very simple solution that will work on any typewriter. Unfortunately, it involves sacrificing one of the keys (I suggest sacrificing the "1/2 1/4" key, which has no equivalent on a modern keyboard). Simply remove the contact underneath that key, and in its place attach a small piece of shim material using superglue. By resting between the key and the crossbar, the shim will ensure that the crossbar is separated from all of the other keys, too. The best source of shim material is the plastic PCB scrap you cut away from the sensor board in Step 5.

### Step 17: Attach the chassis wire

The USB Typewriter works by monitoring the voltage of the chassis of the typewriter (see "Step 2: How It Works). In this step, we will be attaching a wire to the chassis of the typewriter, to connect with the "CHASSIS" input to the interface board.

First, identify a screw or bolt on the typewriter chassis that would make a good connection point. Next, remove this screw and strip away the paint underneath it with sandpaper or a Dremel. Next, crimp a wire onto one of the metal eyelets included with your kit, then lightly solder it for good measure. The eyelet should then be slipped onto the screw, which should then be re-attached.

The loose end of the eyelet wire should then be attached to either of the two "CHASSIS" inputs marked on the Interface board.

Note: If your kit did not come with any eyelets, you have an older version of the kit—in that case you must go out and buy a variety pack of eyelets from the hardware store.

## Step 18: Assemble the reed switch boards
### Why use reed switches?

Certain keys, such as Shift, Spacebar, Backspacer, and Return Carriage do not strike the crossbar, and therefore cannot be sensed by the Sensor Board. To catch these keys, we will mount magnets to them, and then attach reed switches nearby. (Reed switches are special switches that are only closed when they detect a magnetic field). When the key is moved down and up, the magnet will move towards and away from the reed switch, opening it and closing it.

### Assembling the Reed Switch Boards

Because reed switches are very fragile and hard to work with, the kit comes with breakout boards and protective sleeves for each reed switch. After soldering the reed switch to the breakout board, attach two wires—each about 12 inches (30cm) long. Then cover the board with a heat-shrink tube and use a lighter to shrink it in place. (Don't put the flame right onto the tube—you are trying to heat it up, not set it on fire!) You will notice that the glue inside the heat-shrink tube will melt, sealing everything in and protecting the fragile reed switch from damage. This process takes about 1-2 minutes, so be patient. Using a heat-gun or hair-dryer instead of a lighter may speed things up.

Cut off the excess heat-shrink tubing with clippers or scissors.

Warning: The tubes will be extremely hot after shrinking! Let them cool down before handling!

Note: If you don't have the breakout boards, you must have an older kit—email me and I'll send the new parts to you for free!

## Step 19: Flatten the reed switch boards

After the reed switch assemblies have cooled down, you may notice that they are not totally flat underneath. They will be easier to glue in place if they have a nice flat surface. Therefore, you must lightly reheat the bottom of the reed switch assembly with your lighter to soften it, then place it on a smooth flat surface and apply gentle downward pressure. I like to put a few layers of soft cloth between my hands and the reed switch—this prevents me from accidentally smashing the fragile glass reed inside.

## Step 20: Attach the reed switches
### Experiment with positioning

Unless you have worked with reed switches before, it may be tricky to find the appropriate place to attach them to your typewriter. So, some experimentation with a multimeter is required before finalizing the position of each reed switch. First, attach a magnet to the key you wish to detect (for example, the spacebar, backspace key, shift key, or return carriage lever). Next, attach the probes of your multimeter to the wires of the reed switch, and use the "continuity" setting (often signified by a little beeping sound wave) to monitor whether the reed switch is open or closed. The multimeter will emit a beeping noise whenever the switch is closed (i.e. when a magnet is nearby).

Hint: The reed switch can detect magnets in any direction, but it is most sensitive to magnets that are directly in front of it or behind it.

### Finalize the position

When you are satisfied that you have found a good position for the reed switch, so that it opens and closes consistently whenever the key is pressed, use superglue to attach it permanently to the chassis of the typewriter. I like to use hot glue as well—not to attach the reed switch but to tack the wires down.

### Example—space bar

In the example shown above, the switch is normally open, but closes whenever the space-bar is pressed. However, you may decide to use the opposite configuration—so that the switch is normally closed but opens when the key is pressed. It makes no difference whether the switch is normally open or normally closed, because the software is able to figure this out during calibration.

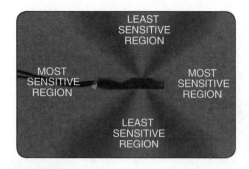

LEAST SENSITIVE REGION

MOST SENSITIVE REGION

MOST SENSITIVE REGION

LEAST SENSITIVE REGION

## Step 21: Connect the reed switch wires

Each reed switch has two wire leads, which must be connected to the correct pairs of solder holes on the interface board. The hole pairs labeled D7, D8, D9, and D10 are multi-purpose inputs that can be used for any key, such as the backspace key, the return carriage key, or the space-bar. The only keys that cannot be connected to the D7-D10 inputs are SHIFT, ALT, and CTRL, which have their own special, reserved inputs.

The picture above shows an example of how the space-bar reed switch might be connected.

TO REED SWITCH

## Step 22: Attach the interface board

After you have attached all the reed switches you need, and you are confident that everything is working correctly, mount the interface board to the side of the typewriter using double-sided foam tape. Don't worry—the tape should peel off easily if you need to remove the board later for some reason.

## Step 23: Perform final calibration

When you first plug in the USB Typewriter, all its microcontroller brain sees is a long row of contacts on the Sensor Board. It has no idea which contacts correspond to which typewriter keys. Luckily, the USB Typewriter has a "Calibration Mode," which sorts this out for you automatically.

To access Calibration Mode:
1. With the USB cable unplugged, open up Notepad (on Windows) or TextEdit (on Mac).
2. Next, hold down the button marked S1 while plugging the USB cable in.
A message should appear that says:
USB TYPEWRITER
REV 2.0
by JACK ZYLKIN
usbtypewriter.com
CALIBRATING...TYPE THE FOLLOWING KEYS:
You will then be prompted to type each letter of the alphabet, all the numerals, punctuation marks, and a few other keys. Just type the corresponding key on the USB Typewriter.

Important: If you come across a character that you don't wish to assign to any of your USB Typewriter keys, press space-bar to skip.

**Some keys are hard-wired**

Note: Alt, Ctrl, and Shift are not assigned during calibration—they are hard wired to specific inputs on the interface board, which cannot be changed.

**How to assign bonus keys**

If you hold down S2 as you assign a key during calibration, the USB Typewriter interprets that key as a bonus key. For example, when the calibration mode prompts you to enter the "F2" Key, you will realize that your typewriter doesnt have one! Instead, you might decide to hold down S2 while entering the "2" key. From then on, S2+2 will send an F2 command. Meanwhile, just pressing 2 by itself will still just send a 2.

## Step 24: YOU ARE DONE!

Huzzah! You now have your own beautiful USB Typewriter! It can be connected to any PC, Mac, or Linux computer. If you plan on using it with an iPad, you will need to buy a Camera Connection Kit (Apple's USB adapter for iPad). It will also work with many Android tablets.

If you have any questions, email me at jack@usbtypewriter.com or leave a comment on this instructable page! I love hearing about interesting problems and successful projects!

**A quick shout out:**

This project was created at Hive76, a rad maker co-op in Philadelphia, PA. Visit them at www.hive76.org—go check out their website for more cool projects going on in Philadelphia.

# Mineral Oil Submerged PC

By glj12

(http://www.instructables.com/id/Mineral-Oil-Submerged-PC/)

The following link is a tutorial on how to submerge a PC in an aquarium filled with mineral oil. The results were quite astounding considering the computer being used is a server for UT2004 and CS:S. It runs at 120 degrees F and is completely DEAD SILENT. This is a fun project, and is most likely best if you use slightly older or spare parts.

## Step 1: Gathering the materials

Alright, so after watching this video you must be thinking either one of two things. 1. Wow, that's really cool! or; 2. I mean, damn, his typing is so freakin' slow! Explanation: My video capture slowed it down a bit, no idea why. Moving right along, since this is so amazing, let's first go over a few things with pretty pictures. Here are the required materials (or the things that we just used).

Materials
- 5 gallon aquarium
- 1 piece of justly fit plexi-glass
- All standard PC components
- Hacksaw
- Hot glue gun
- A lot of minutes on your cellphone (I'll explain why later)
- 5 gallons of mineral oil (or 40 pints, which is more common to find)

## Step 2: Modding the aquarium

So, your materials are gathered, now to the fun part, modding! (To a certain extent). First, we measured all the dimensions to gain the right aquarium, which just so happened to be a classic 5 gallon one from K-Mart. Tester happened to have a sheet of plexi-glass that was a bit longer than the motherboard, so we used that as the back plate to hold it firmly against the side of the aquarium (plus, it will look like nothing is holding the motherboard at all). We then cut it to size, with the plexi-glass touching the bottom of the aquarium. After that, we took it out and drilled 3 holes in proper holding places so that the motherboard would remain secure. From there, we took the spare plexi glass, and broke it into 4 small 1" X 1" pieces, and glued them together with a bonding liquid that was about the strength between superglue and epoxy. After waiting 10 minutes for it to dry for each layer, we had enough time to take the plastic lid that came with the aquarium to have it serve as a slightly moded bufferzone between air and oil. As shown in the image below, a

hacksaw was used to cut the appropriate amount of space for the VGA, RJ-45, keyboard, mouse, etc. to be exposed for connection.

## Step 3: Aquiring the liquid gold and some useless information

After everything was mounted snug, much cleaning was needed. I had completely forgotten that the PSU, system and CPU fans were completely caked in dust. The most difficult part was cleaning out the heatsink underneath the CPU fan. Since this is a server of mine, it has been on for roughly 2 years straight. The hard drive alone has basically been on 9 years; good old Compaq, wish they were as good as they were back then.

The most difficult aspect of this tutorial was, believe or not, gaining the mineral oil. Out of the entire southern region of this state, there is NO MINERAL OIL. We consumed every last bit of it. We had to purchase 40 pints of this liquid gold. 2 Walmarts and 1 K-Mart are leeched. Success.

Once we got back to my house, we placed a lot of bags on the ground, hoping not to mess up the hardwood floor. It is a bitch to get that out of the floor. As we poured in this revolting substance, we held our breath praying that it wouldn't explode in our faces for some odd reason. It posted successfully after filling it completely. Luckily, all went well with this monstrosity. After that, we took a hot glue gun and sealed the top to the best of our abilities while resting the 9 year old hard drive on top. You may ask, "Why can't you place that piece of junk hard drive in the aquarium?!" My answer to you, my friend, is that all hard drives have a little hole on the bottom of it that requires air to maintain proper pressure, if that were sealed, it would not function properly.

## Step 4: Fill 'er up!

Not much skill is needed with this part. All you need is a funnel, and a steady hand. If you have wood floors, odds are it is best to place something underneath your aquarium computer so it doesn't stain the wood. Turn on your computer and quickly fill the area as much as you can. We had to turn off the computer for a bit when it reached the CPU fan since it was disproportioned, and was setting it a bit off kilter. If we had it in gallon form, (the oil) it would have gone much smoother. After filling it up to the top with 37 pints of oil, and seeing that it was functioning properly, we sealed the top off as well as we could.

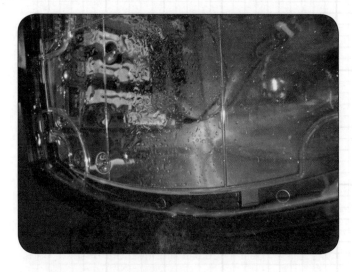

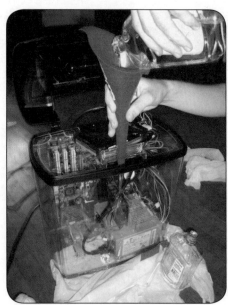

## Step 5: Sealing the Deal

The final step. All we need to do now is to make it as air tight as possible. To seal off the lid, we took a hot glue gun and doused it with glue. We just placed it around the perimeter to the best of our abilities.

## Step 6: Final thoughts

As of now, it seems to be functioning alright, but keep a couple of things in mind; velcro, as I have found out, does not hold down case fans too well. The one black fan started to fall over, but luckily was caught by the other case fan's cord. Phew! One other thing is that the case feels quite hot! Maybe it is because our summers here are pretty warm and humid. I guess certainly no hotter than it was prior in the cirulating air environment. I will certainly keep you posted in the forums about how long this piece of machinery is lasting. I am hoping that if it survives the summer, then it has passed the hardest test on any computer. And by the by, this is one of the heaviest PC's you will ever carry. Since mineral oil is 64 oz. per gallon, and there are 5 gallons plus the weight of the PSU, etc. it should be around 25 pounds. In terms of noise, it would be COMPLETELY silent, if there was no hard drive. Since the HDD is 9 years old, it was not built for silence and performance. Hope you enjoyed this somewhat of a loose tutorial, enjoy the pictures and video, and try this on your own if you have computer parts to spare!

# Mouse Mouse!

By Christy Canida (canida) and Noah Weinstein (noahw), Concept by Noah Weinstein
(http://www.instructables.com/id/Mouse-Mouse!/)

Hacked travel-size (hardware) mouse + taxidermied (wetware) mouse = Mouse Mouse! Fully functional, and furry!

Warning: this project involves taxidermy, dremels, and sometimes graphic pictures of dead animals. While there are no guts in this tutorial, viewer discretion is still advised.

## Step 1: Acquire mice

Obtain a small travel-size (hardware) mouse. This one is a wired mouse that is way too small to use comfortably every day, but perfect for going inside of a mouse.

Obtain a similarly-sized (wetware) mouse. These are commonly available fresh or frozen from pet stores, or any other place that sells reptile food. It's easier to fit a small object into a large mouse than a large object into a small mouse, so err on the side of caution. You can always fill extra space with cotton balls.

If you've got an optical (hardware) mouse, make sure to choose a pale-furred (wetware) mouse for lightest skin pigment—this will be important later.

## Step 2: Dissect (hardware) mouse part 1

Disassemble your mouse.

The mini travel mouse didn't come factory ready to get put inside of a taxidermied mouse. (What were they thinking?)

Thus, you'll need to take your mouse apart and see what's inside.

Take off the spring loaded cable retractor by taking out the screw and then pop the two halves apart with a screw driver.

Remove the little plastic nub that was on the wire so that the wire will thread smoothly through a hole in the (wetware) mouse.

Next, grab a marker and draw lines around all parts of the plastic mini mouse housing that aren't essential. We needed to slim our (hardware) mouse down to fit inside the (wetware) mouse. We used a rotary tool to remove sections from the front of the buttons and the

rear sides so that the (hardware) mouse would fit between the (wetware) mouse's shoulders and hips.

Remove as much plastic as necessary to make your mice fit, but take care not to damage the circuit board. The pseudo-ergonomic styling is really for decoration. You can't make a little mouse like this ergonomic, so go ahead and trim it down to the size of the circuit board.

Make a new slot in the back of the (hardware) mouse for the cord—we need to relocate it to the back to fit with the (wetware) mouse tail.

## Step 3: Dissect (hardware) mouse part 2

In order to pass the USB cord through the tail hole in the (wetware) mouse we had to remove it from the circuit board. This is done by desoldering the connections using a soldering iron. It's easy to do once you have done it before, so maybe practice the method a bit before you give it a shot on the actual mouse. For a quick explanation on desoldering check out the How to Solder instructable. (www.instructables.com/id/EKJGJU1X1VEWP873QK/).

Before you take things apart be sure to write down what wires go into what mounts on the circuit board so that you will be able to put things back together correctly.

Using a soldering iron, gently touch the tip of the iron to the ball of solder that is holding the wire in place. After a second or two the solder will melt and the wire will come free. Leave the ball of solder attached to the circuit board—you can use it to re-attach the wires later on.

## Step 4: Shave (wetware) mouse

Grab a pair of tweezers, your fingernails, a razor, or some wax and remove some fur from your (wetware) mouse's belly. This is where the optical sensor will peek through at the end of the process, so you'll need to clear the fur out of the way.

We started with a sharp scalpel, and then moved onto tweezers and fingernails as they are easier and less likely to damage the skin. Your mileage may vary—go with what works.

## Step 5: Dissect (wetware) mouse

Disassemble your mouse.

Take your mouse apart using the techniques described in my previous Mouse Taxidermy Instructable (http://www.instructables.com/id/Mouse-Taxidermy/).

You should now have a bag of mouse skin; discard the

innards. Remove the tail if you want to run a cord through the opening instead.

Wrap and wire the legs as described for a bit of support, but cut off the wire ends—we'll just let the legs hang loose around the Mouse Mouse body.

Prepare a head-only form, and attach the eyes.

## Step 6: Assembly part 1: reconstitution

Run the cable through the tail hole, and re-solder the four wires onto the surface of the circuit board. Refer to the How to Solder Instructable (http://www.instructables.com/id/How-to-solder/) if you need a refresher on surface mount soldering. Once the wires are in place, plug it in to make sure everything works.

Reassemble the shell and circuit board, and hot-glue the pieces in place.

If you've trimmed any bulky edges of the casing away, you'll want to wrap them in plastic to keep the mouse skin away from the circuit board. We used folded-over kitchen plastic wrap, and hot-glued the edges to the sides of the casing.

## Step 7: Assembly part 2: integration

I inserted the mouse head form just like in the Mouse Taxidermy Instructable (http://www.instructables.com/id/Mouse-Taxidermy/), and trimmed the wires so they wouldn't interfere with the rest of the project.

We inserted the (hardware) mouse into the shoulders first, then pulled the tail region around the back. It was a tight fit—next time we'll find a fatter mouse, as it's easy to fill extra space with cotton balls! Skin is stretchy, though, so long as you keep it moist the mice should integrate nicely.

Sew up the back opening, starting near the tail and working towards the head. Leave a space for the scroll wheel- it won't work properly covered in fur!

Tack the skin down around the scroll wheel with a bit of superglue, taking care not to gum up either the buttons or the scroll wheel. I usually apply the glue with a tool, either a pin or a piece of wire with a small loop on the end.

## Step 8: Optical sensor

If you've got an albino (wetware) mouse, its skin might be clear enough for your optical mouse to work directly through the dry skin. Our mouse had a bit of pigment, so it was necessary to remove the skin flap. Thankfully we had already shaved this area, making the process much easier.

Make sure your completed Mouse Mouse is dry first, or the skin may pull and warp as it dries!

Use your X-Acto knife or scalpel to carefully trim a hole for the optical sensor to peek through, then add just a touch of cyanoacrylate (tissue glue, aka superglue) to the edges of the skin. This will toughen the skin edge and fasten it to the plastic around the sensor.

Use a tool (I used a bent piece of wire) to apply the glue, and do so sparingly—you don't want to drop any on the optical sensor!

## Step 9: Completed mouse mouse!

Now plug your Mouse Mouse into your computer and test things out! Ours worked perfectly—I was really quite surprised.

The buttons and scroll wheel worked beautifully, as did the cursor movement after we trimmed the belly skin away from the optical sensor. You may need to trim a bit of fur around the edges of the scroll wheel or optical sensor, but otherwise it's a wrap!

Keep in mind that this mouse isn't meant for heavy-duty computer use- it's a functional work of art, and should be saved for stylish installations and special occasions. Using the Mouse Mouse on a daily basis will likely cause shedding (the mouse) and RSI (your wrists), so we really can't advise it.

Of course, it's Really Damn Cool—every nerd who's any nerd should have one!

computer

# Duct Tape 20-Sided Computer Server

By flaming_pele!

(http://www.instructables.com/id/Duct-Tape-20-Sided-Computer-Server/)

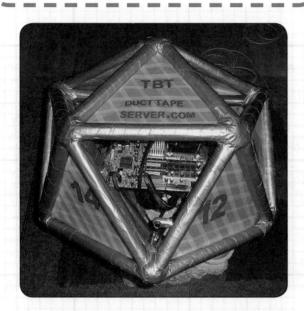

I'm in a group called Team Boom Tape. We are a PC gaming team who also happen to have a certain love for building things with duct tape. In preparation for Million-ManLan 9, we decided to build a computer server housed in duct tape. We've done this before (a couple times, in fact), so we wanted to make something special. We decided to take on a giant duct tape D20.

A D20 is a 20-sided die often used in role playing games like DandD. Geometrically, it is an icosahedron, consisting of 20 triangular sides.

It may seem that sticking server computer components inside is completely random and unnecessary, but this was in fact a machine which we would hook to the LAN and run games (like Team Fortress 2) and apps like Teamspeak and a live video stream. Computer components generate heat, which can be a challenge for adhesives, and everything would need to remain structurally sound for at least the 4 day duration of the summer LAN. As it turned out, it held up for weeks.

Here's a look at the finished product:

## Step 1: Planning

We started with some rough planning. The motherboard was the largest component we'd put in the structure, so it dictated the general size. We aimed at putting the power supply at the bottom and the motherboard in the center. We weren't going for the most compact design possible, but rather something symmetric and decent looking.

The nice thing about an icosahedron is that it's just a series of triangles, which are easy to build and are naturally a sturdy shape. Once we had an idea of the interior space we needed, we figured out the length of the leg of any triangle and got started.

## Step 2: Sheets and tubes

We decided to frame the entire structure from very sturdy tubes of duct tape. To make the tubes we first made a thick duct tape skin by laying down overlapping strips. After the first layer, we'd go over it again with another layer perpendicular to the first. After that, we'd peel up the two-ply sheet, flip it sticky side up, and repeat the process.

Once we had a four-ply sheet, we'd roll it up as tight as possible. Once rolled, we spiral wrapped another layer of tape from one end to the other. When finished the tube was very strong and about an inch in diameter! Just to go a step further—the tubes were usually slightly hollow at the center—we stuffed tiny scraps of duct tape to fill the tubes to add a little more rigidity.

A group of us spent a few nights just mass producing tubes like this.

## Step 3: Making triangles

With nightstick-like tubes of duct tape, we started to build up the structure. It was a relatively simple matter of making a triangle and taping the corners together.

As things progressed we found that our tubes were not all exactly the same length, and that little differences would start adding up and distort our shape. The first few tubes were cut to length with a utility knife, but it was really tough chopping through nearly a solid inch of tape. We also realized that the tubes would look much nicer if they were mitered to fit snuggly together at each corner.

We looked at each other and knew what must be attempted…we had to use a miter saw on our duct tape!

It worked like a charm!*

* Your mileage may vary. Use appropriate caution. Also be prepared to end up with a very gummy saw blade (and maybe more) when you're finished.

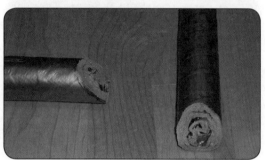

The specs of the machine are pretty low end (we used old gear for the build), but it was plenty to handle its tasks. If you're curious:

- Pentium P4 3.0 GHz
- Intel SFF Motherboard
- 2GB DDR2 RAM
- 80GB SATA HDD
- 475W PSU
- 1 120mm LED fan (rear)
- 1 92mm fan (cpu)

## Step 4: More structure

Construction continued from the bottom up. The bottom face had an extra inner triangle added to support the computer's power supply.

After the bottom half came together, we made a large internal triangle to help support the shape and to hold our motherboard.

As the last of the sides were added, some more tubes were added inside for bracing. At this point, before adding any computer components, the structure was a hefty 20+ pounds of nothing but duct tape!

## Step 6: Finishing Touches

We finished the build by adding some faces made from translucent duct tape. Other sides were left open so people could have a clear view inside.

Remember EVERYTHING that's not electrical is duct tape; anything else would be like cheating to us. Even the letters and numbers we added were cut from red duct tape.

The final tally was a whopping 22 rolls of tape and about 127 man-hours went into this thing. We prefer not to think of the dollar amount behind that—we don't use cheap tape either—but then again it's not every day you build a 3-foot wide duct tape D20!

## Step 5: Putting in the computer components

Turning the D20 into a computer from just a duct tape sculpture was pretty straightforward. The power supply and hard drive were mounted on the bottom face. The motherboard was mounted in the center. We attached one large fan to a side panel made from tape.

As for cosmetics we added a red cathode tube for a little light inside. And for even more needless bling, we charlieplexed a bunch of red LEDs (one mounted at each corner) and programmed them to randomly flash.

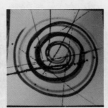
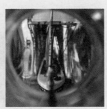

# art

The maker creates a vast majority of his or her projects to serve a specific application or meet a unique need. Making a piece of art simply for the sake of expressing oneself is truly a noble endeavor that we're proud to showcase on Instructables. The projects in this chapter are not only beautiful, but are also innovative in unique ways. Be it the time-honored tradition of ships in bottles, or pioneering a new way to use conductive paint in order to make light-up graffiti, these works of art are amazing because the artists developed original methods and techniques that help them to express themselves through their work in ways that are not only useful, but beautiful.

What can you do with a giant kinetic squid sculpture? Sit back, marvel at its moving tentacles and glowing lights, and let your heart be warmed by the fact that the playful, artistic dreamer inside us all is alive and well.

# Projection Bombing

By fi5e, Agent 005 of the Graffiti Research Lab
(http://www.instructables.com/id/PROJECTION-BOMBING/)

Outdoor digital projection in urban environments is a great method for getting your content up big before the eyes and in the minds of your fellow city inhabitants. This tutorial comes out of trial and error and it works. But please be careful. Helpful comments on safety and alternative methods are encouraged. The majority of this tutorial is aimed toward using a 2500 lumen projector (or smaller); if you have access to something more powerful you might want to skip straight to step 6.

Thanks to Zach Lieberman for, among many other things ,penning the phrase "Projection Bombing." And huge props to Krzysztof Wodiczko for bringing this technology into the streets.

To see examples of this system in use, check out the following examples:

- G.R.L. Drip Sessions (4000 lumen projector), http://graffitiresearchlab.com/?page_id=34#video
- G.R.L. Interactive Architecture (4000 lumen projector), http://graffitiresearchlab.com/?page_id=32#video
- Textual Healing (2500 lumen projector), http://www.txtualhealing.com/
- Graffiti Analysis (4000 lumen projector), http://ni9e.com/graffiti_analysis.php

Textual Healing photos show a 2500 lumen projector in use, while all others show a 4000 lumen projector.

## Step 1: Parts list

**Part: DC to AC power inverter**

Size: 600W-1200W

Average Cost: $80-$150

Note: Power inverters come in a range of sizes. The more powerful your projector the more watts you will need from your inverter. We have had good luck with a 600 watt inverter used with a 2500 lumen projector. Any inverter larger than 1200W will need to be hardwired onto the battery (rather than clips/jumper cables). Power inverters can be purchased online or at auto parts stores such as PepBoys.

**Part: Digital projector**

Note: 2000 ANSI lumens is a recommended minimum value for projecting anything bright enough to be viewed outdoors in the city.

**Part: VGA cable (male to male)**

Average Cost: $10

**Part: Car**

Note: Whatever car you have available should work, but vehicles with larger engines will keep the battery recharging at a faster rate and allow you to project for longer. UHAUL cargo vans work well because they are cheap if you don't drive around much (they bill by the mile), the engines are big, and they are easier to get away with parking in creative locations.

Suggested: UHAUL Cargo Van

Cost: $19.95 + $.99/mile

URL:http://www.uhaul.com/guide/index.aspx?equipment=truck-cargovan

**Part: Laptop**

Note: Any laptop that you can plug into your digital projector will work.

**Optional Part: 200 Watt DC to AC power inverter (with cigarette lighter attachment)**

Note: Powering your laptop from a secondary inverter off the cigarette outlet in your car can be a good way to project for longer than your laptop battery will allow.

Don't try plugging the digital projector into this smaller inverter or you will blow a fuse in your dashboard. Similarly, don't try to plug your laptop and digital projector into a single 600W inverter, overloading can damage the inverter.

Note from RESISTOR: This knowledge comes from first hand experience and involves the element fire.

## Part: DC battery (optional)

Note: This tutorial will focus on describing a process for getting a projection system up with a limited set of common tools. More elaborate projection systems can be created using an additional car battery or a 50-100 watt or more deep cycle marine battery. An additional battery or batteries can be chained in parallel with your car battery. You can make your setup as elaborate as you need it to be. This tutorial will just focus on the basic equipment and process you need to project from your car battery.

## Step 2: Prepare media

### Content:

If you have reached this far in the tutorial you probably already have an idea of what you'd like to project. If not consult your local graffiti writer . . . they tend to have lots of good ideas. If all else fails, project this: http://graffitiresearchlab.com/free_avone/free_AV.mov.

### Media considerations/suggestions:

#### *Go full screen:*

There is nothing hardcore about the Windows or Mac operating systems, so don't let people see them when you are projecting. Launch your files full screen so that your content is the only thing people see. I usually go so far as to keep the lens of the projector covered until my files are up and running.

#### *Hide edges:*

Whenever possible use a black background so that the edges of the projection will blend unnoticeably into the wall in which it is projected on. 4:3 rectangular projections tend to ruin the magic.

#### *High contrast:*

Colors and grey tones often get lost in the ambient light that is inevitable in most outdoor projection situations. To help combat this use true white and black values in your media as much as possible.

#### *Match surroundings:*

Be intentional with where you project. There are lines, edges, curves, and surfaces all over the city waiting to display your message, make sure you don't treat them all in the same way. Projections should fit into the architecture they are projected on.

### Software:

To aid in some of the suggestions mentioned above I have included a simple piece of software, which I have found to be very useful. This simple application allows you to open a Quicktime movie and display it full screen. The app also allows you to scale, drag, and rotate your movie using key combinations. Download the application below. If you are running the PC version ("GRL_qtProjection.exe") place your .mov files in the same folder as the .exe file. If you are running the MAC version ("GRL_qtProjection.app"), CTRL + click the application and go to "Show Package Contents." Place your .mov files in the "Contents/Resources" folder.

When you launch the .exe file it will display the movie in the folder full screen, starting with the first clip in alphabetical order. Other .mov clips in the same directory can be loaded in with the number keys. Once the clips are on screen you can scale, move, and rotate it to best fit the surface you are projecting on. Making these alterations in the software is much easier than constantly having to move the car and projector around. Click and drag the mouse on the screen to move the .mov clip. Keyboard controls are as follows:

'z'—mouse controls rotation
'x'—mouse controls position
'c'—mouse controls scale
'a'—set rotation axis to the Y axis
's'—set rotation axis to the X axis
'd'—set rotation axis to the Z axis
'r'—resets rotation, position, and scale to 0
'1'-'9'—loads in up to nine .mov clips from the applications directory in alphabetical order.

If nothing else this software can save you the $29.99 cost of buying Quicktime Pro just to play your .mov files full screen.

Download PC version: http://graffitiresearchlab.com/projection_bombing/pc/GRL_qtProjection_app.zip

Download MAC version: http://graffitiresearchlab.com/projection_bombing/mac/GRL_qtProjection_MAC.zip

art

Source Code:

Download PC source code/project folder in Code-Warrior: http://graffitiresearchlab.com/projection_bombing/pc/GRL_qtProjection_SC.zip.

Downlad MAC source code/project folder in XCODE: http://graffitiresearchlab.com/projection_bombing/mac/GRL_qtProjection_MAC_SC.zip.

(Written in C++ using the Open Frameworks code library developed by Zach Lieberman and friends at Parsons.)

## Step 3: Choose a location

Finding a good location to project is the most important factor in getting your name up really big and really bright. You can make up for having a less powerful projector by paying close attention to the spots you pick, the lighting conditions, surface color, the distance from your car to the projections surface, every detail down to the audience that will see it. Below are suggestions for picking good projection locations.

Low ambient light:

Street lights, spotlights, illuminated advertisements; these are your enemies. Search for surfaces that are as far from light sources as possible. In some cases you might be able to temporarily cover certain lights with a heavy jacket or blanket, but in general fighting ambient light is a loosing battle. Don't even bother scouting for spots in the day time as you will end up getting your heart broken when you come back at night and find that your perfect spot is ruined by a single street light.

Bright surface color:

White surfaces will reflect much more light than dark ones. White stone, white tile, and painted white walls are ideal projection surfaces. It is possible to project on darker surfaces like brick but you will need to get the projector closer to the wall and hence not be able to get your imagery as big.

No glass:

Avoid walls with a lot of windows and glass. Because light passes through glass instead of being reflected, these areas of your image will appear blank.

Unobstructed view:

Trees, telephone poles, and traffic signage can all pose problems with getting a clear projection path. Placing the projector on the roof of the car will at least get you above most people and automobile traffic that might interfere.

Distance:

How far you are away from your target projection surface has a lot to do with how big you can get your image. At a certain distance, however, you will start to loose brightness. It's a tradeoff but usually brighter and smaller is more noticeable than big and washed out. Depending on the lighting conditions and the color of the projection surface aim to position the projector between 4-10 traffic lanes away from the wall.

Audience:

After going through all this trouble you want people to see your stuff, so make sure to pick spots where there is a lot of automobile and/or foot traffic. Areas near bars and clubs are good bets, especially later when they start letting out for the night.

Available parking:

You will almost never find a legal parking spot that also meets all of the conditions listed above. The good news is, however, that once you pop your hood and start messing around with the battery most people will assume you are having car troubles and give you a break. This is accentuated if you are in a UHAUL van, as people will think you are moving and having car troubles . . . "What a bad day they are having."

Security:

I have never had a problem with people trying to mess with any of the equipment while doing a projection, but that could just be because of my generally thug-ish demeanor. It could be a good idea to bring a few friends. You should always roll deep.

Police:

I have had two encounters with police. One ended with them running my ID and letting me go, and the other ended with the cop saying, "Oh this looks cool, sorry, I had to come check it out because someone called and said there were some Middle Eastern-looking people hanging out by the monument." This was probably because it was a city monument and because RESISTOR was crawling through the bushes with a camera wearing a ski mask. It is my understanding that it is legal to project in NYC as long as it is not over the top of someone else's advertisement.

Go to http://graffitiresearchlab.com/projection_locations to view locations in Manhattan and Brooklyn that I have found to be good projection locations.

## Step 4: Set up equipment

Projector:

Placing the projector on the roof avoids getting a lot of shadows from pedestrians and automobile traffic. If a slightly more clandestine setup is what you are after, place the projector on a box inside the car so it points out the window. Run the VGA and power cable from the projector in through the window.

Inverter:

Place the inverter on the dashboard on the same side as the car battery. Snake the cables through the crack between the door and the car (not through the window). This will avoid ripping it off the dashboard when you inevitably forget about it and swing the door open. If it's your car and you are hardcore, get a drill and make a hole under your dashboard to run your cables directly to the car battery.

Secondary inverter (optional):

Plug this into your cigarette lighter.

art

## Step 5: Hook up power

Open the hood and locate the car battery. Make sure the power switch on the power inverter is turned off and nothing is plugged into it. Connect the red cable from the power inverter to the positive battery terminal first, and then connect the black cable to the negative battery terminal.

If you are careful about closing the hood you can run the cables through the crack between the hood and car. Otherwise, leaving the hood popped open can make it look like you are just having car troubles.

Turn on the power switch of the power inverter. Depending on what model you have you should see a green light come on and hear the soft whir of the fan turning on (if something else happens check the alarms listed below). If you have a green light plug in the power cable from the digital projector into the power inverter. Hit the power button on the digital projector. After the projector goes through its warm up cycle and the bulb turns on you will know you are in business. At this point connect your laptop and you are off and bombing.

**Tip:**

You may want to bring a piece of cardboard to set in front of the projector as you go through the process of booting up and connecting. This is will allow you to see if it is recognizing your laptop, and you will spare your potential audience from having to watch you boot up windows, find your files, and launch your application.

**Alarms:**

Warning alarms and signals will vary on different models, but the warnings for the Vector brand inverters are as follows:

A continuous alarm signals that there is a bad wiring connection. Take this one seriously. One time I tried to ignore it and my inverter starting shooting fire out the back and nearly caught the dashboard of the rental car on fire. Check the connection on the battery to make sure you have a tight connection on both power and ground.

A less constant audio alarm is a signal that the voltage of the battery is low.

A red light with no audio alarm is a signal that there is too much power being drawn from the inverter. Try plugging in less stuff.

## Step 6: Alternative setup: more lumens, more power

If you have access to a digital projector with more than 2500 lumens you will need a more powerful AC power inverter. The system shown here uses a 2000 watt AC power inverter with a 4000 lumen digital projector. This is the projection setup used for Graffiti Analysis, and the projections done by the Graffiti Research Lab.

The only major difference of projecting with more powerful equipment is that you 1) will need more power from your battery and inverter and 2) the connection mechanism between the battery and inverter needs to provide a more reliable connection with a larger contact area than an alligator clip. Most auto shops and places that sell car batteries will sell cables made specifically to be hardwired onto car battery terminals. This allows for a tighter, more permanent connection to the battery.

Because I was using rental cars for my projections and did not want to have to continually hardwire connections to the battery I purchased a secondary battery. This battery sits on the floor of the passenger seat and is connected via jumper cables to the car battery. This makes possible quick on-location connections to the battery under the hood while still maintaining a reliable connection from the inverter to the secondary battery. It also allows for more minutes of projection time since you are running two batteries in parallel. This setup also allows for projection from a moving car.

**Disclaimer:**

This is the system I use most often and it has worked well for me on every occasion, but there are inherent dangers to hooking up a battery. Connecting multiple batteries in parallel can increase this danger and add other complications. Doing so inside a car could cause injury or even death if the battery were to leak, explode, or make the NYPD think you are a terrorist and shoot you. Any thoughts on the dangers associated with this process or alternatives are welcome and encouraged.

**141**

**Step 6a:**

Place the secondary car battery on the floor in the passenger seat. Put the 2000 watt inverter on the floor next to the battery. Turn on the car and pop the hood.

**Step 6b:**

Make sure the inverter is turned off and nothing is plugged in. Connect the inverter to the car battery in the front seat. It's the same process as in the previous page only now, instead of clipping the connection on, you will need to use a 13mm socket wrench to tighten the connection bolts. First connect the positive terminals and then connect the negative. If this was done properly and there is still some charge left in the battery, you should get a green light when you power on the inverter. After testing make sure to leave the inverter in the off position.

**Step 6c:**

Use the jumper cables to connect the car battery to the battery on the floor in the passenger seat. Make the connections in the same order as you would to jump a dead car battery:

1. Connect the red-handled/positive jumper cable clip to the positive terminal (the one with the plus sign) of the car battery.
2. Connect the other red-handled clip to the positive terminal of the battery in the passenger seat.
3. Connect the neighboring black/negative clip to the negative terminal of the battery in the passenger seat (the one with the minus sign).
4. Connect the black/negative clip to the negative terminal of the car battery. You could also try to connect the negative alligator clip to the chassis ground of the car; this may work and can cut-down on the risks associated with arcing caused by connecting batteries.

**Step 6d:**

Turn the power switch of the inverter to the on position, if it shows a green light then plug in the digital projector and you should be good to go. All the setup and warnings from the previous page apply here in the same way.

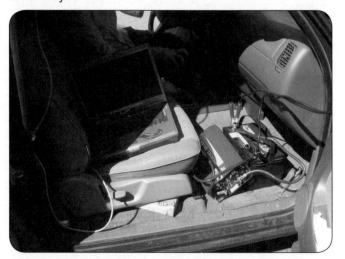

## Step 7: Alternative setup: city powered

One of the easiest ways of powering a projection system in the city is provided by the city itself. This is inherently dangerous and FREE, so we try to do it whenever possible. But be warned: people and pets have been electrocuted before in NYC from just touching the lampposts, so use extreme caution when thinking about reaching inside them. Good luck!

**Step 7a: Find a good projection spot.**

**Step 7b: Look for a lamppost.**

**Step 7c: See if its base panel is open.**

**Step 7d: Open the panel (if locked use a hex key) and see if a three prong outlet has been installed. Not all lampposts have three prong outlets.**

**Step 7e: Plug in and go.**

## Step 8: Alternative setup: no car/deep cycle

A more proper method of powering electronics from a battery is to use a deep cycle marine battery. Deep cycle batteries, unlike car batteries, are designed to provide continuous power for a longer duration. They will definitely outlast car batteries in deep cycle applications (http://www.uuhome.de/william.darden//carfaq7.htm#differences). Use this in combination with an AC power inverter to power your projection system without the need for a car or city-provided lamppost. If you use a 250 watt projector and a 100 Ah battery you should be able to project for two to five hours. You can use a battery charger to recharge the battery. You can put the battery, inverter, and projector in a large rolling luggage bag and pull it around the city from location to location.

Connecting to a deep cycle battery is the same as connecting to a car battery and all the same processes from the tutorial and inherent dangers still apply.

**Materials:**

12 Volt 100 Amp-Hour sealed lead acid battery
10amp deep cycle battery charger
Currently we are testing with a West Marine SeaVolt 12V Deep-Cycle 90, and a West Marine 15A Amp Battery Charger. More to come on this setup soon.

art

# Giant Squid Sculpture

By nemomatic
(http://www.instructables.com/id/Giant-Squid-kinetic-sculpture-from-found-materials/)

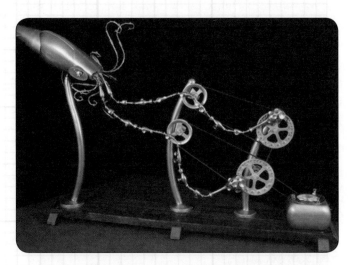

This sculpture grew out of a long-time fascination with the Giant Squid. My name being Nemo has meant a lifetime of "Captain Nemo" references, thus making me aware of these monsters from an early age. I am a sculptor who works almost exclusively with found materials, though typically I like to build things that look more like classic robots. For that reason this project posed several challenges. For one, I really wanted it to be a Giant Squid, which meant finding some large objects, and it would mean breaking a lot of habits to depart from more human-like forms. I also decided not to limit myself to aluminum, as I had been at the time, and to integrate some brass pieces in as well.

## Step 1: Layout

I generally start all my pieces by laying parts out on the floor and arranging them until things start to look right. For this project, large street light covers were going to be the most important forms. These were used for the head, and determined the scale of the whole sculpture. Some rather cheesy brass chandeliers were easy choices for the smaller tentacles. The trick was coming up with the two long tentacles. They needed to look similar to the small ones, but still be flexible and durable. After some fooling around I decided that candle sticks, and fireplace hardware would work if they had aluminum electrical conduit threaded through them. Brass drawer pulls would later be attached to each section to act as suction cups.

It was important to me that the sculpture have a somewhat fluid movement, as it is a sea monster after all. I liked the idea of a sort of antiquated machine look, so I came up with a simple belt drive mechanism based on some nice old belt wheels that I found.

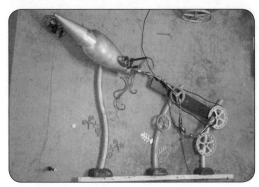

## Step 2: Mechanism

Once I had a decent idea of what the general design was going to be it was time to focus on some specifics. I basically had to work backwards from the mechanical portion of the piece because it required the most precision. The rest could be improvised. From the first stage of laying out the parts, I had determined that the head would be elevated, with the tentacles draping down towards their drive system (no sense fighting gravity). This meant mounting the belt wheels in a fixed position to each other to provid the right angle for the head so it would end up at the right height.

After a good deal of Advil and cursing I had the wheels mounted on bearings welded to stands made from railing sections.

## Step 3: Head

Having worked out the basic mechanics, it was time to make some more decisions about the head. All changes here would affect the weight, and potentially mess with the mechanism, so better to settle it early on. Added to the street light fixtures was a small beer keg, a lawn sprinkler base, and a mysterious aluminum cone. The bag attachments from some old vacuum cleaners made nice oval eye sockets with brass candle stick tops for eyes.

Perhaps the greatest challenge of this project was developing the mount that would hold the head. It had to allow for movement on two axes, support some of the weight, and look cool. Eventually I came across part of a motorcycle frame (I think), and welded some bearing mounts to it that I had turned on the lathe. After some messing around with height and distance from the belt mechanism, the new mount was fixed to the top of some more railing sections.

## Step 4: Structure

Unfortunately, though it may seem that everything was moving along smoothly, I still did not have any way to support all of this moving mass. The temptation was to bolt each of the three railing support pieces directly to the floor. This would have meant only displaying the piece in places with concrete floors and much agonizing alignment issues at the start of each install. I have learned over the years that a sculpture of this size had better be portable if you ever hoped to find a home for it. What was needed was a base of some kind that would allow me to permanently fasten the three posts and the motor to. Then all other parts could be removed for transport.

Fortunately for me my friend Reuben happened to have some huge planks of wood laying around outside his studio. I decided to go with a sort of sunken pier/ships deck look.

## Step 5: Details and wiring

Once all the big dirty stuff was tested and working, it was time to focus on the little details that would make the piece worth more than a glance.

All the lesser tentacles had to be bolted around the mouth opening, leaving room for the large ones to attach inside. I had to machine an adjustable pivot with spring connections so that the head could respond gently to all the random stresses that the motor would produce. I ordered some glass taxidermy eyes to mount in the brass candle holders to give the beast a little more soul. Tiny LED mounts were machined behind the eyes to make them glow. The inside of the mouth got the same treatment.

The motor was concealed with the help of lamp pole base covers, and a timing device was installed to keep it from running constantly.

## Step 6: Results

And here it is. It is difficult to convey all the details and size of this thing. There are a few detail shots attached here, but the video on the intro page probably describes it best. Better yet, visit my website at http://www.nemo-matic.com for a higher resolution file.

# Electro-Graf

## By Q-Branch

(http://www.instructables.com/id/Electro-Graf/)

Dossier #2 from the Graffiti Research Lab: the Electro-Graf. An electro-graf is a graffiti piece or throw-up that uses conductive spray-paint and magnet paint to embed movable LED display electronics. The following pages describe the materials and processes used to create the prototype indoor and outdoor interactive electro-grafs created in the lab at Eyebeam (http://research.eyebeam.org/).

## Step 1: Materials/parts list

The basic materials for building an electro-graf can be purchased using a combination of online vendors and local hardware stores. A small (100 LED, 4' x 4') electro-graf could run around a $100. A large piece could cost as much as $2000 dollars, but thats just a WAG.

Parts:

### Part: Super Shield conductive spray-paint
- Vendor: Less EMF (http://www.lessemf.com/paint.html)
- Average cost: $22 per can
- Note: This is the secret weapon.

### Part: spray-paint, color your choice
- Vendor: I use Krylon from the local hardware store
- Average cost: $22.50 for 6 cans
- Note: Use what you like.

### Part: Magnet paint
- Vendor(s): Less EMF (http://www.lessemf.com/paint.html) for premixed indoor paint called Magic Wall or Magically Magnetic, Inc. (http://lyt.com/) for paint additive. This additive can be mixed with indoor or outdoor primer sealer.
- Average cost: Magic Wall @ $29.95/quart; Magnet paint additive @ $15/quart and primer sealer @ $8.50/quart
- Note: I used Zinnser BULLS-EYE primer 1-2-3 primer sealer (http://www.zinsser.com/subcat.asp?Category ID=1) for the base paint on the outdoor electro-graf

proto. It's the good stuff. Your local hardware store is sure to have a thick outdoor primer that will work. You can get worse paint for less money. Note: Don't believe the hype. The paint itself is not magnetic. It is just metallic and magnets adhere to it.

### Part: 10mm LEDs. The color choice is yours.
- Vendor: Again, it's my crew Denny, Ann, et al. at HB Electronic Components (http://www.hebeiltd.com.cn/?p=leds.9.10mm).
- Average Cost: $0.20 per LED
- Note: You can use smaller LEDs, but it's just not my taste.

### Part: 1/8" Diameter x 1/16" Thick NdFeB Disc Magnet, Ni-Cu-Ni plated
- Vendor: Amazing Magnets (http://www.amazingmagnets.com/index.asp?PageAction=VIEWPROD&ProdID=42)
- Cost: $9.00 per 100 magnets
- Note: Cost reductions for larger quantities

### Part: Power supply
This will vary based on number and types of LEDs, circuit design and environment. You must supply the LEDs with at least 3 volts DC power. Depending primarily on the number of LEDs, you can use anything from a $2.00 9 Volt to a $50 dollar car battery to a regulated 500 watt power supply if the proper current limiting components are used. In the lab I use a regulated DC power supply. We will discuss this more in the following steps.

### Part: Tape
- Vendor: your local hardware store should have painter's tape and masking tape. Get both.
- Cost: $2-$5 per 60 yard roll
- Note: 3M painter's tape is blue and has less adhesion than masking tape. Both tapes are useful in different situations.

### Part: five-minute epoxy
- Vendor: your local hardware store should have five-minute epoxy
- Cost: $5 dollars for one tube
- Note: This is some delightful stuff. Get the kind in the two-part dispenser.

### Part: Stencil materials—acetate, manila folders
- Vendor: Your local art store or office store should have acetate, cardboard, and file folders.
- Average Cost: $10 for a 25' x 12 ft. roll of acetate. Folders and cardboard vary in price and are often found for free.

### Part: Stranded wire
- Vendor: Jameco (http://jameco.com/)
- Cost: $3 per roll
- Note: Any 18-24 AWG stranded hook-up wire will work. Solid core wire is too brittle.

Optional:

### Part: 1/4 or 1/2 watt resistors, the choice of value is yours
- Vendor: Jameco (http://jameco.com/)

- Average Cost: $1 for 100 pieces
  ### Part: 3/4" Foil Tape
- Vendor: Newark In One (http://www.newark.com/)
- Average Cost: $18 per roll
  ### Part: Conductive Epoxy
- Vendor: Newark In One (http://www.newark.com/)
- Cost: $32.00
- Note: The epoxy is optional. It is used to attach magnets to electronic components and wire.

*You can add electronic components to create LED sequences, animation, solar power, etc. You may need stranded wire for connecting your LED traces to various power sources.*

Tools:
- A respirator
- A multimeter
- Paint brushes
- Containers for mixing paints
- Exacto blades
- Clay

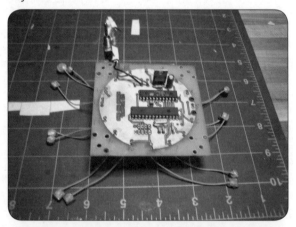

## Step 2: Design your piece

I won't get into any depth regarding designing stencils or graffiti pieces. I will also not go into detail on designing circuits for driving and sequencing LEDs. I will direct you to online and print resources where this information can be gleaned from reputable sources. I will also explain the specific design we implemented with the first two prototype electro-grafs.

Links for basic electronics for non-experts:

- Tom Igoe's Physical computing online resources (http://www.tigoe.net/pcomp/index.shtml)
- Physical computing in print (http://itp.nyu.edu/~dbo3/physical/physical.html) by O'Sullivan and Igoe

### Electro-graf V1:

The first prototype electro-graf, executed in the lab at Eyebeam, is a mash-up of images of the state-of-the-art in military robots combined with quotes from soldiers, officers, and military bloggers. Marine General, James Mattis, said, "It's fun to shoot some people," when discussing his service in Afghanistan, where US forces have killed over 3,500 civilians. That's a lot of fun. More fun than even Bin Laden had on September 11 I bet. The image in this design was taken from promotional material about Foster-Miller's robot TALON. The weaponized configuration is called SWORDS. SWORDS was developed, in part, in a suburb in New Jersey at a place called Picatinny Arsenal.

"The TALON robot is the only mobile platform currently certified by the Department of Defense for remotely controlled live firing of lethal weapons." Read: the first robot licensed to kill.

For this piece we used a Stencil Revolution tutorial (http://www.stencilrevolution.com/tutorials/tutorialsview.php?id=6) to create the stencil in Illustrator CS1 and cut them on a laser cutter. The control electronics were designed, built, and programmed by Twin A in collaboration with a very good LED and video artist named Leo Villareal (http://www.villareal.net/ps1.html). It is currently on loan from A for our experiments in the lab.

### Electro-graf V2:

The first prototype outdoor electro-graf is currently up on the facade of Eyebeam. The design was intended to be minimal and entirely functional: to test the electro-graf capabilities in terms of size, weather-proofing, theft patterns, and public feedback.

## Step 3: Apply magnetic coat

After you have chosen a location and time to execute your piece, you need to apply the magnet paint. If you are using the Magic Wall paint indoors, you can just apply the paint with a brush or roller. You need to paint on two to four coats for a reliable, robust magnetic attraction.

If you are using the paint additive and a primer sealer, you need to mix the powder additive to thick, primer/sealer paint. Follow the instructions on http://www1.ecxmall.com/stores/lyt/posters.html to properly make the magnetic paint. Add one cup of additive per quart of paint. Remember to follow the instructions on the paint can regarding the appropriate temperature for applying the paint.

## Step 4: Apply conductive coat

Now, apply the stencil circuit using Super Shield conductive spray-paint. You will need to apply two to five coats of spray-paint for best functionality. Use the multimeter to test for conductivity and resistance. The trace resistance should be less than 10-20 Ohms per foot. To decrease the resistance, add more coats of paint.

Make sure you functionally test the circuit whenever you can.

## Step 5: Tape contact pads

If you intend to add a topcoat to the electro-graf, like in the case of the prototype indoor electro-graf, you need to put masking tape on the circuit stencil to create contact pads. These are where the LED leads or the wires will make contact with spray-on conductive traces and close the circuit. I used 1/2" by 1/4" pieces of masking tape to make the contact pads. Remember to put these on before you spray your topcoat!

The outdoor electro-graf did not require a topcoat of paint or tape to cover the contact pads.

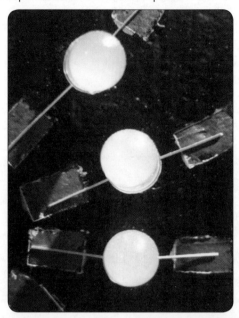

## Step 6: Apply topcoat

Once you have taped the contact pads, you can apply the topcoat. I used Krylon green fluorescent and black ultra-flat spray-paint. You can get specialty caps at a number of online stores. (Here is one: http://www.powderbomb.com/store/spray-paint-caps.php.) Fat caps help reduce the time it takes to cover large areas with a single color. Remember to allow sufficient time for the paint to dry between coats.

Note: Acetate produces a tight stencil with less under-spray than cardboard or thick paper. But acetate is flimsy and requires much more taping to stay flush with the wall.

## Step 7: Remove tape

Now, you can use an exacto blade, tweezer, or small screwdriver to remove the tape over the contact areas. Once the tape is removed, use the multimeter to test the traces, conductivity and resistance. Remember to functionally test the circuit every chance you get, and pay attention.

## Step 8: Make mods to electronics

Every electronic component needs to interface with the wall in two ways: electrically and mechanically.

**Mechanical:**

Components like wire, LEDs, and circuit boards can be taped, epoxied, or screwed into the wall. Another option is to create a metallic surface on the wall (using magnet paint) and then modify the electronic components by adding rare-earth magnets. The magnet mod-ed components then adhere to the section of the wall where the magnet paint has been applied. Wire can be attached directly to magnets using conductive epoxy. Be patient with conductive epoxy and don't speed-up the curing process with heat. Attaching magnets to LEDs is a bit more difficult.

**Attaching magnets to LEDs**

I have developed a simple technique for attaching magnets to LEDs using old, used exacto knives. First, I created a LED holder on the laser cutter. You can also use a little mound of clay, putty, or, I suppose, chewing gum. While holding the LED with its leads pointed up, mix a small batch of epoxy. Place the magnet on the end of a used exacto blade, about 1/4-inch from the tip. It will adhere magnetically. Put a dot of epoxy on the magnet and on the LED. Now, with the magnet facing down, let the tip of the blade slide between the leads of the LED until the magnet is laying face down on the underside of the LED. You can adjust the distance between LED leads and the magnet by moving the magnet further away from the tip of the blade. THE MAGNET SHOULD NOT TOUCH THE LED LEADS. This will create a short since the magnet is conductive. Once one has dried you can repeat the process with a second magnet on the opposite side of the leads. The first magnet will help keep the blade in place for the second magnet. Confused?? Just check out the flicks and give it a try.

**Electrical**

You can connect wires and LEDs to the wall to make electrical connections in many of the same ways. To attach wire to the wall just bond the twisted strand of wire to a magnet using conductive epoxy. Then connect the magnet to a wall that has both magnet and conductive paint applied. The circuit will connect across the conductive magnet. To modify LED to make an electrical connection you can simply bend the LED leads so that they run parallel with the underside of the LED. When the magnet

art

mod-ed LED is adhered to the wall, the bent leads are pre-loaded via magnetic attraction onto the conductive traces. This way you can remove and re-configure the LEDs on the wall at a number of locations by design. Look at the flicks for more details on the process.

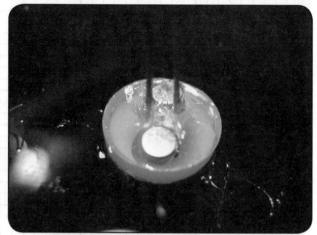

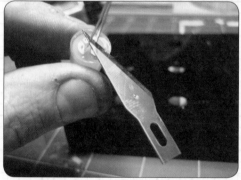

## Step 9: Integrate

Now you can put the LEDs on the wall, connect the power supply and any control electronics and turn it on. Depending on your design this could take a second or hours. If you use the techniques described, your LEDs can be reconfigured along the piece (as in the case of the outdoor electro-graf) or LEDs can be replaced and colors changed (as in the case of the indoor electro-graf stencil).

In some cases you will need to add a resistor directly to the LED cathode lead. This will help prevent the LED from drawing too much current and getting damaged and reduce the voltage drop that occurs in a parallel circuit due to LEDs that are not current limited. To determine your resistor value use the following easy formula.

$$(SupplyVoltage - LEDForwardVoltage)/NominalLEDCurrent = ResitorValue$$

In the case of the outdoor electro-graf we used the following values:

$$(12\ VDC - 3VDC)/.020\ mA = 450\ Ohm\ resistor$$

The main design driver for the magnetic paint and magnet mod-ed electronics was ease of integration. This step should be relatively easy.

## Step 10: Applications and upgrades

The materials and processes discussed in this section will work on concrete, brick, cardboard, paper, and plastic. The cost and complexity of an electro-graf can vary wildly. You can construct an electro-graf that requires days of work and interfaces with complex electronic circuitry or even a networked back-end architecture, or you can make an electro-graf throwie with copper tape and a few LEDs that can be up in five minutes.

art

# Spin Painting Wheel

By matthewvenn

(http://www.instructables.com/id/spin-painting-
wheel/)

A spin painting wheel is a great way to make cool pictures easily. If someone is a not a confident drawer this will allow them the ability to still make something that looks really cool.

I have a gallery of spin paintings here: http://www.flickr.com/photos/matthewvenn/sets/72157600217180863/with/499449311.

## Step 1: Stuff you need
**Tools**
- A saw or jigsaw
- A drill with a range of bits
- Some spanners (ideally cone spanners for wheel bearing adjustment)

**Materials**
- Old bike wheel, I've only used fronts but I'm sure backs would work too
- Some thin board like particle board or mdf
- A short plank of pine or ply
- Long cable ties
- Some large washers that fit round the bolt of the bike wheel

## Step 2: Adjust the wheel

You need to move the whole wheel along the bolt so that none sticks out on one side. This is pretty much the hardest part of the project because it is fiddly, especially without the cone spanners. It's probably worth looking up your local community bike project and going along on one of their open days to do this part.

The bolt has two nuts on each side that are locked together. The nuts closest to the wheel are the cones, and they press against the bearings.

You have two options:

1. Loosen the nuts and take the bearings out, then reinsert them later.

2. Loosen and tighten on the other side, so you can edge the bolt through while keeping the bearings safe inside.

Last time I made one, I tried to do option #2, but ended up having to do #1 when all the bearings fell out! So keep a cloth or something underneath to catch them.

After you've moved the nuts along the bolt, tighten the nuts against each other at one end, then slowly tighten the other side's cone into the bearings. Test the feeling in the wheel, we want a combination of low wiggle (play) and smooth turning. When you've got it right then tighten the other side's lock nut and test again.

## Step 3: Cut and drill the support

You're going to bolt the wheel to a small piece of wood, then mount this on top of a longer plank that can be clamped to a desk.

Because the bolt will have a nut on it, you need to drill a large hole in the long plank so that everything fits together:

Cut a slice off the end of the plank about 10cm wide. Drill a hole through the center just wide enough for the bolt of the wheel.

Put the small slice on top of the longer plank and mark through the hole so you know where to drill the big hole.

While it's all aligned, drill four pilot holes for some screws to screw the planks together. And while you're at it, make a mark on the edges of both pieces so you know which way around it goes later!

Then, on the big piece, drill a large hole (big enough for the nut and washer that you'll use to bolt the wheel onto the small piece.

## Step 4: Mount the wheel

Put a washer on the end of the wheel bolt and then thread it through the small bit of wood. Then another washer and finally one of the wheel nuts. Tighten it all up nicely.

## Step 5: Mount the wheel to the plank

Using the pilot holes, screw the two pieces of wood together. They should fit nice and flat, otherwise your lower hole might not be big enough to take the nut. You can fix this by filing the hole a little bigger.

## Step 6: Cut the painting plate

Now you'll make the bit that you do the paintings on.

Put the wheel on top of the thin wood and mark a square that will fit inside the hub. I usually make the square a little bigger and then slice off the corners so it fits.

Cut it out and check it will fit: if not, adjust.

When it's ready drill another big hole in the middle for the nuts on the wheel. Then drill smaller holes in each corner that fit your size of cable tie.

## Step 7: Mount the plate

Just thread the cable ties through the holes, starting from the bottom side.

Then put the plate on the wheel and tighten up the ties a bit at a time on each corner until everything is nice and tight and not moving when you try to wiggle it.

## Step 8: Test it out!

Use a clamp to hold the long plank onto a table. Then use inks, markers, acrylics, whatever is handy. Apply with brushes, sticks, squeezy pots. The faster you spin the wheel the easier it is to get spirals.

I attach the paper with masking tape.

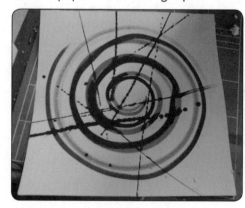

## Step 9: Make a moodlamp!

Here are some moodlamps I made by recycling old phone chargers and then making shades with the bike wheel.

http://www.instructables.com/id/phone-charger-led-lamp/

**151**

# Building a Ship in a Bottle

By Don Hanf (goaly)
(http://www.instructables.com/id/Building-A-Ship-In-A-Bottle/)

Building a ship in a bottle was an old form of maritime art. Sailors of the past would often create things in their free time. They also did not have much room for big hobbies, and from this came old treasures such as scrimshaw carvings and ships in bottles.

I have not made one of these for twenty years. But I thought that this could make an interesting Instructable. I also knew that I could use this opportunity to show my daughter how I used to make them. So I tried again. I was nervous that it wouldn't turn out well, but I was pleasantly surprised.

To start, you need a bottle. The shape of the bottle will determine what type of ship you should build. A tall narrow bottle like this is best suited for a tall ship. A big square rigged clipper would not fit. But a topsail schooner fills the empty space inside the bottle nicely.

## Step 1: The basic hull

I never used a kit. I just use blank pieces of wood that are available at craft stores, and begin with drawing a ship in the size and shape that I want to build.

Holes are drilled through wood that will form the upper and lower parts of the hull. Toothpicks are then inserted into the holes to keep the wood properly aligned during the rest of the construction. Draw a rough outline on the stacked wood pieces.

Now just sand away anything that doesn't look like the boat you are trying to build. I started on a belt sander for the rough shape. Worked a little finer with a sanding drum on a Dremel tool, and finished with a piece of sandpaper.

Take a quick look at the hull next to the bottle. You will be doing this a lot!

You can see that the hull is already larger that the opening of the bottle.

That's why it is not built out of one solid piece of wood.

## Step 2: Adding the keel and rudder

Next, the keel and rudder are added to the bottom of the hull. You can buy really thin pieces of wood at craft stores. This saves you a lot of time. A piece of 1/16 x 1/16 strip was used for the keel. It was also used for the rail on the top of the deck.

Yep, it still looks good against the bottle.

## Step 3: Paint the hull

Add a quick coat of paint to the various pieces. I find this method easier than painting several colors on a single piece of wood once the hull is finished.

At this time the two top pieces and the two bottom pieces are glued together forming the upper and lower halves of the hull.

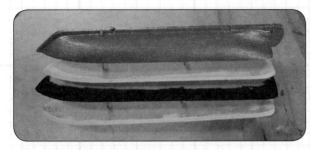

## Step 4: Constructing the mast

Lay out the mast and booms on the drawing of the boat. You need to keep in mind that you are working with a very limited space.

The mast and booms are all made out of toothpicks. I sanded some of them down in order to make them narrower. A piece of leather keeps your fingers from getting burned. This is a delicate process. It will take you a few tries to get the feel of it.

The bowsprit has to be added to the hull. The bowsprit consists of two parts. The bottom stick is inserted into a hole that is drilled into the hull. A top stick is glued to it and two lengths of thread are wrapped around them and glued down. You will also use thread where the two halves of the main mast overlap.

Once again, things should be laid out on the bottle to check the fit.

Lengths of thread are glued to the back of the booms. The thread will act as a hinge later.

A piece of wire is looped through a very small hole drilled into the bottom of the mast. This will be another hinge. You can see that the booms have been attached to the mast by the thread.

## Step 5: Connecting the mast to the hull

Now you need to drill some holes into the hull. I use very small drill bits, only slightly larger than a needle. I keep the drill stationary and I move the hull into the drill. Small sheets of scrap wood bring the hull up to the height of the drill bit.

There are five holes behind the location for each mast. The shroud lines will go into these holes.

The wire hinge on the bottom of the mast goes into two holes on the hull. It is twisted underneath, and the excess is trimmed away.

One long piece of thread goes through the five holes in the hull and through the mast forming the shrouds.

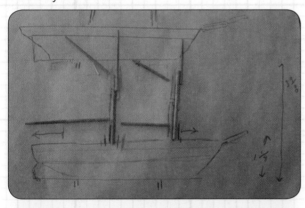

## Step 6: Basic rigging

A wood work stand secures the top of the ship during rigging and detail work. It is held in place by a small screw. The lines that will be used to raise the mast are held tight by wrapping them around the nails at the front of the stand.

Each mast has two lines going forward to the bowsprit. One line goes from the hull, to the booms, to the top of the mast and then forward. The other line goes from the area of the top of the shrouds directly to the bowsprit.

Drilling and threading the very tiny holes in the bowsprit takes a steady hand.

## Step 7: Little details

The anchor was made by bending a piece of thin wire into the proper shape and dipping it into paint. Additional detail was added by dipping the tip of a toothpick into paint and dabbing it onto the hull and mast.

## Step 8: Inserting the bottom half

The hull will rest in the bottle on top of two wood stands. These were made from popsicle sticks and are attached to the toothpicks that hold the pieces of the hull in place. They are not glued yet, so they can rotate and will fit through the opening of the bottle while attached to the bottom of the hull.

Do another test fit. I was going to use the popsicle sticks as the only base for the hull, but I found I had a quarter inch of room inside of the bottle to spare.

I have always tried to make the ship fill as much of the bottle as I could. So I cut, sanded, and stained two additional blocks of wood to put under the ship in the bottom of the bottle. This will raise the bottom of the hull from the glass, and I believe it will give the entire ship a more balanced look.

These were then glued into the bottle. A small piece of tape was used to mark the spot where the glue would go to secure the first piece of wood.

A drop of glue is used to secure the original stand to the bottom of the hull.

The stand is then rotated parallel to the hull in order to fit into the bottle opening.

Using long rods, (one is just a bent piece of wire, the other is some medical probe that I got at a garage sale) I spun the base planks until they were even and then glued them down onto the two pieces of wood already in the bottle.

Here I had accidentally touched the side of the bottle with glue. I cleaned it up using a cotton swab sprayed with window cleaner.

## Step 9: The sails

To create the sails, I first soaked a piece of typing paper with coffee then let it dry overnight. It was then marked with light parallel pencil lines roughly a quarter inch apart.

Plain typing paper was cut to size in order to make a pattern for the sails.

The coffee stained paper is then cut to size, and additional light lines are drawn to create borders. The sails are then secured to the mast or booms. Only glue down one edge of a sail as it has to allow other parts of the rigging to fold away from it.

The rest of the sails are secured. A flag and a couple of pendants are added. Then two deckhouses are placed on the deck. They are NOT glued down at this point!

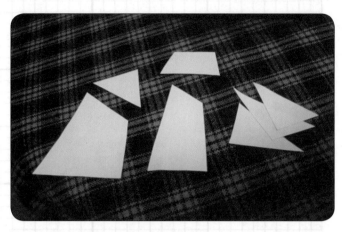

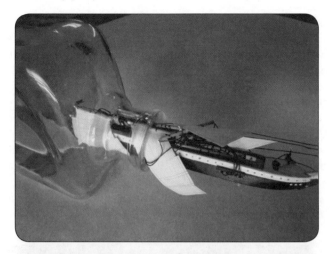

## Step 10: Now, the magic!

Some glue is put on the top of the hull. You are now committed to inserting the top half of the hull within the next few minutes.

Loosen the rigging control lines.

Lower the back mast.

And then the forward mast.

Carefully roll the paper sails around the hull and start slowly feeding the top half of the ship into the bottle.

Once the rest of the ship is in the bottle, pull on the control threads and PARTIALLY raise the mast. You are just trying to get them out of the way while you rejoin the two halves of the hull.

Once you have the two haves together, let the glue dry, and then slowly raise the mast. You may need to reach in and untangle some threads. Take your time.

The rear sail had become misshapen. The masts were slightly lowered and the sail was secured to the bottom boom.

## Step 11: Deckhouses

Two deck houses were built. The top half of the ship would not have fit into the bottle with these installed.

With a little slack still in the mast, the deckhouses were guided to their position.

They were pushed back a little further, and then a drop of glue was put on the deck in front of them.

The deckhouse is edged forward onto the glue.

art

## Step 12: Securing the sails

For ease of identification, the control lines were numbered with dots of paint in relation to their position on the bowsprit.

With a little slack in the rigging a drop of glue is placed where each line will pass through the bowsprit.

The lines are then pulled taught and secured to the bottom of the bottle with a piece of tape.

The sails are then secured to each other with a small dab of glue.

It's a tight fit in there!

When all of the glue is good and dry, a razor blade is used to cut the control threads from the BOTTOM of the bowsprit.

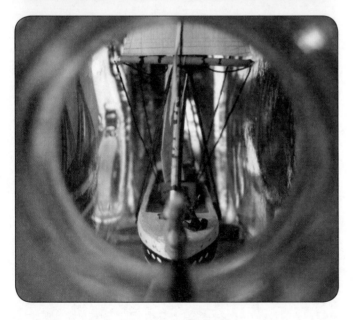

## Step 13: Cork it!

Add a cork... Clean the outside of the bottle... AND YOU ARE DONE!

It seems I've really rambled on during this instructable. I've tried to tell you as much as possible without writing an entire book. Even then I'm sure I left some things out.

Thanks for looking!

## Step 14: Shaping the hull (an added mini-instructable)

After I published the original Instructable, I wished I had posted better instructions on how to carve the hull out of the blank block of wood.

So I am adding this "Mini-instructable." I broke down the entire process into the individual steps that I use to shape the hull. Since this is just a demonstration model I did not worry about getting the dimensions exactly right. (Or this would be a really short and fat little boat. This is also a larger scale than you would use if you were putting it in the bottle.) I just wanted to focus on illustrating the technique.

Note: Although I used a belt/disc sander I used to do the entire process with just the sanding drum on a Dremel tool. In fact, if you are carving a smaller hull to use in a standard sized bottle, the Dremel type tool is a better choice.

1: Draw the basic side profile and top outline of the hull onto the block of wood.

2 and 3: Sand away the front of the block to form the profile of the bow.

4 and 5: Sand away a little from the bottom of the stern. You have now completed the profile.

6, 7, 8, and 9: Form the top outline of the front of the hull. You are just making flat shapes, keeping the block level with the sanding disc.

10 and 11: Rock the bottom of the hull on the sanding belt. This is your first curve. You are just trying to round the bottom of the hull, so that it looks like the letter "U" when viewed from the front or back.

12 and 13: Remove the sharp edges on the front of the hull that were created by the earlier sandings. Just blend everything together.

14, 15, 16, and 17: Using the sanding drum on a Dremel tool, shape the area where the rear of the hull narrows down to the area of the rudder.

18 and 19: Using sandpaper smooth everything out. Notice that I had the sandpaper flat for the soft curves of the bow, and I folded the sandpaper over to create a shape that matched the area of the stern that needed sanded.

20: Finished!

I hope this helps answer any questions that you may have had about shaping the hull. Just take your time, break the process down into simple steps, and you can make this happen!

art

# Steampunk Goggles

By Tristan de Chalain (cutshopguy)
(http://www.instructables.com/id/Steampunk-
Goggles-Personal-Vision-Enhancers/)

These Steampunk Goggles, inspired by, amongst others, the work of Gogglerman on Instructables and Jake Van Slatt at The Steampunk Workshop, are an attempt to combine the Steampunk aesthetic with production of some functional eye-wear that would produce excellent lighting and variable magnification. I use commercial loupes in my day-to-day job and have an old pair for use in my shop as needed, so really this was just an excuse to make something I considered aesthetically pleasing, satisfying to make, and well into the Steampunk genre. I apologize for any lack of detail, but I would think that this would be more of an inspirational jumping-off place to go out and make something of your own, rather than a detailed "how-I-did-it" account.

## Step 1: Making the lens holders

The actual goggles, the part that holds the lenses in front of the eyes, is the body of the design, just as the frame holds the spectacle lenses. I made these from an 1/8" recycled brass sheet thst I got at the metal recycling plant. I annealed the sheet by heating it to red-heat with a gas blowtorch and then quenching it in cold water, before cutting it with tin snips to fit the paper template. Annealing makes brass and copper soft and easier to work with. I used a stainless steel former, again acquired from a scrapyard, around which to bend the sheet and held the curvature with a wire wrap before soldering. The external brass ring was used for aesthetics rather than because it was absolutely necessary.

## Step 2: Bridge and noseguard

To join the two lens-holders I used a solid brass bar, appropriately cut, filed, drilled, and soldered together. On the front, a threaded worm-drive screw was used to raise or lower the nose-guard or footplate, which carries the weight of the headset on the bridge of the nose.

As you can see, my work, which is entirely self-taught, tends to be a bit rough and ready. Due to impatience and haste, holes get drilled off-center and solder is over-used. These sorts of details improve with good planning and a measured approach.

## Step 3: Headband and holding strap

Being made entirely of recycled metal, mainly copper and brass, and some genuine lambskin leather, this device is quite heavy, albeit well-balanced on the head (1.1kg/2.5lbs), so it's not something to wear for prolonged periods, but it does amplify vision really well. To keep it secured on the head, it has a well padded, over-the-top-of-the-head supporting strap, made of a piece of steel from an old clockwork motor spring, which I wrapped in foam to pad it and then sewed into the lambskin leather. It's attached at each end to a box-like extender, which can lengthen the strap for taller heads (vertical adjustment). To keep the eye-cups well secured around the eyes, the two paddles, made of brass sheet covered with foam and leather and secured by a bootlace drawstring, can be tightened against the back of the head (horizontal adjustment). The eyelets on each paddle, through which the drawstring pulls, are old mounting posts from a bronze chest drawer handle, soldered to each paddle before covered with leather. The length of each paddle can be adjusted by loosening the lock nut on the barrel of the earpiece frame and adjusting the stem length to suit before re-tightening and locking the stem in place. This aspect of the construction owes a lot to Gogglerman's ideas.

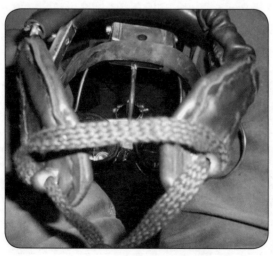

## Step 4: Lights

The principal lighting unit here was from a Cree LED headlight that I bought online and then hacked. I have kept the lens, the push-pull focusing system, and the battery pack with attached circuit-board and micro-switch. To maintain the Steampunk aesthetic I have made from scratch a new brass barrel for the Cree headlight and a brass case to hold the battery pack and micro-switch. This was simply made from folded and soldered brass sheet metal. The lid catch was made by annealing a piece of scrap brass sheet and pounding a steel ball-bearing into the metal to greater than its equator, while the metal was still hot. As the brass shrank, it kept the ball bearing securely in place. This construct was then soldered to the front flap of the box and a dent was made in the face of the front of the box in the appropriate place to accept the ball-bearing catch when the lid is closed. Simple, but it works surprisingly well.

The two sidelights were made from scratch, using three LED bulbs, bright white, in each. These are mounted on a wooden disc, in turn fitted precisely into a copper tube. The LEDs, each soldered to a 67ohm resistor, are wired together and connected to the output of the Cree circuit board, so that all three lights function together. The value of the resistor used will vary depending on the LEDs selected and the power voltage you want to use. I used the power output of 4.5v from the Cree headlight, so tailored my design to that.

The lenses for the sidelights were recycled from an old box Brownie camera I got for $2.00 at the scrapyard. I mounted these in a brass pipe offcut that would just cover the copper pipe in which the LEDs were mounted. I narrowed the end of the brass pipe by heating and hammering over a solid rod former. This enabled the back end to go over the copper pipe while not allowing the lenses, which were the same diameter as the i.d of the brass pipe, to stay in place without falling out of the pipe. The brass pipe was then screwed to the copper pipe shaft with a transverse screw. The completed side-lights were then mounted in a circle of brass, cut from a brass pipe. Screws fix the mid-point of the brass circle to the mid-point of the shaft or barrel of the light, allowing for movement around this central point. The brass circle is then mounted in a friction-fit ball-bearing mount.

Each of the three lights can move about an axis through a range of about 45 degrees in all directions, using a ball-bearing mount. The holders are made from brass sheet, folded into a C-shape and have holes drilled in the ends of the "arms" to take a ball-bearing. Similar holes on the shaft barrel of each light allows a friction grip of the ball-bearings between the holder arms and the light shaft barrel. If the arms of the C-shaped holder are too far apart, the ball is not held securely enough and the light will not maintain its desired position. If the arms are too close together, it's hard to get the balls into position. I found that this design worked best with non-annealed metal for the C-arm holders. The balls were simply

art

harvested from an old ball-race bearing found at the scrapyard.

## Step 5: Earpieces

Just as a pair of spectacles requires earpieces to locate the lenses appropriately, the Vision Enhancer device uses the same idea. The arms of the earpieces are attached to the lens-holder eye cups by brass hinges, which were made from brass rod offcuts and then shaped using an angle grinder and hand files. The stems were made from hollow brass pipe that could carry telescoping flexible ear-hooks (hacked from a redundant piece of eye-wear). The back-of-head pressure pads, held together by the drawstring, were also allowed to telescope into the upper barrel of the earpiece arms. The final position of the stem in the barrel was fixed by a locking screw. This system allowed for some size adjustments between different wearers. The front end of the barrel was formed into a hinge by insetting a short brass rod, soldering this in place, and grinding and drilling this appropriately to

mate with the other hinge component screwed to the side of the lens-holder eye cups.

The main weight is carried on the leather-padded vertical support running over the top of the head and this is attached to the side of the upper earpiece barrel, as is the fixed-length strap carrying the battery case.

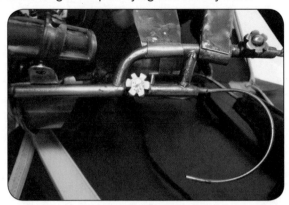

## Step 6: Lenses and magnification system

The main lenses in this Vision Enhancer are simple convex lenses with a magnification of 1.5X and a focal length of 35cm, making them suitable for relatively close-up work such as PC board construction, engraving, or reading fine print. The lenses, which were sourced as surplus stock from an industrial lens and prism manufacturer, defined the size of the lens holding eye pieces. The lenses are held in place by a washer, distal to the lens and soldered to the eye cup, and a simple brass circle made from heavy brass wire or light rod, placed inside the eye-cup proximal to the lens.

To provide further magnification, a pair of redundant Zeiss loupes, 2.5X power, were adapted to fit the Vision Enhancer frame. Making use of the stainless steel frame hinges, these were adapted to be able to be swung down into the visual pathway for enhanced magnification of ultra-fine work, or to be moved out of the way for less detailed viewing. When swung down into the visual pathway, the lenses are held in place by the spring action of the stainless steel stems and a guide-in-hole friction-fit locating system. Interestingly, I acquired these lenses for free after placing an appeal for such a donation through a local surgical society's website. Surgeons use these loupes for doing fine work and they, like eye glasses, are of little use for re-sale purposes once the surgeon retires or stops operating.

# green

While the term "go green" has been passed around from politicians to business executives to marketing specialists, there's no group of individuals who have taken this ethos to heart more than the humble maker. For years the maker/builder movement has cobbled together projects with plucked-from-the-wastestream materials like broken shipping pallets, bicycle inner tubes, old windows, pieces of pipe, and discarded motors.

Many of the projects in this chapter are not only made from green or recycled materials, but are green and renewable energy solutions in and of themselves. These projects are built by pioneers in the green field—individuals who have taken matters into their own hands to develop low-cost and simple-tech solutions in order to generate their own energy and provide sustainable transportation, all in an effort to reduce their environmental impact. Check out these green projects and use the techniques and skills explained in this chapter to inspire your own personal green revolution.

# The Algae Experiment: How to Build Your Own Algae Photo-Bioreactor

By Carolos Charles Mouchtaris (much)
(http://www.instructables.com/id/the-algae-experiment-How-to-build-your-own-algae-/)

In this instructable we will go over how to construct an at-home version of a photo-bioreactor that will use solar energy and artificial lighting with carbon dioxide to produce algae biomass.

The aim of this project is to create a model that harbors an ecosystem fit to help us escape a fossil fuel economy. We are in an era that is experiencing a shift from humanity trying to dominate nature, to trying to preserve parts of nature, to now trying to reach a reconciliation with nature. This is the algae experiment: an idea that is trying to move away from a linear wasteful and polluting way of using resources to a closed loop system where all resources are kept in a closed loop cycle.

## Step 1: Shape, size, and materiality

The over all shape of the photo bioreactor is inspired from a previous project I had been working on and follows a mean summer solar path of the UK. It is meant to be an educational model but should also embody certain architectural elements within, allowing it to possibly be viewed as an informational pavilion.

## Step 2: The ribs

I considered using two materials for the support system.

I tried clear acrylic so as not to detract from the function, which would be the algae tubes containing the algae. However, having to deal with all the transparencies of the materials made the model seem very confusing.

I needed each rib to consist of two pieces of wood in order to provide a stable 'leg' for each segment whilst I would be putting the model together but also to be able

to withstand any rocking from pressure the model would experience during the cultivation hours. I ordered 50 M4 grub screws with a cup point and 150 M4 hexagon nuts and got started on the ribs. (M4 denotes the diameter of the screw: 4mm.) I spaced the ribs apart 20mm, which allowed them to be able to free stand. Together all five sets made a very sturdy model base.

## Step 3: The tubes

I wanted to use a closed loop system, where the algae would travel constantly and safely without getting contaminated, so using clear acrylic tubes was the best option.

I initially wanted to use 15mm outer diameter tubes with an inner diameter of 12mm in order to carry the water required to grow the algae, as well as to match the pump power (4000 liters per hour) that I had obtained for a previous model. However I quickly realized that at every return point of each tube there was no silicone or plastic based hose that was flexible enough to bend around to each connection point.

This wasn't all disappointing as it meant that I could downsize to 12mm outer diameter tubes with an inner diameter of 8mm and save on cost at the same time. Unfortunately, even though I moved down to that size, finding a hose that would fit on the outside of the 12mm seemed impossible.

That is when I decided to try to enter the 8mm inner

area of the tube, something considered very unconventional and 'inconvenient' but, to me, was the only option as far as flexibility was concerned with the materials available to me. I found an 8mm outer diameter silicone tube and it fit perfectly inside.

## Step 4: How it came together

The trouble now was to sort out the frequency and amount of tubes per rib. I needed enough to cover as much of the surface as possible in order for the algae to capture as much light as possible. I therefore ordered 20 x 1m length 12mm outer diameter tubes. This allowed me enough spacing to double up in the future on the inside if I could raise more money to have a second set under the first set of ribs.

Although at first one pair of tubes seemed easy to connect to each other with the 8mm silicone hose, repeating the process 40 times with such a small radius and a tendency to buckle and fold in on itself seemed impractical. I therefore had to come up with a different system of transporting the algae from one tube to the next. This meant either re-designing the ribs to a much larger scale, which would set each tube further apart, or changing the tube to an even smaller size which would allow me to purchase an even thinner hose with more flexibility to achieve that goal.

I decided not to go with either; instead I changed the pattern of transport. Rather than consecutively going from tube to tube, I would skip three tubes on one end and two on the other, three on one, two on the other and so on and so forth. This allowed me to stick with the same design and tubes that were already put together and get a much larger radius, ensuring that the hoses would not pop out of place because of the pressure or their internal positioning in the acrylic tubes.

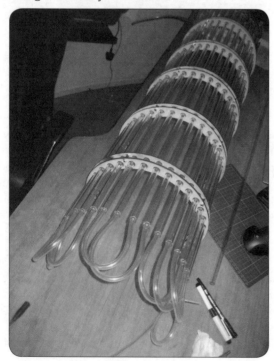

## Step 5: The plinth/base

With the 'above ground' part of the model completed, it was now time for the plinth to be constructed, which would house all the mechanisms that would operate the model 'below ground.' The plinth required to place the model on a height that would be comfortable to be viewed by an audience of both children and the elderly but at the same time not be overstated and detract from the model itself.

I decided to make it 1m tall and allow 15cm for each side of the 1m tubes to have space for the turnaround of the hoses. The final dimensions of the plinth were 1m tall, 1.3m long by 0.3m wide.

As this was going to be both an exhibition piece and a University project I felt that there was a strong educational aspect to it. I wanted to somehow be able to tell the story of the algae with this model. I decided to make viewing holes on the rear side that would show the process, much like the doughnut company Krispy Kreme whom has certain stores where the customers can see the production line of how the doughnuts are made from the dough to the glazing.

On these holes I would label what each component would do. Bio-reactor, CO2 pump, air intake, light source. Once deciding on the location of these objects, I decided that rather than having separate holes with separate names, it would be better to have one panel which would be seen as one object containing all the information one needs to know which would be far less distracting.

This turned out to be a really good choice after all and the laser cutting machine did an excellent job. Etching turned out to be much harder than I thought as every letter had to be converted to an object, which meant that there was a much higher chance for an error to occur. Each letter had to be checked and cleared of any unwanted lines as well as checked for disconnections in the comprising lines.

green

## Step 6: Color

After that the plinth was ready for painting. A clean white look turned out to be the right choice and a color scheme of white, natural ply, and clear proved successful. In hindsight I should have used far less paint quantity on the water tank door as the 3mm ply could not handle the paint and warped. It is purely an aesthetic problem, one that can be addressed after the exhibition is over.

## Step 7: Sealing the bio-reactor

With the plinth drying it was now time to seal the tubes and the hoses shut to make a closed loop bio-reactor. I used the super-instant glue rather than silicone because of its 'instant factor' and because the hose and tube were such a tight fit that silicone would only create clumps inside the tube and probably cause more problems than it was worth.

When trying to fit each hose in the tubes it was extremely hard to get each one in at first. To solve the problem I countersunk all the tubes in order to get a 'start' so each hose could slide in with ease. This was an excellent solution as later I poured glue on the countersunk tube with the hose in place creating a lake that would seal shut. Result: not a single connection out of the 40 connections leaked.

Because the tube was a very small space with a limited air supply, the instant glue would not dry instantly, which created a small puddle inside each connection. I therefore had to try various positions every five to seven minutes to ensure that each connection would seal on all 360 degrees.

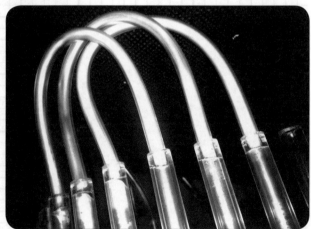

## Step 8: Hose fitting

A minor adjustment had to be made to the pumping mechanism. Due to the fact that 4000 liters per hour was significantly more powerful than the 15 liter water tank I was intending to use, I had to make an outlet where the pump's power would effectively be cut in half, taking the stress off all the plumbing connections so they would not suddenly blow apart from the pressure.

The adjustable handle also meant that I could regulate the speed at which the algae would travel round the model and effectively either accelerate or decelerate the

growth when needed.

Whilst I would be transporting the model, I wanted to have the ability to separate the bio-reactor from the plinth. I used some heavy duty clip-on clip-off fittings which allowed me to completely disconnect the bio-reactor without compromising any connection points.

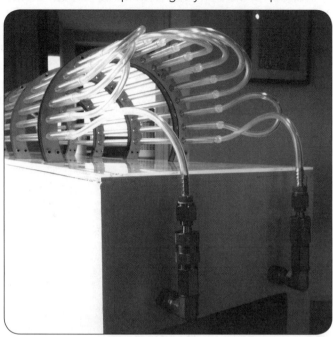

## Step 9: Test runs

After letting the glue settle for 40 hours, the first test run with still water was extremely successful. The air bubbles traveled at a steady pace throughout the model and all the connections held up perfectly. This run lasted four hours. I then proceeded to add algae incrementally over the next week.

## Step 10: Growing the initial algae culture, part I

During the building period, I had started to grow algae using the simple method of a water bottle, algae food, and the sun. This proved successful in the UK but even more successful in Greece where the sun lasted for longer during the day. I started with a culture sent to me by the Algae Depot of 50ml and after a few days I reached three x 100ml travel bottles.

I then proceeded to continue to grow that culture until I eventually reached the required 5.5 liters after approximately two weeks. The algae was growing exponentially quicker due to the limited bottle room I would provide along with excellent sun exposure and feeding regimen.

## Step 11: Growing the initial algae culture, part 2

## Step 12: Test runs

I let the algae run in the bio-reactor for ten days and achieved excellent results.

Perhaps it was the location of the model positioned against a window that received very good sunlight both artificial and genuine, but it had grown at a steady pace, becoming greener every day.

## Step 13: Outcome

Being an ongoing project I do not have the algae biomass output of this experiment yet.

I will keep you posted through my tumblr blog at http://thealgaeexperiment.tumblr.com, where any publications results and other events that will be organized shall be posted.

Thank you for looking through this instructable and please contact me if you need any further info.

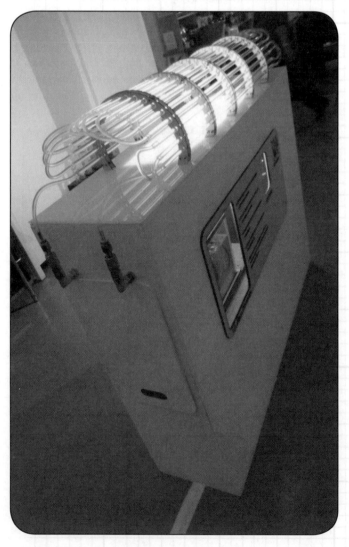

green

# Convert Your Honda Accord to Run on Trash

By jimmason
(http://www.instructables.com/id/Convert-your-Honda-Accord-to-run-on-trash/)

Gasification is the use of heat to transform solid biomass, or other carbonaceous solids, into a synthetic "natural gas like" flammable fuel. Through gasification, we can convert nearly any solid dry organic matter into a clean burning, carbon neutral, gaseous fuel. Whether starting with wood chips or walnut shells, construction debris or agricultural waste, the end product is a flexible gaseous fuel you can burn in your internal combustion engine, cooking stove, furnace, or flamethrower. Or in this case, your DeLorean. Well ok, how about a Honda Accord . . .

Sound impossible?

Did you know that over one million vehicles in Europe ran onboard gasifiers during WWII to make fuel from wood and charcoal, as gasoline and diesel were rationed or otherwise unavailable? Long before there was biodiesel and ethanol, we actually succeeded in a large-scale, alternative fuels redeployment—and one which curiously used only cellulosic biomass, not the oil and sugar based biofuel sources which famously compete with food.

This redeployment was made possible by the gasification of waste biomass, using simple gasifiers about as complex as a traditional wood stove. These small-scale gasifiers are easily reproduced (and improved) today by DIY enthusiasts using simple hammer and wrench technology.

The goal of this project is to show you how to do it—using tools you can find at Sears!

This is a really big project! We split the project into several instructables to make it easier to understand.

This instructable explains how to retrofit a Honda Accord (or nearly any car) with our open source Gasifier Experimenter's Kit (GEK) (http://gekgasifier.com/) to power it. In this project we cover modifications to the standard GEK Gasifier that are needed, details specific to its installation into the Honda, and modifications to the Honda itself.

## Step 1: The goal: Honda + gasifier

We developed the open source Gasifier Experimenter's Kit as a flexible-fuel biomass processor to produce a gaseous fuel (syngas). The syngas produced by our GEK can be used to power generators, heaters, and motors (http://wiki.gekgasifier.com/w/page/24508452/Run-an-Engine-with-the-GEK) (nearly anything that could be run on propane), so we decided to build a concept car powered by our GEK unit.

How does that work?

In a normal car, liquid gasoline is injected into the cylinders while air is sucked in to burn it. The GEK produces a syngas fuel not a liquid—similar to natural gas. So we can't just dump it into the gas tank and run the engine as usual.

What we'll do is to disable the Honda's gasoline fuel injectors and route our syngas in through the engine's air intake. We'll install a somewhat modified version of our standard GEK unit into the trunk area, with a fuel tube going up to the Honda engine in front.

The only modification to the Honda engine is that we disable the fuel injectors, and tee the air intake to allow pulling in our syngas along with the air. In fact, the Honda engine still can be run on gasoline when we are finished—all that's needed is to flip a switch to re-enable the fuel injectors.

Easier said than done! Read on to see how to do it . . . maybe . . .

## Step 2: Tools and parts

The vehicle was built at the ALL Power Labs shop. We've got a lot of fun tools, but you could build this project with just power tools you'd find at Sears. I'll note what your alternatives are below.

Tools we used:
- Power tools: We used all of 'em! Drill, grinder, reciprocating saw, flashlight, belt sander, circular saw, etc.
- Socket set, wrench set, vice grips, etc.
- MIG welder, plasma cutter (hand and CNC). All you really need is MIG and a cutting torch, the rest of it was us just getting fancy. You could also use a reciprocating saw with metal cutting blade instead of a cutting torch, although that would take a bit longer.
- Bench chop saw with metal cutting blade is helpful but not required.
- Sheet metal cutters, benders, rollers. This is because we fabricated entirely from sheet steel. To avoid the bending and rolling the easy thing is to start with a recycled metal tank as described in step 5.
- Car jack: We've got the fancy garage type lifter, but any car jack will do.
- Shop vac to clean up spilled fuel messes, and clean out reactor
- For the electronics: soldering tools, wire strippers, crimper

Parts:

The complete GEK Gasifier is designed so that it can be constructed from the lowest cost and most commonly available parts. It is nearly all common sheet steel and plumbing parts. The Honda conversion also does not use any expensive or hard-to-find components—total raw material and parts cost for this project is probably about $1000 if you build everything yourself.

- You need to supply a working vehicle. We used a 1987 Honda Accord, but most cars should be ok
- Our GEK Gasifier kit. We supply CAD files so you can fabricate totally from scratch, or you can purchase parts kits (http://www.gekgasifier.com/gasification-store/gasifier-systems-and-kits/) from us at various stages of assembly. Fabrication and/or assembly of the GEK using our plans or kits is detailed in our instructables series (http://www.instructables.com/tag/type:id/keyword:gek/).
- Miscellaneous plumbing pipes, tubes, and ball valves
- Sheet steel and a few square steel rods
- Miscellaneous nuts and bolts
- Reactor Control Unit (parts kit available soon from ALL Power Labs)

## Step 3: Safety

There are a lot of potential dangers with this project. We recommend you always have a responsible adult present when building your Trash Powered Honda.

- Cars are big! Heavy! And have lots of moving parts that can squash or grind you up!
- Gasifiers produce gases that are very good for engines, but very bad for humans. Thus please remember the following whenever you run a gasifer.

Warning: A gasifier is a dangerous thermo-chemical device. Like most useful tools, it will do damage if used incorrectly. A gasifier purposely generates carbon monoxide and other dangerous volatile organic gases as an interim step before complete combustion of the gas in a flare or engine. Acute exposure to carbon monoxide can be harmful or fatal. It is colorless, odorless, and will quickly colonize your hemoglobin, leaving no sites left for oxygen to land. Exposure to other VOCs is similarly problematic. In short, it is somewhat like smoking cigarettes, just exponentially worse. In fact, a cigarette is an updraft gasifier, a close cousin to what you are building in steel with the GEK.

Always have a fast reacting carbon monoxide meter in the area where you are working. Ideally, hang one on a tether around your neck. Carbon monoxide meters are available at most hardware stores in the smoke detector section.

And remember that with just one extra oxygen, CO becomes $CO_2$. It is a very easy oxidation pathway, thus why syngas burns so cleanly.

Anyone have a Prius we can challenge at the smog shop?

## Step 4: History, theory, and overview

See here for basic information on wood gas and biomass gasification: http://www.gekgasifier.com/gasification-basics/.

The GEK gasifier design is based on a nozzle and constriction (Imbert type) downdraft reactor. This was the typical gasifier reactor type of WWII, and still the usual starting point for generating low tar wood gas to power internal combustion engines. The GEK design combines all common Imbert type variations into a single configurable reactor, with easy adjustability of all critical dimensions. Gasifier geeks will swoon to know that it supports:

- variable combustion/reduction zone size and shape (tube, bell, inverted V, hourglass)
- variable air nozzle position and size
- air preheating (or lack there of)
- active tar recycling into incoming air
- variable air injection architecture (air from top, bottom, or side annular ring)
- "monorator" type condensing hopper
- rotary grates/stirrer additions

The GEK Imbert reactor standard sizing and configuration is known to produce clean syngas when operated by a knowledgeable enthusiast. This default configuration will run 5-20hp engines. We've expanded the internal sizes for the Honda Accord project so it can support the 70HP or so Honda engine.

The GEK improves on the 60-year-old standard a bit, which we will explore in more detail in the Fabricating the GEK instrucable (http://www.instructables.com/id/Building_the_GEK_Gasifier_in_seven_parts/).

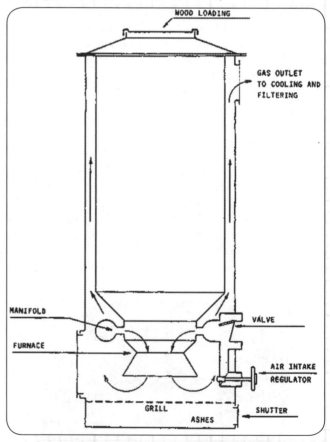

green

## Step 5: Different ways to make the GEK

The GEK building scenario (http://www.gekgasifier.com/wood-gasifier-plans/) lets you decide the relative amount of "effort vs cost" you want to invest towards your finished unit. The basic vessel dimensions are based on common scrap tanks found in North America, so you can choose to build it for minimum money with the dimensions, instructions, and CAD files provided here. The local junkyard will give you all the greasy obtainium scrap tanks you need. Or you can build the GEK from clean and purpose cut sheetmetal, also using the CAD files provided here.

For the obtainium route, you will need scrap tanks of 10," 12," and 14.75," diameters. 10" is typical for hand held air transfer tanks and some truck pony tanks. 12" is typical for 5 and 10 gal propane tanks. 14.75" is typical for a 100lb/25gal propane tank. (Warning: There's a surprising amount of dimensional variation on "standardized tanks" between different tank manufacturers. This can complicate the fit of flanges and end plates to the scrap tanks.)

The more elegant way to build the GEK is from purposed cut and rolled sheetmetal. Sheet metal is still very inexpensive, and you will have better dimensional control than via the obtainium route.

You can cut the sheetmetal to make the vessel tubes, flanges and end plates, using a gas torch or plasma cutter. Potentially even a sawzall, but ugh! Ideally, the tool for the task is CNC plasma cutter, which can run off the CAD files provided here. Many "manufacturing on demand" providers offer CNC plasma cutting services, so you could order in perfectly cut sheet metal to get you started, and not spend all your enthusiasm fighting the prep work. ALL Power Labs can also provide readymade sheet metal and plumbing kits. See http://www.gekgasifier.com/gasification-store for more information about readymade GEK wood gas kits.

Hopefully one of the above scenarios will find a good match with your abilities, time, and money available. Whichever route you choose to build the GEK, the final unit is the same, and thus experiments and customizations are easily sharable across the GEK user community.

## Step 6: Fabricating the basic GEK

The standard GEK gasifier system consists of the following seven components. For the Honda GEK we made a few slight changes to the standard GEK design which are noted below (and detailed in later steps here).

Gas making:
1. Gas cowling and ash grate (for Honda—cowling built into box, grate has motor mount)
2. Downdraft reactor (for Honda: larger reduction bell)
3. Fuel hopper (for Honda: shaped to fit behind rear window)
4. Particulate clean-up
5. Cyclone (no change)
6. Packed bed filter (no change)
7. Gas combustion
8. Centrifugal vac/blower (no change)
9. Swirl burner (no change)

We will be building each of these components separately in a "slight detour instructable" dedicated to the welding project (http://www.instructables.com/id/Building_the_GEK_Gasifier_in_seven_parts/). After we're finished, we'll return right here to consider the final assembly and preparation for the first test run.

CAD drawings for all the sheet metal parts and assembled vessels can be downloaded at: http://gekgasifier.pbworks.com/How-to-Build-and-Run-the-GEK-Gasifier.

And now, get your MIG welders ready, it's time to fabricate your GEK . . .

## Step 7: Assembling the GEK and preparing for fire

With basic GEK welding complete, now we can assemble and prepare for fire. No Honda is required for this. When you are finished assembling your basic (or modified) GEK, it will look like one of these: http://www.gekgasifier.com/wpgallery/.

Well, you might have to apply a bit of paint first. You are welcome to paint your GEK in any manner you like, though we do suggest you use high temp paint commonly found at any auto store. The 500F paint is fine. You do not need the 1200F paint.

Once your paint is dry, there are seven components we'll be assembling, just like there were seven components we just welded together:

- Gas Cowling
- Downdraft Reactor Insert
- Cyclone
- Pack Bed Filter
- Axial Fan
- Swirl Burner
- Fuel Hopper

For the standard GEK: the gas cowling, reactor, and hopper bolt together into a single vertical assembly. The cyclone, packed bed filter, and blower similarly bolt together into a single vertical assembly. These two assemblies attach together via the gas outlet flange to the cyclone. A soft hose attaches the blower to the swirl burner. And then, fire!

The details of how to accomplish this require another "slight Instructable detour" (http://www.instructables.com/id/EW5G8IWFPBKZMMR). You're now through the hard part. It's all downhill coasting from here to 88MPH.

See http://www.instructables.com/id/EW5G8IWFPB-KZMMR/ for the GEK final assembly and first firing preparation instructable.

## Step 8: Proof of concept testing: first fire

With the GEK now together, we hooked it up to a prototype of our electronic Reactor Control Unit (described later) and ran the output to a 2kw 4-stroke generator. This was to simulate more or less what we were planning for the Honda. Somewhat surprisingly, it worked!

Here's the separate instructible for how to start and run a GEK design gasifier (http://www.instructables.com/id/edit?instructableId=ECZWOCAFPKFCSOQ#instructableId=ECZWOCAFPKFCSOQ,stepId=S7EI56XFPKF CSOP).

## Step 9: Prep the Honda trunk mount

The trunk of the Honda seemed like a good spot to put the GEK!

1. Cut out the trunk floor along the inside of the frame struts.
2. Remove the trunk hatch.
3. Fabricate two heavy duty mounting pins. The mount system allows rotating the mounted GEK for access, then pinning in place during driving.
4. Weld/bolt the mounting pins to the frame struts.

## Step 10: Fabricate a frame for the gasifier

When we started out, we were going to get a bit fancy and have a hopper alongside the GEK to hold the fuel. This would be great because the GEK heat would help dry the fuel in the hopper, and the form factor would be more compact. Unfortunately—the alongside hopper requires an auger to move the fuel up and over into the GEK reactor, and this auger proved to be a difficult piece of engineering. So you'll see parts of the hopper with auger bits in them, but ultimately we have not yet gotten the auger fully functioning, though is not needed with a much simpler over-head hopper.

The hopper box frame is sized to hold the GEK, and to fit into the trunk opening in the Honda.

green

## Step 11: Install the cyclone

We started with the standard GEK cyclone and fitted it into the hopper/box as well.

In the photos here we also dropped the box into the car. Actually to be more accurate, we dropped the car onto the box using a car jack, the box just sat in place.

## Step 12: Install the grate, jigglerator, and dump ports

- At the bottom of the GEK cowling is the standard GEK ash grate for holding up the fuel in the gas producing reduction zone and allowing ash to filter out the catch basin. In a standard GEK the grate has an external bar for turning by hand.
- We connected the grate drive shaft to a windshield wiper motor mounted to the bottom of the box, so that it can be turned automatically. We call it the JIGGLERATOR. Although we do love its name, testing of the vehicle showed that, at least in city driving, the car bumps around enough by itself to unclog any fuel jams.
- Also on the bottom are dump ports for ash and water condensation from the output syngas.

## Step 13: Air intake with butterfly valve

The syngas and air are both going into the Honda engine via the original air intake. That means the Honda engine can no longer control its own fuel/air mix. We built a new air intake with a butterfly valve so that we can control the fuel-to-air mix ratio.

The fuel-to-air mix needs adjustment while the car is driving, so we added a servo control that can be operated from the driver seat.

- The new airtake starts with a length of 2" diameter PVC pipe.
- The butterfly valve is a fender washer that matched the ID of the pipe.
- The fender washer is screwed to a 1/4" diameter aluminum rod. The aluminum rod goes through two holes drilled across the pipe.
- The servo turns the rod to open and close the valve.

## Step 14: Syngas piping from gasifier in back to engine in front

- Chop off the end of the air intake tube from the Honda.
- Add a coupler and tee.

- The syngas is routed to the back of the car: Using flexible tubes in front and in the rear, underneath the car we made a rectangular steel tube for strength. Our custom servo controlled butterfly valve is installed as the new air intake. The valve lets us control the fuel to air mix now that both are going into the original air intake.

## Step 15: Solid fuel auger: not used in current design

Originally we wanted to have the hopper alongside the GEK reactor to hold the biomass fuel. It had the advantage of a more compact form factor, plus the GEK heat could help dry the fuel to allow using wetter fuels. But it requires a way to transport the solid biomass fuel up and over to load the GEK reactor.

We built several solid fuel augers, but soon discovered that it is a difficult engineering problem when you want to run an auger up from horizontal, or in our case, about 45 degrees. We currently run the vehicle with the typical top-mounted gravity-fed GEK hopper, which is simple and reliable. We hope to get the auger working eventually but for now you can refer to our prototypes and hopefully learn something about all the ways that the auger cannot work.

We built and tested two different auger designs. Generally, they would work for certain fuel size and shape, but when the particulars changed, they would either jam or fail to move/lift the fuel. The GEK reactor will run on a wide range of solid biomass as long as it is chipped or chopped into chunky bits from about 3/8" to 1.5". All diagonal designs we tested were much more fuel sensitive than the gasifier itself.

green

169

## Step 16: GEK reactor modifications and instrumentation

We made a few changes to the basic GEK reactor design:

- Increased the size of the reduction belt. This increases power output compared to the standard GEK design, which was needed to produce syngas fast enough for the Honda engine.
- Added instrumentation: 4 thermocouples and 2 pressure sensors. These aren't really needed for operation, but we built this as a research design so we like to know what is going on inside.

See the photos for how we routed the thermocouples into the GEK so that they are durable and don't interfere with operation.

## Step 17: Reactor Control Unit (RCU): aka "THE BRAIN 2"

Any modern car has an Electronic Control Unit, or ECU, which monitors and controls the engine function and keeps everything working. It is often called the Brain of the car. One of the Honda ECU's main functions is to properly inject gasoline into the engine and monitor the fuel/air mix. Since we are doing some Serious Monkeying Around with both of those pathways in order to replace the gasoline with our Gasifier produced syngas, we built our own Reactor Control Unit (RCU)—also known as THE BRAIN 2.

The RCU taps into the Honda ECU to bypass its control of the fuel injectors and fuel/air mix. It also has several other functions:

- Sense if the fuel mix is lean or rich. We use the existing oxygen sensor from the Honda and access it where it connects to the Honda ECU (Honda's stock ECU is their brain for running the car).

- Control our new fuel/air mix butterfly valve. We drive a servo from a dial mounted on the dash. We also have a switch on the dash that can toggle between Manual fuel/air mix control and Automatic fuel/air mix control. In Auto mode our RCU uses a closed-loop feedback to automatically adjust the air/fuel mix, just like the Honda ECU does when running on gasoline.
- A control for the grate jigglerator motor (fuel unclogging system)
- A sensing and control loop for steam injection into the gasifier when there is adequate heat. The GEK in the this Honda has a variety of heat recycling systems that result in a surplus of heat in the gasifier, heat which can be usefully consumed via more steam over the glowing char in the reactor, and thus a more hydrogen rich gas output.
- A solid fuel level sensor and auger motor control. Not used in the current non-auger design.
- A USB connection to a laptop, we send all the sensor data to the laptop to display it. The co-pilot can check the readings on all the instrumentation—thermocouples, pressure sensors, oxygen sensor, and all the motors can be activated manually by the copilot.
- A switch to disable or enable the electronic fuel injection. We again tapped into the Honda ECU for this.

Our Reactor Control Unit is built with a SiLabs 8051 devkit with a custom expansion board plugged to it. There are 12 thermocouple jacks, 4 pressure sensors, 4 30-amp H-bridges for motor drive, a USB connection for a data display laptop, etc.

## Step 18: Cockpit

The air/fuel mix knob and manual/auto switch are just next to the wheel for the driver.

The co-pilot can watch all the sensors via the laptop display, and make changes to any of the motors or the air/fuel mix as well.

The laptop also logs the readings so we can see what worked and what didn't.

## Step 19: Final GEK reassembly for Honda

- Install reactor into cowling (standard GEK method with sealing tape).
- Add perlite between GEK inner and outer cowlings (standard).
- Bolt on the gas filtration unit (standard).
- Bolt hopper on top of reactor. We made a thinner hopper than the standard one so it fits behind the rear window.

## Step 20: Blow-off and output syngas valves

When starting up the GEK reactor it's convenient to be able to get it going without having the Honda engine running. We put a tee on the GEK syngas output so we can send it either to the engine or to cyclone burner flare-off. Once the reactor is up to temperature and running well, we can shut off the cyclone and start the car on syngas.

## Step 21: Load solid fuel and ignition!

Hey man, can I borrow your shoes? No? Well, how about some wood chips? Or those peanut shells you are throwing everywhere?

## Step 22: Ready!

## Step 23: GO! 88MPH here we come . . .

Here's a video of us driving the finished Honda Accord around West Oakland. No shots were fired. Fire was kept only in the gasifier. And everyone made it home with smiles on their faces.

green

# Solar Powered Trike

## By dpearce1
(http://www.instructables.com/id/Solar-Powered-Trike/)

Travel for free with the power of the sun!

The purpose of this project is to build a vehicle that:

- Provides free, 'green' transportation for short distances (<10 miles), thus it must never plug into a wall socket, or emit any pollutants.
- Charges while at work.
- Is cheap, simple, and low maintenance.
- Draws attention to the practical application of green energies and promotes fossil fuel alternatives.
- Reduces excess automobile wear and pollution from cold driving/short, in town trips.

## Step 1: Acquire a vehicle

Find a lightweight vehicle with low rolling resistance. A two, three, or four wheeler will do, depending on how much work you want to do, but the concept is the same. Four-wheeled vehicles may be regulated under different laws. Of course the best vehicle is one that you already have, if you happen to have a three-or four-wheeled pedal powered vehicle. In the interest of simplicity, a three-wheeler was chosen for my project. This Schwinn Meridian Trike was $250 new, readily available locally, and the basket provides a convenient location for batteries and solar panels with minimal fabrication.

The first thing to be done was completely disassemble the trike and paint it a bright 'fern' green.

Before painting the frame, I used this stage as an opportunity to reinforce the frame where the Batteries were going to mount. Lead acid Batteries are heavy, but they are relatively cheap. One tube was welded in to distribute the load over 4 points on the axle carrier instead of two. It also ties the rear sub-frame together, which makes the tube the load bearer rather than the weld beads, which may eventually fatigue and fail.

High pressure (65psi) tubes were equipped and the Trike was meticulously assembled in order to minimize rolling resistance.

While the welder was out a battery mount was fabricated and bolts were welded to the basket to be used as battery mount studs making removal easier. Twelve-volt LED's were put in the reflectors and wired as brake lights through the brake levers that cut the motor when you brake. They are wired through only one of the three 12 volt batteries.

## Step 2: Drivetrain/ running gear

The drivetrain consists of your electrical system and electric motor. The Electric Hub Motor kit was purchased from (http://www.goldenmotor.com/), costs $259, and consists of a front wheel with an integrated brushless 36 Volt electric motor as part of the hub, along with the necessary components such as a twist grip throttle, brake levers that are wired to cut power to the motor, battery level indicator, and the motor-speed controller, 36V battery charger and a battery pack connector.

The motor install requires a simple front wheel change, and routing the wires back to the controller which will be mounted under the rear basket. Slack must be left in the wires around the steering tube/fork juncture so they will not be in tension even at the maximum steering angle. The grips and brake levers are replaced with the new ones, and their wires also routed back to the controller.

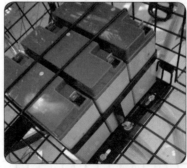

Choosing the right battery is a compromise between price, weight, and range vs. charge time. I took a multi-meter to a local industrial liquidation warehouse and found 3 batteries for $20 each, and they have worked good so far. (3) -12 volt, 20 Amp/hour batteries are run in series to make 36 volts. 20A/hr provides long range, with the trade-off being a longer charge time. A battery cut off switch was added so the rider does not have to unplug the battery pack to shut the electrical system off.

## Step 3: Charging system/solar panels

The solar panels need to be as large as possible to maximize the available wattage, but they also must provide the right voltage. Solar panels produce a range of voltages, which peak and drop, but the nominal voltage of the panel is what matters for selecting the right charge controller. I purchased 3 Q-cell brand mono-crystalline solar panels that I found on Ebay for $110 each. They produce 21.8 volts peak and 17 volts nominal, at about 1.2 amps nominal. With the 3 panels wired in series, this makes around 66 volts peak and 51 volts nominal, which is plenty over the 42V needed to charge the batteries. a basket was added in the front to accommodate the third solar panel.

From Ohm's law Power (P) is equal to voltage (V) times current (I), (P=V*I), so the panels produce ((17Volts*3)*1.2 Amps)= 61.2 Watts nominal, and over 80 Watts peak. A maximum power point tracking (MPPT) charge controller tricks the panels by hiding the battery load from them and allowing them to operate at their peak power when conditions allow.

A charge controller was purchased from www.solar-sellers.com, where Mr. John Drake was very helpful in assisting me and ordering a custom charge controller for my application. The controller basically takes the varying voltage/amperage input from the solar panel array and converts it into a constant voltage (42V) or current, to optimize charging the 36 volt source. Maximum input voltage to the controller is 100 Volts, so the peak of 66 Volts will not harm the controller. The controller is a maximum power point tracking (MPPT) type, which charges faster as more sun is available, rather than at a set rate as most controllers do.

In order to charge the batteries in a practical amount of time, they need to charge about as fast or faster than the provided 110V wall socket to 36V charger/converter,

which charges at a rate of 1.5 amps. At 1.2 amps the panels do not quite achieve this, but with the MPPT Controller it takes right around the same amount of time for a charge. The bike is stored in a location that gets a few hours of sun every day (where I live the sun is pretty reliable), which keeps the batteries topped off and ready to go whenever needed.

And for those of you wondering, the electric motor draws up to 20 Amps, and the 1.2+ Amps added by the solar panels do not make it go faster, since the 1.2 amps are routed through the controller and only serve to charge the batteries.

## Step 4: Solar panel mounts

Now you have to figure out how your going to mount the panels on your vehicle. Hinges were welded on the baskets to mount the panels and allow them to tilt for access to the basket, with rubber hold-downs on the other side to keep them from opening while riding.

Once your wires are all routed and zip tied, your batteries and panels held securely down, double check every thing and you are ready to go.

**Performance:**

This Solar Powered Trike does about 15-18 mph depending on the weight of the rider. The furthest I have gone is a little over 10 miles with small hills and little pedaling, and the battery meter still read full (green) at the end of the trips.

At ten miles, the voltage drops to around 36V, safely above the controller's cut-off voltage. If the batteries are kept from discharging too low the panels take about the same amount of time as the plug in charger, since both the plug in charger and the solar charge controller charge with constant wattage. With constant wattage charging, Power, (P), and Ohm's law again (P=V*I), the charging current goes down as the voltage goes up, as the batteries near their fully charged state.

What this means is if you keep the voltage from dropping too low, the panels provide adequate current to match the charging speed of the plug-in charger, but if it drops below a certain point the panels are slower at charging. This is easily avoided since my typical trip range is around 3 miles or less, semi daily at most, so low voltage is not an issue, but on longer trips I bring the multi-meter.

**Cost breakdown:**

The Trike cost a little over $910 to build.
- Schwinn Meridian Trike: $250.00, www.K-Mart.com
- Q-cell Mono-crystalline Solar panels: $330.00, www. Ebay.com.
- Charge Controller: $95.00, www.solarseller.com
- Electric Hub Motor Kit: $260.00, www.goldenmotor. com, also sells regenerative braking motor speed controllers
- Batteries: $60.00, Earl's industrial liquidation, Hawthorne, CA
- High pressure tubes: $15.00, any bicycle store
  Total: $910.00

green

# Make Your Own Biodiesel Processor

By drinkmorecoffee
(http://www.instructables.com/id/Make-Your-Own-Biodiesel-Processor/)

This instructable will take you step-by-step through the process of making a Biodiesel processor. This type of processor is called an appleseed processor. It uses an old (or new if you feel like dropping the money) water heater. The amount of fuel you can make will depend on the size tank you use. My first prototype uses a 10 gallon tank. Not too efficient if you plan on making large quantities, but great for figuring things out.

Before you run out and buy $100+ worth of plumbing materials, I should say this: As biodiesel becomes more and more popular the resources available become more and more scarce, and people are starting to charge for things that used to be free, specifically Waste Vegetable Oil (WVO). I would suggest securing a source for WVO before you embark on this project.

My instructable on how to use this processor can be found at http://www.instructables.com/id/Make-Biodiesel.

## Step 1: Do some research

Do some research. You can't read too much about biodiesel. I spent about a year researching before I built this and started making fuel.

A book that is a must read is Biodiesel Basics and Beyond: A Comprehensive Guide to Production and Use for the Home and Farm. Much of the information you find on the internet (including this instructable, no doubt) is incomplete information. This book will give you the ins and outs of every step you need to take.

Be familiar with how the process works before you build a processor. If you understand how it's supposed to operate when it's finished, you will make fewer mistakes when you're building it.

## Step 2: Plan

Plan, plan, and plan some more. You can't get too detailed in your planning. Map out every part you'll need, list the functions of every part, and estimate costs. Nothing would suck more than getting half way through and realizing you're out of money and you've

just blown $130 on half a processor. We made the trip to Lowes about 9 times before we had everything we needed.

Tip: Black boards and white boards come in handy, like mine, when you're trying to get a feel for what you need. Things erase easily and you get a larger diagram to concentrate on.

## Step 3: Acquire the necessary parts

You will need a water heater, a pump, and all the plumbing in between. I used a 10 gallon water heater and a 1" water pump from Northern Tool (http://www.northerntool.com/webapp/wcs/stores/servlet/product_6970_7738_7738).

Be sure that the water heater does not leak and has a working heat element. The heat element is very important since you will be heating the oil up prior to making the fuel. You will also want to keep it warm when it settles, in addition to when you remove the glycerin.

You will need about ten feet of 3/4" clear PVC flexible hose (+hose clamps).

The plumbing materials I used were:

- 3 tee Joints 3/4" x 3/4" x 3/4"
- 2 3/4" Unions (these are so you can disconnect your pump without disassembling the whole thing).
- 2 1"-3/4" reducer couplings
- 1 3/4" 90 degree elbow
- 7 3/4" Ball valves
- 11 3/4" x 1.5" male connectors
- 1 3/4" x 2" male connector
- 2 1" x 1.5" male connectors
- 4 3/4" to 3/4" male adapters (Barb to MPT)
- 2 to 3 lengths of 3/4" pipe (this depends on the size of tank you're using. Lowes, the one by me anyways, will cut and thread piping for free. Measure twice, so you only have to pay once.)
- You will also need tape to seal each fitting.

You're going to need some way to secure your processor. We used some adjustable straps and some connectors. Certainly you can secure it however you like, but this best suited us since we plan on replacing the tank very shortly.

One other thing you'll need to get acquainted with are carboys. You can find some good ones here. You need one with a cap that has a 3/4" female threaded port. This will make your methoxide mixing tank, so you will want it to be airtight.

Lastly, you will need 2 power cords. Or just one if your water heater is already wired.

## Step 4: Start assembling

Start putting it together. No doubt you will have leaks the first time you run water through this, so don't tighten things so tight you won't be able to get them apart again.

Start with the bottom of the processor. First attach a

ball valve and work your way to where you'll put the pump.

TAPE EVERY CONNECTION.

The three places you use the Tee joints are essentially identical, so I recommend assembling these before you put them on the rest of what you have. From the tee-connector-> Ball valve->Barbed adapter.

Then it goes—Ball valve-> Connector-> Tee joint (assembled)-> connector-> Ball valve-> Connector-> Tee joint (assembled)-> Connector-> Union-> Connector-> Reducer coupling-> 1" Connector-> Pump-> (now heading up)-> 1" Connector-> Reducer coupling-> Connector-> Union-> connector-> Tee Joint (assembled)-> Connector-> Ball Valve-> Pipe (length depends on how tall the processor is)-> 90 degree elbow-> Pipe back to processor (again, the length depends on how far it is to the processor)-> Malleable coupling-> and you're back!

Be sure to have the unions disconnected when you assemble the upper part, then connect them again to put the pump back on.

This is a good point to start thinking of what to mount it on, and where. Keep in mind you need a place to drain glycerin below the processor, so you'll need it raised some.

The last piece to assemble is the carboy lid. Drill a hole where you're supposed to and screw in the connector. Onto this, add a ball valve and the fourth hose adapter.

Be sure that your carboy has a vent behind the handle, and be sure this vent is drilled out.

### Step 5: Wire it all

Go ahead and wire your pump. A wiring diagram should be included.

Wire the water heater, the next step is testing the element.

### Step 6: Pressure and leak test

Now that you've got it assembled you need to do a pressure test. You can use an air compressor or you can run water through it, which is what we did.

Reasons for pressure testing:
• test for leaks
• gives you an idea of how to use the valves to get liquids where you want them
• to test the heating element
• to be sure everything is facing the right direction (the first time we hooked it all up the pump was facing the wrong way, oops)

Fill a carboy with water and connect a section of hose from the carboy to the intake valve. Use hose clamps to secure the hose. Be sure to have primed the pump.

Now open the valve on the carboy and the intake valve. Turn on the pump and make sure the glycerin drain and out-take valve are both closed, so water doesn't come shooting out. Also be sure that all the valves in the circuit are opened so you don't have any pressure building up. At this point it is very important to have the pressure vent on the tank open.

Mark where you see any leaks with a sharpie.

Go ahead and turn on the heating element, it may take a while to heat up. Mine didn't, 7 gallons of water takes just a few minutes to get hot. You can open the out-take valve whenever you like to get a sample of the water. Be careful, though, we're talking hot water here. You can test it with a quick-read thermometer.

When you're finished, close the valve nearest the tank and let the pump run a few more minutes before you turn it off. There's still some water behind the pump, so open the glycerin drain to drain off the cup or two of water left.

Close the next valve over from the drain and open the first valve. Have something to catch the water as it comes out.

It's probably still hot, so be careful depending on how hot you got the water.

One more thing. After testing all this be sure to open up every connection and let it dry. You don't want a drop of water in there when you make your fuel.

### Step 7: Mount it

Now it's time to mount it. You may find it useful to disconnect the pump at the unions when you're moving it around. You can mount it however you want, and it doesn't have to be able to move, but you do want it raised some so you can drain stuff.

We mounted ours on an existing wooden box, just because we had it. We just took some plywood,

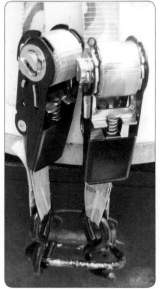

screwed some 2x4s onto that, and attached some wheels to the 2x4s. Two of the wheels are locking, so it won't roll down my driveway, slide around, or generally escape us.

We screwed the pump into a board on top of the box and used adjustable straps to secure the tank.

In my next instructable I will explain how to use this processor. In the mean time, build one!

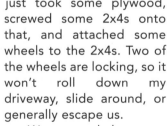

# Solar Kiln

## By Bob Autio (dorybob)
### (http://www.instructables.com/id/Solar-kiln/)

First, kudos to Dr. Brian Bond, students, and staff at Virginia Tech (VT) Department of Wood Science and Forest Products for developing a solar kiln and providing the well-written plans at http://woodscience.vt.edu/about/extension/vtsolar_kiln.

I, of course, modified the VT plans. The solar kiln is basically a box with a greenhouse roof that generates hot air with a internal solar collector. The hot air is blown through the wood with two fans. A load of wood should take approximately one month to dry.

Revision for correct air circulation: I had initially installed the fans on the outside of the kiln, blowing cool, outside air into the kiln. After visiting the sawmill, which had two solar kilns, and rereading the VT plans, I realized that the fans should be installed inside the kiln to recirculate the heated air within the kiln. Blowing in cool air would lower the kiln temperature too much and reduce the drying effectiveness. I constructed and installed an interior baffle with the fans mounted on the baffle and cut holes in the solar collector to allow for recirculation. It would have been easier to construct the baffle prior to installing the greenhouse roof but live and learn. Refer to Step 9 for baffle installation.

The kiln is also made completely solar with the addition of a photovoltaic solar panel shown in Step 10.

The wood is being dried to build an 18 foot Grand Banks dory which will used to haul picnic supplies and picnic princesses to islands off the coast of Maine. Google the Maine Island Trail Association to get a sense of the place. Building a kiln before building the boat in order to haul picnic supplies is my typical, over-zealous approach.

Thanks to all who voted for my instructable in the Green Contest.

List of materials:
- Enough wood to build structure—I used a combination of new and salvaged materials so don't have a list; the longer pieces and treated lumber were store bought
- plywood—3/4 inch thick, exterior grade, 2 sheets
- Polygal and brackets—10 ft x 6 ft piece; cut in half
- flashing—aluminum
- styrofoam insulation—2 in thick, 2 sheets
- Reflectix bubble wrap insulation
- DC fans—2, 16 inch with ring frame
- GRK screws—exterior grade; various lengths
- paint—green for solar collector
- oven thermometer
- photovoltaic solar panel—65 watts

## Step 1: Building the base or floor

The first question when building anything is where are you going to position it. A solar structure needs as much direct sun as possible and your neighbor may not be so keen on you cutting down their trees, even for a "green" project. I also positioned it uphill and adjacent to our workshop/garage to allow future duct work from the kiln to heat the workshop when not drying wood or other items. The position is a compromise between these functions.

The "foundation" is limestone blocks on the uphill side and a treated 4 inch by 6 inch posts on the downhill side. I set the floor level so that future duct work would intersect the adjacent workshop without hitting any wall supports.

Also my relatives on Fogo Island off the north coast of Newfoundland, had a sport of moving houses. Refer to the excellent book titled *Tilting—house launching, slide hauling, potato trenching, and other tales from a Newfoundland fishing village* by Robert Mellin for more information on this "sport." I constructed the kiln so that it could be moved, if needed.

The next question is size. The VT plans use a base with dimensions of 160 inch by 78 inch but I reduced the dimensions to 144 inches by 48 inches or 12 feet by 4 feet. I choose these dimensions to reduce building costs and the roof panels have a combined width of 12 feet and a plywood sheet is 4 feet wide.

The base is constructed of 4 inch by 6 inch treated lumber cut to a length of 11 feet 9 inches. All wood near the ground is treated lumber due to termite issues in our area. I used 2 inch by 6 inch by 4 feet long treated boards and screwed them onto the ends of the 11 feet 9 inches timbers to create a 12 foot by 4 foot box. Measure twice and cut once is the old carpentry policy.

Within this box, I installed cross-members. The 2 inch by 6 inch boards are connected with Simpson Strong-Tie connectors using Simpson nails (http://www.strongtie.com). It won't be to building code without the Simpson nails. (A neighbor's contractor had to remove and replace all the wrong nails on a project of theirs; the weight of the structure is borne by these nails.) I also used leftover 4 inch by 6 inch material and attached with galvanized lag screws. I countersunk the lag screws so that siding could be placed over the screws.

## Step 2: Insulating and installing floor

This was probably excessive but I insulated the floor by making "shelves" to support blue board insulation. The shelving is the light colored wood screwed to the inside of the frame. The insulation is cut into the appropriate sized rectangles and laid on the shelves. I prefer Styrofoam to any fiberglass insulation because the fiberglass is itchy to work with.

Next I installed 3/4 inch exterior grade plywood over the floor frame. This is where you get to see if you built the frame square (i.e., all the corners at 90 degrees) and it turned out pretty well; only about a 1/8 inch out of square. I have been told that all carpenters make mistakes but a good carpenter knows how to hide them.

I painted the floor with some leftover stain to provide some protection.

## Step 3: Building wall frames

The walls are basic, 2 inch by 4 inch stud walls with studs built on 16 inch centers. There are headers built over each of the openings, the door opening on the back wall and two side openings. The side openings were constructed in case I wanted to dry boards longer than the kiln or to extend duct work to the work shop.

I also framed in two openings for the fans that measured 18 inches by 18 inches.

I also cut a 4 inch by 4 inch post diagonally in half and lengthwise to create a header for the front and back walls that would match the slope of the roof. Regarding the slope of the roof, the VT plans state that for the best solar efficiency, your roof should slope at the same degrees as

your degrees of latitude. It would be approximately 39 degrees for us; however, 45 degrees is simpler to build, will work OK, and is what I constructed with.

## Step 4: Wrapping and siding the structure

I am a big fan of wrapping any structure because it allows you to have better control of air flow and air flow is the whole point of this structure.

The house wrap is stretched as tightly around the frame as possible and stapled in place. Wrapping is a two person job. Guess which big box store I brought the wrap at?

Next, I installed siding over the wrap. The siding is poplar boards salvaged from an old barn. The barn had been re-oriented by a tornado to the point where it was unsafe. Thanks to our friends for letting us repurpose the siding. The top of the siding was cut to match the roof slope.

## Step 5: Insulating the walls

I used two kinds of insulation on the walls. Similar to the floor, I cut rectangles of Styrofoam and placed them within the wall studs and pushed up against the exterior siding. Next, I placed a layer of Reflectix bubble warp insulation around the entire interior of the frame. I was attempting to create a dead air space between the Styrofoam and bubble wrap. The seams of the bubble wrap were sealed with aluminum-backed tape and stapled in place. Excessive, Excessive, Excessive.

Since bubble wrap can be punctured, I installed some recycled cedar siding on the inside walls where the drying lumber is placed. The cedar siding protects the insulation during wood handling because you will invariably bump the walls.

## Step 6: Building the solar collector

The solar collector is a salvaged metal roof that was spray-painted dark green. All you graffiti artists likely know about the handle sold by Rustoleum but it makes spray painting much easier.

I cut the metal panels to length using a metal cutting wheel on a 4.5 in grinder with lots of sparks. Wear your safety glasses. . . always.

**green**

I installed a wooden lip on the back wall to support the top of the metal panels and created a 2 inch by 4 inch "shelf" with a back stop to support the base of the metal panels. The metal panels rests on these shelves and can be removed if need be.

I left an 8 inch gap between the panels and the front wall for air flow.

## Step 7: Installing the greenhouse roof

The roof material is called Polygal; it is plastic with 1 cm by 0.5 cm channels. There is even a double channel version available if you needed more insulation. I ran the channels vertically but it seems like you could run in any orientation. There is an outside and inside to the panels, so pay attention when you remove the protective cover. The outside has UV protection of some sort. It is held in place by screws drilled through aluminum brackets. The screws have a neoprene washer to provide a water seal. Puckett Plants & Green Houses (http://www.puckett-greenhouses.com) did a nice job of preparing the panels and brackets, although the shipping cost was almost as much as the material. The brackets or holders are aluminum H-channel to join two panels together and J-channel for the ends.

There are other roof materials but I have been very impressed with how easy Polygal is to work with and how well it functions. During kiln operation, you can feel the heat come through the insulated walls while the roof is cool to the touch. It also seems very durable, as it got whacked by a significant hail storm this spring with quarter-sized hail with no apparent damage.

I also put self-adhesive weather stripping between the frame and roof to reduce air leaks, although the stripping did make it a little more difficult to slide the roofing panels into the brackets. I beveled the edges very slightly with a utility knife and the panels slid into the brackets a little easier.

## Step 8: Initial operation

Revison: Refer to the next step for installation of a baffle for correct air installation.

I initially installed a cheap box fan with an extension cord to push air through the kiln. It eventually stopped working; maybe due to the heat or maybe insufficient electrical supply or maybe some other reason. This setup is NOT recommended because of potential electrical issues like fire. I do recommend getting professional electrical help. In the final slide, I'll show version 2 of the fan system.

The ends of the wood were painted with leftover stain to reduce over-drying of the wood near the ends. The wood is stacked in the kiln with spacers between the boards called stickers. I stapled some Tyvek cloth between the base of the metal panels and laid it across the top of the wood stack to direct air through the stack. Concrete blocks were also placed on the wood to reduce any wood bending.

Based on the oven thermometer, the temperatures are typically run about 50-60 degrees F over the outside air temperature.

The drying process seems to work very well but the real test will come when I purchase a moisture meter. The VT plans also discuss a moisture measuring method using a scale.

## Step 9: Baffle installation

Per the VT design, an interior baffle is needed so that the air can flow across the solar collector to be heated, flow through the stack of wood, and then recirculate to be reheated. Some moist air is discharged through vents in the lower, back side of the kiln. I have read that the vents only need to be opened slightly and also observed this at the lumber mill's solar kiln. There is a balance between enough venting to remove moisture without losing too much heated air.

green

The baffle is a wooden structure that supports the fans and uses Reflectix as the baffle material. The sunny side was spray painted flat black to absorb solar radiation. I built the baffle in two halves because it was easier to handle and then overlapped the Reflectix to create a continuous surface. I attached a framework to the inside of the kiln to support the baffle.

I also cut holes in the solar collector behind the fans, to allow air to recirculate.

It would have been much easier to construct the baffle prior to installing the greenhouse roof and prior to loading the kiln with wood. Don't make my mistake.

## Step 10: Photovoltaic solar panel installation

I installed a 65 watt photovoltaic solar panel to power the two DC motor fans and make the kiln completely solar. The panel was installed on the front of the work shop to be part of a small, awning roof. The angle of the panel from horizontal is 53 degrees, which is our latitude of 38 degrees plus 15 degrees as recommended by the panel manufacturer. I built the roof framework around the 53 degree angle.

A grounding wire was installed fully across the framework for future panels.

Wiring was run from the panel to the kiln in plastic conduit buried just below ground surface. 10 AWG stranded copper wire was recommended and it took some searching to find stranded wire; most electrical suppliers had only solid copper wire. I used terminal strip to split power to the two fans. I could have used a "jumper spade" to send power to multiple terminals but this required a special order, so I fabricated a jumper with excess wiring.

There is no battery or other controls in the solar electrical system. The panel is directly connected to the fans through the terminal strip. The fans only need to run when the sun is hitting the solar collector and heating the air. The operation of the kiln is automatically and naturally controlled by the sun. Bob at Kansas Wind Power recommended this wiring set up. The fans spin with great speed on a bright, sunny day.

I based fan size on the following formula from "Woodweb—Selecting Fans for a Solar Kiln." Air flow in cfm = area of space between wood * 125 ft/min + 50% for leakage. With a high estimate for the volume of wood, I calculated approximately 1000 cfm per fan. The fans were purchased from Kansas Wind Power; the owner, Bob, is a great resource.

I also installed a short metal roof to shelter the fan motors so that the motors could be placed outside the heated box. I screwed together sections of metal roof soffet material to make the roof. The Christmas ornament hanging from the short side is a visual reminder to not run into the roof. Safety first even though this step is next-to-last in this instructable.

## Step 11: Solar kiln operation

I purchased white oak planks from Bonesteel Portable Sawmill & Molding, LLC (rogerbonesteel@bonesteelmillandmolding.com). The planks are 8 inches wide, either 3/4 or 1 inch thick, and 8 to 12 feet in length. I obtained different thicknesses to reduce the amount of planing. The dory plans uses different thicknesses in different locations. I plan to use finger joints to join boards end to end for the eighteen foot dory. Another experiment that will be another instructable. Highly recommend Bonesteel Sawmill if you are within striking distance of Paris Crossing, Indiana. Roger Bonesteel cuts timber on family and adjoining property, uses a small, modern mill, and has two solar kilns for drying wood; a nice operation.

The ends of the wood need to be coated to reduce excessive drying and checking (i.e, cracking) of the wood. VT recommended AnchorSeal shown in photo. AnchorSeal creates a waxy coating on the pores at the ends of the boards.

I measure moisture content, temperature, and humidity on a daily basis to help understand the operation of the kiln. Moisture content is measured with a Lignomat E/D pinless moisture meter. The Lignomat meter measures to a depth of 3/4 inch. The wood was milled to either 3/4 inch or 1 inch thick. I marked the measurement location to be able to get repeatable measurements. Also learned to use the HOLD function to get measurements in locations where it is not possible to see the meter. I take three (3) readings and record the highest value. A dashed trend line was placed through data to estimate when wood is sufficiently dried.

On sunny days, the kiln operates at 50 to 60 degrees F above outside temperatures.

# How I Built an Electricity-Producing Wind Turbine

By mdavis19

(http://www.instructables.com/id/How-I-built-an-electricity-producing-wind-turbine/)

Several years ago I bought some remote property in Arizona. I am an astronomer and wanted a place to practice my hobby far away from the terrible light pollution found near cities of any real size. I found a great piece of property. The problem is, it's so remote that there is no electric service available. That's not really a problem. No electricity equals no light pollution. However, it would be nice to have at least a little electricity, since so much of life in the twenty-first century is dependent on it.

One thing I noticed right away about my property is that most of the time, the wind is blowing. Almost from the moment I bought it, I had the idea of putting up a wind turbine and making some electricity, and later adding some solar panels. This is the story of how I did it. Not with an expensive, store-bought turbine, but with a home-built one that cost hardly anything. If you have some fabricating skills and some electronic know-how, you can build one too.

More details on this project and my other alternative energy projects including my home-built solar panels and my home-built biomass gasifier can be found on my web site at http://www.mdpub.com.

## Step 1: Acquiring a generator

I started by Googling for information on home-built wind turbines. There are a lot of them out there in an amazing variety of designs and complexities. All of them had five things in common though:

1. A generator
2. Blades
3. A mounting that keeps it turned into the wind
4. A tower to get it up into the wind
5. Batteries and an electronic control system

I reduced the project to just five little systems. If attacked one at a time, the project didn't seem too terribly difficult. I decided to start with the generator. My

online research showed that a lot of people were building their own generators. That seemed a bit too complicated, at least for a first effort. Others were using surplus permanent magnet DC motors as generators in their projects. This looked like a simpler way to go. So I began looking into what motors were best for the job.

A lot of people seemed to like to use old computer tape drive motors (surplus relics from the days when computers had big reel to reel tape drives). The best apparently are a couple of models of motor made by Ametek. The best motor made by Ametek is a 99 volt DC motor that works great as a generator. Unfortunately, they are almost impossible to locate these days. There are a lot of other Ametek motors around though. A couple of their other models make decent generators and can still be found on places like Ebay. This web site talks about the virtues and vices of various Ametek motors when used as generators. (http://www.tlgwindpower.com/ametek.htm)

There is more information on how to choose a motor for use as a generator on my web site at http://www.mdpub.com/Wind_Turbine.

## Step 2: Making the blades

Blades and a hub to connect them to were the next order of business. More online research ensued. A lot of people made their own blades by carving them out of wood. That looked like an outrageous amount of work to me. I found that other people were making blades by cutting sections out of PVC pipe and shaping them into airfoils. That looked a lot more promising to me. This web site tells you how to make a set of blades for a small wind turbine using PVC pipe: http://www.yourgreendream.com/diy_pvc_blades.php.

I followed their general recipe. I did things a little differently though. I used black ABS pipe since my local homecenter store just happened to have pre-cut lengths of it. I used 6 inch pipe instead of 4 inch and 24 inches long instead of 19 5/8. I started by quartering a 24 inch long piece of pipe around its circumference and cutting it lengthwise into four pieces. Then I cut out one blade, and used it as a template for cutting out the others. That left me with 4 blades (3 plus one spare).

I then did a little extra smoothing and shaping using my belt sander and palm sander on the cut edges to try to make them into better airfoils. I don't know if it's really much of an improvement, but it didn't seem to hurt, and the blades look really good (if I do say so myself).

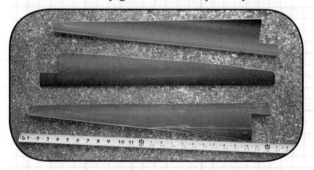

## Step 3: Building the hub

Next I needed a hub to bolt the blades to and attach to the motor. Rummaging around in my workshop, I found a toothed pulley that fit on the motor shaft, but was a little too small in diameter to bolt the blades onto. I also found a scrap disk of aluminum 5 inches in diameter and 1/4 inch thick that I could bolt the blades onto, but wouldn't attach to the motor shaft. The simple solution of course was to bolt these two pieces together to make the hub. Much drilling, tapping, and bolting later, I had a hub.

## Step 4: Building the turbine mounting

Next I needed a mounting for the turbine. Keeping it simple, I opted to just strap the motor to a piece of 2 X 4 wood. The correct length of the wood was computed by the highly scientific method of picking the best looking piece of scrap 2 X 4 off my scrap wood pile and going with however long it was. I also cut a piece of 4 inch diameter PVC pipe to make a shield to go over the motor and protect it from the weather. For a tail to keep it turned into the wind, I again just used a piece of heavy sheet aluminum I happened to have laying around. I was worried that it wouldn't be a big enough tail, but it seems to work just fine. The turbine snaps right around into the wind every time it changes direction.

Next I had to begin thinking about some sort of tower and some sort of bearing that would allow the head to freely turn into the wind. I spent a lot of time in my local homecenter stores (Lowes and Home Depot) brainstorming. Finally, I came up with a solution that seems to work well. While brainstorming, I noticed that 1 inch diameter iron pipe is a good slip-fit inside 1 1/4 inch diameter steel EMT electrical conduit. I could use a long piece of 1 1/4 inch conduit as my tower and 1 inch pipe fittings at either end. For the head unit I attached a 1 inch iron floor flange centered 7 1/2 inches back from the generator end of the 2X4, and screwed a 10 inch long iron pipe nipple into it. The nipple would slip into the top of the piece of conduit I'd use as a tower and form a nice bearing. Wires from the generator would pass through a hole drilled in the 2X4 down the center of the pipe/conduit unit and exit at the base of the tower. Brilliant! (if I do say so myself)

## Step 5: Build the tower base

For the tower base, I started by cutting a 2 foot diameter disk out of plywood. I made a U shaped assembly out of 1 inch pipe fittings. In the middle of that assembly I put a 1 1/4 inch Tee. The Tee is free to turn around the 1 inch pipe and forms a hinge that allows me to raise and lower the tower. I then added a close nipple, a 1 1/4 to 1 reducing fitting, and a 12 inch nipple. Later I added a 1 inch Tee between the reducer and the 12 inch nipple so there would be a place for the wires to exit the pipe. I also later drilled holes in the wooden disk to allow me to use steel stakes to lock it in place on the ground.

The second photo shows the head and base together. You can begin to see how it will go together. Imagine a 10 foot long piece of steel conduit connecting the two pieces. Since I was building this thing in Florida, but was going to use it in Arizona, I decided to hold off on purchasing the 10 foot piece of conduit until I got to Arizona. That meant the wind turbine would never be fully assembled and not get a proper test until I was ready to put it up in the field. That was a little scary because I wouldn't know if the thing actually worked until I tried it in Arizona.

## Step 6: Paint all the wood parts

Next, I painted all the wooden parts with a couple of coats of white latex paint I had leftover from another project. I wanted to protect the wood from the weather. I also added a lead counterweight to the left side of the 2 X 4 under the tail to balance the head.

## Step 7: The finished head of the wind turbine

I never got a chance to properly test the unit before heading to Arizona. One windy day though, I did take the head outside and hold it high up in the air above my head into the wind just to see if the blades would spin it as well as I had hoped. Spin it they did. In a matter of a few seconds it spun up to a truly scary speed (no load on the generator), and I found myself holding onto a giant, spinning, whirligig of death, with no idea how to put it down without getting myself chopped to bits. Fortunately, I did eventually manage to turn it out of the wind and slow it down to a non-lethal speed. I won't make that mistake again.

## Step 8: Build the charge controller

Now that I had all the mechanical parts sorted out, it was time to turn toward the electronic end of the project. A wind power system consists of the wind turbine, one or more batteries to store power produced by the turbine, a blocking diode to prevent power from the batteries being wasted spinning the motor/generator, a secondary load to dump power from the turbine into when the batteries are fully charged, and a charge controller to run everything.

There are lots of controllers for solar and wind power systems. Anyplace that sells alternative energy stuff will have them. There are also always lots of them for sale on Ebay. I decided to try building my own though. So it was back to Googling for information on wind turbine charge controllers. I found a lot of information, including some complete schematics, which was quite nice, and made building my own unit very easy. I based my unit on the schematic of the one found on this web site: http://www. fieldlines.com/story/2004/9/20/0406/27488.

Whether you build your own, or buy one, you will need some sort of controller for your wind turbine. The general principal behind the controller is that it monitors the voltage of the battery/batteries in your system and either sends power from the turbine into the batteries to recharge them, or dumps the power from the turbine into a secondary load if the batteries are fully charged (to prevent over-charging and destroying the batteries). The schematic and write-up on the above web page does a good job of explaining it. Much more information on building the charge controller, including larger and easier to read schematics, can be found on my web site at http://www.mdpub.com/Wind_Turbine/index.html.

In operation, the wind turbine is connected to the controller. Lines then run from the controller to the battery. All loads are taken directly from the battery. If the battery voltage drops below 11.9 volts, the controller switches the turbine power to charging the battery. If the battery voltage rises to 14 volts, the controller switches to dumping the turbine power into the dummy load. There are trimpots to adjust the voltage levels at which the controller toggles back and forth between the two states. I chose 11.9V for the discharge point and 14V for the fully charged point based on advice from lots of different web sites on the subject of properly charging lead acid batteries. The sites all recommended slightly different voltages. I sort of averaged them and came up with my numbers. When the battery voltage is between 11.9V and 14.8V, the system can be switched between either charging or dumping. A pair of push buttons allow me to switch between states anytime, for testing purposes. Normally the system runs automatically. When charging the battery, the yellow LED is lit. When the battery is charged and power is being dumped to the dummy load, the green LED is lit. This gives me some minimal feedback on what is going on with the system. I also use my multi-meter to measure both battery voltage, and turbine output voltage. I will probably eventually add either panel meters or automotive-style voltage and charge/discharge meters to the system. I'll do that once I have it in some sort of enclosure.

I used my variable voltage bench power supply to simulate a battery in various states of charge and discharge to test and tune the controller. I could set the voltage of the power supply to 11.9V and set the trimpot for the low voltage trip point. Then I could crank the voltage up to 14V and set the trimpot for the high voltage trimpot. I had to get it set before I took it into the field because I'd have no way to tune it up out there.

I have found out the hard way that it is important with this controller design to connect the battery first, then connect the wind turbine and/or solar panels. If you connect the wind turbine first, the wild voltage swings coming from the turbine won't be smoothed out by the load of the battery, the controller will behave erratically, the relay will click away wildly, and voltage spikes could destroy the ICs. So always connect to the battery/batteries first, then connect the wind turbine. Also, make sure you disconnect the wind turbine first when taking the system apart. Disconnect the battery/batteries last.

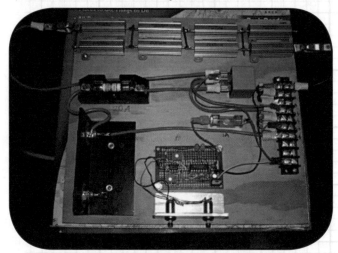

## Step 9: Erect the tower

At last, all parts of the project were complete. It was all done only a week before my vacation arrived. That was cutting it close. I disassembled the turbine and carefully packed the parts and the tools I'd need to assemble it for their trip across the country. Then I once again drove out to my remote property in Arizona for a week of off-grid relaxation, but this time with hopes of having some actual electricity on the site.

The first order of business was setting up and bracing the tower. After arriving at my property and unloading my van, I drove to the nearest Home Depot (about 60 miles one way) and bought the 10 foot long piece of 1 1/4 inch

green

conduit I needed for the tower. Once I had it, assembly went quickly. I used nylon rope to anchor the pole to four big wooden stakes driven in the ground. Turnbuckles on the lower ends of each guy-line allowed me to plumb up the tower. By releasing the line from either stake in line with the hinge at the base, I could raise and lower the tower easily. Eventually the nylon line and wooden stakes will be replaced with steel stakes and steel cables. For testing though, this arrangement worked fine.

I used chain-link fence brackets as tie points for my guy-lines. The fence brackets don't quite clamp down tightly on the conduit, which is smaller in diameter than the fence posts they are normally used with. So there is a steel hose clamp at either end of the stack of brackets to keep them in place.

I used an old orange extension cord with a broken plug to connect between the turbine and the controller. I simply cut both ends off and put on spade lugs. Threading the wire through the tower turned out to be easy. It was a cold morning and the cord was very stiff. I was able to just push it through the length of the conduit tower. on a warmer day I probably would have had to use a fishtape or string line to pull the cord through the conduit. I got lucky.

## Step 10: Erect the wind turbine

The first photo shows the turbine head installed on top of the tower. I greased up the pipe on the bottom of the head and slid it into the top of the conduit. It made a great bearing, just as I'd planned. Sometimes I even amaze myself.

Too bad there was nobody around to get an Iwo Jima Flag Raising type picture of me raising the tower up with the head installed.

The second photo shows the wind turbine fully assembled. Now I'm just waiting for the wind to blow. Wouldn't you know it, it was dead calm that morning. It was the first calm day I had ever seen out there. The wind had always been blowing every other time I had been there. Well, nothing to do but wait.

Finally! The wind was up and the turbine was spinning, and the lovely electricity was starting to be produced.

## Step 11: Connect the electronics

The battery, inverter, meter, and prototype charge controller are all sitting on a plywood board on top of a blue plastic tub. I plug a long extension cord into the inverter and run power back to my campsite. Lots more information of the electronics setup can be found on my web site at http://www.mdpub.com/Wind_Turbine.

Once the wind starts blowing, the turbine head snaps around into it and begins spinning up. It spins up quickly until the output voltage exceeds the battery voltage plus the blocking diode drop (around 13.2 volts, depending on the state of the battery charge). It is really running without a load until that point. Once the voltage is exceeded, the turbine suddenly has a load as it begins dumping power into the battery. Once under load, the RPMs only slightly increase as the wind speed increases. More wind means more current into the battery which means more load on the generator. So the system is pretty much self-governing. I saw no signs of over-revving. Of course in storm-force winds, all bets are off.

Switching the controller to dump power into the dummy load did a good job of braking the turbine and slowing it way down even in stronger gusts. Actually shorting the turbine output is an even better brake. It brings the turbine to a halt right now, even in strong winds. Shorting the output is how I made the turbine safe to raise and lower, so I wouldn't get sliced and diced by the spinning blades. Warning though, the whole head assembly can still swing around and crack you hard on the noggin if the wind changes direction while you are working on these things. So be careful out there.

## Step 12: Enjoy having power in the middle of nowhere

How sweet it is! I have electricity! Here I have my laptop computer set up and plugged into the power provided by the inverter, which in turn is powered by the wind turbine. I normally only have about two hours of battery life on my laptop. So I don't get to use it much while I'm camping. It comes in handy though for downloading photos out of my camera when its memory card gets full, making notes on projects like this one, working

green

on the next great American novel, or just watching DVD movies. Now I have no battery life problems, at least as long as the wind blows. Besides the laptop, I can also now recharge all my other battery powered equipment like my cell phone, my camera, my electric shaver, my air mattress pump, etc. Life used to get real primitive on previous camping trips when the batteries in all my electronic stuff ran down.

I used the wind turbine to power my new popup trailer on a later vacation. The strong spring winds kept the wind turbine spinning all day every day and most of the nights too while I was in Arizona. The turbine provided

enough power for the interior 12V lighting and enough 120V AC at the power outlets to keep my battery charger, electric shaver, and mini vacuum cleaner (camping is messy) all charged up and running. My girlfriend complained about it not having enough power to run her blow-dryer though.

## Step 13: How much did it cost?

So how much did all this cost to build? Well, I saved all the receipts for everything I bought related to this project.

Part, Origin, Cost
Motor/Generator, Ebay, $26.00
Misc. pipe fittings, Homecenter Store, $41.49
Pipe for blades, Homecenter Store, $12.84
Misc hardware, Homecenter Store, $8.00
Conduit, Homecenter Store, $19.95
Wood & Aluminum Scrap Pile, $0.00
Power Cable, Old extension cord, $0.00
Rope & Turnbuckles, Homecenter Store, $18.47
Electronic Parts Already on hand, $0.00

Relay, Auto Parts Store, $13.87
Battery, Borrowed from my UPS, $0.00
Inverter, Already on hand, $0.00
Paint, Already on hand, $0.00
Total $140.62

Not too bad. I doubt I could buy a commercially made turbine with a comparable power output, plus a commercially made charge controller, plus a commercially made tower, for less than $750-$1000.

More details on this project and my other alternative energy projects including my home-built solar panels, and my home-built biomass gasifier, can be found on my web site: http://www.mdpub.com.

## Step 14: Update

I have completed the rebuild of the charge controller. It is now in a semi-weatherproof enclosure and I have also added a built-in voltage meter. Both were bought cheap on Ebay. I have also added a few new features. The unit now has provisions for power inputs from multiple sources. It also has built-in fused 12V power distribution for three external loads.

The photo shows the inside of the charge controller. I basically just transferred everything that I originally had bolted onto the plywood board in the prototype into this box. I added an automotive illuminated voltage gage and fuses for 3 external 12V loads. I used heavy gauge wire to try to reduce losses due to wire resistance. Every watt counts when you are living off-grid.

The setup for the new charge controller is pretty much the same as the old one except for the addition of the Volt meter and extra fuse blocks for the external loads. An easy to read version of the schematic, and more information on the new charge controller can be found on my web site at http://www.mdpub.com/Wind_Turbine.

green

# Plastic Smithing: How to Make Your Own HDPE Plastic Anything (DIY Plastic Lumber)

By Star Simpson (stasterisk)
http://www.instructables.com/id/
HomemadePlastic/

How to make really good hard plastic while reusing and recycling plastic bags at home! Via this method, you can make ANYTHING you want to, out of hard, lightweight, real plastic that's astoundingly durable. It comes out very similar in texture to recycled plastic lumber.

Best of all, this method involves no fumes!

By the end of this, you'll be able to make yourself a knife sheath, mold around your shoes, and make DIY hard-toe sneakers, wheels, bearings, bushings, or any kind of plastic part!

## Step 1: Materials

Collect all the plastic bags you can get, they shrink down a lot. Shredding them will make your final texture finer.

Use an old pot that you aren't going to use for food any more, or get one secondhand for really cheap at a thrift store.

Find a stick or something else you can use for a spatula. I liked the clothespin a lot because I could pick things up as well as stir.

Oh, and oil! (I used canola because it was right there next to my stove. If you're, for example, making a bearing, you can impregnate it with your personal favorite grease.) Cooking oil boils around 350, which is far too hot for plastic, and which you don't want anyway (splashing boiling oil = no fun unless you're a Hun), so I keep it to a nice low-viscosity canola oil heat and things work just fine. If you wanted a smooth, non-oily finished surface, consider using wax instead.

## Step 2: Add oil, and stew

Thanks to reader concern, I will state what may not be obvious from the pictures: there are no fumes. There's no smoke, no fans, no inhalation hazard. If there's smoke or fumes, you're doing something wrong and you're burning the plastic. That's why you use oil for temperature regulation.

## Step 3: Mash it

When it's tacky like chewing gum, start mashing it around to get the different bag-lumps to stick to each other. A hand blender would be exceptionally helpful in this situation, but I chose to merely wreck one of my mom's forks instead.

## Step 4: Get moldy

Now, while it's still pliable, put it into the form you want! Since I'm just experimenting, I grabbed a salsa container that looked about the right shape for a wheel mold, and a wine bottle to make the hole in the middle.

If you were a molding ninja, you could make a plastic positive of your own face!

## Step 5: Freeze

Let it cool like cookies, or if you're impatient, make it cool faster in the freezer.

## Step 6: Enjoy!

There's the finished thing. It's got a lot of visual texture/color swirls, but it's actually a pretty regular surface. The circle turned out very well, and you can carve on this, machine it, turn it, and drill it, if you want something more precise.

Also exciting! If you machined down a brick like this into large-ish chunks, you could feed them to your homemade injection molder! DIY action figures, hooray!

# Building a Vertical Axis Wind Turbine (VAWT)

By Erik van Baarle (rikkiesix)
(http://www.instructables.com/id/Building-a-Vertical-Axis-Wind-Turbine-VAWT-/)

When building this turbine we will be using some powertools. If you are not used to working with power-tools ask someone who knows how to use them. After building this turbine you will still need your fingers so PLEASE BE CAREFUL!

## Step 1: Tools and parts
**Tools:**

- Jigsaw and or band saw
- Hand saw
- Lathe
- Drill press or hand drill
- Drill bits
- Screwdriver
- Tab tool
- Ruler
- Pencil
- Compass
- Sanding paper
- Vise (it makes the work easier)
- Wrenches
- 2 clamps

**Parts:**

- PVC pipe
- Waterproof wood "concrete form plywood is the best" (if you don't have that you will have to protect it with a coating)
- 2 Bearings (bottom one needs to be able to handle a load)
- Grease nipple
- Wire rod (2 sizes) (1 big one and 4 small ones) (Stainless if possible)
- Bolts and washers (2 sizes) (Stainless if possible)
- A piece of 40 mm round aluminium (Alloy) (it will hold the bottom bearing)
- 2 Angle irons
- 3 eye screws

## Step 2: Let's get started
First thing you will do is measure your PVC pipe and cut it in 4 equal pieces. (Mine was 2 meters long, which became 50 cm a piece.)

When you have done that you will cut it over the hole length.

Now you should have 8 pieces (they should be exactly the same size).

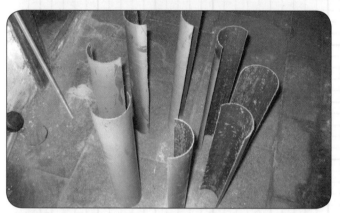

## Step 3: Making the 2 disks of the turbine
Take 2 pieces of waterproof plywood (12 mm). Measure in 2 directions to get the middle of the plate and mark that point.

Take your compass and make a circle of 40 cm diameter. Grab your jigsaw and cut them out.

green

## Step 4: Divide your circle in 8 pieces

Here is a link I have found to do this job quickly and precise: http://www.weborix.com/8.htm.

You only have to do this on one plank. In the next step I will explain why.

## Step 5: Cutting the slots for the turbine blades

The way I did it was to draw the lines on 2 of the planks and then mark all the bows that I had to cut. This I would not do again! I think its better to mark only one.

The bows you draw like this: take one half pipe and hold it against one of the 8 lines you drew before. Draw a line on the inside and the outside of the pipe. The one where you marked the bows on you put on top and then clamp them together. When you cut them they will be exactly the same.

I used a sawblade that's normally meant for cutting metal. That saw blade was just a fraction thinner then the blades.

On the side of the 2 disks you make a marking that runs over both of them. This way when you are assembling the turbine the disks will line up perfectly.

What you also should do when they're still clamped is drill the centerhole to the size of your big wire rod and the 4 holes for the small rods. Divide the 4 rods equally over your turbine. Stay about 2 cm away from the bows. That way you can still place some washers on your rods without them touching the blades. Take the clamps off and mount the turbine blades and the 4 smaller rods as shown in the last picture. It needs to be a tight fit!

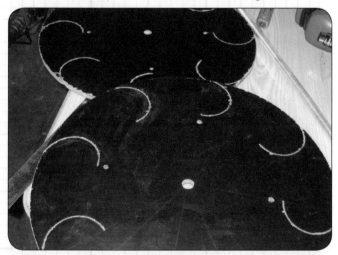

## Step 6: Making the center wire rod to size

First you mount the top of the turbine just as you did for the bottom in the step before.

Pay attention to the markings you made on the sides of the disks when they were still clamped. This way the same cuts will be nicely on top of each other and the turbine will wobble less after its finished. You might want to use a hammer and a little piece of wood to not damage the blades or the disk when you hit it. Make sure the

blades fit tight and the 4 little rods are in the right place. It was not a easy job. Good luck.

Now we will fit the big wire rod with the necessary bolts and washers.

What we're going to do now is mark where we will cut off the wire rod. The first picture is a view from the bottom disk. I put 2 bolts there and they will rest on the bottom bearing. I left the wire longer there so I couldconnect a generator of some sort there. The upper disk is the second picture and the rod will be cut shorter. On that side we will only have a bearing to balance the turbine when it's in place on its frame.

## Step 7: Turning the wire rod down to the right size

If you have a lathe this is a pretty straight forward job. I made the rod 10 mm thick on both sides.

Make sure it fits nicely because this will determine how smooth your turbine will run.

## Step 8: Making the holder for the bottom bearing

The bearing I used is made out of 3 parts as shown on the first picture.

This bearing is made to cope with vertical weight.

If you watch closely you will see that the 2 disks don't have the same inner size hole.

The disk with the biggest hole (the one on the right) is the top part of the bearing where the turbine will rest on.

I cut the hole out on the lathe just the diameter of the bearing. Do this according to the size of the bearing you will use.

Don't make the hole too deep!

Make sure that the top part of the bearing is just sticking out of the holder.

The reason for this is that the top ring will spin together with the turbine and would otherwise rub against the inside of the holder and would slow your turbine down and wear it out quickly.

You will also have to drill a hole through the bottom of the holder so the wire rod can fit through.

Make it slightly bigger then the size of the rod so

once it's mounted it will not touch the sides.

You have seen that this bearing has no grease in it so we will have to install a grease nipple.

Use a thread cutting tool to do so.

First drill a hole according to the tread and the nipple size you will use. Mine was M6.

Use some cutting oil because you're cutting in aluminum and otherwise it will get all rough on the inside. Run the cutting tool for about 1 turn and then run it back for half a turn. This way the metal is cut inside and you will not brake your tool. Use the 3 stages of cutting until you reach the right tread.

## Step 9: Making a frame around your turbine

First you get two pieces of wood that are exactly the same length.

Make sure they are wide enough so you can make a strong structure.

Look for the center of both of them and make a hole the size of the bearing holder for the bottom one and the size of the top bearing for the top one. I was lucky I had a big drill to do so. If not, take your biggest drill bit and drill it out and then cut the rest out with a round axe.

For the bottom one you have to drill the center of the hole through with a drill one size bigger then the size of the big wire rod that will fit into the bearing. For the bottom one you will have to cut out a little slot so the nipple can fit inside and so that you have enough space to put in the grease pump. You can see what it should look like on the pictures.

Take two more straight pieces of wood for the sides. (I had some plywood so I used that.)

Take the bottom piece with the bearing holder inside and put it on a flat surface.

Use one of the side pieces and screw it on there. First drill some holes in the side so the screws will go in better. Make sure it's perfectly square (90 degree angle).

Do the same thing for the other side.

Now take your turbine that's completely assembled and lower it into the bottom bearing.

Now take the top piece and slide the bearing over the big rod. Measure on both sides of the turbine and make sure you measure the same distance; that way your frame will be perfectly square.

## Step 10: Building the support for the turbine

This stuff I did not really measure.

I made sure that everything was in perfect line with the axel of the turbine.

Just build it as you can see from the pictures.

Just make sure it's strong cause there will be a lot of power on it.

I did not connect any generator yet.

Had no idea what to connect to it.

I was thinking of another power generator (coils and neo magnets).

Ideas are welcome.

I hope you enjoyed building this turbine.

Keep me informed on your building.

## Step 11:

I connected some ropes to the turbine to hold it stable. I used some old pins from a tent to connect the ropes to the ground and at the side of the turbine I used 3 eye screws. Works well.

When you put up your turbine make sure to have someone that can hold the turbine while you connect the wires to the ground.

   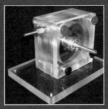

# science

When fundamental principles of science are combined with DIY creativity and ingenuity, there's no limit to the astounding projects that can be created. The following science-based projects help illuminate and unlock inspiring scientific principles in a tangible way. Use the projects in this chapter as teaching tools for educational purposes about such topics as air quality and light refraction. And whatever the motivation was for the builders of these projects to involve some kind of science in their work, we're glad that they did, and always excited to see what instructables users come up with next.

# Star Map

By Patrick Barnes (MrTrick)
(http://www.instructables.com/id/Star-Map/)

Light up your home with this breathtaking piece of sky!

I made this star map last year for my wife, and everyone who sees it wants to know how it was made.

Be warned, to build something like this is a big project. You should expect to know:

- Basic woodworking skills
- How to handle a soldering iron
- How to design LED-based circuits
- How to safely deal with AC voltages

And above all, you'll need plenty of spare time.

This star map is a little over 2m wide, and 1.2m tall. It weighs 12-15kg and has somewhere between 1500-2000 optical fiber stars and 108 LED stars.

You could quite easily use some of the techniques in here to make a small version, and it would still look really nice. This instructable, then, can be used as a general reference for building star maps, not just how to replicate mine exactly. There is some additional info for small maps in the Addenda section.

## Step 1: Materials: optical fibers

Note: You can't use fishing line. Don't even think about it. It just doesn't conduct light in the right way. (http://www.cockeyed.com/incredible/fiber/fiber1.php)

You can buy optical fiber by the reel, but there are better and cheaper ways to get it. For large star maps, a fake Christmas tree works very well!

For smaller star maps, the retro-tastic 'UFO Lamps' are a great source of fibers and are pretty easy to find in dollar stores.

Both of these sources are great! They are cheap, and they terminate all the fibers into one place, so it is easy to light the stars.

Just consider:

- The more stars you have, the better it will look. Try to find a tree or lamp with plenty of 'points.'
- The size of the tree/lamp will determine how large your map can be. For example, if you have a 120cm/4ft tree, you can build a map about 2m/6.5ft wide. (Of course, the exact shape of the tree and your frame will affect the maximum. Get your measurements right before you buy/cut anything expensive.)

## Step 2: Materials: light sources

Trees and lamps come with a light source, of course—typically a small halogen bulb. These are hot, inefficient bulbs, and they don't last very long. You will not want your masterpiece to catch fire or break down, so use LEDs!

For smaller maps, you might find an array of 5mm high-brightness LEDs quite appropriate, but I needed something bigger: a 3W LED spot (http://www.dealextreme.com/details.dx/sku.15070). This bulb runs off AC voltage, and generates a narrow beam—perfect for illuminating the terminator. Unlike a halogen bulb, it will last for years, and use about a tenth of the power.

It is not ideal to have all of the stars be the same brightness. In my case I wanted to highlight the constellations, so those brighter stars had a small 3mm or 5mm LED dedicated to each one. A smaller star map may be better off using LEDs with a small integrated light-pipe for constellation stars.

As poster Little Red suggested, you could alternatively use a store-bought string of LED lights if you're not confident in designing your own circuit. This might work out well, just remember that LED strings are usually a constant distance apart, so there could be a lot of splicing to do to make them reach your constellations.

## Step 3: Materials: everything else

The other main components are:

- A frame: If making a small map, you can use a store-bought picture frame. At large sizes, you'll need to make it yourself.
- Substrate: something that the fibers will be poked through. I used a large piece of double-thick corrugated cardboard, covered in black cloth. You could

also use thin plywood, or as commenter **astack** suggested, foam-core board.

- Backing: something to stop light leaking out behind the frame. I used black cloth.
- Power supply and control circuitry: This depends on your light sources. It could simply be a battery and an on/off switch. Mine is a little more involved, read on for more info.

**To build a map just like mine, you will need:**

- Lumber: Lengths in the frame width you want, and smaller pieces for the inner frame.
- Fasteners: Screws and right-angle brackets
- Stain: Black stain to get the frame the right color.
- A refrigerator or air-conditioner box—something big and cardboard.
- Cloth: Black cotton drill, or anything that doesn't stretch and blocks light well.
- Fiber-optic Christmas tree
- 3W LED spotlight
- 108 white LEDs, other associated components (wire, resistors, etc)
- 30V DC power supply (or similar)
- RF switch module
- Heatshrink and acrylic rod
- Tools: Hand-saw, clamps, screwdriver, box cutter, side-cutters, pliers, a needle, plenty of tape, wood glue, stapler, multimeter, bench power supply, breadboa
- Lots of patience.

## Step 4: Planning and design

As mentioned earlier, the maximum size of the star map is determined by the fibers you have—the most effective place to mount the terminator is flat in the center of the board, and the longest fibers need to reach into the corners of the map. Some simple trigonometry will determine your maximum dimensions. (*Allow 5% extra, because the fibers will not always be perfectly straight.*)

Due to the large size of this star map, the frame is built in two pieces—an inner and outer frame. The outer frame is what the audience sees, and will be stained black. The inner frame supports the cardboard substrate and fabric front, and is hidden behind the outer frame.

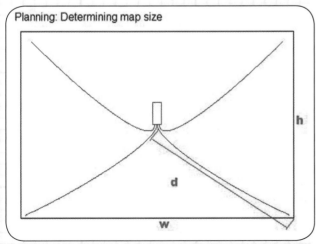

Planning: Determining map size

## Step 5: Planning and design: it's full of stars!

One *could* use a random pattern of stars, but where is the fun in that? Making your stars an accurate replica of the sky is easy! Celestia is a fantastic sky-searching program, and among other things, you can use it to generate a high-resolution star map.

- Download and install Celestia. (www.shatters.net/celestia)
- Go to *Render->View Options*, switch off Planets, and show Constellation diagrams.
- Go to *Render->Star Style*, and select 'Scaled Discs'

Now, find the area of sky that you wish to display. Using "[" and "]" you can adjust the number of stars shown, and using "," and "." you can adjust the field of view (FOV). To capture the image, go to full-screen mode (**Alt+Enter**) and press **F10**.

Getting the right number of stars might be a bit tricky. If you have too many stars visible you may run out of fibers three quarters of the way through construction. If you have too few you'll end up with a sparser star map, and lots of left-over fibers. I suggest taking a sample image, counting every star in a small fraction of the image, and extrapolating from that to estimate the total number of stars.

So, find yourself a pretty section of sky, and save a nice high-resolution image. How do you get that design onto the star map? Read on.

## Step 6: Building the frames

The inner frame:

From 42x19mm pine, build a butt-jointed frame so that the internal space is equal to the map area. Screw together using countersunk screws.

The outer frame:

From 200x19mm pine (or a decorative wood if desired) build a flat miter-jointed frame, with the same internal space. Again, this frame will be seen, so it can be decoratively built if desired. These pieces are kept together with angled plates. A taut strap around the outside of the frame will help keep it square until the angle plates are attached.

Turn the outer frame over.

Place the inner frame on top of the outer frame. Drill pilot holes and screw the two frames together from the back (so that no screws or holes will be visible in the front when the frame is completed).

## Step 7: Painting the Frame

*(Only the outer frame needs to be painted, but it helps to keep the frames together for now because the inner frame elevates the outer frame off the ground.)*

Paint or stain the frame according to your preference and the instructions on the can. I put a coat of sealant on the wood, then five coats of black stain to get a nice almost-black finish.

## Step 8: Attaching the substrate

Place the substrate (cardboard or thin plywood) over the inner frame. It helps if the material is slightly oversized. Using a staple gun, fix the material to the inner frame. (Take care to avoid placing staples over the screw holes)

Once secured in place, trim around the outside of the frame to make the substrate flush with the edges.

## Step 9: Attaching the front material

*(If the substrate you use will take a nice finish, you may be able to just paint it black instead of attaching cloth.)*

I covered the front of my star map in black cotton drill. To stretch the material over the frame is fairly simple, and is done in the same way as stretching canvas. An instructable by **Gburg_06** (http://www.instructables.com/id/How-to-Stretch-a-Canvas-Painting) shows in more detail how to do this, but put simply:

- Stretch the canvas out flat and staple to the back of the frame.
- Start at the center of each side, and gradually move to each corner.
- Again, avoid placing staples over the screw holes.

Cotton drill is not as tough a material as canvas, so it may also help to fold the edge of the fabric over before stapling through it.

## Step 10: Attaching the map to the back of the substrate

Now that you have the view of the night sky you want, here is how to transfer it to the back of your frame. Open the Celestia screenshot in a graphical editor (I use Gimp, but even MS Paint will do), invert the colors, and mirror the image.

Then, using PosteRazor (http://posterazor.sourceforge.net/) or a similar tool, scale your image up to the right size

for the map, print it onto multiple pieces of paper, and trim off the margins. Using thinned wood glue, glue each page to the back of the frame. Now you can use the enlarged image as a template to place all the star points.

*(Remember, it must be mirrored, or you will end up placing all of your constellations backwards!)*

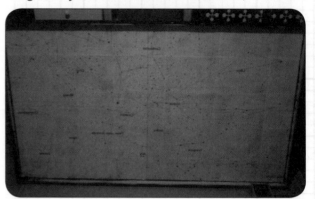

## Step 11: Chop down the Christmas tree!

You will need:

- Pliers
- Box cutter
- Patience
- Patience
- Patience

The goal here is to remove the tree from the fibers. Most trees are constructed from steel rod (the trunk), wire (for the branches), and the leaves; stuff that looks like, but is not quite, tinsel. The fibers run right up the middle of everything (of course), so to remove the fibers you have to disassemble the whole tree.

Starting at the bottom, carefully break open some of the material wrapped around the trunk, and start unwinding. There will be lots of sticky-tape holding it in place, but just carefully peel the 'leaves' back. Each branch will have a similar arrangement, just continue peeling back the 'leaves' until there is none left. Now, you will have to remove any other sticky-tape holding the tree together, and the fibers should be left on their own. Many many many hours later, you will have something like this left.

When the tree has been taken apart, try to group fibers of similar lengths together—this will make it easier when building the map.

## Step 12: Mounting the terminator and light source

The termination point of the fiber bundle needs to be fixed in place in the center of the frame. Cut a short piece of pine and screw it to the top side of the inner frame—this means that it will 'float' over the substrate, but still be strong enough to support the light assembly and keep it in place.

Screw a clean food tin to the support, and mount the LED spotlight so that it is centered inside the tin. Using a centering spacer made of wood and a pipe clamp, fix the terminator to the support so that it lines up with the spotlight, at a distance so that the entire terminator is lit, but there is not too much light spillage. It will help to determine this optimal distance *before* attaching anything together!

*(The LED spotlight is fixed inside a standard GU10 AC socket and attached to a bracket I happened to have lying around. You could use a wooden spacer and a pipe clamp to achieve a similar effect.)*

## Step 13: Initial fiber placement

Spread out the fiber bundle over the inner frame. Using masking tape, organize roughly where each bunch of fibers belongs, so that you have good coverage over the entire map.

It may help to use highlighter pens to divide the star map into radial 'sectors.' Each sector thus needs approximately the same number of fiber bundles at each distance.

## Step 14: Poking through and gluing the fibers

There is no way around this—placing the fibers takes a *long* time! **(Read the next step, though, before you start this.)**

For each small point of light, poke a hole through the substrate with a heavy-duty needle. Thick cardboard is tough, so you will need to push the needle through with the help of a pair of pliers. (If you are using something tougher, like plywood, you will need to drill hundreds if not thousands of tiny holes with a drill. Good luck.)

Gently feed a single fiber through the hole you have just made. If you have thick cardboard or fabric on the front you may need to twist the fiber carefully to poke it through. If you push too hard, the fiber will kink. If this happens, trim below the kink and try again. Once through, keep pushing the fiber in until there is just a little slack left on the back side. It helps to feel on the other side so you know when the fiber has gone through properly. (Take care that the fiber doesn't get misdirected down a corrugation of the cardboard)

Using wood glue, apply a drop to the fiber where it feeds through the back of the hole. (IT MUST BE WOOD GLUE! If you use anything with solvents, like super glue, the fibers will craze internally and stop transmitting light properly.)

Of course, it is best to punch lots of holes in one go, then poke through lots of fibers, then glue a lot, then repeat. And repeat. And repeat. Take breaks occasionally, because constantly gripping the pliers and poking the fibers through will start to hurt after an hour or two. (The Mk II hole poker, with the needle taped to one jaw, the jaws taped shut, and the handles squeezed together and similarly taped is **very** handy.)

Eventually, you should have placed every fiber into your star map. Take a deep breath, and relax. It's quite pretty, even viewed from the back.

## Step 15: Secondary light sources: planning

**Note**: *You will have an easier time if you place all the secondary lights before you place the fibers. The steps are still in this order, because I placed the fibers for half of*

science

*the map, placed the secondary lights, then finished up with the fibers.*

To light the brighter and constellation stars, it works well to use individual LEDs. These need to be driven by a power supply of their own, as the LED spotlight I use only has an internal power supply. I had an old printer power supply that supplied 30V, 400mA. This is ideal, as the high voltage allows me to drive multiple LEDs in series.

This next bit is somewhat technical. If you aren't confident with LED circuits, consider reviewing some of the simpler LED-based instructables on this site, or consider whether it would be appropriate to use LED Christmas lights instead.

For a given power supply voltage, you can run up to **N** LEDs in series, where **N**\*forward-voltage-drop is less than that of the voltage. At full brightness, the LEDs I used have a forward voltage drop of 3.15V. If I have a 30V power supply, I can run up to 9 LEDs in series with a small ballast resistor. (Don't forget though, in most cases a ballast resistor will still be needed)

For a given power supply amperage, you can run up to **M** LED chains in parallel, where the current through one LED \* **M** is less than the power supply amperage. If I have a 400mA power supply, I can run up to 20 chains of LEDs. (In practice though, you don't want to have a power supply running at its maximum capacity in an enclosed space for long periods of time—the lifetime of the power supply will be reduced.)

Count the number of brighter stars on your map. In my case, there were 108 constellation stars. Inside the space of possible LED array arrangements, I chose to have 12 chains of 9 LEDs.

If you have a large number of LEDs to power, it may help to build a junction board. This simple circuit board splits the 30VDC supply into 12 sockets, each with an appropriately-sized ballast resistor. It makes wiring much easier!

## Step 16: Secondary light sources—planning II

One important feature that I did not immediately implement in the junction board was brightness control. In hindsight, that was a mistake—108 x 20000mcd white

LEDs, plus the 3W primary light source, is just blinding! However, it is not a difficult feature to add.

As the schematic below shows, a potentiometer controls the voltage, and thus the amount of current flowing into the base of an NPN transistor. The transistor then allows a proportional amount of current to flow across it, thus controlling the brightness of any LEDs attached. My test circuit was controlling a single LED from a 5V source, but the principle for 108 LEDs was exactly the same; just connect the negative ends of the LEDs/resistor chains to the transistor, instead of straight to ground.

Choose a transistor able to cope with plenty of power, and attach a heatsink.

## Step 17: Secondary light sources: assembling light pipes

I did not want the LEDs to poke straight through to the front. For one thing, 5mm is too wide! Also, the substrate was too thick for an LED to reach all the way through. Instead, obtain a few meters of clear acrylic rod. It conducts light like an optical fiber, only it's 2-3mm in diameter.

Put together a pile of as many LEDs as you'll need, a pile of 2cm-lengths of heat-shrink large enough to go over an LED, and a pile of 2.5cm-lengths of acrylic rod. (You can quite easily cut the rod with a good pair of side-cutters)

Assemble the LED, heat-shrink, and acrylic rod together, then using a soldering iron or a heat gun shrink them together. Try to avoid getting the LED too hot, as it can kill them. Repeat until you have a hundred or so of these assemblies. (This is, believe it or not, another step that takes a long time.)

**Note**: *I initially tried melting acrylic rod directly onto the LED. The LED is a different type of plastic so the rod does not 'stick' properly, the acrylic starts to darken when it is heated, and lots of noxious gases are produced. Not recommended.*

## Step 18: Secondary light sources: installing

Drill a hole through every large star to the same diameter as the light pipes. (Don't forget to go through the fabric as well) Place each of the LED/pipe assemblies into the holes.

For your array layout (in my case, 12 chains of 9), plan the best way to wire up your chains. Then, carefully solder each LED in a chain together, from the shorter negative lead of the previous LED to the longer positive lead of the next. At the ends of each chain, there should be a clearly indicated red (positive) and black (negative) end, and ideally have some sort of keyed connector back to the junction board to make life easier.

At this stage, you should test your LED chains to make sure all the LEDs work, and are connected the right way around. Ease of access is one reason it is better to wire in the secondary light sources *before* you put the optical fibers through. The other reason is that optic fibers are made of thin filaments of plastic, and tend to melt right through at the slightest touch from a soldering iron, so keep them well apart from one another.

Once everything is working, apply some wood glue around the outside of each LED assembly to keep them in place, and make the connections neat.

## Step 19: Narcissism

What is a work of art without a signature? Using a piece of veroboard as a spacing template, I poked a signatory pattern through one corner of the map. Then, I set up a colored LED for each row with some heat-shrink, lighting some left-over fibers.

These LEDs are connected into the same 30V power supply as the other secondary light sources. The circuit is simply three LEDs in series with an appropriate ballast resistor, soldered to a small piece of veroboard.

## Step 20: Trimming

You may have been wondering what happened to the extra lengths of fiber that have been pushed through to the other side. Well, it's a pretty sight, but it doesn't look like stars yet.

Turn the frame around so you can access the other side. If your working area is carpeted, put down some newspaper. (Trust me, I'm still finding stray fibers stuck in the carpet.)

With a pair of side cutters, cut off every fiber and light pipe so that only about 2-3mm is still poking through the front of the substrate. You don't want to cut it completely flush, or the fiber might pop back through the fabric.

This stage is disappointingly *much* quicker than placing all the fibers. When finished, gather up and dispose of the thousands of short fibers you have cut. (*I tried to think of a use for them, but other than those in the signature I only ended up using one as a cat-taunting toy.*)

science

## Step 21: Wiring

I needed a way to switch the whole map on and off, but the outlets nearest to the star map would be very hard to reach. To make it just that little bit cooler, I used a R/F controlled AC switch. (http://www.dealextreme.com/details.dx/sku.3072) This gadget has exposed AC terminals, so it must be safely housed inside the frame of the star map.

As a bonus, the switch module has two channels, so another AC circuit can be controlled, up to 500W.

The top-level schematic shows how all the components of the system are connected.

*WARNING: A good portion of the wiring is at mains voltage and can be very dangerous. If you don't know what you're doing, don't. Even if you think you know what you're doing, make sure that the outlet you are using is protected by an RCD (Residual Current Device, also known as a Ground Fault Circuit Interrupter). Do not lick wires.*

Commenter **static** asked why an RCD on the outlet's circuit would be necessary for a device like the star map— because if while you are wiring it up you accidentally do something stupid it's better to have the RCD trip and say to yourself, "I just did something stupid," than to risk electrocution.

The switch module and power supply should be placed inside the edges of the frame, and secured with screws and wire as appropriate. Ensure that the power cables have some kind of strain relief, and if possible use a terminal block with an insulating cover.

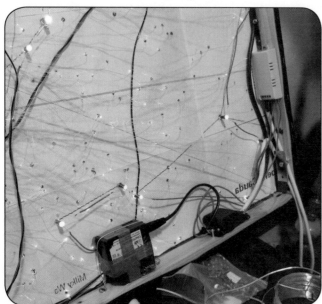

## Step 22: Putting it all together

Now that the map is all wired up and all the fibers have been glued and cut, it can go back together! Mount the inner frame back onto the outer frame, and screw it back together. The screws will now go through the inner frame, through the substrate and fabric, then into the outer frame.

Next, staple more black cloth to the back of the frame to block out any light leakage, and to protect the fibers and electronics.

## Step 23: Hanging around

In my estimation, the frame weighs between 12 and 15kg. It is going to hang above my head while I sleep. **Don't skimp on the hardware that stops it from falling!** I'm using a heavy-duty dyna-hook straight into a brick wall; it would probably hold my entire weight, albeit uncomfortably.

Put two long screws into the top edge of the inner frame, and put some fairly heavy-duty wire between them. Hang the frame up on the wall, do not knock any ornaments over in the process, plug it in, and done!

## Step 24: Bask in the glow

Totally worth it.

*(That second RF switch channel? It runs the lava lamps on either side of the star map.)*

# Homebuilt 6" F15 Refractor and Mount

### By Astrochef

(http://www.instructables.com/id/Homebuilt-6-F15-Refractor-and-Mount/)

Hello fellow Instructables. What better way to celebrate space than to look at it through a really big telescope? I have been an ATM for quite a while and this is my latest project, a big refracting telescope on a big mount.

## Step 1: Gathering parts

The mount is made from mostly easy-to-find scrap parts I found on line. I spent a lot of time looking for scrap pieces that were close to sizes I needed until I found that the metal merchants would cut pieces to size for pretty cheap. I used common power tools such as a small drill press, router, circular saw, and chop saw. Working with aluminum is a lot like working with very hard woods, the cutting feels the same but slower.

The chassis is made of 1/2" sheet aluminum. The bearings are pillow block bearings. The Main(RA) shaft is 2-5/8" diameter aluminum and the smaller(dec) shaft is 1-1/6" steel. The large worm gear was purchased cheaply from an astronomy website.

## Step 2: Routing aluminum

This is a step that I thought about for a good long while. An equatorial mount has to have some adjustment for the angle of altitude in order to track properly. The angle for your location is your latitude. Where I am, the mount needs to be set at 42 degrees. I decided to make the angle adjustable about 5 deg either way. To make these small arcs I used a circle-cutter attachment on my router and made quick 1/8" passes until I cut through each side of the chassis.

## Step 3: Basic chassis assembly

I trimmed the mounting tabs from the large pillow block bearings and ground down the sides with an angle grinder. After some drilling and some tapping, I bolted the base chassis up.

I added a brace and tapped a hole for an adjustment bolt. Turning this bolt allows the angle to be adjusted then clamped down when it's right.

## Step 4: The RA shaft

My large pillow block bearings were sold to me as 3"ID. However, when they arrived they were closer to 2-5/8"ID. I was able to find 2-5/8" aluminum cylinder and had it pressed into a 6" dia 1" thick disk. Pressing the shaft in is a very strong and stiff junction and is a job for a metal shop with a press. My local machine shop charged me $20.

## Step 5: The Dec shaft

I had the 1-1/16" dia x 24" long dec shaft pressed into a 2-1/2" x 2" x 10" aluminum bar. For the correct alignment of the tube, this unit has to be trued on a lathe. Another $20 to the machine shop.

I felt like Thor when I carried this into the house.

## Step 6: The Dec shaft assembly

The dec shaft rides in two 1-1/16"ID pillow block bearings mounted to a 1/2" aluminum plate, which is bolted to the RA shaft. I added a 4"wx14"l aluminum bar to mount the tube rings.

## Step 7: Mounting of the large drive gear

In a big scope the accuracy of the tracking is directly tied to the size of the worm gear. Big worm gear means smaller errors. A big worm gear also needs a smaller drive motor. This gear is clamped between two circles of HDPE, which is actually cutting board material. I routed two 12" circles to act as clutch plates as well as a smaller 6" donut for the gear to ride on. This assembly is clamped tight via two threaded shafts. This clutch arrangement allows the tube to be moved anywhere while the motor turns for effortless pointing and tracking.

## Step 8: Worm drive assembly

The worm drive is built from pieces of aluminum bar cut from left over material. The worm gear came from another smaller drive and happened to fit. The shaft rides in oilite bushings. Gear slack is taken up by a screw that presses the shaft from the side and prevents lateral movement of the gear. Each piece of this unit took a couple of tries because, to avoid binding, some precision was involved. By precision

science

I mean drilling holes over and over until finally the shaft stopped binding!

The motor is a synchronous timing motor that runs at a set speed from household voltage. These are used in older or simple telescope drives because it uses the frequency of your house voltage to keep accurate speed.

Adjustments of the speed can be accomplished by the use of a square-wave frequency generator, a simple circuit that allows you to speed up or slow down the motor for tracking.

### Step 9: Tripod hub

The tripod hub is made from two disks of aluminum bolted to three leg mount bars. The top of the hub is machined flat. The bolt holds the chassis to the hub.

### Step 10: Oak tripod legs

The tripod legs are built up from oak flooring boards discarded as scrap by a neighbor. They are as long as the shortest piece so about 48".

### Step 11: Mount assembled

All the different assemblies together as a mount head.

### Step 12: Finished mount

After some fiddling, refitting, stiffening sanding, and painting, the finished mount.

### Step 13: The heart and soul

Ah, now it's time for the cool stuff The Objective! This lens was made by Istar Optical, at the time a relatively new manufacturer of telescope optics. The lens has shown itself to be an excellent performer, especially for the price. Currently the objective in cell costs about $515.

### Step 14: The tube

The tube is a section of aluminum tube made by Hastings Irrigation. I had to special order the size as shipping an 8' tube costs as much as the tube itself

The focuser is a Synta refractor focuser painted blue for looks.

The interior is baffled via 7 knife-edge baffles spaced 12" apart. The baffle assembly was built from plans I drew of the optical path. The baffles are kept out of the light path by about 1/4" or so.

### Step 15: Objective cell mounting

The objective needs to be mounted in a collimatable ring. This ring was routed from three pieces of HDPE drilled and tapped for three push-pull screw arrangements.

### Step 16: Sliding dew shield

Traveling with a 9' tube is tough, traveling with an 8' tube is much easier, fits right in the mini-van. To make things easier the dewshield slides over the objective to shield the lens from stray light.

### Step 17: How does it perform?

This refractor is an achromat, which normally would not be suitable for photography. Due to it's large focal ratio (f15) and long focal length (2276mm) this scope is a superb planetary performer.

# Air Quality Balloons

### By Stacey Kuznetsov (staceyk)
(http://www.instructables.com/id/Air-quality-balloons/)

This instructable will show you how to make giant, super cool, glowing balloons that react to surrounding air quality. Inside each balloon is a tri-colored LED. This LED reacts to data from an air quality sensor, turning green, yellow, or red based on low, average, and high values.

## Step 1: Gather materials

Here are the materials you'll need to make a single balloon:

- Air Quality Sensor from Figaro (I recommend the VOC [http://www.figarosensor.com/products/2620pdf.pdf] or the diesel/exhaust [http://www.figarosensor.com/products/2201pdf.pdf] sensor, $10/$20 each)
- PICAXE micro-controller (http://www.sparkfun.com/commerce/product_info.php?products_id=8308)—8 pin ($2.95)
- DIP-socket for the PIC: http://www.sparkfun.com/commerce/product_info.php?products_id=7937 ($1.50)
- Rechargeable lipo battery: http://www.sparkfun.com/commerce/product_info.php?products_id=341 ($8.95)
- Tri-colored LED: http://www.superbrightleds.com/pdfs/RGB-1WS_new.pdf ($7.95)
- Either a 10Kohm resistor for sensing VOC or exhaust, or a 100Kohm resistor for sensing diesel
- Weather Balloon: http://www.world-costume.com/p4290/BALLOON-36-IN-WEATHER-WHITE/product_info.html ($3.95)
- Access to Helium (you can probably go to a party store, or rent a tank from a welding supply shop)
- rubber band or string to tie the balloon once inflated
- (optional) connector for battery: http://www.sparkfun.com/commerce/product_info.php?products_id=9749

You will also need to use:

- Picaxe starter kit (http://www.sparkfun.com/commerce/product_info.php?products_id=8321) and cable (http://www.sparkfun.com/commerce/product_info.php?products_id=8312), or some other way to program the pic
- wire
- solder/soldering iron
- electric tape
- heat shrink/heat gun
- pliers/wire strippers
- power-supply or some power sources around 5V to preheat the sensor

## Step 2: Preheat sensors

Data sheet for both sensors suggests 48 hours of preheat to make the elements most stable. I've run them for about 24 hours and it seemed to work fine.

All you have to do is hook up the Power and Ground on the sensor to a power supply (at 4.5Volts) or battery (3.7-4.5 volts should work). If using a power supply, make sure it's not current-limited because multiple sensors will draw a lot of current.

You can do this on a breadboard or using alligator clips and leave it on over night.

## Step 3: Program the PICAXE

First, you need to install the PICAXE IDE and drivers for your computer from www.picaxe.com.

Second you have to assemble your PICAXE programming board or whatever you choose to use to program

science

the pic. Refer to http://www.rev-ed.co.uk for details on starting out with the PIC.

The code is very simple. It samples the sensor output, and if it's below, within, or above certain thresholds, it turns the LED green, yellow, or red. Each sensor might have slightly different thresholds. Here are the values I used, based on collecting data around my city:

```
main:
'w5 = 270 'DIESEL GREEN'
'w6 = 295 'DIESEL RED'

'w5 = 448 'VOC GREEN'
'w6 = 470 'VOC RED'

w5 = 360 'EXHAUST GREEN'
w6 = 380 'EXHAUST RED'

goto runsensor
runsensor:
readadc10 4, w3 'SENSOR VALUE'
if w3 < w5 then 'GREEN'
high 1
low 2
endif

if w3 >= w5 and w3 < w6 then 'YELLOW'
high 1
high 2
endif

if w3 >= w6 then 'RED'
low 1
high 2
endif
pause 500
goto runsensor
```

An easy way to guess what the green, yellow, and red values might be after you already wired up the circuit is by using a voltmeter. You can see what voltage the sensor is giving off at different locations and translate that into analog values:

1023 * sensor voltage/your battery voltage

## Step 4: Solder the circuit (VOC sensor)

This is the trickiest part of the project. All connections must be very solid or they will fracture from the movements of the balloon. I recommend lots of heat shrink or electric tape around each joint.

Solder the pic socket (not the pic itself to allow easier programming). Leave about 6 inch wires between the LED and the picaxe. Solder the picaxe, sensor, and battery close together.

Sensor pins:

1—ground (this could be the battery ground or the picaxe ground)

2—picaxe pin 4, with a 10K resistor across ground

3 & 4—VCC (this could be the picaxe VCC or the battery VCC)

LED pins:

Green—picaxe 1
Red—picaxe 2

## Step 5: Solder the circuit (diesel or exhaust sensor)

This is the trickiest part of the project. All connections must be very solid or they will fracture from the movements of the balloon. I recommend lot's of heat shrink or electric tape around each joint.

Solder the pic socket (not the pic itself to allow easier programming). Leave about 6 inch wires between the LED and the picaxe. Solder the picaxe, sensor, and battery close together.

Sensor pins:

1—picaxe pin 4 with a 100Kohm resistor across ground (for diesel)

OR

3—picaxe pin 4 with a 10Kohm resistor across ground (for exhaust)

4—ground (this could be the battery ground or the picaxe ground)

3—VCC (this could be the picaxe VCC or the battery VCC)

LED pins:

Green—picaxe 1
Red—picaxe 2

## Step 6: Lots of tape

Put electric tape all around the sensor and picaxe, without blocking the sensor element from getting air. Tape is a DIY container for this circuit (this way you don't need any other enclosure).

Put some tape around the LED too; it could get too hot or too sharp and make the balloon pop.

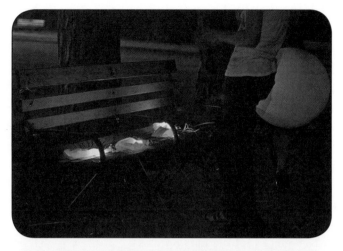

## Step 7: Insert into balloon

Insert the LED into the balloon, but keep the picaxe, sensor, and battery outside.

Most likely, your sensor will float at this point and the LED will turn red no matter what threshholds you set in step 1. Give it some time, it'll settle back to normal in 20 minutes.

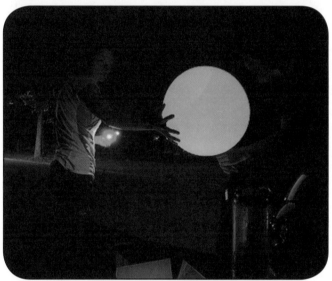

## Step 8: Inflate the balloon!

This step is awesome. You can now inflate the balloon! We used rubber bands to tie them off since tying the actual balloon might break the already-fragile wiring. If you're planning to set up a balloon installation, I recommend inflating the balloons on-site. They will not fit into a car.

## Step 9: Write sensor name on balloon

Write the name of the sensors on your balloon in thick marker.

## Step 10: Go out and show off!!

You can walk around with your balloon(s) or leave them in some place. Make a video, and take some pictures!

# Giant Fresnel Lens Deathray: An Experiment in Optics

By Matthew Pearson (DrSimons)
(http://www.instructables.com/id/Giant-Fresnel-Lens-Deathray-An-Experiment-in-Opti/)

So you don't have access to your own rail gun or military space laser but never fear, we'll use the 1000 Watts/m2 of free sunlight in your backyard! But how?

**A 13 square foot magnifying glass!**

Seriously. A solid glass lens that size would be silly, but instead we can use a 4 foot wide Fresnel lens. You know, those clear, flat things with the ridges, you find them on overhead projectors and rear windows on some buses? The idea is pretty simple: a Fresnel lens is just a normal curved lens chopped into thousands of little rings, but just as effective.

**Disclaimer:**

This device is extremely dangerous, and will **INSTANTLY** set things on fire! It's extremely cool, but I'm not responsible for anything that happens if you decide to ignite yourself, your house, the forest, or anything else. Also, if you decide to skip the eye protection step, I hope you like Braille.

## Step 1: Acquire the lens

For many future scientists, the destructive power of magnifying glasses provide hours of fun in the backyard (although I do not believe in burning living creatures, whatever the size). But everybody already has a magnifying glass. Where are we gonna get a 60-inch Fresnel lens?

They can be had online, but only for substantial piles of cash (from **$80-$150 on Ebay**), which is why few

people ever enjoy these devices. Traditionally, the actual lens is by far the biggest cost in a project like this, with lumber and hardware being almost nothing if you already have the tools. And now, I will impart to you the ultimate source of **FREE** giant Fresnel lenses:

**Rear Projection TVs.**

Every rear projection TV uses a Fresnel lens the exact size of the screen to focus the image. The screen has **several layers**:

- Outer cover (optional): Some TVs have a clear layer on the very outside keep it; it could be useful in another project.
- Lenticular lens: This is the hideous outer screen with 1000s of vertical lines. The purpose of the lines is to spread each pixel outward so you can see the screen from the side. It will probably rip apart as you separate the layers.
- Fresnel lens: this is the innermost layer—clear with millions of circular ridges on one side. The crown jewel of the TV.

Two excellent sources of free rear-projection TVs:

1. Craigslist!
2. The Dump.

Once you have your TV screen, peel the layers apart (you may need to cut some tape along the top) and extract the precious Fresnel. Admire your plunder, and dispose/recycle the TV carcass.

## Step 2: Build a frame

The first thing you'll notice about your lens is that it flops around and refuses to stay straight. The lens absolutely must be flat in order to work right, so we need to build a frame. This will also prevent it from being bent or cracked.

*Note*: The ridges on one side of the lens are **extremely delicate** and scratch effortlessly. A few scratches won't affect performance, but look terrible. Try not to drag the lens against anything.

**Materials required:**

- At least 15 feet of lumber—I recommend 1x2" boards
- Plywood or miscellaneous scrap wood
- 20-40 wood screws
- Power drill
- Tape measure and pencil

**Holding the lens:**

The goal here is to secure the lens in a frame. The most elegant way to do this is to cut a groove down the length of each piece of wood, so the lens fits into the slot. By lowering the saw blade on my table saw so it only stuck up about half an inch, I was able to cut perfect grooves down the boards.

**Cutting the frame:**

Once you have your grooved beams, you'll need to cut them just long enough to come together with the lens nested into the grooves. Make sure the grooves are all on the inside, and after measuring exactly how long each side should be, cut the sides at 45 degree angles so the corners look nice. I used a miter to get the precise angles here.

**Assembly:**

Once the frame pieces are positioned around the lens you can pull everything together. We sandwiched each corner between two pieces of plywood and put screws through all 3 layers, but there are lots of options for this part.

It's a little complicated, and the method varies depending on what tools you have available. If you don't have a table saw, there are other ways to make a groove, or you could trap the lens with multiple boards. If you have any kind of workshop you should be able to rig up something. I don't advise screwing directly into the lens though, because it might crack.

**Once your frame is done, you can move the lens around safely.**

Now **BEFORE** you go out and start burning stuff, I must urge you to wear the strongest sun glasses you can find, glacier goggles are better, but nothing short of welding goggles are really going to protect your eyes.

*The light spots these lenses can produce are literally as bright as the sun.*

On that note, be extremely careful where you put this lens. If it's sunny out, the thing shouldn't even be left outside; you never know when it might decide to focus and set your house on fire! Once again I am not liable for anything, including forest fires, so use your head.

## Step 3: Eye protection!

This is such a good idea, I decided to make it a whole step. Let me tell you—throughout this project you will spend a lot of time playing with this device, and you'll want to look at the focus a lot to see the results.

However, you will find that after a few seconds, spots linger in your vision when you look away. The center of your retina will become more and more desensitized until it starts taking permanent damage. Then you won't be able to see anything.

When you're looking at this spot, it may not seem so bright. That is because your eyes are already being desensitized. Thus, you have to wear at the *very least* some dark sunglasses. With welding goggles, you can't really see anything except the focal point, so I recommend glacier glasses (used in mountain climbing so you aren't blinded by the sun reflecting off of ice).

## Step 4: Measure the focal length

Rather than proceed with building the rest of the device, at this point you need to measure your lens' focal length. This is the distance from the lens to the spot of light it will produce. This distance will only be correct when the light rays hitting the lens are parallel to each other, and perpendicular to the lens. In other words, the light has to either be sunlight or two parallel laser beams, and hit the lens dead on. Unless you live at the equator, with the sun straight up, measuring the focal length is actually quite difficult. After a lot of frustration I decided to use lasers.

**Materials required:**
- 2 (or more) laser pointers
- A level
- Some flat ground
- A T-square
- A tape measure
- A large, rigid screen

We want to find the point in space where parallel light beams bending through the lens intersect. This is the focal point, and it will be straight out from the center of the lens.

**Laser setup:**

To set up our parallel beams of light, put your two laser pointers on either side of a book or something so that they're parallel. The goal is for the lasers to be perpendicular to the lens, so make sure they're on a level surface. Turn them on and aim the whole setup straight at the lens.

Meanwhile, have someone hold the lens straight up, using a T-square to make the lens perfectly vertical. You'll get two weird diffraction patterns on the wall behind the lens.

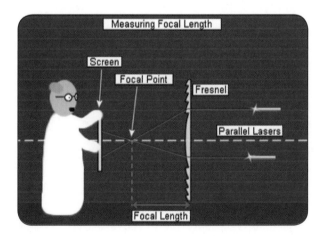

**Finding the focus:**

Now, with your tape measure extending out from the base of the lens, hold your screen up so the two lasers hit it. Move it back and forth until the two spots converge. When they do, see how far from the lens your screen is.

This may sound confusing, but the pictures should help. I recommend trying several times, maybe moving the lasers around, so you can see whether your results are consistent. For my lens, the focal length was about 40 inches (about 100cm), which is average for especially large Fresnels.

## Step 5: Acquire focusing lens

Now that you know the focal length of your Fresnel, it's time to get a diverging lens to bend the light into a beam. This will go right at the focal point, so you get as small a beam as possible.

**Benefits of creating a beam:**

- Objects don't have to be right at the focal point to burst into flames!
- The beam can be further manipulated—magnified, reflected, put through a prism, whatever floats your optical boat.
- Ridiculously intense light beams are like lasers—*they're awesome*.

**Optics refresher:**

In optics, the strength of a lens is measured by its focal length (stronger lenses have shorter ones). To cancel the converging effect of the Fresnel lens, we need to either diverge the light before it gets to the focal point (use a **diverging lens** with a negative focal length) or converge it after the light spreads out beyond the focal point (using a **converging lenses** like a magnifying glass).

**Diagram 1:**

When two lenses are far apart, it's useful to think of light in terms of geometry and angles: the focusing lens has to be strong enough that its focal length is small so that the light spreading out from the Fresnel's focal point is completely captured by the second lens.

From basic geometry, we know that the second lens has to have a ratio of diameter to focal length at least as big as the Fresnel lens in order to capture all the light. This means if the second lens has a focal length fB, it has to have a diameter of at least

$$dB = fB (dA/fA)$$

where dA and fA are the diameter and focal length of your Fresnel (use the larger width since the Fresnel is not a circle).

**Diagram 2:**

With a strong enough lens (the one I got had a focal length of 35mm), you put the lens 35mm (or whatever) past the Fresnel's focal length. The light will then be bent inward, forming a beam. Of course, this will only be approximate, so you'll have to move the lens back and forth until you find the correct distance.

**Optics Applet:**

An excellent resource for basic optics is this Optics Applet I've found: http://webphysics.davidson.edu/physlet_resources/dav_optics/Examples/optics_bench.html. You can't really use it to get real-world numbers, but

it's very handy for planning and understanding how lenses interact. Place a "beam" on the x-axis, then a couple lenses (you can adjust the focal lengths by dragging the little white squares).

You can find lenses in lots of random places online, and the closer the focal length is to your measurement, the better.

Also, **bigger lenses are preferable** because giant Fresnels typically don't create a very small focus spot (between 1 and 2 inches wide) so you'll need at least a 2" wide lens to capture all the light.

**Where I bought my lens:**

Surplus Shed: http://www.surplusshed.com/pages/category/lenses_1.html

There are other places I'm sure, especially educational sites and the like but it may be hard to find the exact lens you need. I should also mention that you want a glass lens, plastic simply won't do for this intensity of light.

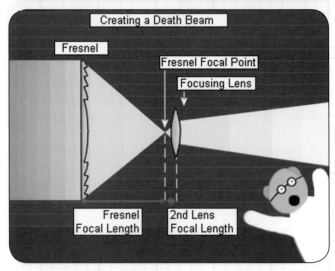

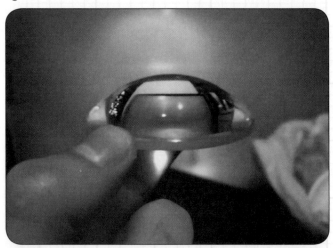

## Step 6: Lens scaffold

Now that we have a set of focusing lenses, we need to devise a scaffold to hold them in place out in front of the Fresnel lens. After a good deal of thought we conclude the easiest way is to use thin (1x1) wooden stakes held together by plywood gussets.

Materials required:

- 4 1x1 stakes
- Scrap plywood
- Woodscrews
- Drill, countersink if available
- 2x4 plank
- 2" hole saw (or larger)
- Several right-angle brackets

Basic structure:

Odds are you're going to do this your own way if you try it, so I won't go into too much detail about the construction. I assembled the sides first (minus the 2x4s) by cutting the 1x1 stakes with a miter saw to get the necessary angles, then cut plywood gussets to hold these together. We used 2 right-angle brackets (inside corners) to attach these gussets to the plywood crosspiece that will eventually hold the lenses.

Note: A very important thing here is the orientation of the Fresnel lens. I found out the hard way that when the flat side of the lens is facing the sun, it doesn't work right (but well enough that you might not notice). So make sure the ridges are facing out, away from the scaffold—that means they'll be facing down if you build this with the lens on the ground, as I did.

After the sides are completed, two long plywood gussets secure them onto the side of the frame. Since we

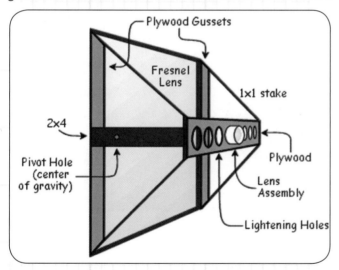

want the whole device to rotate about its **center of gravity** (somewhere between the Fresnel and the small lenses), we need a strong beam that passes through that point (hence the **2x4s** in the diagram), so we screwed the 2x4s onto the necessary gussets, providing a substantial increase in strength.

Finding the center of gravity

To find the center of gravity of this whole scaffold (it will be along the centerline of the 2x4), you and a friend each grab one of the 2x4s and see where the thing balances. You'll want to choose a point closer to the Fresnel (so the Fresnel wants to hang down) because the

lens assembly hasn't been installed yet. Finally, drill 1/4" or 5/8" holes (depending on the carriage bolt in the next step) through the points you choose.

Note: When using wood screws in the small wooden stakes, you definitely want to pre-drill/countersink holes, because wood this thin is very easy to crack.

## Step 7: Support base

This lens scaffold we now have needs to rotate around so it can aim up at the sun. To accomplish this we came up with a super simple, super sturdy base made from 5 blocks of wood.

Materials required:

- One 8 foot 2x4
- Around 8 feet of 2x6 board
- 8 medium lag bolts
- 2 big lag bolts
- 2 carriage bolts and nuts
- 6 washers
- 2 wood spacers (use the lightening holes you cut out for the scaffold)

The design:

The planks are held together with large lag bolts—to use these, drill clearance holes through the first part (as wide as the part of the bolt without threads) and a pilot hole through the second part (not as wide, so the threads can bite into the wood). Then you screw the bolts in with a ratchet. It's very tight, and very strong. A few of these should hold each part together.

You'll want to **measure the lens scaffold first**, then slightly overestimate the width for the base so you can get it between the two supports easily (the spacers will take up the rest of the width).

Mount the lens scaffold:

We want to put a couple holes at the top of each support and insert a suitable collection of a spacer, washers, a nut and carriage bolt.

Once the pivot is together, you can use a wrench to tighten the bolts and lock the scaffold in position.

## Step 8: Lens mount

Clearly, our death ray is missing something. If you swivel the lens up so it's perpendicular to the sun's rays, you'll just get a spot of bright light on the piece of plywood at the focus. Once you do this (yes, I recommend it—but don't let the thing catch on fire), you'll know just where to put the focusing lens.

**Materials required:**

- 2" PVC expansion joint
- Your favorite epoxy
- Miter saw or hack saw
- Sand paper (60, 150)

**Lens tube:**

The easiest way to set up the optics here is to mount the main focusing lens on the end of a tube around 2 inches wide. This will do exactly what this instructable (http://www.instructables.com/id/Home-Made-Collimator) does—collimate the light into a smaller beam. In a sense, the entire device is already doing this with the sun's parallel rays, but we want the smallest beam possible.

Up until now, I was troubled and lost as to what I would use for this part. What was needed was essentially two tubes inside each other, the inner one allowed to telescope in and out easily, but be able to stay put. Then, while wandering the aisles of Home Depot I found the perfect part: a **PVC expansion joint for 2" conduit pipe**. It consists of two pipes, the inner one having two o-rings and a lot of silicon lube, allowing it to slide in and out of the outer pipe beautifully. It also happened to be a perfect fit for my 57mm focusing lens.

**Preparing the tube:**

This was fairly straight forward—the inner tube had a rim sticking out past the ridge where the lens wanted to sit, so I made quick work of it with a miter saw (a hack saw would work equally well, just take it slow and rotate the tube as you're cutting). After a quick sand, the tube was ready for the lens.

**Epoxy:**

I rifled through the adhesives toolbox, found something appropriate for both glass and plastic (Duco Cement) and glued down the lens. A day later someone knocked the tube over and the lens popped off, so I decided to use epoxy to seal the lens in. This worked better (the specific epoxy isn't that important, just pile it up around the sides of the lens to keep it in).

**Note**: Since diverging light is entering this lens, we want the least curved side of the lens (assuming your lens isn't symmetrical) facing out so the angle of incidence is lower, minimizing loss of light by reflection. Imagine a stone skipping off a pond versus a stone dropping straight down (which is what we want in this case).

## Step 9: Installing the lens mount

One morning I woke up and found the sun actually out. The past week had been mostly overcast, with almost no sunlight hitting the deck where this project sat. So I ran out, put on my glacier glasses and pulled the tarp off the device.

**Aiming:**

A simple way to aim at the sun is to rotate the device until its shadows are parallel to the supports on the ground (if the ground is flat). This means the sun is directly forward. Then all you have to do is rotate it so the lens is closer to the sun, and an intense spot of light should form on the lens scaffold.

Even in the middle of winter at this latitude, a 1-inch charred spot formed in a few seconds. It wasn't exactly in the center of the plywood beam, meaning the device wasn't facing perfectly towards the sun.

**Lens mount:**

I didn't expect the light spot on the plywood to be so small. This meant that the focus was right on the plywood—farther than I expected. And since the lens assembly can only extend forward (towards the Fresnel), I had to recess the tube past the plywood. We accomplished this with a primitive housing made of 2x4 beams and plywood sides.

The 2x4s were ripped to a width slightly less than that of the lens tube, so the plywood sides squeezed the tube in place. If you decide to mount the lens this way, be careful not to accidentally crack the tube. But even better, think of a better way to attach it, and make the lens scaffold stick out at least 4 inches past the focal point.

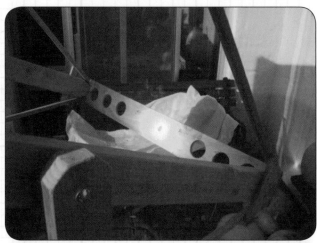

## Step 10: Testing

Despite it being December 22, winter solstice, the shortest day of the year, I proceeded to test out the completed lens system. But even with the least possible sunlight to work with (several hours before noon, at 37 degree latitude, we got a very satisfactory spot of blinding energy at the focus. When the device was aimed so that this spot fell on the secondary lens nothing happened.

**Failure analysis:**

Despite moving the lens tube back and forth through the focal point, no beam of light formed beyond the lens mount. To find out why the light wasn't cooperating, we decided to do a beam visualization by blowing dust to reflect the light. We first used flour, but then switched to water mist (from a sprayer) since it's not as messy.

The light funnels into a highly concentrated point, as expected, but then basically fizzes out. If your Fresnel deathray is doing this, most likely the Fresnel lens is backwards and flat side is facing the sun, rather than the ridged side. Getting this right is essential to getting a good beam profile (which we'll see in the next step).

Since the secondary lens is convex, i.e. it bends light inward, the incoming light has to be diverging in order to form a straight beam. Since the light from the Fresnel seems to disperse randomly past the focal point, almost no light even entered the secondary lens. Other Fresnel lens devices on the internet demonstrate good beam shapes.

## Step 11: OK—let's burn something!

Update: at the suggestion of foobaz utne, I flipped the Fresnel lens around so the ridges are facing the sun, and found a dramatic increase in lens performance. The secondary lens still isn't working right, but I was able to upgrade from melting zinc pennies to liquefying solid copper ones and destroying nickels!

**First test:**

Inspired by similar Fresnel experiments floating around the net, I decided to try melting a penny. On winter solstice, I found that a zinc penny melts within a minute when held in the focus. Solid copper pennies (from 1982 or earlier) wouldn't melt, but probably would during summer. Copper's melting point is almost 2000 degrees Fahrenheit compared to Zinc's 790 degrees Fahrenheit.

**Round 2:**

With the Fresnel lens oriented correctly, I had another crack at melting those coins. MUHAHAHAHA!

**Note**: Copper's melting point is about 2000 degrees Fahrenheit, but Nickel's is 2600 degrees Fahrenheit. So it's highly possible that only the copper in the coin (75% copper, 25% nickel) melted, resulting in the mutilated pitted surface.

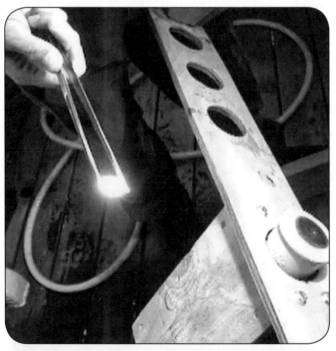

## Step 12: Conclusion

**Conclusion:**

Clearly, a giant Fresnel lens with an area of ~1.2m² is a powerful asset. Assuming the maximum available solar energy hitting the ground is around 1000W/m², this lens could theoretically concentrate 1200W of power into a square centimeter. Of course, at this latitude and time of year, around half of the maximum sunlight is available so this would make an excellent summer project. But even during winter, the fact that I could easily melt solid copper and make a nickel red hot is pretty damn cool.

**Other uses:**

Perhaps the most valuable thing you can get out of this instructable is the source for these giant lenses. There are loads of of them heading for landfills, or recycling, or god knows what else, so reclaim these things and put them to use!

**Note**: You may think, as I did, "Gee, I bet I could make a super efficient solar panel with one of these." But according to this discussion board (http://www.other-power.com/cgi-bin/webbbs/webbbs_config.pl?noframes;read=4434) that isn't a very good idea, and could ruin your expensive solar panel. You could certainly power a small heat engine like this sterling engine (http://www.instructables.com/id/The-Sterling-Engine-absorb-energy-from-candles-c) though, by trapping all the light in a black container thermally connected to the boiler. A company working on this technology, but using reflectors instead of lenses, is Sterling Energy Systems (http://www.sterlingenergy.com).

Thanks to everyone for your comments and suggestions.

Special thanks to foobaz utne for solving my problem with the Fresnel lens focusing properly.

I hope you enjoyed this project, and I will either update this if I further develop it, or post other solar-related projects in the future.

# The Rubens' Tube: Soundwaves in Fire!

By Nik Vaughn (yourtvlies)
(http://www.instructables.com/id/The-Rubens—Tube%3a-Soundwaves-in-Fire!/)

What could be more entertaining than fire and good music? How about fire that will dance to that music? The following will not only cause flames to pulse to a beat, but it will also allow you to see different wavelengths of audio frequency. The following is my first instructable, and my entry to the instructables Science Fair contest.

In addition to documenting the build steps to create something called a Rubens' Tube, I'll also go over some of the basic concepts and science involved with sound waves.

From the moment I discovered what a Ruben's Tube was, I wanted to build one and, considering I was in a physics class at the time, there couldn't have been a better excuse than extra credit.

## Step 1: What is a Rubens' Tube?

Heinrich Rubens was a German physicist born in 1865. Though he allegedly worked with better remembered physicists such as Max Planck at the University of Berlin on some of the ground work for quantum physicists, he is best known for his flame tube, which was demonstrated in 1905.

This original Rubens' Tube was a four meter section of pipe with 200 holes spaced evenly along its length. When the ends are sealed and a flammable gas is pumped into the device the building pressure will have only one route to equalize. The escaping gas can be lit to form a row of roughly even flames. Upon introduction of a loud speaker to one of the sealed ends, standing waveforms can be seen in the flames.

Within the Rubens' tube, as soon as gas is ignited generally uniform flames will be seen. This is because there is very little pressure differential between any given area of the space inside the tube. Once sound is applied from one end, pressure will change within the tube. Should the sound be an easily measurable frequency, the wavelength will be visible in the series of flames, with the highest flames being where condensation is occurring and the lowest where rarefaction is occurring.

## Step 2: Nerdy stuff: a bit on waves

Visualizing sound as a wave can be a bit misleading. Sound is often portrayed as a sine waveform because it's easier to illustrate than the longitudinal compression wave that it actually is.

The first image shows the typical way a sound wave, or just about any wave, is portrayed visually. Because sound is basically a vibration created by changes in air pressure, the peaks on the waveform correspond to the highest pressure and the troughs correspond to the lowest pressure. The wavelength is measured by the distance between two peaks, or two troughs.

The second image is a more accurate way to visualize compressional waves, including sound waves. Each dot could represent a molecule of the matter (such as air) that the wave is traveling through. At the points where the pressure is highest you can see that the density of the material is relatively higher than the areas with lower pressure. These are called condensation and rarefaction, respectively.

The third image shows the previous two stacked, it's easy to see how the peaks of the wave correspond to condensation, and how the troughs correspond to rarefaction.

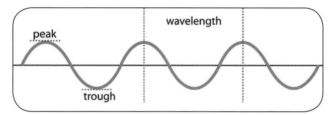

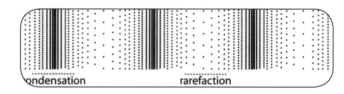

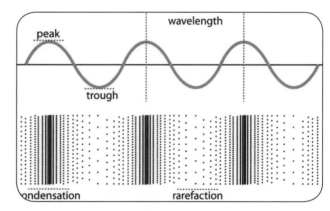

## Step 3: Nerdy stuff: the application

In step 2 we were able to grasp some of the basics on sound waves, and although the concept isn't all that abstract, I thought it might be nice to take it from the theory level to the application level as it applies to what's going on inside a Rubens' Tube. I've made a few diagrams to help illustrate the concept.

The first image represents a functioning Rubens' Tube under normal conditions. We can assume that in this

science

image an arbitrary, constant tone is being played into one end of the tube. But what might we witness if we were able to peer inside the tube, and see the sound waves?

The next image gives us an idea what's going on if we were able to see the sine wave of the tone. But what's critical to remember is that what's actually occurring is a change in pressure between different amplitudes of the waveform.

The final image illustrates these pressure changes as a compressional wave. Understanding sound in this way makes it clear as to why we have the varying flame height. The taller flames correspond directly with the higher pressure. This higher pressure in the compressional wave is what's pushing the gas out of the holes with more force than in the areas with lower pressure.

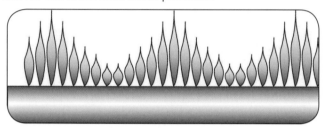

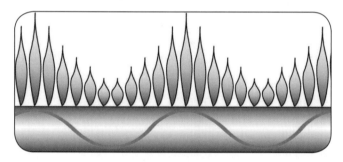

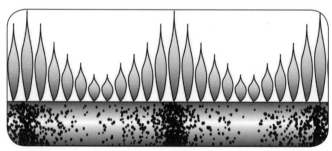

## Step 4: Nerdy stuff: measuring sound

The speed of sound is roughly 340 meters per second at sea level, but this is when air is the medium through which the sound waves travel. But because propane is of a different density than air, the velocity of sound is also different, and like all gases, the density changes with heat or pressure changes. For our purposes, we can work with a velocity of 257 meters per second.

As mentioned in the last step, sound is a vibration. We measure the frequency of this vibration in hertz (Hz), which is the number of cycles of the vibration per second. Wikipedia tells us that "The frequency (f) is equal to the speed (v) of the wave divided by the wavelength (lambda) of the wave."

So in other words, frequency = speed/wavelength or:
f = v/lambda

To find the wavelength, we use basic algebra—multiply by lambda and divide by f to get.

lambda = v/f

To test this we can take the sound wave used to demonstrate the device in the video as an example (360Hz), and use or rough speed of sound for v.

lambda = 257(m/s)/360Hz

This gives us a value for lambda of about 0.71 meters, which should be close to the distance between the peaks of the flames. (Though the actual measured value may differ from what is calculated given the above mentioned scenarios.)

## Step 5: Materials and tools

The materials required to build this Rubens' Tube are fairly inexpensive, most of which can be found on Amazon. com, or your local hardware store. Note that some of the recommended are not identical to the parts that I've used, they will however, serve the same, or superior function to what I've used. That being said, the materials you use, and the build process is extremely flexible and forgiving.

Building materials:
- Ventilation ducting: Ducting used for HVAC, though any thin-walled metal pipe should work. My tube uses 4 inch ducting, I'd imagine success using anything from 2 to 6 inch material.
- Brackets x2: These are brackets used for supporting the ducting. Obviously the same size as the above ducting.
- Propane: This is the fuel source. Anything with a valve so you can turn it off and on safely should work.
- Tubing: Nothing too insightful here, 1/4 inch inner diameter, or whatever fits your fuel source.
- Hose T connector: I used brass, but something like this would work fine.
- Hose splicers x2: Used for fuel delivery. This will work much better than the small piece of copper tubing I used.

science

- Latex sheets: This will serve as our diaphragm. I used polyethylene sheeting; however, latex should perform much better as it's thinner and more pliable, but either will work and it just goes to demonstrate the flexibility of the build.
- Scrap wood

Tools and supplies:
- Drill: You'll also need a 1/4 inch bit and a bit between 1/16 and 1/32
- Hammer
- Tape Measure
- Knife or Scissors
- Silicone Sealant
- Epoxy Putty
- Duct Tape
- Masking Tape
- Teflon Tape
- Miscellaneous: Various hardware for attaching the brackets to your wooden base. Simple wood screws should work fine. A nail or similar may be needed for pre-drilling. And finally some hot water for working with the tubing.

## Step 6: A note on the sound source

For this project, any sound source should work. I used my iPod with the driver from old 3 computer speakers I got from Goodwill. But nearly anything should work, from a do-it-yourself setup, to an old radio, to a hi-fi sound system, to a boom-box.

I also have three recommendations:

Whatever speaker you use should be able to reach volumes to move the diaphragm.

The speaker should be placed or mounted close enough to the diaphragm to easily move it, without making physical contact

The speaker's diameter should be as close as possible to the tube's diameter to ensure maximum diaphragm movement.

We're even lucky enough here in the instructables community to have projects (http://www.instructables.com/id/ELCGX5TJ7MEPOK92AF/?ALLSTEPS) that would work wonderfully as a source of sound with little to no

modification.

If you're interested in getting your hands on sine wave audio tones, they can be had by Googling for "Audio Test CD" or "Audio Test Tones." The one I used for this project was found here (http://virtuelvis.com/archives/2004/09/audio-test-cd).

## Step 7: Construction part 1: marking and drilling

**Step 7a:**

Determine what will be the top side of the tube. If you're using ducting like I did, there's a seam on where the ends of the tube connect, this will be the bottom.

**Step 7b:**

Run a piece of masking tape along the top of the ducting. Using a tape measure, mark off every half inch running down the center of the tape. I came 14 inches out from the center in both directions—this left 4 inches on each end of the tube without markings.

**Step 7c:**

Using a nail or other object carefully tap a point in each marking with a hammer. The goal is to create a small depression at each location to facilitate drilling.

**Step 7d:**

Remove the tape and carefully drill through the ducting at each depression.

## Step 8: Construction part 2: sealing and diaphragm

Obviously, in order to get this thing to function the way we want it to, we're going to have to seal up the tube and create a diaphragm.

**Step 8a:**

Use duct tape to cover the potentially sharp edges of the tube—this will prevent the ducting from ripping through the diaphragm. You'll probably want to use more than one layer, but again, this is coming from my experience with the ventilation ducting. Depending upon the type of material you're using, it may not be necessary.

**Step 8b:**

Cut a latex sheet to serve as your diaphragm. You'll definitely want to cut it large enough to completely cover the end of the tube with enough extra to tape down and pull taut. The size I selected was roughly 6 inches square. It's also worth noting I used polyethylene sheeting. This will work, however latex will provide additional flexibility. It's also worth noting that latex will slowly oxidize, and may need replacing over time.

**Step 8c:**

Start taping the sheeting down to create the diaphragm. The concept here is to basically emulate the head of a drum. It needs to be tight enough to allow it to easily vibrate, but not so tight that it will tear. Once satisfied tape down, or trim the excess, and tape around the circumference of the tube in order to create an airtight seal.

**Step 8d:**

On the other end, repeating the processes will allow for later experiments using a "stereo" Rubens' Tube. However, simply sealing it off with duct tape to create a good seal is a perfectly acceptable method to create a functioning device. In either case, be careful what you set the opposite end on to make sure you preserve airtight seal.

**Step 8e:**

Finally, if you're using ventilation ducting like I am, it's worth while to run a bead silicone sealant down the seam of the tube. I pressed it into the joint using my finger, and then cleaned up the excess. Now we have our tube completely sealed where we want it to be.

## Step 9: Construction part 3: fuel holes

Now it's time to build the fuel delivery system. The basic idea is to evenly distribute the fuel within the tube.

**Step 9a:**

Determine the location(s) where fuel will enter the ducting. I recommend using what will be the "back" of the tube—this is simply a right angle from the line of holes on the top. Additionally, depending upon whether or not you choose to have fuel delivered at more than one location, a bit of advance planning should go into where these locations are.

In my case, I chose two locations—at distances half way out from the center hole and the first and last hole. It's also worth noting, again in retrospect, that one point for fuel delivery would probably work equally as well, so long as this location is centered.

**Step 9b:**

As in the prior step, tap your marked location with a

nail, and drill a hole large enough for your hose splicer to fit. In my first attempt, I didn't use hose splicers, but rather 1/4 copper tubing. Using hose splicers will make hooking everything up **much** easier, and I highly recommend it.

**Step 9c:**

Using a utility knife, nail, or other sharp object, lightly score the ducting around the hole, or holes. This should allow for the epoxy to create a more secure bond.

**Step 9d:**

Install the hose splicer(s) in the hole(s). Mix up some epoxy putty, and apply liberally. You'll want to create both an airtight and secure bond.

## Step 10: Construction part 4: fuel supply

This step's all about hooking up the propane to the tube.

**Step 10a:**

Teflon tape on the areas where you'll be attaching the tubing is a good idea to make sure you won't have propane leaking. This includes the propane nozzle, the tee connector (if you're using multiple delivery points for fuel), and end of the hose splicer(s) that will connect to the tubing.

**Step 10b:**

Hooking up the fuel is a pretty straight forward process. Simply cut and attach the hose. To do this, you'll want a cup of very hot water close by to soak the ends of the tubing in, this will warm and soften it up so you can easily get it over the connections.

If you're using one entry point for fuel, you'll only have one connection to make right now, if you're using a tee connector for two entry points, connect both ends to the connector, and to the Rubens' Tube.

## Step 11: Construction part 5: mounting

Considering the Rubens' Tube is round, it's a good idea to mount it on something so it won't roll around.

**Step 11a:**

Attach the brackets to the base using screws. (I used a piece of scrap wood, I think it was part of a shelving unit once).

**Step 11b:**

This step may or may not be required depending upon how your tube fits in the brackets. During construction I found that the brackets were slightly larger than the ducting. To aid this, I used some scrap hosing and zip ties to put around the ducting, thus adding to the circumference.

science

**Step 11c:**

Finally, mount your Rubens' Tube inside the brackets. Tighten up the brackets and you should be left with a fairly stable setup.

**At last!**

Your Rubens' Tube is ready for action! Please read the safety notes before hooking up the propane and continuing.

## Step 12: Safety first!

As with anything dealing with fire and flammable gas, there's some important, although fairly obvious things to consider. And although I am fairly confident that this is a sound design, just as with a propane grill, heater, or lantern, I must urge on the side of caution, and cannot take any responsibility for any accidents or mishaps that may occur. In order to minimize the possibilities of an accident, do not operate the device without keeping in mind all of the following.

**Step 12a:**

As alluded to above, propane is flammable! When using your Rubens' Tube, make sure you're in a well ventilated area or outside. In addition to the potential fire hazard, there is also a very real danger of carbon monoxide exposure from propane being less than completely burned. Carbon monoxide is DEADLY.

**Step 12b:**

Take note of the way you orient the propane tank. If the tank is not right side up, the propane may flow in unpredictable ways. Even a regular propane tank, used for a lantern or torch, turned on it's side, is likely to start spurting liquid after it's been turned on for some time— this can be extremely dangerous. Also allow for a safe distance between the Rubens' Tube and the fuel source.

**Step 12c:**

Even after the propane is shut off, the tube and hosing will still contain fuel. After turning off the fuel, you'll see the flames slowly start to lower. However, even after they're no longer visible, it's possible that they're still burning within the pipe itself. After shutting off the gas, remove the propane tank from the hose and allow plenty of time for the remaining fuel to burn off—there's more fuel than one would expect inside the tube itself!

**Step 12d:**

While the entire Ruben's Tube isn't likely to reach very high temperatures while being operated for reasonable lengths of time, the top part of the tube will become hot, even after short runs. Be very careful to allow adequate cooling time before handling the device.

**Step 12e:**

In case of emergency, be sure a fire extinguisher is close by at all times. Finally, if you're a minor, never operate your Rubens' Tube without the supervision of a responsible adult.

**Finally:**

Use common sense! As dire as the above warnings may sound, assuming you use common sense and play it safe, your Rubens' Tube will serve as an amazing scientific toy!

Let's move on to how to use the device.

## Step 13: Using your Rubens' Tube

Assuming you've already gone over the safety notes, the first step in using the Rubens' tube is to "prime" the tube.

**Step 13a:**

Attach the fuel source. Again, make sure there's a safe length of hose between the propane tank and the tube itself.

**Step 13b:**

We're going to want to create some positive pressure inside the Rubens' Tube. Because the flow of propane is fairly slow, and there's a lot of volume within the tube, we need to seal it up temporarily. To do this, use a strip of masking tape to cover all the holes on top of the ducting. Then turn on the gas.

Wait about two minutes, by this time enough propane should be in the tube to create a decent pressure differential. Depending upon the size of your tube, and the pressure of your fuel source, it may be necessary to wait a shorter or longer period of time.

**Step 13c:**

Remove the tape covering the holes. Then, using a long match or fireplace lighter, try lighting the gas by one of the holes. Assuming there's enough pressure, each hole should ignite down the tube. However, it may be necessary to light the tube in several places.

If the flame is very small, it may be indicative of lack of pressure within the tube, so you'll want to wait a bit longer the next time around before removing the tape.

The tube's ready for prime time when each flame is roughly an inch in height.

**Step 13d:**

Introduce an audio source near the diaphragm. You should be able to excite the flames by lightly tapping on the diaphragm, or even snapping next to it. However, for the most fun, and scientific pursuit, you'll want to use a speaker. See step 5 for notes on the sound source. Refer to the safety notes for turning it off.

You should be able to literally see the wavelengths of various audio sources. Head back and take another look at steps 2 and 3 to get a better understanding of exactly what's happening. As entertaining as dancing fire can be, there's a lot of science behind it too.

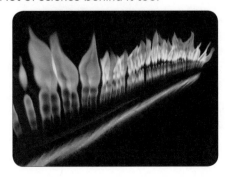

# Build a 15,000 rpm Tesla Turbine Using Hard Drive Platters

By sbtroy

(http://www.instructables.com/id/Build-a-15%2c000-rpm-Tesla-Turbine-using-hard-drive-/)

Here's a project that uses some of those dead hard drives you've got lying around.

In the Tesla Turbine, air, steam, oil, or any other fluid is injected at the edge of a series of smooth parallel disks. The fluid spirals inwards and is exhausted through ventilation ports near the center of the disks.

A regular blade turbine operates by transferring kinetic energy from the moving fluid to the turbine fan blades. In the Tesla Turbine, the kinetic energy transfer to the edges of the thin platters is very small. Instead, it uses the boundary layer effect, i.e. adhesion between the moving fluid and the rigid disk. This is the same effect that causes drag on airplanes.

To build a turbine like this, you need some dead hard drives, some stock material (aluminum, acrylic), a milling machine with a rotary table, and a lathe with a 4 jaw chuck.

Wikipedia has a good review article (http://en.wikipedia.org/wiki/Tesla_turbine), as well as articles about
- Nikola Tesla (http://en.wikipedia.org/wiki/Nikola_Tesla),
- the boundary layer effect (http://en.wikipedia.org/wiki/Boundary_layer),
- and Reynolds number (http://en.wikipedia.org/wiki/Reynolds_number), which determines if the fluid flow is laminar or turbulent.

I run my turbine on compressed air (40 psi), and it easily reaches speeds of 10-15,000 rpm. While the speed is high, the torque is low, and it can be stopped with your bare hand.

I have more details on my webpage (http://staff.washington.edu/sbtroy/turbine/turbine.html).

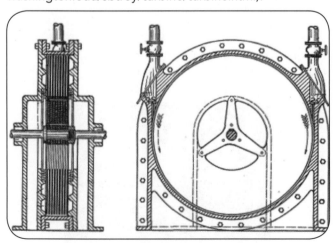

## Step 1: Make ventilation holes in the platters

Step 1 should probably be to disassemble some hard drives but I assume that if you read Make, you've already figured out how to *un*-Make a hard drive.

The easiest way to make vent holes in the hard drive platters is with a milling machine and a rotary table. Center and clamp a stack of several platters to the rotary table and then you can cut any radially symmetric pattern fairly easily. Just be sure that you use aluminium platters because ceramic platters will shatter when you drill into them.

I made two sets of platters; one with a radial array of holes, and one with radial arcs. The platter with radial arcs in the picture was on the top of the stack and took the

most damage. The platters beneath it have very little tear-out and look much better.

## Step 2: Make or reuse spacers

The ideal spacing between the platters depends on several variables including the fluid viscosity, velocity, and temperature. You could go through the calculations (http://en.wikipedia.org/wiki/Navier-Stokes_equations) and make a set of spacers, or be lazy and just reuse the spacers from the disassembled hard drives.

I was lazy and reused the spacers that were originally in between the platters. The advantage to this is that they'll have the same inside diameter as the platters. They're about .05" thick where the ideal spacing is closer to .012" but the increased distance doesn't make that big a difference in this case.

## Step 3: Make the shaft

This is just a piece of aluminum stock turned on a lathe. The center diameter is about .98" (which is the inside diameter of the platters) and about 1.77" long (so it will fit in a piece of 2" thick acrylic).

The thinner sections on each end are turned to fit the ball bearings I pulled from a box of scrap.

## Step 4: Make collars

The collars are made from more aluminum stock are wider versions of the platter spacers. The inside diameter is also .98" but they're about .3" thick to hold a #10-32 set screw.

## Step 5: Rotor assembly

Center the platters, spacers, and collars on the shaft and tighten the set screws to hold everything together. I used 11 platters, and 10 spacers. Try to line up all of the ventilation ports. If there isn't enough tension between the two collars, the platters can rotate around the shaft instead of with it.

## Step 6: Make the chamber

This is a 4.75" x 4.75" x 2" piece of acrylic that was bored out on a lathe using a 4 jaw chuck. The intake hole is taped for a 1/4" pipe fitting and all of the other holes are 1/4-20.

I used acrylic because it's what I had around and because it's going to be used for lecture demonstrations. You can use metal or even wood. However, if you plan to use steam instead of compressed air, wood might expand too much.

## Step 7: Make the side panels (stators)

The side panels are 4.75" x 4.75" x 0.47" acrylic with untaped .25" holes to screw to the main chamber. The center hole is 0.6" and the counterbore is 0.28" deep.

The two 0.6" holes (one on each side) are the **ONLY** exhaust ports. The air spirals inwards across the face of the platters, through the ventilation ports, around the air spaces in the bearings (2nd picture), and finally out through these two holes.

However, more exhaust holes in the side panels might improve efficiency.

## Step 8: Assemble everything

## Step 9: Complete turbine

See http://www.youtube.com/watch?v=d-sq92Z-igM&feature=player_embedded for a video of the complete turbine.

# tools

Humanity's ability to create and wield tools has allowed us to increase the power our bodies can exert. It's not hard to marvel at the ease with which a band saw can cut through a steel plate, or at how a stubborn bolt is easily overcome with an impact wrench. These feats are nothing short of superpowers!

Many people are familiar with the hand and power tools you can buy at the store. Fewer people are familiar with more advanced tools, but there are a select few who don't just use complex tools, but invent them.

If their creative process demands a tool that doesn't yet exist, they make it. It is these people, the tool-makers, who are able to alter existing tools, or fabricate their own tools in order to meet new and specialized needs that deserve our thanks. These meta-inventors give us new powers, pushing not only tools, but humanity itself forward.

# Pocket Laser Engraver

## By Otto Hermansson (Groover)
(http://www.instructables.com/id/Pocket-laser-engraver/)

I feel it's time to share my latest project—a low cost laser engraver. The workspace is a bit small but none the less it works and comes so cheap that most will be able to replicate the result. I did take a few shortcuts; as I feel I don't have the knowledge to do all the electronics, I opted for readymade but low cost in favor of trying to make my own (and most likely failing). All parts used are, however, easy to find.

I am pleased with the end result even if there is room for improvements. The small size and low power is a bit limiting but I have made a lot of fun things already: Paper cutouts, plant markers, and stamps among some.

A word of warning is in place. This instructable is using a ~200mW red laser. It might not cut through chunks of wood, but it will make you go blind if you are not careful. Never look into the beam; even reflections can be dangerous if focused. Please be careful.

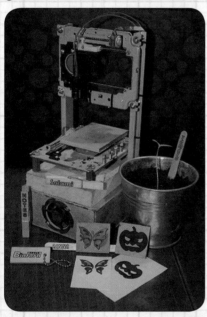

## Step 1: Acquire the parts

Most of the hardware comes from my junk bin. The aluminum profiles, the piece of MDF and various nuts, bolts, and wires. But some things need to be acquired. Most of the electronics can be found over at Sparcfun and the rest on e-bay or a swap meet.

- Arduino (http://www.sparkfun.com/products/9950): this is the heart of the control electronics.
- Easydrive (http://www.sparkfun.com/products/10267): stepper driver.
- Two DVD-rom drivers: Maybe more if you're unlucky, and at least one DVD-R to salvage the laser from.

- Laser housing (http://aixiz.com/store/product_info.php?cPath=40&products_id=72): singles can be found on e-bay.
- Laser driver: There are lots of alternatives here, I use a simple LM317 based circuit.
- Various nuts, bolts, and other building materials.

## Step 2: Rip apart the DVD-Roms

All you need from the DVD-Roms are the stepper motor assembly and one laser diode. I had a bit of bad luck and found that one of my DVD-Roms had a plastic assembly that would be very hard to work with. Thus I ripped apart three DVD-Roms and only used parts from two of them. It is pretty straight forward and most DVD-Roms I have opened work more or less the same way.

After removal of the screws at the bottom of the drive you can lift it off like a lid. Underneath you will most likely find two circuit boards that are not any use to us. But remember to salvage other useful parts that can be used for other projects. For example, under the front circuit board there is a small DC motor worth saving. This is when it is time to remove the front together with the front of the tray; the front comes loose after you pull out the tray (just use a hairpin and the small hole in the front). The next step can include some screws and/or mild force. Remove the two circuit boards. Be careful with the ribbon cable to the stepper motor. If you turn the DVD-Rom right side up and remove the cover, you should find what we are looking for, the stepper motor assembly. Remove the screws and just lift it out.

Now that we have the assembly out it needs to be cleaned up a bit. Remove the spindle motor; it could be useful but I feel they are hard to drive and so I don't keep them. They are usually held in place by three very small screws but sometimes they are part of a larger assembly, so be careful that removing it won't compromise the two rods holding the lens.

The lens is another story, just remove it in the best possible way, we need a smooth surface to attach other parts to later. Be careful to not harm the DVDR laser diode. It can come to good use if you don't want to buy a new powerful laser later. See the next step.

## Step 3: Putting a laser together

Removing the laser from the DVDR is not hard but most lens assemblies look different. Locate the diodes (there will be two, one IR and one red) and remove them from the assembly. There are some optics and two magnets that can be saved for future projects. Once you have removed the two diodes you must be careful. The two diodes are very small and fragile. Remove the small connecting PCB strips from the diodes and use two AAA batteries to check for the red diode.

Now that you have the bare diode it is time to mount the diode in the housing. Place the diode in the housing and use the back of the housing to press down the diode very carefully using a vice. When you get this far you are on the home stretch. Solder the wires to the positive and negative pins, screw in the lens, and you are done.

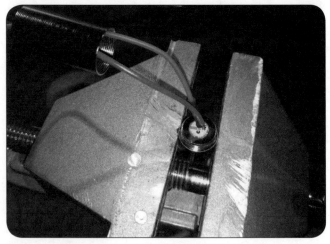

## Step 4: Construct the mechanics

To make this as easy as possible I got hold of a piece of MDF just a little bit larger than the DVD-Rom stepper assembly. This will work as the base to hold both the X

and Y axis. I found some spacers to hold the Y axis but bolts with a couple of nuts would work just as well. The measurements here are not critical but it is important that every axis is square to the other entire axis. I found that mounting the first assembly level with the MDF would make it easier to align everything.

The workspace is mounted on the old laser diode assembly. Make sure it is flat and level then glue something on that will serve as workspace. I found a piece of 1/4" acrylic that worked out just fine. It made this workspace stable enough but, as the laser can shine through it, I was not sure if this would be a security hazard or not. Later I found the solution I think works out for the best. I cut a piece of the DVDR metal case to the same size as the acrylic and glued it on. This way it is still very stable and you get a workspace that will be tough. One positive side effect is that you can secure whatever you are engraving with small magnets.

For the X axis I found some aluminum profiles in my junk bin, but just about anything could be used as long as it is stable. Measure the height you feel will be right for what you want to engrave. I opted for 7.5" long pieces for the support. This would give me a little under 2" clearance.

One important thing, the mounting holes on the assembly are not symmetrical. Be sure to measure the distance from the bottom end of the supports to the linear guides. That way you will be sure to get everything aligned. Where you mount the X axis will be dependent on the laser mounting. The laser should be in the center of the work area when the Y axis is in the middle position. When you mount the axis to the base plate, drill a small guide hole for the screws after you make sure that everything is square.

Now you should have the X and Y axis done and square to each other.

The laser mount does not have to be very sophisticated; mine is made from a small piece of plastic sheet and a clip with everything is glued together. Using a clip to hold the laser lets me change the focus point by simply sliding the laser up and down. As with all other parts the size is not that important as long as everything is square. There is just one measurement you need to think about here: the laser should be in the center of the work area when the Y and X axis is in the center position.

tools

## Step 5: Electronics

I started soldering the steppers. I used a ribbon cable to connect the steppers and solder them to the existing connections from the DVD boards. On the other end I soldered a four pin header so that it could be used with a breadboard. The same thing goes for the Easydriver; solder pin headers and use them with the breadboard. Ribbon cable can be found in abundance around old computer shops and service centers. All those old disk drive cables can be of good use.

In the schematics I have added a relay for use with a fan. This can come in handy as the engraving produces some smoke.

The Easydriver have two pins called MS1 and MS2, these set the step sequence. Tie them both to the five volt output from the Easydriver. This sets the step sequence to micro stepping. The four pins from the stepper connect to the motor output. All steppers I have found have all had the same pinout on the small connecting PCB. Connect the pins in the same order to the Easydriver as on the connecting PCB. The control pins (step, dir, gnd) goes to the Arduino. Besides this the Easydriver needs motor power connected. I use a twelve volt wall wart that drives the motors, fan, and Arduino. There is a potentiometer that controls the power to the motors, I just set this to the lowest setting and turn it up a tad if the steppers don't have enough force. I don't know the rating on the steppers. If they get too hot you're driving them too hard.

The fan just needs to be connected to the fan output. A small computer fan works well, just connect the positive and negative leads to the correct output.

The laser driver is an LM317 based circuit with no specials. This will work fine but it is far from optimal. I am driving the laser diode far too hard at about 300mA and if you do that you can't expect a very long life for the diode. The best solution would be to find a stronger laser and better driver, but to keep to the spirit of things, I wanted to use the laser from the DVDR itself. Laser on/off is controlled by the same relay as the fan.

If you want to simplify you could skip the whole laser driver and use a readymade driver. Then all you would have to do would be to connect the power to the fan relay. Of course this would probably be a little bit more expensive.

The whole thing evolved into a new Arduino shield, the Laser Shield. I have included the schematic and board layout in Eagle format (http://www.cadsoft.de/download. htm). Creating a circuit board is a bit out of the scope for this instructable, but there are lots of really good guides here on instructables.

If you want to make your own layout with Easydrivers I have made an Eagle library with the driver. It can be downloaded at http://www.slackersdelight.com/instructables/easydriver.lbr.

## Step 6: Prepare the Arduino

For the Arduino I started out writing my own software. But while searching for a good way to control movement from the serial port I stumbled upon something called "Grbl" (http://dank.bengler.no/-/page/show/5470_grbl). This is a g-code interpreter with lots of nifty functions. As I already had everything connected to the Arduino I had to either change my connections or change the software. Luckily it is easy to change control pins in the software. I did however have to download Winavr (http://winavr.sourceforge.net) and then the code from github.com. It is not that hard to do. After downloading and extracting the code you have to change the port numbers in config.h and make sure you get them in the right order. Then all you have to do is start a command window, enter the correct folder, and type "make." If all goes to plan you should end up with a .hex file ready for the Arduino.

[Ed. note: Arduino software can be a little tricky. If you'd like to follow all the details, please see this project's online Instructables page.]

You should see 10mm movement on each of the axes.

## Step 7: Getting the software ready

I will just go through the basics, including the software you'll need. For detailed instructions on how to set everything up, please visit this project's online Instructable page: source vector editing software (download at http://inkscape.org/download/?lang=en).

- Laser engraver extension: This generates the g-code needed to control the laser (download at http://www.slackersdelight.com/instructables/laserengraver.zip).
- G-code sender: A small windows program I wrote to communicate with Grbl (download at https://github.com/downloads/OttoHermansson/GcodeSender/gcodesender.exe) (source: https://github.com/Otto-Hermansson/GcodeSender).

## Step 8: Final assembly and extras

To finish the small engraver I made a small box from the Masonite board I found in a picture frame. It is just glued together. In the front there is a small fan from an old graphics card. The cooling is necessary for the Easy-

tools

drivers when you mount them in any kind of housing. They get hot when out in the open and even hotter in some sort of housing. In the box I glued some threaded spacers; this allows me to screw on the bottom. The Arduino is in turn screwed to the bottom. It makes the engraver into a useful and easy to handle little tool.

Some small extras have been added along the build. First off is the fan that keeps smoke away from the workspace. This is a small 40mm computer fan connected to the laser relay that I wrote about in the electronics step. The fan is pointed away from the workspace and gently sucks away smoke.

Another small but very useful extra are the magnets to hold down paper and other light weight objects. I got these from an old toy (http://www.amazon.com/Magnetic-Metallic-Geometric-Bridges-Chemistry/dp/B003LOVFUQ). After gluing some nuts on top of them they are done.

To change the focus you can screw the lens in and out. Or you could set the focus once on the workspace and then slide the laser up and down in the mount. This is how I do it. I have a set focus when the laser is at the lowest possible position in the mount. Then all I have to do is measure the thickness of the material and raise the laser the same amount. Most times I just hold the material next to the laser mount and move the laser to the correct height.

## Step 9: Final results

Here are some of the things I made with this little engraver so far. I will let the images tell most of the story. The only limit is your imagination (besides the low power and small work area).

**Key chain:**

I found some paint stirrer sticks at my local DIY shop. I liked the look of the wood and they were cheap. I sawed off a piece and drilled a small hole. After some sanding I engraved the Binford logo from the sitcom *Home improvement*.

**Plant marker:**

A normal Popsicle stick engraved with the plants name.

**Personalized matches:**

I'm just trying to show off.

**Memo note holder:**

A clothespin engraved and with a small neodymium magnet glued to the back makes a great way to stick a bunch of notes together on the fridge or any other metal surface. I like clothespins they are very versatile.

**Stamp:**

Cut out of a small foam sheet and glued to a piece of Masonite.

# Revive Nicad Batteries by Zapping Them with a Welder

By Tim Anderson (TimAnderson)
(http://www.instructables.com/id/Revive-Nicad-Batteries-by-Zapping-with-a-Welder/)

Nicad batteries often die in such a way that they won't take a charge and have zero voltage. This usually means they're shorted out by crystal dendrite growth.

Here's a method of bringing them back to life by zapping those shorted crystal dendrites away with too much current and/or voltage. We'll use a welder as a power source.

**WARNING:** If you get killed by a poisonous explosion it means you did something wrong. Electrocution is a real possibility also. Ask your parents how to not electrocute yourself with a welder.

Watch the video online and see how zapping is done.

## Step 1: Gather your materials
- Dead Nicad batteries
- Nicad battery charger
- Multimeter
- Voltage source: We'll use a welder.
- Insulated gloves
- Safety goggles

## Step 2: Check your battery

Charge up your battery up for a few hours or overnight to make sure that it is charged. If you suspect your charger isn't working you can trickle-charge it from a different voltage source. To make sure you don't overcharge it put some little lightbulbs from christmas lights in series so the current is below 1 amp. I use 1/2 amp usually.

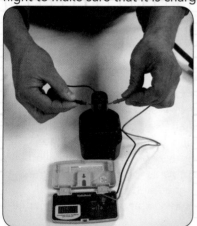

When you're sure your battery has had a fair chance to charge, check the voltage with your multimeter. Since you're reading this, the voltage is probably a lot lower than the label says it should be.

To see how much current your battery can put out, run the drill. Grab the chuck and stall it to get a feel for how much power it has.

## Step 3: Check your welder

Use your multimeter to make sure your welder is supplying DC and whether the gun or the clamp is positive and negative. Welders are sometimes AC and sometimes the polarity is backwards.

Turn the knobs to see what voltage range the welder puts out when no current is flowing. This one puts out about thirty volts at the max setting.

## Step 4: Zap the hell out of the frickin' battery!

The title says it all.

Tap the positive end of your welder to the "plus" terminal of your battery while holding the negative end to the battery's "minus" terminal.

You should see some sparks and nothing should get welded to anything.

No welding please. If you get killed by a poisonous explosion it means you did something wrong. It should feel like something good is happening.

## Step 5: Try out the battery and see if it worked

Try out your battery. It ought to be much better almost immediately.

## Step 6: Zapping individual cells

Pete Lynn dropped this battery pack in salt water. It shorted out the cells and it has been fully dead for a year or so. We peeled it apart to get at the individual cells. We scraped the salty cardboard off them and zapped them with a car battery. After that it worked fine.

It's easier to zap an individual cell than the whole pack at once.

Sometimes you can't revive a cell. You can cut or unsolder it from the others and replace it with a good one.

221

# Mini Metal Lathe

### By Gavin Wolchina (Random_Canadian)
(http://www.instructables.com/id/Mini-Metal-Lathe-1/)

Hack a power drill into a mini metal lathe with precision speed control.

I used a couple of broken power tools for the drive components in this mini lathe.

It features a powerful motor and small size.

The speed control hack is shown in step 5.

I am starting to think that I need a laser etcher to make a micrometer tool holder for the next round of tweaks.

## Step 1: Materials

There are some specialized items needed for this instructable.

The base materials are from Bosch Rexroth. The extruded aluminum base, t-nuts, inside brackets, end caps are all Bosch Rexroth. The extruded member is 45X90 and 14 inches long.

The support blocks are from VXB.COM Part number WH12A.

The Skate bearings are form VXB.COM Part Number 608ZZ. Yes I know that these are not taper bearings (ideal choice) but they do work for this application.

The flex motor couplings and rubber spider are from PrincessAuto.com.

I used a 12V DC motor from a Black and Decker cordless weed trimmer.

I used a variable speed switch from a Milwaukee 18V Li-Ion cordless drill.

The rest of the materials are presented as needed in the instructions.

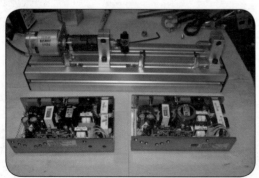

## Step 2: Make the supports

The shaft support blocks have an ID of 3/4 inch. You will need to bore/drill to 7/8 inch for the skate bearings. This was done gradually with increasing size drill bits and a hand drill.

The bearings are set flush to one face of the blocks and tightened into place.

The tailpiece support is a 1/2 inch counter bore bit that will be running in reverse. The shaft on the bit is 1/4 inch and a copper tubing adapter was used to increase the size to 5/16 inch for the inner race of the bearing. This is a friction fit shaft and you are done with this piece.

The drive side is a flex coupler mated to a 5/16 inch rod. The flex coupler was threaded to accept the rod then two hex nuts are placed on the shaft for spacing. You may need to add a spacer or washer for clearance. The shaft is then fed through the bearing and the assembly is clamped down with a nylon lock nut. The assembly should be snug but not binding.

## Step 3: Assemble the lathe

Install 2 inside supports and set the drive side bearing side on the base. This is to mark the position of the drive motor. I used 10-24 counter bore screws to allow for minor adjustment instead of the metric bolts needed for attachment of the angle supports.

The motor mount was marked and drilled with a 3/8 inch hole then fastened loosely to the inner angle supports. The motor shaft was smaller than the drive coupler so I had to build up the shaft diameter with aluminum foil tape. The drive spider is now installed and the drive bearing assembly is placed, then tightened securely. The motor is aligned and fastened securely.

Place the tailpiece support and snug the bolts into place.

I placed 2 additional angle supports between the bearing blocks for use as a tool rest.

You can finish the base with end caps if you desire.

tools

## Step 4: Make a 3 Jaw Chuck

Now is the time to make a 3-Jaw Chuck. A 4 Jaw Chuck is shown in my pocket lathe instructable. You will need to know how to braze or weld.

Begin by selecting a 1/4 inch fender washer. This is the base plate for the chuck. You will now need a 5/16 inch nut and a set screw that is 1/2 inch long. Place the set screw into the nut so that the bevel is protruding enough to center the nut in the 1/4 inch hole of the fender washer. The nut should sit flat on the washer and not move about the hole. Braze the nut in place. Then remove the set screw and flip the assembly over.

Place a 1/2 inch hex nut in the exact center of the washer and equally space three 5/16 hex nuts around the perimeter of the 1/2 inch hex nut.

Braze the 5/16 inch hex nuts in place and remove the 1/2 inch hex nut. Remove any slag with a wire brush and finish as desired. I chose to prime and paint flat black.

Install the three 5/16 inch 1/2 inch long set screws and you now have a 3-Jaw chuck. You might want to use a thread locker on the set screws. Be sure to completely tighten the screws before you use the chuck. This lathe will throw materials at a high velocity under full speed. Play safe. . .

## Step 5: Make the speed control

I highly recommend a speed control for this motor. It rotates insanely fast and if operated without a guard will represent a safety hazard.

You will need the trigger assembly from a cordless power tool. Preferably not a Li-Ion type as these can be fiddly to work with due to the safety circuitry inside of the switch.

I used some scrap materials to quickly put together a clamping mechanism as shown, in a pinch a C-clamp will work for this.

The drill that I used had a blown motor but the switch was still good. Since this was a Li-Ion type tool there is control circuitry in the switch. The fine wires shown on the inside of the larger wires are for that control circuitry. I placed the battery mating plug onto the battery and determined that the control circuit is 3.6V in reverse polarity. That means that you will need a small Li-Ion battery connected red to negative and black to positive for this switch to work. The switch is hand held and squeezed to adjust power as needed.

The switch has a direction lever and if your motor is running clockwise the chuck will not stay on the threaded shaft, so reversing the direction will correct this. Run the motor so that the chuck is tightened onto the shaft by rotational force.

I put a quick jig together to allow for setting the speed at a desired level, so you can have your hands free. I used a small section of the Bosch tubing and some 5/6 inch bolts. The switch was taped to the tubing and a lever was brazed together from scrap pieces. The adjustment is accomplished with a 5/6 inch threaded rod joiner. Tightening the joiner squeezes the trigger and increases the motor speed, while loosening the joiner releases the trigger and the speed reduces. With no tension on the trigger the power stops.

Previously I hacked a motion sensor for a switch, the main control board had a 3.6 Li-Ion cell as a backup source. I used this to trick the switch into working. Now when the power supply is attached the switch gives variable power to the motor to control the speed.

The power supply inlet wires go to the bottom of the trigger as do the control circuitry wires. The motor is directly connected to the terminals at the top of the trigger.

**tools**

223

## Step 6: Test the power and lathe

I wanted to use a 12V supply for this project but needed one that was in excess of 10A. I connected two 5Volt supplies in series to accomplish this. The supplies allow for adjustment in output via a small pot. I got 11V with what I had. Yes it will run on the battery but only about 20 minutes of continuous use will deplete it.

You might want to place a safety guard over the rotating motor and shafts for safety.

I used metal files and HSS cutting tools to work the aluminum. This was done at fairly low speed and dry. The tool rest in from the workpiece is a 1/4-20 bolt.

The motor coupling that I used was horribly out of balance and I had to clamp the lathe to the workbench with a C-clamp.

I am currently working on a better tool holder for more accurate cuts.

## Step 7: Build a 2 axis tool holder

This is a long step, read carefully and look at the pictures when possible.

You will need a 5 inch long piece of steel and a 1 inch by 1/8 inch bar stock as a base. You can use a slightly longer piece if you have it and I will explain this part later.

You will need two 6 inch 5/16 bolts and an 8 inch 5/16 bolt that is threaded the full length.

You will also need 11 5/16 nuts.

Begin by drilling out 8 of the nuts with a 5/16 bit to remove the threads. Grind one flat on 4 of the drilled nuts slightly.

Place 3 of the drilled nuts on the 6 inch bolts then thread on a regular nut fully.

Place 2 of the drilled nuts on 8 inch bolts.

Lay the bolts on the steel bar stock and braze the 6 end nuts to the steel bar. The alignment of the bolts is critical and must be as parallel as possible. Make sure that the ground part of the 2 center nuts on the 6 inch bolts is facing toward the plate.

Do not braze the 4 drilled nuts on the 6 inch bolts as these need to move freely; these will be called slide nuts later.

Remove the 8 inch bolt.

Grind one face of a 5/16 nut slightly then braze this nut in the center of a square piece of steel bar stock, keeping the face of the nut parallel with an edge and the ground flat opposite to the plate.

Place this small plate nut side down in the center of the previously brazed piece then feed the 8 inch bolt back into the piece, threading it through the nut on the smaller piece. Make sure that extended threads of the center bolt are towards the right. This is critical for use later.

Position the upper piece in the center of the 6 inch bolts, then move the slide nuts to the corners of the 1 inch piece and carefully braze them to the 1 inch plate, making sure that they do not get brazed to the bolts.

Test that the small plate moves freely along the 5/16 slide bolts. It may be a little tight but it will work and move freely as long as your slide bolts are parallel. You may have to tap the center bolt with a hammer to break any slag off of the bolts.

The heads of the 6 inch bolts were not brazed in place to allow for a little play if the slide bolts were not completely parallel.

Cut the ends off of the 6 inch bolts but not the 8 inch bolt. The 8 inch bolt is an adjuster bolt.

This whole process needs to be repeated using 1/4 inch bolts.

You will need 6 slide nuts, two 2 1/4 inch bolts and one 3 inch bolt that is threaded the whole way.

Make the 1/4 inch slide nuts the same way as before using a 1/4 inch drill bit. Grind one flat on 4 of the drilled nuts slightly.

Place 2 slide nuts on each 2 1/4 inch bolt and thread a regular nut the whole way on.

Place 2 slide nuts with the ground flat on the 3 inch bolt.

Align the bolts on the upper plate at a right angle to the 5/16 inch slides. Make sure that the slide nuts have the ground flat facing downward. Carefully braze the 6 end nuts in place leaving the slide nuts free.

Remove the center bolt and grind the head round.

Cut the slide bolts off flush to the brazed nuts.

Place a threaded nut on the center between the 1/4 inch slides. Thread the center bolt through the nut with the threads extending towards you with the lower adjuster bolt toward the right. This is your upper adjuster bolt.

Take a small piece of the bar stock that is as long as the slide bolts, this is the upper plate. Drill and counter bore the exact center of the upper plate. Place the plate on the center of the upper slide. Align the slide nuts so that they are about 1/4 inch apart in along the center of the upper plate edge.

Braze the center nut through the counter bore hole. Make sure that is brazed in place and the threaded adjuster moves freely. Then braze the slide nuts in place. Test for freedom of operation.

Finish the upper plate by brazing 4 small headed 10-24 1 inch bolts to the corners, threaded side up.

The clamp is a small piece of aluminum that has 4 holes drilled in the top. This is held in place with standard 10-24 nuts. The tool is clamped in place between the upper plate and the upper clamp.

The adjuster bolts will need to be locked in place firmly but not binding. I used a lock nut and threaded rod joiner for the lower adjuster. This was drilled and pinned in place. I did not have a roll pin so I used a small nail cut and pinned in place. The upper adjuster had 3 standard nuts installed on the threads then brazed in place.

As a final step I brazed 4 fender washers to the bottom plate for clamping to the lathe. It is held in place with standard T-nuts.

I primed and painted it flat black.

## Step 8: Tweaks

Due to the height of the tool holder I had to adjust the height of the motor by drilling new holes for the mount. Then I had to increase the height of the drive bearing blocks by placing a 1/4 inch shim of aluminum under the support blocks.

More importantly I removed the foil tape from the motor shaft and pressed a small section of 1/4 inch copper tubing onto the shaft. Then I used the new tool holder of the machine, the tubing, to make an exact fit for the motor coupling, which greatly reduce the vibrations.

Note the cutting tool looks like it is on upside down. This was done due to the lack of stores being open at 4 A.M. The cutting tool was too thick to meet the shaft properly so it was installed upside down and the motor was run in reverse to get a proper cut.

## Step 9: Still more tweaks

I have made some updates to the mini lathe since the first one was posted.

While the first one was functioning fine I wanted to improve the operation. I have added a second bearing on the main shaft along with soft clamping jaws on the chuck. The motor coupling still is producing some vibration.

tools

## Make a Good, Cheap, Upgradeable Sheet Plastic Vacuum Former

By **drcrash**

(http://www.instructables.com/id/Make-a-good%2c-cheap%2c-upgradeable-sheet-plastic-vacu/)

In this instructable, I'll show you how to make a cheap but good vacuum former, using mostly things you have around the house, or can buy very cheaply. The whole thing shouldn't cost more than about $30 to $50, maybe less depending on what shortcuts or substitutions you choose, and what materials and tools you have lying around. It also shouldn't or take more than an hour or two to make. (Plus a shopping trip to a home improvement store and an office supply store, and letting some silicone cure overnight; you can use epoxy if you're in a big hurry and want to do it all in an evening.)

Relatively few people know about vacuum forming, or how easy it is. They are mostly radio control model builders—who use it for making thin plastic parts for airplanes, or bodies for cars or helicopters, or hulls for boats— or they're Star Wars fans who use it for making their very own costume armor.

It's unfortunate that vacuum forming know-how is mostly limited to these little niches, because vacuum forming can be used for many purposes, artistic and practical. If you like making stuff in general, and especially if you like non-rectilinear stuff that doesn't look "home-made," you should know how to vacuum form.

For vacuum forming at home, the main limitation is usually space for the equipment—the size of your vacuum former is proportional to the size of plastic sheet you need to form. The $30-50 vacuum former described here doesn't take up much storage space at all, and can handle thin plastic sheets as big as will fit in your oven.

The vacuum former described here will work very well with an inexpensive high vacuum system, getting professional quality results for thick plastic, for under $100. If you want a standalone vacuum oven, so that you can use it somewhere besides your kitchen, you can make a medium-sized one (12 x 20 inches) for $30.

### Step 1: Understand the design

Our vacuum former consists mostly of:

- a board (called a "platen") with a hole in the middle of it
- a vacuum cleaner that sucks air through that hole
- a pair of frames we can clamp together around the edge of a sheet of plastic, and
- a kitchen oven.

To use it, we'll do three basic things:

- heat the plastic in the oven until it's soft and rubbery and stretchable
- stretch it over the shape we want to copy, and
- suck it down around that thing, and let it cool in that shape

In more detail, we'll:

#### Setup

- Support the board on something near the oven. The support(s) can be pretty much anything, or any convenient pair of things that is reasonably sturdy, allows us to route the hose to the vacuum cleaner without kinking it, and can be put very near the oven we're using.

- Put some things in the oven that we can support the plastic-holding frames on. (Glasses made of actual glass, for instance.)
- Preheat the oven. This usually gives us more even heat.
- Position some object that we want to shape plastic over on the board, over the hole, but with some spacers under it, so that air can flow from around the the object, under it, and to the hole in the board.
- 

### Heat

- Clamp a sheet plastic between the pair of frames and support it on three or four things in the oven (such as glasses made of actual glass)
- Wait a few minutes for the plastic to get hot and rubbery and stretchable. For most plastics, we can tell how stretchable it is by how much it sags under its own weight. When it sags about the right amount, we know it's ready.

### Form

- (Turn on the vacuum cleaner, open the oven, and) QUICKLY but carefully remove the plastic from the oven with gloved hands.
- stretch the plastic down over the shape we're copying, until the frame meets the board, creating a kind of "tent" of hot rubbery plastic over our form and stretching down to the board, and
- let the vacuum cleaner suck air out from under the "tent," by sucking air from under the form, and in turn from around it. This will suck the stretched, rubbery plastic inward into the desired shape, in about one second, and the plastic will cool enough to solidify in the new shape in about 10 to 20 seconds.

To make this work well, and flexibly, we'll add a few basic enhancements:

- We'll put a foam rubber gasket on the board, the size and shape of our plastic-clamping frames. That way, when we stretch the plastic over our mold, we can press the frame against the gasket to make a seal.
- We'll use a 3/4" galvanized floor flange (plumbing fitting) under the hole in the platen, as part of our connection to the vacuum cleaner hose. This will let us replace the vacuum cleaner with a more powerful—but surprisingly cheap—vacuum system later, if we want.

## Step 2: Gather materials and tools

You'll need:

- A kitchen oven or some other way of heating plastic.
- A good vacuum cleaner, preferably a powerful (1000 watts or more) canister vacuum. If you don't already have one, you can get one for $5 at the Goodwill Outlet Store (a.k.a. Blue Hanger Store).
- A 3/4" MDF (medium-density fiberboard) at least 2 inches bigger than the inside dimensions of your oven, cut down to 2 inches bigger each way.
- A 3/4" galvanized floor flange (plumbing fitting). (Less than $3.00.)

- A 3/4" x 2" threaded pipe nipple (or "riser"); PVC plastic or galvanized is fine. (That's just a short piece of pipe threaded on both ends, about 50 cents.)
- A little PTFE tape, a.k.a. "Teflon tape," used for sealing plumbing joints. (About $1.)
- Four 3/4" long wood screws, fairly large diameter but small enough to fit through the holes in the floor flange. (About $1.)
- 8 aluminum windowscreen frame corner braces, for 7/16" or 3/8" thick frame material. (5/16" will do for small frames and thin plastic, but thicker is better for larger or thicker plastic; small differences in thickness have a significant effect on stiffness).
- 2 or 3 sticks, 6 or 7 or 8 feet long, of aluminum 3/8" or 7/16" windowscreen frame material that goes with the aluminum frame corners. You'll need enough for four frame sides in each of the two dimensions of the plastic you'll be using, plus a couple of inches extra per stick. (About $4-5 per stick.)
- 1 box of a dozen binder clips, large size, from an office supply store. (Three or four dollars.)
- A sheet of thin plastic 2" bigger each way than your chosen plastic sheet size, or just 1" bigger in a pinch, maybe a flimsy GARAGE SALE sign or a piece of the thin plastic you intend to vacuum form. (See step 7.)
- A little silicone caulk or silicone sealant, or maybe epoxy, or rubber cement. (Any kind of gap-filling glue will work, if it doesn't set extremely quickly like hot glue. Tacky putty will do temporarily, in a pinch.)
- A 10-foot roll of foam rubber weatherstrip, at least 1/4" thick and 1/2" wide, preferably 3/8" thick and 3/4" wide. You want the kind that's just foam rubber self-stick tape with a rectangular cross-section. (Three or four dollars at Home Depot.)
- Some washers or coins to use as spacers.
- Masking tape or (preferably) blue painter's tape.
- Duct tape may come in handy, as it often does. (See Step 8.)
- Some aluminum window screen material is also nice to have, but optional. Screening from a junked window screen is fine.

You should probably take your vacuum cleaner hose to the store, and look for a plumbing fitting that adapts 3/4" pipe threads to roughly the size of your hose (inside or outside). It doesn't have to fit well, but anything that gets you closer is good. (See Step 8.) If you already have a shop vacuum with a large hose, and will be using that, you'll want an adapter from the large hose size to the small hose size. (About four dollars.)

You'll also need some basic tools:

- a drill and a reasonably large bit (such as 1/4"), plus a bit that's somewhat smaller than your screws
- a screwdriver that fits your screws
- an electric saw such as a portable jigsaw or circular saw, unless you have the board cut to size at the store. (That's usually free; see Step 3.)
- a hacksaw

tools

- a miter box you can use the hacksaw with
- scissors

## Step 3: Make a platen

The heart of your vacuum former is the platen, which is just a piece of MDF (medium-density fiberboard) a little bigger than your kitchen oven—about an inch bigger all the way around. The extra inch will be useful for taping down a sheet holding the frame gasket.

Measure the inside dimensions of your oven, side to side and front to back, and add two inches to each measurement. That's how big your platen board should be. (A little bigger isn't a problem, unless it makes it hard to fit your board and yourself near your oven in your kitchen.)

Now make a hole 1 1/2" in diameter in the middle of the board. I used a hole saw attachment on my drill to make a neat hole, but it doesn't actually matter. If you have a drill and a portable jigsaw, you can drill a starter hole with the drill to get the jigsaw blade through the board, and cut out the 1 1/2" hole with the jigsaw.

(Don't make the common mistake of making the hole the same size as the diameter of your pipe. That creates an air flow bottleneck right around the hole, where the air must squeeze under the mold to get into the hole. You want a hole with a larger circumference than your pipe.)

The platen shown is actually 1/2" MDF, because that's what I had around. 3/4" MDF is nicer; it's more than three times as rigid.

## Step 4: Attach the floor flange to the platen board

Now you need to attach the floor flange to the bottom of the board, over the hole. Center the flange over the hole, and mark the spots where the screw holes are with a pencil.

Drill pilot holes into the board at the centers of those circles. (The pilot holes should be about the diameter of your screws' shafts, not including the threads, or a shade smaller.) Drill most of the way through the board, but not all the way.

Clean the surface of the flange where it meets the board, using soapy water and then non-soapy water. Galvanized fittings often have a thin protective layer of oil

on them, which can keep sealants and glues from bonding well to them.

While you're at it, dampen the area around the hole just a little, maybe pressing a damp paper towel to it. (This will make silicone set up faster. You don't want it really wet, which may make the MDF swell; you just want a touch of moisture.)

Put a bead of silicone caulk or silicone sealant around where the flange meets the board, going on both sides of each screw hole.

Press the flange to the board, and screw it down. Wipe around the edge of the flange with a paper towel or something to remove excess silicone.

(You can use epoxy instead of silicone, if you're in a hurry, or if that's what you have handy. In that case, don't dampen the MDF, but do make sure the flange isn't oily.)

## Step 5: Make a matched pair of clamping frames

Now you need to decide what size frames you want to make and use first. You can make different-sized frames later, any size from a few inches across to whatever size will fit in your oven. (That's probably about 16 x 22 inches.)

For many reasonably small items, 12 x 16 inches is a good size for frames. You can divide sheets whose dimensions are 2 x 4 or 4 x 8 feet into 12 x 16 in sizes with no waste, and 12 x 16 inches will accommodate most RC plane canopies, most full-size masks, many enclosures for small electrical and mechanical projects, etc. (You can also cut 12 x 18 inch sheets of craft foam down by a couple of inches, and not waste much foam.)

Have a look at your windowscreen frame material and the aluminum corner braces. See how the ends of the corner pieces fit INSIDE the frame material, with a funny groove going along the inside edge of the frame on one side. (That groove is for a rubber strip that holds windowscreen in, and it's useless to us, but you should know where it goes.)

The groove has to be along the inside edge of the screen frame, or the corner things won't go in right. (They have a little alignment tab on them that fits in a small slot in the frame material.) When making your miter cuts, make sure that the non-groove edge is the long edge, and the grooved edge is the short one.

Each piece is shorter on the inside edge (where the groove is) than on the outside. It's the longer outer edges that should have the same dimensions as your plastic. Cut four pieces the size of the shorter dimension, and four

tools

pieces the size of the longer one. (This will require a separate miter cut for each end of each piece—16 cuts—because the frame material is asymmetrical and the remaining piece is always mitered the wrong way.)

Use a miter box and a hacksaw for these cuts, because you want the pieces to meet pretty closely. Be sure to clamp the material you're cutting. That helps make a reasonably precise cut.

Now put the two frames together, sliding the cut pieces on over the corners.

Look at both of them, paying particular attention to the corners. Pick the one whose fit is best, with the least gap at the joins on both the top and bottom, to use as your bottom frame—that's the critical one for making a seal. (The plastic needs to be flat against the top of the bottom frame, and the bottom of that frame is what will meet the gasket.) If they're both about the same, but with a sloppy fit on some corners and a good fit on others, mix and match the parts to make one neatish frame and one sloppyish one.

Mark the bottom frame BOTTOM FRAME with a permanent marker or something.

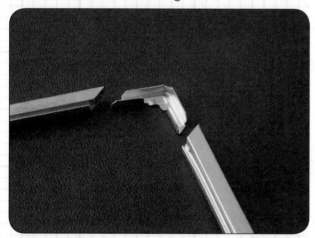

## Step 6: Clamping plastic

Orient both frames so that the useless groove is on top, so that the side with the wider flat area is on the bottom. You may want to mark each frame on the top, so you don't forget. (Maybe "BOTTOM FRAME, THIS SIDE UP" and "TOP FRAME, THIS SIDE UP.")

Take a sheet cut to your frame size, put it between your two frames, and clamp the frames together around it with binder clips.

For most thin plastics, and sheets up to about 12 x 18 inches, 6 binder clips are sufficient—one at the middle of each shorter ends, and two spaced about 1/3 and 2/3 of the way along each of the long sides. (For thick plastics, larger sheets, or difficult-to-form plastics like acrylic or polycarbonate, you may need more clamps. A clamp every few inches is generally enough.)

Because our clamps go on the outside of the frames, they can interfere with the seal between the bottom frame and the gasket if we're not careful. If they don't sit flat against the bottom, there can be a gap that the gasket

doesn't seal, and if they're too far out, the rolled edge of the binder clip can hit the gasket, which may cause an air leak. (And if you do it a lot, you'll tear up your gasket.)

Look at the bottom of each clamp. Make sure the rolled edge sticks inward around the plastic about 1/4" past the frames, and the bottom is flat against the bottom of the bottom frame.

(Unless you plastic is just the right thickness, the clamps won't be quite flat on both top and the bottom; they'll usually taper in a bit, or for thick plastic they'll flare out. Just make sure they're flat against the bottom, and let the top do whatever it wants.)

Now remove the bent-wire handles from the binder clips, at least on the bottom, so that the handles won't get in the way of making a seal. (Just squeeze the handle so that the ends come inward away from the rolled edge of the binder clip at the ends, and pull it away.) Put those aside in a pile.

If you don't have a tight fit in your oven, you can leave the top handles on, flipped back and outward. If you do have a tight fit, remove them too, so they won't stick outward past the frames and be a problem.

## Step 7: Make a removable weatherstrip gasket

Now make the gasket for your chosen frame size. You want it easily removable, so that you can use different-sized plastic and frames for different projects, so don't just stick the weatherstrip right down on the platen.

Instead, use a thin sheet of flexible material, such as 1/32" plastic, maybe the same stuff that you'll be vacuum forming. (You might think it would stick, but it won't.) One of those cheap flexible "garage sale" signs from a hardware store will do fine, too.

You'll put the gasket on this "tape-down sheet," and tape the sheet to the platen with masking tape or painter's tape over the edges. (You might think this would make a lousy seal, but it works fine; vacuum sucks the tape in so that it seals better. Positive pressure would blow it right off.)

Cut the plastic 1/2" or 1" bigger than your frame size all around—only a half inch if it's almost the size of your board (or the plastic sheet you're cutting it from), but an inch otherwise. An inch is nice, but a half inch will do fine. You don't want it way oversized, because that just makes a bigger edge you have to seal with tape.

Now cut a hole in the middle so that your tape-down sheet won't block the vacuum hole in the middle of the platen.

Mark the rectangle where your frame will meet your gasket, both the inside and the outside edges. That's where you want the gasket.

I like to make mitered corners in my gaskets, cutting a 90-degree vee out of the material at the corners, but not quite all the way through—leave about 1/8" of foam at the outside edge, rather than cutting all the way through it. Other people cut theirs square.

The weatherstrip is flexible and stretchable, which can make it difficult to apply neatly, evenly, and in a straight line, if you peel the backing tape off of it too quickly. So don't. Peel the backing paper off a few inches at a time, and carefully smooth it down without stretching it. (There should be some slack.)

That's especially important at the corners. Don't cut your pieces too short, or cut your vee-notches too soon. Lay the stuff down almost to the corner, and then cut it a shade too long, maybe 1/16," rather than a little too short—lay it down slightly scrunched at the corners, so that the foam presses against the joint and holds it closed, rather than being stretched and having the joint gape open.

(Don't obsess about this, either, though—if you get it wrong, you can fill the gap with silicone, or re-do it, and it will be fine.)

If you're in a hurry, don't bother to seal the corner joints. You can go back and silicone them later, when you won't be using the thing overnight. (Or use rubber cement, which sets up quickly.)

You probably don't want to actually tape the sheet to the platen at this point; wait until you've adapted your vacuum hose. If you do tape it down, be careful not to damage the gasket when you're fiddling around with the bottom side of the board.

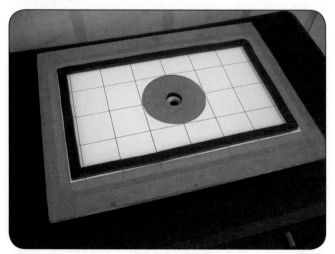

## Step 8: Adapt your vacuum cleaner hose to the nipple

This is the only part I can't give you precise instructions for, because vacuum cleaner hose diameters vary somewhat by brand.

You should probably take your vacuum cleaner hose to the hardware store, and find some plumbing fitting that adapts 3/4" pipe threads to something that fits your vacuum hose (inside or outside) reasonably closely. Then

you'll have less shimming or packing or taping to do.

If you're using a shop vac with a standard large (2 1/2") diameter hose and an adapter to the standard small (1 1/4") diameter, the adapter will likely fit right over 3/4" pipe nipple, with the pipe threads going inside the (unthreaded) adapter. (That's not how it's designed to work, but it works.) You can just screw the adapter over the nipple, with epoxy on the threads and around the outside where they meet, to permanently connect them and seal the joint. (If you don't want to commit to permanently joining them, you can pack the threads with tacky putty, screw them together, smear a little tacky putty around the outside of the joint, and wrap duct tape around the whole mess.)

For most household vacuum cleaner hoses, the hose will fit loosely over the nipple, and you need to shim it out a little so that it fits snugly. A few wraps of duct tape may fill the gap. If the gap is very large, you may want to wrap some craft foam or leftover weatherstrip around it first.

## Step 9: Tape the gasket to the platen

Once your silicone or glue has set up, center the tape-down sheet holding the gasket on your board, and carefully tape it down with masking tape or painter's tape. 3/4" masking tape will do fine, but 1" wide painter's tape is nicer.

Apply the tape carefully to each edge, unrolling it and smoothing it halfway on the tape-down sheet, and halfway off (on the platen). If you get a wrinkle, lift the tape up back to the wrinkle, pull it taut, and smooth it down again.

tools

## Step 10: Screw the nipple to the platen flange

Wrap several layers of PTFE tape (teflon tape) around the threads of the pipe nipple, where it will screw into the floor flange. You need several layers, because the tape is very thin, and you want to build up enough thickness to fill any mis-fits in the threads and make a good seal.

Now screw the pipe nipple into the flange, hand tight.

## Step 11: Tips on using your vacuum former

I won't give detailed instructions for vacuum forming here—that's for another instructable I'm working on.

For more information on vacuum formers and vacuum forming, check out my web site, http://www.vacuum-formerplans.com (It has links to several other good sources of information.) I will give a few tips that are somewhat specific to this design, though:

- Pick a size of plastic that's appropriate for what you're making. You need some "extra" plastic between your mold and the inside edge of the gasket. A good general rule of thumb is that if your mold has steep sides, the extra area should be as wide as the mold is tall. If the sides are more rounded or gently sloping, you don't need as much. If you have too much extra plastic around the mold, you may get webbing. (Wrinkles caused by the plastic stretching too much and not being able to suck inward onto the mold without folding over on itself.)

- Be careful about the binder clips; remember to make them flat against the bottom of the bottom frame, with the rolled edge a bit inward from the frame so that you don't tear up your gasket. You will sometimes bring the frame down a little out of alignment, and dent the inner part of gasket with the rolled edges of binder clips. That's no big deal. You can add guide rails to prevent this, and bring the plastic down straight every time. All you need is three strips of something reasonably stiff, sticking up just outside the gasket. If you put two along one edge and one along an adjacent edge, that defines a corner that you can nestle the frame into just before bringing it down, and press it lightly into the "corner" as you lower it. L-shaped guide rails can be clamped to the platen anywhere you want them, for different sizes of plastic.

- Put your mold up on spacers such as washers or coins, about the thickness of pennies, to ensure that there's room for air to flow under the mold and to the platen hole. You can also use a piece of aluminum window screen under the mold, to keep the mold from sitting quite flat against the platen. For plastic up to about 12 x 16 inches, I often use a piece of window screen folded once each way, to make four layers, and no other spacers. This makes one thick, porous "spacer" under the whole mold, which air can flow right through. In effect, it makes thousands of platen holes, including hundreds right around the edge of the mold, where

they count most. (Even if you have a many-hole platen, one layer of window screen is a good idea. It keeps the mold from blocking the holes it's sitting on, and keeps the plastic from sucking quite flat to the platen and blocking the holes right around the mold.)

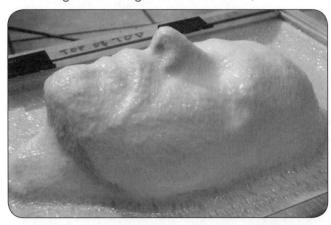

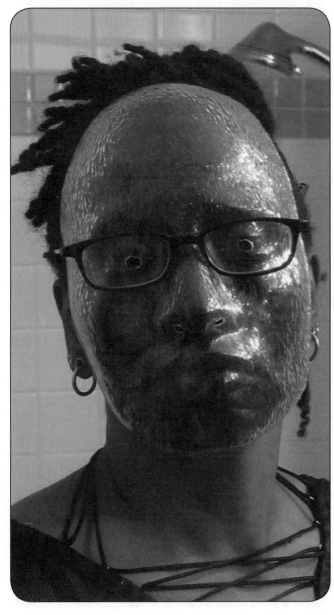

tools

# Converting an Inkjet Printer to Print PCBs

By Ryan Pourcillie (pourcirm)
(http://www.instructables.com/id/Converting-an-Inkjet-Printer-to-Print-PCBs/)

Recently one of my focuses has been to find a way to make the PCB (Printed Circuit Board) creation process easier. I like being able to design something based on what I want in a circuit and just making it myself on the random weekend. While the toner transfer method has been my go to in the past it's just not nearly as consistent as I would like it to be. The specific pressure of the iron and timing both make it a hit or miss approach. I'm not a fan of hit or miss. I like to know something is going to work every time I try to do it. This sentiment got me exploring new ideas for PCB creation, which is the topic of this project.

## Tools and materials

**Materials:**
- Obviously you'll need some form of an Epson inkjet printer probably of the C80 family as those are the ones I have seen modifications to in the past.
- A sheet of aluminum or steel or some metal sheet (about 9 inches by 14.5 inches roughly)
- Approximately 4 feet of 1/4 inch bent (90 degree corner piece) aluminum rail
- Some type of brackets and screws to secure them with (I used 3)
- Some 4–40 screws (I used 1/2 inch long ones)
- Nuts for said screws (I used about 16)
- A small piece of scrap plywood and some other random scraps of 2x4 or something of the sort
- Epoxy and/or hot glue
- The drivers for whichever printer and operating system you decide to use
- An ink kit from Inksupply.com (more details on this later)

**Tools:**
- A Dremel tool with grinding wheels to cut through metal
- Various screwdrivers
- Pliers or a socket wrench that fits the nuts or screws you'll be using
- A drill of some sort to attach the brackets
- A hot glue gun
- A heat gun

Once you've gathered all of those things you're ready to begin.

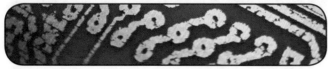

## Step 1: Panel removal and breakdown

Step 1 is a pretty easy one and is somewhat self explanatory. The first thing I did was remove the paper feeder sticking out of the back of the printer and toss that aside. Once that's gone you can just use the tabs in various areas of the printer to pop off the front tray, the side panels, and ultimately the main printer casing. I chose to keep the main casing so that I have something to cover the printer with later for storage purposes.

Once you get all that done you'll end up with the internals of the printer ready for modification.

## Step 2: More removal of parts

After removing all the covers there are some parts that you should remove and set aside for later. You'll need to relocate the paper feed sensor because the feeder no longer sends paper in from the top rear of the printer. I'll talk more about how this system works later, but you'll want to remove that sensor from the back of the printer and unplug it from the circuit board. Set this aside and we'll work more with it later.

Next up is the pressure wheels in the center of the printer. You don't really need all three sets and the center set could cause clearance issues when you send a circuit board through the printer. So to avoid this problem I simply removed the roller leaving a clear area for the circuit board to pass through.

Finally you'll want to remove the print head cleaning station. You'll want to be careful here! This station simply pops out from the press fit connectors it's sitting on, but it will have a tubing system connected to it. This tubing is necessary so make sure not to break it or remove it. Once you have those three things removed we can start looking at the heart of modifying this printer, the lifting process.

## Step 3: Removing the print head assembly

The next step is where you roll up your sleeves and start the cutting and modifying process. It's also the step where you need to pay attention to what you're doing as you could seriously injure yourself and/or ruin your printer modification completely. As such you should be wearing safety glasses or goggles during the cutting process and keep your hands away from the cutting disc. Also for those unfamiliar with using a Dremel tool, when you cut through the metal sections of the printer body you will create a rain of sparks and small flakes of sharp metal. As I said before be careful and wear safety glasses, you don't want any of this stuff in your eyes.

So on to the modification...

Let's start with the easy areas first and work from there. Starting with the front rail of the printer you will see two screws that you will want to remove. Once you do this the rail lifts away and you can set it aside for later re-installation.

Next you can focus on the two screws near the print head cleaning mechanism. By removing these two screws the right side of the printing assembly will be lose and removable. However you cannot remove this entire piece yet as the left side is one large metal piece and there is a small hidden tab that also holds the assembly in place.

This is where the Dremel tool enters the picture. You first want to look at the metal areas and plan out exactly where you would like to cut. I tried to minimize the area I had to cut because, as I mentioned, the sparks flying in your face is something you want to experience as little as possible. That being said you'll want to cut through the small interior tab to release the right side of the assembly before finally cutting around the entire left metal corner, so that you can lift the print head assembly and remove it completely from the printer's base.

If you've been careful and followed the directions thus far you should have three pieces laid out in front of you.

## Step 4: Cleaning the print head (optional)

This step is optional depending on what shape your printer is in, but since mine was a little older and had been sitting around I decided to clean the print head. This is a pretty easy process since you've now removed the entire assembly and you can just place it on the table while cleaning the head. My print head was pretty dried out and had a lot of old ink stuck on it so I did some research to find out the best way to remove it. What I found to be the best suggestion was to use some cotton swabs to knock some of the larger gunk off before spraying the cotton swab with Windex glass cleaner to really remove the dried out ink from all the surfaces. I used quite a few cotton swabs to clean the print head really well.

Like I said this step is optional, but it really helped my print head work like new again.

## Step 5: Reinstalling the print head assembly part one

Now that everything is taken apart and cleaned up it's time to start the process of lifting and reassembling the print head. This process will ultimately depend on what you're hoping to print on and the thickness of the material you're planning on using. For my modification I plan on using a metal carrier tray onto which I will attach some copper clad board I'm hoping to print on. As such my materials are just under 1/16th of an inch for the metal carrier and a little over 1/16th of an inch for the copper clad. However I don't want the print head to be too close to the copper clad or hit anything so I went ahead and lifted the printing assembly almost 3/8ths of an inch for guaranteed clearance. This is also a good idea in case I decide to print double-sided boards in the future as the copper clad for that is a bit thicker due to the extra copper layer.

Now that I've decided on the amount I want to lift the printing assembly I can begin inserting spacers to get the desired height. The easiest place to start is with the front rail system. As it is attached with two screws I simply bought some longer 4–40 screws and used two of the nuts that came with them as spacers. Once that rail is screwed back in it's done with and you can move on to the more complicated print head assembly portion.

## Step 6: Reinstalling the print head assembly part two

The reinstallation of the print head assembly is a bit more complicated because you will need to create some sort of bracket piece to hold together the corner section that you cut through. For this I purchased some corner brackets from the local hardware store and cut them in to single smaller pieces that I could use. I just chose them because they were cheap and I figured they'd be easy to modify, but you can make other brackets as you see fit.

Once I had the brackets made I needed to mark where I wanted to drill for the bolts to hold these brackets in place. This process was simple for the bottom section. I just decided where I wanted to put the supports and then marked for the holes and drilled. Once I had those holes drilled I attached the bottom portion of the brackets so that I could line up the print head assembly and mark where the top holes should be drilled.

To make sure the top holes were in the right spots I went ahead and inserted the 2 spacer bolts on the right hand side where the two screws attach to the printer base. Once those where attached I aligned the brackets with the cut corner and used a level to make sure the assembly was in the correct position before marking the hole locations. At that point I removed the assembly again to drill those holes and then reattached the entire piece this time using screws and the brackets I had created to secure the entire assembly in place.

## Step 7: Lifting the print head cleaning station

This is a step I think gets overlooked a lot, but is actually quite important for your printer to function well for a longer period of time. When you turn off your printer the print head moves into the cleaning station to help prevent the ink from drying out and clogging the nozzles. This station is also what's used to perform a nozzle cleaning cycle so you need to make sure you raise it just as you raised everything else in the printer.

To make sure the cleaning station was raised the right amount I used a somewhat indirect method of measuring. You can obviously choose your own way to lift this, but what I did was reinstall it in the normal position before using two of the leftover brackets that I had to mark where the screw holes fell on the printer base and the cleaning station itself. From there I measured 3/8 of an inch down from the marks on the cleaning station and drilled pilot holes at those marks and the marks on the printer body. Once I had those holes I lined up the brackets to the printer body and attached them with screws before lining up the cleaning station and screwing it to the brackets as well.

When I turn the printer on and run cleaning cycles the cleaning station is lined up where it needs to be and works as it should.

## Step 8: The feed system

At this point in the modification you've got most of the straight printer work done, but if you look at what's in front of you, you'll notice that there's still no good way to feed material into the printer, and you also still have a sensor sitting off to the side of your work. Since you'll ultimately be using a heat gun on your printed work it's a good idea to create a system that can feed your carrier and copper clad material into the printer pretty much hands free. As such I built a rail system that supports the carrier and allows the printer to function without me having to hand feed it.

Again you can devise your own system, but here's what I've done with my printer. My first consideration was where I wanted to attach the feed sensor. This sensor is absolutely necessary or the printer will not function. What it does is it senses when material passes through its gap and relays that message to the printer so it knows exactly where the printing material is. The second important thing to know about this sensor is that it expects a delay between the time that the rollers of the printer start feeding paper in and when the sensor is triggered. I'll go into detail about that more later, though, when I talk about the carrier piece. Since the sensor needed to be mounted in a place where the carrier would pass through it, and I was already planning on making a plywood deck area to level the back of the printer body, I decided it would be best to hot glue the sensor right into that decking near the edge of where the carrier piece would travel.

As you can see in the images I basically used a few layers of scrap plywood to create a level area in the rear of the printer. This decking area covers the large felt waste ink reservoir you'll see and also the metal power supply area. Basically all I did for this area was to measure out those two enclosed areas and cut layers of plywood until they were level. That took two additional layers in the waste ink reservoir, and then I was able to lay one larger piece over the entire surface. Once I created this decking I cut a corner off of the top layer and lined up the feed sensor with where the carrier material would travel. This ensures that the material can travel through the sensor and set it off as the printer expects it to.

The main point of the decking area however was to create something to which I could attach support rails to. Using these rails I can simply lay the carrier and copper clad in the tray and let the printer take over. What I did for that was to take some aluminum that was bent into a 90 degree corner and cut it to the length of my expected carrier piece. From there I epoxied the rails to the decking and a third piece across the back for extra support.

With the feed system taken care of I wanted to test and make sure everything was functioning properly. To do that I finally cut my carrier material. I had a sheet of anodized aluminum lying around so I decided it would make a good carrier. To start I measured the width of the print gap, which in my case was around 9 inches. With this in mind I decided to aim for something similar to paper size and drew out a 9 inch by 11.5 inch rectangle. Luckily however I read more information about the feed sensor before I cut that sheet because as it turns out that carrier would not have worked very well. From what I've learned the carrier piece needs to have a notch cut out of it that is about 3.5 inches long to allow for the proper delay between the feed rollers activating and the sensor triggering. So with this new information I modified my carrier outline to be a 9 inch by 14.5 inch rectangle with a 3.5 inch section cut out of one corner.

After cutting this carrier I installed the printer drivers on my computer and taped a piece of paper onto the carrier before running a print cycle to check for complete functionality. Everything came out and the printer functioned normally, so I began to look forward to the printing of PCBs.

### Step 9: Filling the ink cartridge

The final modification to the printer is in the ink. While this printer can still use regular ink cartridges from Epson the ink in those cartridges will not resist the chemical etching process used to make PCB's, so it has to be replaced with ink that can. This actually brings the entire modification full circle because this ink replacement is why an Epson printer was chosen in the first place. Aside from the somewhat easy modifications Epson uses a special print head known as a piezo print heads, which allows them to print a replacement ink called Mis Pro yellow ink (http://www.inksupply.com/product-details.cfm?pn=MISPRO-4-Y). This ink would clog most other printers as they use a different type of print head system.

So the Epson is of double importance to the entire project.

If you follow that link above it will take you to inksupply.com which is where I bought everything I used for the ink replacement. All you really need if you have an empty cartridge is the Mis Pro yellow, but I bought a few things to make the process easier. The first thing I bought was an empty ink cartridge that they sell which will make filling the printer easier and I won't have to clean out an old cartridge. Secondly I bought a fill kit from them that supplies you with two syringes and a set of tips to fill the ink cartridge with. Finally I bought a device from them that resets the small chip that's on Epson print cartridges so that you can convince your printer there is still ink in the cartridges after they run dry and you refill them.

So using these things and my yellow ink I filled up the cartridge and got it prepared for installation in my modified printer so that I could run a final test and etch a circuit board to see the results of my work.

### Step 10: Printing test

Recently I've been testing various techniques for creating PCBs so I created a test board in CadSoft's Eagle that features the three pad types and traces in various different measurement sizes, so I thought it would be an appropriate gauge of how well this printer works also.

Also for those of you who are curious about how detailed this thing can get I've also printed drj113's Ethernet Arduino board (http://www.instructables.com/id/A-credit-card-sized-Ethernet-Arduino-compatable-co/). This thing is packed full of little details and a few surface mount parts so that will give you a very good idea of what you can print with this system.

Make sure to check out the next page for some important etching information before you proceed any further or you may ruin your boards!

### Step 11: Notes on etching

First, everyone should know that if you go this route you need to use ferric chloride to etch the boards. I know it's nasty for the environment and a lot of people are trying not to use it, but the Mis Pro yellow ink will only work with ferric chloride as far as I know. I tried to etch my first set of boards in a mixture of hydrochloric acid and hydrogen peroxide, but the etching solution ate right through the Mis Pro ink and I ended up with those nice green boards of junk (oxidized copper) when I got frustrated and washed them off with water. Ferric chloride however does not eat away the Mis Pro ink and the etching will work as expected provided you follow the next suggestion.

Second, the thickness of the copper layer on your copper clad board is somewhat important. If you choose a copper clad board with a thinner copper layer of 1 ounce per square foot the Mis Pro ink will survive the shorter etching process and give you a better PCB in the end. (If you're looking to buy PCB material check out

tools

eBay as it's a great source for bulk material at a good price.)

Lastly, my "Trace and Pad Test Board" was poorly designed. Yes that's a shot at myself, but I thought it was worth admitting. I realized during the etching process that there is way too much copper on that board that needs to be etched away. As such I thought about redesigning it with less open space, but then decided to stop trying to etch a nonuseable test board because I didn't want to waste more ferric chloride when I knew the process was working already. Also the Ethernet Arduino (http://www.instructables.com/id/A-credit-card-sized-Ethernet-Arduino-compatable-co/) serves as much a better measure of printing and etching with this new printer modification as it will be a functional board that I can solder parts to and test traces on.

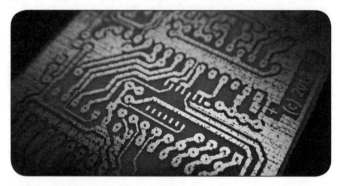

## Step 12: Etching revisited

As many people in the comments have noted my boards had pinholes all over them and I was just as unsatisfied with that as anyone. As such I started to do some more research and try to find ways to correct this issue. Among the many suggestions I received I put two at the top of my list for researching. Firstly, I looked into a better etching setup as I've been considering this for some time and this seemed like the right project for the upgrade to heated, aerated tanks. Secondly, a few people mentioned the ink I am using and that the proper setting temperature may be higher than I am actually achieving with my heat gun. Since those two things seemed easy enough to remedy I focused on them first to try and solve my pinhole problem.

To start I began looking at a few different etching tank designs and thinking about what I wanted out of my design. I came to the conclusion that I wanted something nice, but not overly expensive and building my own setup was the best option. As such I took a plastic cereal container that I found lying around the house and decided to use it as my tank base. This container is nice because it's large enough to fit bigger boards and has a snap on airtight lid, but not too large that it takes a whole gallon of etching solution to fill. From there I visited the local pet shop and purchased an air pump, some plastic tubing, a bubbling rock, and a small aquarium heater. With all the materials together I hot glued the bubbling rock into the

bottom of the container and the plastic tubing up the wall of it. Finally I inserted the heater and was ready for the etching solution.

My second improvement was to heat the boards hotter and set the ink better in hopes it would adhere to the boards better. This was an easy fix as I found a coupon for a dual temperature heat gun at Harbor Freight Tools. This heat gun cost me $10 and has two settings of 570 degrees (F) and 1110 degrees (F) or so. This is more than enough heat, as through some research I found the ideal heat for setting my ink is around 425 degrees (F). This is also great because at about 425 degrees (F) the copper clad board will start to turn a bit purple due to oxidation and the heat.

With my two problems solved I printed 2 new boards and tried out the new heat gun. This is where I must issue a warning. As much as you may think the higher 1110 degree (F) setting will heat your board faster and set the ink more easily do not try it. If you heat the board too fast it will warp. If you heat it too much, as I did with my first board, the adhesive holding the copper to the board will melt and the copper will bubble up. All that bubble took was a second on 1110 degrees (F) and the copper popped off.

My second board however I was patient with and used the 570 degree (F) setting and slowly heated the entire board until it started to turn purple. You have to keep your eye on your boards as you do this. Once the ink was set at this higher temperature, I filled up my etching tank with some Ferric Chloride and let it heat up and bubble for a bit. When the solution was nice and warm I dipped my board into it and checked it every 30 to 40 seconds for progress. After about 3 minutes my board was done etching. (This type of tank and etching method is so much faster than rocking a container around by hand so I'd recommend the upgrade to everyone.)

After my board was complete I rinsed it off. These two tweaks in my method produced results that are significantly better as this board has crisper traces and none of the pinholes that plagued the first few boards that I etched.

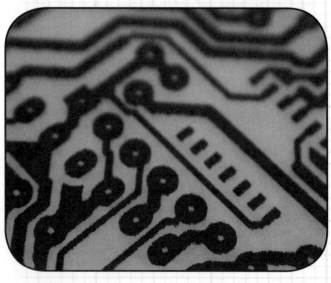

tools

# The Smallest Workshop in the World

By Stelios L.A. Stavrinides (steliart)
(http://www.instructables.com/id/The-Smallest-Workshop-in-the-World/)

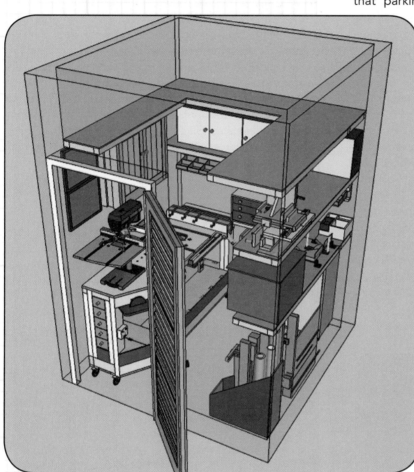

Being a woodworking enthusiast is not enough especially if you don't have a place to work and you live in an apartment court.

In my case, this was not the only issue but I also had no budget or space for big machines, so I came up with the impossible.

I live in Nicosia, Cyprus and woodworking is not best here. The woodworking accessories they sell here are very basic and everything is mostly oriented for cabinet makers. Even a simple miter track I needed had to be imported from the UK or USA, most of my things are from there. As for wood; Oak, Beech, Swedish pine, low quality plywood, cheap-boards, and MDF it's mostly all you can get and their price is ridiculously high.

Everything was designed using Google Sketch-up which has been proven to be a valuable tool to woodworkers.

The sketch-up image shows the whole idea in theory. And I will provide detail photos of throughout the project.

So, at my open air parking space that I have in my building there's a small storage room with dimensions a bit greater than 5X5 feet (1.6X1.6 meters). In that space I decided to keep my workshop and work openly in my parking area.

The problem is that, I can spread things around in that parking space but everything has to be stored, locked, and cleaned when you are done.

Fortunately my neighbors had no problem with this project, but I have to be careful running the power tools only at selected hours.

## My multi power-tool bench

I decided to build a multi power-tool bench 59X20 inches (1.5X 0.5 meters) that will fit into my storage room and hold simple hand tools that will allow me to work on any woodworking project I want. Made out of 2X4" and 2X2" for the body, plywood for the sides and an 3/4 MDF top laminated with Formica for better strength.

The tool bench holds 5 major tools, drill press, sander, jigsaw, circular saw, router (with a lift device), and the possibility for a lathe (later addition).

It also has a vice, 5 small drawers (one for each tool's small accessories), under storage space, and 8 electrical sockets with wiring. The bench sits on 5 casters with stoppers so that it can easily roll into and out of the storage room.

You will also notice that there is an angle cut on the bench design, that was done so that it will allow me some space to pass through into my storage room even when the bench is inside it.

tools

## Step 1: Drill press

My bench top drill press was modified a bit for better workability. I changed the old pole to a stainless steel one, which is taller and allows me easier up-down movement. Also I attached a drill press accessory bar made from a piece of aluminum angle and two shallow boxes from 1/4 inch MDF, and it has been proven to be a very useful asset to the drill press.

I have also made a drill press table from an old office shelf together, with a plywood fence that pivots at one point and a stop block. Some homemade hold-down clamps run into the two T-tracks, which are nothing more than simple curtain aluminum tracks. The drill press table has two frac14; (6mm) plate inserts are on top of each other, one has the standard drill press hole opening and the second plate has a larger hole to fit my drill press spindle sanders.

Another accessory I made for my drill press was to attach over the drill press table a piece of plywood base with two homemade knobs to hold onto the t-tracks and my drill press vice mounted on it.

The old depth-stop system with the 2 nuts was so unfriendly to use, so I came up with an easier way to work around this problem. A small piece of hardwood and a threaded iron base with a small knob, made the depth-stop now very easy to adjust and use. Then I replace the broken plastic depth ring with the one made out of clear 3/8 acrylic. I used two magnets, one holds the drill press chuck in the right place so I don't lose it all the time, and the other one on the top holds my plastic bit cleaning brush.

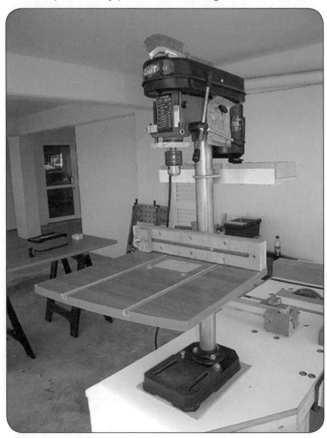

## Step 2: Disk sander

My very old drill became my disk sander. Mounted under the table with a sanding wheel Velcro attachment and a sanding table makes the perfect job.

With the help of a friend we rewired the drill's electrical functions and put everything in an electrical socket box. On and Off switch, Forward and reverse, Fast and Slow fixed speed, adjustable speed control, all functions run smoothly and it's so handy.

The sander's table is attached with two threaded inserts on the tool-bench, bolds and wing nuts through the table to tighten it to the bench.

The sanding table has several functions. One is the use of a simple T-square for parallel sanding and it has an angle guide for sanding miters and a circle sanding jig attachment for cutting perfect circles from very small ones up to 12 inches (30cm) diameter circles.

## Step 3: Jig saw

The jig saw is mounted upside-down under the tool-bench with T-nuts and 8mm bolts, and over the top a hold down arm design system (ShopNotes #23 Magazine) with a blade guiding system, which guides/holds the blade with the help of two bearings, can cut very good as high as the blade you use.

Very practical for cutting patterns near the line and finishing them with your sander. Also the use of a good quality wood blade like BOSCH which can cut very straight and give precise perfect finish results.

tools

## Step 4: Circular table saw with fence and miter gauge

I mounted a circular saw under the bench and hold it with 4 bolts and wing nuts. I made 4 holes on the circular saw base, 3 of which are elongated for fine adjustment. I also cut a space for insert plates from 0 degrees to 45 degrees clearance and added 2 miter track slots to the left and right. The circular saw is powered by a safety stop switch and can hold a riving knife also on the blade (not shown here).

My wooden rip fence is made out of 3/4 MDF body and hard wood for the round center piece and the off center handle; also a small aluminum angle is used to run on the fence guide rail. It's design is based on Biesemeyer fence. Left site of the fence is used for ripping with the circular saw and the right site is used as the router fence with an opening and dust hole.

The fence guide rail is simple, a 2X2" attached along the side of the bench with an aluminum angle across it so that the fence locking mechanism won't damage the 2x2" when tightened. UHMW tape is used to help the 2 aluminum angles to run smoothly.

Some push sticks have also found there way on my tool-bench. Even though almost everything here is home made, security was always in my mind before anything.

My miter gauge is a mixed idea from various DIY designs (one is from Phil B instructables). Hardwood bar piece to run into the miter track slot, plywood for the body, a clear protractor, a piece of thick clear acrylic, and a wooden handle with a T-nut at the bottom to act as a tightening handle and keep everything tight in place.

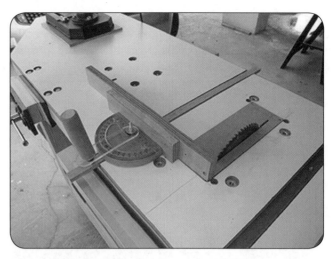

## Step 5: Router with fence and lift

Installing the router is no different than other tutorials. I made my own router table plate from 11/32 clear acrylic on which later I put red plastic adhesive for color (the clearness of the plate was distracting me from the work piece). A miter track slot is also there and on the joint circular saw and router fence I can now attach an external 2 piece fence with the use of special clamps.

An inexpensive router lift method is used with the help of a scissor car jack. Mine is a replacement out of my car's jack as it is very smooth to turn and has accuracy down to the millimeter.

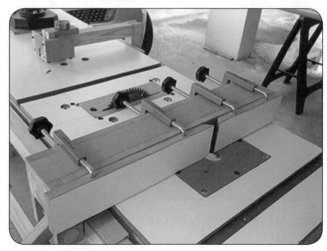

## Step 6: Bench vise

An inexpensive bench vise always comes in handy on any bench.

## Step 7: Cross cut sled

My cross cut sled is 2X2 feet of 1/2 plywood, 2X4" fence, and an acrylic piece for safety. A mixed design from various ideas runs on metal miter track bars and its true 90 degrees, can't do without it.

## Step 8: Miter sled

The miter sled I built is based on the David Marks aluminum one and is made basically from plywood and

tools

some scrap pine wood. The T-tracks are from aluminum curtain tracks (try them, they work perfect) and 2 metallic hold downs and a stop block complete the project. Perfect 45 degree miters every time.

and keep things from rusting. Over the door I install a strong light that tilts to face inside or outside.

## Step 9: Bench extensions

I have made 2 extensions for my multi power-tool bench. One piece serves as an extension to the circular saw and router area and the other one as an extension to the front side of the router.

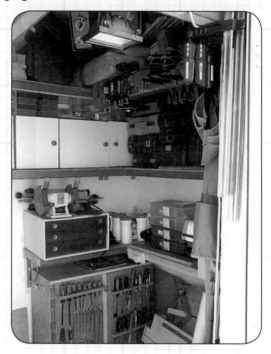

## Step 10: Assembly table

Using a kitchen counter top and 2 saw horses I have a mobile assembly table that serves me well.

## Step 11: 5X5 feet storage room

Some thrown away shelves from a friend and some 2x2 made my shelving system. A few drawers and lots of plastic containers keep me organized as much as I can.

One wall mounted cabinet keeps accessories inside. An old narrow bookcase thrown sideways plus a few doors serves me as small cabinets to keep my essentials.

I keep all my power tools in there plastic cases to keep them safe from humidity (we have lots of it here). I had to screw a double layer nylon to the inside face of the storage room aluminum door to keep the humidity out

## Step 12: Tool storage cabinet

A simple idea from the WOOD Special magazine. Its dimension are W32XH32XD13 inches and is a very clever idea to have lots of storage in a tiny space. About 7 square feet of wall area will give you about 26 square feet of storage space.

At the bottom of the cabinet there are 7 removable screw bins (2 divided in half), which holds most of the common screws I need. Bins are made out of 3/4" plywood and 1/4" MDF.

Made of 3/4 plywood it rolls on 4 casters so that its mobile and I can roll it out to the open if needed. The only trick here is to organize it correctly—plan it on paper before putting up the tools on the wooden surface. I think it's one of the best storage ideas I have ever seen.

Basically that's about it. The Smallest Workshop in the World!

tools

# food

At Instructables HQ we often say that food is many people's first experience with making something. While there are thousands of great recipes and informative food prep techniques available on the site, the editors thought it would be fun to showcase some of the more whimsical and wild food creations in this chapter. You might think working with only food as a building material might be a limitation to constructing amazing creations, but these projects definitely prove that's not the case.

Not only are the following food projects each unique and fun in the way that only a rose made out of bacon can be, but they taste great too!

# Bacon Roses

By Kevin Kittle (kaptaink_cg)
(http://www.instructables.com/id/Bacon-Roses/)

Flowers make a nice gift to the friend that needs a smile or for that special someone in your life. Roses are even better. But sometimes even roses don't cut it. Sometimes you need something a little more non-cliché, something...extraordinary... Sometimes, you need BACON.

## Step 1: Materials
- BACON: I like to use one regular pack and one thick cut pack
- Rose Stems
- Glass Vase
- Mini Muffin Pan
- Broiler Pan
- Drill with bit (I used an 1/8" bit, but any similar size will work)
- Gravel or marbles for vase

## Step 2: Preparing the pans
Drill holes in the bottom of the muffin pan. This will allow the grease to drain when cooking the bacon.

Place the muffin pan on top of the broiler pan.

## Step 3: Prepare the rose buds
Preheat the oven to 375 degrees Fahrenheit.

Open the bacon and begin tightly rolling the roses, one piece at a time. Start with the widest end of the bacon, with the fat edge down. I like to use a combination of thick and thin bacon so I end up with a variety of rose shapes.

Place all of the bacon in the muffin pans pushing down slightly to "seat" them. The bottoms will flair out a bit.

Place in the oven and cook for 30-40 minutes. Check in on them occasionally. Sometimes you will have to lift the rose so the grease will drain out the pan.

## Step 4: Prepare the rose stems
While waiting for the buds to cook you can start working on the stems. I found the stems that work best can be purchased at Walmart in bunches of 7, for under a dollar each.

Pull all of the roses off from the stems.

Pull the green backing off from the rose and then separate it into individual parts.

Discard the petals and center red piece. Reassemble the remaining green parts as shown.

Put the green piece back on the stem, but force it down so that roughly 1" of the stem protrudes.

I like to tape the stems together at this point, but this is optional.

Put the stems in your vase and fill with gravel or marbles to hold them in place.

## Step 5: Assemble and present!
When the bacon buds are done, remove from the oven and place on paper towel to cool.

You'll now have a variety of rose buds to choose from. Pick your favorites and slide them onto the protruding stems. Arrange the roses to your liking and then present the aromatic bouquet to your favorite bacon fanatic!

food

# Rubik's Battenburg Cake

By Vicky McDonald and
Nelius Phelan (stasty)
(http://www.instructables.com/id/Rubiks-Batten-
burg-Cake/)

### Why make this cake?

The Rubik's cube is close to my heart as I am a child of the 80s and the Rubik's cube always brings me back to a time of joy and wonder. It's hard to imagine kids today being as fascinated as I was by such a simple but clever toy. I wanted to make a cake that epitomizes this ingenious and timeless invention. I knew it would have to be a clever cake that would make you question how it was made.

Thankfully I had the help of my other half and his engineering brain to assist with the planning and general math of this cake. It took an entire day to make but was definitely worthwhile, especially when we cut the first slice.

## Materials list:

One Basic Battenberg cake:
- 6 oz. of butter
- 6 oz. of castor sugar
- 3 eggs
- 6oz of self-rising flour
- A few drops of food coloring for each color.

To finish:
- 14 oz. of blackcurrant jam, sieved
- 14 oz. of plain white marzipan to cover the entire cake
- 2 oz. of icing sugar for rolling out the marzipan

## Step 1: Baking the cakes

Pre-heat the oven 180 degrees Celsius. Grease and flour a Battenberg tin. My Battenberg tin was 8 inches x 6 inches and had 4 individual sections to put the different colors.

You'll need to make three cakes and each cake will comprise two of the colors needed—white/yellow, then red/orange and finally blue/green.

Cream together the butter and the sugar until it becomes light and creamy. Gradually add the beaten eggs. Then, carefully fold in the sieved flour.

Next split the mixture to make the two different colors. Take half of the mixture out, and place in another bowl. Add a few drops of food coloring to one batch. To the other half, add a few drops of a different food coloring. For the white sections of the cake. I slightly over-beat the egg mixture and didn't add any coloring. This achieved a pale off-white effect. Spoon the mixture into the separate sections of the tin.

Place in the oven for 30-35 minutes. To test if it's ready place a clean knife through the center, the knife should come out clean when it is fully cooked. If the cake rises over the tin, use a serrated knife to even off the top. Let the cake cool in the tin, once fully cooled, remove from the tin and place on a wire rack.

Repeat twice using the same method, ingredients and remaining food colors for the red/orange and blue/green cakes.

Optional: You might want to flavor the cakes as well as color them. I used lemon zest for the yellow, orange zest for the orange and vanilla for the white. You want to find complimentary flavors that will work as a cake, so it's probably best to resist the temptation to put mint flavoring in the green as it could taint the whole cake.

## Step 2: The grid

Decide on the color combinations. It is important that each slice is different. Each section overlaps so each slice of the cake reveals a differing combination.

I have included the map we created that would guarantee that each slice was different to the one previous.

Note: I've used the color black on the map to represent white in the cake, because white looked clearer as the background of spreadsheet.

food

243

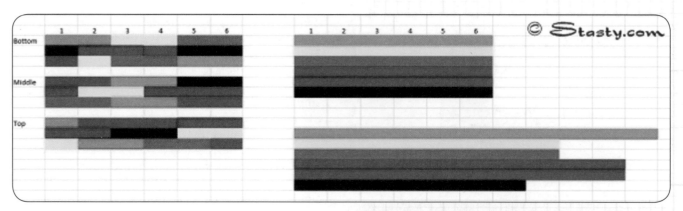

## Step 3: Cutting Guide

With a ruler draw out a cutting grid that is the size of the tin. (Our tin was 8 inches x 6 inches.) We drew our grid with pen and ruler on a sheet of A4 paper and measured all our cakes piece with this.

Cut out the cake pieces using your paper grid. We did this all together so we were left with deconstructed cake pieces of different sizes.

## Step 4: Building the cake

Roll out a long even slab of marzipan. We rolled ours out to be about 10 x 26 inches (10 = 8 inches plus another 2 inches spare to work with, 26 = 4 x 6 inches plus another 2 inches).

This will depend on your cake and tin size. Place the jam in a saucepan and warm over a low heat. Next, sieve the warm jam into a separate bowl to remove any seeds in the jam.

Begin with the bottom layer. With a pastry brush coat all the outside of the cake cubes and arrange on top of the marzipan with unjammed face pointing outwards.

## Step 5: Sticking it all together

Continue building using your spreadsheet to figure out where all the pieces go and applying the jam to stick it together.

## Step 6: Wrapping in marzipan

Once you have all three layers of cake in place, ensure that the outside of each piece of cake is covered in jam so the marzipan will stick.

Gently place the marzipan over the cake and cut off the spare on the edges.

## Step 7: Slicing

To cut the cake use the grid to figure the correct place to slice to ensure you reveal a different color slice. Voila!

food

# Tooth Cupcakes

By Erica Knee (ericasweettooth)
(http://www.instructables.com/id/Tooth-Cupcakes/)

They're ironic but fun—teeth molded out of a cake frosting mixture and fondant! Don't forget to brush after enjoying these!

## Step 1: Fondant

Prepare a half-batch of homemade marshmallow fondant and let it sit overnight in the fridge until you're ready to make the cupcakes. You can also buy the pre-made kind at a craft store.

### Ingredients for the fondant:
- 1/4 cup butter, at room temperature
- (1) 16 oz package of mini marshmallows
- 4 tbsp water
- 1 tsp vanilla extract
- 2 lbs powdered sugar

Directions for the fondant:
1. The night before you plan on building the cake, make the fondant by first placing the marshmallows in a large microwave-safe bowl, and microwave for 45 seconds to start melting them.
2. Stir the water and vanilla into the hot marshmallows until smooth.
3. Add the sugar slowly and beat together until the dough is well combined but sticky. Reserve 1 cup of sugar for kneading.

4. Using the butter to grease your hands, sprinkle the fondant with powdered sugar and begin kneading the sticky dough for 5-10 minutes. This should help make the dough more pliable and no longer sticky.
5. Form the fondant into a ball, wrap tightly in plastic wrap, and refrigerate overnight.

## Step 2: Baking the cupcakes

Bake your cupcakes in pink liners. Use whatever recipe you want—boxed mixes work too!

## Step 3: Making the cusps out of cake ball mixture

1. Set aside half of the cupcakes, and crumble the rest of them into a large bowl to create coarse crumbs.
2. Mix a few scoops of canned frosting into the cake crumbs to make a malleable, yet not too wet, mixture.
3. Form cusps on top of cupcakes with the cake-frosting mixture, using your clean fingers and an offset spatula to create the anatomy.

## Step 4: Finishing the tooth cupcakes

1. Once you're done with all of the teeth, let them chill in the fridge for about an hour so they solidify a bit.
2. Roll out the fondant to ¼" thickness, using powdered sugar for dusting.
3. Cut out fondant circles that are a bit wider than the cupcake diameter and drape them over the cusps.
4. Use a sharp knife to trim the edges and an offset spatula to tuck in any remaining fondant.
5. Enjoy!

food

# Bowl of Worms, Anyone?

By cpacker1

(http://www.instructables.com/id/Bowl-of-Worms-Anyone/)

Create tasty, edible worms. This recipe is simple and great for Halloween, April Fool's, or anytime you feel like snacking on wormy goodness! If you can make Jello, then you can make these cool looking worms.

## Ingredients

- 2 packs (3 oz) Raspberry Jello
- 1 pkg unflavored gelatin (for extra firmness)
- 3/4 cup whipping cream
- 3 cups boiling water
- 15 drops green food coloring
- 100 flexible straws (or enough to fill your container)
- Tall container (1 quart or 1 liter carton of milk)

## Directions

1. Combine gelatin in bowl and add boiling water.
2. Let it cool to lukewarm and then add the whipping cream and 15 drops green food coloring.
3. Gather your straws (don't forget to flex them out) and put them in the container. It's important that the straws have a tight fit so the Jello stays in the straws. For this reason, a 1 liter carton may be better; you will probably get longer worms since there is a tighter fit. If you have a bigger container, a rubber band around the straws is helpful. Or you could just add more straws to fill the container.
4. Add the gelatin mixture to the straw-filled container and let it set until firm.
5. There are multiple ways you can remove the worms from the straws. You can roll a rolling pin over the straws and squeeze them out or you can hold the straws over warm water. The worms will slip right out.

And voila! Jello worms are served.

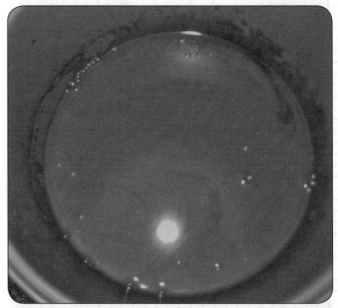

# Chocolate Nut Assortment

By Lauren Ryder (annahowardshaw)
(http://www.instructables.com/id/Chocolate-Nut-Assortment/)

Chocolate hearts aren't for everybody...

## Step 1: Form mold

**Make wooden frame:**

Cut two 3.5" wood strips.

Cut two 5" wood strips.

Tape all pieces together. Tape the last corner with a tab of duct tape to use as a clasp. (You will need to attach and remove it for each batch.)

**Silicone putty setup:**

Measure out equal parts of silicone putty components and mix according to instructions.

Spread out evenly in the frame.

Place hex nuts.

Wait 10 minutes.

**Cut mold:**

Remove nuts from mold. This can be tricky since you will have to unscrew them off the silicone.

Cut each section in half. Trying to unscrew less-than-solid pieces can result in accidental cracking.

To make filled chocolate, cut out middle piece of silicone and sand to even out both sides.

**Variation:**

I also made a smaller mold with different size nuts... and a wing nut.

## Step 2: Chocolate shells

Once the mold is all set, it is time to fill it!

Melt chocolate over stove or in the microwave and stir until smooth. I used a small pitcher so that the chocolate could be poured directly from it. I added a silicone sleeve to the side in lieu of an oven mitt.

Pour into molds.

For the molds that will have filling, pour in enough to cover the bottom and use a spoon to push chocolate against the sides of each section.

Sections for the solid sections should be filled in 3/4 of the way.

Tap mold against the table to push air bubbles up and ensure that chocolate spreads out evenly.

Place mold in the freezer for 5 minutes.

food

247

## Step 3: Solid chocolates

A few variations for solid chocolates. Try stirring in...

- Dark and white chocolate together
- Chopped pistachios
- Coconut flakes
- Drizzle with contrasting chocolate

## Step 4: Amaretto truffle filling

Remove molds from freezer and fill with...

Amaretto Truffle Filling
### Ingredients:
- 6 ounces Chocolate
- 1 Tbs Butter (unsalted)
- 1/4 Heavy Cream
- 1/8 cup Amaretto
### Directions:
- Melt chocolate in a double boiler.
- Add butter and cream and mix.
- Once smooth, add Amaretto.
- Pour mixture into a glass dish and set in the fridge for about an hour.
- Use small spoon to take some truffle out and place in a chocolate shell.
- Cover in chocolate and allow to set.

## Step 5: Additional fillings

Try out different fillings! Nutella is great in anything, and peanut butter is a natural choice.

Now what other candy hardware to make...?

For an instructable on the Tiny Toolbox: http://www. instructables.com/id/Tiny-Toolbox/

food

# LeGummies Brick-Shaped Gummy Candies

### By SFHandyman

(http://www.instructables.com/id/LeGummies-brick-shaped-gummy-candies/)

In this Instructable, I'm going to show you how to make gummy candies.

I made a silicone candy mold using Lego bricks. You don't need to make a custom mold. There are many commercially available silicone molds, or you could just skip the mold completely, and cut them with cookie cutters, a knife, or even scissors.

## Step 1: Tools and ingredients

When I made the candies in the picture, I experimented with many, many different techniques and recipes to figure out how to get the best flavor, texture and clarity.

I made them in small batches so I could do many experiments.

The recipe is for a small batch (one full mold for me). You will probably want to double, triple, or quadruple it.

**Ingredients:**

- 1 package of flavored Gelatin (Jello)
- 3 packets of Unflavored Gelatin (Knox is most common in the US—they come 4 packets to a box)
- 1 500 mg Vitamin C (optional but it adds some great sour flavor)
- 1/3 to 1/2 cup of water

**Tools:**

- Pyrex Measuring cup
- A cooking pot that the cup will fit into
- Some kind of spatula.
- Mold or a flat bottom pan to pour the candy into
- Mortar and Pestle (or a hammer?) to grind up the Vitamin C

**Directions:**

In the photos you see me using a shallow pan with just about an 1"–1 1/2" of water to melt the syrup. You should go ahead and use a pot with higher sides, so you can get the water level up another inch or two.

I used the shallow pan so it would be easier to see what was happening in the photos.

The syringe I used to fill the mold in the photos is optional. You can just pour the candy in.

I have a metal and plastic trigger activated frosting gun. It is used to decorate cakes. I don't remember when, or where I bought it. I tend to buy tools when they are on sale, and think up a use later. I decided to try it out with the gummy syrup and it worked great. That is what I use now.

(The wire strainer in the photos is not needed. I reviewed my notes on the experiments and the clearest candies—the green and red, didn't use the strainer.)

## Step 2: Making the candy

To make gummies the only essential ingredient is unflavored gelatin.

For flavor I used flavored gelatin (Jello is one brand) plus a Vitamin C to bump up the pucker power.

The amount of flavored gelatin you use is up to you. I'm recommending a full package of flavored gelatin for each batch. It gives the candy a pretty intense flavor.

Use an extra packet of unflavored gelatin, and they will be even chewier. Use one less, and they will be softer. **Here we go:**

If you don't really care how clear the candy is, just stir the powders in the water, put it in hot water on the stove and melt it, then pour it in the molds.

I use a little over 1/3 cup of water (you can use even more for softer candies). Measure 1/3–1/2 cup of cold water into your measuring cup.

**Mix it up:**

SPRINKLE the gelatin powders into the water, as you continuously and gently stir it. Don't let the dry powder pile up. Sprinkle, stir, sprinkle, stir... If you get a pile of gelatin and stir that in, it will make a lump, and lumps are hard to dissolve once you've made one. Do this rather quickly. The gelatin will immediately start absorbing the water. If you move too slowly it will get pretty dry towards the end and it will be very difficult to avoid lumps.

**Let it rest:**

Cover the Pyrex cup with plastic wrap and let it rest for 10 minutes. The gelatin needs time to absorb the water before we heat it.

You can leave the spatula in the gelatin while it is resting, but don't leave any chunks of gelatin on the back of the spatula where it will dry.

**I'm melting...**

Put a pan of water on the stove and bring it up to a slow boil/fast simmer.

After the resting time, remove the plastic wrap and put the measuring cup in the water. The lump of clay or slushy material will melt but it does take several minutes. Occasionally stir it. Stir it gently. Don't get too vigorous and mix a lot of air in it, or you will have cloudy candy. (If you are adding vitamin C to sour them up, add it at the very end.)

Once it melts, you will see that it has a layer of foam on top. Try to avoid mixing that foam back into the melted syrup. When it is hot enough you will see there is a very thin layer of clear on the bottom, a layer that isn't as clear, then the layer of foam on top.

Now stop stirring and just let it sit in the water for about 2 minutes. We are letting bubbles rise at this point.

**Finally we fill the mold:**

Now I put my syringe into the bottom of the cup and suck up all that clear syrup.

I use the syringe to squirt the candy into my mold.

(Step 4 has other ways of molding the candy).

If your mold won't hold all the syrup you made, turn the heat off and let the cup sit in the water while your first batch of candy is setting up. When you pull the first batch out of the mold, just turn on the stove and melt the syrup that is still in the cup the same way we did it the first time.

You don't need to use any kind of release (no oil or cooking sprays) with gummies. They will peel off of anything that is smooth. If you get some on your stove, floor, or counter, don't bother to try to clean it up while it is wet and hot. It's much easier to just let it set up and peel it off.

Most of the time when you make gummies you will not try to mold them in 360 degrees. The top side (which will be the bottom of the candies) is just left flat. I wanted to mold in little holes on the bottom of in my bricks so I could actually stack them.

The syrup contracts quite a lot as it cools. I had to fill the mold, then go back through and top them all off again as it would shrink way down. When I got them all full, I took the base plate (the same one I used when making the mold) and pressed it on the top of the mold, squeezing any extra goo out of the sides. Then I let it sit on the counter top for a couple of minutes.

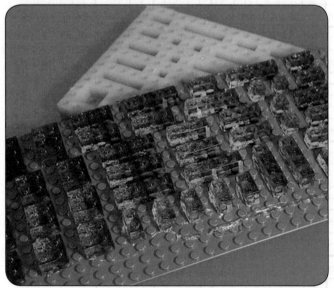

I put the mold with the lid (base plate) into the freezer. You only leave it in the freezer for 10 or 15 minutes.

These candies actually do not need to be refrigerated at all to set up. You can just leave your mold on the counter at room temperature and they will still set up. I use the freezer to get them done faster.

Once they are set up, take them out of the mold. Clean them up if they need it, and you are done.

food

## Step 3: Add some pucker power—Sour Gummies

I really like sour flavors in gummy candies.

The official way to make sour gummies is to add Ascorbic Acid Powder. Other powders that will add sour are called Citric Acid or Vitamin C powder. You can buy it in a cooking store, a health food store that sells supplements, probably some pharmacies and I think it's even available at some bulk food stores.

Just stick to plain cheap generic Vitamin C if you are going to grind your own. For pure sour pucker power, the cheaper the better.

I add the powder of one 500mg Vitamin C to a batch of gummies.

The easiest way to sour up gummies, and to also give them more concentrated flavor is to add unsweetened Kool-Aid powder! There are a lot of flavor experiments you can try by mixing different flavored gelatin with different flavors of Kool-Aid. They don't come out very clear though.

After it is melted and almost ready to go into the mold, stir in the Vitamin C, then let the syrup sit in the bath for a couple of minutes.

This info applies to candy making in general: When making candy, you will almost always add the flavorings right at the end. The reason is, sometimes flavorings can change flavor or breakdown completely when they are heated. When you are making candy, you will usually cook your candy first, then stir in flavorings right after you take it off the stove.

Have fun and experiment.

## Step 4: Molds

You don't need to make a custom mold like I did to make gummy candies. There are many great silicone molds available. They are used for making candies, baking, molding butter, making ice...

It doesn't have to be made of silicone either. A regular Ice tray will work too. Any thing that has a flat and smooth surface should work fine. I read a suggestion, by a Mom on some recipe site, to pull the rack out of your toaster oven, put a piece of foil on it, and push the foil down through the slats. She made a gummy worm mold that way.

This stuff is very forgiving.

Mold options:

Pour the candy in a flat pan and after it has gelled, then just slice it into squares, rectangles and triangles with a knife. You could cut shapes out with cookie cutters. You could even peel the sheet off in one piece, and cut it up with scissors.

Whatever you do, I'd recommend you keep them pretty small. If you are using an ice tray, or a butter mold, or any mold with large compartments, don't fill it to the top. Just fill them up to around 1/4 or 1/2 an inch.

You can make Mega-Gummies if you really want to. Ever wanted a gummy the size of an Ice Cube? Go ahead. It will work fine. Want one shaped like a Banana? Go ahead—just don't tell me what you plan on doing with it.

### How I made the silicone mold:

I purchased Food Grade Silicone from Douglas & Sturgess (http://www.artstuf.com/).

The number I used is FGS-2237 Food Grade Silicone. (There is a new number MC-1287.)

You need two parts. Part A is the silicone gel and part B is the catalyst. They sell it as a set. This is a 1 lb. set.

The silicone must be weighed to make sure you put in the right amount of catalyst. It's 10 parts Silicone (part A) to 1 part Catalyst (part B). Buy yourself a gram scale to do this. You really want to be accurate. You don't want to waste this stuff because you measured wrong.

I made my positive (the part that I made the mold from) out of—you guessed it—Legos!

### How to make the mold:

I wanted my tray to not waste any space. If I left more than a single peg between each candy piece I'd be wasting the silicone.

food

When I got the Legos—I built the Taj Mahal (http://www.amazon.com/LEGO%C2%AE-Creator-Taj-Mahal-10189/dp/B002EEP3NY)- I couldn't resist! Have you seen it? It's amazing. 5,922 pieces.

So three days later, after I finished the Taj, I started taking it apart to get my candy mold pieces.

I put the pieces on a tray, and ringed the tray edge with a double stack of pieces to act as a wall and hold the silicone in. Legos are made so well, that they really fit tightly together. I found that I didn't have to seal any of the cracks between the pieces inside.

Silicone will not stick to Legos. So you don't need to put any kind of mold release on the positive.

### Weigh the silicone:

To measure how much silicone you are going to need to fill the mold, you can measure it a couple of ways. The standard way is to fill the positive with water, pour the water into the plastic cup you are going to mix it in, and just draw a line on the cup at the water line. That is how much silicone you will need to fill the mold.

Put your plastic container—with the line marked on it, on your gram scale and set the scale to zero. That way you won't be weighing your plastic cup, just the silicone. Now pour enough of Part A to get up to your marked line. Don't just glop it in there, try to avoid causing any air pockets. Check to see how much the silicone weighs. Let's say it measured 350g. Because you use 10 parts A and 1 part B, you will need 10% of that weight in Catalyst or 35g. Zero (sometimes the button you use to do this is labeled "Tare") your scale out, with the silicone still on it. Then add the 35g of Part B right into the same container.

### Mix it up:

Mix your Part A and your Part B with something plastic. The catalyst is blue and the silicone is white so you can tell if you have it mixed. Scrape the sides and bottom as you do it. You want to be careful not to mix any extra air into it. Does that sound familiar? Just like the Gummies!

### Pour it in your tray:

You will pour the mixed silicone over the positive. Fill the tray up until you cover the tops of the pieces.

Pour slowly and don't move the Silicone back and forth like you are drizzling on frosting. That will leave air bubbles in the corners around your pieces. Pour it in a stream that hits the bottom of the tray—not over the Lego pieces, and let it flow around the tray and fill it up. This will help you avoid trapping any air.

Silicone is pretty good about releasing bubbles so you probably will get a pretty good mold.

### Let it set up:

Don't try to clean up the cup and tools right now. Let them sit overnight. Most of it will set up and you can just peel it off. If you find you have any sticky spots of silicone gel, you can clean those off by dabbing them with a little Catalyst. That will make them set up and you should be able to peel it off.

Let the silicone set at least overnight, then just pull the Legos out of it. They will come out very easily. Let it set up for 24 hours before you use it. I put mine in the oven at 175 degrees for about 15 minutes after it had already been curing for 24 hours, just to make sure. It might not have been the right thing to do (I should have asked Douglas and Sturgess) but I knew they did that with some of the other silicones.

After you get the Legos out, just trim off any of the little bits that squeezed between the pieces. Wash the mold and you are ready to go.

Now if you will excuse me, I have to go rebuild the Taj Mahal.

## Step 5: Addendum: How to get really clear candies

I figured out how to get really clear candies with almost no bubbles.

I started by straining my vitamin C through a paper coffee filter so I got most of the solids out. I ended up with a very sour liquid that looked like water.

The secret to clear candies is to melt it twice.

After the first cycle of heating, let it rest, and cool off in the refrigerator. Almost all of the bubbles will rise to the surface while it is cooling. When it is cool enough to handle, take it out of the cup (the foam layer sticks to the cup, just cut through it around the edge of the cup with a knife). Put some water in the cup to get that foam to soften up so you can clean it out before you heat the candy again.

Now take your lump of clear candy with the foam layer and cut the foam layer off.

Melt all of those clear chunks. No real need to stir it while it is melting. I leave it alone so I don't add any bubbles. I just give it a gentle stir at the end before I suck it up into the syringe.

This technique makes amazingly clear candies. I have two pyrex cups so I make a second batch while the first one is cooling, then while No. 2 cools, I cut the foam layer off No.1 and melt it for casting.

food

# Lactofermented Granola

## By Ben Bennett (Tarps)
### (http://www.instructables.com/id/Lactofermented-Granola/)

We're going to make granola by soaking all the ingredients together, letting lactic acid bacteria ferment everything, then dehydrating it rather than baking it.

Lactic acid bacteria are a group of bacteria including the genus Lactobacilli and others, that can tolerate a lower pH than other bacteria. They occur naturally on food and in your gut where they help you digest food. They eat up sugars and produce lactic acid. "Probiotic" foods contain certain species of lactic acid bacteria intended to aid digestion and promote healthy "gut microflora."

## Step 1: Ingredients

Of course you can use any ingredients that you want in your granola. Basically we want grains, nuts, seeds, dried fruit, etc. As for amounts, just eyeball it. Or you could use a granola recipe as your basis.

Here's what I'm using:

- rolled oats—Oat groats that have been rolled flat. Rolled oats are sometimes lightly steamed or baked to pasteurize them, and often have the nutritious bran removed. Since I'm using organic Amish-grown oats, I trust that nothing too weird has been done to them. Quick oats will work fine as well.
- raw almonds—Use whatever nuts you like. They don't have to be raw.
- raisins
- raw sunflower seeds
- flax seeds
- sesame seeds
- blackstrap molasses—Molasses is the byproduct of extracting sugar from sugar cane or sugar beets. There is light, dark, and blackstrap molasses. Blackstrap is the one with the most sugar removed, so it has the highest amount of vitamins and minerals relative to the sugar content. I'm only putting in a spoonful. I think the molasses will be a good food for the bacteria and help it get started fermenting, but that's just a feeling.
- stevia—An herb that's really sweet but doesn't contain sugar or calories. I haven't tried it in granola but I like in other stuff.
- cinnamon

Other ingredients you might consider:
- honey
- ginger
- nut butter
- shredded coconut
- fruit—dried or fresh. I bet blueberries would be good.

- oat bran—This would replace nutrients lost in the removal of the bran from the rolled oats.

## Step 2: Smash nuts, grind flax

Any nuts or seeds that you want in smaller pieces, grind or smash them however you want.

For the almonds, I'm smashing them into largish chunks inside a bag with a hammer.

I always grind up flax, because whole flax seeds will pass right through you without giving you any nutrition. I use a small coffee grinder. You can also get flax meal. (They grind up the flax for you and hike up the price).

I'll leave the sunflower and sesame seeds whole.

## Step 3: Mix it up, add water

Put all your ingredients in a glass or ceramic container like a jar or bowl. You don't want to use plastic because the increasing amount of acid can react with it. I'm not sure about what metals are reactive, so I'm avoiding metal containers, too.

Stir it up.

Add water—Use non-chlorinated water, because it will kill the bacteria that we are trying to promote. I used tap water that I set out in a bowl for a day to let the chlorine evaporate out. Maybe you have some better water.

Pour water over the dry ingredients until it just covers the surface. In a few hours the oats, nuts, and seeds will absorb some of the water and expand, so the water will not cover the surface anymore. We want a consistency of a thick oatmeal (it basically is just thick oatmeal).

Cover the container with a cloth to keep dust and flies out.

food

253

## Step 4: Ferment

Put the container somewhere that's about room temperature. Slightly warmer temperatures may speed up fermentation and cooler temperatures slow it down.

As this stuff soaks, Lactobacilli and other lactic acid bacteria will consume sugars and starches producing lactic acid, lowering the pH of the mixture. This acid environment is inhospitable to the bacteria that cause spoilage and food poisoning.

You'll want to let it soak for at least 24 hours, or let it go for as long as a week (maybe longer, but I'm not sure what will happen to it). The longer you let it ferment, the more acidic it becomes and the more sour it tastes. It will begin to smell sour, too. Bubbles may form, because Lactobacilli also create $CO_2$ as a waste product.

You may want to stir up the mixture every day or so, mainly so the stuff on the top doesn't get dry.

At any point along the way, you can just eat this stuff as oatmeal. In fact this is the same way I make oatmeal, I just don't dehydrate it.

### Why ferment?

- Grains, nuts, and seeds contain phytic acid, a form of phosphate that is not bioavailable to humans (we can't absorb it). Additionally, phytic acid binds up minerals like magnesium, calcium, iron, and zinc, and the vitamin niacin. Because of this it is considered an "anti-nutrient." Lactobacilli contain the enzyme phytase which breaks down phytic acid, freeing up nutrients so we can absorb them. According to Wikipedia, lactofermentation is more effective than cooking at removing phytic acid.
- Nuts contain enzyme inhibitors which prevent them from sprouting in adverse conditions (dryness). If eaten in great quantity, this can supposedly strain your digestive system. Soaking the nuts neutralizes the enzyme inhibitor (the nut thinks it's getting rained on).
- Starches are broken down into simple sugars and into lactic acid which are more digestible. It's the same thing that happens in your digestive tract, but this way we get it started in a jar first.

### Step 5: Put the batter on the dehydrator

I let this batch ferment for about 48 hours. It smelled good and sour, and I could see bubbles of $CO_2$ in it.

Once you've decided that it's fermented enough, stir it up so the consistency is even, then spoon globs of it onto the dehydrator trays. If you don't have a dehydrator, or even if you do, it would be sweet to build a solar dehydrator (http://www.thefarm.org/charities/i4at/surv/soldehyd.htm). It looks pretty easy to make.

Last time I made this stuff, the dried granola stuck to the trays a bit, so on one tray I'm spooning the glop onto wax paper and poking some holes to let the air circulate. We'll see if that helps. I suppose a nicer dehydrator with Teflex sheets would be ideal for this. If you wanted, you could just put a portion of the glop on the dehydrator and let the rest ferment longer. You could put more on

each day, so you could taste how it changes as the fermentation progresses.

### Why dehydrate?

If you were to bake this instead of dehydrating it, it would still be more nutritious and digestible than its unfermented counterpart, but by dehydrating it we get all the benefits that come with not cooking food. Cooking destroys digestive enzymes, adds carcinogens, and so on and so forth, blah, blah, blah.

### Step 6: Done

It took almost 2 days for the globs to dry out completely. The ones on the wax paper took slightly longer, but they did come off the paper easier than the other ones came off the tray.

The end product is crunchy and tasty. The raisins retained their chewiness and sweetness which is good. This is good travel food. I'll take some on a bike trip. It should keep pretty long, but again I haven't waited long enough to find out. I would assume that most of the bacteria die without having moisture, so I would hesitate to call this food "probiotic."

food

# Quilt Cookies

By wold630

(http://www.instructables.com/id/Millefiori-
Inspired-Icebox-Cookies/)

These cookies are inspired by a glasswork technique called "millefiori," which translates to a "thousand flowers," but I think the cookies look like little quilts. The glass technique involves creating rods with multicolored patterns that can only be seen at either end of the rod. The rod can be cut in cross sections, or beads, and keep the pattern throughout.

The possibilities are truly endless using this technique. These will "Wow!" almost anyone and make great gifts. I hope you enjoy this instructable and its "mille" steps!

## Step 1: Make the dough

I mostly love this cookie recipe because it is a one bowl cookie dough! You will be kneading and mixing in food coloring so the dough will be well mixed without needing to sift the dry ingredients separately.

Icebox Sugar Cookie
- 1 c. butter
- 1 c. sugar
- 1 egg
- 1 t. vanilla
- 3 c. flour
- 1 1/2 t. baking powder

In a large mixing bowl cream butter and sugar until combined. Add egg and vanilla mixing well. Sift flour on top of wet mixture and before stirring add the baking powder. When you start to combine the wet and dry ingredients, the flour and baking powder will incorporate well enough throughout the dough.

Dump dough onto a piece of waxed paper and divide dough into six equal pieces. You can obviously use more or less colors but I chose six.

## Step 2: Color the dough

After dough is divided choose food coloring colors and mix into dough using your hands. I find that there is enough butter in the recipe that your hands don't take on the food coloring but you could use gloves if you want make sure you don't have rainbow hands when you are finished!

## Step 3: Shape the dough

Turn your imagination on high and start making your patterns. This is a relatively easy process but it does take some time and patience.

To make a bullseye shape:
1. Choose a color and form a cylinder.
2. Roll out another color large and long enough to wrap the cylinder.
3. Gently press or squeeze dough to make sure the pieces stick together well.
4. Keep wrapping with colors until you have the bullseye you want.
5. Roll the completed bullseye into a longer log shape.
6. Cut in half, thirds or as many as needed.

To make a flower shape:
1. Choose a color that will be the center of the flower and form a cylinder.
2. Roll out another color large and long enough to wrap the cylinder.
3. Gently press or squeeze dough to make sure the pieces stick together well.
4. Make a coil of dough and pinch the top to make a triangular shape. Repeat for amount of petals you want.
5. Stick the triangles on the sides of the covered cylinder.
6. Press another color of dough in between the triangles.
7. Wrap the entire cylinder again with an outer color.
8. Cut in half, thirds or as many as needed.

Those are the two basic techniques I used but be creative and make anything you want!

food

## Step 4: Choose a cookie pattern

Once you have all of the patterns of dough made, arrange them together to get the final pattern that will be the finished cookie.

Roll patterns into longer logs if you want the pattern to be smaller in the final cookie. If necessary cut logs so they are all the same height.

Wrap in plastic wrap and freeze until hard—2 to 3 hours.

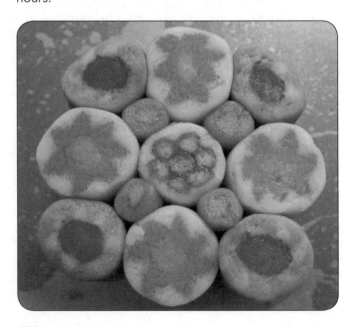

## Step 5: Cut the cookies

Preheat oven to 350 degrees F.

Remove cookie dough from the freezer and slice in 1/4 inch pieces. Repeat with all of your patterns (if you have more than one).

## Step 6: Bake the cookies

Bake for 7-9 minutes depending on how soft or crisp you like your cookies. Remove cookies from oven and let cool on baking sheet.

Color will not fade while baking.

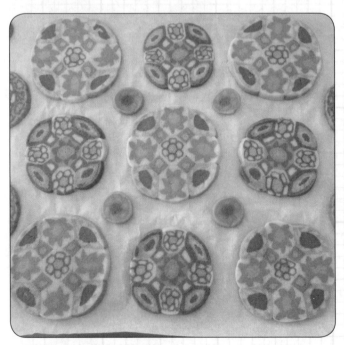

## Step 7: The final cookies

Eat and enjoy! Yum!

food

# furnish

The items that furnish our homes are often the first place that makers look when it comes to customization. Home furnishings are a great scale to work on, in that they're complex enough to get the creative juices flowing, but so long as things go mildly according to plan, the end is usually in sight. What's better, once the project is done, they can be shown off right in the gallery of your own home and used each and every day, so that everyone can enjoy and benefit from your hard work.

The following furnishing projects push the limits of form and function for the built world we inhabit. Innovative, playful, and well designed, these are pieces of furniture that also do double duty as art. It's hard to look at these projects and not want to cast off the boring conventions that we've grown accustomed to—right angles, dull colors, and store-bought cookie-cutter furniture that looks just like your neighbors'. Let these projects lead you to question why your bed looks just like "a bed." Let these projects inspire you to make something that shares your creative passion right in your own home.

# Rubik's Cube Chest of Drawers

By makendo

(http://www.instructables.com/id/Rubiks-cube-chest-of-drawers/)

Rubik's cube is not just the quintessential hand-held puzzle though: it's also an iconic piece of design, so I co-opted it when making a new chest of drawers for my son's room. This cubic piece of furniture has only one of the three required axes of rotation, so is unsolvable in the conventional sense, but can be arranged in any configuration you like by non-sporting means. The drawers do pose a brain-bending challenge: the first thing you have to solve is detecting that they're there, and all three have hidden locks in different locations.

## Step 1: Design

Unsurprisingly, there are lots of bits of furniture around that are based on the Rubik's cube; coffee tables (http://www.jellio.com/store/cubetable.html) are particularly popular, and for 980€ (!!), you can even buy a Rubik's cube locker (http://freshome.com/2010/09/20/rubik-cube-locker-a-puzzling-furniture-item/). I wanted to do something different, and use lazy Susan bearings to

achieve at least one axis of rotation—they're cheap, really strong, and add a wacky dimension to a chest of drawers.

The design is simply three boxes, each containing a single drawer. Their construction is basic—they're made of 1/4" and 1/2" plywood (which you should get precut at the lumber yard into two 2'x8' sheets), and assembled using a brad nailer and wood glue. This method of construction is super fast and precise, and results in really strong objects. The main challenge in this build is cutting the pieces with high precision—if you can't cut plywood to within 1 mm, you should probably practice on something simpler until you can.

I was going to simply glue the "stickers" on to decorate the outside—or even just paint them on—but the future owner insisted he had to be able to scramble and "solve" the cube, so I enabled this with the help of rare-earth magnets for holding power and short dowels for positioning. I'm glad I did—it's more fun now, and the colors can be selected to match your mood or decor, including impossible combos of color (insofar as the real cube goes).

The puzzle is a little under 60 mm across, and this chest of drawers is exactly 600 mm across, so it is in approximately 10:1 scale. 1000 regular Rubik's cubes would therefore fit inside.

## Step 2: Materials and tools
Materials:
- One and a half sheets of 1/2" plywood
- One and a half sheets of 1/4" plywood
- Two 12" lazy Susan bearings (http://www.leevalley.com/en/wood/page.aspx?p=44042&cat=1,250,43298,43316)
- Three pairs of 22" full extension slides (http://www.leevalley.com/en/hardware/page.aspx?p=46576&cat=3,43614,43616)
- Shorter screws than those provided with the above, say 60 1/2" flat head screws
- 45 3/8" rare-earth magnets (in hindsight, the 9 on the top are not really necessary, so 36 would be enough)
- 54 3/8" steel washers
- 54 6 mm x 30 mm dowels (http://www.leevalley.com/en/wood/page.aspx?p=32733&cat=1,250,43217,43228), cut in half
- Wood glue
- Epoxy glue
- Brad nails
- Undercoat
- Gloss paint in six different colors of your choice. I used spraypaint, as it's a relatively cheap way of getting small quantities of paint, they keep well, and they're handy to have around.
- Black gloss paint
  Close to $200 all up.

Tools:
- Circular saw
- Table saw

furnish

- Miter saw
- Router
- Orbital sander
- Cordless drill with a 3/8" forstner bit (http://www.leevalley.com/en/wood/page.aspx?p=63566&cat=1,180,42240)
- Brad nailer

## Step 3: Cut your plywood

Cut the plywood into the following dimensions. You'll notice that my extra half sheet of 1/2" ply actually came from offcuts I had lying around from other projects (yes, even after making the Lego construction table (http://www.instructables.com/id/Lego-construction-table/), I still had a few old cupboard doors left over).

1/2" plywood (11 mm thick)
- 6 of 600 x 582 mm (tops and bottoms of cases)
- 6 of 582 x 178 mm (sides of cases)
- 3 of 600 x 200 mm (drawer fronts)
- 6 of 543 x 160 mm (sides of drawers)
  1/4" plywood (7 mm thick)
- 3 of 600 x 200 mm (backs of cases)
- 3 of 550 x 550 mm (bottoms of drawers)
- 3 of 550 x 160 mm (backs of drawers)
- 54 of 165 x 165 mm (the "stickers," see later for more detailed instruction on these)

I always cut using a straightedge with the circular saw, which gives you a perfect straight line but requires a few clamps. Get a decent finishing blade, you'll save yourself a lot of sanding. I use Freud thin-kerf blades in all my saws—the quality is excellent, and it reduces the load on the saw and the amount of sawdust produced. I used the bench saw and miter saw wherever possible, because the setup is quicker. Cut to a stop using the miter saw to ensure reproducibility.

## Step 4: Add drawer slides

These are best attached BEFORE you assemble the individual cases. The exact height doesn't really matter, but make sure they're square, parallel to each other, and 5 mm back from the front edge.

## Step 5: Assemble cases

Assemble the cases with wood glue and brad nails, as shown. Leave to dry overnight, then sand, fill any imperfections with wood filler, and sand again.

## Step 6: Build drawers

Build three more boxes, without a top or front, that fit nicely inside the runners. I made the base and back with 1/4" ply and the sides with 1/2" ply. Nailing into the edge of 1/4" ply is perfectly doable, but you do have to be a fair bit more precise than for 1/2." Sand and fill.

## Step 7: Add drawer faces

Attach the drawers to the slides, and check the fit (whether they slide in and out nicely). Put the case on the end, and drop something in behind the drawer so it will sit slightly proud when closed. Line up your drawer front, and mark and cut to fit. Glue and nail to the drawer, again taking care with the nailing (I recommend transferring the lines to the front to avoid errors). Round the edges of the drawer front to match the case, remove the stop, and sand, fill, and sand again.

## Step 8: Groove the faces

To create the illusion that the cube can spin conventionally (i.e. on three axes, not just one), I faked it using a router with a V-shaped bit to cut grooves in all the exposed faces. Use a guide—because it's hard to clamp on to a face, I just tacked the guide in place temporarily using the brad nailer the correct distance from the desired groove. I ripped a piece of wood exactly the right width so I could rout both sides using the same guide (with my router, it needed to be 56 mm). The groove doesn't look exactly like the horizontal gaps, of course, but the visual illusion holds at least at first glance.

## Step 9: Cut squares

I measured each cubie to be 19.1 mm on a side, and each sticker as 15.6 mm, about 81% of the size. So I rounded up to the nearest 5 mm (165 mm for a "sticker" for a 200 mm cubie) and ripped much of one sheet of 1/4" plywood into 170 mm strips. I then set a stop on my miter saw to 165 mm and made two cuts for every square,

to ensure the 54 squares were as close to perfect as possible. I ganged them all together with a strap, and routed and sanded the corners of all squares simultaneously. This step was pretty quick, and all the components were done now. Just painting and hardware to go!

## Step 10: Paint case and drawers

Remove the drawers, and take the hardware off them. Undercoat everything except the inside of the cases (you don't see them), then sand. Paint the cases and drawer fronts gloss black to give it a shiny plastic look. Three coats should do nicely, sanding lightly between coats with very fine sandpaper.

## Step 11: Washers and dowels

Make a template for this step. Drill two dowel-sized holes part way into each "sticker" (about 3/4 the way through), and with the Forstner bit, drill a shallow (just deep enough for your washer) hole in the center. Repeat 54 times! You really need two drills, or the swapping of bits will drive you nuts. Now cut 54 dowels in half by taping them to a scrap piece of plywood and running them through the bench saw. Glue the half-dowels into the holes. Epoxy the washers into the shallow holes in the center.

## Step 12: Paint stickers

Undercoat, then spray paint the edges and top of each sticker in whatever combination of colors you like— we stuck with the conventional white/yellow/orange/red/green/blue. I let the future owner pick exactly which shade

furnish

of each he liked of each. I spent a few minutes painting one coat, then returned about 15 minutes later and did another. I used about half a can per set of nine, I reckon.

## Step 13: Holes and magnets

You'll need to use a template again. Use the previous template to make this one; it needs to be 200 x 200 mm. Make the dowel holes slightly bigger (I used 15/64" for the dowel holes, and went to 17/64" for these). Drill just deep enough for the magnet to sit flush with the surface (conveniently, this was just into the second layer of ply, so I just eyeballed it), but bore all the way through for the others. Repeat 45 times (you don't need to do the base, for obvious reasons!). Glue the magnets in the holes using a thin layer of epoxy.

## Step 14: Lazy Susans

The 12" lazy Susan bearings are pretty low profile (9 mm), but I reduced the gap between cases further by routing out a layer of plywood from the cases (3 mm from each) to set them into. I just freehanded it after marking the lines carefully. I greased the ball bearings—this makes it stiffer but quieter, both desirable for this application. The lazy Susan bearing has to be PERFECTLY centered. I screwed one side on and just epoxied the other.

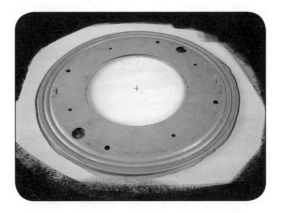

## Step 15: Add locks

I added a simple hidden lock to each drawer, all in different places. I just drilled holes through case and drawer from the side, and stuck a dowel in. To unlock, you just remove the correct sticker and push in the dowel. It's low tech but effective, and I don't anticipate it spending much time locked, but it's nice to know you can.

## Step 16: Solve the cube!

Add the "stickers" however you like to get the design you want (store the leftover nine stickers in one of the drawers, of course!). Change the stickers and make a new piece of furniture. Take it for a spin. Play some Scrabble (or 3D Settlers of Catan [http://www.instructables.com/id/Custom-3D-Settlers-of-Catan-board-from-scrap-plywo/]). Leave it in the middle of your living room as a coffee table. Bring it with you to a park and confuse strangers. Organize your underwear in high geek style. Talk to it. Sit on it and slowly orbit. Put your favorite boardgames in it. Challenge people to solve it one handed, and/or blindfolded, and time them. Use it as a stand for your prize-winning laser-cut, LED-lit, Arduino-controlled, solar-powered, steampunk-themed, EL wire-crocheted Halloween cupcakes...

Many thanks to the following sites for featuring this build: make, boingboing, hackaday, neatorama, ohdeedoh, geekosystem, technabob, manmade, babble, wins.failblog, design-milk, storagegeek and others; thinkgeek for tweeting about it, and of course instructables users for all the great feedback. Cheers!

furnish

# Building a Dump Truck Bed

By djmccray

(http://www.instructables.com/id/Building-a-dump-truck-bed-with-front-loader-book-s/)

Here is how to make a bed that your son will love. I made this bed for my son's third birthday. The goal in making the coolest dump truck bed was so my son would give up his crib to his 6 month old sister without a fight. My daughter was quickly out growing her bassinet and I didn't want to buy another crib that would only be used a couple months. My wife and I searched for store bought beds but they were all over priced laminated particle board without character. So I decided that my son was going to have to deal with a homemade bed, well the coolest dump truck bed he has ever seen.

## Step 1: Specs/features of this fully loaded truck

The dimensions are 101 L X 49 W X 60 H inches. It hauls a twin sized mattress with plenty of capacity for your precious son. It has a F. River Tilt Steering Column with working steering wheel, horn, blinkers, and flashers. Headlights, turn signals, parking lights, dome light, cargo light, and caution lights are all LEDs for a total of 242 LEDs. Roughly 203 feet of wire is routed throughout the truck and power is turned on by a keyed power switch in the dash. The storage area is roughly 45 cubic feet under mattress. Both doors open and close on industrial looking stainless hinges. I think the weight is about 650 lbs because I broke my harbor freight furniture dolly.

## Step 2: Tools/safety and bill of materials

**Tools required:**
- Circular saw, router, reciprocating saw, belt sander, hand sander, drill, paint brush/roller
- Optional equipment
- Table saw, chop saw, nail gun, paint sprayer

**Safety:**
- Always wear a dust mask or preferably a respirator when cutting MDF.
- Wear your safety glasses.

**Materials:**
- 2 sheets of 3/4" laminated particle board 75lb each
- 2 sheets of 1/2" MDF 60lb each
- 3.5 sheets of 3/4" MDF 90lb each
- 2 Sheets 5/8" MDF 75lb each
- 2 sets handicap hinges
- 24 14-20 T-nuts
- 2 1/2" diameter aluminum rod
- 8 3" 1/4-20 wood bolts
- 16 1" 1/4=20 wood bolts
- 4 1 1/2" 1/4=20 wood bolts
- 1 box 1" wood screws
- 1 box 1 1/2" wood screws
- 1 gallon safety yellow paint
- 1 quart black paint
- 1 quart silver paint
- 1 gallon primer
- 2 spray cans primer
- 2 spray cans black tool dip

**Optional material:**
- Steering column/wheel
- Lights, switches, wire, power supply
- Hub caps
- Horn/buzzer

## Step 3: Getting started
### Base:

The base is comprised of 6 large pieces. The top and bottom pieces are the same size. See picture. The mattress will rest on the top piece and the bottom piece will be the floor in the storage area. The top and bottom pieces are 3/4" laminated particle board for easy cleanup and a slick sliding surface. These pieces should be cut 2 inches larger than your mattress. Make sure you measure the actual mattress. I measured the showroom floor mattress thinking it would be the same but it was 1 1/4" different in the width. Based on this dimension you can determine the sides and ends. The 5/8" MDF side pieces overlap the 3/4" MDF ends. The back end piece will need an opening to access the storage area. The top and bottom pieces rest on 1 1/2" strips 3/4" MDF attached to the ends and sides with glue and 1" screws. The side height dimension is controlled by the needed storage height and 2/3 the mattress height. I choose the height of a Rubbermaid container plus 3" for the storage height. Screw pieces together with 1 1/2" wood screws dry fitting and disassemble for facade fitting.

### Dump truck sides:
#### Cab sides:

The cab's left and right sides are mirror images with the exception of a routered groove for wiring if wanted. They are made of 2 layers of 3/4" MDF. Where the sides attach to the base they are only one layer thick. The fender attaches in the single layer area to provide extra strength. The fender is two layers of 5/8" MDF. The fender shape is sculpted with a belt sander. I cut the straight edges of the windows out with a circular saw and finished the radius cut with a reciprocating saw. I cut the door out with a 1/16" blade on my reciprocating saw. This gap plus sanding was plenty for door operation and alignment. Going back to wiring, router a 1/2" by 1/2" groove on the inside panel so the wire will lay between the panels. Lay the wire in before gluing, brad nailing, and screwing them together. Use a 1/2" radius router bit on all outside edges. Use a 3/8" router bit on all inside edges including the door and window areas.

#### Dumper sides:

The dumper is 1/2" MDF with the exterior corrugated ribs two 5/8" X 3" layers MDF. There is a single interior corrugated layer of 5/8" MDF. The corrugated pitch is 6". The top rail is two 3/4" X 3" layers exterior and a single layer of 3/4" MDF interior. This top rail thickness is perfect for hot wheel cars.

For the dimensions, the lower portion of the dumper is 8" above the top of the mattress. I am not sure if there are any codes on a bed rail height recommendation but this looked good to me. If you are concerned you may want to check. The dumper is 2/3 of the entire bed length. It is best to lay the pieces out on the base side pieces to confirm fitting. Proportion is everything when you are making a simplified copy of a real thing. If the proportions are off too much it will look goofy.

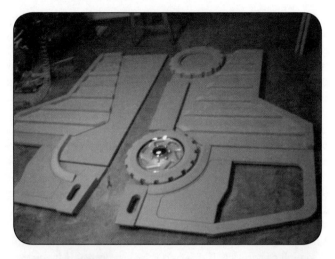

## Step 4: Components
### Doors:

The hinges on the door took me a while to figure out what I wanted to do. The door is the only moving part and I wanted it to be as kid friendly as possible. I would feel really bad if my son hurt himself on something I made if I could have made it better. I finally decided on handicap hinges with one of the hinge sides flipped. This way in the closed position the hinge forms a 15 degree gap. This gap minimizes pinched fingers by allowing a space but the outside is not noticeable. If finger pinching becomes a problem I will install webbing in this gap to end it once and for all. For the center screw on each side of the hinge I installed a 1/4-20 screw and T-nut to guarantee the screws do not strip out if a neighbor kid pulls down or hangs on the door. My kid would never do this. A plunger stop is used to hold the door in the closed position. The door stops against the base portion of the bed. I limit the amount the door opens to help climbing into the truck with 1" webbing under the hinge screws. The door handle is a 6" SS drawer pull recessed half way into the surface of the door. A small pocket was routered 1" depth into the door for your fingers.

### Tires:

In the interest of saving time I designed the tires so standard 16" hub caps would fit. This way I didn't have to make wheels too. The tires are three 3/4" MDF and one 5/8" MDF layers of 24" diameter circles. The top layer I cut the ID to the outermost diameter of the hubcap using a circle cutter attachment to my router. The next layer I cut the same diameter 1/4" depth. This is so the hubcap is recessed into the tire for a more natural look. I then cut the holding hubcap diameter the remaining thickness through the 2nd layer. I cut the 3rd layer same holding tab diameter to the depth of the holding tabs. The 4th layer is not cut. For the 20 lugs I drilled two 1/2" holes at the base of each lug corner and used a reciprocating saw to cut them out on the 4th layer. Then I glued the 3rd layer to the 4th layer. I used a tracing bit on my router to cut the lugs into the 3rd layer. You could use the reciprocating saw for all layers but the router cut surface will require less prep for painting. I then repeated this for the 2nd and 1st layers. And finally I used a belt sander to shape the side wall of the tire. If the bed is going up against the wall like mine you will only need 2 tires.

I used tool dip paint for the tires over standard rattle can primer. The rubber texture makes the tires more realistic. It took 1 can of primer per tire. That's MDF for you.

### Cab roof:

The cab roof is two layers of 3/4" MDF. To make things as safe as possible I added two 1/2" diameter aluminum rods between the layers. I drilled and taped the rods 1/4-20 thread at both ends. I drilled a hole and placed a nail through the rod so it will not spin. I used wood bolts to attach the cab top to the cab sides into the rods. This way if someone somehow breaks the 1 1/2" of MDF by sitting on it they will not fall though into the cab. Say like the neighbor kid again. The aluminum rods will bend but it will not be a catastrophic failure. I added two handles with a router. The wiring is added between the MDF layers so there is no wiring visible for little fingers to get to. Notice the extra area for the connector. Once connected the connector gets pushed into this area so it is not smashed. For all hidden wires I used 16 gauge wires just in case.

### Cab front and dash:

The front of the cab is a single layer of 3/4" MDF. The grill is glued to this piece and it is two layer 3/4"MDF. It has 7 slots cut with a router only one layer deep. The dash is two layers of 3/4" MDF. I made a small box for gauges. The gauges and switches were bought off ebay for 40 dollars. They are for a boat and came on a plastic dash that I modified to look more like a truck dash. The wiring travels down to the electronic compartment via a routered 1/2" by 1" slot behind the grill. I needed 21 wires.

### Cab floor:

The cabin floor is 1/2" MDF with scrape strips glued to it to reduce noise. The floor surface is 1/2" below the door opening to minimize tripping while exiting the vehicle. I used a dado cut to secure the floor to the cab sides but you could use 3/4" MDF strips. The steering column I used bolted though the floor. I used a custom hot rod steering column to minimize design time. It has

telescoping, tilting and angle adjustment so I can easily change it based on the size of the cab. I could have bolted the steering wheel to the dash but that would not be as cool, plus I get blinkers, flashers and horn all in one.

The compartment under the floor is used for the electronics.

### Step 5: Electronics

The electronics compartment has a key latch so no little ones can access the wiring. The electronics are 12 volt so I could buy automotive lights and have a very large selection. I chose a 12 volt power supply from superbrightleds.com as well as two pulse width modulators (PWM) to dim the lights. The LED lights are far too bright to run at 12 volts and reducing the voltage or adding a resistor does not really work that well with LEDs. I used two PWMs so I could selectively dim two circuits. If you do this make sure you separate the grounds too. I ran 12 volts through the fuse panel, to the key switch, to the blinks/flashers, and to the two PWMs. The flasher must have a 12 volts input to work properly but the lights can run off of a different voltage and ground. All the running lights and head lights are on one circuit with the dome and cargo light on the other PWM circuit.

## Step 6: Paint and book shelf

### Paint:

You should use the safest child safe paint you can find. Do some research, your child is worth it. I chose Behr premium latex paint. I chose high gloss and have some regrets. I knew that I would be bolting painted panels together and I wanted them to be able to be disassembled without sticking together. This is not what latex paint is known for and especially not full gloss. I searched for a paint that would dry without being tacky but they were either toxic or had a complex prepping process (similar to painting a car). I asked at more than one home improvement store and they all said that latex will dry and would not stick together within a week. Wrong. I waited 4 weeks and still tacky. To get around this because high gloss was a must for my son's truck I masked all mating surfaces from high gloss paint. I also placed drawer liner between surfaces just in case the primer sticks together. I used blue tape for small 3/4" mating surfaces.

### Front loader mural with book shelf:

Although the front loader is not a wood project it is an integral part of the functional wood book shelf. Painting a mural is fairly simple if you cheat a little, like finding someone to help that has painted a mural, my dad in my case. This is my first mural or painting for that matter and it turned out better than expected. First I went down to my local Caterpillar dealer to take a few pictures and then I borrowed a projector from a friend. I figured out the best place for the mural where it was not blocked by the truck. My son's room is very small so I had only a few options. I initially wanted the bucket over the dumper but I thought my son might bonk his head on the bucket. So I placed it over the cab as if the truck is rolling forward and the loader is waiting to dump the dirt into the dumper. Not dump on

the cab. My dad did a little photo shop to get things looking right, then its paint by numbers. You can trace the projected image then paint or paint with the projector on. We used left over latex paint from the dump truck. This way I could paint it over if I can ever afford another house.

### Book shelf:

The book shelf is very straight forward. I made a bucket tooth out of scrap wood then patterned it onto the book shelf with the router tracing bit. The bottom piece and side leading edges are 3/4" MDF. The rest is left over 1/2" MDF.

## Step 7: Mission accomplished

The bed cost was $430 dollars without the electronics and steering column/wheel. This is a little pricey but worth every penny. With everything it was around $1020 dollars. Ok I went way over budget but in the interest of keeping schedule and coolness factor I had no choice. I guess I will need to eat a bag lunch for the next six months. I did reduce a few options because of the accumulating cost like: Humidifier smoke stacks, rotating tires, shaker motors, dumping dumper, etc. The time to produce this truck was 2.5 months.

I hope you are inspired to create something.

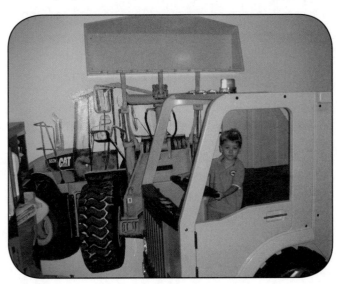

**furnish**

# High Functioning Coat Hooks

By Brian Jewett (BrianyJewett)
(http://www.instructables.com/id/High-Func-
tioning-Coat-Hooks/)

Back in Los Angeles, any old coat rack or a few hooks by the door would do. Most of us would just toss a jacket in the back of the car in the winter months. But here in Vermont we need a little more. Many of the vernacular farm houses I visit have at least a half dozen hooks per person lined up in their mud rooms. My wife and I each will have several different coats, jackets, and vests in play all winter long. Add to that assorted scarves, hats, and gloves, several of each for both of us, and your average coat rack doesn't stand a chance. The bench by our door spent the whole winter covered in coats hats and gloves with the overflow often spreading to the back of the sofa in the living room.

**Materials, for each hanger you'll need:**
- One cleaned or refinished paint can.
- 2 screws long enough to reach into wall studs.

**Tools:**
- Long handled screwdriver or screw gun with sufficient extensions to reach bottom of can.
- Punch or small drill
- Stud finder (optional)

## Step 1
With the handle in a horizontal position, lay out and make 2 small mounting holes at the top and bottom of the can within an inch or less of the edge.

## Step 2
Locate and mark stud position on wall for upper screw position.

## Step 3
Screw through the upper hole of the can into the wall stud but not quite snug to the wall.

## Step 4
Straighten the can and screw through the lower hole of the can into the wall stud snug to the wall.

## Step 5
Snug up first screw.

## Step 6
Hang, stuff, drape, and regain control of your entry space!

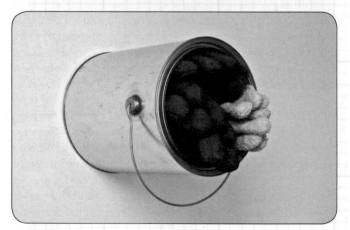

furnish

# The Micro-Bus Bunk Bed and Playhouse

By Bryan Upton (Uptonb)
(http://www.instructables.com/id/The-Micro-Bus-Bunk-Bed-and-Playhouse/)

My brother recently decided to have a new house built to better suit his family. I thought an appropriate house gift would be a bunk bed for his 3-year-old son. Since my brother is a huge Volkswagen fan, what better than a VW themed bed. After scouring the web for ideas, and not finding anything up to my expectations, I decided to just design my own. This is the end result. I am pleased with how it turned out, and better yet my nephew just loves it.

The inside will be used as a play area here, but it will easily fit a single mattress for when he is old enough to have a friend over for a sleep over. I am designing bench seat futons at the moment.

I didn't start taking pictures until I was 3/4 of the way through the project. Kind of spaced it out to be honest. I will provide illustrations up to the point pictures were started.

A side note. Using the same basic design of this project, I am sure you could tweak some measurements and convert a boring old bunk bed frame into something great.

## Step 1: Materials

Overall cost of the bed was just over $500, sans the mattress. It seems like a lot, but any store bought bunk beds are close to this price, and often times higher. I did find a couple online sites selling a "VW" bunk bed. These ran from $1200 for one style, and $2800 for the other. And to put it as humbly as I can, they are not as nice as this one.

All materials can be purchased from most any home store. The only items not purchased from the home store are the VW accents. They can be found online, at auto parts stores, and at local junkyards.

Measurements are in inches and feet.

Lumber:
- 5 sheets of 4'x8' 1/4 inch plywood. I used a premium floor underlayment. The price was really good and of durable quality. (These are for outer skin.)
- 2 sheets of 4'x8' 3/4 inch MDF or plywood. (In my project I used 1/2 inch thick and needed to add extra bracing underneath it. I would definitely use 3/4 inch for better stability and less bracing.) (These are for the floors of top and bottom bases.)
- 11 sticks of 3/4"x4' dowels. (These are for the safety railing/faux cargo rack.)
- 7 pieces of 1"x2"x8' firring strips. (These are for safety railing/fuax cargo rack.)
- 3 pieces 1"x3"x8' firring strips. (These are for the ladder.)
- 9 pieces of 2"x2"x8' firring strips. (These are for the frames of doors and safety rail/faux cargo rack.)
- 2 pieces of 2"x6"x8' studs. (These are for ribs of curved front end.)
- 12–14 pieces of 2"x3"x8' studs. The amount is dependent on how much bracing you are comfortable with. (These are for the majority of all the framing.)
- 1 piece of 4"x4"x4' post. Some home stores will cut this for you. If not, a full 6 or 8 foot stick may need to be bought.
- 4, pre-cut 16" diameter, 3/4 inch thick plywood circles. Some home stores sell these. Otherwise you will have to cut your own.
- 1 piece of 3/4"x12"x44.5" pine board. Try to get a nice knot-free piece here.

Hardware:
- 1 box of drywall screws.
- 1 box of 2" deck screws.
- 1 box of 2.5" deck screws.
- 1 small box of 3.5" deck screws.
- 4, 1/4 inch x 3" carriage bolts.
- 4, 1/4 inch washers.
- 4, 1/4 inch nuts.
- 4 hinges for the doors
- *12 "L" brackets 4"x4" These can be found in the door and hinge section of home stores.
- *12 "L" brackets 1"x1" These can be found in the home store area that contains framing hardware, such as hurricane straps.

    *Pictures supplied in The Wall Frames step of this instructables.

Tools:
- Jigsaw and/or Band-saw if available. (Wishlist for me)
- Power drill

- Countersink bit
- Compound miter saw
- Table saw, if available
- Hand sander and sand paper
- Wood filler
- Paints of whatever color you prefer
- Clamps for when you need that 3rd or 5th hand to hold pieces up.

Accents:
- Hubcaps
- Steering Wheel
- Headlights
- Pin striping
- Little decals and stick-ons

## Step 2: Bottom frame

This bed is designed to knock down to help facilitate moving. It is easier to start from the bottom and work your way up. I have pre-drilled and countersunk every screw used.

You will need the following size pieces of lumber for this step:
- 2, 41 inch 2"x3"s
- 2, 79 inch 2"x3"s
- 3, 38 inch 2"x3"s
- 4, 8.5 inch long 4"x4" legs
- 82"x41" sheet of 3/4" MDF or Plywood.

Assemble the frame as shown in first picture. Space the 3 inner braces 18 5/8" apart.

Attach the 4, 4" x 4" to the inside corners using 3.5" screws as shown in second picture.

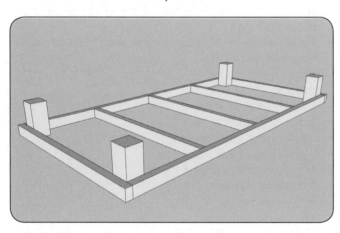

## Step 3: Wall frames

There are 5 parts to the left and right walls of the bus. One side is a continuous piece. It's the side with no doors. The side with the doors consists of the front, back, and two doors. Now depending on where you plan on putting the bus in the room, this is the step you decide which side is which. This instructable shows the build with the doors being on the "passenger" side of bus.

The pre-cut lumber needed here is:
- 4 pieces of 41.5 inch 2"x3"

- 4 pieces of 27 inch 2"x3"
- 2 pieces of 25.5 inch 2"x3"
- 1 piece 27.5 inch 2"x3"
- 2 pieces of 19 inch 2"x3"
- 1 piece of 14.5 inch 2"x3"
- 2 pieces 14.5 inches long 2"x3" with the end cuts being parallel 82 degrees.
- 2 pieces 15 inches long 2"x3" with the end cuts being parallel 76 degrees.
- 1 piece of 75.75 inch 2"x2"
- 2 pieces of 19 inch 2"x2"
- 2 pieces of 25.5 inch of 2"x2"
- 4 pieces of 40 inch 2"x2"
- 4 pieces of 13.5 inch 2"x2"
- 2 pieces of 10.5 inch 2"x2"

The pictures explain the layout of these pieces of lumber. Remember to pre-drill and countersink your screws.

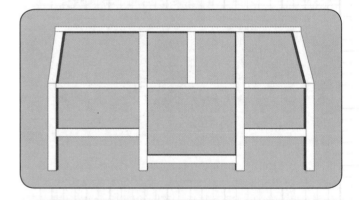

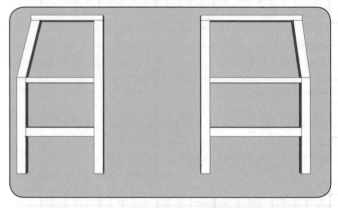

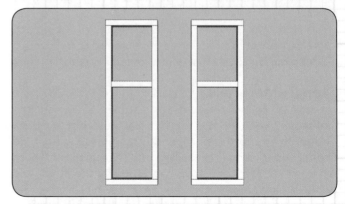

furnish

## Step 4: Front curved frame

The main aspect of this build that determines the uniqueness of the VW Micro-bus is the rounded front end. This is actually not too hard to accomplish. I did my curve free hand. If you can find a compass large enough or something to use as a pattern, please feel free.

Cut 3, 44 inch length pieces from the 2"x6" studs.

Use a jigsaw and cut the arc out of this wood. Use the arc to trace onto the remaining two 44" pieces. Clamp the 3 pieces together and sand the curves until each are identical with each other.

Use one of these as a template also to trace the same arc on the piece of 3/4"x12"x44" piece to be used later as the top cap of the front end.

Pre-cut materials are:
- 3, 44 inches long 2"x6"
- 2, 39 inches long 2"x2"
- 2, 23.75 inches long 2"x3"
- 1, 44 inches long 2"x3"
- 2, 10 7/8 inches long 2"x3" for bracing the arcs

Use the pictures provided for the layout and assemble. Place screws anywhere you feel is appropriate for strength.

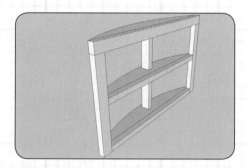

## Step 5: Rear frame

This is one of the more simple frames to assemble. The only difficult part is the angles of the upper pieces. They are cut at 82 degrees.

Pre-cut list is:
- 2, 27 inches long 2"x3"
- 2, 14.5 inches long 2"x3" with parallel cuts at 82 degrees. The angle cuts are on the wide part of the 2"x3."
- 2, 39.25 inches long 2"x3"
- 1, 44 inches long 2"x2"

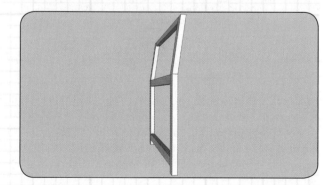

## Step 6: The top frame

The top frame is a little bigger than the top of the bus, due to the size of a single mattress. I don't think it takes anything away from the finished project though. You'll also notice a couple of the 2"x3" braces inside are on end instead of flat like the outside border is. I did this to help brace and space the middle area of the side walls.

Pre-cut list is:
- 81"x46" sheet of 3/4" plywood
- 2, 46 inches long 2"x3"
- 2, 76 inches long 2"x3"
- 2, 41 inches long 2"x3" (Pay attention to how these pieces are positioned)
- 2, 16 inches long 2"x3"
- 2, 26 inches long 2"x3"
- 1, 31 inches long 2"x3"
- 2, 10.5 inches long 2"x3"

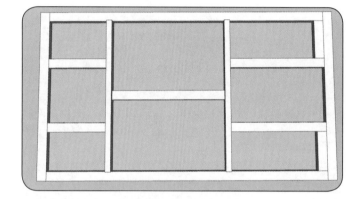

## Step 7: Assemble the frames

Assemble all the frames. Another person is very helpful here. If going at it alone during this step, clamps will do. Start with the wall containing no doors. Attach this wall with 4 of the 4"x4" "L" brackets in the correct position. The wall will support itself after the brackets are installed. You now can move one to installing the two walls on the side with the doors. Use 4 more 4"x4" "L" brackets here.

Then move on to the rear section. Install with the smaller bracket.

Time to place the 4 tires. See illustrations for placement. You might want to sand and paint the tires before install.

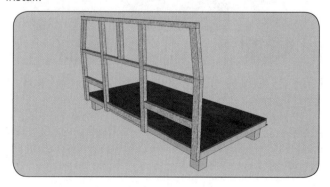

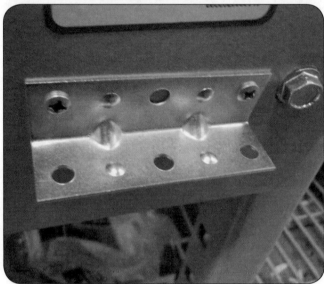

front and back angles, and also around the wheels for wheel wells.

Use the jigsaw and cut out the pieces not needed. For the rear wheel well, measure up 8 inches on both sides of drawn line. Make a straight line to give you the guide to cut the flat top of wheel well. You will repeat this on the other sides rear wheel.

Apply wood glue along the outside of frame where the plywood skin will attach and clamp skin to frame to hold it while using drywall screws to attach.

Measure the areas to be skinned on remaining walls and doors, cut out accordingly, and attach with glue and screws.

## Step 9: Attach the front frame and skin

Attach the front frame with 4 small brackets.

Use a tape measure to measure the front surface of the curved ribs on front frame. Take this measurement as well as the height of bottom to top and this will be the size of front skin.

Apply wood glue to the surface of the three ribs. Now starting from either left or right side line up skin to edge of ribs. Place some screws in to begin the wrap around attachment. Once you have a few screws in, start to push the skin in against the ribs and place more screws in. Continue this process all the way to the other side until you have attached the skin. The 1/4 plywood should be pliable enough to wrap well.

You now have two narrow strips left to skin. The two sides where the ribs attach to frame. Should be 1.5 inches wide by 27 inches long. Finish this and you are now done with outer skin.

Take the piece of 3/4"x12"x44.5" and cut the pre-traced arc out. Now you will have to notch the two inner sides to fit around the wall frame. See illustration for final look of top cap.

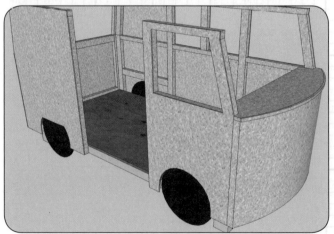

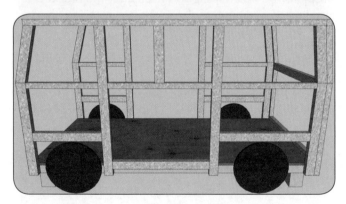

## Step 8: Apply the outer skin to sides and rear frame

Rip one of the 1/4 inch plywood pieces to make it 83.5 inches long and 43 inches wide. Use the clamps and place it on the frame with no doors. Using a pencil, trace around the frame where windows need to be cut out, the

Attach this piece to top of front end with about half inch overhang. This is the dashboard.

Measure, horizontally, across the front of the skinned front end. Add 1 inch to this length and cut a 2"x3" this length, this gives you about half inch overhang on each side. This will be the bumper. About every 1.5 to 2.5 inches you will be making cuts approximately 1" in depth. (See picture.) This will allow you to bend the 2"x3." Find the center on the front end and the piece of 2"x3." Use these center marks to line up the bumper. Glue and screw the bumper in place.

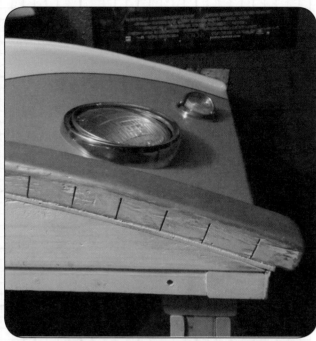

## Step 10: Place the top frame

Get some help here, unless you are He-Man/She-Ra. Lift the top frame up and set onto walls. You'll now notice the two 41 inch 2"x3"s you set on end fit nicely between the left and right walls. This is the junction you will place the "L" brackets to help secure top to bus. Four small brackets in the front and back will finish securing the structure. You will now find this bunk bed to be extremely sturdy and stable.

## Step 11: Security rail/faux cargo rack and ladder

I had already finished this part of the bus, but I will do my best to explain the position of pieces in the attached photos.

Material to pre-cut:

Rails:

- 10, 12" pieces of 2"x2"
- 2, 79" pieces of 1"x2"
- 2, 60" pieces of 1"x2"
- 4, 42.5" pieces of 1"x2"
- 8, 20.5" pieces of 3/4" dowel
- 6, 25" pieces of 3/4" dowel
- 4, 29.5" pieces of 3/4" dowel

  Ladder:

- 2, 66.5" pieces of 1"x3"
- 4, 14.5" pieces of 1"x3"

I have the railing spaced one inch inside from edge. See the pictures for spacing and placement of uprights. To install the dowels a drill press is handy and more precise, but not necessary. On the 2"x2" pieces make two lines 4 inches apart and one line down the middle of wood. These intersections mark where you need to drill out the 3/4" holes to glue dowels in.

The ladder is best to actually build piece by piece onto the rail. The measurements are just generalized. The angle I chose seemed to be the best for strength. Your angle may vary.

## Step 12: Inside skin

Take measurements of the inside walls and cut out 1/4 plywood skin accordingly. Be sure to cut around any brackets holding frame together to keep the knock-down available in case you win the lottery and need to move into a bigger place. Glue and screw these in place.

## Step 13: Accents and paint

Now the real work begins. Sand the entirety of the bus. (Don't want the kids to get any splinters.) Apply wood filler to all the countersunk screws, and any gaps you may have where the skin edges up with the frame.

Choose some great colors, designs, or decals and have fun painting this beast. I noticed as I was building this, I kept thinking about green with flowers and "The Mystery Machine" on the side.

Add your accents, and take a deep breath. You are finally done. This project is time consuming and can be frustrating at times, but when you stand back and look at your finished project, ahhh. Such a good feeling!

furnish

Create your own shabby chic candle chandeliers for your wedding or other great space.

My fiancée and I are getting married October 15th of this year. We met at summer camp six years ago, started dating just over four years ago and as of this spring we are set to be married. Erin is a wonderfully stylish woman and she has a great eye for design (she's a budding photographer and took most of these pictures for me) and I appreciate her love for shabby chic design because it's all stuff I can build and make for her. Our wedding will take place at the camp where we met and then we will have the reception at a great venue called Brookside Farms in Louisville Ohio.

Besides being a beautiful venue, they are also exceptionally accommodating with decorations and this led to among other great ideas, a wonderful set of chandeliers made from mason jars, a wagon wheel, barrel hoops, wire and some twine.

### Step 1: Forming the wire hanger

Safety is a big issue when you have open flames in a huge wooden building, so we decided that making a wire hoop to hang the jars on would be the safest way to go. We tested the first run with taller candles then we plan to use so the flame would get as close to the twine as possible.

The results: We could not get it to burn even after letting it go for 6+ hours.

For this step you will need a coat hanger or other piece of wire as well as a pair of needle-nose and lineman pliers.

- Cut and straighten your coat hanger (don't worry about length—we will trim it later)
- Bend a small hook into one end of the wire
- Bend a loop the diameter of your wire (approximate). The loop should be opposite the hook you just bent when you wrap the wire around the jar's neck (this distance just happened to be the length of the grip on my pliers)
- Bend the wire between the hook and the loop into a 'C' shape

### Step 2: Finishing the hanger

Finishing the hanger:

- Wrap the wire around the jar's neck and bend the end of the wire up through the hook you bent earlier
- Bend the wire that is now sticking straight up into a 'basket handle' shape and trim off the excess wire with your cutters
- Insert the wire end into the small loop and bend the end upwards to lock it on
- Repeat 200+ times . . .

## Step 3: Hanging the jars

The finished chandelier will incorporate a center wagonwheel support and 2-4 barrel hoop wingmen to hold the 250 or so jars that will make up the final product. This example uses 36 jars suspended on twine and hanging from a doubled twine rope. The finished product will be suspended from a set of wooden barn pulleys using a 3/8" sisal rope, which will allow for lowering and lighting.

Hanging the jars is a simple but tedious process that requires tying quite a few knots. I used simple overhand knots and made sure the ends were cut short so they don't catch fire.

The jars are hung at various heights and it seemed easiest to just start by tying short to long.

- Begin by hanging your wagon wheel or barrel hoop from strong rope tied to at least three evenly spaced points and hang it from something sturdy.
- Tie your first level of jars and don't spend too much time making everything even
- Move on to tying the next levels and make sure to space the jars out well and don't leave any dangling ends to catch fire later on.

*This step can be modified for easier transport to your venue later on by tying hooks to the ends of the twine instead of tying directly to the jar hangers. This way the jars can be stored in boxes until it's time to hang everything.

## Step 4: Light those candles

Once your chandeliers are hung, go ahead and drop in some long burning tea lights (if you haven't already), light them and enjoy your handiwork.

*Note: the pictures show votives being used but 6 and 8 hour tea lights are available in bulk from party and restaurant supply places and are much safer because they keep the flame as far from the twine as possible. (I just had a pile of lavender votives a friend had leftover from their wedding that we used for the pictures.)

furnish

# Moresque Lampe

By stregoi

(http://www.instructables.com/id/Moresque-lampe/)

Hey everyone, this is my first instructable, and I would like to share with you how to make this Moresque inspired lamp.

Like most instructables, this project is easy to make (no special skills needed), looks good, and costs virtually nothing! (It will look great even with cardboard.)

I tried to make something original. Searching on the internet I found this website (http://www.storeystreet.com/smlglobe.html) selling a nice looking lamp, so I wanted to make something similar!

For those who are lucky enough to have a laser cutter, that is an advantage, but for me, I cannot afford one, so I will use the traditional way!

The lamp can be made with any material (cardboard, aluminum, plastic, plywood), but the principle is the same.

I will use plywood with a 3mm thickness for this project.

This is my first instructable. I will try to do my best explaining things, but if something is unclear, bear with me, and feel free to ask!

## Step 1: The design

So what was my inspiration? The amazing old mosaics of southern Spain and Morocco. I was always fascinated by these, drawing them all the time. A quick search on the internet produced the patterns (just search in Google for: "Arabic patterns" or something similar).

I used 3Ds max to model the sphere and texture it. To see how it would turn out, when it was done, I tried to copy the model on paper, and with some adjustments, here and there it worked out.

## Step 2: What do you need?

For lampshades made from thick paper:
- some sheets of paper
- scissors
- glue

For lampshades made from plywood:
- some plywood sheets (no thicker than 3 mm)
- many brads (no less than 288!)
- material to saw your patterns

And of course, you'll need the patterns! To follow along with this exact project, visit this Instructable's website for links to the exact patterns shown here.

## Step 3: Cutting the patterns

You can cut them the traditional way by printing the patterns and gluing them to the wood. Use a drill and a saw, or if you own a CNC machine or a laser cutter—I am not that lucky—it will make the job much easier.

If you are using carton or paper, print them and use your scissors.

Once cut, we proceed.

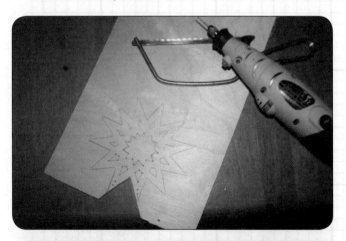

## Step 4: Connecting things together

Before connecting the pieces together I put them in a sink filled with water for 10 minutes, just so they bend easily. But if you are using very thin plywood (1 mm–1.5 mm), you don't need that!

Then to connect them:

IMPORTANT: Make sure to connect the stars to the triangles first in such a manner that the shortest "arm" of the star should connect to the middle arm of the triangle.

And then use the brads to secure them in place together or use the glue if you are using paper.

Then finish by cutting the sticking part of the brads.

## Step 5: Keep connecting pt I

To make the "skeleton" of the lamp, you need 8 square patterns in a row (they will bend at the end to make a circle).

The patterns are connected together with the part we made from the earlier step (you will need 8 of these in total—4 at the top of the "skeleton" and 4 at the bottom of the "skeleton")

Finish the step by connecting the end of the "skeleton" to make a circle.

## Step 6: Keep connecting pt II

Connect all the pieces together to finish the lamp, and secure it with the brads or the glue if you are using paper.

## Step 7: The finished lamp. Enjoy

Here is a picture of a new model, which follows the same principle (working on it).

## Adjustable Modular Furniture

By theRIAA

(http://www.instructables.com/id/Adjustable-Modular-Furniture/)

This is a piece of furniture that can be bent like a snake and is screwed solid with nuts. You can create lots of different tables and chairs. I will make 8 sections but you can choose to make as many sections as you want. You can always add sections later.

### Step 1: Materials to make 8 sections

- 32–1 foot sections of 2x4
- 9–15" sections of threaded rod (I used 5/16" rod)
- 18–grade 8 nuts (size of rod)
- 100–1 1/4" outer size fender washers (size of rod)
- 300 in2–60gt sandpaper
- Wood Stain
- Glue

### Step 2: Cut the boards into 8 pieces

I cut my 8' 2x4s into 11 3/4" pieces with a chop saw. Just try and pick a length that you want that uses your wood efficiently.

### Step 3: Cut 3" in on each side

There's probably a better way to do this (like a band saw), but I set up a jig on my chop saw. You SHOULD cut slightly to one side to compensate for the blade thickness, but I will just fill in this gap with washers.

Note that the chop saw will not cut 3" straight all the way down. I had to flip the boards over and even them, and there was a "V" shape left inside.

### Step 4: Cut off the blocks (or try)

I clamped 8 together at a time and ran them through the table saw at the right height to cut out the blocks. Notice they still stay in because of my faulty technique in the previous step.

### Step 5: Pop 'em out and sand smooth

They snap out with a hammer easily and left less of a problem than I thought. I just sanded the "V" smooth with a circular sander.

### Step 6: Drill holes

A drill press and quick jig would make simple work of this but I was without one. Marked the spot and just eyeballed what's straight. Make sure to use a bit that is quite larger than the threaded rod, don't use the same thickness, it'll be too tight!

furnish

## Step 7: Make sandpaper washers

The friction of wood against wood alone will not support much weight so washers covered with sandpaper are put in between all the cracks; 63 needed, I made 70.

## Step 8: Sand and stain

I sanded with a random orbit sander and stained them with black walnut danish oil.

## Step 9: Cut your rods and bolt your pieces together

Cut the rods to 15" or however short you feel conferrable (the width of 4 2x4s is 14"). Screw the nut on the end, slip two washers on, and push the rod though the pieces, adding sandpaper washers in between each piece. Finish the end off with 2 fender washers and another grade 8 nut.

Tighten the nuts at least a quarter inch in on each side and it will be rock solid. To change the shape, unscrew the nuts until they're loose and it will move around easily.

## Step 10: Imagine the possibilities, all infinity of them

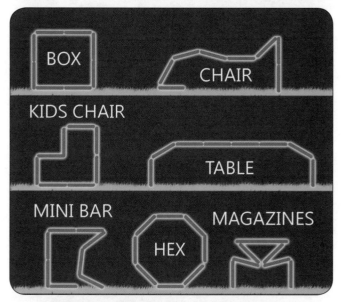

BOX

CHAIR

KIDS CHAIR

TABLE

MINI BAR

MAGAZINES

HEX

furnish

# Wine Barrel Beer Table

By Warrick Smith (liquidhandwash)
(http://www.instructables.com/id/Wine-Barrel-
Beer-Table/)

I found half a wine barrel that the local pub was throwing out, so I grabbed it because it was made out of oak, and I would hate to see that in someone's fireplace.

## Step 1: The barrel

As I said I found the barrel that someone had cut in half. It was almost ready to fall to pieces as 2 of the bands had fallen off and the top one was also ready to fall off. It would be very difficult to reassemble, so I carefully put the bands back on, and took it home.

I was not sure what to make until I saw the nice graphics on the top, so I sanded the top back and put furniture oil on it. It looked good so I decided to keep the graphic, which would mean keeping the top intact. My first thought was a coffee table, but as the project progressed the misses said she liked the height of the table and would like it on the deck next to her chair.

## Step 2: Stuff you will need
- Sand paper grits 40, 80, 120, and 240
- Matte black paint
- 3 or 4 coach bolts with washers and nuts
- Drill and dill bits
- 3 or 4 wood screws
- Small nail or tacks
- Hammer

- Jig saw (reciprocating) saw
- Clean rags
- Your favorite timber finish
- Angle grinder, with sanding disc.
- About 2 hours
- Beer

## Step 3: Mark out the legs

I decided to make the table with three legs as they don't rock around on uneven surfaces so I marked out the three slats that we are going to be used for legs.

I then made sure the bands were straight and tight and drilled and screwed the three slates to the bottom band so nothing would move in the next steps.

## Step 4: Remove the sharp bits

The top band had quite a sharp edge on it so I used a grinder with a sanding disc to remove the edge and make it smooth.

## Step 5: Remove the bands and paint

I removed the top 2 bands with a hammer and a block of wood and then cleaned with thinners. I hung them from the roof with wire and spray painted matt black. I also painted the heads of the coach bolts.

furnish

## Step 6: Sanding

I used 4 different grit sand papers starting with 40, then 80, 120, and 240.

I only sanded the top and the top of the sides and the legs.

Sanding is boring so I got some free child labor to do most of it.

## Step 7: Oiling

You could probably do this step last, but I put a coat of my favorite furniture oil on, so it would be under the bands, helping protect the timber from spills and moisture. Just use a rag to rub the oil on.

## Step 8: Refit the top band

I put the top band back on and knocked it down with a hammer.

## Step 9: Cut out the legs

Next I drilled 3 holes big enough for my jig saw blade to pass through, and cut around the bottom of the line the 2nd band had left.

I found that oak was very hard and difficult to cut with a dull blade. I should really have put a new blade in the saw, but the store was closed.

Don't forget to leave the legs uncut. The waste wood can then be removed.

## Step 10: Fitting the second band

The second band can now be fitted. I knocked it down with a hammer and a block of wood and drilled three holes through the band and the legs into which the coach bolt were fitted.

To help keep the top band in place I drill 3 small holes and nailed in some carpet tacks as they had an old style black head that matched the look of the table.

## Step 11: Remove the bottom band

Now that the table has been bolted together the bottom band can be removed and the legs sanded and finished off.

The misses likes the height of the table but it could be cut down for a coffee table.

## Step 12: Other stuff

I think that now its finished that it would look better with four legs, and it needs to be a bit shorter as the curve on the end of the legs make it look a bit odd. But it is very stable, doesn't rock around and the ring around the top stops my drunk friends from putting there glasses on the edge of the table, so that stops their beer getting knocked over.

furnish

279

We've been collecting bottle caps for what seems like forever anticipating this table. After moving our collection with us to 4 different homes in 3 different states, we now have enough caps for this table plus a few matching stools. What makes this project different than a simple mosaic project is that we covered the table with a thick resin, creating a look quite similar to the tables at your favorite pub.

### Step 1: Collect bottle caps
**Tips:**
- Become friends with bartenders.
- Cheap date night: Visit alleys behind local bars.
- Buy microbrews based on how cool the caps are, not how good the beer is.
- Get your friends to help you collect.
- When traveling overseas, buy beer instead of souvenirs.

### Step 2: Find the table
You can do this on any sized surface. I've seen huge bars covered in pennies or old photos, but unless you want to deal with storing wheelbarrows of bottle caps, a bistro-sized or small end table is good for starters.

We used a Noresund IKEA table purchased in the As Is area at our local IKEA. I believe it is now discontinued. Sorry.

Link to Ikea store: http://www.ikea.com/ca/en/catalog/products/10073835.

### Step 3: Lay out your design
We started out with a random design, featuring just one bottle cap from every kind we had in our cap stash. This left room for some repeats, so we arranged a pattern around the circular shape of the table.

### Step 4: Begin gluing
You might be thinking that you can just lay caps down and pour resin over them, but don't skip this step.

Since we were covering our table with clear resin, we weren't too concerned with the type of glue used. I started out with contact cement, moved on to furniture glue, then Liquid Nails for small projects, and even tried siliconized caulk. I ended up using plain old super glue. This was the best option and the one I suggest for you. Since the caps are going to get covered with resin, they just need to stick to the table, so a couple of dots are all you need. Don't go crazy, because messy excess glue will show through the resin when you're done.

**Extra information regarding this step:**
Although I suggest super glue for this project, the contact cement was truly the strongest adhesive. However, it took some time to use and was less forgiving. The silicone-based glues (Liquid Nails and caulk) seemed to shift or expand as it dried, which ultimately threw our design off. Super glue was the least elegant choice, but it dries relatively quickly and was rigid enough for this project. One note of caution: I discovered that Super Glue reacts with the hexane/toluene base of contact cement. They discolor and create a crystalline growth that resembles a fuzzy, white mold that must be removed with acetone. So pick one glue and go with it to avoid this kind of situation.

### Step 5: Prepare your surface
Once everything was glued down, I used blue painter's tape to cover the edge of my table just even with the surface of the table. This is usually recommended to avoid drips of resin from drying to sides of your project, but I did it to keep the duct tape from getting my table all sticky (see Step 6).

Don't forget to also tape up any holes on the surface of your table. I did this from underneath so that the blue tape wouldn't show once the resin was applied. If you have a table surface with lots of openings (like a metal mesh or expanded metal), you may want to get a piece of Plexiglas or MDF and use that for your tabletop.

## Step 6: Build a barrier

If your table has a rim, you can skip this step. Since mine had no rim, I had to create a way to keep the resin at a depth that would cover the bottle caps without running off the side. I needed something sticky enough that it would create a barrier against resin, yet slick enough that it would not stick to the resin.

### Step 6a:

I decided to use aluminum foil and duct tape. First, cut some long strips of duct tape to go around the edge of the table. Next, cut strips of foil about 3" wide and 1" longer than your strips of duct tape. Laying the strips of duct tape sticky side up, carefully cover about half of the duct tape with a strip of foil. The straighter you do this the better. You could also do this with wide painter's tape and eliminate the need to cover the edges of the table with painter's tape in Step 5.

### Step 6b:

Tape the foil/tape strips around the edge of the table, making sure that the bottom edge of the foil falls just below the surface of the tabletop (the actual table, not the bottle caps). See photo for details. The reason: If the sticky surface of the duct tape is above the tabletop, the resin will stick to it and defeat the purpose of making an easy-release barrier. If the foil is too far below the tabletop, resin may seep over the edge, trapping blue tape underneath.

## Step 7: Cover with resin

I won't get into how to mix the resin since there are instructions in the box, not to mention ample tutorials available online. (The resin I used was Envirotex Lite Pour-on High Gloss Finish). You will, however, need to spread the resin to get into the gaps between the bottle caps as well as out to the edges. This is why your caps need to be glued down, as you will be running a rigid piece of paper or plastic over the surface of the caps. This is a great opportunity to use those fake credit cards that come in your junk mail. I used an old insurance card, but any stiff plastic or cardboard would suffice.

Remember that the resin will level itself out, so just make sure you have enough to fill in the gaps and even out any high areas. You may want to cover your work to keep any random hairs or dust from getting stuck. Now walk away for about 7 or 8 hours.

## Step 8: Remove the tape

After the resin is fully set, carefully begin peeling away the foil/tape. If the foil was kept relatively smooth and the tape was not touching the resin, it should peel away from the hardened resin easily. The only area I had problems was where some resin seeped between overlapping ends of the foil/tape. Also, there were a couple of spots where the resin seeped over the edge of the blue tape slightly. These were both easily remedied using a hobby knife.

## Step 9: And voila!

You have a great new conversation piece for your home or patio.

**furnish**

**281**

# Compass Table

By Noah Weinstein (noahw)
(http://www.instructables.com/id/Compass-Table/)

One day I was playing around with a compass and a magnet noticing how much fun it was to manipulate the compass rose as I moved the magnet around. I'm of the mindset that when it comes to fun, more is usually better, so I rounded up 500 compasses and some rare earth magnets and decided to turn what started as just a little silly but entertaining play time into an actual piece of furniture.

The compasses are inlaid into a custom table top underneath a piece of glass. The coasters were made to match—they also provide an inconspicuous home for the powerful rare earth magnets that affect the compasses.

Now I always know which way is north, and exactly where my cup of coffee is ... er, so long as it's always on my compass table.

Note: the reliability of compasses in mass quantities and close proximity decreases somewhat since compasses themselves are magnets. It still works, and actually results in some pretty cool patterns, but if you're looking for the table to be 100% accurate, I'd recommend not designing a table that places them so closely together. I'm a big fan of the way the table came out, as it's a toy just as much as it is about the science of magnetism.

## Step 1: Materials

To make a compass table you need supplies for the top, the legs, and the tools to put it together.

**Table:**
- 12mm sanded plywood
- table legs—I used 4 Ikea Vika Oleby prefab legs
- 16 7/16" x 1/8" thick glass circular top (I had this custom cut)

**Coasters:**
- a couple square feet of 6mm sanded plywood
- 2 cork coaster inlay
- 2 rare earth magnet

**Compasses:**
- approximately 500 "mini compasses." I got mine for around 20 cents a piece off Ebay. It takes 500 20mm compasses to cover a 16.5" circle—crazy I know!

**Tools:**
- router
- circle jig
- drill
- wood glue
- brush
- polycrylic—water based clear satin wood finish
- speed square
- clamps
- random orbital sander

## Step 2: Modify the legs

The Vika Oleby legs from Ikea look cool and aren't too Ikea-trashy, so I saved myself some building time and went for them. The circular table that I built is a bit too small to fit them all on there in their store-bought form so I modified them slightly.

Using a speed square I marked and cut two 45 degree lines on the end of the table leg where it mounts to the table top so that I could fit 4 legs on my 18" table top.

I removed about 1.5" of material off the corners. No need to be precise here so long as you don't affect the mounting bracket.

## Step 3: Route out the tabletop

The table top is made from three different layers of 12mm sanded plywood in order to get the right depth for the compasses and overall table top thickness.

Two 18" circles were routed out using a Jasper Circle Jig (a tool that I'm quite fond of: http://www.amazon.com/Jasper-270J-Router-Circle-Cutting/dp/B00009K77B). A third circle of the same size was cut, and then had a slightly smaller circle inscribed inside of it to create the rim for the table. The rim turned out to be 1/2."

## Step 4: Glue and clamp

I used a brush to spread some wood glue between the layers, stacked them all up, centering them carefully, and then clamped and weighted the entire sandwich between some stiff maple boards until they dried.

## Step 5: Sand and finish

Once the glue dried I used a random orbital sander with some 220 grit paper to smooth everything out and take off any rough edges.

Then, I brushed two coats of polycrylic, a Minwax brand water-based clear wood finish, that's a whole lot easier to clean up and is more forgiving than Polyurethane, onto the table top.

I sanded lightly with 220 grit paper in between the two coats for a nice smooth finish.

## Step 6: Attach legs

With the table top finished, it was time to mount the legs onto the table.

Using the supplied mounting brackets as a guide, I marked and drilled the mounting holes for the legs into the top.

The supplied Ikea allen wrench tightens the bolts into place.

furnish

## Step 7: Arrange compasses

If the table were a square or rectangle I would have arranged the compasses in a grid, but since it was a circle (to match the circular form of the compasses themselves), I had to come up with other arrangement options. After fiddling around with them for a short while I was able to find something that worked well—concentric circles.

Arrange the compasses as tightly as possible working from the outside in, getting the final few in place takes a bit of a massaging, but once they all go down, it's a nice symmetrical tight fit that can adjust to whatever size circular table that you have.

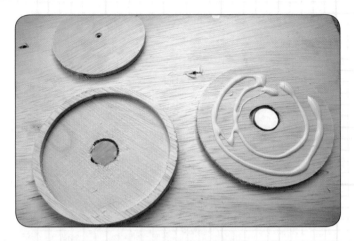

## Step 8: Coasters—route out

The coasters are made in almost identical process to the table top itself, just smaller.

One base circle was cut from the thinner 6mm plywood and then one ring was created to become the coaster lip. The ring is a bit more tricky to route than it's big brother was with the circle jig because it doesn't have enough friction to hold itself in place as the router passes by. A little tape does the trick so you can complete the cut.

The rare earth magnets that I bought were 3/4" by 1/8" thick, so I routed out a small inset for them in the coaster base using just my eye, since that hole was going to get covered up anyway in the next step with the cork coaster pad.

When you lay the magnet down in its pre-cut hole, make sure that you've got the pole facing the right way, we want to attract the north end of the compass, so flip it around until you've got it the right way.

## Step 9: Coasters—glue and clamp

Spread glue on the rim of the coaster and the coaster base and make a coaster sandwich. The cork pads can be cut, or, pre-bought from Ikea as well and glued into place inset within the rim in order to cover the exposed rare earth magnet.

Clamp them between some of those pieces of maple from before and allow them to dry.

## Step 10: Coasters—sand and finish

Once the coasters were dry I sanded them smooth with some more 220 grit paper and put two coats of polycrylic on them as well.

Finding things to dry them on is easy since they've got a magnet embedded in them.

## Step 11: Glass top

I was toying around with the idea of pouring epoxy or polyester resin into the table top to finish things off and permanently secure the compasses into place, but upon learning more about the process, I decided that cutting a simple glass top would be safer since I didn't want to jeopardize my 500 compasses in case something went wrong with the resin pour.

I got the glass cut at East Bay Glass (http://maps.google.com/maps?q=east+bay+glass&oe=utf-8&client=firefox-a&ie=UTF8&hl=en&hq=east+bay+glass&hnear=San+Francisco,+CA&z=10&iwloc=A&cid=912852194416034974) at exactly 16 7/16" so that would perfectly fit inside the rim of the table. It sits directly on top of the compasses nicely and has virtually zero play. As a result, I'm not worried about scratching the tops of the compasses, but if whatever you were inlaying was more vulnerable for some reason, putting in some kind of supports for the glass could be a good idea.

furnish

# Tennis Ball Chair

### By Will Holman (wholman)
### (http://www.instructables.com/id/Tennis-Ball-Chair/)

I made a pair of these chairs a few years ago while I was in school, and had access to a nicely-equipped shop and, most importantly, a laser-cutter. The tennis balls you see are not glued in place; they are held only by different-sized holes in the top and bottom sheets of plywood. The holes on the bottom are smaller so the balls don't push through when you sit on it. To create the contoured effect, the sizes of the top and bottom holes vary in specific ratios. The balls can still freely rotate and some of them can come all the way out. That said, it is much easier to make without all the contouring, but decidedly less comfortable. I made a prototype version in which the balls do not contour.

Everyone always asks me if it's comfortable. Yes. The key here is that the balls are not glued in place or screwed through somehow, so they can flex and deform. With the body distributed over fifty of them, no single one makes a pressure point; the slope on the seat pan, and the U-shaped contour on the back, match butt and back as closely as possible, giving spine and tailbone some breathing room.

The fact that they are not fixed in place also means that they shrink and expand from their holes with changes in heat, humidity, and altitude, as the air trapped inside the balls changes in volume.

## Finding a chair frame
1.  Find an old chair frame.
2.  Unscrew the cushions, which are held in place by four metal straps that span the frame from side-to-side.

Use a Dremel or an angle grinder to cut the straps off the frame, and then grind down the weld spots smooth. The frame should now just be two sides, only held together by the crossbars on the legs. The cushion straps acted as a brace, so the frame will now be lacking stiffness.

## Substructure
3.  Cut two pieces of 3/4" MDF 16-1/4" by 14-1/2." These will become the substructure underneath the plywood, and give the frame its stiffness back. The square cross-section tube that composes the frame of this chair is 3/4" thick, thus this thickness for the substrate. You could also use plywood, but that is substantially harder to drill through, especially holes this big.
4.  The 16-1/4" dimension is side-to-side, the 14-1/2" dimension is from front-to-back. Draw a grid on the MDF that has lines every 3" from front-to-back and 3-1/4" from side-to-side.
5.  Using a hole-cutter bit and a drill press, bore a 2-5/8" diameter hole at each of the twenty-five intersections on each grid on each piece of MDF. This size hole is slightly bigger than the maximum diameter of a new tennis ball (approx. 2-1/2").
6.  3-1/4" inches down from the end of the chair frame top, drill a 1/8" diameter hole from the side of the frame. Drill another hole eight inches below that one. Take care to make the hole as straight as possible, because you're really drilling two holes—one through each side of a hollow section of tube. If the two holes are misaligned because you didn't drill straight, it will be hard to get the screws through. Repeat a total of eight times, two holes on each side of each eventual cushion.
7.  Insert the MDF between the sides of the frame 1/4" shy of the ends of the frame and screw stainless steel,

1/8" diameter metal screws with washers through the holes and into the MDF. You should now have two pieces that are secured with four screws each in the approximate position of the old cushions.

## Plywood finish sheets

8. For this step, I used a LaserCamm rapid prototyping machine that uses a laser to cut sheets of flat material. This step can be done by hand, but thin plywood tends to chip and scar at cut edges—the laser leaves a clean, burnt edge and is also perfectly accurate. To avoid this, another sheet material such as masonite, could be used. Cut four pieces of 1/4" plywood or other suitable sheet material 17-3/4" across and 15" front-to-back. That leaves a quarter-inch of overhang to the front and back of each cushion, and 3/4" overhang on each side, which overlaps the steel frame.

9. Starting from the center instead of the sides, mark the same grid as you did on the MDF, 3" front-to-back and 3-1/4" from side-to-side.

10. Mark each piece with a number, one through four. From front-to-back, the balls will slant downwards. Starting with piece number one, which will be the bottom plate of the seat pan, use a hole-cutter bit to drill the following diameters of holes, each centered on the appropriate intersection on the drawn grid. The first row, side-to-side, should be 2-7/16" in diameter. The next row, again side-to-side, should be 2-3/8" in diameter. The following rows should be 2-5/16," 2-1/4," and 2-3/16." If you want to save the time and trouble of all the contouring business, just make two pieces where all the holes are 2-7/16," and another two pieces where all the holes are 2-3/8."

11. Piece number two will be the top of the seat pan. From front to back, the rows should be 2-3/8," 2-7/16," 2-1/2," 2-9/16," and 2-5/8."

12. Piece number three will be the back of the back cushion. From side-to-side, the balls make a U-shaped contour. This time, each column of holes will be the same diameter, instead of each row. Using a hole-cutter bit, drill a column of holes 2-3/16" in diameter on the outside two rows. On the two rows just inside, the holes should be 2-5/16." The center column should be 2-7/16."

13. Piece number four is the top plate of the back cushion. The two outside columns should be 2-5/8" in diameter. The two columns right inside those should be 2-1/2" in diameter. The center column should be 2-3/8."

14. Sand, stain, and seal the pieces as desired.

## Finish up

15. Drill a total of twelve 1/8" diameter holes through the chair frame from top-to-bottom, again taking care to align them as straight as possible. The holes should be centered on the rows of holes in the MDF, the two edge rows and the center row.

16. Drill a matching set of 1/8" diameter holes through the pieces of plywood.

17. Take piece number one, the bottom of the seat pan, and attach it to the underside of the seat piece of MDF with glue and stainless steel screws. It should be aligned so that all the holes in the two pieces are centered on one another, allowing for a 1/4" overhang of the MDF on each end front-to-back, and 3/4" of an overhang side-to-side, which overlaps the steel frame.

18. Do the same with piece number three, the back of the back cushion.

19. Insert a tennis ball into all fifty holes. They are available used, quite cheap, on eBay. If you have done everything right so far, all of the balls should fit snugly and none should push through.

20. Fit piece number two over the balls in the seat pan. Again, everything should fit snugly, trapping the balls in between two retaining edges created by the plywood. Glue and screw into place.

21. Do the same with piece number four, the front of the back cushion.

22. Now use twelve 1/8" diameter machine screws with washers to go through the holes drilled in step 15 from top-to-bottom through the frame and both pieces of plywood. Tighten nuts and washers on the underside, snug against the frame. Use a Dremel or angle grinders to trim any excess screw length down flush with the nut.

23. Cut four strips of plywood that are 3/4" by 16-1/4." Sand, stain, and seal as desired. Glue on the four remaining exposed edges of MDF.

24. Sit down and take a well-deserved rest.

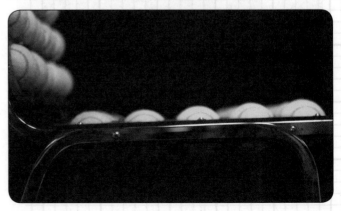

furnish

# Pacman Pouf

## By allesflex
### (http://www.instructables.com/id/Pacman-pouf/)

Browsing the Internet I found a link to an Italian design site that creates hockers (pouf) in the shape of the so ever loved Pacman creature!

When I saw the picture on the internet, I thought, well . . . that shouldn't be so hard to make it myself! I dove into the adventure of designing, creating, and (for the first time) doing upholstery. I hope you like it and comments/suggestions are welcome.

## Step 1: Design

First thing I always do when I start a build or a project, I create some Autocad drawings on scale, so in later stage during the build, I can easily measure the angles and sizes of the woodwork I need.

**The requirements for the design I restricted myself to:**
- low cost (was about €120)
- low weight
- easy to build
- sturdy (should be able to hold 2 people at least)
- in metrics (of course, it is the world standard!)

**Then the following process was to determine the size of the Pacman:**
- For the height I took my current couch as the best height (40 cm). Keep in mind that the foam/padding determines the height of the woodwork!
- The radius of the Pacman was defined in proportion with the height. It looks quite large (d=80 cm) but proportionally the Pacman will look strange if the height (40cm) was set to a 50 cm diameter.

**Material list:**
- 15 mm MDF, depending on the size, you will need at least the C-shape to be created from one piece.
- 9 mm multiplex (plywood)
- 32mm*40mm timber (count number needed * height for total length needed)
- larger ones (for example 40mm*40mm) for the corners and block

- upholstery: I used sky to get that leather-look, but it is not so flexible. Mine had already some sliding-stuff on the inside, so it can slide over the foam. If you get other stuff, inform if you need additional stuff.
- cardboard strips. I had special ones, but you can cut some yourself
- lots of staples!

**Equipment needed:**
- workmate/bench
- Jigsaw
- drill
- drill-bits
- countersink
- screws (about 30mm in length, 3,2*30mm would be ok)
- wood glue (read instructions!)
- needle (curved one special for this type of work) and thread (special sturdy one!)
- sewing machine [if available] (I don't know if a regular sewing machine is able to get through the upholstery)
- foam and other filling
- a stapler! (I had a pneumatic one, but an electrical or whatever is a must. I don't thing the manual ones will be able to enter the MDF deep enough).
- knife
- markers

**Tips/remarks:**

In the design the top (9mm multiplex/plywood) of the Pacman was created separately because I was not certain if the upholstery required a top that was not connected. Only when doing the upholstery I found out that it was better that the top was fixed, but also for the weight reduction it is a good solution!

## Step 2: Create the base structure
### Creating the C-shape:
- First draw the C-shape on the MDF. I used a nail in the middle and a piece of wood and pencil to create the perfect round shape.
- Measure the inner edge of 7.1 cm.
- Mark the points where the vertical timber for the frame will be glued and screwed between top and bottom C-shape.

### Creating the block:
- Draw the square top/bottom.
- Jigsaw to cutout the pieces.
- Mark the edges where the timber will be mounted (glue and screw).
- Attach the sides.
- Drill holes all over.

**Tips/remarks:**

The holes drilled in the wood structure are to prevent air from getting stuck under the upholstery. When you sit down on the pouf, the air can escape through the holes.

Work precise and get rid of all imperfections using files and sanding paper, because a lot will show when you put on the upholstery.

## Step 3: Eye of the beholder

Ok, now the hard part.

A Pacman looks nice, but is only complete with an eye to scout for the blocks to eat. I have measured out where I wanted the eye to be and how large it will be, all relative to the size of the whole set of course.

Test the sewing of the eye:

As I have tried some examples first to create the perfect round eye and sew it to the red cloth, you might see that it is a good step to test some examples from material you have spare after cutting the basic cloth.

I used a professional sewing machine for this, but as you might see in a detail picture, it has quite a high start resistance, so it might 'shoot' its way in a straight line. Practice is a must!

Maybe it is better to do it manually, but then you will have to work precise in the distance between the stitches.

Tips/remarks:

Stitch just on the edge of the white 'eye' so when the pouf is going to be used, the edge will not curl up and take it loose from the red cloth.

## Step 4: Block upholstery

Ok, after all the preparation, it is time to start the upholstery. I first took the small block for the test, because it is cheaper to buy a new small piece of cloth when it goes wrong instead of the C-shaped piece.

Glue the foam:
- Use appropriate glue for the foam (I used Bison Tix). Let it dry for the required time (15/20 minutes) before mounting it together!
- Start pushing the edges together, lifting the center piece. Work your way from the edges in.

    The edges will look chamfered, something like this: \\_/

    When the upholstery is put on, it will get it back into the shape, creating straight edges.

Mounting the top part:
- Measure the rough shape and keep about 10 cm extra to pull it into shape.
- Use the staple gun (in an angle, see Tips) to get the first stretching in place. Start at the corners and make sure to see that the curving is ok. Continue with the sides.
- Check if everything is straight and if tension is high enough. You can check this by placing your hands on the side and move to the middle. If the upholstery curls up, there is not enough tension. If the edges are not even, there is probably too much tension.
- Because of the non-stretch of the cloth I used, no corners with even tension and no wrinkles were possible, so I decided to use folded corners (see pictures).
- Finish the top by stapling it. Use one staple length between staples to get even tension.
- Cut the remainder part by marking it evenly. (I used a piece of wood again with a mark on it and a pen to trace the line whole around.)

Continue with the sides:
- I used one length of cloth for the sides, getting one sewing edge at one corner.
- Mount the white cloth inside out and use a strip of cardboard, which will create the sharp edges.
- Put the inner padding on, some extra on the edges.
- Fold down the cloth and staple it on the bottom. Use the same technique as described above (using angled staples). Finish the bottom part first for the three edges that can be fixed. Leave the sewing edge open.
- Fold the last corner in shape and use pins to keep it in shape. Staple it on the bottom with temporary staples. Check if the corners are not too bulky, else fold it in further and remove cloth that is not needed/out of sight (be careful cutting! ).
- Start the sewing at the top by creating a knot at the end, pull it through both corner-ends with the special curved needle and get it back through the knot. If you

furnish

want to make sure it stays put, sew it fixed to the red top cloth.

From there, get from the back from one side to the other side and push the needle through, bending it back so it pops out 4 to 5 mm in the other side. Something like this:

_ _)(_ _)(_

Continue your way down with even stitches and finish at the end.

- Finish the bottom by stapling it fixed and cutting the remaining cloth around 5mm from the line of staples!

Tips/remarks:

- Use the staple gun in an angle for the 'tagging.' It is easy to remove the nails when you make mistakes, as only one 'leg' of the staple is in the wood.
- Stretch all corners and sides evenly. Use a lot of views to see if the lines (curves) are even and straight. View it from eye-height, turn it around, put it on the floor and do the same!

## Step 5: C-shape upholstery

Now the first part is finished, start with the C-shape.

With the experience from the 'block' you use the same technique for the C-shape.

### Difficulties:

- The center of the top-part is quite difficult. Use a spare-piece of cloth to test the cuts you will need to make. Note: Be very careful cutting, as you will cut too deep quite easy. Don't underestimate, cut, test, cut a bit more, test again!

- Use same folding edge corners like the 'block.' If it leaves marks from the wood, fill it with extra foam where needed.
- I used it like with the block, a piece of cloth for the outside of the C-shape and stapled it in the C-cutout.
- I used a small piece for the cutout with overlap. Mount it like all other side-walls and fold in the edges for sewing. Use same sewing technique as mentioned before.
- I finished it by putting in 2 nails so the corner-sides wont be able to be ripped down.

Tips/remarks:

Be careful with your cuts. Use small v-shaped cuts at the end to divide the tension better.

## Step 6: Enjoy finished project

Now the fun part.

Put it in your living room and enjoy!

Beware of couch eating abilities.

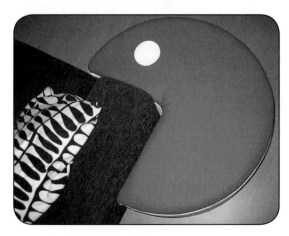

furnish

# Skateboard Table

By Wade Wilgus (wilgubeast)
(http://www.instructables.com/id/Skateboard-Table/)

For those of you who were told not to skate in the house as a child, here's a lazy Susan coffee table that rotates on skateboard wheels.

Think of the possibilities: Play board games where nobody has to look at the board upside-down. Bring the remote within reach without getting up from the couch. Epic tea parties.

## Step 1: Design inspiration

I wanted a design that met the following constraints:
- Less than $100
- Made from wood and parts available pretty much anywhere
- Requires minimal power tools
- Easy to assemble

I ended up spending around $70 for everything but the glass top. The glass put me over my intended budget by around $60. Had I waited for a good yard or estate sale, I imagine I could have gotten the glass much cheaper.

After cutting and drilling, assembly is more or less Ikea-style. All inserting dowels into slots. Then some screwing. Just like Ikea.

## Step 2: Materials

Parts:
- Redwood board—2x $14 each
  - 2 x 6 x 8
- Dowel pins—$2
  - 12 pack

with channels in the side for extra glue hold
- Dowel centers
- Simpson strong-tie T-shaped strap—$4 at HD
  - 6" x 6"
  - and screws to install on the bottom
- Krown Rookie Complete Skateboard x2—$44 at Amazon  full set of trucks/wheels/bearings cheaper as full set than individually
  - save deck for future projects
- Wood glue
- Semigloss polyurethane
- #8 1" wood screws

Tools:
- Miter saw
- Palm sander
- Drill
  - with brad point bits
  - 5/16" and something teeny-tiny for your pilot holes
- Speed square
- Protractor
- A band clamp (you could use any ratcheting tie, it's pretty much the same thing)
  - with brad point bits
  - 5/16" and something teeny-tiny for your pilot holes
- Rubber mallet
- Palm sander
- Sponge for applying polyurethane

## Step 3: Saw

Cut your 2 x 6s to length. I had the guys at the lumberyard cut the boards into 24" segments, then I cut them to size in the shop.

The length of the radial portions on the top of the table base may vary. Customize it to your space. (I made my table a little smaller than the original by shortening the radial boards from 20" to 18.") Just make sure each board end is absolutely square by trimming the last inch or so from each side of the 2 x 6 prior to working with them. Not every cut at the mill or the lumberyard is going to be to your specs. Here's what I did for a 36" diameter table:
- Radial boards for the top of the base: 18"
- Leg boards: 14"

## Step 4: Saw 2

Now that all of your boards have been cut to length, it's time for the fiddly part: that central joint. We'll need to know where to make the cuts to give you a beautiful set of 120 degree pointed boards, and that might require some math. I've broken it out into three options for you:
1. For students of the humanities and children, use a protractor to mark a line from the center of the end of the board. Draw a line along the 60 degree mark from that midpoint to the side of the board. That'll give you a lovely line that you may cut along.

2. For those of you who fully trust the angles along the bottom of the miter saw, just go ahead and mark the midpoint of your board, then set the saw to 30 degrees, align with the midpoint, and cut.

3. For those of you who know trigonometry, just puzzle it out. [Hint: x = .5(width of the board) * tan(30)]

The measurement from the end of the board came out to around 4.01 cm or 1 17/32." But do this part for yourself to ensure that everything lines up properly. Trig will be most accurate. Trusting your miter saw is fastest.

Now that you know where to make the cuts, get to it. I made a few practice pieces to get a feel for a new saw, figure out the size of the kerf, and because I am on the obsessive side of cautious. I also struggle with simple math.

Things to remember: make your marks as exactly and as consistently as possible. Use the speed square. Use a ruler. Check with a protractor. Then cut.

## Step 5: Treat the wood

You can save this step till last, but I like my pieces to be done before I assemble everything. It gives me that Ikea feel of ready-to-assemble furniture. And it makes me concentrate extra hard on not allowing any dings to the wood. And forces me to glue very, very carefully later on. For those of you unsure of your polyurethaning abilities, you might want to do this just before installing the skateboard parts.

I chose polyurethane because it has good protective qualities and has a matte finish. I don't want a glossy table with a glossy top, that's a little too much shine for me. The semi-gloss is good for my needs and hides mistakes better than a gloss. You will be fine with an oil or wax if you want to go that route. The Minwax tung oil gave me the same look as the semi-gloss poly, in case you are curious. (It was also approximately a zillion times easier to apply.)

For the brave and/or foolhardy, let's put on some polyurethane. First, follow the directions on the can. Then, because the can directions sometimes suck, try this:

- use as matte a finish as possible to avoid having a tiny mistake force you to start over

- use a disposable sponge brush (or just a sponge like I did)
- don't over-do it, you will regret it later when you have to scrape off the bubbles/drips with a razor
- follow the grain
- allow plenty of drying time
- hand-sand between coats*
- if any of that sounds too hard, just use oil or wax

I used two coats, sanding with 220 after each. I could have gone for a finer grit, but I like the ever-so-slightly unfinished look of the 220. Play with it. It's your table, after all.

*The palm sander moves too fast and melts the finish. Then you wind up having to sand everything back to zero and start over. Bad news. Get close with your wood. Touch it. Caress it. Then rub it with abrasive paper. Lovingly. John Henry will appreciate the triumph of man over machine. So will your finish.

## Step 6: Joint

Now that everything is cut to size, it's time to mark our holes for doweling.

You'll really want some dowel centers for this. (If you don't have any, a thumbtack should do in a pinch.)

Mark your drill locations in the following places:
- each side of the pointy bit on the radial supports
- two equidistant marks on the underside of each radial support
- two equidistant marks on the top of each leg

Using the dowel centers means that you don't need a doweling jig for this. It does mean, though, that you will need to keep track of which boards fit together. Each dowel joint done this way is slightly different, so label your boards (on a spot that'll be covered) in such a way as to be able to know which radial support fits perfectly with which leg. This is, as they say, important.

Use a brad point bit. It will make this easier. If you don't have one, drill pilot holes, then use your normal bits. You shouldn't need to buy anything special for this. Be sure to wrap your bit so you don't end up drilling too deep.

Measure twice, stay away from the edges of the wood so as not to split your board, take a deep breath, then drill perpendicular to the face you are working on.

furnish

Use the dowel center to mark the drill location for the board you will attach to the board you just drilled into freehand.

## Step 7: Glue

To glue, put a small dab of wood glue on both sides of your dowels. Then align the corresponding board. You'll have to glue and push in all three boards at once for the interior joint. Once you've pushed everything together to your satisfaction, put the strap clamp around the whole shebang. Tighten to the point that everything is pushed together, but not so tight that it starts to pull your joint apart. Then wait for it to dry.

Bonus cheating step: screw the T strap onto the base of the joint after the glue has dried. I don't fully trust the dowels, so some surreptitious metal makes me feel better.

Then glue on the legs. Clamp them in place.

## Step 8: Attach trucks

Your trucks may vary in size, so I'll give approximate directions for attaching your skateboard apparatus.

Center the trucks on the board. You'll want your outermost wheel to be even with the edge of the radial board. Measure, measure, measure. Mark the center of the holes with an awl or pencil tip or paper clip or something else thin and pointy.

Use the same technique as before to create drill stops with tape, using the length of your screws as a guide. Then drill each mark that you made. Go in as straight as you can to keep the screwheads parallel to the radial boards. It'll be prettier that way.

Put on all the trucks facing the same direction. Look at the pictures. Then screw 'em on.

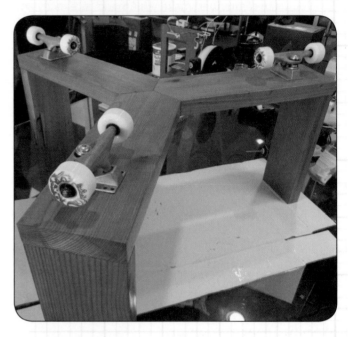

## Step 9: Tabletop

Glass tabletops can be pricey. Check for cheap ones at thrift stores, garage sales, and flea markets, or just cannibalize one from another table.

Put the glass on top of the skateboard wheels. Centering the table is a bit of a challenge (aka nightmare), so I decided to just eyeball it to get it as close as I could. You'll notice in the video that the glass hangs over one set of wheels a bit further than the others, but it's not too much of a hassle to move it back into place. I imagine that a real set of skateboard wheels with proper bearings might prevent the eccentric motion, but I chose not to check. Or I could have just picked up a bigger piece of glass for an extra $10.

You're welcome to experiment with the placement of the glass, the bearings, or the glass size. Tell me what worked for you.

furnish

# Nine Square Chair

By wholman

(http://www.instructables.com/id/Nine-Square-
Chair/)

With a road sign and some geometric shenanigans, the Nine Square Chair was born on a garage floor in Baltimore in early March.

Classical architecture, especially in plan, was derived, generally speaking, from a four-square grid: bilateral symmetry. Modern architecture was/is derived, generally speaking, from a nine-square grid, which allows for asymmetry.

A road sign 48" to a side breaks down neatly into a nine-square grid of 16" squares. Seat height for side chairs is usually in the 16"-17" range. I made a bunch of 1" to 12" scale models out of cereal box cardboard before I settled on a form that would turn into a chair without the need to add anything for bracing or stiffness—purity of concept. I made a full-size mock-up out of cardboard to make sure of all the dimensions and folding sequence, then worked on the sign.

This bad boy is 100% recycled except for fasteners, and is virtually waste-free in its construction. Later in the instructable there is a picture of all the waste generated in the process, and it was only one dustpan full of aluminum shavings, which are recyclable.

## Step 1: Mock-up

This sequence of steps shows the general layout and folding sequence of a cardboard mock-up. Lay out with a marker or pencil, starting with a grid of nine 16" squares. Number the grid to keep track of pieces as you begin to fold.

To hold the chair together, triangular fins are positioned such that adjoining squares will have overlapping fins, which can be through-bolted to hold it. For the model,

use brads or staples. This folding scheme is one of many possibilities using this general geometry and working method, so you may want to explore other designs.

Cut slits where appropriate, and perforate the seams that need to be folded. Then, fold squares seven, eight, and nine under squares four, five, and six. Pin seven to four, eight to five, and five to six. Fold 7/4 and 5/6 up ninety degrees from 8/5. Bend out the triangular fins from seven, eight, and nine, and they should overlap. Pin through them to secure the legs.

Flip the chair over and bend up the back and pin it by joining the fins from squares two and five.

## Step 2: Signs!

Now it's time to butcher a real sign. Find them in junkyards, alleys, and through friends. Do not steal signs. The one I have has graffiti on it, which I didn't clean off—it shows that the chair is one-of-a-kind, and I don't think you should cover up the scars it gained out in the world.

Start by laying out your sixteen inch grid again, this time with masking tape. Mark out the triangular fins. The fins on the underside of the seat in the finished chair are cut from squares seven, eight, and nine. You can see how they are laid out in the pictures: those fins are 12" by 6" and are creased along the hypotenuse.

furnish

293

The fins that secure the back are 12" by 4" (attached to square 2) and 8" by 4"(attached to square 5), creased along the 12" and 8" sides.

The fin that holds the back of the legs together is made from squares three and seven and is 12" by 6," creased along the hypotenuse.

Along all the folds, strike a center line and, measuring from the centerline towards the corners, make a tick every 3/4." Drill out each tick with a 3/8" bit to make the perforations that will allow the sign to bend. This makes 3/8" diameter holes that are 3/8" apart.

Where cuts are necessary, use a jigsaw with a fresh metal blade. Aluminum is very strong, but rather ductile and soft. I dulled the drill bit considerably—there are an awful lot of holes to drill.

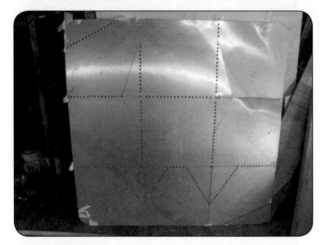

## Step 3: Fold

Once the perforations and cuts are done, find an old two-by four and start folding. Do the fins first, by laying the two-by along the seam and standing on it, then pulling the aluminum up. Use a rubber mallet if necessary. The fins only need to come out to about 45 degrees.

Next, fold squares seven, eight, and nine underneath squares four, five, and six. Drill through and pin seven to four, eight to five, and nine to six with number ten by 3/4" long machine bolts. Bend 7/4 and 9/6 up ninety degrees. The fins protruding from these three panels will overlap. Drill through the overlap and bolt to hold the legs in place.

For the back, fold square one 180 degrees to match up with square two. Bolt through. Bend 1/2 up ninety degrees to form the back. The fins attached to that piece should overlap the fins coming up from the seat, square number five.

Last, bend square six ninety degrees so that its fin overlaps with the fin coming off of panel seven, forming the back of the legs. Bolt through twice.

You might want to run over the seams with some eighty-grit sandpaper on a block or use a bastard file to take off any burrs and sharp edges.

Sit down.

furnish

# photography

The field of photography, be it still image or movie, digital or film, requires a specialized set of often expensive tools and equipment. Driven by a desire to bring professional photographic and cinematic techniques to the masses, DIY photography enthusiasts have made it their mission to produce solutions that deliver the same cinematic effects as their Hollywood counterparts at a fraction of the cost.

From time lapse dollies to aerial video balloons, the photo-tech inventors responsible for the projects included in this chapter are literally changing the way in which low-budget filmmakers and photographers make high art.

# Super Awesome Digi-Cinema Camera Rigs!!

By MattosaurusRex

(http://www.instructables.com/id/Super-Awesome-Digi-CInema-Camera-Rigs/)

I'm a film teacher and photographer, and I've learned that most photo/video accessories are tremendously overpriced. This instructable will teach you to make a variety of camera rigs that can improve the technical quality of your images and digital video. Most or all digital cameras now have video capability, and these rigs are most useful for that application—shooting video on your point and shoot or dSLR.

Mr. Shiny is great for 2 reasons. First, you can hand-hold your camera more smoothly at many angles, allowing better and safer handling and smoother handheld shots. Second, if you have other accessories (like flashes, lights, microphones, etc) you can mount them all to its frame.

The Lumber Dolly is a great little dolly. It can be used without a track, rolling on a smooth surface, or it can use lumber up to 6 inches wide.

The coolest thing with my design is the SPRING MECHANISM. It grips itself to the board, and can be used with less than perfect, cheap lumber you find or buy for this use. One rail of the wheels is removable, and if you flip that rail over, you can have it ride the edge of a table or counter-top. Also if you just switch which side the mounting screw is on (effectively flipping the unit upside down), you can use this design on any smooth surface without a track.

The Shoulder Mount, is sort of a hack on a ready-made solution. The ROI on designing and building a DIY shoulder pad just wasn't worth it for me, but feel free to make your own of course! My modification is built on a self-gripping shoulder pad that is sturdy and cheap, and only $30 from Amazon (CowboyStudio Shoulder Support Pad). My modification makes it much more useful and

customizable for the digital cinematographer. By customizing this design for your own cameras and applications, you'll have a cheap, extremely handy, and somewhat macho looking, piece of equipment.

Together, the professional versions of this equipment would cost over $1000, and you can build all of this for under $200!

## Cage/Fig Rig AKA Mr. Shiny

Mr. Shiny is a very versatile and durable rig. I'd suggest making a cardboard cutout of the size you think you want for your camera before cutting metal. The sizing is completely left to your preference—the size I built is great for a standard sized dSLR (like a 7d).

Parts required:
- 2- 12" Aluminum 1" square tube
- 2- 9 3/8" Aluminum 3/4" tube
- 1- 5 1/2" Aluminum 3/4" tube
- 2- 5/16"-18 All thread, 12" long
- 4- 1" Square End Caps (furniture tips)
- 2- 3/4" Round End Caps (furniture tips)
- 4- 5/16"-18 Cap Nuts (acorn nuts)
- 5- 5/16" washers
- 1- 2 1/2" 1/4-20 thumbscrew or bolt
- 2- 1/4-20 wing nuts
- 1- 1/2" Two-Hole Strap (for EMT conduit)
- 2- 8-32 x 1-1/2 machine screws with nuts

Assembly info:

The box channel/square tube will be the top and bottom. The round tube will be the sides, and they will enclose the all thread. The all thread will go through holes in the box channel, and will secure everything together. The top handle is attached with a two-hole strap, that is too small for our pipe, and the camera will mount inside onto a 1/4-20 threaded thumb screw, that will we have "float" with the rig.

### Step 1: Measure and cut the tubing
a.  Cut the square tube or box channel into 12" sections.
b.  Cut the all thread into 12" sections.
c.  Lay out the square tube and all thread. The all thread will go through the square tube, and have a washer and cap nut at the other end. The round tube will enclose the all thread, between the square tubes. Verify the length of the round tubes you will need (9 3/8")
d.  Cut the round tubes

### Step 2: Deburr or file your cut edges
Cutting metal makes sharp little edges, Make sure you deburr or file them.

### Step 3: Mark and drill holes
- You will need 4 holes at the edges of the box channel/square tube for the 5/16" all thread. You will want the holes in about 5/8" or so, so that the 3/4" tube's edges

don't extend over the edge. The holes need to go through both sides of the box channel.

- You will need 2 holes that go all the way through for the two hole strap, on one of the box channels. You should center these holes, and verify hole placement with your hole strap. The holes on my rig are 1-3/4" apart. Make sure the holes are on the same sides as the all thread holes. For my design, I used 8-32 machine screws.
- You will need one hole for the camera mount location. The bolt is 1/4-20, and you will need to drill all the way through. Again, make sure the holes are on the same sides as the all threads' holes.

## Step 4: Lay it all out

## Step 5: "Float" the camera bolt

The wing nut is too wide to complete a rotation within the box-channel, so that means you can thread into it and it will hold the camera bolt!

a. Thread a 1/4-20 wing nut onto the thumb screw, with the flat part towards the top of the threads, not towards the thumb screw part. Put a washer on it. This is what will tighten the camera to the rig.

b. Place a second 1/4-20 wing nut in the box channel that has the singular center hole for the camera bolt. Shimmy it down until it is sitting over the hole you drilled.

c. With patience, carefully and slowly try and thread the bolt into the suspended wing nut.

## Step 6: Attach the hand grip to the other square tube

It doesn't matter which side, but the grip should be on the top of the rig when it's finished.

a. First attach the strap tot the round tube. It is "too small" for it, but it turns out it should work perfectly. You'll need to slightly force it onto the tube. You want 1/2" to 5/8" of tube to extend behind the strap, and the rest out in front for the grip.

b. Bolt it down, you should need to go back and forth tightening, again because the strap is too small. Why use one that is too small? Because it will be super tight and I bet you don't want your camera-loaded rig to slip away from that hand grip.

## Step 7: Final assembly

a. Thread and bolt up the all thread. A washer and cap nut on each end please. Lookout for over-tightening, you will start to squash your square tube.

b. Push in the plastic end caps. You may need a rubber mallet, or just use a hammer and a magazine.

c. TEST FOR STRUCTURAL INTEGRITY.

## Step 8: Attach camera and go nuts!*

*NOTE: You could break your camera if you thread the bolt in too far. Thread it gently until it won't go any farther, back it off a 1/4 turn, then tighten the wing nut. This will protect your camera and still have a super-strong connection.

This is a great rig for attaching accessories to, you just need to modify it as you wise. You can simply drill holes and thread 1/4-20 thumbscrews to them, or you can drill holes and attach flash-shoe posts. You can use rubber bands if you want, but in the meantime, the rig will be useful for steadying hand-held shots, and it will be shiny.

photography

# Lumber dolly

This lumber dolly is great! It's compact, works well, and it is really easy to set up and use.

## Parts list:
- 2- 1" x 12" square perforated tube
- 2- 5/16-18 x 12" all thread
- 8- 54mm Skateboard Wheels[1]
- 8- Skateboard Wheel Bearings[1]
- 8- 5/16-18 x 2-1/2" hex bolts
- 8- 3/4 x .385 x 13/64 Nylon Spacers
- 16- 5/16 washers
- 10- 5/16-18 Lock Nuts
- 6- 5/16-18 Nuts
- 4- 1/4" Nylon clamps (5/16 works too)
- 4- 8-32x3/4" machine screws with nuts
- 4- 3/16x2-1/2 J bolts (with nuts)
- 2- Extension Springs 1/4 x 1-916 x .032"
- 4- 1" square end caps (furniture tips)
- 1- 3-1/2" x 7-3/4" base plate: 1/4" inch plywood or similar material (Jigsaw) OR 3/16 or 1/4 Plexiglas (box cutter + Ruler, but be careful!)
- 1- 1/4-20 x 5/8" thumbscrew (or steal one from the CowboyStudio Shoulder Pad)
- 2- 1/4x1-1/2" fender washer
- 1- 3/8 to 1/4 tripod head adapter bushing. (Amazon link, or go to your camera store)

## Step 1: Cut and arrange materials
a. Cut box channel/perforated tube into 12" pieces
b. File/deburr the edges

## Step 2: Assemble main wheels on first rail
These will be the wheels for support (vertical orientation).
a. Insert bolt into the last hole of one of the tubes.
b. Put on a spacer, wheel, washer, then lock nut. Tighten/loosen according to your preference.
c. Do the same thing at the opposite end. Note, the wheels should be oriented the same way, and be as far as possible from each other.

## Step 3: Assemble side wheels on first rail
a. These wheels will hug the edge of the lumber. alMove to the other set of walls of the tube, and see how many holes you need to move down. For my 54mm wheels, I needed to leave a hole empty and use the next one (my second bolt is 2 inches and 90 degrees from the first bolt).
b. Put on a spacer, wheel, washer, then lock nut. Tighten/loosen according to your preference.

c. Do the same thing at the opposite end. Note, these side wheels should be oriented the same way, and should be closer in than the other set of wheels.

## Step 4: Assemble second rail
Follow above steps. It actually doesn't matter about the orientation of the second wheels, you can rotate the rail until it's correct for assembly.

## Step 5: Layout the rails
The horizontal rails should be on the bottom, and the vertical wheels should be inside the box channel.

## Step 6: Attach the frame to the "front" rail
This is the one that stays stationary, the other rail could be adjusted in or out.
a. Slide the all thread through holes parallel with the main wheels, as close as possible to the edges of the rail, just past the side wheels bolt.
b. On the outside edge (the side opposite the main wheel (see illustration if needed) slip on a washer and a lock nut.
c. Repeat on other side of the rail.
d. On the inside of the rail, slip on a washer and thread a nut. Tighten up.

## Step 7: Spring hooks on rails
a. Front Rail: through the adjacent hole to the all threads, place the J hooks. You want the hook on the inside (same side as main wheels), and a washer and nut on the other side.
b. Back Rail: place the J hooks in a similar orientation, leaving a hole on each side for the all thread to go through. The hook part should be on the same side as the main wheels.

## Step 8: Attaching back rail to front rail and frame
a. Thread another nut onto each all thread, a little more than halfway up. These nuts will be a stopper for the Back rail.

---

1 Buy the wheels and bearings online for some savings. You will need to press the bearings into the wheels, you can follow instructions online, or take them to a skate-shop. I bought mine from a shop and they pressed them for me.

b. Slide Back rail onto the all threads. Make sure the Main wheels are on the inside, and the side wheels are on the bottom.

c. Thread a nut on the back end of the all threads

d. Connect the J hooks with the springs.

## Step 9: Attaching the base plate

a. Slip 4 nylon clamps onto the all threads, inside the two rails, with the flat side of the clamps facing up (away from the side wheels which are the bottom), and with the hole on the outsides of the all threads.

b. Adjust each all thread's set of clamps to be 2-1/4" between holes. Measure the distance from one all thread's set to the other. The holes should be about 6" apart.

c. Mark and drill holes in your base plate to match the measurements of your clamps.

d. Find the center of the base plate by drawing a diagonal line from each corner. Drill a center hole for the thumbscrew.

e. Bolt up the base plate to the rod clamps. Have the screw heads on top, so it looks nicer.

## Step 10: Attaching the attachment bolt.[2]

a. Place a large fender washer onto the thumbscrew.

b. Slip through the hole in the base plate.

c. Slip on the other fender washer.

d. Thread on the 3/8 to 1/4 Tripod head adapter bushing. At full tightness, the 1/4-20 post must not extend past the bushing.

---

[2] Depending on the bolt/thumbscrew you use, and the thickness of your base plate, you may need to make alterations. You do not want too much screw post sticking out than your camera or tripod head can accept. Over tightening could ruin equipment. You can simply add washers to take up some of the extra length, but you need it to be as low profile as possible, in case you want to flip the thumbscrew assembly upside down to use the dolly on a flat surface (the side wheels would be facing up, disengaged from anything).

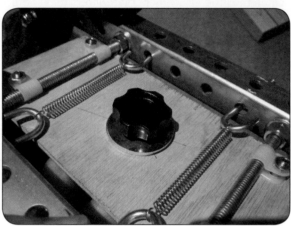

# Shoulder mount

This Shoulder Mount is very handy, incredibly adjustable, and super useful. You can additionally mount other gear to the horizontal bar, and the vertical riser can quickly be swapped out and adjusted for different used. If you use CowboyStudio's shoulder pad as a base, it can also be hands-free! Of course you can build your own, or use another, but realize you'll need to modify the lengths of materials too.

## Parts list:
- 1- CowboyStudio Shoulder Support Pad
- 1- 1" x 12" perforated square tube
- 2- 1" Square End Caps (furniture tips)
- 3- 1/4-20 Flange Nuts (you could use other nuts, such as 1 cap nut and 2 regular nuts)
- 3- 5/16 washers
- 2- 1/4 x 1-1/2" Fender Washers
- 2- 1/4-20 Wing nuts
- 1- 1/4-20 x 2-1/2" all thread (for horizontal bar)
- 1- 1/4-20 x 5" all thread (for vertical riser)
- 1- About 12" worth of 1" Aluminum Square Tube, cut to your sizing preference.

## Step 1: Cut your materials
a. Cut the perforated square tubing to 12"

b. Cut the Aluminum square tube into other lengths for different uses applications with this mount: 1", 1-1/2", 2", 2-1/2", and 3". This will allow you to adjust the vertical raise from the platform of the shoulder mount to your eye level. Personally, I use the 2-1/2" piece for using the Shoulder Mount with Mr. Shiny.

c. Cut all thread for the vertical riser and for the horizontal bar.

## Step 2: Disassemble the CowboyStudio unit

a. Remove all thumb screws. Use needle nose pliers to grip the nut hiding under the rubberized grippy material, and unscrew thumbscrew.

b. Ditch the little attachment plate/lifters that came with unit.

c. On the platform attached to the main unit, lift up the rubberized gripper, and remove the nut.

## Step 3: Attaching the horizontal bar

a. Decide how far you want the bar to extend to the side, based on your shoulder pad, body, and preference, and slip the shorter all thread though the hole you choose.

b. Put a washer and wing nut on one side, that side is now the top.

c. Thread the harvested nut from the shoulder pad's platform onto the other side of the square tube.

d. Push the nut through the rubberized gripper pad, and thread the bolt down.

e. Underneath the shoulder pad, slip a washer and Flange Nut (or Cap Nut), onto the all thread and tighten down. For adjustments, you can loosen and tighten the wing nut.

f. Hammer in the 1" end caps

## Step 4: Attaching vertical riser

a. Decide how far out you'd like the riser. Directly above the riser would be whatever you attach, a camera or rig.

b. Slip the loner all thread through the hole you choose, top/bottom.

c. On the Bottom, place a washer and wing nut, you will adjust this to tighten into whatever you put on top, and to adjust for different length vertical rises.

d. On the top side of the channel, slip on a large fender washer, a nut, and leave room between nut and washer. This will need to be adjusted and left loose for each different riser you insert.

e. Slip on the Aluminum Tube riser piece of your choice. I assembled this with a 2-1/2" inch riser for attaching Mr. Shiny and camera.

f. On the other side, slip on another fender washer.

## Step 5: Attach whatever you want

a. If you want to just attach a camera, adjust the nut inside and the wing nut on the bottom until you have a proper amount of all thread sticking past the top

fender washer. 1/4 inch is almost always safe. Again, you must be careful to not over tighten the bolt into the hole, instead, you thread it in, and tighten the other end, the one with the wing nut.

b. If attaching the Cage Rig through its camera mount hole, you will first need to un-thread it. Don't worry about re-aligning the wing nut inside, it's pretty easy.

c. Attach it and tighten it up.

In the picture attached, I've got the Shoulder Mount supporting Mr. Shiny, who is holding my 7d, with an LCD viewfinder attached. The great thing about these units is that they're completely customizable and have a good amount of adjustment possibilities, allowing you to use them for many different applications.

I hope you have a great time building these, and find these rigs helpful for making better photos and videos.

Best to you! and your DIY spirit! Long Live instructables!
-MattoSaurus Rex

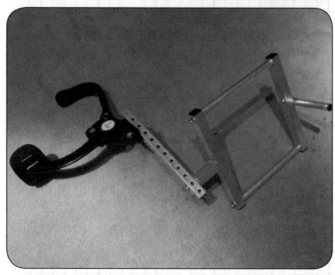

# Budget Launch: Aerial Video Balloon

## By killbox
(http://www.instructables.com/id/Budget-Launch-Aerial-Video-Balloon/)

The Hackerspace I "work" at, Quelab.net, just marked its 1 year open point. And so we thought about combining our usual monthly/bimonthly event with a bit of a larger scale project. And that was to fly a balloon with a camera.

But we have a pretty limited budget and a short time frame to get it done. Here is how it went.

## Step 1: The parts

• 1 36" latex balloon, $3.85 got it at (balloons-fast.com)
• 1 Tank of helium (was able to borrow my dad's otherwise rent one. the disposable tanks are overpriced)
• 1 6" x6" square of foam-core board
• 1 spy pen video camera. $30
• 1 Kite reel (I had one already, but they go for about $4)
• 1 postcard $0.25 and $0.29 stamp
• 1 Ziploc bag
• 1 Dollar bill (prize)
• 1 sticker prize
• Tape, used both scotch and 3m double sided sticky tape

## Step 2: Assembly

I cut a slot on the foam core board, it's a little less than 1/2CM wide. The balloon just above the know will go here

I cut it off center to allow for the prize/postcard Ziploc to counter balance the camera.

Prize pouch contains, Ziploc baggie, full of 1/2 of a dollar bill (part of the prize if they return the postcard with an address) a sticker from Quelab, and a postcard pre filled out and stamped, requesting where it was found and a return address to send other 1/2 of the bill.

Camera is double sided taped down, and also had a thing of tape around the board to make sure it didn't fall off.

## Step 3: Launch day

We had a large event involving local rocketry experts, and astronomers, and all sorts of paper airplane testing/contesting.

I was worried that the afternoon storms had whipped up some wind, but we got a little calm, so I decided to go for it.

I was worried that the wind might catch the balloon as I was filling it or tying it, so I had friends hold a netting over me while I inflated it. It was a good idea.

It had more lift than I thought. (Was not totally full probably only 80% of the way to being frighteningly full)

Slid the platform on the bottom of the balloon, and turned on the camera.

## Step 4: More photos

Ok, so first off it was a little windy, and apparently the kite reel I had lets out line a little jiggly.

Next time I hope it's a more calm day, I may also put a wide angle lens on the camera, maybe a fin or tail on the camera so it only looks one way.

When we were all done I retrieved the camera from the platform, taped the platform to the balloon, and set it free! It was visible for about 11 minutes until it started to kiss the clouds. Let's hope someone mails back the postcard!

photography

# Time Lapse Dolly

by Derek Mellott (DerekMellott)
(http://www.instructables.com/id/Time-Lapse-Dolly/)

This is how I built my time lapse dolly, it was made with a whole bunch of trial and error, hopefully this will help you build yours.

A lot of the stuff I used I had on hand, don't know where I got it, or have no idea what it worth but I'll do my best at giving you a complete list of what I used and where you might get it.

## Step 1: Doin' rails

I will start with the rails because I found it super simple to set the width of the dolly cart if you already have the rail made.

**Parts and Tools (All costs are an estimate. I didn't pay close attention to costs because it scares me.)**

- 2 x 8ft 1" square aluminum tubing $30 each here in Canada probably much cheaper down south.
- 1 x 4ft 1/4 20 threaded rod $2
- 6 x 1/4 20 sex bolts yeah (aka barrel nuts or Chicago bolts) $1 each.
- 6 x 1" steel hinges $2-3 a pair.
- Drill bits and a drill and a 1/4 20 tap/ thread cutter, preferably a drill press to keep things straight.
- Something to cut the aluminum tubing, I used my compound miter saw.
- Hack saw
- Allen wrenches

**Cut the rails to length**

I originally used the full 8ft but found it a pain to move around and handle in general so I cut mine down to six feet leaving me with two 2ft pieces to use for other parts.

**Cut the cross members**

The overall width of my rails is 6.5 inches so my cross members are 4.5 inches long and I used 3 of them.. You make these any size you want, remember the width of your rails determines the size of your cart. This is also a good time to drill the holes where you will attach the tripods. Measure out the center of the cross pieces and drill a hole, I used a no. 2 drill bit then ran the 1/4 20 thread cutter bit into the hole. This will be the bottom of your cross members. test this on a piece of scrap first.

**Attach the cross members to the rails with the hinges**

I clamped it all together and then put the hinges in place to mark where to drill the holes. This is very important to get right so take your time and make sure everything is square and the hinges are flush and your holes are marked out correctly. After you have marked the holes for the hinges go ahead and drill your holes. You are going to want to drill the right size hole for the screws that came

with the hinges. Test it out on a scrap piece of aluminum, if the hole is too big the screws won't bite enough to hold it all together and the hole is too small you will strip the screw head or break the screw trying to get it in.

**Drill the holes for the "clamp bolts"**

These bolts are what make the rails rigid. You have to drill a hole big enough for the shaft of the barrel nuts to fit in. Mark the center of your cross members and transfer that mark to the side of the rails.

*IMPORTANT* DO NOT DRILL YOUR HOLE FOR THE BARREL NUT IN THE MIDDLE OF THE RAIL!!!!! Make the hole as low as you can without the lip of the barrel nut going below the bottom of the rail, you need the top of the rail to be clear for the bearing to roll on.

Now you cut a length of the 1/4 20 threaded rod that will reach in between the two barrel nuts. You may have to trim it down or cut a new piece if it's too short, no worries this stuff is cheap. Make sure you get a good fit and you can tighten good, you don't have to tighten too much but you don't want any movement in the rail. You want to do this for all three cross members.

There you go! You now have a foldable rail!

## Step 2: Laying tracks

This is the part that you will need to figure out for yourself. I will show you what I did but the parts I used I don't know what they are or where they came from.

The good news is that there are cheap parts made for this purpose but I wasn't going to spend $20 to ship a $3 chunk of plastic to Canada.

## Parts

- 1" square aluminum tubing. I used the bits cut off of the rails when I shortened them.
- 1 1/2 inch 1/4 20 bolts x 4 $.50 each
- Timing belt clamps. I used some mystery things but you can get real one here: http://www.sdp-si.com/web/html/newprdbelts5.htm. Just make sure you get the right one for your belt.
- Timing belt. I used a HTD 5m 9mm belt. It cost me about $15 You can get one here, https://sdpsi.com/eStore/PartDetail.asp?Opener=Group&PartID=30471&GroupID=343

I used the chunks of aluminum to attach the clamp to the rail. The trick here is to make sure the belt is level with the pulley on your cart. That above all will determine how you mount your clamp, this is just how I did mine.

You will also notice that there are a bunch of bolts occupying a small space, keep this in mind when you are making your holes.

This step is simple. Attach clamp to chunk of aluminum, attach that to the rail, DONE! Just make sure it is level with the pulley.

## Step 3: Pickup truck for your camera

The title of this step is accurate, you need to build this like a truck: it starts with a frame, you put on some wheels and a motor, add some electronics then load up your gear.

## Parts

- 3/8 threaded rod $3-4 bucks for 3-4 feet
- 3/8 lock nuts
- 3/8 nuts
- 3/4 aluminum angle $10? for 4 feet
- 10x30x9 bearings $1 each. You will need 10 of them. I have no idea what those numbers mean, it is what was on the box.
- 3/8x1/2 x1 bronze bearings. $4 for the pair of them. These are oil impregnated sleeve bearings that the belt slides past by the pulley
- Pulley $17 I used one of these. https://sdp-si.com/eStore/PartDetail.asp?Opener=Group&PartID=59827&GroupID=346

- 1 1/2 inch 1/4 20 bolts. I used a bunch, buy a bunch, they are handy
- Wire rope clamp. I used 4 of these, I'm not sure what size I used just make sure that the 3/8 threaded rod fits nicely in it. http://www.homedepot.com/h_d1/N-5yc1v/R-100299148/h_d2/ProductDisplay?langId=-1&storeId=10051&catalogId =10053
- Washers that fit the 1/4 20 bolts, you can never have too many
- 1/4 20 nuts
- 1/4 20 lock nuts
- Shoulder bolts? I lucked out and found these bolts at home depot and the sleeve bearings fit perfectly on them there is a picture below.
- 1/4 plastic pluming pipe, the whitish flexible stuff used on sinks? 12" is more than enough
- Motor $50-60 PLUS SHIPPING. I used a .45 rpm Dayton gear motor. Notice that it is .45 rpm not 45 rpm. I got it from http://www.servocity.com
- Ball head. I used a Benro BH00 it's cheap and works great, use what ever you want just make sure is has a quick release plate.
- Some sort of metal to use as a base. I used a steel electrical box cover, make sure whatever you use that it is big enough to mount everything on.

## Cut the 3/8 threaded rod to length

7.5 inches or so should do

## Cut your 3/4 aluminum angle to length

This can match the length of whatever you use as a base plate.

## Drill the holes for the 3/8 rod in the angle

Now the placement of these holes is very important. I had mine centered but there was no way to make the motor to fit like that so I had to offset them. The measurement in between the rods was arbitrary, I just chose a stable looking width, you may want to put some more thought into it.

Make sure you make your holes in the exact same spot on both pieces of angle, this must be straight so it can be square.

## Add the bearings

It doesn't really matter where you place these—just put them in the same place on both sides. Don't worry about the "outrigger" bearings yet; we will get to those.

On the bolt goes the washer, plastic spacer, bearing, washer, locknut. Now this you might want to play around with to fine tune the placement of the bearing on the rails add washers or nuts as spacers as needed. Remember that the bearings that go on the outside of the rails have to track above the flange of the barrel nuts.

## Put the frame together

This is where the threaded rod shines. Place some nuts on the rods then slide on the angle pieces and adjust the nuts so the bearing sit flat on the rails and the frame is square. It is a good idea to use lock nuts here because you don't want this to move after you have it set up.

**Mount the other two bearings on some sort of material**

I used some aluminum plate I had. Drill some holes on the angle to mount the outriggers. Place the frame on the rails, make sure the the bearings are tight to the bottom of the rails and tighten down the bolts to hold them in place. Now the frame is locked on to the rails. you can slide it off of one of the ends or collapse the rails to remove it.

**Add the top plate**

Place the top plate on top of the frame and mark the location of the rods, then get your wire rope clamps and figure out where to drill the holes. I should mention that I had to add nuts on the clamps below the top plate to lift the plate over the bearings. After you mark your holes go ahead and drill your holes. It is a pain to clamp this together but if you are taking on this project then I'm quite sure you can figure it out.

**Mount the motor and sleeve bearings.**

You want to place the bearings as wide as you can to lower the angle to the pulley. Pick your spot for your motor, drill your holes. Very straight forward.

**Blast a hole to mount your ball head**

Remember to leave room for your electronics.

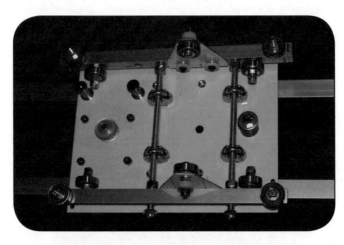

## Step 4: Kill the PWM

This is how you control the speed of the dolly and stop it from tearing itself apart.

**Parts**

- Bidirectional PWM. I bought this one: http://cgi.ebay. ca/DC-Motor-Speed-Controller-Forward-Backward-Switchable /140357279325?pt=LH_DefaultDomain_0 &hash=item20adf21e5d. This PWM came with the directional switch and the POT.
- Enclosure I used the 1591SFLBK from Hammond Manufacturing.
- Hook up wire. 20' will be lots
- 4 switched DC power jacks
- 4 DC barrel plugs
- 2 micro switches

REMEMBER TO CHANGE DIRECTIONS BEFORE YOU UNPLUG THE SWITCHES. When the micro switches are unplugged the system will be live with no safety.

Basically the goal here is to shut off the power to the system when the cart is out of track. Before the positive from the battery reaches the PWM I ran it through some switched jacks and micro switches. The reason for the switched jacks is that once one of the micro switch is tripped there is no longer and power to the system so you can't move the cart, I have it set up so that if you diconect the switches they will be by passed and the power will go straight to the PWM.

REMEMBER TO CHANGE DIRECTIONS BEFORE YOU UNPLUG THE SWITCHES.

Find a place on each side of your cart to place a micro switch so that it will contact something at the end of the run. Connect your wires to the common and normally open pins. Once the lever contacts something the positive to the PWM will be cut off and your cart will stop moving. When you are adding the barrel plug to the wires going to the micro switch it doesn't matter what post you connect them to.

photography

For the straps I used some shoulder straps from some old camera bags and used 4" hose clamps to attach the straps. Find the balance center and go from there making sure the straps are long enough to use as a back pack, I left one strap a bit longer than the other, this tilts the pipe at a bit of an angle so it's not dragging on the ground.

**Carry case for the cart**

Here I lucked out big time, I found a $10 tool box that the cart fit in perfectly. It is made by Plano and is Model 761. I simply cut wood to raise the "outrigger" bearing off the bottom drilled some holes for the bearing bolts to fit in and all done. I know the case protects well because the handle came off once and the case went crashing to the ground, the cart was 100% fine. P.S. I discovered that the handle can come off so watch for that.

## Step 5: Extras

Here are a few extras you might want for your dolly system.

**Stubby little legs.**

I made these for simple low, level shots, my cheap tripods wobbled too much in the wind, these are solid.

I used two 8" chunks of left over aluminum tubing and some fiberglass pole I had lying around. I would recommend using aluminum pipe instead but I'm broke and already had these.

Drill two holes about and 1 1/2" in from each edge with a #2 drill bit and thread with the 1/4 20 bit, this is where the legs attach. Next mark the center of the top the square tube and drill a 1/4" hole straight through. I added a 3/8 piece of HMWP (high molecular weight poly-ethylene, hockey boards) as a spacer for two reasons. 1 I needed to raise the track a bit so that the top of the legs would clear the rails. 2. The HMWP keeps the bolt from falling out when not attached to the rails. I simply drilled a 1/4" hole in the center of a 4"x3/4" strip and drill and counter sunk two hole for screws to attach it to the tubing.

Now the bolt. Cut 2 3" pieces of 1/4 20 threaded rod. What I did was sandwich a wing nut in between two lock nuts to "lock" the wing nut in place to act as a handle. what I do is I give the bolt assembly a couple of turns into the bottom of the rail then tighten the second wing nut for a very snug bond.

Lastly I added some wood into the ends of the legs to stop the fiberglass from getting crushed when tightening the adjustment bolts.(this is why I would recommend you use aluminum.) by loosening these bolt you can adjust the legs in order to level the system, I am impressed with how well these work.

**PVC container**

This is very simple. I used the white drainage PVC for two reasons, it is lighter and cheaper than the black stuff. Cut the length a bit longer than your rail, it gets longer when it is folded and I added some Styrofoam at each end for some padding. after its cut glue on a solid cap on one side and a screw cap on the other, Dry fit everything first to make sure your cuts are good.

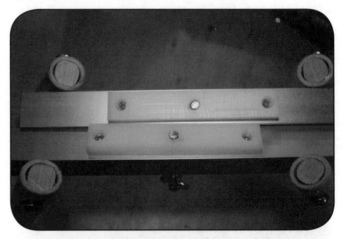

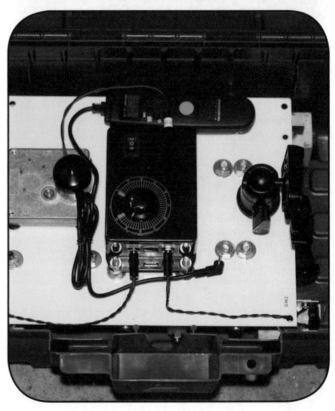

# How to Make a Snorricam

by Carter Marquis (Cartemarquis)
(http://www.instructables.com/id/How-to-Make-a-Snorricam/)

The Snorricam, named after Einar Snorri and Eiour Snorri, or the "Snorri Brothers," is a body mount for a camera which is used to create an interesting point of view, which can be seen in such movies as *I Am Legend*, *Slumdog Millionaire*, *The Hangover*, and most impressively, *Requiem for a Dream*. I work for a small video production company, and with much enthusiasm from my boss, I designed and built my own version of the Snorricam, which is very adjustable and versatile. For about $30 in parts, and around a day of labor, you can have yourself an adjustable Snorricam of your own!

## Step 1: Tools and Materials

My design is fairly simple, and requires only a few simple tools. All materials can be easily obtained at your local home improvement store (Home Depot is our favorite) for around $30. That being said, the more tools you have, the easier this build will be.

Tools:
- Drill with basic set of drill bits
- Handsaw
- Router with 1/4" roundover bit (optional)
- Jigsaw
- Circular saw
- Hack saw with metal blade
- Sandpaper. I actually used drywall sandpaper cloth stuff, but use what you have around
- Compass with pencil attachment
- Small framing square (the kind with the lip and a 45 degree angle)
- Tape measurer

Materials:
- One 1"x3" @ 8' long
- 3/4" plywood (You'll need 3 pieces no larger than 12" x 8" each)
- 1/2" plywood (a piece no larger than 8" x 6")
- Matching nuts, bolts, and washers (Use what you have, I didn't have to buy any new hardware when building mine)
- 1.5" angle iron or angle aluminum
- Qood screws
- Two 2-packs of Tiedown straps(~$7 each)

## Step 2: Building the Chest and Back Boards

First cut twos 8"; x 12" pieces of ¾" plywood. You could also probably get away with using ½" plywood here, but I went with ¾" because the chest piece will be supporting weight, and I didn't have enough ½" plywood. Scribe lines 1 inch in on the two long sides and one short side. From the unmarked edge, measure and mark at 1 1/2" and 2 1/4". Measure and mark at 1" and 1.75" across the top line. Lastly, measure and mark at 2" and 2.75" down the side lines. Take the other board and clamp the two together one on top of the other. Next, drill out the holes with a 3/8 diameter drill bit and cut the pieces in between them with the jigsaw. If all goes well, it should look like picture 5. Route all edges with a 1/4" roundover bit.

## Step 3: Building the Shoulder

Scribe a line 1.5" into a piece of 3/4" ply. Take your compass and make a 4" radius semicircle starting from the line. Draw a 3" radius semicircle. Next, draw lines coming out of the center of the semicircle. I had my lines be 22.5 degrees apart, meaning there are lines at 90 degrees, 45 degrees in both directions, lines in between those, and lines 22.5 degrees further than 45. I decided not to put lines at 0 and 180 degrees.

This next portion I did slightly in reverse. I built the lower arm first, then used the hole in that to drill the holes in the shoulder, ensuring that the holes would line up perfectly. If you feel confident in your precision drilling, continue reading. If you want to go the way I did, drill the center hole and go onto the next step, then return to this step to finish the shoulder.

Drill holes at the intersections of the rays and the 3" radius, as well as the center. Use whatever size bit you want to fit the hardware you're using. I used 5/16" for the radial holes and 1/4" for the center. Now cut along the 4" radius line and cut straight out of the board. Next, cut out 2 right triangles from 3/4" ply. The short sides should be 3" long. Screw them into the piece you just cut out 2" from each end of it. Next, screw the triangles and the shoulder piece into the chest plate 1 inch from the top with the shoulder piece centered.

## Step 4: Building the Lower Arm and Elbow

To build the lower arm, start with a 1"x3" that is 17 1/4" long. Mark 1 1/4" inches down both ends, and make a semicircle radius 1 1/4" at one end of the piece. At the center of that semicircle, drill the same size hole as the center of the shoulder piece you made in the previous step. 3 inches further down the board (at 4 1/4"), mark a center point on the board. Drill a hole the size of the holes in the shoulder piece. Now cut the semicircle out of the end of the board. If you skipped drilling the holes in the last step, now is the time to put a bolt through the center hole and use the lower arm as a guide for drilling the holes in the shoulder. Drill another hole (the same size as the center of the shoulder) centered on the 1 1/4" line at the other end of the arm.

To build the elbow, start with a piece of 1/2" plywood that's 8" by 5 1/2". Draw a line 1 1/4" from the 8" side, and make 2 semicircles coming out from the center of that line. The radii should be 4" and 3". Make marks every 22.5 degrees (just like the shoulder piece). If you want to use the upper arm as a guide for drilling the holes, Drill the center hole and skip to the next step now. If not, go ahead and drill the holes on the intersection of the lines and the 3" radius. Cut along the 4" semicircle line and line up the hole in the center with the hole at the end of the lower arm. Use a bolt to keep the center hole aligned and use screws to attach the 2 pieces. Make sure your screws are flush with the semicircular piece.

## Step 5: Building Upper Arm and Camera Mount

To build the upper arm, take a piece of 1"x 3" that's 13 1/4" long, and draw a line 1 1/4" up the board. Draw a semicircle (just like the lower arm) and draw another line 3" further up the board. Cut out the semicircle at the end of the board (just like the lower arm). Drill a hole at the mark closest to the end of the board the same size as the center hole for the elbow. Drill another hole at the mark 3" further down the same size of the radial holes in the elbow piece.

If you skipped drilling the holes in the last step, now is the time to put a bolt through the center hole and use the upper arm as a guide for drilling the holes in the elbow.

Lastly, take your angle iron or aluminum and cut a 2.5" piece. Drill a hole for your camera; either 1/4" 20 thread for a direct mount or 3/8" 16 thread for mounting a small tripod head like I did. Depending on how you want to mount your camera, you might need to make this mounting plate adjustable. I would suggest finding some kind of small tripod head to put on the end of the snorricam. Without one, it's difficult to fine-tune the shot once the snorricam is set up.

## Step 6: Final adjustments and Improvements

Lastly, use adjustable straps to attach the two plates to each other. I used 1 strap for each shoulder and 2 straps for the rest of the body. Put bolts through the center of the shoulder and elbow pieces and tighten them down. The lower arm attaches to the shoulder, the upper arm attaches to the elbow as in the picture in this step. Use your other bolts to set the arms to their respective radial holes to get the shot you want.

And that's it! Here are some possible improvements I've thought about since I finished building it.

- Make the upper arm longer, as the camera is pretty close.
- Make more holes in the shoulder and elbow for more adjustments.
- Make this rig out of aluminum for durability and weight.
- Make an adjustable camera mount on the end, using a similar style as the shoulder and elbow.
- Add some kind of counterweight system to the back plate to help counter the weight of the camera.

# Digital Holga
by frenzy
(http://www.instructables.com/id/Digital-Holga/)

Lomography and Toy Cameras are fun cameras to play with, yet most of these cameras use film so you can't see your finished product right away and you might end up spending a bunch on film and processing. The Holga is one of the more popular versions of this camera, and at such a cheap price it's easy to see why people would gravitate towards such a camera.

This Instructable will show you how to make a simple holga lens for your digital camera so you can share in the toy camera awesomeness.

## Step 1: Supplies
You will need the following:
- A DSLR camera (I'm assuming if you want to do this, you already have one)
- Holga Camera
- Body cap for your DSLR
- Drill w/ 5/16" drill bit
- Screw Driver
- Hot Glue Gun

## Step 2: Open Up The Holga
First step is to open up the holga and locate the screws. Once you find the screws, unscrew them and the first part of the lens will fall off.

There will be two yellow wires, just clip or pull those out to get the lens part off

## Step 3: Removing the shutter
Next you want to remove the shutter assembly; again there will be 2 screws. Unscrew them and the shutter will fall off.

## Step 4: Removing The Lens
Lastly to free the lens, you want to unscrew it from the square piece. Just turn the lens counterclockwise, till you hear a click. It should then screw right off and you have your holga lens.

## Step 5: Drilling the body cap
Next you want to drill the body cap. Try to center it to the best of your ability.

## Step 6: Gluing the lens to the cap
Lastly you want to use a bit of hot glue to glue the lens to the body cap. The lens should line up with the hole for it to work right.

## Step 7: UPDATE Moving the lens closer
I found that the original placement of the lens was too far away to get good enough pictures so the following pictures show you how to move the lens more forward.

I basically removed the plastic lens from the holga by prying up on the melted points.

Then I hot glued the lens directly to the body cap, then glued on the rest of the holga lens to complete the look.

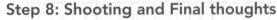

This method makes taking pictures that are farther away much easier.

## Step 8: Shooting and Final thoughts
Now it's time to take it out and try it out. The lens works pretty well, yet the focus point is about 2 feet from me, so it's hard to get good pictures.

It is wonky like a standard toy camera, but this project was pretty easy for the effect. I could see this lens doing well for portraits, but not so well for landscapes. To operate the camera it has to be in manual mode. I can control the speed of course.

After getting the lens closer, the pictures seem to be a lot clearer. The next step to this project would be to introduce some vignetting.

Hope you enjoyed this Instructable!

# Laser Triggered High-Speed Photography

by Brett Coulthard (Frivolous Engineering)

(http://www.instructables.com/id/Laser-Triggered-High-Speed-Photography/)

In order to consistently photograph something like milk drops the usual method uses a high-end camera ($500 and up), Speedlite flash ($300 and up) and an optical electronic delayed flash trigger ($120 and up).

There are lots of DIY circuits for this purpose, but they still require a good camera and a high-end flash unit.

And you have to manually open the shutter requiring the photo to be taken in a darkened room.

Here's how you can consistently take the same photos with an simple circuit, inexpensive point and shoot camera, no additional flash unit, all without fumbling around in the dark.

I've concentrated on milk drops, but this can be used for many different things. The separation between the laser and the detector could be hundreds of feet apart, or bouncing off mirrors.

©2009 SASKVIEW.CO

## Step 1: Materials

I got the following at my local dollar store. (Each item was actually $1.25: talk about misleading advertising!)

- Laser pointer
- Door chime
- USB Cable
- Magnets
- Clamp
- Shelf brackets
- Mini-tripod
- Self-Adhesive backed Velcro
- Small picture frame (for the plate glass insert)
- Eye drops

- Here's what you'll need for the circuit (I don't think your local dollar store will have these so you might try an electronics distributor like Digi-Key):

Part/Value Digi-Key Part #
- 4 .01 uF 50V metal film Caps P4513-ND
- 3 1.0 uF 50V Ceramic Caps BC1162CT-ND
- 1 10 uF 35V Electrolytic Cap P818-ND
- 1 1K Ohms 1/4 W resistor 1.0KQBK-ND
- 1 22K Ohms 1/4 W resistor 22KQBK-ND
- 2 120 Ohms 1/4 W resistors 120KQBK-ND
- 2 200 K Ohms .5W Multi-turn Pots CT94EW204-ND
- 1 Green LED P14228-ND
- 1 Red LED P14224-ND
- 1 LM556CN timer IC 296-6504-5-ND
- 1 7404 inverter IC 568-2921-5-ND
- 1 Photodiode PNZ300F-ND

Please note that the schematic has been revised to use new photodiode.

## Step 2: The Camera

You'll need a Canon camera because we're going to temporarily modify its firmware using the Canon Hacking Development Kit. CHDK is loaded onto the memory card inside the camera, allowing us to override most of the camera's functions, turning a cheap point and shoot into a highly adjustable way-cool time freezer.

A great tutorial to help you get CHDK running on your camera can be found here.

Installing CHDK didn't harm my camera, and it's temporary. I can revert back to the original firmware simply by turning the camera off and restarting it without CHDK.

Of course I can't guarantee you won't blow up your camera by attaching home-made electronics to it. Do so at your own risk!

©2009 SASKVIEW.COM

## Step 3: The Circuit

To trigger your CHDK enabled camera we'll be using the USB remote function. In this case we have to use it via the "syncable" method, which is lightning fast compared to the normal USB remote.

The syncable remote also operates differently. It triggers the camera on the falling edge instead of the rising edge of the 5-volt signal. When the camera detects the 5 volt USB signal, it gets ready to take a shot, waiting for the voltage to fall to zero.

There are high-speed camera trigger circuits floating around the 'net but I couldn't find any for syncable USB. So I cobbled together the circuit below.

It uses a 556 timer IC, an inverter, a photoresistor and some caps and resistors.

The dollar store had a USB cable identical to the one my camera uses. I lobbed one end off of it, instead of wrecking the one that came with my camera.

A 5-volt power supply is needed to power the circuit. If you don't have one, pick up a cheap USB charger, or add a 7805 voltage regulator to the circuit.

The photoresistor is not on the circuit board; it's mounted on a small piece of perf board at the end of a short cable. Glue some magnets onto the back for easy alignment with the laser.

The circuit should be built first on a bread-board and tested. Once you're sure everything is working then either etch a circuit board or use a prototype board like I did. Or just continue using the circuit on the bread-board.

## Step 4: The Laser

The laser pointer has a momentary switch but I wanted a slide switch that would allow the laser to remain on without me holding the button.

The dollar store magnetic door chime not only had the slide switch that I wanted, but also it used the same kind and number of batteries that the laser does. This was cheaper than buying just a switch from an electronics supplier.

I removed the tiny circuit board from the door chime and installed the working guts of the laser in its place using the chime's switch and battery holder.

You don't have to go to this extreme if you don't want to. Just use a rubber band wrapped around the laser pointer to keep it turned on.

Like the photodiode, I hot-melt glued some magnets on the back.

## Step 5: The Drop Rig

Below is a photo of my setup.

Some pieces of wood and some steel shelf brackets clamped to a TV tray.

The laser is mounted with the magnets on one of the brackets, and the photodiode on the other. In between and slightly above I've Velcroed the eye dropper bottle filled with milk.

## Step 6: CHDK Settings: Enabling Synchable Remote

In order for the USB cable remote to work, you have to enable it.

With CHDK installed on your camera go into the Main Menu and at the very bottom you'll see Miscellaneous stuff. Enter that menu and at the very bottom of it you'll find the Remote parameters menu. In that menu set Enable Remote [.]

Make sure there is a dot inside the square brackets, meaning it's enabled.

Below that is Enable Synchable Remote. Enable it.

Next is Enable Synch, enable this too.

photography

Also on this screen are settings for synch delay. They didn't work for me, and that's another reason I built the delay circuit.

## Step 7: CHDK Settings: Extra Photo Operations

Now go into the Extra Photo Operations menu at the top of the main menu and set:

- Disable Overrides [disable]
- Include AutoIso and Bracketi [.]
- Override shutter speed [1/10000]
- Value factor [1]
- Shutterspeed emun type [Ev Step]
- Override aperture [5.03]
- Override Subj. Dist. V [350]
- Value factor [1]
- Override ISO value [80]
- Value factor [1]
- Force manual flash [.]
- Power of flash [1]

In order to get the right exposure you will have to adjust the aperture, ISO, and flash power settings.

Lower aperture numbers will brighten the shot, higher numbers will darken the shot.

Keep in mind that the higher power of flash, the longer the flash's duration will be. You will want to use the lowest flash power that provides sufficient exposure. Flash power of zero is very feeble and you may need to use 1.

For the ISO you will want to use a low ISO value because higher ISO's cause more noise and the resulting pictures look grainy. The overall ISO is the value times the factor. Factor can be 1, 10 or 100 giving you an ISO anywhere between 0 and around 32000. Keep in mind that ISO's lower than 40 or higher than 800 are most likely beyond what the camera can actually achieve.

## Step 8: Adjusting the Camera Settings

Normally you would be triggering an external flash, while the shutter is open using a cable release with the camera in 'bulb' mode. Once the flash goes off, you let the shutter close. This requires the room to be darkened because the shutter will be open for many seconds.

In this setup you can have the room lights on because the flash and shutter are triggered at the same time, and the exposure is set for 1/10,000th of a second.

Before we hook the camera up to the trigger circuit we first adjust its settings, manually taking pictures until we get the exposure correct.

Mount your camera on a tripod and place a stationary test object right where the drop is going to land. Frame the test object, and adjust zoom to your liking. Use the macro setting if your camera is close enough to do so.

Keep in mind that you will most likely get milk splashed onto your camera and lens, so the sollar store glass plate should be placed in front of the lens to prevent this. If the glass plate is in front of the flash it may reflect back into the lens, causing unwanted glare.

Now take a test shot and revue how it turned out. If the shot isn't properly exposed adjust the exposure, flash and ISO until it is.

You can also adjust the shutter speed, but keep in mind that it's mostly the flash that's freezing the action. I set the shutter speed to 1/10000 of a second and left it alone.

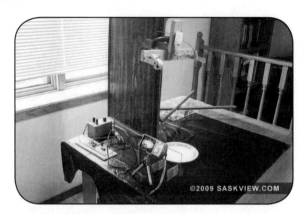

©2009 SASKVIEW.COM

## Step 9: Adjusting the circuit

With your drop rig in place mount the photoresistor to one of the steel brackets and the laser on the other one. Adjust the position of the laser so that the droplets fall through the beam. Adjust the position of the photoresistor so that it's illuminated with the laser.

Power up the circuit. LED1 will light up, indicating power.

Before we begin using the eye-dropper, we should set the photoresistor's sensitivity using VR1. Momentarily interrupt the beam. LED2 should blink indicating the circuit has tripped.

Adjust the sensitivity so the circuit triggers consistently. You may find ambient room light is interfering with the circuit, either preventing or causing false triggering, so you may need to dim the room lights, or mount a shade around the photoresistor.

Make sure that the delay potentiometer is set somewhere around the middle. If it's set to the very end of its limit, the circuit won't work.

Once the circuit is working, power it down and plug the USB cable into your camera.

Turn on your Camera with CHDK running, then power-up the circuit. A 5-volt signal will be fed to the camera. Sensing that signal, the camera will pre-focus, and then its LCD viewfinder will blank. The camera is now armed and ready, waiting for the 5 volt signal to fall to zero.

Interrupt the laser beam, and after a very short delay the camera will take a high-speed flash photo.

Interrupting the beam a second time will re-arm the camera for its next shot. Once the circuit is working, interrupting the beam alternates between arming the camera, and tripping the shutter.

Now it's time to start spilling milk. All that's needed is to dial in the proper amount of delay.

# crafts

Crafts as we have come to know them on Instructables.com could not be further from the feather and glue collages that some people might remember from first grade. As one of the largest categories on the site, encompassing everything from airbrush gun mods to soft circuits, with of course lots of creative knitting and painting in between, craft projects help us to create items for our lives.

The projects included in the craft section of this book showcase how it's possible to take even the most conventional hobbies or materials, and make something truly extraordinary with them. Working on a unique project like a handmade wedding ring forces us to remember that, while it's important to stay focused on what we make, how we make it matters too, and that's where the field of crafts can really shine.

crafts

# Quilted Mad Tea Party Set

By technoplastique
(http://www.instructables.com/id/Quilted-Mad-Tea-Party-Set/)

This tea set is made with quilting done in a dimensional way. It's a set of 4 teacups, 4 saucers, and a teapot. This version is made with a striped fabric so that each teacup has a different design, perfect for a mad tea party. The set is entirely hand sewn, so it's a super project for keeping your hands busy in front of the TV.

## Step 1: Supplies and Equipment

- Fabric – a yard will get the job done. I used three different fabrics. One was a bubbly print that I used inside the cups and pot, one was an all over that I used for the saucers, and one was a stripe that I used for the outsides of the cups and pot. A variety of florals or more simple stripes would have given a more traditional look.
- Thread – match your fabric, mine is ordinary white sewing thread.
- Sewing basics – needles, scissors, etc.
- Fray Check – use this when you intentionally or unintentionally cut a seam allowance smaller than you like. It will help stabilize the edge of the fabric so it doesn't fray out when you need it.
- Iron and ironing board – iron on interfacing with this, and the more often you press things in place as you work, the nicer your finished pieces will be.
- You will need to choose to either use an iron-on interfacing OR use freezer paper and batting.

- Fusible interfacing – 2-3 yards, relatively lightweight if this is for display, heavier weight if some dolls will be making regular use of it.
- OR
- Freezer paper – you'll need several feet. Cut the interfacing shapes on the pattern, iron it in place, and pull the paper before sewing things closed.
- Batting – cut pieces to match the interfacing patterns, and put the batting in before sewing things closed.
- I used the interfacing for a smoother, simpler look (and the directions focus on this method), but feel free to switch it up and use the paper piecing and batting method for a softer, cuddlier tea set.

## Step 2: Pattern

I've included my pattern pieces here, it makes a smaller than life tea set. I developed it by looking at a lot of pictures of tea sets and making models. If you would like to try patterning something different I would recommend designing it, printing/tracing it onto paper, and taping together a mock-up before committing to sewing it.

The numbers on the pattern are the number of pieces that should be cut from interfacing.

Each piece has a number of pieces to cut. In the handles and the teapot you may want to layer two thicknesses of fusible interfacing to give the pieces a bit more strength. Iron one piece onto the fabric, then stack on the next piece and iron that.

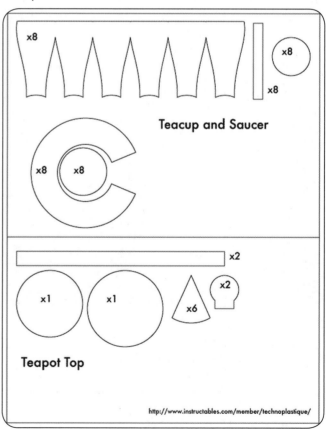

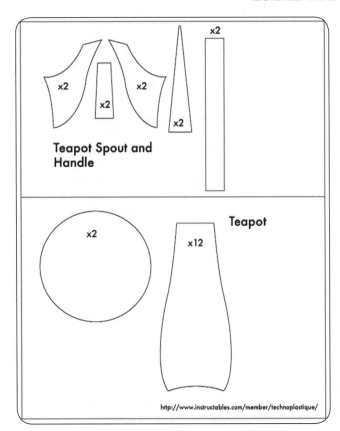

Teapot Spout and Handle

x2
x2
x2
x2
x2
x2

Teapot

x2
x12

http://www.instructables.com/member/technoplastique/

## Step 3: Fusing

Fuse your interfacing onto the fabric, leaving a solid 1/4" seam allowance around everything (more if you're nervous, you can trim it down after you sew things together.) Cut the pieces out loosely around the interfacing, stack them up by category.

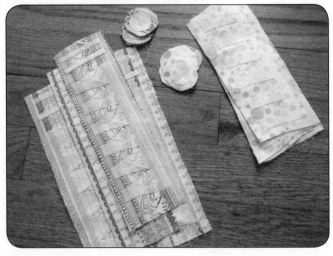

## Step 4: Sewing tips

Backstitch is a super choice for this project. Running stitch can gather the fabric a bit if you're not careful. Lots and lots of tiny stitches will give you your best finish. Use the interfacing as a guide, sew along the edges as neatly as possible.

When you're sewing a circle into a round opening it's a good idea to put pins in at 1/4" or 1/6" marks on each

piece. Matching these pins as you sew around will help make sure everything lays smoothly and evenly.

## Step 5: Sew the Saucers

These are the easiest, so start with them.

1. Sew the seam at the side of each "c" shaped saucer piece. Press the seams open.
2. Sew the circles into the round openings. Trim any extra bulk.
3. Match pairs of these pieces, sew most of the way around, turn them, and then sew it closed the rest of the way. Bury your knots in the seam.
4. Press them so that they "cup" and the edges are smooth.

## Step 6: Sew the teacups

1. Sew pairs of handle pieces together – sew a short side, a long side, then a short side. Trim an extra bulk. Turn it, and sew the remaining side closed.
2. Sew in the darts on all of the cup pieces.
3. Sew each lining to an outer at the "rim." Press this seam open.
4. Sew up the side seams.
5. Sew the bottom into the lining side of the teacup.
6. Turn the outer over the lining.
7. Sew the handle onto the sides of the outer teacups. This is tricky, but you can kind of push the lining up and out of the way a bit.
8. Sew the bottom of the outer onto the teacups.

crafts

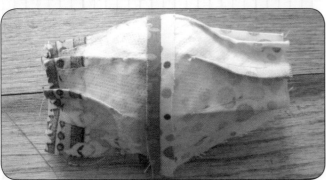

3. Sew the two halves of the dome together with the handle between them.
4. Sew the two long strips together along one edge, and then into a loop. Turn and press.
5. Sew this to the smaller circle.
6. Sew this circle to the larger circle.
7. Sew the top dome to the larger circle.

## Step 7: Sew the top of the teapot

1. Sew the two topper handle pieces together, turn and press.
2. Sew the pie shaped wedges together in groups of three. Press the seam allowances open.

## Step 8: Sew the teapot

1. Sew five of the six vertical seams of the outer teapot together, press seams open. Do the same for the lining.
2. Sew the four pieces of the spout together on the long sides, both outside and lining.
3. Sew the ends of the nozzles together. Trim any excess seam allowance. Turn it right side out.
4. Sew the outer and lining together along the end of the spout that attaches to the teapot.
5. Sew the handle pieces together in the same way the teacup handles were constructed. Sew the handles onto one panel of the outer teapot.

crafts

315

6. Sew the spout onto the outer of the teapot.
7. Sew the inside and outside of the teapot together along the rim edge.
8. Sew the teapot together along the one remaining vertical seam.
9. Sew the bottom of the lining in place.
10. Turn the teapot right side out.
11. Sew the bottom of the teapot outer in place.

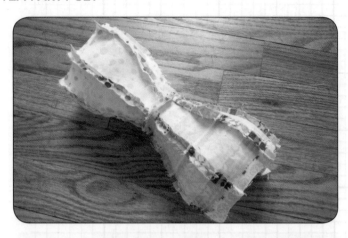

## Step 9: Quilting and finishing

I had originally intended to do this set in a floral or solid, and quilt patterns into the side. If you've added batting you can easily add quilting stitches to any of the pieces. If you're expecting these to see a lot of play you might want to embed washers into the bottoms of the teacups. With handles, they're slightly off balance so they might be a bit tippy.

# Carving a Lattice and Acanthus Pattern on an Emu Egg Shell

By bbstudio
(http://www.instructables.com/id/Carving-a-lattice-and-acanthus-pattern-on-an-emu-e/)

I created this project with the amazing Faberge eggs in mind. My approach was to combine the precision and beauty of the famous Faberge eggs with modern tools and possibilities. I used an emu egg because of the natural layers and colors that it contains. Nothing on this egg shell is painted or dyed. This piece is meant to be contemplated up close.

The columns are stylized acanthus leaves carved in relief using the mainly the turquoise layer. The lattice is formed by removing multiple layers from around the outermost layer. The white negative space was made this way intentionally. I thought it would provide the best background for the darker colors of the foreground. In addition, when displayed where light is allowed to enter the pierced areas, that very light will show through the thin white portions of the design.

## Step 1: Safety first

I give the egg a quick wipe down with alcohol to reduce the chances of Salmonella existing on the eggshell.

Then wash the shell in water and dry thoroughly. Be sure to wear a surgical mask to help prevent breathing the dust created. It is not healthy at all to inhale this stuff.

## Step 2: A good design starts with basics

Begin by marking a grid pattern on the egg. This can be done by stacking various household items like books or blocks of wood. A better method is to use an egg marker.

## Step 3: Begin drawing the design

Step 3 is to draw the lattice pattern on the egg using the grid as a guide to keep the lines of the lattice evenly spaced

## Step 4: Draw in Acanthus

After the lattice is complete, draw on the acanthus columns. I draw the pattern on paper first. This gives me a guide to use when getting the image on the egg. If a person does not think they can draw the things over and over the same then there are other options. I know many people who use a stencil film (I buy mine on-line from Profitable Hobbies), which can be run through a copier or printer and then applied directly to your project as it has an adhesive on one side. I have used it in the past and still do from time to time.

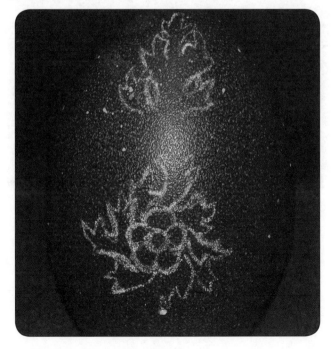

crafts

## Step 5: Cut in light outline, remove drawn on lines

Next, using a #171 bit in a high speed engraving tool, I lightly cut each line of the design that will need further attention later in the process. By doing this I am able to remove all the pencil marks before the egg shell becomes too fragile to be sanded or otherwise cleaned. The surface of the emu egg is not smooth, nor is it even in hardness, so be careful while marking the pattern so you dont end up with deep cuts. Another reason I pre-mark the design is the eggs can chip as the cutting bit is drawn through the shell. By making a first pass chipping is reduced.

## Step 6: Begin carving the acanthus

The acanthus columns are now begun. They will be the thickest part of the egg after it is carved. By carving these first the shell remains as strong as possible while it is handled. I first carve with a #2 carbide ball burr. All the rough-out as well as the majority of the detail is done with this bit.

## Step 7: Add details to leaves

Change to a #0.5 carbide ball to begin adding the undercuts and the finer details.

## Step 8: Continue detailing leaves

Again move to a smaller carbide ball burr #1/16. This is used to finish the undercutting. It is really too small to do much carving of large areas. At this time, the flower is left alone as it is to be taken to the white layer.

## Step 9: Time to carve the lattice pattern

We now will begin the lattice. Because the outer-most layer varies in hardness and surface texture, I will remove it before making the effort to take the turquoise layer away. I realize this is a lot of work but I do it so I have a much reduced chance of punching a hole completely through the egg. I use a #171 tapered flat carbide burr to remove the dark green layer. I do this by carefully following the outline previously drawn to roughly the depth of the outer layer. After the diamond shape is marked I remove the remaining dark shell just outlined.

## Step 10: Remove the turquoise layer

Time again to change bits. Now I will use a fairly large carbide ball burr #6 to remove the turquoise layer. You will not be able to remove a small amount where the white layer meets the lattice. Don't worry we will take it out next. Care must be taken here as this burr is pretty aggressive for the small area and thickness we are removing. The parts of the shell that are to be pierced can be left alone at this point. I mark them with a Sharpie pen so I know where they are and so I won't waste time continuing to carve in areas that I will be removing later.

## Step 11: Touch up the edges of the lattice

When all the diamond shapes are roughed out to the white layer we change burrs yet again to a #699 tapered flat carbide cutter. The end of this burr is flat so it can be stood straight up and it will cut like a router bit. This burr is used to remove all the turquoise layer that remains next to the lattice lines It can also be used to remove any remaining large pieces of the turquoise layer.

## Step 12: Finish removing any signs of the turquoise layer

After cleaning up all the diamond shapes between the lattice lines the burr is changed to a green conical sanding stone. We now remove the small thin portions of the turquoise layer that remain in each of the spaces between the lattice. And to smooth the white surface. BE CAREFUL!! Not much thickness here for errors.

## Step 13: Completion of flowers

Time to finish the flowers. The center is left alone in the dark outer layer. The petals are carved with a #4 carbide ball burr by first removing the dark layer. Second, strokes are drawn from the edge of the center circle to the edge of the petal through the turquoise layer down to the white layer. We don't need a lot of precision here in the stokes except to avoid cutting too deeply and breaking through. The randomness of varied stokes will more closely match those created by nature.

## Step 14: Undercutting the flower petals

When you are satisfied with the petals of all the flowers, change to burr back to the #1/16 and undercut the petals.

## Step 15: Time to punch some holes

Time to remove the pierced portions. Either the #699 or the #171 can be used for this. The end of these bits will cut so they can be carefully pushed straight through the shell then drawn along the edges of the design that are to remain.

## Step 16: Beginning to prepare the egg for display

After you are satisfied with the carving and cutting portion of this project, prepare a solution of bleach and water. You will hear many different ideas on the correct proportions of bleach to water. I have used straight bleach and a mixture as diluted as 50/50. Obviously the diluted solutions will take longer to accomplish the task at hand. We are going to remove the film that is inside the egg. If you are patient enough you can put a piece of dental floss in one hole and out another to help you put the egg in the bleach. I just use a rubber kitchen glove since it gives me more control over how the egg enters the liquid. This process will raise a strong bleach smell as the bleach eats away the proteins. I wait until the surface of the liquid no longer has any bubbles or foam on it before examining the egg for any remaining inner film layer. (Steps 16 and 17 can be ignored if you choose not to pierce the shell.)

## Step 17: Wash, Wash, Wash

After the film is removed, wash the shell thoroughly with lots of water. The point is to be absolutely sure all the bleach is removed. Allow the shell to dry over night then you can begin applying light layers of polyurethane. Don't hurry here as a run or drip will be basically impossible to remove.

## Step 18: Time to finish the egg for display

Find a stand that you feel is appropriate to your work. I use a super glue style adhesive to hold the egg in it stand. My opinion offered here is to choose something that will compliment the design and not overpower. After spending countless hours creating your project, it seems to me that saving a few pennies and putting your work on the cheapest base you can find is detracting from your work of art.

## Step 19: Photo time

Photograph your project to your heart's content.

## Step 20: Protect your hard work

Glue the stand containing your egg shell to the center of the base that comes with a glass dome. Place glass dome over the entire project. I use professional modeling clay to hold the dome in the base. The clay never dries and will hold the dome in place nicely. Never pick up this display by the dome, always the base.

crafts

# Making a Custom Platinum Diamond Engagement Ring

by chrisparry
(http://www.instructables.com/id/Making-a-custom-Platinum-Diamond-engagement-ring./)

So, I am a professional jeweler. (http://www.chris-parry.co.uk). I also sell some items on http://www.chris-parry.etsy.com.

If you are really bored, you can visit my flickr page (http://www.flickr.com/photos/chris-parry/).

A client wanted a traditional design for his engagement ring.

This instructable shows you how his ring was created using the lost wax casting system.

To begin with, I cut a section of jewelers wax (a special wax that has great properties for cutting, sawing, and carving) into the basic ring shape. I created a hole the same size required for the finished ring.

## Step 1: Seating the diamond

The 5mm princess cut diamond is set into its position in the ring.

I decided how high the diamond was to sit, then using small engraving tools, I cut a square hole for the diamond to sit in.

You can also make out lots of faint white lines on the wax ring blank. These will determine which parts of the wax are to be cut away to form the shape of the ring.

## Step 2: The basic shaping

I have now cut away the major excess parts of the wax, and the ring begins to take shape.

## Step 3: The setting is begun

I have now carved out the setting for the diamond.

Once this was complete, I scribed the central part of the ring shank, so that I could determine how wide the ring was to be.

## Step 4: The ring shank is cut back

I have now used the scribed lines to cut the ring shank back to the required thickness.

The wax is now beginning to look more like an engagement ring.

## Step 5: The prongs revealed

The client wanted a four claw prong setting for the diamond.

Here you can see that I have cut back the wax in the mid section of the setting to reveal the four corner prongs.

## Step 6: Making it visually lighter

The ring shank and setting were too "heavy" VISUALLY. So I created some airholes, to make the ring more delicate.

crafts

## Step 7: Making a mould

I could have taken this ring directly into the "lost wax casting" process, but I decided to make a mould first.

Sometimes in the casting process, there may be a casting failure, where the item doesn't cast perfectly. By making a mould, I can create duplicates of this ring.

If the first wax produced, fails to make a good platinum cast, I can simply go to this stage and create another wax model using the mould.

During the "lost wax casting" process, the wax is lost in the process when it melts in the kiln. By making a mould I wouldn't have to re-carve the model should a failure occur.

## Step 8: Pouring the mould

I use a simple two part RVT silicone molding compound when I create my moulds.

You can see that I have half poured the liquid rubber into the mould box. I stopped to take the picture, and the mould box was filled to completely cover the ring model.

## Step 9: The finished mould

Here is the finished mould 24 hours later.

Encased inside is the wax model.

I use a sharp blade to cut the mould open, to remove the wax model.

The cavity left in the mould is a perfect copy of the master wax model.

To produce more wax models, liquid wax is injected into this mould. Within 30 seconds, it cools and the mould is opened to reveal a wax duplicate.

If I wanted to produce hundreds of this design, I would simply use this mould again and again. That however is for the "high street." I make unique items for each client, so I won't re-use this mould again.

## Step 10: A ring is finished

The wax model is then sent off to the platinum caster.

Whilst I cast my own gold and silver items, platinum casting requires specialist equipment. So the wax is used in the "lost wax casting process" and the platinum ring is returned.

I then clean up the cast piece, I file, sand, and polish it and set the diamond.

Here is the finished item.

crafts

# Conductive Fabric: Make Flexible Circuits Using an Inkjet Printer

by mikey77

(http://www.instructables.com/id/Conductive-Fabric-Make-Flexible-Circuits-Using-An/)

Extremely flexible and nearly transparent circuits can be made using conductive fabrics. Here are some of the experiments I've done with conductive fabrics. They can be painted or drawn on with resist and then etched like a standard circuit board. Conductive glue or conductive thread is then used to attach the components to the fabric circuit board.

To make this clear, the inkjet printer is not used to directly print resist onto the fabric. Instead, it is only used to print the circuit design onto the conductive fabric. You will then have to hand paint a clear resist over the inkjet image before the circuit can be etched. Alternately—an inkjet printer is not necessary—you can just freehand paint or draw on the resist where you want the conductive traces to be.

## Materials

- Performix (tm) liquid tape, black
- Carbon Graphite, fine powder—Available in smaller quantities at your local hardware store. It's called lubricating graphite and comes in small tubes or bottles.
- Conductive thread
- Conductive fabrics
- Clear Nail Polish
- Crayons
- Ferric Chloride etchant
- Inkjet printer
- Toluol solvent—Available at hardware stores

- Wax paper
- Picture 2 shows the three conductive fabrics that were used in this instructable.
- VeilShield—A mesh polyester plated with a blackened copper. Very light and 70% transparent.
- FlecTron—copper plated nylon rip stop
- Nickel Mesh—Semi-transparent copper and nickel coated polyester

Picture 3 shows the back of the circuit and the glued components.

## Step 1: Print the circuit pattern with an inkjet printer

Create a black and white image in a drawing or image program that will be the pattern for your circuit. Print it out onto the center of a piece of copy paper and adjust the image size until you get the exact printed circuit size you are looking for. The final traces should be 1/8" to 1/4" wide. Make them wider if you plan on carrying more than 100ma of current through them.

Next is to glue a square of conductive fabric onto the center of a standard piece of copy paper (pic 4). Clear nail polish works well as it dries thin and fast (about 5 minutes). Glue all the way across the top of the fabric (the side that feeds into the printer) and then put a blob of glue on the bottom of the fabric to keep it stretched tight.

Then, print the pattern of your circuit board (pic 5) onto the conductive fabric. Sometimes it takes a couple of passes to easily see the pattern on the fabric.

Wax is very hydrophobic. As you can see in the next step, even wax crayons can be used as resist on conductive fabrics. So, one good possibility for printing resist directly onto the fabric is a Xerox Phaser or Tektronix Phaser printer that uses a melted wax ink. This very good instructable (http://www.instructables.com/id/DIY-Flexible-Printed-Circuits/) by ckharnett shows how he used such a printer to print wax ink resist on special copper-clad polyimide plastic sheet to create flexible circuits. These are expensive, hard to find, business printers, but if you can get access to one, it may just work to directly print resist onto conductive fabrics.

## Step 2: Paint or draw on the resist

Nail Polish Resist

For putting resist on the FlecTron (pic 6) or VeilSheild, I painted on clear nail polish. If you put it on thick enough, it will saturate the fabric and resist the etchant on both sides. To keep it from sticking, I painted it on a flat surface with wax paper underneath the fabric. After about 5 minutes it should be dry enough to flip over and touch up any dry spots on the back side.

Draw A Circuit With Crayons As The Resist

See picture 7. It turns out that you can simply draw your circuit pattern on either the FlecTron or Nickel Mesh fabric with crayons. The wax in the crayons is water resistant enough that, even though coverage is not 100 per cent, it works extremely well. The nickel fabric works best with crayons as it is stiffer and fairly transparent. You can place it like tracing paper, over a pencil drawing or printout of your circuit pattern, and then draw on it. The traces should be 3/16" or wider. After you have solidly drawn on one side, flip it over and draw in the back side. It must be coated with crayon on both sides to resist the etchant well.

 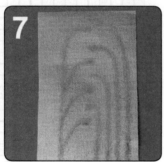

## Step 3: Etch the conductive fabric

For those who have never etched a circuit board, here is how it works. Ink, paint, tape, or some other material (called a resist) is used to cover parts of the copper clad circuit board and seal it from the etchant. The etchant (usually Ferric Chloride) reacts with any copper that is uncoated and chemically removes it. So, wherever there is resist, the copper will remain. The resist is put on in the pattern of conductive traces that you want your circuit board to end up with.

The process is the same with conductive fabrics, with the exception that we are dealing with a porous woven material that is plated with copper and/or nickel. Conductive fabrics have an extremely thin plating of metal, usually over nylon or polyester. It is so thin that they can be etched in from 5 to 60 seconds. This is with a strong Ferric Chloride solution at room temperature.

Soak the fabric in the Ferric Chloride solution for the following times:

- VeilShield-5–10 seconds
- FlecTron 30–60 seconds
- Nickel Mesh–60 seconds

Remove the etched fabric and rinse VERY WELL with lots of water and then blot on paper towels and hang to dry.

Picture 9 shows VeilSheild fabric that has been etched with 3 conductive traces to form an almost transparent, flexible cable. Picture 9b shows the cable with conductive glue and conductive thread.

Picture 8 shows the nickel fabric with crayon resist after etching. The Ferric Chloride etches nickel nicely. Even though there are tiny gaps in the conductive traces, they conduct extremely well. The fabric was soaked in toluol solvent to remove the crayon. Soak in a glass container for about an hour and agitate it occasionally.

  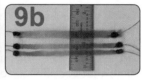

## Step 4: Completing the circuit

It turns out that nail polish resist puts on a very thin insulating layer over the conductive traces. You can make a simple conductive paint that will melt through this insulating layer to create a conductive glue joint. This means you can glue components such as LEDs, Integrated Circuits, resistors, conductive thread, or wire anywhere on the conductive traces.

Make Conductive Paint

It is easy to make a conductive paint that is simply conductive glue that has been thinned down. It is thinned down with a solvent in order to stick well to the fabric and melt through the nail polish resist.

Mix the paint 1-1/2 powdered Graphite to 1 Liquid Tape to 1 Toluol by volume. Mix it fast and mix it well. Have everything you need to glue set up and ready to go as this paint dries fairly fast. Because it is so thinned out, you may have to apply two or three coats to get a thick enough connection to your components. This mix has strong solvent fumes. Do this in a VERY WELL VENTILATED ROOM or do it outdoors.

The conductive traces themselves will usually only add an ohm or less to the resistance. Each conductive glue joint to a component will add about 3 to 5 ohms.

Picture 10 shows the crayon resist circuit with one led lit. the Nickel Mesh fabric is transparent enough that the LEDs can be mounted on the back and the LED glow will come through.

Picture 11 shows the back of the crayon resist circuit.

# Identity Preserving Balaclava

by Andrew Salomone (snag hazard)
(http://www.instructables.com/id/Identity-
Preserving-Balaclava-all-the-warmth-with/)

It's pretty easy to wear warm clothes on just about every part of your body except for your face. As far as I can tell, the main reason that cold-weather facial attire is somewhat socially taboo is because it generally obscures the identity of the person wearing it. Despite all of the progress our society has made towards accepting and treating all people fairly, we still have yet to escape the notion that a person in a balaclava (or ski mask) is generally up to no good. The "Identity Preserving Balaclava" is my solution to the social stigma associated with the identity concealing effect of the average balaclava.

Here is the method and pattern that I used to make my own "Identity Preserving Balaclava." Hopefully other people will be able to use this to liberate their cold faces from social repression!

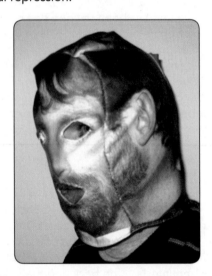

## Step 1: Stuff you will need

Ok, here's a list of all the stuff I used to make this project:

- Digital Camera
- Photo Editing software (pretty much any program that you can crop images with)
- Inkjet printer
- Inkjet Iron-on transfer paper (at least 6 pieces)
- Light-colored sweatshirt material (from a cut up sweatshirt or from a fabric store, 1/2 a yard is more than enough)
- An iron
- A good pair of scissors

- Needle (or a sewing machine if you know what you're doing)
- Thread
- Straight pins
- A flat surface to iron on and a pillow case to lay on top of it
- A ruler or tape measure

## Step 2: Take pictures of your head

The pattern I came up with uses 6 digital images that are 8 x 10 inches. Each image is taken from a different angle of the head, so that when they are sewn together properly they will make a mask that displays everything that it is covered up.

Here are the angles that need to be photographed:

1. Face straight on
2. Left profile
3. Right profile
4. Back of the head straight on
5. Top of the head straight on
6. Neck and upper shoulders straight on

## Step 3: Editing your images

Once you have images of all the different angles of your head you will need to edit them so that they will print properly onto iron-on transfer sheets.

Probably the best way to do this step is by trial and error. Take a ruler or tape measure and try to measure the dimensions of your head.

Crop your images to a ratio of 10 x 8 inches, which will fit easily onto the 8.5 x 10 inch Inkjet iron-on transfer sheets.

Try to match the printed out images to the dimensions of your actual head, keeping in mind that they will probably need to be a little bigger than your head in order to fit over it.

You will probably want to print test images on scratch paper to make sure that the images are the right size before printing on the inkjet iron-on transfer sheets.

Remember to reverse all of your images before printing them onto the inkjet iron-on transfer sheets.

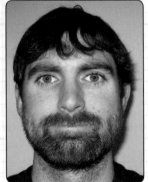

crafts

## Step 4: Ironing on the images

Just follow the directions that come with the Inkjet iron-on transfer sheets.

Note: It may help to wash the fabric after the iron-ons have been applied. I didn't do it because I was worried they might shrink a little and I had them measured to just the right sizes. You can try it though. It might work better because the iron-ons can be kind of tough to sew through and washing them is supposed to soften them up.

## Step 5: Sewing the pattern together

I made my own pattern for this project, and even though it seems to have worked pretty well, it can only be used as an approximation of what it should look like because everyone's head is different. So you will probably need to adjust this pattern to fit your own head, but here is what I did and here is what it looks like.

Starting with the straight-on image of the face, cut out the eye hole and the mouth hole and make sure they line up with your eyes and mouth. To do this cut a cross-shape and sew down the flaps.

Then line up the profile images with the straight-on image of the face. To make sure you get it right, first line up the jaw lines on either side, then use the straight pins to pin them together at the seams.

Stand in front of the mirror and try wrapping the pinned together pieces of fabric to make sure they accurately line up with the features of your face and head.

This process will probably take a lot of trial and error.

Try and line up the images of the face straight-on, the left profile, the right profile, and the back of the head, so that they make a straight line that can been eventually sewn into a tube.

Once those images are lined up and sewn together, cut the fabric with the image of the top of the head into thirds the long way. Then cut the middle third in half, like a hamburger. Line up the four pieces with the strip of images you have already sewn together so that the image of the top of the head is the same length as the rest of the strip. Make sure to line up the image of the hair from the top of the head with the hair from the other angles of the head.

Finally cut up and sew the image of the neck and shoulders onto the bottom of the images that you have already sewn together. This part will take a few more judgment calls than the rest, because the main purpose of this is to add enough fabric to the bottom of the strip of images so that later you will be able to make an even hem at the bottom of the balaclava.

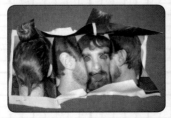

## Step 6: Fitting

At this point it's pretty much all trial and error.

Pin the pattern you have made into a tube and make sure it fits over your head properly.

Once you have the right fit, sew the seam that you have pinned together.

Go through the same process sewing together the seams of the fabric that cover the top of the head.

Once you have everything sewn up and fitting well enough, you should be able to hem the bottom of the balaclava so that it is all even and none of the back side of the fabric is showing.

Finally, you can trim all the left-over fabric from the seams you've stitched together.

## Step 7: Liberate your face!

Now you can go out in public without having to worry about people thinking you might have criminal tendencies just because your face is hidden behind an average balaclava. Tell convenience store clerks not to worry, the police will still be able to identify you if you do decide to commit a robbery. And maybe if you are walking down the street a friend of yours will recognize you and offer to give you a lift, knowing that you are not just some creep walking down the street in a ski mask. Nope, you will not look creepy at all.

But before you go out, don't forget to brush your teeth.

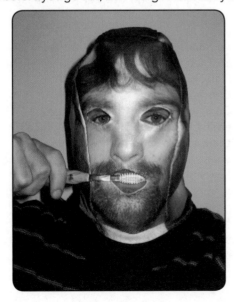

# Rhino Trophy Head

## By mezcraft
### (http://www.instructables.com/id/Rhino-Trophy-Head/)

I began this adventure by being involved with a craft swap on craftster.org. My partner had wanted a stuffed rhino head, so I decided I would give it a go. I also made one for my husband for Christmas in the process! I had seen on websites and in stores these amazing leather rhinos, often used as stools and I thought I could approach my rhino in the same way.

## Step 1: Supplies

This is what you will need to this:

- A toy to build off of, preferably one you don't mind wrecking.
- Cellophane
- Masking tape cut into thin strips
- Fine tip marker
- Sharp exacto blade
- Dark or not white paper
- Use of a scanner/photocopier with ability to blow things up (hahaha, wouldn't that be crazy!) bigger
- Scissors
- Quilting ruler (clear ruler) or just a ruler.
- 2 yards of fabric (I used a grey velour and I also did this with a faux black leather)
- Thread to match fabric colour
- Glue Gun
- Cardboard, or cardstock, or even a piece of wood (to close the back up with)
- A wooden plaque from the dollar store (or if you are more savvy and have access, cut a shape out of wood and router the edge cause that's really all the dollar store plaque is.)
- Paint (to paint the plaque)—I used black for the rhino of faux leather and brown for the rhino with grey velour
- A screw eye

## Step 2: Steal the shape from your toy rhino!

To start, take your toy and figure out what part you want to "steal the shape" of. I was only doing the head, so I began by covering it all in a thin layer of cellophane, making sure to get all of the crevices, and trying not to bulk it up to much. I found it easier by cutting it into smaller pieces. You put this on so that the next step, the tape, does not get stuck to your toy.

Then I took my exacto blade and cut into some masking tape, creating thin strips of masking tape.

I then covered the rhino head in these, making sure to get all angles and all spots, also making sure that there were no creases in the tape. This part is fun, because once you have all the tape on you can really see the shape of the toy.

## Step 3: Create your pattern
### Lay down the lines

Now comes the part where you really have to think. Place lines on your rhino to create your pattern pieces. What you are looking for are curves and high and low points. For those of you who don't know much about fabric, if you want there to be a curve in your pattern, then you need to create either a pleat, a dart, or a seam. In this case, by making each curve a pattern piece, you are making a seam to encompass that curve. That way the shape of what you are making will come out exactly like your original. It might just be easier to look at the pictures in this case.

### Labels and registration

I then labeled each piece so that when I took it apart I would be able to figure out what each piece was. I also added registration marks. Those are the ticks, circles, and triangles I used on the lines, which I will then transfer to my fabric allowing me to match up the pieces precisely.

### Cut it out

Now take a sharp blade and cut along each one of these lines making sure not to go over. Remember the sharp blade part! Dull knives are the cause of most injuries with an exacto blade.

*Enlarge*

Once you have them all cut out, Lay them down flat on several pieces of dark paper leaving a bit of space in between each piece of your pattern. Either scan them into your computer, or take them to a photocopier and increase the size of the shapes. I increased them by 300 percent to get the size I wanted (he still is a tiny rhino).

*Create Seam Allowance:*

Next you need to add a seam allowance, so using a clear quilting ruler, measure out 1/4 inch around all edges.

## Step 4: Transfer your pattern to fabric and cut 'em out!

*Iron*

Before you lay down your fabric, if applicable, give it a bit of an iron to flatten out any creases. I didn't need to do that as I was working with a velveteen and a leather (I did this twice).

*Pin Down and Cut out of fabric*

This part's pretty easy! Just lay down your pieces onto your fabric, pin them down and then cut them out. The only time this would get more complicated is by what fabric you choose . If I really cared I may have wanted the pile of the velveteen to all sit the same way; then I would have to think about which way is up on each of my pattern pieces. Also if you chose a fabric that had stripes or a very disincentive repetitive pattern, I might want to orient my pieces in such a way that they would all look good together.

The green bits on my pattern pieces are where I had to add seam allowance, as I made a mistake when making the pattern by putting my pattern pieces too close together on the dark paper, forcing me to use tape to create the seam allowance.

## Step 5: Sewing it all together!

Sewing this was soooo easy. There are a lot of pieces but each section was really only 2 inches long or so. It took me about 2 hours to sew this whole thing together. The only tricky parts are the ears and the horns.

I began by sewing all the sides together, then the section under the chin. I sewed the horns and ears separately and attached them by hand, because with all the layers of fabric, my wuss of a sewing machine said "heck no" and wouldn't sew through them. I did a quick stitch of that, then clipped any corners that were going to bulge once I turned it out.

I may have over simplified the sewing of this but it really was very straight forward. As long as you follow the registration marks it should work out fine. And the beauty of fabric is you can just unpick something that doesn't work out. Can't do that with glue!

## Step 6: Stuffing and finishing off your head!

*To stuff*

Starting with the sticky outy bits, like the horns and the ears, push stuffing up into them so that they push on the seam. I like my rhinos to be stuffed to the hilt with polyfill. (I use the eco friendly reused pop bottle stuffing).

*The backing*

I then cut out a cardboard oval that I approximated for the hole at the back. I checked it against the head several times, trimming where I felt it would make the most sense. I then glued it with hot glue to the rhino, bringing the fabric over the edge of the cardboard by about 3/4 of an inch all the way around. I did leave one spot to shove a bit more stuffing through, as I wanted it to be stuffed tightly.

## Step 7: Painting the placard and finishing the whole thing!

*Paint*

For the black rhino I painted my dollar store plaque black and for the grey rhino I painted it brown. I let that dry.

*Screw eye*

I screwed in a screw-eye at the top of the plaque to hang it on.

*Rhino onto Plaque*

I then Glued the cardboard backing of the rhino head to the plaque making sure it was centered and then VOILA! You have your stuffy, plushy, not cruel to animals rhino head!

# Nickel Ring/Pendant

## By Mrballeng
### (http://www.instructables.com/id/Sweetheart-Nickel-RingPendant/)

Use a nickel to make a ring or pendant for your sweetheart.

**Tools**
- Sliding square
- Razor blade
- Center punch
- Small hammer
- Large hammer
- Mandrel (I used a pry bar)
- Rotary tool
- File
- Drill press
- Sockets
- 80 Grit sand paper
- 400 Grit sand paper
- 2000 Grit sand paper
- Polishing Compound

### Step 1: Mark the center

Center the coin in the carpenters square. Using a razor blade score a line in the center. Rotate the coin 90 degrees and score another line. Where the lines cross is the center. Now use a punch to mark the center. This helps you in the next step.

### Step 2: Clamp and drill

Clamp the ring. Starting with a small drill bit, drill through the pre-marked center. Progressively drill a bigger hole until it will fit on the mandrel you're using. I used a pry bar as the mandrel.

### Step 3: Start hammering

Place a large hammer on a flat surface to serve as an anvil. Next, place the coin over the mandrel. Using a small hammer, hammer the edge of the coin. As you hammer rotate the mandrel and apply slight pressure towards the anvil. This hammering and pressure helps elongate the coin as it moves down the mandrel. As the coin stretches, check it against the finger measurement it's being made for.

If you want a thicker ring, hammer the edge at a 45 degree angle toward the mandrel. The ring will form a cone shape. Continue to hammer until the cone forms a cylindrical ring.

### Step 4: Keep hammering

Place the coin/ring flat on the anvil and hammer the edge. Eventually you will see the seam between the inner smoother surface start to close up against the outer hammered surface. Next, clamp the ring and use a rotary tool to grind out the seam. CAUTION!!! The ring will get hot! Spray it with water before handling. Wear safety goggles, not glasses. Airborne metal dust can fall behind your glasses.

## Step 5: Mount the ring

Find a socket bit just barely smaller then the ring. If you can't find a socket that's just right you can use a smaller socket and use something to wedge between the ring and socket. I use parachord when I need to. You'll better understand on a later step.

After you press the ring on the socket, use a nut and bolt and secure it through the female end. The protruding end of the bolt will be used for mounting in the drill press. Mount the assembly in the drill press and spin it round. Use a file to shape the ring. You will shape the bottom side first.

Now you have to start being careful not to mar the ring. Use the clamp and a smaller socket to remove the ring from the socket. Flip the ring over and press it back onto the socket. Make sure you use a soft work surface when you hammer the ring on and off. I used the clamp itself.

## Step 6: Final shaping

With the assembly spinning in the drill press, use progressively finer sand paper to make the ring its final shape. I start with 80 grit, then 400, then 2000. Spray the 400 and 2000 grit sand paper with water. This prevents the sand paper from getting clogged with metal particles. Again, this gets HOT! And don't breath the metal dust.

Flip the ring as needed. Use polishing compound to buff it to a shine. Now that the outside is nice, time for the inside.

## Step 7: Repeat the process

To buff the inside of the ring place it inside a larger socket. If it doesn't fit use a "filler" to wedge it in there. Parachord works well because it stands up to the heat. Electric tape works too but if it gets too hot it liquefies the adhesive causing the ring to fall off. Plus adhesive makes a mess on the ring.

Repeat the same process from the outside to the inside. The 80 grit is not necessary here. The 400 will do to start.

## Step 8: Done

Depending on how much you file off, you can make it a men's or women's ring. A women's ring has rounded edges while a men's ring is more rectangular in profile.

Several different size rings can be made; thick or thin. I made this pendant out of 3 nickels.

crafts

This instructable will teach you how to wrangle brass sufficiently enough to create a flattering and practical dress that doubles as a functional bird cage.

It's perfect for casual Fridays at the office. Steer clear of cats, coal mines, ferrets, and weasels.

## Step 1: Beginnings

Creating a functional birdcage dress was something I had wanted to do for quite a while. Most illustrations of the concept that I had seen lacked legs, which made the idea of creating the real thing quite appealing. It seemed like a fun challenge.

I began by scouring the mighty internet for birdcage and crinoline photos in order to consider potential shapes and see what might actually be feasible. I also started thinking about materials and researching how actual bird cages are built. Sketching helped to conceptualize the ideas that were running around in my head.

## Step 2: Brass is a worthy opponent (i.e., picking a material)

I highly recommend picking a material that is near impossible to work with.

I decided to go with brass because I loved how the antique brass cages had a bit of sheen. I did not, however, realize that this decision would make the project a thousand times more difficult than working with steel.

After a bit of searching online, I was able to order a small quantity of different sized brass and copper rod and strap samples to see what options might work. Some of the online metal shops don't charge a cutting fee for small pieces, so it's worth tracking down one of those.

I opted to go with 1/16" brass round rod for the cage mesh and 1/8" x 1/2" brass strap for the majority of the dress. I also picked up some 1" strap for the belt so there would be a little more substance there. Industrial Metal Supply in LA was kind enough to order a bunch of 1/16" round rod for me, as it wasn't something they generally carry.

At this point, I went back to sketching. Once the materials are settled, it's generally easier to figure out what can and can't happen with the originally conceived idea.

## Step 3: Attaching shiny bits

I played around with the samples quite a bit. Since brass was a new material to me, I spent some time researching its properties and just getting a feel for the metal.

I wanted to make sure that I could attach the 1/16" rod to the 1/2" strap before I got too far down the design road. I asked around and was told that brazing it would probably be the best bet. I tried simply welding the rod to the strap with an oxy-acetylene rig and just made a mess. Regular plumbers solder didn't stick at all. I took a sample of the materials to the welding store and asked the guys there. They set me up with some brazing rod that seemed to do the trick. Seemed is the key word here. I thought I was in the clear and had found something that worked, however, the attachment story does not stop there.

For any larger, structural joints I opted to drill holes and use brass rivets. I picked up some of the old-style rivets that you actually pound out, because they look really amazing when they're placed.

The design ended up working best split into two separate pieces. This would make it possible to actually get it out of my front door (a good thing) and worked as a perfect way to get the person inside of it.

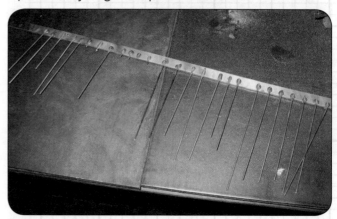

## Step 4: Bending shiny bits

Figuring out the outer shape of the skirt was next, since it seemed like the shape of the whole thing would stem from that.

I worked on measuring and bending a prototype of the belt and outer skeleton. The 1/2" brass strap turned out to be malleable enough to bend by hand with the help of a vice. Hurray! I was very thankful, because I had a ton of bending in my future. I wanted the circumference of the circle to be 16', so worked out the geometry from there [2 * (pi) * radius = (pi) * diameter]. The design morphed slightly and did affect the numbers, but that's at least where it started.

I cut and bent the waist band to try to get an idea of how many vertical lines the skirt would require, then drilled holes to attach pieces so that I could get a decent idea of how it would look.

## Step 5: Cutting, drilling, and bending brassy bits

After a bit of wrangling, I decided upon a swooping, bell-like shape for the skirt. It was inspired by some of the old Victorian birdcages from days of yore. Working from that size, I created the other component—the internal skeleton shape (so that birds would not peck at the wearers legs) and the bottom skeleton pieces so that both sections would (hopefully) meet appropriately.

I then proceeded to cut and drill individual pieces

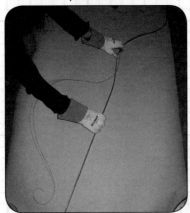

following the pattern. This was a leap of faith—I was counting on the fact that I did the math correctly. Brass is pretty pricey, so messing up on a grand scale wouldn't be cool at all.

I found it very helpful to use a metal punch to mark the spots I needed to drill. The devices are conveniently called 'metal punches' and will save you a lot of frustration by not letting the drill press wander all over the place.

After cutting and drilling the pieces, I used a bench grinder to smooth out the surface on each piece.

Be sure wear safety goggles because your eyes are important! Guaranteed, you're going to need your eyeballs throughout this entire project.

## Step 6: More bending of brassy bits

Thus began many, many days of bending. Though the brass is relatively malleable, getting consistent curves just takes time. Ironically, I am not a patient person. I think (hope) this project taught me in that regard, but it remains to be seen.

So, the great bending phase continued . . . on and on and on and on . . .

It became remarkably apparent that this dress was going to consume A LOT of time.

## Step 7: Still bending shiny bits

And then—huzzah! The bending was complete! Now it was time for hardware and actual attachment. This was exciting because the shape came to life with dimension and for the first time actually felt real. I was thrilled.

## Step 8: Shiny bits with dimension!

It was really rewarding to attach everything and see the shape come to life.

I ended up needing to re-drill a lot of the holes to

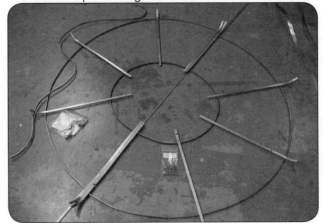

make them slightly larger to compensate for the hardware.

Attempting to drill some of the bent pieces was like playing an unruly game of Twister with the drill press as an opponent. Caution was of primary concern and I used a lot of clamps at some really weird angles to make sure that the ol' drill press and I were on an even playing field.

## Step 9: Brassy floor

After attaching all of the pieces, I measured, cut out, and drilled the pieces that would compose the floor of the cage.

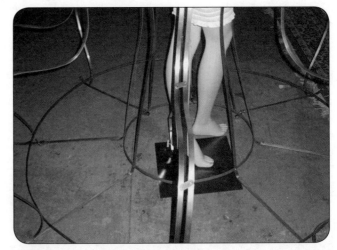

## Step 10: Brassy caster bits

The dress was going to be quite heavy, so I decided to put it on casters. I found some small brass casters online and ordered a few to try them out.

As the dress grew, I kept ordering more and more so that it could actually hold the weight. A total of fourteen casters were used in the piece.

I ended up cutting off the metal attachment piece that came with the caster and using a bolt to attach them to the brass strap.

## Step 11: Hammering brassy bits

I purchased a ton of brass rivets, thinking that I would rivet as much of the dress as possible. That was a mistake on my part, though, because after bending all of those pieces, it was impossible to wrangle them on or around the anvil to hammer appropriately.

I ended up using brass hardware (machine screws and acorn cap nuts) in all the spots I couldn't hammer. Just a good thing to note: riveting large, unruly things doesn't work. Some of the random positions I tried were pretty funny - a third arm would have been really helpful. If anyone has a suggestion as to how to pound rivets into unruly objects, I'd love to know.

## Step 12: Frustrating brassy bits

Once the basic shape was formed, it was time to start bending and placing wire to make the actual cage. I had done some attachment testing earlier to make sure that I would be able to attach the metal properly; however, when it came down to actually doing it on the shape itself, some unforeseen problems arose—it wasn't working at all. Ack!

I tested and tried numerous brazing and soldering combinations in an attempt to find a solution. Alas, nothing was working. It was incredibly frustrating. Finally, a combination of Harris Stay-Clean flux and lead solder heated with a propane torch worked.

Hallelujah! And huge thanks to Syd and Steve for their help in figuring that out.

The successful process was as follows: I clamped the pieces together with C-clamps, then used a paint brush to apply the flux, heated the joints with the propane torch, and applied the 60/40 lead solder.

Be sure that you're working with clean metal. If it's dirty, it just won't bond properly.

Thus began a multiple week adventure of clamping, fluxing, and soldering.

NOTE: Wear a respirator and gloves when dealing with this stuff. Wash your hands often. Lead in the lungs or anywhere on your skin is no good.

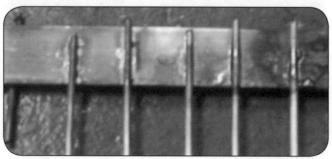

## Step 13: Clamping shiny bits

Truth be known, I had not anticipated having to individually clamp down each of the nearly 2000 attachment points. It was a daunting task, but I had put so much work into it already that I decided to press on.

Finding a solution for clamping was more difficult than it seemed like it should be because the attachment points were so close to each other (15mm apart). I would have loved to have used spring clamps, but the heat from the propane torch was too much for the little guys. The solution ended up being some small 1" C-clamps. I replaced the turning apparatus on each of them with smaller screws since the attachment points were so close.

Ideally, I would have created a jig to make this process easier, however because all of the bends were different, I couldn't think of a jig option that would work. I resigned myself to the fact that I would be spending a lot of time clamping.

## Step 14: Clamp, flux, solder, repeat. Clamp, flux, solder, repeat . . . .

Thus the great soldering marathon began with the outside of the dress. The process was incredibly time consuming, but it was pretty thrilling to see it coming together.

## Step 15: Flip it over, clamp, flux, solder, repeat. Clamp, flux, solder, repeat . . . .

In order to be able to solder the bottom, the dress needed to be flipped over. I rigged up a contraption with a stool, an anvil, and a few zip ties to hold it in place. It was fairly rickety, but did the trick.

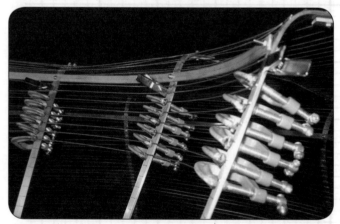

## Step 16: More clamping, fluxing, soldering and repeating . . . .

Then it was time to start the internal cage so that the wearer would be safe from pecking critters.

## Step 17: Then came the tricky part . . . .

Soldering the top of the cage was a real challenge due to the double layers. The heat from the propane torch would separate joints that were already soldered, so I had to clamp down completed joints and try to absorb some of the heat with a wet cloth. It was pretty painstaking and progress was slow.

Many a tiny spring clamp gave its life for this part of the process— the C-clamps were too large to use in the tight areas. The spring clamps just couldn't take the heat, but were thankfully strong enough to temporarily hold down the sections that were catching indirect fire.

## Step 18: And the first half was done!

Brief celebration, then onward to the second half . . .

## Step 19: More clamping, fluxing, soldering and repeating . . . .

Repeat steps 13 through 16. Take lots of breaks so you don't lose your mind.

## Step 20: Voila! The cage portion of the dress is nearly complete!

'Twas a joyous moment indeed.

I recommend grinding off the edges of the wire to get rid of the poke-y bits. 226 individual brass wires circle the entire dress, so there are plenty of sharp pieces worth sanding down.

This is a good time to round up your hardware. I was able to order brass machine screws through smallparts. com for a much better price than I could find them locally. I also found some brass plated magnetic catch strips that I used as attachment pieces for holding the two sides of the dress together.

Casters were placed in their appropriate positions and I went through and made sure all of the hardware was where it needed to be.

## Step 21: Sewing the silky under dress

The dress design morphed quite a bit. I initially had wanted to use pieces of brass in the top section, but everything I tried just plain didn't look right. I opted to go with silk fabric instead and picked up a variety of silk fabric that would complement the brass.

I started by cutting fabric and fitting it to the dress form. For me, a large part of designing with fabric is trial and error. I had picked up a few different variations and hues of silk and wanted to mix them up in an organic way, so I just started cutting and sewing.

The lining of the dress is form fitting and the outer layer of silk is sewn to it by hand. Silk ribbons provide the final touch and wrap around the entire dress.

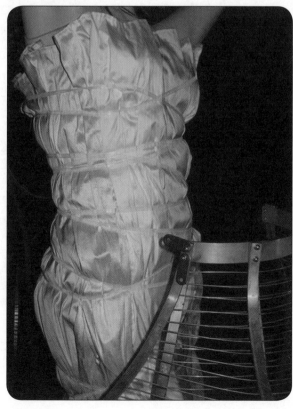

crafts

333

## Step 22: Bejeweling

I wanted to create some jewelry to accent the piece, so tracked down some interesting stones and played around with bending and nesting the wire to create a necklace and bracelets.

## Step 23: Creating shiny accessories

The cage needed perches and a door, so I messed around with different possibilities before deciding how I'd like them to look. I went with pretty simplistic designs for both.

I was exceptionally nervous about cutting the door. I put it off as long as possible. It became *very important* that I had a clean work area and that all my ducks were in a row.

I practiced soldering the brass wire together before doing it in place on the dress. It went fairly smoothly and the door turned out alright, albeit somewhat janky. It was a one-shot thing, so I am thankful that it turned out decently.

With the door in place, the bird cage is officially fully functional!

I'm thrilled to have found a place that will rent doves to put in it for the first show.

## Step 24: Add birdy bits

I really, really, really want to put chickens in the dress at some point, but for the first show, it's going to have four doves flying around in it. I can't wait :)

## Step 25: Putting it all together

Suzan and Kelly Jones were kind enough to photograph the dress.

Emmeline Chang looked amazing in it.

Juli Gudmundson handled hair and makeup and created the beautiful hairpieces for it.

Many thanks to all involved with the final shoot. It was so wonderful to see it come together.

crafts

# Tatted Mask

## By TotusMel
(http://www.instructables.com/id/Tatted-Mask-1/)

My tatted mask is made with cotton thread, Swarovski crystals, and a few small pieces of wire. You will need an intermediate to advanced knowledge of needle or shuttle tatting to complete this project, including split rings, josephine knots, and adding beads to tatting.

This project uses size 10 crochet cotton thread, size 5 tatting needle (or shuttle), 45 3mm/4mm Swarovski crystals, 1 piece of wire at 6.5cm and 2 pieces at 17.5cm, jewelry pliers, scissors, steel crochet hook (optional for joins).

Happy tatting!

## Step 1: Wire eyes

Using your own eyes as a guide form an almond shape with the 17.5mm wire. Fold over at the corner and use the pliers to tighten down. You may cut off excess wire if desired, but it's not necessary as the wire will be covered by thread in the last step.

## Step 2: Center medallion

Center: 8 picots(p) separated(sep) by 2 double stitches(ds), tie, cut, and hide ends.

Outside: ring(r) 8ds join to center picot(+) 8ds close(cl) reverse work(rw), r 4ds 1p 3ds 1p 1ds cl do not reverse(dnr), r 1ds+3ds 1p 3ds 1p 1ds, Split ring(sr) 1ds+3ds/4ds cl rw.

Continue in this way around the center ring joining the top picots of the 2nd and 4th clovers to the eye wires. Join the 8th clover to the first by the side picots.

## Step 3: Side medallions

Make 2 side medallions. First load 6 beads onto the thread for each medallion using a beading needle. Make the medallion in the same manner as the center medal-

lion, except there are only 6 clovers around leaving 2 free picots on the center ring. Add beads to the top picot of each clover as you tat.

Set these aside and they will be joined during the next step.

## Step 4: 1st round

Starting at the top right of the center medallion:

r 3ds join to top picot of clover 3ds join to wire 3ds 1p 3ds cl rw, chain(ch) 6ds 1p 3ds 1p 3ds 1p 6ds cl rw, 3ds+3ds+3ds 1p 3ds cl rw, ch 6ds 1p 3ds 1p 3ds 1p 6ds cl rw, r 3ds+3ds+3ds 1p 3ds cl rw, ch6 cl rw, r 3ds+3ds+3ds 1p 3ds cl rw, 6ds 1p 3ds 1p 3ds join to side picot of side medallion 6ds cl rw, r 3ds 1p 3ds+3ds+3ds cl rw, ch6 cl dnr, r 4ds join to 1st free picot of the center ring of the side medallion 2ds join to next picot 4ds cl dnr, ch6.

Continue around mirroring the top edge, after last ring: ch6 cl rw, r 3ds+3ds+3ds 1p 3ds cl rw, ch 5ds 1p 3ds 1p 3ds 1p 5ds, r 3ds 1p 3ds 1p 3ds 1p 3ds cl rw, ch 5ds 1p 3ds 1p 3ds 1p 5ds cl rw, r 3ds 1p 3ds+3ds 1p 3ds cl rw.

Continue around the other eye in the same manner .

## Step 5: 2nd round top

First load 21 beads onto the thread.

Begin at the left side of mask:

3ds 1p 3ds join to first empty chain (see photo) 3ds 1p 3ds cl rw, ch 5ds+3ds 1p 3ds+6ds cl rw, r 3ds+3ds 1p 3ds cl rw, ch 6ds1p 3ds 1p 3ds 1p 6ds cl rw, r 3ds+3ds+3ds 1p 3ds cl rw, ch 6ds cl rw, r 3ds 1p 3ds+3ds 1p 3ds cl rw, ch 6ds 1p 3ds 1p 3ds 1p 6ds cl rw, 3ds+3ds+3ds+3ds cl rw, ch 6ds cl rw, 3ds 1p 3ds join in between clovers 3ds 1p 3ds cl rw, ch 6ds 1p 3ds 1p 3ds 1p 6ds cl rw, r 3ds 1p 3ds join to top clover 3ds 1p 3ds cl rw, r 4ds 1p 4ds cl rw.

Continue the second side as a mirror to the first.

## Step 6: 2nd row bottom

First load 12 beads onto the thread for the bottom edge.

Make a chain of 6 clovers, the same as the ones on the medallions, across each side of the bottom, attaching where shown in the photos and adding beads to the top picot.

## Step 7: Floating rings

You will need to make two rings to finish the nose portion. The rings are 4 picots separated by 3ds attached by side picots.

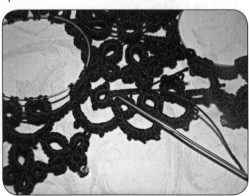

## Step 8: Nose Wire

Take the small piece of wire and weave into the back of the mask as shown. Fold over and attach to the eye wires. Make sure to stretch the lace a bit before attaching to give enough space to bend the wire over your nose.

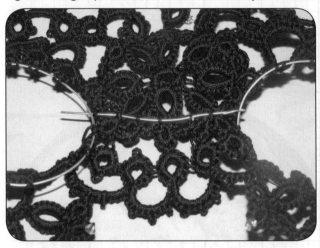

## Step 9: Finishing

This is perhaps the most time consuming step of the mask. Cut a long piece of thread and, using the tatting needle, knot the thread over the wire repeatedly as a Josephine knot or first part of the double stitch. Use the needle to go through the edge of the rings where it looks appropriate.

You will need to go around both eyes as well as wrap the nose wire to hide as much of the metal as possible.

You will need to iron the mask with steam, taking care to lay all the rings and chains down well. You may use a fabric stiffener to help the mask stand up. Use a long ribbon to thread through the side medallions to wear the mask. Youmay want to try the ribbon in several places to find your perfect fit and press the wire to your face to shape it.

# DIY Cufflinks
## By Mrballeng
(http://www.instructables.com/id/DIY-Cuff-Links/)

What better way to show a brother you care about them by making custom cufflinks for each of his eight groomsmen. Each will receive cufflinks unique to their personality. No special tools are required and materials are well within reason.

So to get started, this is how to make the backings.

## Step 1: Rivets repurposed

The backings are made out of clothing rivets. Each is composed of 3 pieces, the button side, the anchor side, and a short section of coat hanger wire to join them. Solder keeps it all together. I got these and all my other materials at the hardware store.

Now that we know how to make the backings, let's move on to the business side of the cuff links.

## Step 2: One likes Rasta music
Materials
- 16 gage steel wire
- 22 gage sheet metal
- Polymer clay

I made these cuff links by taking wire and shaping a square and a spiral. I then soldered them onto a piece of sheet metal. Next I filed the wire flat and polished it. I filled the recesses with polymer clay the same colors as Rasta and baked it in the oven.

## Step 3: Another likes his Corvette
Materials
- 22 gage sheet metal
- 18 gage brass

I cut a Chevy symbol out of brass and chamfered the edges with a file. I then soldered it on to a piece of sheet

metal, cut out the excess, and continued to file in the Chevy shape.

crafts

### Step 4: Another likes Dasani Water
**Materials**
- 3/8 carriage bolt
- Photo paper

This I made by turning a bolt in my drill press and filing until it looked like a bottle. I used a printed bottle for size reference. After I polished it I printed out the label on photo paper and super glued it on. I used an engraver to texture the cap.

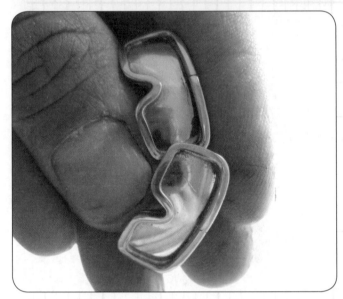

### Step 5: Another likes dirt bikes and snow boarding
**Materials**
- 16 gage wire
- 18 gage brass

First I formed the goggle frame with pliers. I then made it into a curved shape by striking it with the head of a carriage bolt. I used the same process to dome out a piece of brass. I then soldered them together and filed the wire flat. A small piece of brass covers the seam to the wire.

### Step 6: Another likes firearms
**Materials**
- Shell casings
- Coat hanger

To make these I pressed shell casings on a socket bit and then used a pipe cutter to cut the primer section off. I then filed the backs flat and soldered them together with a piece of curved coat hanger wire. The lettering is filled in with paint pen. The photos are from ".223 ammo pin" but the idea is the same.

crafts

I made these basketballs by embossing pennies with paperclips. The paper clips were shaped to match the curves of a basket ball and them hammered onto the pennies. The relief lines are filled with paint pen.

## Step 7: Another likes DJ Tiesto
Material
- 2 nickels
- DVDR compact disk
- Photo paper
- Hot glue

I first printed out the symbol. Then I separated the layers to a DVDR and removed the silvering with packing tape. I placed some hot glue on a piece of DVDR, placed the paper, added more glue, and then pushed on another piece of DVDR. I double stick taped the piece onto a socket bit and used 100 grit sand paper and a razor blade to shave it to size while spinning it in my drill press. I used epoxy putty to set in to the nickels, which are made the same way as in "vintage locket" and "polished granite pendant." At the right angle the cuff links are iridescent.

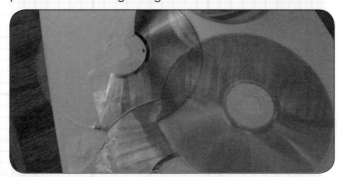

## Step 8: Another likes basketball
Materials
- 2 pennies pre-1983
- Paper clips for embossing

## Step 9: Another likes Xbox
Materials
- 2 nickels
- Polymer clay

I hammered out the detail on two nickels and super glued the photo image of Xbox controllers onto them. I then used a center punch to mark where I would drill. I drilled out the holes, and shaped and polished the controllers with rotary bits. I filled in the holed with polymer clay and baked them.

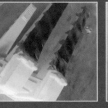

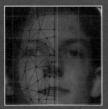

# costumes

Fully Functional Camera
Costume

Full-Size Power Loader
Costume from Aliens

Inspector Gadget Costume
with Motorized Helicopter

[Real Life] Big Head Mode

Werewolf Costume

Can Suit

Catahedron Costume

The Ultimate T-Rex Costume

Whether it's for Halloween, fancy dress parties, Burning Man, or just to scare the neighborhood kids, people who make their own costumes consistently produce some of the most impressive and extraordinary creative work. The secret lies in completely transforming oneself into the new costume identity, so much so, that everyone around you believes what they're seeing is real, even if it is something as wild and crazy as a 14-foot T-Rex skeleton walking around the local downtown shopping district. If the costume is truly convincing, there's almost no limit to the awe that it can produce.

As children, many people dress up at one time or another. Limited by their parents' closets and a still-developing body simply too small to carry the heavy weight of a Full Size Power Loader costume from the movie Aliens, many kids never get to wear the costume of their dreams. It's important to remember that dressing up in costume isn't just for young people going trick or treating, and that as adults, equipped with tools, greater resources, and healthy imaginations, there's no limit to the fun we can have, not to mention how much easier it will be to carry the heavy support structures when you finally actualize your Alien Loader.

# Fully Functional Camera Costume

By tylercard
(http://www.instructables.com/id/FULLY-FUNC-
TIONAL-Camera-Costume/

For Halloween 2011, I made a fully functional DSLR camera costume. That's right, it really takes pictures, and comes complete with LCD display, pop-up flash, and shutter release button. I built this entire costume in one week, for only $35 dollars (excluding the cost of the camera equipment and laptop), with materials located at any local hardware store.

This instructable contains detailed instructions on exactly how I made mine. With some simple modifications, anyone can make their own with any digital camera and laptop.

Seen on The Discovery Channel, Yahoo! News, Huff-ingtonPost, Gizmodo, Gizmag, Mashable, BuzzFeed, WINS.failblog, DPReview, PopPhoto, Wired, LaughingSquid, The Metro, PetaPixel, Geekologie, and many more.

## HERE'S WHAT YOU'LL NEED:

For the body/structure:

- Black duct tape
- Black spray paint (semi-gloss)
- Plexiglass (16"x18")
- Window fogging spray
- Glue/spray-tack
- 5 gallon bucket with lid
- Utility knife
- Scissors

To make it work:

- Any DSLR*
- Any External flash
- Hot-shoe flash extension cord
- Remote shutter release button (wireless or not)
- A laptop (that you don't mind disassembling)

*any digital camera can be used, but may not be capable of having the external flash, and shutter release button features.

## Step 1: Construct the main body

I started by making a rectangular box with no top or bottom, that fit my body (shoulder width and body depth is the main measurements you'll need, but remained proportional to the dimensions of my camera. Remember that you'll need room inside for the computer body too. I put two small squares of cardboard on both the left and right side, top and bottom, to make sure the box stayed rigid and square. From this, I added the the flash base/viewfinder part, and the angled top on each side. It takes a little measuring, some simple multiplication, and trial-and error. If you're not comfortable making some of the angled contours, don't worry, just stick to basic geometry like squares and rectangles, and it will still look great, and still function the same.

For this step you will need:
- Cardboard
- Duct tape
- Utility knife
- Scissors

Tips:
- Use a straight-edge and utility knife to cut the cardboard.
- For the round pieces, use scissors.
- Tape both sides of every joint. You'll need the strength or the costume will fall apart! USE GORILLA-TAPE brand duct tape. It is MUCH more durable than any other brand I could find, and only slightly more expensive.
- Save the painting until the very last step, or your tape won't stick.
- The more precise your measurements are, the easier the costume is to make, and the stronger the structure will be, so measure twice and cut carefully.

costumes

## Step 2: Construct the lens-mount/flash-mount

There will be a lot of pressure on the joint where your lens (bucket) attaches to the main body of the camera. The weight of the bucket, and your camera/tripod inside,will create a lot of leverage pressure on the joint. What I did was made a double-layer mount to eliminate the pressure from being held by only one joint. If you don't understand what I mean, that circular piece of cardboard on the front of the main rectangular body is the second mount. The bucket mounts to the rectangular piece, and a ring cardboard around the bucket is taped to this extension so the pressure of the bucket isn't held just by the joint of rectangular body.

You will need:
- More cardboard
- More tape
- Compass/circular object to cut cardboard ring
   Note: Don't mount the bucket yet/flash assembly yet! It will make installing the monitor very difficult.

## Step 3: Unhinge laptop screen

Warning: Only proceed with this step if you are comfortable with possibly causing irreversible damage to your laptop!

To make the LCD screen, I simply unhinged my laptop screen, and flipped it around backwards, so the screen shows on the outside when the laptop is "closed." I also removed the keyboard so no keys would accidentally be pressed (since the body of the computer is mounted directly behind your back, inside the costume.)

The position/length of your monitor cable (the part that plugs into the computer body) might make mounting difficult. Luckily for me, I was able to align the screen and body almost perfectly after it was flipped.

For this step, you will need:
- A small screw-driver
- Parental help/permission

Warning: the monitor cable can be quite delicate, so be careful not to pull on the cables too much, especially near the socket end. The small wires/pins can easily be bent and/or pulled out, and render the screen useless.

## Step 4: Mount the LCD display

Your monitor should be unplugged and separated from the computer body for this part. You do not want the screen to move around at all, to prevent the cable from being pulled out/damaged. I taped the monitor down to the body of the costume, and built a small cardboard housing around it. This cleans up the look and provides additional support. The tape alone may not hold the weight of the screen. I cut a small hole in the body of the costume so that the cable could easily run through to the computer (which will be mounted inside the costume.)

For this step, you will need:
- More cardboard
- More duct tape
   Warning: Duct tape and duct tape residue on the monitor/monitor housing of your laptop may be very difficult to remove.

## Step 5: Mount the lens (bucket)

First of all, remove the metal handle on the bucket, if it has one. Next, you need to cut the bottom out of the bucket. I used a utility knife, but a saw would be faster and easier.

WARNING: BE VERY CAREFUL CUTTING THROUGH THE PLASTIC WITH A UTILITY KNIFE, AS IT CAN BE DIFFICULT AND TENDS TO SLIP.

I left a small ¼" lip around the edge, again, to help prevent pressure on the joints.

As I mentioned in Step 2, you want to reinforce the bucket as well as possible, so be sure to tape both the inside and outside of each joint. Any place that the bucket touches the cardboard, should be taped.

Note: I did not tape the side of the ring that is visible on the outside of the camera, to make it look cleaner, but doing so will prevent the lens from drooping over time. I also mounted the bucket before the flash-assembly was put on, but these pictures were taken after.

For this step, you will need:
- More tape
- A utility knife/saws-all to cut the bottom from the bucket

**Tip:**
- Use a black bucket if you can find one. I used this orange one from Home Depot because it was only $2, but scratches are very noticeable, and the paint scratches easily on the plastic bucket.

## Step 6: Create the flash assembly

For this step, I started by making the sides first, then the long back. Start with two long pieces of cardboard for the sides, hold one up at the approximate angle it will be secured, and then draw your detailed cuts, such as the curves at the bottom and top.

**Sides:**

I made my sides hollow so the flash extension cord could be hidden inside. This also helps hold the whole thing up. Depending on your height, you may have to adjust your measurements and try a few times to make sure the opening for your head is large enough. I was lucky and got it right on the first try.

**Flash compartment:**

Make a rectangle box, with no front or back, to fit inside the sides. Cut an angle on both sides so that the box sits level when it's mounted in the angled sides. I secured this piece to the top so it can be hinged open to access the flash without having to remove the plexiglass front. This is useful for changing batteries/turning the flash on/off and hooking up the extension cord.

Next, line the insides of the compartment with tin foil, so when the flash goes off, the light is efficiently bounced out.

**Diffuser:**

Cut a rectangular piece of Plexiglas to fit the front of the flash compartment. Using window frosting spray, coat one side evenly. This will not only help hide your actual flash that will be mounted inside, but acts as a diffuser to soften the light/radiate the light evenly. When you mount the plexiglass, mount the coated side facing out, for the best results.

For this step, you will need:
- Cardboard
- Tape
- Plexiglass
- Plexiglass cutter
- Window frosting spray
- Tin foil

Note: A relief cut will have to be cut in the flash compartment, for the flash cord.

**Tip:**
- Don't mount your flash diffuser until you paint the costume.

## Step 7: PAINT!

It's finally time to paint everything. Be sure to cover up your LCD display!

Give the whole thing a few good coats, especially on the bucket. The paint tends to scratch easily on the plastic. Coat the inside of the bucket too.

**Tips:**
- Do not use flat black. It will show dirt, finger prints, and look dull. Also, the shiny duct tape will stand out badly.
- I found a semi-gloss that looks most like the finish on the actual camera.

## Step 8: Wire it up

All that is left to do is wire up everything, which is not as difficult as you might think.

**Shutter release:**

Mount your shutter release button inside the costume where the shutter button will be. Cut a hole over the button so that when you press down on the costume's button, the shutter button is clicked. You'll have to use a lot of tape, and/or build a little shelf for it to sit on, to keep it from coming loose when it is pressed. Run the wire through the back of the bucket, to the inside of the camera.

**Flash:**

Run your flash extension cord up through one of the hollow sides of the flash assembly. Mount your flash on the back, as far from the diffuser as possible for the best possible diffusion of light. Tape the cord along the way, so the tension of the cord doesn't move your camera off-center once it is mounted inside the bucket. You want some slack inside the bucket.

**USB:**

Run your USB through the back of the bucket, inside the costume, around to the back. This might best be done after the computer is installed on the inside, but you should wait until the very last step to install the computer body, because you don't want to risk the weight of it pulling too much on the monitor cable.

**To install the laptop body:**

Install the body of the laptop vertically on the inside of the costume, directly behind the LCD screen, but ensure that the screen cable will reach correctly. Plug the laptop screen back in, and tape the computer body up VERY HEAVILY. There won't be much holding the computer in the compartment, other than the bottom edge of the costume, the tape, and your body pressed against it. You do not want the computer to come loose,

because if it comes loose, the monitor cable can break, and if it comes really loose, it can fall out completely. Be sure to cut holes around the fan units and leave them uncovered from tape. Also, make sure you leave clearance for your USB, and power cable.

**Mount the camera:**

I used a small tripod to mount my camera inside the bucket. This kept the camera lens near the middle of the costume lens, to prevent the edges of the bucket from showing in the photos, and also provided a solid base for the camera, so it wouldn't twist/tilt after it was installed. I just glued and taped the legs of the tripod down to the inside of the bucket.

Be sure to mount it far enough inside the bucket that your camera lens doesn't touch the costume's plexiglass lens when it rotates during auto-focus. Be sure not to mount it too far in though, or you'll see the edges of your bucket in the photo.

**For this step, you will need:**

- Lots of tape
- Glue (optional)
- Hot-shoe extension cord
- Remote shutter release button
- USB cord.
- Laptop Body

## Step 9: Details

You can find vector logos for different cameras online. If you print out these logos onto paper, you can glue them onto your costume with glue or sprayable tack. This will look a lot cleaner than painting them on, but if you don't have the option, paint works too. I used a vector for my logos, and I took a picture of my selector dial so I wouldn't have to bother with painting the detail of that, but for the small buttons, I just used paint.

**Lens Cap**

Paint your bucket lid black, attach your Logo, and use a black shoe-lace or string and tie it so it dangles from the end of your lens. This is a nice touch that people really seem to enjoy.

**Plexiglass Lens**

Make your plexiglass lens by cutting a circular piece of plexiglass slightly smaller than the inside diameter of your bucket. You will want this to be very snug, so you don't have to tape it in. Accessing the camera from the back of the bucket (through the inside of the costume) is very difficult, so you will want to make this piece removable. This was the most difficult part for me, because I didn't have the proper tools.

After you get your piece to fit properly, cut a thin ring of cardboard to fit on the very edge of the plexiglass. Paint the cardboard ring black, then use glue or tack to fasten it down to the plexiglass.

**Tips:**

- Pad the shoulders of the costume—the first night I wore this costume, my shoulders were bruised from

costumes

the places the vertical pieces of cardboard rested. The costume will weigh about 20-30 lbs by the time you're finished, so having padding on your shoulders will make it much more comfortable. I used some thick bubble wrap, and that worked well.

- Don't use real companies' logos—you will have to get permission from them to use them if you plan to use the costume to make money in any sort of way.
- Make a compartment inside—I made a compartment on the inner side of my costume to hold things like my USB mouse (which you will need unless your mouse pad is accessible), a roll of tape for spot-repairs, a black marker for touch ups, extra batteries, and whatever else you might need on the fly.

## Step 10: Make the pictures show on the LCD

This is the part of the costume that most people who inquire are curious/stumped about, but it is not difficult at all.

Since your camera is hooked via USB to your computer, you simply need to open the drive for your camera as "explore" and go into the folder that contains all the images on your camera's SD card. As you take photos, they will automatically load into this folder. You can then simply click on the first photo, and play them as a slideshow in full-screen mode.

There is also a program called "Camera Control Pro 2" for Nikon that will allow the pictures to be instantly viewed in full-screen mode on your computer. I experienced glitches with this program for my camera, so I ended up just going the slide-show route. Most people find it a little cooler when the picture shows instantly, so they can instantly see how their picture turned out, but using the slideshow feature works well and is very entertaining too.

## Step 11: Put it on, and click away!

You're ready to start taking pictures!

Get out there and click away. Remember to refresh your slideshow if you go that route. It's best to have a friend there to help you with that so you don't have to take your costume off all the time. Also, occasionally check to make sure your photos are turning out correctly.

### EXTRA TIPS:

- Use a wide-angle lens if you have one. It makes framing the pictures a lot easier, because it is hard to aim the costume just right. With the wide-angle, there is a better chance you will get your subject in the frame. The photos can then be cropped down later.
- If you use the costume in a really hot environment, your actual camera may fog up, making messy/unusable pictures, and disable your auto-focus. You may have to remove the plexiglass lens to solve this problem.

## How can I make a costume like this without a DSLR?

- Any digital camera can be used to make a costume that will take pictures. If you don't have the ability to use a remote shutter release, you might just have to keep one arm inside the costume and use the shutter button manually.
- If your costume doesn't have a hot-shoe for an external flash, that's okay too. You can use your camera's built-in flash. Just mount the camera near the end of the costume lens so the flash can work properly, and don't use plexiglass over the end of the costume lens, as it will reflect the flash back to the camera and the pictures won't turn out.
- Any laptop or tablet PC can be used with any DSLR. The photos on any digital camera should be accessible on the computer, regardless.

# Full-Size Power Loader Costume from Aliens

By Alex Walton (alexthemoviegeek)
(http://www.instructables.com/id/Life-Size-Power-Loader-Costume-from-Aliens/)

Shortly after I started making my life-size Alien Queen statue (http://www.instructables.com/id/Life-Size-Alien-Queen-Statue-from-Aliens/), I began to wonder if it would be possible to make a Power Loader to go along with it

Before we get into this, I'll say that I borrowed some ideas from flaming_pele!'s Power Loader costume: http://www.instructables.com/id/Aliens-Powerloader-Halloween-Costume-1/. I will give him credit where it is due along the way.

There have been many Power Loader costumes before, but this Instructable will show how I made mine on a modest budget in a pretty short time.

## Step 1: Inspiration and goals

At one point or another, I remember having seen all of the Alien movies in my youth. I'd always remembered the xenomorphs, but specifically the Alien Queen, and the awesome fight between her and Ripley in the Power Loader. As the the beginning of the school semester neared, I wanted to make something really cool to finish off the summer break. I made the Alien Queen in the first 2 weeks of August. Then I figured with the last few weeks I could make a Power Loader as well, using a lot of the same cheap and lightweight materials that I used for the Queen (mainly foam boards, hot glue, and spray paint). I was titillated at the idea that I could be the only person

who had ever made a life-size Power Loader and Alien Queen. Yes, I am truly a geek.

Shortly before beginning construction, I looked around to see what other Power Loader costumes had been made before. There were many awesome ones on YouTube. And, of course, I saw flaming_pele!'s cool one on here. After looking at these previous attempts, I made observations and decided on some goals that I wanted to achieve in making my own:

First, I wanted mine to be truly life-sized. A lot of other Power Loaders were slightly scaled down, and the foot stilts especially weren't as tall. That's completely understandable, especially in terms of balance and movement. But I wanted mine to be the same size and proportions as the original. I also wanted it to be screen-accurate on all other details. I wanted the exact same shapes, colors, and structures that the original had. I wanted it to match it as closely as possible in all physical details. If I was going to bother making a Power Loader at all, I wanted it to be the Power Loader. All or nothing. And, of course, I wanted mine to be practical. I wanted to be able to walk in it and move the arms, all with a reasonably stable balance and control. I'm not mechanically inclined enough to have figured out a way to make the pincers move, but other than that, I wanted joints to be articulated, complete with pumping hydraulic cylinders.

And finally, for the ultimate challenge, I wanted my Power Loader to have two qualities, when compared to other attempts: made cheaper and easier. Most other attempts didn't have any budget estimate, so I had to figure the always-assumed standard of spending as little as possible. But I also wanted this to be made quickly. Other attempts had been made over the course of several weeks, even months. I wanted mine done by the first week of school (beginning construction in mid-August). In the end, I wanted the best of all categories: cheap, quick, functional, and accurate. I then began to make the machine.

Good research and reference was critical. I used the Sideshow Diorama of the Power Loader as a constant template, taking precise measurements and scaling them up 8 times to be full sized. I also went through the movie and took screen-caps from its featured scenes, and also gathered behind-the-scenes images. It's always fun to understand how the original was made.

## Step 2: Materials and cost

Foam boards, which form the basis of the suit, have been a staple of many of my projects. They're light-weight, strong, smooth, and easy to work with, when compared to something like cardboard. I had seen them at craft stores before for about $3 per 20 in by 30 in sheet, but I also found them at a local dollar store. Great catch.

Wal-Mart was great for glue, tape, and spray paint. Lowe's was good for the critical PVC pieces. Other parts were found either at thrift stores or craft stores, save for a few parts ordered from eBay. A rough budget estimate on the materials of the costume:

- Foam Boards (60) - $60
- Racing Harness - $39
- Revolving Amber Light - $31
- PVC Pipe and Connectors - $30
- Spray Paint - $21
- Hoses, Cables, and Wires - $21
- Hot Glue Sticks, Foamie Sheets, Aluminum Tape, Metal Grate - $23

A grand total of about $225. All things considered, a pretty modest budget for a full sized, accurate and functional costume like this. As you can see, about $70 went into the light and harness, which, in order to make them as accurate and functional as possible, I had to order specific parts off of eBay. High quality will cost you, but it does add great touches to the finished product. If one wanted to, they could probably make a Power Loader (or similar costume) with basic detail and function for about half the cost.

## Step 3: Foam board body pieces

This is where most of the time gets devoted to a project like this: cutting and gluing together pieces of foam boards. There's not much to explain. I simply measured out specific proportions from my reference statue and scaled them up. Drew the outlines on the foam boards and cut them out. Hot glued it all together. It's pretty simple, it just takes a lot of time. Adding all manner of smaller details also takes a lot of extra time, like the letters on the arms and legs. Thin cardboard, like cereal and soda boxes, also comes in handy for more specific details. Containers that were already cylindrical, like Pringles cans and oatmeal containers, are also very useful.

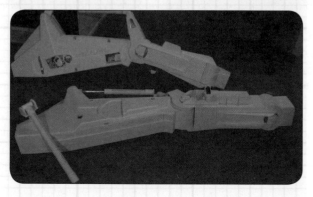

## Step 4: Stilts and cage

Two-foot tall stilts need to be very specific. I learned that first-hand. I went to my dad's garage where he had plenty of spare wood. I made my own design out of whatever pieces I could find. I ended up having to use an air-powered nail gun to secure the pieces of wood together. I could then build up the foam board pieces around the stilts.

The cage was also a challenge. I'd seen other Power Loader costumes that used connected pieces of PVC pipe, but the problem with that was you could tell it was just pieces of PVC pipe, instead of a single piece of welded metal. I decided to used 1" PVC pipes and 3/4" connectors, both with an outer diameter of 1.25", so that they'd have a singular diameter and look like a solid piece. I had to add some small wooden dowel pieces and hot glue to help strengthen the connections.

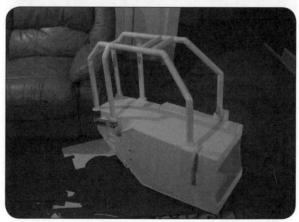

## Step 5: Joints and hydraulic cylinders

PVC pipe is like duct-tape; it has a million uses. For the joints, I would cut a hole through the area when I wanted the rod to go through. After sliding the PVC pipe through the hole, I glued the ends of the pipe onto the other parts of the costume and secured the joint, able to swing freely. The elbows, knees, and ankles were all made in this way.

**347**

The shoulders simply had a T connector that I could attach to PVC pipe that was sticking out of the shoulders of the arms (free to rotate). The hips had a piece of PVC pipe that could attach to a connector piece on the upper legs (this proved difficult, more on that later). The top piece of the cage and headpiece was attached to the torso with wooden dowels aligned in joint holes. The pincers attached to the forearms with a PVC pipe connector.

Hydraulic cylinders were basically a piece of wooden dowel covered with aluminum tape (idea credited to flaming_pele!), that could slide in and out of a larger piece of PVC pipe. Making these light enough and aligned well enough to actually "pump" in and out during motion was difficult.

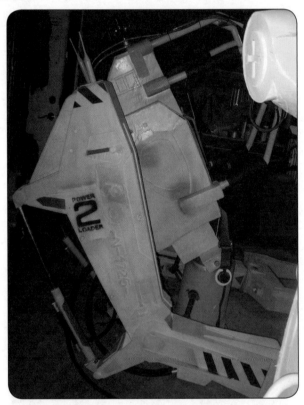

## Step 6: Paint and other details

Painting was pretty straightforward, just a bunch of yellow spray paint. Then the black stripes would be made with the help of painter's tape masking out striped areas and then spraying black on top. Decals on the sides of the arms and legs were made in a similar manner; I printed out images and then cut out the symbols or text and then spray painted to add them on.

For a spinning amber warning light on the top, I found one that was for parties that plugged into a wall outlet, and also happened to be just the right shape. The harness on the torso turned out to be pretty much the same thing as a 4-point racing harness (knowledge discovered from flaming_pele!). I found one in the right color on eBay, and then added a label on the buckle to match the one seen in the movie. I added wires onto the feet that go from the cylinders to the legs. I added blue and red wires

that go from the torch along the cage, complete with cable ties. The wire mesh on the top of the roll cage was a metal grate I found at Lowe's. I made the back and leg padding out of black foam board and added "cushion" pieces, cut out of foamy sheets. I also made the keypad on the left arm with the foamy sheets. I added some phone cords onto the handles to attach to the arms.

## Step 7: Suiting up

The process of getting the whole thing put together is very meticulous. I'd start with the torso and arms sitting on top of a bucket and the tail sitting on the floor. After attaching the arms, I'd then slip into the cage from the underside and get my torso buckled up in the harness. I could then stand up and walk.

Next was getting onto the stilts. I'd have to step on a bucket in front of the legs and then step backward onto the stilts. I had to bend over forward while stepping up so that the tail didn't hit the legs (you can see this process in the video on the intro page). After that, I could have an extra person attach the legs to the torso, slip my toes into the straps, and walk around. The connection of the legs to the torso wasn't perfect, so I ended up using some bungee cords to keep the upper legs stable for the first suiting up. Have an extra person plug in the revolving light, and voila, I was in the Power Loader.

The final product is about 9 feet tall. The torso weighs 20 pounds, the legs 10 pounds each, and the arms 5 pounds each, for a total of 50 pounds.

As for being able to move around in the thing, well, I was able to "walk" in it. The steps were pretty small, but I could lift my feet off of the ground and take a step. The arms were hard to balance (the size of the pincers made them very front-heavy), but I was surprised at how high I could lift them. I could get the pincers as high or higher than my head. The handles had to be reinforced to make sure the PVC pieces didn't just slip out of the connector when I lifted the arms.

Also, I had planned to have the cables that ran from the arms, hydraulic cylinders, and other places and onto the tail (I made them out of soaker hose), but they weren't flexible or long enough to be able to work with the practical movements.

pressure on the joints. Also be aware that if you leave them in the sun, the glue can heat up again and become weak.

- When attaching a PVC pipe or dowel to somewhere where it will take the burden of weight, it needs to be on VERY securely. Don't be afraid to add extra pieces of foam board and hot-glue the crap out of it, or whatever you need to do, to make it stable.

- I might have put the handles on the forearms further down on the arms. Because of how high they are, I can't really bend the elbow joints, and it displaces the weight in a very uncomfortable way, making them awkward to move.

- The cage could have been stronger and lighter. It was the hardest part of suiting up; slipping into it without putting too much pressure on a spot and breaking it.

- Also, it should go without saying, but if you're going to make 2 foot tall stilts, make them strong. A slip-up there could be pretty devastating to you or your project. If you have to, sacrifice some height to make them more stable.

- The little details can make a huge difference. It's a great challenge to make something look just like the original. That's my purpose in being a geek and trying to replicate movie-magic. It's frustrating to add details that take tedious, time-consuming work (details that most people won't even notice), but it's definitely worth it in the end.

Good luck to any and all who might attempt a similar project. Or, at the very least, I hope you enjoyed this look into my crazy project.

## Step 8: Final thoughts and advice

Overall, I would have liked it to have been easier to move around in, but other than that, I was able to call my Power Loader a success. I'd done it; it was made in 2 weeks even, for less than $250, and I could walk in it, and it was pretty darn accurate.

If anyone else is attempting to make one of their own, or anything similar, I give these points of advice, things that could be improved, and problems that could be avoided:

- Make it as cheap as you can. You don't have to have a practical rotating light or functioning harness. If you have the money, great, but just know if you do want them to be that accurate, it's going to cost you.

- I definitely should have used thinner and lighter PVC pipe. Most hardware stores will have schedule 40 and schedule 80, try to get schedule 40.

- Make sure joints are secure. If you're using hot glue, make sure it's completely dry before you try to put any

# Inspector Gadget Costume with Motorized Helicopter

By Laura Skelton (prixprix)
(http://www.instructables.com/id/Inspector-Gadget-Costume-with-Motorized-Helicopter/)

Go go gadget COPTER!

This moving Halloween costume was made almost entirely from recycled and thrifted materials. It was a serious crowd-pleaser— I walked into a bar and everyone started chanting "Go Go Gadget" until I switched on the helicopter and the entire bar started cheering. You too can be this awesome!

I started collecting materials for this costume the weekend before Halloween. It probably took 8-12 hours to construct, over the course of a few days as the spray paint needs to dry overnight.

## Step 1: Tools and materials

To make this costume, you need:
Thrifted, found or borrowed:

- A gray or beige trench coat
- A blue necktie
- A white collared shirt
- Blue pants (I wore jeans)
- Mens' dress shoes (it looks properly cartoonish if they are a bit too big)
- Brown gloves (I wore my work gloves)

Thrifted:
(These will get destroyed, so don't borrow them)
- A classic fedora (~$3-$8) (If you can't thrift it, get a cheap foam one from a costume shop.) Brown, gray or beige will look gadget-astic.
- A 1980s-era battery operated shoe polisher with detachable heads (~$3)
- (check on ebay if you can't thrift it)
- Two old bike grips (see if a local bike shop has some they don't want)

From the hardware store:
- Two 3' long, 1/2" diameter aluminum rods (~$8 each)
- Glossy orange spray paint (~$5-7)
- White universal primer spray paint (~$5-7)
- A tiny amount of gray or silver universal spray paint (optional)
- Three wooden paint stir sticks
- A screw (I used a random drywall screw I had around)
- A small electrical flip switch ($3)
- 8 feet of relatively thin, flexible copper insulated electrical wire (~$2)
- A roll of electrical tape ($1)

From the recycling bin:
- A cardboard box about 16" long
- An empty cereal box
- Two empty plastic 500-yard thread spools
- Three empty jars or oatmeal tins with lids
- A wire twist tie

From a craft store or your stash:
- Around a 20"x20" piece of black faux fur ($1)
- A small sheet of sticky-back felt ($.50)
- A bunch of hot glue sticks
- A tube of strong glue (like e6000)
- Four AA batteries (for the shoe polisher)

Tools:
- Needle-nose pliers/wire cutters
- A tiny Phillips-head screwdriver (you can find it at a hobby shop)
- A regular-sized screwdriver
- A hot glue gun
- A dremel tool
- Structured Tooth Tungsten Carbide Cutter attachment for dremel (cone or taper)
- Cutting attachment for dremel that will cut aluminum and plastic
- Drill bit attachment the size for your screw for the dremel (or just a separate drill)

costumes

350

- A vise or vise grips
- A sturdy table or workbench
- A piece of scrap wood of some kind, at least a foot long (I used a mini ironing board)
- An xacto knife
- A utility knife
- A ruler
- Sewing pins
- Helpful: a smartphone and an angle-measuring app

Safety:

- A spray paint mask (this is under $20 and really important for your health)
- Safety glasses

This took around 8-12 hours over the course of a week to fully construct. I'd set aside several evenings to work on this costume.

## Step 2: Hack the shoe polisher

Before you get started on this epic costume, pop in some AA batteries and make sure the shoe polisher is working properly.

Take your length of electrical wire and cut it in half. Take off the battery cover and remove the batteries from the shoe polisher. Use your tiny screwdriver to remove the two screws holding the plastic case together (I had to pop off a plastic circle from inside the battery area to get at the second case screw). Remove the 3 screws holding the motor in the case (your shoe polisher might be slightly different, but same idea). Don't lose the tiny screws! Put them in a Ziploc or something. Pop out the motor and remove the on-off switch.

Find the two metal tabs that the on-off switch makes contact with in the "on" position. Strip one end of each of your pieces of electrical wire about 3/4". Bend the stripped ends into little hooks and hook each one onto one of the metal tabs. Pinch securely with pliers. Use a bunch of electrical tape to keep them from touching.

Try putting the motor component back in the plastic case with the wires coming out of the hole where the on-off switch used to be. If it doesn't fit, mark on the case

where the wires are blocking it. Use the dremel cone grinding (tungsten) tool to expand the switch opening in the top and bottom pieces of the case so it can close around the wires.

Carefully put the motor back into the case and reattach all of the screws. Put the case back together with the screws you have carefully saved. You can test if the hack is working by putting the batteries back in and touching the far ends of the electrical wires together. (Don't leave the batteries in while you're working, though.)

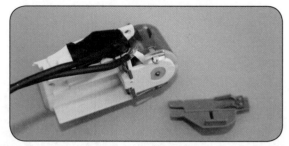

## Step 3: Keep hacking the shoe polisher

Take the two empty thread spools and your dremel tungsten grinding cone and cut out the cross-bracing ribs from the inside of the spool (between the inner and outer tubes). Cut as far down as you can from one end of each spool with the dremel without cutting through either tube. Try to get at least 1/3 down the height of the spool. Leave the opposite end of the spool intact.

Take one thread spool and thread your electrical wires through the inner tube, so that the intact end of the spool ends up against the shoe polisher. Put the wire twist tie on the under-side of the shoe polisher and stick one end into the thread spool (between the inner and outer tubes). You probably will have to fold the tip a bit to fit the twist tie inside. Use a ton of hot glue on the base of the spool and stick it to the shoe polisher. Let it set and then add a bunch more all around the base to really secure it.

Place the other spool opposite the first spool, with the intact end against the shoe polisher, stick the other (folded a bit) end of the twist tie into the spool, and hot glue it like crazy to the shoe polisher as well. After it has set just add a ton of hot glue until it seems really secure. Add some glue over the twist tie as well.

## Step 4: Hack the hat

Cut out the top of the lining of the fedora. Start cutting a small hole in the crown of your fedora with your x-acto knife. Put the shoe polisher (attachment tip up and towards the rear of the hat, batteries towards the front) into the hat and see how much bigger the hole needs to be for the polisher to stick up through the hat. Keep cutting the hole bigger until it fits the part of the shoe polisher that sticks up.

## Step 5: Keep hacking the hat

Put the hacked shoe polisher into the fedora. The spools should make it fit really tightly inside the hat, and they may even push the fedora out a bit.

costumes

Take an end of one the aluminum tubes, find where the spool is pushing against the hat, and use the tube to mark on the outside of the hat where the center of the spool is placed. Do this on both sides and take the shoe polisher out of the hat. Cut holes the size of the aluminum tubes where you marked on the hat using the x-acto knife.

Put the shoe polisher back into the hat so the spools line up with the holes you just cut. Pull the electrical wires through the hole they're near. From the inside of the hat, go totally crazy with hot glue to secure the spools and the shoe polisher in place. Put glue all over the place but avoid putting it on the battery cover, which should be hard to reach anyway. Let the glue set thoroughly before doing anything else to the hat.

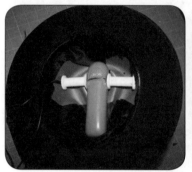

## Step 6: Make the battery opening

Cut a flap from the top of the hat from where the shoe polisher is sticking out to the front crown of the hat. This will be over the battery cover of the shoe polisher. The flap should stay down on its own but you can use a piece of double-stick tape to hold in in place as well.

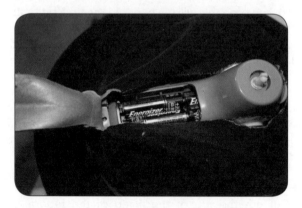

## Step 7: Make the helicopter blades

Use your utility knife to slice 3 of the long flaps (2 top, one bottom) from your cardboard box. Make a template for the helicopter blades that is about 4" wide (2" at the narrow end) and 16" long (see photo for shape). Trace the template onto the cardboard flaps and use the utility knife to cut out the shapes (don't use scissors they will make the cardboard bend).

Use strong glue to attach a paint stir stick to each helicopter blade so that the stick extends 4" from the end of the blade. Let the glue set thoroughly before proceeding.

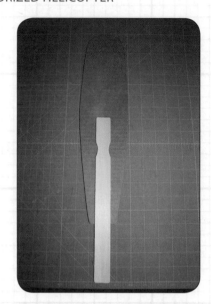

## Step 8: Paint the helicopter blades

Take three 4" x 4" scraps of cardboard and cut a 1.5" slit in the center of each. Take your empty oatmeal canisters and cut a 1.5" slit in the lid of each. Put something heavy in the bottom of each oatmeal canister. Put each helicopter blade through a cardboard scrap slit and then through an oatmeal lid slit. It should stand up vertically and extend about an inch into the canister.

Paint 2 or 3 thin layers of primer onto the helicopter blades, then spray a couple thin layers of glossy orange paint. (Go outside and use cardboard or newspaper to avoid getting paint everywhere.)

## Step 9: Make various helicopter bits

Take one of the shoe polisher attachment heads and attach the plastic cap to the head using strong glue.

Take another cap from a shoe polisher attachment. Place it on intersection of the helicopter blades and mark where the edges of the paint stirrers meet the cap. Use the dremel cutting tool to cut out 1/4" high slots from the cap so that it will fit over the center intersection of the helicopter blades.

Take a piece of cereal box chipboard and trace around one of the empty thread spools. Put an aluminum tube end in the center of this circle and trace around it. Cut out the donut shape and cut a slit to the center hole. Make two of these.

Mask the top face of the shoe polisher attachment with the glued-on cap using tape or a piece of cardboard.

Use the silver or gray spray paint to paint these pieces (attachment with cap, notched cap, and the two cardboard donuts).

## Step 10: Construct the helicopter

Once the paint has dried, overlap two of the helicopter blades at the unpainted end. Adjust them so that there is a 120 degree angle between them. Make sure that the paint sticks are both against the table and not facing up. Use strong glue to attach them together.

When the glue has set, attach the third helicopter blade, also with a 120 degree angle between it and the other two blades. You may want to clamp the attachment with a vise while it sets.

Take the shoe polisher attachment with the glued-on cap and attach the unpainted top face of it to the center of the helicopter blade intersection with strong glue. Make sure it is attached to the side where the cardboard blades are in front of the paint stir sticks.

When it has set, use a drill to make a small hole in the center of the helicopter intersection down into the plastic cap. Secure the connection with a screw.

Place the notched cap over the intersection, covering the screw. Glue it in place to the paint stirrers and the lower cap using strong glue.

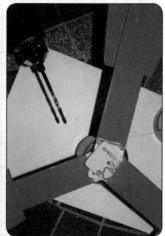

## Step 11: Make the handles

Cut 5 ½" off from each aluminum tube using the dremel cutting attachment. (Use safety glasses and a dust mask for this.)

Thread both of the electrical wires through one of the aluminum tubes.

Put the aluminum tubes onto a work table so that they overlap the table by about 7". Put your scrap wood on top of them and use the vise to hold them securely. The hat will have to be on the table as well because it's attached to the wires.

Pull and bend each of the tubes carefully (you really don't want to pinch the wires). When you are done bending you want them to be at a bit greater than a right angle. Work slowly and get the tubes to be at the same bent angle.

## Step 12: Attach the handles

You might want a friend for this step.

Take the handle with the wires in it and start gently pulling the wires through the tube, so the handle gets closer to the hat. Be really careful not to pull too hard or scrape the insulation off the wires as they go into the tube.

Attach both handles to the hat by putting the shorter ends of the handles into the space between the inner and outer tubes of the spools of thread you hollowed out. They should fit pretty snugly.

Put on the hat and stand in front of a mirror. Hold the ends of the handles at a comfortable angle from your body. After wearing it for awhile, I found it was most comfortable when my elbows were touching my sides. Either eyeball how far from vertical the handles are pushed, or have a friend with a handy-dandy smartphone with an angle-measuring app get the exact angle that you're pushing the handles in front of you. I found 17 degrees from vertical to be a good angle.

Stack some boxes on a low table and put the hat on top with the handles inserted. Either eyeball it or use the angle-ometer smartphone to get the handles rotated at the same angle (17 degrees or so) that was comfortable. Adjust the angle by inserting supports under the hat to make it higher from the ground, until the handles are at the correct angle. The handles should touch the ground.

Use a ruler to check that the handles are reasonably symmetrically placed. Mark on the ground with electrical tape where the ends of the handles are.

Use the hot glue gun to fill up one of the thread spools (in the space between the inner and outer tubes) with glue. Stick the handle into the spool as far as it will go, and make sure that the handle is at the correct angle you just figured out. Let it set, then do this on the other side. The side with the wires will be a bit finicky. So have the handle very close to the spool but not inside when you fill it with glue, then smoosh the handle into the space all the way.

Go crazy with the hot glue and thoroughly glue all around the spool-handle attachment point, filling in any gaps. Hot glue the silver spray-painted cardboard donuts from earlier over the attachment point of the handles to hide the glue.

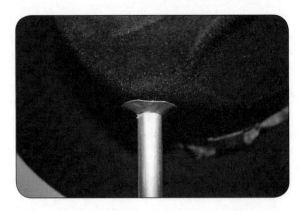

## Step 13: Add the switch

Take one of the bike grips and cut a 1.5" slit in one end. At the top of the slit cut a square hole big enough for your switch. Put the switch in from the slit end and pull the switch's wires through the bike grip.

Cut the hat's electrical wires so they extend about 1.5" out of the aluminum tube. Strip them 3/4" from the end. Make them into little hooks with your pliers, and do the same for the switch wires. Connect each switch wire hook to one hat wire hook and pinch securely with the pliers. Cover the exposed wires with electrical tape so that the two separate connections don't touch each other.

Push the aluminum tube into the bike grip, letting the wires either push into the tube or fold up inside the bike grip. Push the tube in as far as you can with the switch in the square hole you cut into the grip.

Use hot glue inside the top of the grip to secure it to the tube, and glue the slit closed as well to hold the switch in place.

Hot glue the other grip onto the other handle at the same height. Hot glue a bit of weight into the bottom of the grip opposite the switch side— I used 15 pennies. This will help the hat to balance evenly on your head by counterbalancing the weight of the switch and wires. You can glue a few pennies at a time and keep checking the balance of the hat until it's even.

## Step 14: Add padding to the hat

Cut an oval of sticky-back felt big enough to fit snugly inside the top of the hat, and put it over the shoe polisher inside the hat.

Move outside to cut the fur— the fibers get all over the place.

Cut 1 piece of black faux fur about 5"x6", and two pieces 5"x4". Round the corners. Hot glue the large piece to the inside top of the front end of the hat (fur on the hat-side). Hot glue the other two pieces on top of the first piece at the front of the hat. This will help the hat to rest evenly and not tip forward, and also add comfort.

The black Inspector Gadget hair is optional, but if you decide against it you should still use fur padding around the perimeter of the hat just to make it fit more snugly. (Because the shoe polisher makes the hat sit higher on your head, it gets really loose).

Cut a piece of faux fur 20" long by 4" high. Orient it so the fur hangs in the short direction (so the fur points down if you hold the piece horizontally). Cut a curve from one side so the piece is 2" high at each end and 4" in the center. Attach the piece to the inside of the hat, fur facing out, with pins (pins pointed out!) and try on the hat. Adjust the "hair" until it looks right, then hot glue it to the hat. If you don't want the "hair" to show, trim it at the hat brim— it will still help hold the hat on your head.

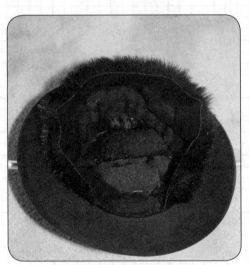

## Step 15: Put it all together!

Open the battery flap in the hat and put in the batteries.

Get dressed in the Inspector Gadget clothing. Gently attach the helicopter to the shoe polisher in the hat. Put on the hat (you can tuck up your hair inside if it's long) and turn on the switch! You are now totally awesome.

Tip: Make sure you're clear of people and walls before you go go gadget copter.

If you're going to be in really crowded spaces the whole time you're in costume, you could try making the helicopter blades a few inches shorter to give you some extra clearance.

# [Real Life]
# Big Head Mode

By Philipp Stollenmayer (ddi7i4d)
(http://www.instructables.com/id/Real-Life-Big-Head-Mode/)

A, B, Up, Left, A, B, Up, Left??

A, B, Up, Left, A, B, Up, Left??

Damn, this doesn't work. Is it because I'm in real life?

In case this also doesn't work with you, but you don't want to miss such a moronic feature in real life, you can get help now.

But who should feel the desperate urge to carry around a ridiculously big paper head?

Here's the story: Eric Testroete, 3D artist, had the idea of a very unique Halloween costume last year. He presented it on the web and a few people, including a music video producer, copied the idea. Nevertheless, no one had the ambition to write instructions, especially for the main street that has ordinary computing and crafting skills.

So let me introduce the Instructable of the big paper-craft head, which I modified only a bit, because the basic idea is undeniably genius.

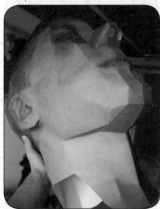

## Step 1: Preparation

The 3 phases of the project require the following stuff:

**Photographing**
- Camera: The better, the better. DSLRs are perfect, compact cameras also work
- And a tripod can never be wrong.

**Modeling**
- A modeling program: I use Anim8or, which I will introduce later.
- An image editing program: I use Paint Shop Pro X, but any other one will work, too.
- An unfolding program: You have no choice. There's nothing but Pepakura.

## Crafting
- Paper: The best paper for crafting weighs between 160g/m&sup2; (40 pound) and 250g/m&sup2; (66 pound) and is matte. Glossy paper is conducive to physical aggressions.
- Glue: Please don't use a glue stick or double-sided tape. On the long run, your head will bow itself off. I use UHU (liquid, because you need to fill gaps), but as this isn't available anywhere else, I recommend Gorilla Glue (of course).
- A printer
- A zip lock or Velcro (eventually)
- Regular crafting stuff: scissors, cutter, tweezers, those little clothes-pins, ruler

As you may have noticed, the costs are really assessable. It won't probably be more expensive than 15$.

## Step 2: Photo session

You will need at least 3 photos.

1. Face, front (The whole head should be on the photo)— texture

   Head, side (If you have a remarkable characteristic only on one side, you need pictures of both sides)— texture

2. Whole body, front (This is important for the right size later) — reference

**How to take the pictures:**

Put your camera on a tripod and make sure that your face is fully and evenly lighted. Avoid dark areas, the best way to get the right result is to put the camera in front of a window, camera facing you, you facing the window.

Consider that the camera will probably set a wrong focus when you trigger the self-timer.

## Step 3: Preparing Anim8or

Right here, the déjà vu part starts. Modeling the head is exactly the same process as in the Paper Clone Instructable, so the description is also pretty much the same.

If you don't have any experience with modeling, I recommend you to use Anim8or, which you can download for free. There are a few functions which make you able to model your head.

When you are not familiar with the program, please make at least the modeling a hand-tutorial first, so that you get into the program.

At first load the 2 head-pictures (front and side) into the scene. Go to front view and load the first one with Build – Reference Image. Go to a side view and load the other one. Put the images a bit away from the middle, but first make sure that your head has the same size on both of the images. Scale the images with the scale-tool if necessary. It should look like the image below.

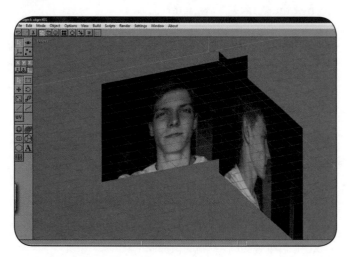

## Step 4: Modeling the head

In my eyes, Eric's head is a little too angular, which is caused by the low poly-count. So I made the UV-faces a bit smaller, the size of coins in the face and the size of credit cards on the rest of the head.

I recommend doing the head with line-modeling instead of box-modeling. That means that you draw a grid of lines along the "edges" of your face, fill them and move the points to the right place. A whole head-model-tutorial can be found here. This head-model is a bit too non-detailed. These are the tools you need for modeling a detailed head:

- The Arc-Rotate-tool (Ctrl R): Move the camera around the model.
- Hide (h): if an object is in the way, click on it and hide it. Shift H lets it reappear.
- The Add-Edge-tool (left side, middle): Draw the contours of your face first with this tool.
- The Drag-Select-tool (d): Select a few points in the front view mode, switch to the side view, and move (Move-Tool ; m) the points where they belong. Using more than one perspective at a time (view - All) is very helpful.
- The Cut-Faces-tool (Shift C): This is for adding details. When you cut a face, points are added. When you cut a line, the line is divided into 2 lines. You often have to turn the camera in order to prevent wrong cuts, i.e. on the backside of the object.
- The Fill-Holes-tool (Shift J): Select your wire-frame in edge-select-mode (e) and fill the holes to add faces between the lines.
- The Extrude-Faces-tool (Shift Y): Select a face in face-select-mode (g) and extrude it, so that you can add an ear for example. You could also do that with adding edges, but this is much faster and more accurate.
- The Merge-Points-tool (Shift J): Merge 2 points that are close together.

Summing up, the process is: Draw a few lines, move the points where they belong, fill the holes. Add lines, move points, fill holes, etc.

Try to use a structure with many triangles, because then nothing can go wrong with bad folds in rectangles (because you can fold a rectangle along 2 different diagonals).

Model all the way along the neck, and keep a notch where your shoulders go. You can still cut away a bit when the paper model is done.

**Variety 1:**

For the variety of eyes that will follow the observer (see step 8), draw the edges of the eyes clearly and make the eyes a bit more popping out (compare pic. 4).

**Tip:**

Do only one half of the face. Then mirror it, select both sides and "join solids", select the points in the middle and merge them.

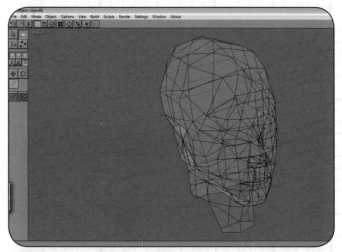

## Step 5: Texturing the head

Color the head with the following material:
Ambient: 1
Diffuse: 0.5
The rest: 0
And a color of your choice.

This creates a material without shades, what makes it easier for you to compare the textures and prevent clipping mistakes.

Now you can prove your Photo Shop skills. Go into the Flat-Shaded-view (Ctrl F) in the side perspective and make a screenshot. Crop the image, so that you only see the head. Then make the image 500 - 600% bigger, copy your head-photo over it, and make the 3D-image a bit more transparent, so that you have it as a reference. Use the warp-brush to adjust your photo to the model (without making it look ridiculous). Additionally, I made the ear a bit smaller.*

Very important: The head must everywhere be bigger than the original model, or you see the background on the model.

costumes

Save the photo, which is now a texture, but don't forget to make the reference image transparent. You can't use a png or tiff, so just save the best jpeg possible.

Go back to Anim8or and open the material you colored the head with. Click on texture, load the texture and save the material. It should look weird now, so choose Texture UV (v) in side view and adjust the texture to the head.

**Quick UV-guide:**

- Right click within the circle moves the image
- Left click outside the circle turns the image
- Middle mouse button zooms the image (inside circle: x/y not constant)

*Select only the ear in Face-Select-mode (g) and press UV again. Then zoom in a bit and make it look real. This prevents that the texture of the ear is also behind the ear, which would be wrong.

If you want a face like a pixel-zombie, you can go to the next step. If not, make a screenshot of the front and paste it into your image program. In Anim8or, select your face's faces and color them with a new (here: green) material that has the same values as above. Make the same screenshot as before and paste the images on one image. It should look like below now. Make them again 500 - 600% bigger and copy your face-front-photo in. Now adjust the image in the green area to the model, using the warp brush. When the form is right, use brushes like darken/lighten, tone, or saturation to make the edge of the texture fit to the other and create a non-visible transition. Save the cropped image and put it on the face instead of the green material like before. After you have checked your head for mistakes (you can still change the textures), you are done with it.

## Step 6: Finding the right size

Insert the full-body-image with Build - Reference Image and change the size until the model-head and the head on the picture have the same size. Copy and paste the head with Ctrl+C, Ctrl+V, select one and make it as big as you want. I suggest about double size, this has the disadvantage that you eventually can't pull it over your head when you have a slim neck, so you will have to attach a zip lock later.

When you are satisfied with the size, draw a rectangle that has the height of your body, delete the original-sized head and put the head beside the rectangle, like in pic. 3.

Save the head as a 3ds-model (Object - Export).

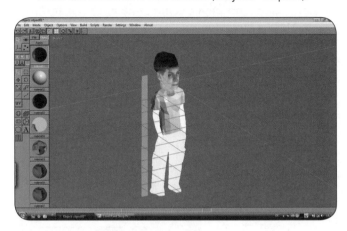

## Step 7: Unfolding the head

For the next step you need Pepakura. Download the trial for free, but include enough time for the unfolding, because you unfortunately can't save it.

Open the 3ds-file with Pepakura and deny every question except that of joining the edges. If you don't see any textures, click on 3DModelWindow - Texture Configuration and load them again. Navigate around your model with the mouse (zoom is on the middle button) and specify the open edges: Click on the cutter on the toolbar (it should be selected already) and click on all the edges of the head that you want to cut along later. You don't have to specify all open edges, only the ones that need to be open. Choose a more vertical structure, that makes you thinner.

Edges where the textures change should always be open.

Unhook Auto and click on Unfold. Choose Specify Value. The size should be your actual size, therefore you have the rectangle beside the head.

Now you see a bit of chaos in the right area that you have to get under control, using the right-click-options, especially Join/Disjoin Face. Finding out by yourself what they all mean is the easiest way to learn to make comfortable unfoldings. Put the big size-rectangle anywhere on the left of the screen, so it won't be printed.

What is also really important for comforting crafting is that the flaps are alternating on one side and the next one on the other side of the open edges. Do this as the last step. This keeps the parts in their forms and makes everything more stable, because the parts intertwine better with a zip-lock-effect.

When you are done with organizing the parts, click Configuration - Line Style and hook "Hide Lines that are almost flat" with a value between 0 and 180 degrees (a higher value means more folding lines, which doesn't look nice — 140 degrees is a good compromise). Don't forget to hook "Color flaps with neighboring face colors" in the

**costumes**

357

Flap Configuration, otherwise your papercraft will have white edges.

Then print your papercraft on the thick paper. You may want to change all quality values to maximum in printer setting and paper configuration, to get the best result. Make a few screenshots of the open model, so you see where the parts go.

Printing it a second time with concept settings on normal paper can't be wrong.

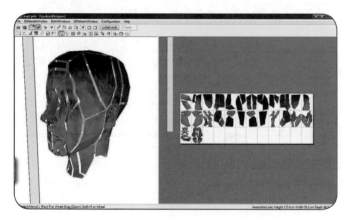

## Step 8: Crafting Time

Finally it is time to glue your stuff together! I suggest beginning with the nose and gluing the face around it piece by piece. The middle line on the back of the head should be left open. You can try if the head fits you without opening that line after holding it together with a bit of tape, and if it does, you can glue it together. If you need to open the gap, you can cut the flaps away and glue a zip lock or Velcro strip on the inner side, so you can open and close the head.

**The following things may be helpful:**

Cut the part out and fold only the vertical folds with the aid of the tweezers. Dotted lines mean mountain folds, dotted and lined lines mean valley folds. Of course you can use tape on the inside. Use the mini clothes-pins to hold something together.

How to glue: you should always have some kind of a narrow piece of paper. Rip it and you have something like a glue-brush. Do a bit glue on it or the flap and arrange it with that piece. You often need less than expected. Press it together for 5 seconds and it should hold together. Don't do more than one flap simultaneously. When you have trouble with the last parts because the flaps are inside, you can cut a hole into a face, print it again on normal paper, and glue it over the hole again.

When you don't know where something belongs, take your model as a reference.

**Variety 1 - Glossy Eyes:**

Cut out the eyes before you glue the parts together. Cut out another pair of eyes and glue them behind the eye-holes in the head after you have put a piece of transparent sticky tape over them.

**Variety 2 - Dynamic Eyes:**

The dynamic eyes always look at the observer; they work like the Dragon Illusion or the Look-at-me-Boo.

Simply fold the eyes inverted, that they go inside the head. The result is that the head looks at everyone, where ever they stand (obviously not behind it).

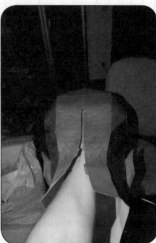

## Step 9: Finishing

Your papercraft head is finished!

You may want to make the neck edges smoother with the scissors to adapt it to your shoulders.

The papercraft head fits best when you wear a jacket and pull the collar over the neck. When you use it open-air, please consider that the head suffers from severe aquaphobia. When you wear it, you may notice that you see absolutely nothing. When you grant your head a pair of real nostrils, you can not only see which time of day it is, but also huge obstacles. Another option is putting brown transparent tape on the inside of the nostrils, to make them a bit more invisible. So when you walk with the head on, please let a blind person's guide accompany you.

Have fun!

# Werewolf Costume

## By missmonster
(http://www.instructables.com/id/realistic-were-wolf-costume/)

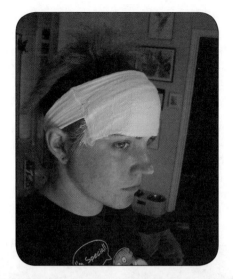

Create your own werewolf costume! Moving jaw, padded body, lots of fur!

I'd like to express how excited I am to see this posted around the internet. This is my second full crazy costume, the first being an armored demon. I do costuming as a hobby but I am a full-time artist.

Had I known so many people would be looking at this, I would have documented the steps a little better. If you have any questions, feel free to ask via commenting on this site and I'll try to answer them as best I can.

Thank you for checking out my Instructable. I hope it inspires you to make a big mean creature of your own!

Have a great Halloween!

## Step 2: Add the snout and jaw
You will need:
- Cell-u-clay
- Aluminum armature wire
- Pourable plastic resin (optional)
- Resin epoxy glue
- Hot glue

Okay so I skipped a few steps, here. Basically I formed a little wire armature for the snout, nice and ugly. I then glued it down with the epoxy and glued some foam over the wire armature with hot glue. Snip the foam snout down to the shape you want. Make it a little skinnier than needed since we are going to add to it.

I then coated the entire thing with resin to make it super strong!

Mix your cell-u-clay and create a basic snout. Let this dry for awhile.

## Step 1: Start the head
You will need:
- Upholstrey foam
- Plaster gauze strips
- Lotion
- Elastic
- Hot glue
- Needle and thread

Using plaster strips, make a little half mask. Don't forget to lube your face with some lotion!

When the half mask is done, start adding some foam to protect your noggin. Nothing too thick, you don't want the wolf to have a huge balloon cranium (or maybe you do, whatever). With the foam added, now make a little elastic bit to hold it on. Sew it into a ring and add a little hot glue to the sewn parts to make sure it stays. Add some strips over the foam to make it more solid.

## Step 3: Add the jaws and teeth
You will need:
- Sculpey
- Dremel tool or sand paper (dremel tool will save a ton of time)
- Aluminum wire armature
- Key ring (minus keys)
- Elastic
- Epoxy glue

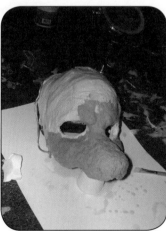

Once the clay dried I went and dremeled down a lot of the texture. I didn't think I'd be covering the whole thing with fur, my plan was to hand glue hair and then leave most of it smooth, so I really got into smoothing the face, which was sort of a waste. Oh well, that's what happens when you make it up as you go along!

I also added wire ears and the jaw. The jaw was also made with plaster strips molded onto my actual chin. A wire serves as the support for the foam mandible, just like with the upper head.

The jaw works by making a little ring that attaches to the upper head. The lower jaw hooks in and is removable. I made the hook with some wire formed into a hook shape, attached to an elastic loop.

## Step 4: Detailing the head and making the teeth

You will need:

- Sculpey
- Oven to bake sculpey
- Sharpie marker
- Dremel
- Spray primer
- Epoxy glue

I added plaster strips to the ears as well as paper clay. Lots of shaving, sanding, and swearing later and we kind of have a werewolf on the way.

Sculpting with paper clay sucks. I just did a little, let it dry, sanded, added more . . . repeat until happy. It's frustrating but it's worth it to me. This paper mache clay is REALLY light and really strong. It takes patience. I'd work on it between other projects so I didn't get too annoyed.

Oohhhh man, this is where it got fun. The teeth are sculpey, which I molded to the jaw, then baked, then

glued in. I also put a little snarl over them in paper clay later on.

I also used a ton of primer on this thing while I was obsessing over the smoothness. (That's why the whole thing is suddenly grey.)

I marked the teeth so I could glue them in easier later on. I didn't detail the teeth as much as I could have but it works anyway.

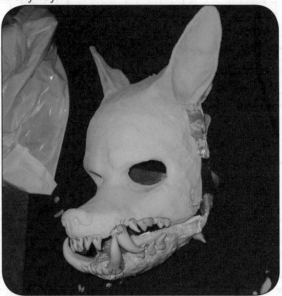

## Step 5: Finish up the head

What you need:

- Acrylic paint
- Brushes
- Clear epoxy
- Hot glue
- Fake fur
- Scissors
- Exacto knife

Time to paint him! Again, I had thought most of the front face would be naked so I cared way too much about painting it all nice. It's not a total flat black, there's actually a little shading and highlighting. That red stuff in the jaw is tool dip, I figured I'd seal the inner face since it would get pretty nasty in there with all the sweating I'd be doing. Easier to wipe off and makes it a little smoother.

I also have some black eye make up to blend things a little better and a balaclava to hide my mouth (ninja mask type hood).

The teeth have been sealed with a glossy clear epoxy. Do a test on your epoxy first, because the brand I used for the bottom teeth yellowed within a month or two and they no longer matched.

The teeth are not a pure white, either. I did stain them a little but it doesn't show up too well in the flash.

The hair was weird. At first I added mohair that I dyed and glued in piece by piece. Like I have mentioned I was going to have a somewhat naked face and was going to blend the hair into the skin. Dumb waste of time. I ended up hot gluing on fake fur and trimming it to become short

costumes

on the face and snout . . . and blended that into longer hair towards the top of the head. I also bought some long high quality fur from National Fiber Technology for the back of the head. I used hot glue to attach all of the fur onto the face and head.

## Step 6: Make some paws

You will need:

- Baseball batter's gloves
- Epoxy
- Dremel
- Plastic craft claws
- Foam
- Scissors
- Needle n' thread
- Fake fur
- Armature wire
- Opera gloves
- Acrylic paint
- Clear polyurethane

Foam over a baseball batters glove. Hot glue it on. The wires will make the claws sturdy on top of my fingers (the claws will fit over the wire, create a hole in the claw with the dremel tool). The foam makes my hand look like it has different stubbier joints and hopefully a little less human.

Glue the claws onto the finger wire with epoxy. Paint your claws and seal with the clear epoxy. I painted the paw pads first with the latex to reduce to pores of the foam, and then went over that with black tool tip. (There are better ways to make paw pads but this is what I did). I shaved down the finger tip fur and let it fade into longer fur on the back of the hand.

Cut the fingers off of the opera gloves, put one on and insert it into the glove. Using hot glue, (yes, hot glue) glue on strips of fur up to your elbows. The trick is to use a low heat glue gun (NOT the large high heat!) Apply your glue onto the strip of fur, let it cool for a minute, and then apply it to the opera glove. It will be warm but won't burn you. You just need it to stick enough to hold in place. Once all the fur is attached, remove the opera glove with the paw still attached and sew all of the fur seams together. Lower arm done!

## Step 7: Make the werewolf feet

You will need:

- Shoes
- Foam
- Hot glue
- Exacto
- Plastic claws
- Epoxy
- Acrylic paint
- Dremel
- Clear polyurethane

Add Velcro around the top to your shoe then some around the sides for the end of the fur legs to Velcro on to. I also made a strap for this brand of shoe, which also has Velcro on top of it for the legs to attach to.

I riveted AND glued the Velcro on—you don't want it going anywhere! Plus rivets are fun to install. Toes! Basic block of foam, carve with scissors to round them out a little. Don't bother too much with making it super smooth, it's going to be covered with fur anyway. I glued my claws in by cutting a slit into the foam, filling it with hot glue, and inserting the claw.

Paint your claws, varnish them with polyurethane. Add strips of fur, hot glue it all down, trim the toe fur, and you are done!

## Step 8: Make the body
You will need:
- Fake fur
- hot glue
- Leotard
- Under Armor type shirt
- Foam

I used a duct tape dummy to help out with sizing. I put a leotard with an under armor shirt over it. Then I hot glued foam shapes over the shoulders, chest, and back to make a beefy upper chest. Then to create a digitigrade leg (dog leg appearance, not a backwards knee like everyone thinks; they just have shorter lower legs, longer feet, and stand on their toes). I added foam to the front of my top leg and the back of my calf to make a shape like I'm bending my knees even when the leg is straight.

Try the suit on every so often with the head on to make sure the proportions are okay. Trim accordingly. Get the foam right because you don't want to have to go back a step to fix things. Remember you will be adding fur on top of the foam. This will add more bulk, so slight shapes are best. The shirt and leotard connect with Velcro. I sewed and then glued the corresponding sides to the inside of the shirt and outside waistline of the leotard. Also add some Velcro to the elbows of the shirt. This is where the lower arms will connect.

Cut shapes of fur with your exacto (cut the back as to not mess up the fur) and hot glue it all on. Place the pieces close together, fill gaps with smaller pieces. After you are satisfied, sew all of the glued-on pieces together so when you flex and bend, the fur does not show seams and gaps.

I also included a photo of all the parts we have covered so far.

## Step 9: Try it on!

You are pretty much done. Get some colored contacts to look less human and really freak people out! I blended my face into the black of the mask with some Kryolan aqua makeup (sillyfarm.com). It mixes with water and can be applied with a finger or brush and does not rub off too easily.

Add a tail if you feel like it! I didn't document that process but just sew some fake fur, stuff it then sew it to your wolf's butt. Try on your new suit! You may need to make some changes and adjustments...but congrats! You are now a werewolf. Stay hydrated and be very careful, this suit gets really hot. You will lose a lot of water and moving will take a little more out of you. Take frequent head breaks (take off the head and hood) in front of a fan and have someone around to help you get in and out of the suit AKA a wrangler. A wrangler can also help you spot trouble where you can't see it (people tugging on the suit from behind or kids getting a little too aggressive), or do simple things like open doors for you when your claws can't. Most people will be really cool and want to pose for photos or pet you, but be aware of people just wanting to make trouble with an easy target. Especially drunk people! Having some back up can make the difference between having a great time out or getting your costume damaged and you possibly hurt. I have had some bad experiences being out alone with another costume and I'd hate for anyone else to have the same trouble.

But don't let all that scare you. It's going to be awesome and you will have a great time! Go scare some kids and have a great Halloween!

For more costumes and cool stuff check out miss-monster.com!

# Can Suit

By Benjamin Senger (Prototyp81)
(http://www.instructables.com/id/Can-Suit/)

## Step 1: Cans

At first you need a lot of cans . . . about 350-400!

I decided to use RED BULL COLA cans for two reasons.

First: I like the colors and their combination in this diagonal design.

Second: some cans are made out of aluminum; others are produced out of tin-foil (coca-cola). Red Bull uses aluminum.

The advantage of aluminum is that you have no corrosion (rust) at the cut edge and it's much easier to cut and to punch!

The disadvantage of aluminum is that it's not that ductile; tin-foil is more ductile, and, therefore, it breaks easier when you start buckling it 2 or 3 times at the same place, but if you act carefully with your suit, this is not a problem.

## Step 2: Tools

This image shows the most important tools and materials I used.

Before you start connecting, you need holes. Therefore, use a puncher or a special bin rail. The hole-diameter has to be larger (1mm) than the grommet-diameter (5mm). This is necessary because the grommets fit better and the pieces stay flexible towards each other. The connection of the pieces works well with grommets (do you call them grommets?). For more solid connections, especially between the can pieces and the steel band, use blind rivets. The steel band helps you to strut some parts like the helmet or the shoulder components.

## Step 3: Cutting

Remove the cap and the bottom of the can, and then cut the cans if you want to give your suit a special optic. I chose the diagonals where the colors change. Be careful and use gloves, otherwise you will hurt yourself at the cutting edge!!!

## Step 4

Here you see an inside view to the shoulder and front component. Based on my body size, I used a chain to get the most important data; I constructed something like a frame out of steel band and tin-foil. After that, I took the can pieces and connected them bit by bit with the frame.

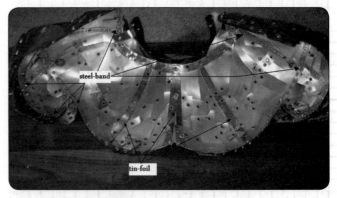

## Step 5: Connecting

For the legs I made a frame out of tin-foil and connected everything with grommets.

costumes

## Step 6: Knee

For the vertical stabilization I used elastic band, which is, in addition, flexible enough to allow you to angle your knee. For covering the gap between the thigh and the shank, I connected the elastic band in the middle with some loosely riveted strips (next step).

## Step 7: Knee

This picture shows the loosely riveted strip which is very flexible. It can be banded in every direction without being destroyed.

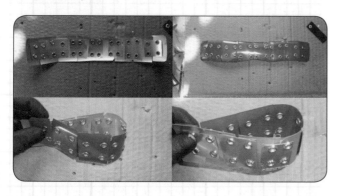

## Step 8: Connecting

I needed about 2800 grommets to connect all the pieces.

## Step 9: Legs

On the backside I connected the pieces with zippers.

## Step 10: Pants

It fits like a glove . . . partially.

## Step 11: Helmet

The helmet is made out of two parts. On the top these parts are connected with a hinge. I chose a hinge that you find in your kitchen unit. Good choice because it's cheap and it has a snap fit so after opening the helmet it stays in that position.

## Step 12: Join them

All together the suit consists of 12 pieces.

2 shoes: Each shoe has two parts which are connected with hook and loop fastener so under your "new shoes" you can wear your "old shoes."

2 legs: The pieces for the legs are connected on the backside with zippers. They fit very good at the thighs (work exactly with the diameters) so they don't glide off.

2 pieces for the hip: On the inside of these pieces I added nooses for a belt. What is more, a hook and loop fastener helps to join the pieces.

1 piece for the torso: With a piece that looks like a mat you surround the torso. On the backside you connect it with a wide loop and hook fastener. Advantage of the wide one: it still fits after eating too much.

1 component for shoulders and front: Look the previous step.

2 arms: The arms are joined to your body with elastic bands. At the elbow they have an articulated joint.

1 piece for the neck and a helmet.

## Step 13: Ready to go!

costumes

# Catahedron Costume

By Lilli Thompson (maicoh)
(http://www.instructables.com/id/Catahedron-Costume/)

What's cuter than a platonic solid? A cat dressed up as a platonic solid for Halloween!

This instructable details the making of a soft quilted tetrahedron costume for the more patient of my two cats.

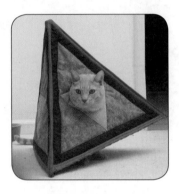

## Step 1: Choose fabrics and preprocess them

The first step in any quilt is to pick out fabrics. You will need at least 4 colors, two for the contrasting triangles, one for the outside border, and one for the backing. I was working with fabric scraps from other quilts, so I used more colors, but whatever you've got will work. Be sure to wash, dry, and iron all fabrics at least once before you start working with them. There's nothing worse than finding a finished product ruined in the wash by runny dyes or fabric shrinkage.

You'll also need an attractive color of quilt binding. Binding can be purchased at most fabric stores (I use Joanne's). The binding is a cloth strip that will sandwich the outer hem to create a finished edge. Also make sure you have a color of thread that matches your fabrics.

## Step 2: Cut triangles and piece them together

Using a rolling cutter, measure and cut equilateral triangles from the chosen fabrics (the size will vary depending on the size of your cat). You will need 9 of one color and three of the other. Pin the triangles together one pair at a time, sew, and iron the seams flat immediately. Never skip the pinning or ironing steps! Quilting is all about patience; you will get far better results if you are methodical.

Measure a strip of your 3rd contrasting fabric for the outside edge; the border shown in the pictures is a 2" strip. When the 4 triangles are sewn together and ironed into a bigger triangle, pin the border on the edge and sew in place. Once one edge is attached, cut the edges flush, iron flat, then repeat for the other edges.

## Step 3: Attach batting and backing fabric

Take the backing fabric and lay it flat on your work surface, right side down. Place a layer of quilt batting over the fabric, taking care to smooth out any wrinkles. I used polyester low loft batting in a "child's blanket" size. Anywhere that sells quilting supplies will have a ton of options for batting lofts (how thick it is) and material (cotton, polyester, etc.). A lower loft is better for this project because it will keep the overall product lighter and be easier for the cat to wear.

Place each pieced top right side up on top of the batting, making a batting sandwich, and pin it into place with basting pins (which are like safety pins, but shaped more conveniently for this purpose). Once the batting is pinned on, cut the sides of both the batting and backing fabric flush with the quilt top. It's easiest to use a rolling cutter and straight edge to do the trimming all at once.

## Step 4: Attach binding, quilt along the color borders

For ease of construction the triangles will all be independently finished and then sewn together later.

Pin the binding strips to sandwich all three edges of each triangle. Fold the edge of the binding under at the corners to hide any unfinished edges. With your sewing machine set to very slow, carefully stitch the binding in place on all 9 edges. As you sew the binding you should aim your stitches at the very edge, no more than a millimeter from where the binding meets the quilt top.

I also chose to quilt another line a quarter inch out from the binding seam. This gave it a nice visual border and took care of holding the binding on at any of the points where I messed up on the initial seam. Specifically, it's easy to have stitches that are accurate on the top, but that miss the binding edge on the underside. The second line of stitches takes care of these cases and reinforces the final product.

While I was at it, I stitched across the seams where the black border met the large triangles, and along the color borders between the inner triangles. This sort of stitching is what gives it that classic quilted look, and also keeps each triangle together flat as it flexes. Try to use one long line for all your quilting stitches; you want as few loose thread ends as possible.

## Step 5: Cut head opening, assemble tetrahedron

Pick one of the finished quilted triangles and cut a smaller upside-down triangle out of it, as an opening for the head. Use a wide sewing machine stitch to finish the cut edges. This was the part of the project I was least happy with the finished look of. If had it to do over again I would have made the head-triangle out of three smaller triangles with finished edges, rather than cutting into it and attempting to finish with sewing machine stitches. However, fortunately the border doesn't really ever show while the cat is wearing the costume.

Using a color of thread that matches your binding, sew the edges together. Place triangles back to back (right sides out) and simply stitch along the edge. Though this will create a lip on the outside (showing edge) of the final product, because the triangles are already finished with binding I consider it aesthetically acceptable. Repeat process with the final triangle and the last two edges. After the edges are sewn together you should have a soft pyramid, almost capable of standing on its own.

## Step 6: Initial fitting

At this point I stopped to test how the tetrahedron would look on my cat. My hope had been that the stiffness of the edges would be enough to make the soft tetrahedron stand on its own once it had a cat inside. However as he started walking around it became apparent that a frame was required for it to maintain its shape, especially when you consider how the tail deforms the soft sides. I had thought that the tail could go under the bottom border, but my cat had other ideas.

## Step 7: Create wire frame

After the initial fitting, I decided the costume needed a frame for full effect. Take three wire coat hangers and bend completely straight using either your bare hands or pliers where necessary. Once you have a long length of straight wire, measure it against the tetrahedron edges and bend it into a triangle, duct taping the edges together.

Make sure that the beginning of each wire is not at a corner, but is in the middle of an edge. This will make it much more stable and easier to tape safely in place.

Make three wire triangles the size of the tetrahedron sides and duct tape them together into a pyramid. Make absolutely certain that all sharp edges are firmly duct taped in place so that there are no unpleasantly pokey parts to injure your cat. Forming the pyramid out of three finished triangles has the benefit of creating nice smooth pieces,

and also having two wires along each edge will give it extra support because coat hanger wire isn't that strong.

When the frame is ready simply pull the cloth over it and use safety pins or basting stitches to hold it in place. You don't want to permanently attach the frame because you may want to wash the costume in the future. All that you need is something to hold the bottom edge of the cover to the bottom edge of the frame, and safety pins hidden on the inside work perfectly for that.

## Step 8: Final fitting

Once the frame is attached to the quilt the costume it's ready to go! Gently coax your cat into it and admire your work!

At first I was worried that my cat would be unhappy wearing the costume, but as it turns out he really likes it. Like many cats, he's got a strong instinct to sit inside of things so even when I took the costume off of him he got right back in. I would worry about him injuring himself if he wore it while I wasn't directly supervising him, but he definitely seems to appreciate the concept. Also, he appears to be able to walk around freely while wearing the costume, which is adorable!

While your cat is not wearing the tetrahedron it can be placed on its side to make a quilted cat tent-nook-bed thing, which both my cats (even the one that's far too skittish to be costumed) like very much. Happy Halloween!

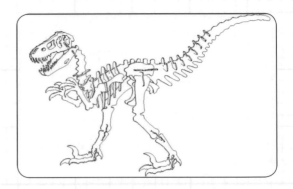

# The Ultimate T-Rex Costume

By James (Jamie) Price (jamiep)
(http://www.instructables.com/id/The-Ultimate-T-Rex-Costume/)

This Instructable documents the construction of Jamie Price's dinosaur costume. It is over 10 feet tall and 14 feet long! There are over 140 individual parts that were created. It is built from a flexible foam with a welded steel/aluminum support substructure. Most of the parts were cut using a CNC router with a few cut by hand using a dremel and regular router. Total build time was around 130 hours at a materials/machine time cost of $550.

## Step 1: Design

I wanted to build a large-scale dinosaur costume that would standout. First, I found several 3-D dinosaur puzzles on the internet. Once I found one to my liking (look, geometry, etc), we scanned the parts into a design software (can be anything as long as you can output a .dwg file for the machine shop later). Once scanned, the parts were output onto heavy card stock and constructed into a prototype model. From there, you have to figure out what parts are going to move, where you will be within the structure, and how you will hold it up.

Since most of the models are designed to be static with no moving parts, it takes several revisions to the parts to make mounting plates, get rid of parts that impede movement of parts, etc.

Once you get this all done, the parts will be ready to be cut by the CNC router (a spinning tool that is computer driven that can cut out exact parts from large sheets). The machine shop will "nest" the parts (get as many parts onto a sheet as possible, which saves waste and money).

You could cut these out by hand, but that would take FOREVER. Best to use a CNC Router for this!

## Step 2: Cutting parts

Once the design is finalized and you have your machine file (check with your machine shop for type of files that may be used), it's time to get the foam. I used ½" thick white closed cell poly foam plank. This stuff came in 4' x 8' sheets and this project took about five of them. I paid around $150 for the foam and another $100 for shipping (ships flat in huge box via truck).

Once I got the foam delivered to the machine shop, we were ready to cut! The CNC router cuts this stuff like butter as long as you cut around the part in a counter-clockwise method (same with the hand routers). Below is a pic of the first batch of cutout parts.

## Step 3: Structure

You will notice that the foam parts are quite limp without any structure and won't support their own weight. You have to build a skeleton for the skeleton.

I used ¼" thick steel rod for most parts and 1/8" for the smaller parts that weren't load bearing. For this step you need a welder, a vice to bend the rod, and a method of cutting it.

The steel rod was shaped to match the part, a groove is made part way through the foam piece to house the steel rod, then an overlay part glues over it to hold/hide the steel. To cut the grooves, I used a router on the larger ones and a dremel router on the small ones. You could also make the grooves part of your file for the CNC router.

For some overlay parts, I used 1/8" thick white abs plastic. For others, I used ½" foam to cover up the steel structure. You can see examples in the pictures of different structural parts. Every dinosaur is different, so different pieces will need to be reinforced, but the methodology is the same. For extra heavy parts (like the neck that supports the ribs, arms, and head) I doubled up the 1/4" rod to make a structural beam. This still allows some movement, but supports the weight nicely.

Note: Superglue (cyanoacrylate) is the ONLY glue that will adhere this closed cell poly foam!

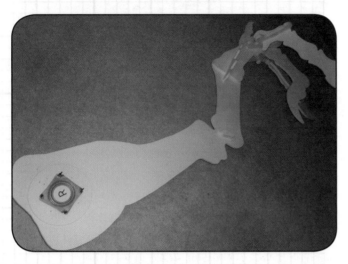

## Step 4: Supporting rig

As your pieces start to slowly come together, you will next be faced with the challenge of how to support/wear the costume.

I acquired a used military surplus backpack that was then modified. As most of the weight of the dinosaur is over the front, you need to add a belt to the front of the backpack so that the pack is attached around your torso. This allows the weight to ride properly on the waist and shoulder straps.

I used aluminum square tubes to create the frame that attaches the dinosaur to the backpack. I fired up the chop saw and welder to create the parts. After welding, the parts were then taped off and painted either white or black depending on what needed to be seen or disappear.

Note the slanted aluminum plates on each side. This is where the lazy susan bearings plug into that allows the legs to move.

## Step 5: Final assembly

Now that you have tons of parts, it's time to put them together! LOTS more superglue! Some of the parts that were structural (legs, pelvis) had to be permanently assembled as they were load bearing. The rest of the parts are made to friction fit into the slots. Other than the legs/pelvis, the other parts can pack flat in a large zippered carry bag.

The neck and spine attach via two aluminum angle plates that attach with large bolts and wing nuts. This then attaches to the backpack frame.

Note: Some hardware was fabricated to help take the weight off of certain parts. I used steel fishing leaders to help carry the overhung load that the arms placed onto the rib. The leaders were connected from the rib to the neck.

## Step 6: Finishing touches

This costume plays on the use of light and dark to make certain parts of it "disappear."

For the outfit, I bought a black military surplus flight suit. I also bought black cotton gloves, black socks and shoes, and a black mesh head cover.

Any part that you want to be not noticed, make it black!

Also, to cover up the spine attachment hardware, I created pieces of white foam that Velcro over it.

A good project is all about the details!

costumes

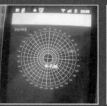

# games

USB Biofeedback Game Controller

Who doesn't like playing games? Games are a great way to take a break from the busy and sometimes challenging task of creating and making things. However, some people just can't seem to turn their creativity off—even when they are supposed to be relaxing. Luckily, this results in amazing new versions of our favorite games. Makers love reinventing and tweaking the games we all grew up with to reflect new technology and new ideas.

Think the claw-the-stuffed-animal game and pinball machine have lost their luster along with the midway, or think you've seen all the possible variations on a Rubik's cube? Think again! In this chapter we cover games as you've never seen them before, from a ball maze controlled with a cell phone to an Arduino-controlled chess set. Makers are leading the way to keeping the rich history of games alive, and keeping you from getting any work done!.

# USB Biofeedback Game Controller

By Brian Kaminski (Gundanium)
(http://www.instructables.com/id/USB-Biofeed-back-Game-Controller/)

This tutorial will teach you to build a USB Biofeedback Game Controller. Use it to play any computer game (that uses keyboard inputs) using your muscles as the controller.

Drop by our web store to purchase muscle sensor circuit boards, sensors, kits, cables and electrodes.

## About Advancer Technologies

Advancer Technologies is a company devoted to developing innovative game-changing biomedical and biomechanical technologies and applied sciences. Additionally, Advancer Technologies promotes all forms of interest and learning into biomedical technologies. To help cultivate and educate future great minds and concepts in the field, they frequently post informative instructions on some of their technologies. For more information, please visit www.AdvancerTechnologies.com.

## Step 1: Materials
### Basics

- 1 x Arduino Uno R2 (needs the atmega8u2 USB chip which is only available on newer Arduino MCUs)
- 1 x Arduino Project Enclosure
- 1 x USB cable for your Arduino
- 4 x Advancer Technologies Platinum Muscle Sensor
- 1 x Advancer Technologies Muscle Sensor Power Supply (without headers)

- 1 x 12V Power Supply (Wall wart)
- 4 sets of EMG Cables and Electrodes

### Miscellaneous
- Jumper cables or solid core wire
- 3 x 1" length pieces of 24-30 AWG wire (1/8" stripped off each end)
- 3 x 2" length pieces of 24-30 AWG wire (1/8" stripped off each end)
- 3 x 3" length pieces of 24-30 AWG wire (1/8" stripped off each end)
- 3 x 4" length pieces of 24-30 AWG wire (1/8" stripped off each end)
- 3 x 3 position Female Receptacle
- 1 x 3 position Female Housing
- 3 x Crimps for Female Housing
- Plastic board (ABS)
- 1 pack x 3/8" 4-40 Screws (91772A108)
- 2 packs x 4-40 Nuts

### Tools
- Soldering Iron
- Scissors or Tin Snips
- Crimping tool
- Screw driver
- Drill with 1/8" bit
- Sandpaper
- Dremel tool or other cutting tool

### Software
- Arduino
- Processing

## Step 2: Constructing the plastic insert

First we will need to create a insert to attach the Power Supply board and three of the Muscle Sensors. This insert will fit inside the project enclosure and rest on top of the Arduino UNO and the last muscle sensor.

All four
L. Bicep    R. Bicep
L&R Bicep    L. Forearm    R. Forearm
L. Forearm    R. Forearm

If you're using relatively thin plastic board material, you can probably use a set of heavy duty scissors or tin snips to cut out the insert.

After you construct the insert, try sliding it into the bottom of the enclosure and putting the top on. If it doesn't fit properly, get the sand paper out and sand down the parts that are interfering.

## Step 3: Preparing the bottom of the project enclosure

Next we'll prepare the Arduino project enclosure.

First, trim down the two middle supports on the bottom of the enclosure. Leave enough height so that they will still go through your Arduino mounting holes but not go past the Arduino headers.

Next, place one of the muscle sensors in the bottom left of the enclosure by sliding the bottom left support through the muscle sensor's mounting hole (the one near the female headers). Straighten the sensor by rotating it around the support such that its sides are parallel with the enclosures. Gently and such that you don't jostle the sensor board, slide your plastic insert onto the enclosure and hold it above the sensor. Now, look down the rectangular cutout on your insert and verify the three male headers of your sensor are directly below. If not, remove the insert, adjust the sensor position and repeat until it is in position. Once it is in position, mark the location of the muscle sensor's second mounting pin, remove the sensor, and drill the hole.

Note: If you don't get the hole in exactly the right position, it's OK you can just widen the cutout more to compensate.

## Step 4: Preparing the top of the project enclosure

Next, you'll need to modify the top portion of the enclosure as well. Using a Dremel tool or some other cutting tool, completely cut off the reinforcement wall near

the front of the enclosure. Additionally, completely cut off the two middle supports that complement the supports you cut on the bottom portion of the enclosure. These both need to be removed to give us some more head room for the muscle sensors and plastic insert.

## Step 5: Soldering the power supply connectors

We now need to create a way to connect the Power Supply board to each of the sensors. Grab your power supply board, the four sets of wire lengths, and the female housing and receptacles.

On the Power Supply board, there is a grid of through holes in a 3 column x 4 row pattern. Solder the three 3" wires to the holes in row 1, solder the three 2" wires to the holes in row 2, solder the three 1" wires to row 3, and solder the 4" wires to the holes in row 4.

Next, grab your 3 female receptacles and bend all the solder tabs so that they're at a 90 degree angle. For the 1"-3" wire sets, solder the female receptacles (with the ports facing downward) such that the wire soldered to the +5V column is soldered to the right solder tab, the GND wire is soldered to the middle solder tab, and the -5V wire is soldered to the left solder tab. For reinforcement, dab a glob of hot glue on the joints.

Using a crimping tool (you can also choose to solder instead of crimping), crimp the crimp tips to each of the 4" wires with the tabs pointing upward. Now insert each of the wires' crimp tips into the female housing, again following the +5V right, GND middle, -5V left order.

Your power supply board should be ready to go. Double check each solder and crimp to make sure they'll good and solid.

## Step 6: Mounting the muscle sensors and power supply board

Now it is time to mount your sensors using the 4-40 screws and nuts.

Grab three of your sensors and the power supply board and put a screw into each mounting hole. Thread a nut on each screw but leave it slightly loose. These nuts will be used as standoffs.

Next, place each sensor's mounting screw into each corresponding mounting hole. Remember to keep the muscle sensors' female headers on the same side as the shelf's offset. Thread another nut onto each screw until they are nice and tight. Tighten more with a screw driver and a wrench, holding the second nut secure.

Next, follow this same process for the power supply board. Make sure the power jack is facing the front side of the shelf.

For the last muscle sensor, insert a screw up through the bottom of the enclosure and secure with a nut. Then slide the muscle sensor down the support column and insert the screw into the sensor's mounting hole and secure with a nut.

games

Check to make sure you can fit the female housing through the gap between the sensors and down into the rectangular cutout and onto the male headers of the sensor below. If the gap is too tight, remove one of the top sensors and sand one of its mounting holes on the shelf until the gap is wide enough.

For the remainder of these instructions we're going to refer to the sensors as follows:

Sensor 1 = Closest to Power Supply
Sensor 2 = Middle
Sensor 3 = End
Sensor 4 = Bottom

## Step 7: Connecting the power supply to the muscle sensors

By this time, your muscle sensors and power supply should be mounted and your Arduino should be in the project enclosure. Now you should be ready to start connecting everything together and set up your electrodes.

First you'll want to give all your sensors power. Insert the plastic insert into the project enclosure and then connect each

female receptacle and housing to the corresponding sensors. (Hint... the 1" wire goes to the sensor closest to the power supply, the 2" wire goes to the middle sensor on the insert, the 3" wire to the last sensor on the insert, and the 4" wire goes through the rectangular cutout to the sensor on bottom.) MAKE SURE THE CORRECT VOLTAGES ARE CONNECTED TO THE CORRESPONDING SENSOR PINS (+Vs = +5V, GND = GND, -Vs = -5V). IF NOT, YOU CAN POTENTIALLY BURN OUT YOUR SENSOR BOARD.

DOUBLE CHECK.... BETTER SAFE THAN SORRY!

## Step 8: Decide which muscles are going to control which button(s)

Now, you're going to have to decide which muscles/muscle combos you want to use for your button(s) layout. We've opted to go with the following layout. If you want to go with a different layout, you'll have to make some modifications to the Arduino code we'll get to later on.

**Function buttons:**

Button A à Right forearm muscle
Button B à Left forearm muscle
Start Button à Not muscle controlled
Select Button à Not muscle controlled

**Directonal pad:**

Right à Right bicep muscle
Left à Left bicep muscle
Up à All four muscles (combo)
Down à Left and right bicep muscles (combo)

## Step 9: Attaching the electrodes to your muscles

Next, you'll need to attach the electrodes to your muscles. The image above illustrates where to place the electrodes for our button layout. You can use any muscle you want (bigger muscles have stronger signals and surface muscles are easier to detect) but for our example we've gone with the ones shown.

games

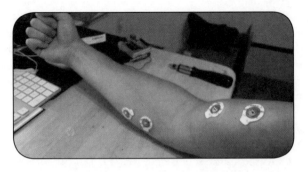

## Step 10: Connecting the electrodes to the muscle sensor(s)

Now, we'll attach the electrodes to each muscle sensor using the EMG cables.

Sensor 1
Dark green- M.Mid Pin
Light green - M.End Pin
Sensor 2
Dark pink- M.Mid Pin
Light pink - M.End Pin
Sensor 3
Dark red - M.Mid Pin
Light red - M.End Pin
Sensor 4
Dark blue- M.Mid Pin
Light blue - M.End Pin

Each muscle sensor needs a reference electrode to be connected to the Ref pin. For our example, we are going to place them on the back of the forearm near the elbow. The reference electrodes should be placed on electrically neutral areas of the body such as the bony area by the elbow.

## Step 11: Connecting the muscle sensor(s) to the Arduino

Now we're getting close. By this step, your muscle electrodes and power supply should be hooked up to your muscle sensors. We just have to connect the sensors to the Arduino.

Using the solid core wire/jumper wire, connect the Vout pin of each muscle sensor to the analog pins on your Arduino.

Sensor 1 Vout --> Analog pin 0
Sensor 2 Vout --> Analog pin 1
Sensor 3 Vout --> Analog pin 2
Sensor 4 Vout --> Analog pin 3

Then connect the GND pin of muscle sensor 1 to the GND pin on your Arduino and the GND pin of muscle sensor 2 to the Analog pin 3 of your Arduino. That last part will keep the remaining two analog pins from floating along with your sensor 4's output.

## Step 12: Upload visualization sketch to your Arduino

By this point, your USB Biofeedback Game Controller should be completely assembled and hooked up. Before we go any further, we'll need to test out your muscle sensors to make sure everything is setup properly.

To test your setup, we're going to use the same visualization software as we used in our muscle sensor demo video. If you haven't already, download and install both the Arduino and Processing software.

Next, download and unzip the visualization program files: Arduino, Processing. Open the Arduino sketch and upload it to your UNO. If you're new to Arduino, check out the information on Arduino's website to help you on this step. Once uploaded, plug in the wall adapter to the barrel jack to power up your muscle sensors.

Next, open the Processing sketch and hit the Run button in the top left. Another window will pop up with 6 colored bars on it. Flex your right forearm, left forearm, right bicep, and left bicep and watch the bars move accordingly. If while at rest, your sensors value is below or above 150 then adjust the gain of your sensor using a screwdriver and turning the poteniometer on the corresponding sensor so that they are around 150 at rest.

As you flex each muscle, the bars should move past the 300 mark. This is important since the software to follow uses the 300 mark to trigger a "button press." You can adjust the gain of your sensor and this threshold level in the code to fine tune your desired button press sensitivity.

Once everything appears to be in working order, close out Processing and you're ready to hack your Arduino into a keyboard.

## Step 13: Upload keyboard sketch to your Arduino

Now, we'll work on turning your Arduino UNO into a HID keyboard.

First, Download the zipped Arduino project from our Google Docs page. (https://docs.google.com/file/d/0B8Wy2qiwirwyZWJiMWQzNDMtM2U5YS00NDc0LTlINDctOGZlMWFlNWRkYTlw/edit?hl=en_US)

Then unzip, compile and upload the sketch to your Arduino.

This is the code that, if desired, you would modify the threshold value in to adjust the "button" sensitivity.

## Step 14: Hack your Ardunio to load new atmega8u2 firmware

To play video games on your computer with the Arduino, we're going to turn your Arduino into a HID USB keyboard to interface with your computer; to do this you'll need to upload new firmware.

## Introduction

I attended Google I/O 2011 and managed to get my hands on an Android ADK demo board. ADK is the Accessory Development Kit, an Arduino-based interface board whereby you can connect your compatible Android device (2.3.4 and any device from 3.1 onwards) to virtually any hardware and use the phone to control a device, or vice-versa. It's called the Android Open Accessory platform, and it's totally cool.

To introduce the concept to the Google's keynote speech they produced a regular ball maze toy, familiar to many, which was controlled by a Motorola Xoom tablet. This Instructable is kind of two Instructables in one: First, I'll be illustrating the steps required to set up the ADK from scratch and then I'll be reproducing Google's ball maze on a Nexus One phone to demonstrate a simple use of the ADK board (I'll keep the massive bowling-ball version for another Instructable).

## Concept

The idea is relatively simple: monitor the phone's accelerometer, and translate the three-dimensional acceleration vector (i.e. which way is "down") into a coordinates on a two-dimensional plane — one dimension for each servo or axis of rotation on the maze. This is mapped to two absolute positions between 0-255 for positioning the servo arms. These values are passed to the ADK board which acts as the servo controller and controls the tilt on the maze.

In other words, you can now play the ball maze game by using your phone as a remote controller!

## Step 1: Materials and tools
### Materials
- A ball maze / labyrinth game
- Google's ADK Demo board or compatible ADK board with 2 servo outputs

- Two small servos (eg. mini servos found in small RC cars/helicopters)
- Google Nexus One or Nexus S with Gingerbread 2.3.4 (not tested on Nexus S)
- Short cable with female 3x2 or larger box connector (an internal USB panel patch cable works well)
- Male box connector pins - either: one 3x2 or two 3x1 (for connecting to servo sockets)
- 0.5mm aluminum or other pliable sheet metal (for servo brackets)
- Small springs or springy metal (e.g. I used stainless steel strips found in some wiper blades)
- A small block of wood (For mounting the "inner" servo to the ring)
- Thin stiff wire, e.g. paperclip wire (for servo lever arm fixtures)
- Assorted small screws (to secure servo brackets)
- Small tacks, nails or a staple gun (to secure springs in place)
- Cable ties
- A few drops of oil or grease, particularly if your maze is 30+ years old like mine

### Required tools:
- Drill and drill bits (I used 1mm, 6mm bits)
- 1-2 pairs of small needle-nosed pliers
- Wire clippers
- Screwdrivers
- Soldering iron
- Sharp knife / craft knife

### Other useful tools:
- Drill press
- Small hand-held rotary drill/grinder tool (Dremel or similar)
- Diamond-tipped engraving bit or drill bit (for drilling holes in stainless steel spring strips)
- Bench grinder
- Small hammer / tack hammer

## Step 2: Setting up Android development software (Eclipse)

To compile the source code you'll need an Android development environment, and the easiest one to set up and use is probably Eclipse. The entire installation process is well documented on this page, but here are the basic steps:

1. Download the appropriate installer for your operating system and install (choose the "Eclipse Classic" version).
2. Download the Android Software Development Kit (SDK) and install it.
3. Download and Configure the Android Development Tools (ADT) for Eclipse.
4. Add Platform support for the Platform APIs and Google APIs. If installing on a Nexus One or Nexus S you will need the following (whatever is the latest revision is for each):
- SDK Platform Android 2.3.3, API 10
- Google APIs by Google Inc., Android API 10

## Step 3: Install ADK components and setting up DemoKit

"That's a lot of software to set up," I hear you say... But you want your maze, so press on!!

### ADK Components

Now that you have a functional Eclipse environment, you are ready to set up the ADK components and test the board. The process is well documented here so I'll only outline the three steps briefly here. Once you've done this, you are ready to test:

1. Install Arduino Software (contains libraries and an IDE for coding and installing firmware to the ADK board).
Install the CapSense library (not strictly required for this project, but if you're going to be tinkering with the ADK — which I'm sure you will — you should install this now. It contains the libraries to sense human capacitance. This is needed for the capacitive button that is located on the ADK shield).
2. Install the ADK package (contains the firmware for the ADK board and hardware design files for the ADK board and shield).

### Setting up USB Debugging

While we're not going to actually use USB debugging, enabling it provides a quick, easy way to quickly compile, install and test apps on your device. Follow steps 2 and 3 outlined here to enable USB debugging.

### Compiling and Running the DemoKit app

Finally, follow the steps outlined here to get the DemoKit application working on your Android device (if you've followed my steps then you've already done the first step). When it says "Install the application to your device," do the following:
On the device, go to the home screen, press MENU, select Applications > Development, and make sure USB debugging is enabled. You may get a warning—

that's fine, it just means that when connected via USB you will be able to install and run applications from Eclipse without any user interaction on the phone. If you want to be super-protective you can disable this when you're done.

3. Connect your device via USB
4. With the DemoKit code open in Eclipse, select Run > Run or press Ctrl-F11. If you see the Android Device Chooser, just select your Android device and click OK. Eclipse will upload the compiled package and run it automatically.

Now finally you're ready for some fun!

## Step 4: Setting up the ADK board and testing with DemoKit

Without the ADK board the DemoKit application you've just compiled is a little pointless, so once it is running on your phone (you'll see an Android robot with a front panel open), disconnect the USB cord from the computer and (with the other end still attached to the phone) plug it into the ADK board's USB host port.

Plug the power into the ADK board and you should see a power indicator light up on the main Arduino board (under the demo "shield" board which is on top).

Now that DemoKit is installed on your phone you can run it as often as you like — you no longer need to recompile unless you want to make changes. When connecting the phone to the ADK board, you should get a message like the one shown in the second image — be sure not to check the "Use by default for this USB accessory" because we also want to use the RealMaze program with the ADK board. Simply click OK to start using it.

The initial screen has a number of hardware input indicators — showing the status of buttons, temperature, light sensors and more. tap "Out" tab at the top to show the controls for ADK outputs — relay switching, LED brightness controls and servo controls.

Connect the servos to the ADK board, taking care with the polarity — Black = Ground or -, Red = +, Grey = Signal.

Now you can control the servos using the sliders (second image). If it's not working check the power light on the board, USB connection, and re-check the servo polarity. Test the other outputs on the demo shield: lights and relays.

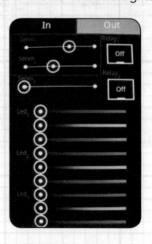

## Step 5: Compiling and running RealMaze

Now for installing and compiling the RealMaze code. RealMaze is just a severely and shamelessly ripped, hashed-up and duct-taped-together-again version of DemoKit with a bit of code from around the web (sources cited in the code). It's called RealMaze because all the other accelerometer-based ball maze games are fakes onscreen. This one controls the real thing.

1. Download the RealMaze.zip file attached to this Instructable and extract the files (with paths intact) in a suitable source code location.
2. In Eclipse, select File > New Project, then choose Android > Android Project and click Next.
3. Type the project name "RealMaze" choose "Create project from existing source."
4. Check that the Build target is correct for your device (Using Google APIs version 2.3.3 for Nexus or 3.1 for tablets)
5. Click Finish
6. Reconnect your phone to the PC then in Eclipse under Package Explorer, right-click RealMaze and select Run As > Android Application

Similar to the DemoKit installation, you should now have the RealMaze program installed on your phone. Disconnect the phone from the PC and connect to the ADK board. You'll see a message similar to the one you got with DemoKit, click OK and you should now be in control of the servos using the tilt on your phone.

(Note: One known bug is that RealMaze does not resume well if you start another activity then try to go back to it. Simply start it again from the programs list.)

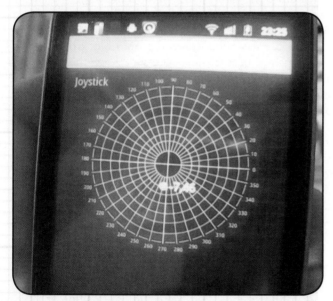

## Step 6: The maze hardware - preparation

### Basic preparation

If the maze you're using is anything like mine was, it might need a bit of thought. I had to dust it out, oil up the pivot points, and remove hot glue that was used to stick the back on (after it had been dropped many years ago).

Remove the panel on the underside to get at the maze mechanics — this may require removal of screws, wood staples, or in my case an old hot glue repair job. The two tiny servos were easily strong enough to move the tilting deck and the string, rods and knobs that were attached to it. If your controls are still stiff after oiling you may have to disconnect the old mechanism for this to work more smoothly.

Important note: When referring to the connected wooden parts that make up the tilting maze I will hereafter refer to the outer box as the "casing," the slightly smaller square wooden ring inside the casing as the "ring" and the actual maze which sits inside the ring as the "table."

### Servo location

You now need to identify where to put the servos (but we're not mounting them just yet!). You don't want the ball to hit a servo, spring or any wiring when it drops through a hole

- You also don't want the ball to get stuck behind anything if it drops though a hole and starts rolling back to the exit
- You need to have enough space for the table to swing through both axes, plus clearance for the servos.
- You need to consider where to put your springs and how they will be attached. Springs are not critical, but they are a very good idea if you want your servos to last.
- One servo will have to be mounted on the casing, this will control the ring in one axis. The other servo will actually be attached to the "ring" (it moves when the other servo moves), and this controls the table top tilt in the other axis (which is always relative to the ring).
- Consider what orientation works best — the servo arm can be adjusted, so you may want to flip or rotate them to find the best position.

For these reasons, I decided to put my servos on the opposite side of the maze to the exit hole as shown. There's not quite enough clearance there to replace the sloping base panel, but I've decided not to for now.

### Spring shape, size and placement

My springs came from wiper blades — some blades are reinforced with flat stainless steel rods and these make a perfect springy lever for attaching servos to the board. You will have to experiment a bit with size and shape, and consider where they might be placed. Here are some pointers:

- Add a 90 degree twist near the top end of the spring, this increases the strength of the spring and ensures the servo linkage can be attached.
- The springs should be soft (i.e. long) enough to provide the servos with some protection. With a servo arm screwed onto the servo pivot point, you can test this by cutting a length of metal and using it to (very gently) try and turn the servo arm at the furthest point from the pivot. Ideally you should probably have about 10-15mm of flex in either direction without the servo arm moving.

Be careful when doing this, as some servos don't take external forces well and this could strip the gears.

- The springs should be stiff (i.e. short) enough to move the table with very little flexing. This probably comes down to adequate lubrication, but you can test this by taking the same piece of metal above and (with the maze the right way up) using it to tilt the table in each axis. There should be no more than a few mm of flexing anymore and your maze will be "sticky" and very hard to play.

- The springs also allow you to raise the pivot point away from the table — you need some separation to ensure the spring has room to flex and the table has room to move through the full swing (or at least as much as the servos will allow).

Shape is less important, but with springs like this it is the total length from mounting point to lever arm pivot that gives it its "spring." Watch how each spring moves in relation to the servo arm when the table is tilted in each axis, and look for a good place to mount the spring. Mark it with pencil.

Each spring will need a small hole at the top end to connect the servo linkage to, plus it may need 2 more at the base as I did depending on how you decide to mount them. Stainless steel does not drill well at small diameters, so I used a diamond-tipped engraving bit to slowly drill my holes (approx 1mm diameter), a drill press will work best for this.

If you find drilling the stainless is too hard, you may wish to use epoxy glue or similar to mount them instead, and on the top end you could glue a small piece of plastic with the hole for the servo linkage instead.

### Cable placement

Like the servos, you don't want the cables interfering with the ball or table movement. Decide where you are going to locate the cables — if the servos are apart from each other you may need additional connectors or extensions. Don't drill or cut anything just yet until you actually have your servos in place.

## Step 7: The maze hardware - putting it together

### Mounting Servos

Using the sliders on the DemoKit app, move each servo as close as possible to the midpoint of its 180 degree rotation, then disconnect from the board. Holding the first servo roughly in its mounting position, attach the plastic lever arm to the servo pivot so that it's roughly horizontal. Screw the lever arm to the servo pivot. Repeat with the other servo in its place.

Now mount the servos in place. I used thin strips of sheet metal cut to size as straps around the servos and screwed them into the wood. In my case the "outer" servo is mounted to the casing near the corner, and it is used to tilt the ring. The "inner" servo is mounted on a block of wood, which is mounted to the ring, close to the ring's pivot with the outside casing. This servo is used to tilt the inner maze table.

If you are mounting a servo on a block of wood for clearance as I have done, make sure when this block and servo are mounted that there is enough clearance for the maze table to move full swing in both directions, as well as pivot on the opposite axis without hitting anything.

Once you've mounted the servos, you'll need to identify the relationship between servo arm swing and the displacement of the maze table (via the spring). Image 2 depicts the servo arm swing (most servos turn 180 degrees, I allow for slightly less). A full clockwise rotation pushes the spring "down" (at least from this perspective), while a full counter-clockwise rotation pulls the spring "up" approximately the same distance.

### Mounting the springs

Now you can mount the springs. If you didn't drill the holes in the springs, find the optimum position and glue in place. If you managed to drill the holes in the base of the springs, you can now position them one at a time, mark and pre-drill the holes slightly undersize with a Dremel and perhaps 1mm drill bit. You can then use small tacks or 1.5mm diameter nails which have been cut down to approximately 10mm long and re-sharpened on a bench grinder. A small tack hammer works well here. If

games

drilling/nailing make sure you're nailing into some wood on the other side, not just through the maze surface!

### Adding linkage

Now that servos and springs are in place (and assuming servos are still center-swing), with the table level you can start preparing the linkage. Put a small Z-shaped bend in the wire close to one end and feed this through the hole in the spring. Measure or mark where on the wire the server arm hole is, then make another Z bend in the wire at that position and cut just marginally after the second bend, as shown in the third image. You should now be able to feed the bottom Z-bend into the spring and with only slight bending you should be able to gently click the top into place on the servo arm. Repeat with the other servo linkage.

### Wiring it up

Finally, you need to add the wiring. I used a USB cable that is often found inside PC's to connect the motherboard to a USB port panel. This works well because at least one end is wired with a block connector which will fit onto the ADK board. You can carefully trim the plug (usually 8-10 pin) down to 6 pins with a craft knife, and trim the unused wires back.

Bring the servo plugs together and this is where you can drill a hole to feed the cable through. Drill a hole the same diameter as the cable, cut any plug from the other end of the cable, and feed it through the hole, with the female box connector on the outside.

On the other end (the inside), we actually want a male 6-pin block connector to plug the servos into, that is if you don't fancy cutting off the servo plugs and soldering them to this cable. I used one from an old sound card. Solder it on, being very careful to get the wiring of the pins right so that they match the female plug on the other end. Test with a multimeter if necessary.

I then used a couple of cable ties to hold the wires out of the way of the ball and stop the cable slipping and damaging things if it was tugged from the outside. I plugged the servos into the male connectors, I then separated the servo plugs and bent the two sets of 3 pins apart so that there was minimal pulling on the relatively fragile servo wires.

Finally, check and double check the servo cable wiring and polarity, then plug the cable into the ADK board. You should hear the servos move into place if they've been moved off center at all (and hopefully the maze table will move too), and that means you're good to move on to the next step.

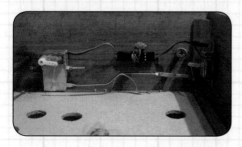

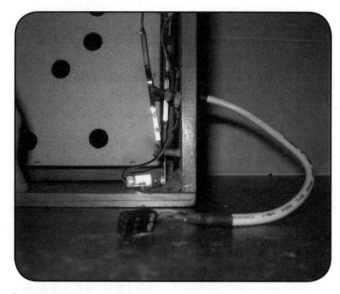

## Step 8: Fine tuning

Wow — you now have a fully functional maze that you can control from your phone... but chances are that it's not quite playable yet.

### Axis swapping

The first thing to adjust is if the axes are the wrong way around. If your maze moves side-to-side when you tilt your phone forward and back then that's a simple fix - swap the servo plugs over.

### Inverting an axis

If, for example, you tilt your phone forward and the maze tilts back then you need to invert the movement on one axis (or both). This is done by making a change in the RealMaze code in Eclipse. Open RealMazeActivity.java from the Package Explorer > RealMaze > src > com.google.android.RealMaze. Edit the lines highlighted in Image 1 (about line 110) by changing the (x*1.5) to (x*-1.5) if you believe the x axis needs flipping, or change the (y*1.0) to (1*-1.0) if the y axis needs flipping.

### Changing sensitivity

If the servos are moving too wildly or not wildly enough for you, then you can change the multiplier on the commands sent to the servos. For some reason the x axis needed multiplying by 1.5 for me (which is pretty significant — I still don't know why), but it may be dependent on hardware. Simply adjust the 1.5 or 1.0 in those same two lines to adjust sensitivity. You probably won't have to change either one lower than about 0.7 or higher than about 2.0.

Recompile, redeploy and retest. Rinse, repeat. When it's working better, move to the final (and most important) step....

## Step 9: Play!

Fire up RealMaze again, connect to the ADK board, and enjoy the fruits of your hard work!

# LED Pinball Coffee Table

By Zieak

(http://www.instructables.com/id/LED-Pinball-coffee-table/)

I found an old pinball machine at the dump. I promptly took it home and out it in the house where it sat in my living room long enough to put rust stains on the carpeting where the metal feet sat.

It wasn't complete enough to make it work without spending a lot of time and money on it. I live too far away from a market to sell it as-is. And honestly, the wife didn't seem too keen on starting a game parlor with our limited space.

So I decided to make a coffee table out of the main playing surface.

## Step 1: Tools and materials
This will largely depend on what you have available...
- A pinball machine
- Lumber
- Plywood
- Screws
- Staples
- Hot glue
- Tempered glass
- Aluminum stock
- Wood glue
- A few strings of LED Christmas lights
    Some suggested tools...
- Screwdrivers
- Drill and bits
- Pencil
- Tape measure
- Glue gun
- Staple gun
- Small nailgun
- Belt sander
- Miter saw
- Table saw
- Bench grinder
- Reciprocating saw
- Pliers
- Wire cutters
- Bolt cutters

## Step 2: Disassemble the pinball machine
Once you have a derelict pinball machine the hard part is over. Now start taking the thing apart.

NOTE: Vintage pinball machines are collector's items. Make an effort to get parts into the hands of people working to restore these collectible machines. You won't be using all of the parts in this project so save the rest and don't send them to the dump! (Note that this machine was salvaged from the dump before you blast me for cannibalizing it in this way.)

Remove the scoreboard area, the legs, and then get to removing the guts — well, most of them. You'll want to leave in the flippers, and any other items that project onto the play surface. If the mechanical system extends too far below the play surface you might want to fake it by cutting off a part and reattaching it later.

games

## Step 3: Replace lights with LEDs

I carefully went through the machine and replaced with LEDs where there had been incandescent light bulbs.

First you need to remove the plastic ends put on the light strings to make them "icicle-like." I found that some came off easily with just a twist of my fingers. Others needed pliers to be worked loose and some needed to be clipped off with wire cutters.

I then used a combination of staples and hot glue to affix the lights to the back side of the board. Be extremely careful not to pierce the insulation of the wires when using the stapler. I used the stapler mostly to position the lights that penetrated through the play board. I used the glue-gun to position the ones that needed to be glued in place against the transparent plastic indicators.

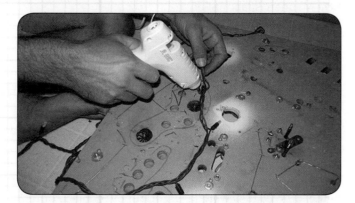

## Step 4: Build a frame for the table

I had two dimensions I had to work around — the size of the pinball play field and the size of the tempered glass that I had on hand. You might live somewhere that you can just order a piece of glass to fit the same size as your machine. Or you might have the glass from the machine you're working with. I had to use two pieces that I had kicking around though. And I don't have the tools to cut tempered glass. (And will not ever, I suspect.)

I used yellow cedar for the frame. I notched out a groove for plywood on the bottom side for rigidity. I used

stainless steel screws that were countersunk in the wood for the frame corners. And I used some strips to support the sides of the glass just above the play field.

## Step 5: Add legs

I have a problem figuring out the legs for the tables I want to build. But I had some aluminum rectangular stock kicking around that I decided would do the trick.

I drilled pilot holes and then used screws to attach the legs to the frame on the inside. By using rough-cut lumber I had almost a full 2 inches of thickness to work with on the leg attachment points.

## Step 6: Enjoy it!

Now to put an electric outlet in the middle of the floor of the living room so that extension cords are not necessary.

games

# How to Build an Arduino Powered Chess Playing Robot

By Max Justicz (mJusticz)
(http://www.instructables.com/id/How-to-Build-an-Arduino-Powered-Chess-Playing-Robo/)

Judging by the sheer number of chess related Instructables, I think it's safe to say the community enjoys the game. It can be difficult, however, to find someone who plays on the same level you do. To solve this dilemma, and to increase my playing skills, I built this Arduino powered chess playing robot.

The board works like any other xy table, with a few key differences. First, the x axis has an extra servo attached to it, which raises and lowers a magnet. The magnet is attracted to pieces on the chess board above, allowing them to move. Second, embedded in the board are 64 magnetically activated reed switches, allowing the arduino to know the location of each piece.

## Step 1: Parts and materials

You may have many of the parts for this project already, but if you don't, the whole list costs about $350, depending on where you get your parts from. Many, many of them can be salvaged, so look to recycle before you buy!
• 1 Arduino Uno or Diecimila

We'll be using this arduino to drive our stepper motors and servos. You can pick these up just about anywhere online. I got mine from Adafruit. $30
• 1 Arduino Mega

This is the most expensive item in the project. It'll be dealing with the inputs from each chess square to let the computer know where you've moved. We're using the mega here due to its speed and number of inputs. Adafruit $65
• 1 Mux Shield

The mux shield (short for multiplexer) gives us even more inputs for our arduino mega. We'll need 64 inputs in total, one for each square. Sparkfun $25
• Motor Shield

The motor shield will be controlling our stepper motors and servo. You'll need to solder it together. Adafruit $19.50
• 1 Large chess board with pieces

This one is a little more self explanatory. We want a large chess board here because the pieces need to be able to move in between each other with disrupting others. Make sure you measure the diameter of the bottoms of the pieces. We'll need that in a moment. I'm not sure where mine is from, but you can pick them up from a flea market for a bargain. The playable area of my board is 24".
• 64 NO Reed Switches

Reed switches are magnetically activated switches. They'll help us find the location of moved pieces. "NO" stands for normally open, that is, the circuit is disconnected Digikey about $30.
• 16 10K 1/4 Watt Resistors

These are the pull up resistors for the built in digital pins. The mux shield, luckily, has integrated pull downs, so we don't need to worry about those. Digikey about $2.
• Roughly 90 feet of 30AWG Wire

This is the hookup wire for all of our sensors. About $16.
• Neodymium Magnets to fit your pieces

This is where the measurements from the bottoms of your chess pieces come in handy. You'll need disc magnets to fit underneath each piece. For proper strength, they should be about 1/8" think. A great source for these is K&J Magnetics, about $55
• 1 Large Neodymium Magnet

This magnet will be attached to the XY table underneath the board, to move each piece around. K&J Magnetics $19.
• 2 Pairs of 24" Drawer Bearings
• The size of your bearings will depend on the playable area of your chess board. These allow for the stepper motors to move back and forth underneath the board. Amazon, about $30
• 2 Stepper Motors

Stepper motors can move in very precise increments. In the late 90s they were in just about every piece of tech you could find. The best place to get these are in old dot-matrix printers. You can them at the flea market for next to nothing!
• 2 Vex Rack and Gear Sets

The rack gears allow the stepper motors to travel on the drawer bearings. See Step 4 for a more detailed explanation. Vex Store $40
• 1 Standard Hobby Servo

This servo will be raising and lowering the powerful magnet below the board. You can find them at a hobby shop for about $10.
• 1 2' x 2' Perf Board

The perf board is super thin and will be the mounting surface for all of our reed switches. The price will vary greatly on this one.

- 1 2' x 2' x 1/2" MDF Board

  Similar to the perf board.

- Various lengths of scrap 1"x2" wood

  This wood forms the bridge between the X-Axis drawer bearings. Go behind any hardware store and you'll see dumpsters full of this stuff for totally free!

- 5 Minute Epoxy

  This stuff is a godsend. It's used for just about everything in this project, from mounting motors to attaching the rack gears. I'm in love.

- 1 Wood Saw

  You probably already have this one, but if you don't.

## Step 2: Design and code explanation

That parts list is a bit scary if you're not sure what everything is going to do, so here's how many of the pieces will be used.

You can see in the images below that each stepper motor can move freely about its axis thanks to the drawer bearings. On the Y Axis, each rail is connected with the wooden structure, so that the X Axis may sit atop it. Also on the X Axis is the servo that raises and lowers the powerful magnet, so that it may position itself before moving pieces.

Feel free to download the sketch up file and mess around if you're not sure of anything.

Another interesting element of this design is how to code talks with the Arduino and motors. We need to address each square as a set of coordinates so that we may find slope and distance, however the traditional method of labeling squares A1, A2, etc. doesn't work particularly well in code. Standard (x,y) coordinates are much friendlier. Those coordinates, however, need to be in the form of a single number. What I ended up doing is assigning each square to a number Those numbers don't really work as coordinates on an 8x8 chess board, however, because we use a base 10 number system.

To solve that issue, we take the base 10 number of each square and convert it to base 8 using the modulus operator in C. 27, for example, is 33 in base 8, with the first digit being the x coordinate and the second the y. If you count over three squares and up three squares, voila! You end up on square 27.

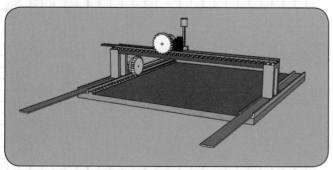

| Base 8 | | | | | | | |
|---|---|---|---|---|---|---|---|
| 7 | 17 | 27 | 37 | 47 | 57 | 67 | 77 |
| 6 | 16 | 26 | 36 | 46 | 56 | 66 | 76 |
| 5 | 15 | 25 | 35 | 45 | 55 | 65 | 75 |
| 4 | 14 | 24 | 34 | 44 | 54 | 64 | 74 |
| 3 | 13 | 23 | 33 | 43 | 53 | 63 | 73 |
| 2 | 12 | 22 | 32 | 42 | 52 | 62 | 72 |
| 1 | 11 | 21 | 31 | 41 | 51 | 61 | 71 |
| 0 | 10 | 20 | 30 | 40 | 50 | 60 | 70 |

## Step 3: Mounting the drawer bearings (Y Axis)

The drawer bearings are what allow the axes to move in their respective direction. The mounting instructions may vary slightly depending on the brand, but usually it's as simple as driving a couple of screws.

The only reason I've made this its own step is that aligning the bearings perfectly is key. Should you fail to do this, and they both point slightly outwards, they'll stop at some arbitrary point and refuse to move once you connect them. Save yourself a lot of trouble and use something you know is square as a reference for alignment. The corner of a book is perfect.

## Step 4: Building the motor mount (Y Axis)

The stepper motors we'll be using have fantastic torque, but are circular. This means mounting them to our bearings later on will be nearly impossible, unless we build a square mount. To build one, find a hole saw with a similar diameter to your motor. You'll want to use a drill press rather than a portable drill for this, so I borrowed my school's.

Once you've cut the hole, slice the circle in half to get two mounts. This chipped the tips of my semicircle, so I used some 220 grit sandpaper to clean up the edge.

My steppers came with mounting screw holes, which line up well with the wooden frame. I used the smallest screws I could find. Mine fit so well that it wasn't necessary, but you might consider adding a bit of epoxy to strengthen the bond.

## Step 5: Installing the rack gears (Y Axis)

The rack gears are what allow the motor to latch onto a surface to pull itself along. Your physics teacher probably defined them as a way to convert rotational energy to linear.

Again, we use the epoxy to attach the gears onto the MDF. In addition to heavily applying epoxy to the board itself, make sure some is spread on the side of the drawer bearing, that way there is stability in two dimensions. Do your best to prevent epoxy from getting in places it shouldn't be — you may gum up your motor.

It works out that the rack gears extend a little bit off of each end. This is a good thing — it enables the gear to travel the full length of the board without running off. The stepper motor will be offset just enough that if the gears only covered the board's length the whole motor assembly would get stuck at one end.

Also install the circular gears onto your motor at this time. Mine had a set-screw, but you may wish to use some JB weld to hold your gear in place. If you go that route, the joint needs to fully cure before you try to use it, or you risk the gear popping off!

## Step 6: Wiring and mounting the motor (Y Axis)

The leads that come attached to the stepper motors are very short. Because the Arduino is mounted off the board, the wires need to be at least the length of one side. That made mine about 2' 5" long. Heat shrink tubing is your friend here — we're using enough power that it might arc if you're not careful.

If your stepper motor has 5 wires, you're all set. If there are 6, however, it means you have to connect your center taps. Jason Babcock has a great tutorial on reverse-engineering your motors. In my case, however, the wires were the same color.

After extending the wires, the center taps go into the center of one of your motor hubs. The wires from one coil go to one terminal on the motor shield, and from the other coil to the other terminal. At this time we also hook up our 24v 1A power supply to the motor shield. If you get the polarity wrong on this, your motor shield is toast.

After trimming the motor mounting block to about 4 inches, it's time to attach it to our bearings. Mix up the epoxy, and liberally apply it to the area of the bearing the block will touch.

Also, if you have any pets, be sure to animal-proof the room you're working in. Cats seem to have an affinity for knocking over things that are drying.

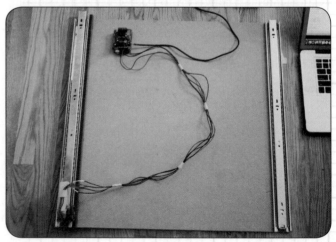

games

## Step 7: Mounting the crossbars (X Axis)

Atop the Y Axis sits a cross-bar which will hold the X Axis. To do this, we mount another block on the opposite Y Axis bearing. This will across from the motor mounting block.

Then we cut two 2' lengths of 1"x2" wood and mount them to the blocks with wood screws. Make sure these screws are in tight, or the bearings might not move at the same time. You might consider adding some wood-glue to lock them more tightly in place. While these cross bars need to be large enough to support our X Axis bearing, we want to use the least amount possible to avoid unnecessary weight. If the entire X assembly weighs too much, our Y Axis stepper motor won't have enough torque to move efficiently, or, if it's really heavy, at all.

Test that your bearings move evenly with each other. The crossbars should be as close to perpendicular with the bearings as possible.

## Step 8: Mounting the drawer bearing and rack gears (X Axis)

We are going to mount this drawer bearing in the same way we did on the Y Axis. Using the included mounting screws, attach it to the crossbars, making sure to leave room on one side for the rack gears.

This time, however, we have some options for mounting the rack gears. We can choose which side to mount them on. This is going to vary depending on how your motors are placed on their blocks. Once you've decided where to place them, though, they are glued in exactly the same way as on the Y Axis. Extend the rack gears slightly off of each end to make sure we have full travel on our steppers.

Again, make sure to try and keep any glue out of the sliding mechanism. If you do allow some glue to enter the mechanism, all is not lost. Fortunately for us, drawer bearings come in pairs, so we'll have one left over anyway. Mount it to the same screw holes and you're set! Just don't do it again!

## Step 9: Attaching the magnet to the servo (X Axis)

The chess board needs to be able to move into position and grab a piece. To accomplish this, we achieve a pseudo Z Axis by mounting a magnet to a servo on top of the X Axis. Use epoxy to attach your large magnet to a small piece of wood (Jenga blocks work wonderfully). Once that has dried, attach the wooden block to your servo.

If you're concerned about the torque of your servo, you might consider adding a counterweight to make lifting the magnet less difficult.

At this time you should also extend the leads on your servo motor. Do this the same way you did for your stepper, going one wire at a time and covering it with heat-shrink tubing or electrical tape.

Epoxy bonds best when there is a significant weight holding the two bonding surfaces together. Keep in mind that while 5 minute epoxy dries in 5 minutes, it may not cure for several hours.

## Step 10: Wiring and mounting the motor (X Axis)

We mount and wire our X Axis motor as we did earlier, however we also need to attach our servo assembly. We need to mount the servo as closely to our motor as we can get without interfering with the gearing. This way we are guaranteed to have maximum coverage underneath the board.

Using a piece of wire or cotton swab, carefully apply epoxy to the block where you've decided to attach your servo. If you aren't careful, some epoxy may end up on your stepper motor, rendering it useless. It's a real pain to clear mixed epoxy out of motors, so it's worth the extra time it will take. Firmly hold your servo in place for several seconds, and leave it clamped to dry.

Once your servo is mounted, we can attach the motor block to our bearings. Being cautious as to not get glue in the sliding mechanism and, like earlier, apply the epoxy to the exposed metal the block will touch.

After that is dry, wire the motor like you did before, extending each lead. This time, however, we'll connect it to the other motor terminal. Congratulations, the XY Table is done!

## Step 11: Wiring the sensors

Each chess piece has a magnet embedded in its bottom, which makes detecting location really simple. Underneath each square is a magnetic reed switch hooked up to our Arduino mega. When a change is detected, the Arduino spits out the coordinates.

Pull up resistors make sure we don't get false readings from our sensors. 48 of the 64 switches won't need pull up resistors, because the multiplexer has them built in. Unfortunately, we still have to solder 64 sensors. To make this go a lot faster, tin your wires before you try to solder them to the switches. Basically, just add solder to the wire alone before soldering with it. Label each switch with tape as it is completed to avoid a wiring nightmare later!

Hook up each switch to the Arduino as you go along. The multiplexer has a built in ground next to each input, which is really convenient.

To wire the pull-up resistors to the built in pins, connect one resistor end to 5V and one to the pin you're using. Then, skipping the resistor, connect one end of your switch to ground and the other directly to your pin.

Find a comfortable chair, because this is going to take a while!

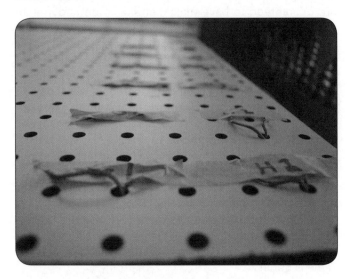

## Step 12: Place the magnets

Each chess piece has a magnet embedded in its bottom to trigger the reed switches. The only thing that's important here is that every piece on one side of the board has one polarity (like north), and every piece on the other side has the opposite (like south). If you'd only like the computer to play one color, make sure it is the opposite of the magnet attached to the servo, so they will attract each other.

Other than that, though, this only takes a few minutes.

## Step 13: Code, final assembly, and reflection

The code for this project is surprisingly simple. It takes the reading from the chess board out of terminal, plugs it into a chess algorithm already built into Mac OS X (look inside the Chess.app bundle), and spits out the coordinates back into the Arduino window with some fancy applescript. The algorithm is a fantastic open source project called Sjeng, meaning this will work cross platform as well.

The final assembly for this project is fairly simple. Find something to hold up your sensor grid, and lay that down. Next, place your chess board and pieces on top. You're done! Run the software and give it a whirl.

### Reflection

There are changes I would make to this project if I revisit it. First, the mounting of the gears should be improved; a few times the gears would pop off due to the heating of the stepper motors. Proper mounting with screws would fix this. Second, the board gets (fairly severely) out of calibration after a few moves, presumably due to skipped steps, and must be manually moved back to the origin to avoid misalignment. Some potentiometers allowing the board to know its absolute position would fix this. The rails, despite my best efforts, were misaligned, making the last few rows of squares very difficult for the stepper motors, causing them to skip steps and click loudly (bigger steppers would be better). Sometimes the motors would stop altogether and wouldn't be able to make it in those rear squares, rendering a game unplayable without human intervention. Aligning the rails better would fix this. Third, the code could probably be streamlined further; I completed this project when I was relatively new to C and Arduino. I'm sure there's a better way to do this than having an applescript copy and paste into the Arduino environment!

# Magnetic Acrylic Rubik's Cube

### By gfixler
(http://www.instructables.com/id/Magnetic-Acrylic-Rubik-s-Cube/)

27 ¾" clear acrylic cubes are drilled with 108 3/16" holes, fitted with 108 D32 neodymium disc magnets with proper polarities facing out from each, and assembled into a size-matched magnetic version of the original Rubik's Cube.

## Step 1: Plan out polarities

Before I devoted my time to this idea, which came to me while imagining a version of the cube that didn't need the intricate connecting tabs found inside a cube, I checked Google for magnetic Rubik's cubes, finding none (though a friend found one, theoretically, available in China by removing the 's from Rubik the day before I finished this thing). Then I mocked up a 3D version in Maya to figure out the polarities of the magnets to see if it would remain sound as faces were spun all around. It appeared that it would.

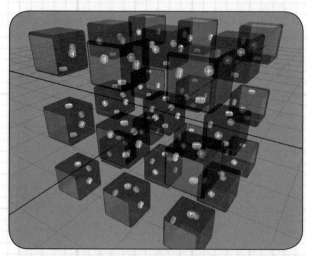

## Step 2: Get some cubes

I researched cubes of all sorts online, including wooden blocks, "learning cubes," cubes of ABS, PVC, etc, and finally settled on ¾" clear cast acrylic cubes from Tap Plastics: http://www.tapplastics.com/shop/product.php?pid=136&.

I got 3 sets of 10, as I needed 27. The extra 3 helped me test things out, which saved me some big trouble. These aren't all that precise, with romboid and trapezoidal angles aplenty, but in the end, they work well, especially as they're nicely rounded.

## Step 3: Get some magnets

I settled on their D32 3/16" disc magnets, which are 3/16" tall.

I got a pack of 100, and a pack of 25. I needed 108 for the cube prototype. If I build another, I'm going to beef up 12 of the magnets — the 6 pairs that form the axles off the center cube, probably to twice the width, perhaps to the D63.

## Step 4: Set up the drill press

I don't have a shop at the moment, so I had to settle on a cheap drill press on the dining room table. I used a needlessly high-precision CNC-milled clamping.

I held the clamp guides in place with some small Irwin Quick-Clamps, and later, for some more stability, with standard metal C clamps.

To align things, I eyeballed it: I'd get it about right, clamp it down, then press the non-spinning bit into the acrylic to make a tiny dent, then turned the cube 90 degrees and pressed again.

## Step 5: Get your polarities straight

It's crucial that all these axially-polarized disc magnets are put in the right way, and I'm glad to say I didn't mess this up once in all 108 magnets. To keep me straight as to which side of each magnet was which, I stuck them all together in one long rod, then drew a Sharpie dot on one end, and peeled that magnet off, and repeated, all the way down. Now they all had a visible polarity, though I don't know still which was N or S.

## Step 6: Drill out the central piece

The central piece requires 6 holes, one per side, dead center. At first, I tried using a drill stop clamped onto the bit itself, but this is disastrous. The acrylic going up the flutes gets caught in there, and becomes a heated spinneret of fibers that instantly wraps around the bit, creating a solid acrylic chamfer between the bit and stop that then immediately cuts conically into the plastic. Once I remembered that my drill press had a stop built in, I got perfectly clean holes every time.

I drilled all holes for the project a little shallow first, then tested with a magnet as I slightly drilled more each time, up to the stop value I set in, until the magnet was just a hair's width lower than the surface of the cubes. As the cubes aren't all exact, I couldn't just rely on the stop itself.

The trick is to not let the magnets touch. In that last hair's width, their force becomes tremendous, and it's much harder to shear them apart.

The magnets themselves slid in to an almost air-tight seal. Their slippery nickel-plating helped a lot here. To get the magnet back out after I tested it, I simply pushed the block up against part of the drill press, and it flew out and stuck to the metal. In this way, I could keep drilling just a bit more and dropping the magnet back in to test for the right depth. Many times, however, the holes were the perfect depth after the first drilling.

### Step 7: Glue in the magnets

Without prior testing, I settled on Duco Cement from my local hardware store. I'd put a bit of the glue in the hole, then push the rod of magnets into it, and slide the rod sideways to leave the tip magnet in the hole — always remembering to check the polarity.

Be sure the 6 magnets you glue into the central piece have matching outward-facing polarities.

### Step 10: Drill and fill the 8 corner pieces

The corner pieces have 3 sides that face out, and shouldn't be drilled, and that means they have 3 sides that should. Just be sure they're all connected at one corner, and that your outward facing polarities all match, and mate properly with the edge pieces.

### Step 11: Put all the pieces together - you're done!

Now you have a working magnetic cube. It's exactly the same size as an official one, too, but you can make it do many more things, pulling pieces apart, connecting

them in new ways, finding weird ways things pivot, and playing with the flexibility of the magnetic connections.

### Step 12: Optional step - labels!

My newly-acquired cubing habit has not only spawned a bunch of weird project ideas like this, but has also seen me gather lots of official cube junk to me, and as such, I have a stack of nice PVC labels (the polypropylene are crap — steer clear of these immediately-peeling night-mares).

Many people, including me, prefer the beauty of the clear cube, but as this one is my first, and kind of home-brew looking, and because it got boring having nothing to solve, I applied some official labels and made it a real cube, albeit satisfyingly heavier.

The only thing to note here, besides making sure you center them carefully, is that if you want it to be official, you need to put orange opposite red, green across from blue, and yellow on the flip side of white. Also, you need to get the winding order correct.

Enjoy your new cube, labeled or not, and remember that if you want to apply imagery to the faces of the cube, the edges and corners will always work out again when you solve it, but the centers can end up in 1 of 4 rotations, which greatly increases the number of possible solutions, and makes solving it by traditional methods all kinds of way harder.

Luckily, the magnetocube is easy to take apart and put back together, either way.

# Giant NES Controller

## By Spencer Beauchamp (thisissafety)
(http://www.instructables.com/id/How-To-Giant-NES-Controller/)

Here is my Instructable on how I built a giant (working) NES controller/trunk.

## Step 1: What you need

I added a downloadable file of the basic parts and measurements you need for this project so you can print it off if you'd like. If not here is a list of the basic parts needed.

Hardware:
- Bolt/Screw - 14
- Washers - 24
- Switches - 8
- Spade terminals (4-6 stud) - 30 or more
- 5 pin plug (both male and female) - 1
- P-Clamps - a bunch
- Locking Nuts - 14
- Small Springs (must fit over bolts) - 10 - 14
- Non-Skid Protectors (felt) - 14 or more
- "Piano" Style Hinges - 2 ft at least
- Different Colour Wires - 9
- NES Controller - 1
- Various amounts and sizes of screws

The Controller:
- 48 x 21 in. - 1 (&frac34; in. MDF)
- 48 x 3 1/2 in. - 2 (1/2 in. MDF)
- 20 x 3 1/2 in. - 2 (1/2 in. MDF)
- 48 x 21 in. - 1 (1/8 in. MDF)
- 47 x 20 in. - 1 (1/8 in. MDF)

The Trunk:
  (all 1/2 in. MDF)
- 48 x 16 in. - 2
- 20 x 16 in. - 2

- 47 x 20 in. - 1
- 47 x 2 in. - 2
- 19 x 2 in. - 2
- 48 x 3 ½ in. - 2

I also made up some blueprints for myself to follow. I photocopied my controller and placed a sheet of tracing paper on top of the regular paper that the controller was copied on to. the reason I did this was so I could write and erase measurements and whatnot. I then took calipers and measured the actual controller in millimeters and just transferred that to centimeters. These measurements are more of a guide line than anything.

## Step 2: The controller

Depending on where you get your wood at you can usually get them to cut out the sizes for you. When I first started this project I had only a small idea of how big I wanted this thing. I don't have a table saw, or one that works rather, so I had to rig up a jig so I could make straight cuts with the skilsaw.

Then I took the 1/8 in MDF and cut out the raised parts of the Nintendo controller. I relied on my blueprints and a rough estimate to get the spaces between the placing of the 1/8 MDF.

For the sides of the controller I got a trim that was 3 1/2 in tall and 1/2 in thick. All I did was glue and brad those pieces to the bottom of the top piece to form a box. Once I got the sides on I then glued down the 1/8 MDF that way I had no nail holes to deal with.

## Step 3: Controller 2

Once you have all the 1/8 MDF in place and glued I took the router and recessed the space for the start and select buttons. I also routed out the hole for the D-pad. I then routed the edges of the whole top to give it a cleaner look.

I then took some fill to all the edges and later sanded it to clean up all the unwanted lines and imperfections.

The next step was to prime the lid.

games

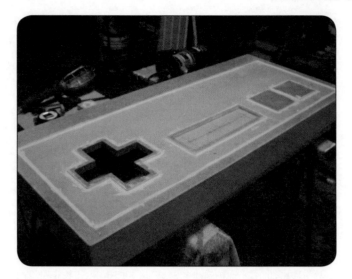

To make the buttons actually work I needed switches. I found some momentary switches which you can get at hardware stores or tech shops.

For the D-pad I used a ball joint type bolt that my Dad found at work. It acts as a pivot point for the d-pad since it has to move in 4 directions. On the bottom of the D-pad I drilled a small dip so the ball could sit in comfortably.

Once all the buttons were done I set them into the table to measure them for mounting and adjustments.

## Step 4: The box

I'm not going to take too much time on this part since all you're doing here is building a box.

If you have any questions on building a box check out some of the instructables here.

The only major things I did to the box were routing all the edges for a cleaner took and I also added a lip on the inside to give it a little more strength and room for hinges.

I then sanded, filled and primed the box to get it ready for paint.

## Step 5: The buttons

The buttons were tricky but fun to figure out. I got hold of a 10cm hole saw bit and cut out my A and B buttons. Then got a 1in bit and cut out the holes for the start and select buttons.

The d-pad was cut out of 3/4in MDF and the arrows were cut out of the 1/8 MDF then glued them together and routed the edges.

To mount the buttons I cut out square pieces of MDF and used the Bolt/Screw to mount them with washers and springs giving it resistance and keeping it level.

games

## Step 6: Wiring

I made up a wiring diagram for soldering to the board and to the plug, see below.

Cut off the chord that runs from the board in the controller to the console and solder those wires to one end of the plug. The rest of the chord that you cut off gets wired to the other end of the plug. This way you don't always have a chord coming out of the chest and when you want to play your favorite NES games all you do is plug in the chord.

Now solder your wires to the other side of the board and run the wires out to its corresponding switch. I used P-Clamps to hold my wire harness down and I used spade terminals tightened down by screws for easy removal if I need to fix or change anything.

I cut a hole and mounted the plug roughly where a real controller's chord would come from.

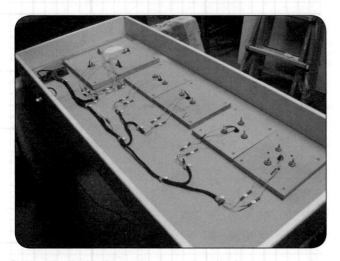

## Step 7: Painting

Time for painting! For the body of the controller I unfortunately couldn't use Krylon products because I needed to color match the ones from the controller. I did use Krylon paint and clear coat on the buttons though. It was wanting to spray paint the buttons in the beginning since they are funny shapes and would be easier.

Once I had a few coats of the light grey on the controller I masked off a small portion and rolled on the dark gray.

Then I masked off the rest of the controller and rolled on the black. When I peeled of the masking I was pretty stoked!

The box I put the light gray on the inside and the black on the outside. I didn't want to do the whole thing black cause that just didn't feel right, but do what you like to yours if you decide to make one!!

Now that it was painted I needed to get the decals. I tried cutting them out myself but it just wasn't coming out how I wanted. So rather than take away from all the work I had done by using crappy decals I just went and got them professionally done.

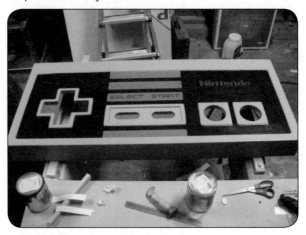

## Step 8: Final touches

I wanted to make a cover for the underside of the table so you couldn't see all the wires and stuff. I added these spare pieces of wood to the inside and got some more 1/8in MDF and made a backing. It's held on by 6 screws so you can access the wiring fairly easily still.

I also routed out a recess for the hinge to sit in so it would be flush. I also added a chain to both sides so the lid wouldn't fly all the way back when you opened it.

## Step 9: DONE!

So there it is! How to build a giant NES controller.

If you have any questions about this or how I did something just leave a comment or message and I'll try to answer it the best I can!

Happy Gaming!

| NES Coffee Table Wiring Diagram | | |
|---|---|---|
| Button Wire Colours | NES Board Diagram | Plug Wiring |
| Up ~ Yellow | Ground ~ o o ~ | Y B R O W   W O R B Y |
| Down ~ Grey | Right ~ o o ~ | o o o o o   o o o o o |
| Left ~ Orange | Left ~ o o ~ | o o o o     o o o o |
| Right ~ Brown | Down ~ o o ~ | ( I only needed to use 5 of the 9 |
| Select ~ Purple | Up ~ o o ~ Start | pins so i just used the top 5 ) |
| Start ~ Blue | ~ o o ~ Select | |
| B ~ Green | ~ o o ~ B | |
| A ~ Yellow/Green | A ~ o o ~ | |
| Ground ~ White | | |

# fun

It is a true testament to the playful nature of the creative mind that some of the most extraordinary projects in the book are contained within this chapter, which we've simply called Fun. In the sometimes task-driven world in which we work and live, it is imperative to remember that enjoyment should be a powerful motivational force. Makers have spent long hours at the workbench, sewing machine, and in the garage in order to create something that's main purpose is to crack a smile and make us laugh!

There is plenty to feel good about when you're launching a vacuum cleaner powered bazooka, or when the kids declare you as Super Parent when you've defied the weather and created a snow-day in the backyard with a homebuilt snow gun. If you've been looking for a reason why you should make something cool this weekend, perhaps the following projects will convince you that "because it's fun" is as good of an answer as any.

# Gigantic Bubble Generator

By Zvika Markfeld (zvizvi)
(http://www.instructables.com/id/Bubblebot-
Gigantic-Bubble-Generator/)

Here is one grand weekend project!
Make this awesome Bubble Bot.

While being a bit lengthy and requiring experience with Arduino, this contraption is bound to grant you infinite glory among your friends, toddlers and grownups alike!

Avast, then!

## Step 1: What you need

Here's a list of the materials and parts I used:

**The Frame**

- 5 x 4-feet long rectangular profile (0.5" x 0.5") pieces of wood, as solid as possible.
- Although you could probably get away with plywood if you wanted to, I always like to go for something sturdier than what I actually need, to compensate for unexpected shortcomings.

- 2" x 4" x 0.5" piece of wood for holding the fan and servo. From now forth I'll refer to it as the wooden shelf. Please excuse my English, I am Israeli.
- 2 hinges, mine were about 1.5" in length.
- 4 Colorful plastic floats a.k.a "Wacky Noodles", ~5 feet long.
- 20 medium-size zip ties for securing the plastic floats to the wooden frame, alternatively, you could go with glue...
- 5 tiny-size zip ties for attaching the opening-closing arm to the servo Make them colorful if you can, to go with the rest of the design!
- Some bolts, nuts, washer, I used 1/8" diameter ones, various lengths. Sorry for being somewhat vague, it'd take quite a coincidence for you to get exactly the same parts, do your scavenging and adjustments.
- 6 feet fishing line. This will be used to connect the motor to the arms, so better get a strong one
- 6 feet thick thread for making the bubbles, preferably made of cloth. Use a thread that is absorbing and flexible - important for bubble making, as you'll find out. I actually used a mountaineering thread I had, about 5mm wide. The important features you want are: a. that it would be able to absorb the soap and b. that it would be flexible enough and not form knots. One of the reasons I like using distilled water, is that the thread will never hardens.
- 2 round wooden sticks, 2 feet long, 3mm in diameter. (Or zip-tie together two 1-feet sticks). These will be used as the poles holding the threads that create the bubbles. One of them will be fixed to the piece of flat wood, and the other will be mounted to the servo - this means they need to be as light-weight as possible.
- 1 round wooden stick, 2 feet long, 5mm in diameter. (Or - zip-tie together two 1-feet sticks!). This will be used as the lever allowing the motor to bring the arms up and down, using the fishing line. Therefore, it should be sturdier than the others.
- 10 1.5" long wood screws, 3-4mm in diameter
- Plastic tub for the soap fluid

**The brains**

- 3 feet of ordinary 1-lead wire
- A levered micro-switch, something like this one: http://parts.digikey.com/1/parts/977112-lever-switch-pcb-spdt-3a-80gf-d2f-l.html
- A Servo, preferably not the lamest one you can get. I got mine for free in a time of blissful need from someone during geekcon2010, but it was roughly similar in size and torque to this one: http://www.dealextreme.com/p/dynam-34g-servo-b2232-4504.
- 6V Geared motor
- This one's responsible for raising and lowering the arms that go into the soap bucket and spread open in the air, so it better be geared to take some load. I used a geared motor module I disassembled from a scanner/

printer, but you can use anything, as long as it's 6v, around 5-10 RPM.

- A roller/pulley, used to collect the wire. It should be attached to the motor's shaft, so make sure you get parts that can play nicely together. I got mine by taking down all solder from my soldering kit's roller (see photo). Not the best option, I'll admit.
- 12V Tower-rack computer fan. I used a 4.7" X 4.7" one. You can always slow down a fan by rapidly switching it (using PWM or otherwise), but not the other way around.
- 10 feet of 3-pin servo leads extension cables. I used these ones, which are hassle-free
- Circuit Prototyping board, I use something that looks like this: http://www.123rf.com/photo_3476690_macro-detail-of-a-circuit.html
- 1 Arduino or an Arduino-clone. I use this RBBB from ModernDevice (http://shop.moderndevice.com/products/rbbb-kit), which is pretty cheap and easy to work with. Instead of the supplied transistor I install a 7805 regulator to take down my 12V input (moped battery)
- 1 plastic kit-box for the electronic components. Mine was 5" x 3" x 2".
- 12V battery / Power adapter. I use my moped's battery when outdoor or the adapter when in civilization.
- H-Bridge components:
- 2 x TIP107 PNP Darlingtons
- 2 x TIP102 NPN Darlingtons
- 4 x 2N3904 transistors
- 4 x 1/4W 1K resistors
- 4 x 1/4W 10K resistors
- I am grateful to Chuck McManis, who wrote this must-read piece on H-Bridges which I pretty much implemented as written: http://www.mcmanis.com/chuck/robotics/tutorial/h-bridge/bjt-bridge.html. See schema in photos.

## Soap Mixture

I used the instructions published by these guys: http://www.soapbubble.dk/en/bubbles/bubblemixture.php, quantities multiplied by 4:

- 4 liter of distilled water
- 3.2 liters of a pre-made bubble mixture
- 1 deciliter of detergent (I used regular green Fairy with great success)
- 1 deciliter of glycerin

## Tools

- Solder iron and solder
- Hot Glue Gun: Although abominable when overused, there aren't many engineering problems that cannot be solved with enough hot glue.
- Electric screwdriver/drill
- We will drill some holes and screw some screws when building the frame
- 3mm and 5mm wood drills
- Wood Glue

- Hand Saw, Awesome!

## Step 2: Building the frame

OK, there are 2 ways of starting up:

**"By Hand"**

1. Screw together two sticks into a V shape. Then do another pair, making sure they come out as similar as possible, for maximum stability.
2. Connect them with one another with a horizontal stick.

When sawing the horizontal piece of wood, you may want to leave some room for the Arduino box, to be attached to it, taking extra 5-6" that will stick from the side.

You are now supposed to get two triangles, connected by their vertexes.

See main image for an example of the outcome.

**Premade**

Just buy separately one table stand. It probably makes more sense unless you enjoy any kind of wood-work (like me).

Now, onto that horizontal stick:

1. Evenly attach hinges. I am such a pretty bad carpenter; hinges are my all time nemesis. I hope you do better.
2. Attach their other end to the little shelf. Yes, that's the last piece of wood on the list -keep in mind that you should be able to drill a 5mm hole in it's width, so double check you chose a piece thick enough; this hole is going to be used for the round pole that is connected to the motor with a fishing line.

Onto the wooden shelf's profile, drill holes for the needed peripherals:

Facing backwards
- 5mm hole for the stick mentioned above
Facing forwards

- 3mm hole for the fixed bubble-making arm
- 2 holes for attaching the fan via screws.
- Depending on the servo's size: Holes for attaching the servo or saw a socket for it, which is what I did

## Step 3: Adding the bubbling subsystem

Includes: servo, arms and thread loop

1. Attach the servo to the wooden shelf. Either use the socket you sawed or drill it in. At any case, servo should be leveled with the shelf so that when the shelf is facing down, pulled by gravity, the servo's arm should also be on a plane almost perpendicular to the ground
2. Stick (and later glue) the 3mm round wooden stick in the hole you made for it.
3. Attach the second 3mm stick to the servo using zip ties. Servos are designed to control little RC airplanes, and their physical arrangement is somewhat awkward when it comes to things other than that, in my honest opinion. Just do the best you can to get a stable, fixed-as-possible, arrangement. Alternatively, if you're up to it, you can make better fittings with a piece of tin and 0.5mm drill
4. Cut the 6 feet of string to 2-feet piece and 4-feet piece. Minor size adjustments may be made later on, but these sizes should put you in the safe zone.
5. Tie each end of the string to each end of the wooden sticks. So, now when the arms are open, a loop is formed.
6. Tie a zip-tie on the long thread, creating a smaller, 8" loop just below the bigger one. This will make sure that when the arms are down, dipping in the bucket of soap, the loop will not be partially covered with soap and not develop bubble. Also, it helps the loop go back into the bucket when the arms are brought down. (In BubbaBot 1.0, the arms just dropped back into the soap bucket by gravity, movement it was much more abrupt. perhaps you don't really need that last knot here)

And now, a message from our cheerleaders:

Voila! Forward arms are ready!

Now stick the 5mm round wooden stick in the hole facing backwards. As said, later glue it in. Then, tie a fishing line to its end. You can grind a small crack that will keep the line in its place. Test manually how much power it takes to pull the shelf, arms and thread. It shouldn't be too hard, if your hinges are right. If they are slightly crooked, try oiling them. If more than slightly, you're up for some alignments.

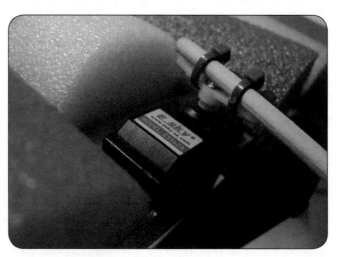

## Step 4: Fan

Attach the fan to the wooden shelf, so that it blows air just below the spreading arms. You may need to adjust it later, so don't drive the screws all the way in.

For the first version at Geekcon2010, I used an ordinary household fan connected to AC that blew air continuously. Later I found a computer fan big enough to push enough air through the loop so that decent bubbles are created.

The mechanical motion of air is a pale imitation of the free flow of air that is created when you make bubbles manually with two sticks and a string, as in this Instructable, but it does the trick. (Any improvements welcome, of course.)

Take a break. Get a beer, you deserve it.

## Step 5: Attach feedback switch

Take the levered micro switch and hot glue it to the top frame wood, but first, solder leads to its terminals, yes? Glue it so that when the wooden shelf is brought up, the switch clicks - just before the shelf is hitting its maximum range.

I used an on-on switch, meaning, 3 terminals.

In case you use an on-off, you'd need to pull down - just add to the pinout a grounded 10k resistor.

## Step 6: Installing the motor

Depending on what you have in store, size of motor, its docking points, power ratio, packaging, etc.:
**Attach the motor with a pulley/roller to one of the back legs.**

I tried a few motors here; you may also need to do some careful experimenting too. Printers and scanners are great to salvage, as they come with paper-feeding speed gears, like mine, I suspect.
**Fix the fishing line to the roller.**

The line's other end should already be tied to the 5mm wooden stick. Do you see it now? As the roller collects the fishing line, wood stick is pulled down, lifting up the wooden shelf on the other side of the frame. Software then spreads the arms, creating the initial soap surface. Then, the fan blows air, arms close and Voila! A bubble is born.

Some Arduino motor shields exist for that purpose, too. But then you'd probably need to tweak the code. At any case, my circuit does not use the consolidated control lines (FWD, REV, ENA in the schematics below). I just access all 4 bridges from code, keeping the right order not to short switch.

Also, I did not use an opto-isolator, although safer, as they were too expensive. Instead, I used the modified circuit

Driver code looks like this:

```
void HBridge::forward() {
  idle();
  digitalWrite(_positive0, LOW);
  digitalWrite(_negative0, LOW);
  digitalWrite(_positive1, HIGH);
  digitalWrite(_negative1, HIGH);
}
void HBridge::backward() {
  idle();
  digitalWrite(_negative1, LOW);
  digitalWrite(_positive1, LOW);
  digitalWrite(_positive0, HIGH);
  digitalWrite(_negative0, HIGH);
}
void HBridge::stop() {
  idle();
}
void HBridge::idle() {
  digitalWrite(_positive0, LOW);
  digitalWrite(_positive1, LOW);
  digitalWrite(_negative0, LOW);
  digitalWrite(_negative1, LOW);
}
```

## Step 7: Building the H-bridge

I don't have an awful lot to say here, other than:

fun

## Step 8: Connecting the Arduino

House the Arduino and H-Bridge comfortably inside a kit box and attach that kit box to the frame - using screws, zip locks or your favorite bonding technique.

Drill holes for the wires to come out and voltage come in. I secured the Arduino inside of the box and drilled a hole next to the RBBB's DC-in terminal. That proved convenient.

Connect the peripherals using the following configuration:

```
// scan limit switch pin
const int switchPin = 2;
// arms spread servo pin
const int servoPin = 3;
// fan source pin
const int fanPin = 4;
```

Connect the motor, switch and servo to the Arduino. Use the 3-wire extension cables, or any other wire you like. During prototyping I used a small matrix like the one in the second photo, later I soldered the RBBB onto a PCB similar to the one I used for the H-Bridge. When working with such a PCB, which I recommend, disconnecting conductivity is easily done by gently drilling the copper out (I use 3mm drill) and removing residue on that line with a good blade.

Connect the Fan through a relaying transistor or another Darlington. See here for serious documentation: http://www.electronics-tutorials.ws/transistor/tran_4. html, or here for shorter version of it: http://www.kpsec. freeuk.com/trancirc.htm. I used shrinks to protect the transistor's terminals from closing circuit with anything when squeezed inside the kit-box.

Load the attached software onto the Arduino and dry-run.

Modify servo boundary values, depending on servo type and physical arrangement. Yes, I mean this code:

```
// Servo boundary values
const int min_pos = 85;
const int max_pos = 127;
```

## Step 9: Finishing colors

Apply the Wacky Noodles on the frame. I cut the noodles on their length, about 2/3rd deep, consistently. Then I wrapped a wooden leg and just pushed the noodle onto the wood. It kind of wrapped it, and then came a zip tie to secure it. I know. Call me superficial.

Add even more wackiness, apply differently shaped noodles on all other exposed wood surfaces.

Congratulations! You've Made it!

Prepare the bubble mix using these ingredients (http://www.soapbubble.dk/en/bubbles/bubblemixture. php):

- 1 liter of water (Preferably distilled, demineralized or rain water)
- 8 deciliters of Bubbles (which is a pre-made bubble mixture you will find in most toy stores in Denmark and other European countries. If you cannot find Bubbles in your local toy store, you will probably find an equally good brand. We have used different brands with success)
- 1 deciliter of detergent (If you live in Denmark, then use Fairy Ultra.)
- 1 deciliter of glycerin

Fill tub with soap mix and place below the Bubblebot. You'll need to do trial and error here, to get the right height and placement

Activate the bot and make final adjustments.
- Modify source code for arms spreading speed and duration, number of spreading iterations
- Heighten / Lower the soap tub
- Try Indoor / Outdoor

Now, you bring this colorful bliss to any birthday party and be thrice as welcome!

I have loved model rockets since I was a kid, but instead of building from kits I prefer to make funky ones from scratch. About a year ago, I got the idea to make a dual-engine model rocket in the shape of Iron Man. The idea presented a lot of unique challenges—which I've enjoyed working on—but this was one project I was happy to finally get out of the way.

I spent many nights lying awake trying to figure out how to make a man-shaped model rocket flight-stable, how and what to make him out of (to keep the weight down), how to construct the parachute deployment system, how to mount him onto a launch rod, what kind of launcher I would have to make, and on and on. I resolved most of the issues, and I'll show you how all of these ideas came together.

There were plenty of missteps and failures along the way throughout this project, but I've cut most of that out in order to keep this as straight-forward as possible. Please excuse the shoddiness of the exterior details on the finished rocket. This is less about the actual Iron Man character, and more about my journey and the process of trying to make and fly a crazy man-shaped rocket. In the end, you'll see that I had mixed results with this project.

I began by making the head, which I figured would be the hardest part.

## Part I: Hand-carved Iron Man head

This is an Iron Man head I carved out of balsa. From chin to crown, it is about 145 mm tall, and about 90 mm wide at the widest part. It weighs about 150 g (a little over 5 oz.).

### Step 1: Balsa block glue-up

I purchased blocks of balsa from a craft store and glued them all together as shown with wood glue. The individual blocks were approximately 3" x 5" x 1.5". When the glue was cured, the large resulting block was trimmed so the final dimensions were 6" x 5" x 3.5".

I made a side-view template of Iron Man's helmet by tracing a side photo of an Iron Man toy using basic drawing tools on my computer. I've included a template just in case you are so inclined to make one of these.

### Step 2: Carve basic shape, lay out details

Using the template, I traced the outline of the helmet onto the wood. I hacked off some of the excess balsa to get down to the basic shape using a small wood saw.

Using the tip of a mechanical pencil, I traced and impressed the details of the mask into the balsa on either side of the block of wood. Then I drew in the details with sharpie to work as guide marks on the sides and front of the mask.

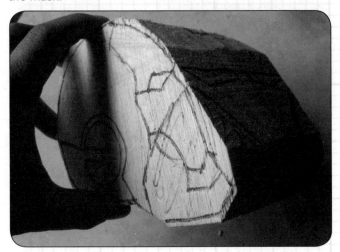

fun

## Step 3: Begin carving

Using a heavy duty snap-style utility knife with the blade mostly extended, I began to carve out more of the basic shape.

If you use a utility knife in this manner it can be very useful, although EXTREMELY dangerous. You could do some serious damage to yourself or someone else if you're not careful.

## Step 4: Continue carving, drawing in details as a guide

I continued carving and redrawing in details with a sharpie as I removed material.

Continually adding details with a sharpie as a guide and inspecting carefully after every couple of cuts kept me from making any drastic mistakes, like removing too much material.

## Step 5: Begin working on details

I started working on more intricate details using a combination of coarse sandpaper, exacto blade, and a 1/4-inch chisel.

## Step 6: Finish carving, sand smooth

More fine details were added, and I gave the bare wood a final sanding.

As balsa is quite soft, it was easy to gouge and make little mistakes. These were fixed in the next step.

## Step 7: Use wood filler to smoothen, fix blemishes

I rubbed wood filler into the wood with my fingers, and then sort of burnished it into the wood with my palms. Working in small sections at a time, this created a smooth, non-porous surface.

I lightly sanded the surface and continued shaping areas that needed additional work. Once completed, the entire surface was smooth with no bare wood showing.

## Step 8: Prime, add wood filler, sand, repeat

I gave it a coat of spray primer, which revealed many little blemishes. These little cracks and holes and such were filled with wood filler, rubbed in really well, and then the whole thing was sanded and primed again. I went through this process three or four times.

More difficult details were added by carving out small areas of wood, refilling the void completely with wood filler, and then shaping the filler while it was still soft.

## Step 9: Final priming

Once I was happy with all the details, a couple of final coats of primer were added with a light sanding in between and afterward.

## Step 10: Final painting

I spray painted it with three or four coats of crimson red. When that was dry I added gold paint by hand, and then white to the eyes.

## Step 11: All done (with his head at least...)

That's it. Thanks for looking!

fun

re-sized the lay-out, and waited a few months till I was ready to work on it again.

For my second attempt, I decided to build the body up using foam board (1/4-inch foam sandwiched between papers). This proved to work very nicely for making a lightweight skeletal-type structure, but led to some difficulties in covering.

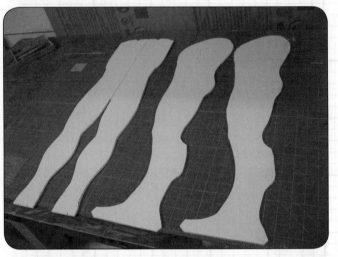

## Part II: Iron Man Body
### Step 1: Body

I laid out a design for the body by copying details from photos of Iron Man and an Iron Man toy I borrowed from a friend. If you're feeling ambitious, I've included a template with the front and side lay-outs that I created. The total height of the finished rocket is 36 inches.

I ordered rocket supplies from apogeerockets.com, which has been a very nice company to work with. I ordered a bunch of 24mm tubes (which hold D- and E-size Estes model rocket engines), some tube couplers, engine block rings, launch lugs, and Kevlar cord.

My first attempt at making the body was with layers of pink insulation foam glued together with the rocket tube structure sandwiched inside. I used a sharp knife to carve out the body shape, which was tedious and messy. In the end it weighed too much to use and I had miscalculated the proportions, so the head which I had already finished was too small for the body. After plenty of cursing, the pink foam body ended up in the trash... in very tiny pieces. I

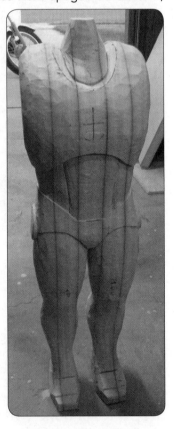

## Step 2: Rocket tube structure

The rocket tube structure was assembled with regular white glue. The 45-degree cuts were made using a miter saw.

The parachute deployment system I came up with is basically a hatch attached to the back of the rocket with a long cord that is shot off when the engines backfire. The parachute is attached to the cord, but is stored in a compartment all its own outside of the actual rocket tubes. This is a technique I've used on other oddball rockets and it seems to work well, if I make sure there is no way for the parachute to get stuck once the hatch is blown out of the way.

## Step 3: Exhaust tube

The two main tubes lead to one exhaust tube. Prior to gluing, surfaces of the tubes were roughened up with sandpaper.

## Step 4: Building up the body

The foam board body cross-sections were glued to the rocket tubes to build up the body. White glue was used for this. Notice the slight space left at the bottom of the tubes where the foot pieces were added.

There was a lot of shaping, reshaping, and moving things around from this point on. This was very much a sculpture, and required quite a bit of eyeballing and continually adjusting things to suit my tastes.

## Step 5: The launcher

Before I got too far on the body, I had to figure out how this was going to be launched, and where to put the launch lugs (the little tubes that hold the rocket to the launch rod to guide the rocket on take-off).

I paused here and built a launcher, and figured out how to have the rod go right up through the middle of the rocket without coming out the top of Iron Man's head.

This launcher design was made specifically to accommodate some giant removable fins I was going place underneath Iron Man's feet when it was time to fly. These were going to be added to increase flight stability.

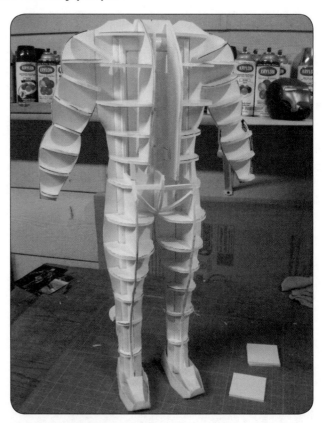

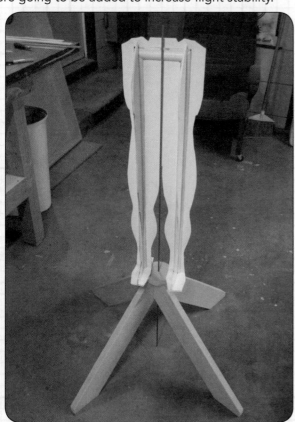

## Step 6: Finishing up the skeletal structure

I made individually shaped pieces out of foam board to fill-out and define the body. I tried lots of things prior to this, but this method seemed to produce the lightest, most effective results. These pieces were all glued on with hot glue. This step required some modifying to the body cross sections to get a shape I was ultimately satisfied with.

## Step 7: A layer of skin

I used masking tape to create a skin over the body shape. This took two rolls of tape, and added quite a bit of weight.

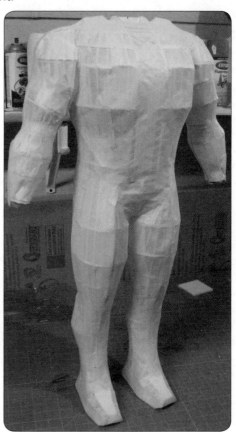

**fun**

401

## Step 8: Craft foam covering

I probably should have just painted the tape and called it good. But I thought it would look nice to give him a clean covering of craft foam.

I cut individual pieces to fit and used 3M 77 spray adhesive to glue them in place.

I thought the legs turned out looking pretty slick. But I realized how dumb it was to add this extra weight to a thing that was probably going to crash, so I didn't completely finish covering the body with the craft foam.

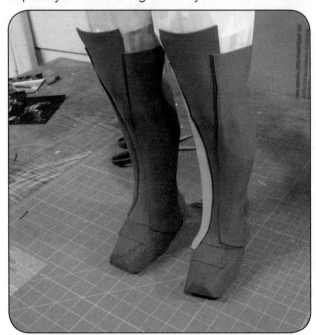

## Step 9: Painting

I'm pretty good with a spray can, and I prefer Krylon specifically because of the adjustable fan-spray nozzle that they started using in the last few years. It helps you make nice, even coats, and that's the key to a nice paint job.

However, this is not a good example of my spray skills, or the niceness of Krylon paint, for which I apologize. This was a messy, heavy, primerless single coat of crimson red, immediately followed with a few spots of gold and spot of white. I used a thick permanent marker to draw in some details, and glued the head in place.

## Step 10: Launch

I couldn't wait to launch this to see what would happen. I didn't even put a parachute in it, which actually negates the whole point of calling this a "model rocket" (and violates the model rocketry code...), but I figured it wouldn't go that high anyway. It ended up weighing so much that I wondered if it would even get off the launch pad.

I used two E engines, and went to a place way out in the middle of a dirt field away from buildings and anything flammable. I was secretly hoping for a spectacular, fiery crash.

## Step 11: Flight damage

The rough, parachute-less landing broke his neck. That was about it. (Luckily, he missed my car.)

I was surprised at how he flew. If I had made and attached some giant fins extending below his feet, I'm sure he would have flown much more straight. Still, excessive weight is the real issue I would have to overcome if I ever revisited this project.

Since the original posting of this Instructable, I have removed the head piece and all the tape covering to examine some things. I found that the rocket tubes had blown out at the 45-degree angles near the shoulders. That's another problem that will need to be re-designed around if I were to revisit this project. Overall however, aside this and his head, he was in pretty good shape for the crash landing he took.

# Magnetic Silly Putty

By mike warren (mikeasaurus)
(http://www.instructables.com/id/magnetic-silly-putty/)

Thinking Putty (also known as Silly Putty) is a silicone polymer children's toy. Silly putty is fun because it has some unique properties: it is viscoelastic, meaning it can be stretched and shaped and mashed back together again; and as its apparent viscosity increases directly with respect to the amount of force applied (read: it can be torn or shattered with impact). Silly putty is a non-Newtonian viscoelastic polymer, better characterized as a dilatant fluid. Also, it bounces.

Ok, enough science. I'm sure we've all played with Thinking Putty in our youth, but how about magnetic silly putty?

By adding a ferrous component to an already wacky toy we can keep all characteristics of the original putty, but now have the additional dimension of magnetism! I've seen magnetic thinking putty for sale on other websites, but I'll show you how you can make your own for a fraction of the price and in about 20 minutes.

## Step 1: Tools + materials

Tools:
- Disposable gloves (latex or other)
- Disposable face mask
- Disposable work area (paper plate)

Materials:
- Thinking Putty ($2.00 or less) - any color
- Ferric iron oxide powder (artist supply stores)
- Neodymium magnet

The secret ingredient that makes the putty magnetic is an iron oxide powder, which is ferric (magnetic). Ferric iron oxide is a fine powder used as black pigment and can be found at art stores. If your local artist supply store doesn't carry it, you can always purchase it online.

## Step 2: Prepare putty

Iron oxide powder is very fine and inhaling it is probably not such a good idea. Put on your gloves and face mask before you begin.

Open the thinking putty and remove from the container. Work the putty in your hands a little to warm it up, then stretch it out like a sheet and lay it on your disposable work surface (sheet of paper or paper plate).

## Step 3: Add iron oxide

Thinking Putty comes in different sizes, depending on where you purchase it. I found mine in a local toy shop, it comes in an egg-shaped container and is about 24 grams (0.8 oz).

For this size, I used about a tablespoon of iron oxide, you may require more or less depending on your putty

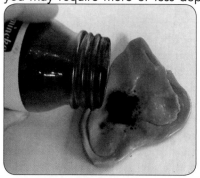

size and amount of magnetism desired.

Carefully spoon the iron oxide into center of putty sheet, then close lid on iron oxide powder to reduce excess iron dust escaping.

## Step 4: Work it

Gently fold edges of putty sheet into center and work the powder into the putty. Go slow, the powder produces lots of dust.

After a minute of massaging the putty it will lose it's color and begin to look black as pitch. Keep massaging putty for about 3-4 minutes.

## Step 5: Experiment and have fun!

That's it, you're done! Grab your magnet and start experimenting with your new magnetic putty.

Caution: Putty has been known to leave a residue on some surfaces, even more so with the iron oxide powder. Use caution when playing with your magnetic putty. If you get magnetic putty stuck to fabric you can try placing the magnet on top of the fabric and the putty may work its way out (wait 24 hours). Alternatively you can apply rubbing alcohol to area and work out the putty, try a concealed test-area first. WD-40 may also work. If all else fails, take the fabric to the dry cleaners and tell them it's a silicone-based stain.

fun

I will show you how to build a net gun out of materials available at any big box home improvement store. This net gun is capable of firing a 90 square foot net 15 to 25 feet using 80-100 psi of compressed air. The net is reusable, assuming your prey doesn't destroy or run off with it. The launcher section is modular and can be removed in case you want to use a different design or add attachments. Thread on some 1" PVC pipe and you have a Christmas Cannon, or check step 11 for how to build a tennis ball launching attachment.

The net gun is similar to many pneumatic launchers, but instead of launching a single projectile, it launches four tractors that pull the net through the air. The tractors are based on the fact that the neck of a standard soda bottle fits very well over the outside of 1/2" PVC pipe. The cost to build this will range from approximately $40-$75.

## Step 1: Materials

Before you begin be aware that this project uses PVC pipe in an application it is explicitly not intended for. PVC is meant for water, not pressurized air or other gases. The problem is not the pressure, this project uses pressures less than half the working pressure of any PVC component, but the failure mode when pressurized by gas. If the PVC is compromised, by dropping, impact, or other means, it shatters into sharp pieces that are ejected by the pressurized gas.

Nearly all of these items can be picked up at your local home improvement retailer. It is probably worth buying a full 10' length of 1/2" pipe, for all the other sizes see if you can buy shorter lengths or scrap. Alternatively, get some friends together, share the costs of the full length pipes, and build a lot of net guns. The tire valves

are available at auto parts stores. The net is addressed in detail in the next step.

SUPPLIES
- All PVC fittings are slip fit unless otherwise noted
- All PVC pipe and fittings must be SCH-40 (Schedule 40) unless otherwise noted
- All PVC pipe should have a PSI rating of 200 or greater,
- Absolutely no cell core ABS DWV pipe

    Pressure chamber parts
- 1 1" MPT (Male Pipe Thread) to 1" slip street elbow
- 1 1" elbow
- 1 2" to 1" reducer bushing
- 1 2" cap
- 1 2" coupler
- 1 foot of 1" pipe
- Minimum 9" length of 2" pipe
- 1 valve stem, prefer a .453" as it corresponds to the readily available 7/16" drill bit
- Optional 1 pressure gauge

    There are two standard size automotive valve stems, one for a rim hole sized .453" the other .625". These two sizes correspond to fractional drill bit sizes of 29/64" and 5/8" respectively, the much more common 7/16" bit can be substituted in place of the less common 29/64". Additionally, most common drill indexes stop at 7/16" or 1/2" and do not contain the larger 5/8" bit.

Trigger valve parts
- 1 Orbit Model 57461 1" sprinkler valve
- 1 Blow gun similar to this
- 1 1/4" NPT hex nipple, like this

Bending jig
- 3 2"(ish) wood screws
- Wood scrap for base, a 16" length of 2x4 should work fine

Launcher section
- 4 13" lengths of 1/2" pipe
- 1 1/2" cross
- 2 1/2" tee
- 4 1/2" street elbows
- 4 1-1/2" pieces of 1/2" pipe (coupler joiners)
- 1 1-1/2" pipe 9" long
- 1 1-1/2" coupler
- **1 1-1/2" to 1/2" reducing bushings
- ** 1 1" MPT to 1/2" slip
- 1 nickel

These transitions usually can't be made with one adapter, just make sure the starting and ending dimensions are correct.

Net
- Memphis Net and Twine sku# 263 1lb minimum order is enough to make 7-8 nets
- OR a substitute net computed using the net math spreadsheet and instructions in step 2
- Nylon mason's twine (#15 or smaller), kite string, or some other thin durable rope
- 4 per net 16-20oz carbonated soda bottles
- 4 per net zip ties > 4" long

- Hot glue/silicone/wax to pour in bottles to add weight
- Optional additional items needed for high performance net tractors
- 4 per net 3/4" couplers
- 4 per net 3/4" caps
- 4 per net 8" lengths of SDR-21(Class 200) 3/4" thinwall PVC note: regular 3/4" SCH40 will NOT work!
- 4 per net 12" lengths of non-adhesive 1" ID foam pipe insulation. Pipe insulation is generally sold in 6' lengths.

Consumables
- PVC pipe cement and primer
- PVC safe pipe joint compound (pipe dope) such as this
- Teflon tape
- Sand, at least two cups worth (for bending the launcher arms)
- 2 1/2" PVC caps (for bending launcher arms, not part of gun)
- Epoxy for modifying sprinkler valve
- Thread locker (Loctite)

Tools and Safety
- Saw, for cutting PVC pipe
- Heat gun, propane torch, or candle for bending PVC
- Drill
- 3/16" and 7/16" (or 5/8" see the **note in the pressure chamber section) drill bits
- Tape measure
- Utility knife
- Dremel tool, or similar, with a sanding drum
- Wrench for 1/4" npt hex nipple
- Large adjustable wrench or channel-lock pliers, for tightening the trigger valve
- A compressor or pump capable of attaching to a Schrader tire valve and attaining at least 80 psi
- Safety glasses
- Leather gloves

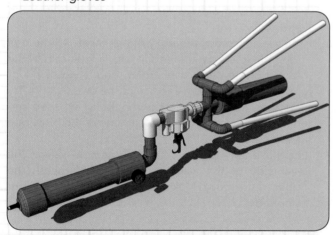

## Step 2: Net procurement and math

I ordered my net from the Memphis Net & Twine Company. If you have your own favorite gill net vendor, you can probably order an identical item from them. I have NO financial ties to MN & T other than being a satisfied purchaser of their retail products.

- Here is the link to the product page on the MN & T website: http://www.memphisnet.net/product/187/netting_multi_208. Below is the exact info from my order information page, shipping is not included in the price. One pound of this net (minimum order) will make 7 or possibly 8, 9-1/2 foot square nets.
   Sku: 263
   Description: 3 in. sq. mesh, 12 ft. deep
   Qty: 1lb
   Price: $12.65

## Step 3: Build the pressure chamber

The pressure chamber is assembled first. It should be allowed to cure a full 24 hours before applying pressure. PVC pipe assembly is simple and is covered in other Instructables as well as on YouTube. A brief refresher on solvent welding PVC pipe. Use in a well ventilated area, make sure both pieces to be assembled are clean and free of burs, prime both pieces, put glue on both pieces, assemble with a twisting motion and hold for 15 seconds. For brevity's sake, solvent welding will be referred to as "gluing" PVC.

Pressure chamber supplies
- 1 1" MPT (Male Pipe Thread) to 1" slip street elbow
- 1 1" elbow
- 1 2" to 1" reducer bushing
- 1 2" cap
- 1 2" coupler
- 1 foot of 1" pipe
- Minimum 9" length of 2" pipe
- 1 valve stem
- PVC primer and cement
- Drill and 7/16" bit (or 5/8" if you purchased the larger base valve stem)
- Optional- 1 pressure gauge

Assembly
1. Drill the correct size hole in the center of the 2" cap. 7/16" for the smaller (.453" base) valve stem, or 5/8" for the larger (.625" base) valve stem. Pull the valve stem through this hole.
2. Cut a length of 2" pipe at least 9" long. Keep in mind that the longer it is the more time it will take to fill up if you are using a manual air pump.
3. Glue the 2" to 1" reducing bushing into the 2" coupler
4. Glue the 2" cap with tire valve to one end of 2" pipe.
5. Glue the coupler to the other end.
6. Glue a short piece of 1" pipe into the bushing, glue the 1" slip elbow onto that.
7. Cut a piece of 1" pipe for the pistol grip, something between 3" and 6" should work. Glue the 1" MPT street elbow to one end of pistol grip pipe.
8. Glue assembled pistol grip pipe into 1" slip elbow on pressure chamber. Ensure that the threaded fitting aligns with the axis of the pressure chamber and doesn't point off to the right or left.

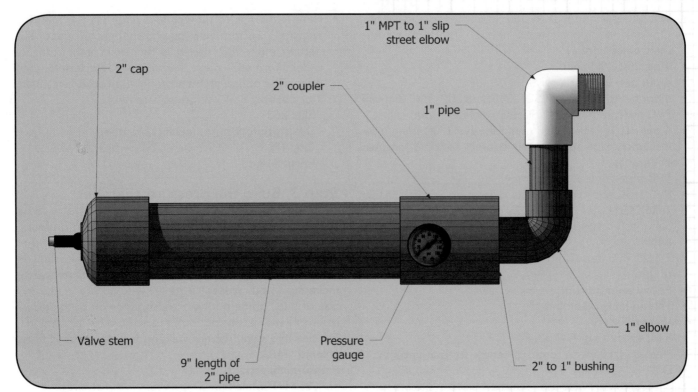

- 1" MPT to 1" slip street elbow
- 2" cap
- 2" coupler
- 1" pipe
- 1" elbow
- Valve stem
- Pressure gauge
- 9" length of 2" pipe
- 2" to 1" bushing

9. Optional: Drill a hole of slightly smaller diameter than the fitting of the air valve, locate the hole 3/4" into the pipe side (NOT the bushing side) of the 2" coupler. Use the air valve to cut threads into the hole, then thread back in using thread locker on the fitting.

## Step 4: Build the trigger valve assembly

In this step we will modify an Orbit Model 57461 1" jar top sprinkler valve, making it a pneumatically actuated trigger valve. I found this particular model to have a number of advantages. It is the cheapest 1" valve I've found. The air valve is installed in the center of the cap allowing easy orientation of the trigger. Finally, the "jar top" construction makes it extremely easy to work on. Here is a link to a page devoted to modifying this exact valve, I left out the safety ball valve in this design. Here is a link to a visual explanation of how the sprinkler valve works.

Trigger Valve Supplies
- 1 Orbit Model 57461 1" sprinkler valve
- 1 Blow gun or similar
- 1 1/4" NPT pipe/hex nipple, like this
- Epoxy
- Teflon tape
- Wrenches
- Dremel or drill
- Threadlocker

Assembly
1. Remove solenoid and bleed screw, they will not be needed. Save the solenoid for future diabolical inventions.
2. Disassemble valve by unscrewing the "jar" ring. Be careful, as under the top is a spring under tension.

3. Cut, grind, or drill out the center of the top, make sure to leave enough plastic to thread the 1/4" NPT fitting in. Grind or cut down the lip of material around the center hole to the level of the ribs This will allow you to get the fitting deep and tight.
4. Use the 1/4" NPT fitting as a tap for cutting threads into the hole you just made, try to keep it as perpendicular as possible.
5. Once you have the threads cut, put Teflon tape on one end of the fitting and thread that into the blow gun. Apply some thread locker to the other end of the fitting and tighten the whole assembly into the valve top.
6. You are now ready to epoxy three places. A little dab in the bleed screw hole in the top, a little dab in the bleed hole at the valve outlet, and a good bit of epoxy around bottom and top of the brass fitting. Try and leave the wrench flats of the fitting exposed and epoxy free in case you need to remove the blow gun at some point.
7. Let the epoxy dry and then reassemble valve. The lever side of the valve should be underneath the outlet of the valve. Make the securing ring is as tight as possible.

## Step 5: Assemble and test valve and pressure chamber

Once your pressure chamber has cured for 24 hours, and your trigger valve has cured long enough for the epoxy to reach full strength, you are ready to assemble and test the trigger valve and pressure chamber.

Supplies
- Assembled pressure chamber from step 3

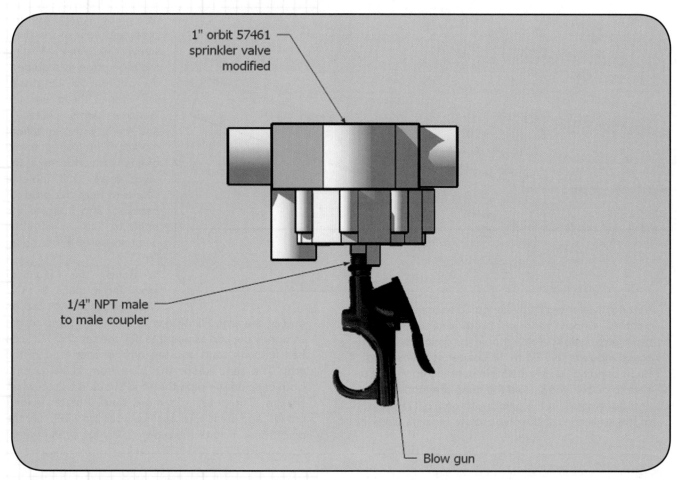

1" orbit 57461
sprinkler valve
modified

1/4" NPT male
to male coupler

Blow gun

- Assembled trigger valve from step 4
- PVC pipe joint compound (pipe dope) such as this:
  http://www.oatey.com/Channel/Shared/ProductGroup-
  Detail/90/Great_White__Pipe_Joint_Compound_with_
  PTFE.html
- Source of pressurized air
- Wrench or channel lock pliers
- 5 gallon bucket filled with water (optional)

Assembly

1. Thread your trigger valve onto the pressure chamber
   for a test fit. The arrows on the side of the valve point
   in the direction of the airflow, they should be pointing
   away from the pressure chamber. The goal is to get
   the blow gun situated vertically in front of the pistol
   grip to act as a trigger. Use the channel lock pliers or
   adjustable wrench to get the trigger valve as tight as
   possible. If the sprinkler valve bottoms out before the
   blow gun trigger is vertical, you can file off small
   amounts of plastic from the end of the threaded
   street elbow until it fits perfect.
2. Fill the chamber to 80 psi. Aim in a safe direction and
   briskly pull the trigger, you should get a loud POP
   and feel a bit of recoil. Here is a great troubleshooting
   guide if your valve does anything other than go bang:
   http://www.spudfiles.com/forums/viewtopic,p,95154.
   html#95154

3. Once you have a successful test, remove the trigger
   valve. Apply the pipe joint compound to the street
   elbow threads and tighten down the valve once more.
4. Optional: perform a leak test. Pressurize your chamber
   to 80 psi. Fill a 5 gallon bucket with water and dip the
   assembly, look for any bubbles. Tighten and add pipe
   joint compound to areas with leaks. If the PVC joints
   are leaking on the pressure chamber, you can apply a
   vacuum and suck super glue into the voids.

## Step 6: Bend launcher arms

In this step we will build a bending jig, and use it to
bend four launcher arms to a specific angle. Make sure
annotations are turned on when viewing the video.

Launcher arm supplies
- 4 13" lengths of 1/2" pipe
- 2 1/2" PVC caps DO NOT PRIME OR GLUE THEM
- Sand, at least two cups worth
- Heat gun, propane torch or candle
- Wood scrap and 3 2" screws to make bending jig
- Leather gloves

Assembly

1. Choose a launcher tube angle. A 17 or 19 degree
   angle will give you longer range but you may need
   the high performance tractors. A 21 or 23 degree
   angle will give you quicker opening shorter range

fun

**407**

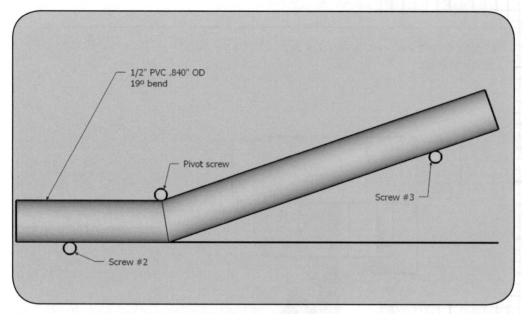

1/2" PVC .840" OD
19º bend

Pivot screw

Screw #3

Screw #2

using the edge of the pipe as a guide. Again, with the pipe held against the pivot screw, sink screw #3 using the pipe edge as a guide.

3. Cut four 13" lengths of 1/2" pipe, these are the launcher arms. Measure and mark, with permanent marker, 3" in from one end of each arm. This mark, the pivot mark, will indicate where to heat the pipe for bending, and indicate the point to line up with the pivot screw of the bending jig.

4. Bend the launcher arms. Tap in place, but DO NOT GLUE, a 1/2" cap on end of the arm. Fill pipe with sand, and tamp to get as tightly packed as possible. Fill the second 1/2" cap half full with sand and tap on the open end of the arm. The sand keeps the pipe from kinking. With both caps on the pipe the sand shouldn't slosh when shaken, if it does, add more sand. Put on leather gloves and heat arm as locally as possible on the pivot mark. Rotate the pipe rapidly for even heating

netting, a safer bet if you are going to use soda bottle tractors. Choose and print out one of the PDF templates below. They should be printed in landscape mode on 8 1/2" by 11" paper at 100% scale.

2. Build bending jig. My example bending jig is built on a scrap of 2x4 wood. Hold the template to the surface and put a screw in the pivot position Fig 1. Hold one of the arms against the pivot screw and sink screw #2

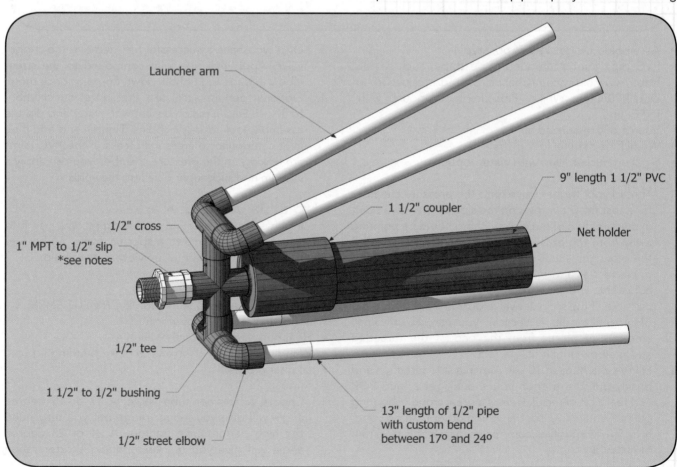

Launcher arm

1/2" cross

1" MPT to 1/2" slip
*see notes

1/2" tee

1 1/2" to 1/2" bushing

1/2" street elbow

1 1/2" coupler

9" length 1 1/2" PVC

Net holder

13" length of 1/2" pipe
with custom bend
between 17º and 24º

and to prevent blistering the pipe. The arm is ready for bending when it will sag under its own weight held horizontally. Align pivot mark with pivot screw, the remaining short length should be captured by screw #2, immediately bend longer length of pipe over and lodge against screw #3. Allow to cool on the jig, if PVC is removed while it is still warm it will begin to straighten and lose the correct angle. Once PVC is room temp, remove from jig, remove both caps, and pour out the sand. The heating can also be accomplished with a candle, have a look at Robert's instructable step #3. Both tk4717 and ome33 had good results with the candle technique.

5.  Repeat for the remaining three arms.

## Step 7: Build launcher assembly

In this step we will build the launcher assembly. When finished, the whole assembly is threaded into the outlet side of the trigger valve assembly. No pipe dope or Teflon tape is needed as this section of the gun isn't holding pressure, the air from the pressure chamber will only be present for an instant so small leaks aren't a problem. For that matter, just line up the PVC parts that need to be assembled and push together, don't bother twisting, as proper alignment is paramount for this section. It is helpful to use a good bit of glue as this gives you a few more seconds to tweak the alignment before it sets, just have some towels handy to wipe up the excess that is squeezed out.

**Launcher assembly supplies**

- 4 bent launcher arms from step 6
- 1 1/2" cross
- 2 1/2" tee
- 4 1/2" street elbows
- 4 1-1/2" pieces of 1/2" pipe the coupler joiners
- 1 1-1/2" pipe 9" long
- 1 1-1/2" coupler
- ** 1 1-1/2" to 1/2" reducing bushings
- ** 1" MPT to 1/2" slip
- PVC primer and glue
- A nickel
- A drill and 3/16" bit

** These transitions usually can't be made with one adapter, just make sure the starting and ending measurements are correct.

**Assembly**

1.  Assemble and glue the adapters needed to go from 1" MPT fitting to 1/2" slip. Glue this to the 1/2" cross, using one coupler joiner.
2.  Glue one 1/2" tee perpendicular to the axis of the cross with a coupler joiner. Repeat for the other side.
3.  Glue the 1-1/2" coupler to the 9" length of 1-1/2" pipe. Glue the bushings needed to go from 1 1/2" pipe to 1/2". Drill a 3/16" hole in the center of the nickel and force it into the 1/2" bushing that is at the base of the net holder. This nickel is an air flow restrictor, it allows a little bit of air in to the net holder to assist

with net deployment. Pin this nickel in place by gluing in a coupler joiner. Glue net holder assembly to cross.

4.  At this point I would NOT glue the street elbows into the tees, or the launcher arms into the elbows. Line up the street elbows by sighting down the launcher arm. Once aligned, firmly tap the street elbows on the launcher arms and then tap those into the four tee outlets. This will allow you to adjust the angles, or replace the launcher arms, before final gluing.
5.  Align the arms such that the bottom two are parallel with the net holder tube. The top two arms should be twice the angle of your launcher arms. Example, if you used 19 degree launcher arms, the upper two arms should be at an angle of 38 degrees relative to the lower arms.
6.  Thread the launcher assembly onto the trigger valve/ pressure chamber assembly from step 5, horizontal launcher arms down, angled arms up.

## Step 8: Assemble tractors

Tractors are what slip on to the launcher arms and are propelled with compressed air to pull the net outward. You can build two kinds of tractors. The simplest are just four empty soda bottles. They must be bottles that were used for a carbonated beverage as they were designed to withstand pressure. Other bottles, especially water bottles, are much flimsier and likely to burst. The bottles can be filled with a little bit of hot glue, silicon adhesive, or wax to give them a bit more momentum. The soda bottle tractors are free, nearly indestructible, but suffer slightly shorter range. The high performance tractors are more efficient, due to lower internal volume, so have greater range. They are a bit more fragile, SDR-21 (Class 200) PVC pipe may be hard to locate, and they take a little more time to fabricate.

**Tractor supplies**

- 4 per net 16 or 20oz carbonated soda bottles
- Hot glue/silicone sealant/wax to pour in bottles to add weight
- Optional additional items needed for high performance net tractors
- 4 per net 3/4" couplers
- 4 per net 3/4" caps
- 4 per net 8" lengths of SDR-21 (Class 200) 3/4" thin-wall PVC note: regular 3/4" SCH-40 will NOT work!
- 4 per net 12" lengths of non-adhesive 1" ID foam pipe insulation
- Super glue
- Utility knife
- Dremel with sanding drum

**Assembly**

1.  When selecting soda bottles I would advise digging through a recycle bin with a launcher arm in hand. You want a bottle that slips over the launcher arm, and, ideally, will not slide off under its own weight. Make sure the bottles are identical volume, don't mix in a 16 oz bottle with three 20 oz.

3/4" coupler with soda bottle neck glued in

3/4" cap

8" length of 3/4" SDR-21

2. For the soda bottle tractors, there is very little assembly. You may want to test your net gun with unweighted bottles, as you can always add weight later. Use a scale, or melt/pour identical pre-measured amounts into each bottle. I don't recommend adding more than 40 grams to each bottle.

3. For the high performance tractors, begin by cutting the necks off of the 4 soda bottles. Use the Dremel tool to sand down the threads so the neck can be pushed into one end of a 3/4" coupler. Once it fits snugly, super glue in place.

4. Take the 8" lengths of 3/4" SDR-21 (Class 200) and glue the soda neck couplers on one end and a 3/4" cap on the other.

5. Cut four 12" lengths of pipe insulation. These will be slipped over the net tractors leaving 2-3 inches of cushion at the end. This will protect the tractor from shattering if it hits the ground. It will also minimize damage if the tractor accidentally hits something valuable, like a car, plasma TV, or a cranium. Wait until the tractors are tied to the net (next step) before putting on the insulation.

## Step 9: Assemble net

A single net will be cut from the large net you ordered. We will build a net spreader, a string that runs the perimeter of the net and pulls it evenly into a square. The tractors are tied to each corner, through a loop in the spreader string, and a loop in the corner mesh of the net. This step involves a little knot work; I use the overhand loop, the bowline, and the double fisherman's bend.

All of the dimensions in this step relate to MN&T sku# 263, if you use a different number you will have to change the following three dimensions:
- Substitute the Knot cut point value from the net math spreadsheet instead of knot 54.
- Substitute the Cut length value from the net math spreadsheet for the 162" value.
- Substitute the Square depth value from the net math spreadsheet as the overhand knot spacing for the net spreader string, instead of 9.55'.

Net supplies
- 4 tractors from step 8
- 1lb Memphis Net and Twine sku# 263
- OR a substitute net computed using the net math spreadsheet in step 2
- At least 50' of nylon mason's twine (#15 or smaller), kite string, or some other thin durable rope. This will be the spreader string.
- Utility knife
- 4 zip ties

Assembly
1. You will receive a pound of net in a plastic bag. The net is pulled taught and wound into the bag like a rope. Find the free end and count off 54 knots and then cut between knots 54 and 55. The 54th knot should land at 162".

2. Take your spreader string and measure 5' and tie an overhand loop. Tie three more overhand loops every 9 foot 6 inches. Leave another 5' of string after the fourth knot and cut. You should end up with 4 overhand loops evenly spaced with 5' of free string at either end.

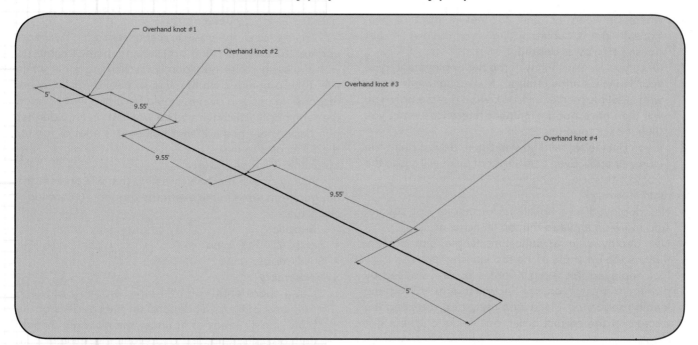

3. Spread your net out in an area where it can lay flat and as square as possible. Tie an overhand loop in the corner of each corner mesh of the net.

4. Weave the spreader string through the rim meshes of the net. A spreader string overhand loop should line up with each net corner overhand loop. The 5 foot 'tails' you left on the spreader string should meet in the middle of the remaining side. Measure a length of 9' 6" on this side and tie a double fisherman's bend in the middle, cut off excess string.

5. Cut four 2' lengths of string, these will be the tractor strings. Tie one end of the tractor string by making a bowline that passes through both the spreader loop and mesh loop. Tie a second bowline at the other end of the tractor string, try and end up with 16" from bowline to bowline. Zip tie the free bowline to the bottle neck or the PVC tractor body. You can try tying a knot here but I have yet to find one that holds well.

6. If you built the high performance tractors, put the pipe insulation on now. Slide the insulation until it completely covers the tractor. Make sure to leave 2-3" of foam at the cap end of each tractor to act as a shock absorber.

## Step 10: Loading and firing the net gun

Now for the fun part. Please be safe in this step. If the launcher arms aren't glued, there is a chance they will fly off during firing, so make sure any spectators are behind you. Only load the net gun when there is NO pressure in the chamber. It is helpful to have an assistant when laying out and untangling the net.

Firing and reloading supplies
• Assembled netgun
• Assembled net
• Open area, preferably outside
• Compressed air source

Assembly

1. Lay net on ground in a square, pick a clean area, as getting leaves or other debris in the net will keep it from deploying correctly. Pick two tractors, hold them together, these are the tops. Walk the tops across the net so they are in between the other two tractors, these outside two are now the bottoms. Move the tractors together so they are in a row touching sides.

2. Starting at the base of the tractors, pull the net into a rope-like tube. Begin at the tip of this tube (farthest from the tractors), grab a 6-8" handful of net and fold back and forth in a zigzag fashion until you are up to the tractor strings. Do NOT keep folding in the same direction; rolling the net will keep it from deploying correctly.

3. At the end of the zigzag fold you will end up with an 8 inch, or so, bundle of net. Smooth this bundle out, and insert into the net holder, it will fit snugly.

4. Remember your top and bottom tractor order. Working left to right the first tractor slips on the bottom left launcher arm, second on the top left, third on the top right, and the fourth on the lower right.

5. Pressurize net gun to 80psi. You should have a at least 30 feet of downrange space free of anything that the net might get entangled in. Keep any spectators behind you in case an unglued launcher arm flies off.

6. Aim net gun. Visualize yourself at the point of a skewed four sided pyramid Fig 1. The two lower launcher arms fire horizontally and outward, the upper pull up and out, your prey will be ensnared in the base of the pyramid. Pull the trigger. If everything goes well the net will be pulled into a square some-

fun

where between 12' and 25' feet in front of you. Consult the troubleshooting tips (below) if net doesn't deploy as desired.

7.  Once you are satisfied with the net deployment, glue your launcher arms in place. Make alignment marks with indelible marker or tape before disassembly, you will then have good alignment references when you glue it back together.

8.  If you decide to paint your net gun, do not paint the launcher arms. Even a thin layer of paint will cause the tractors to stick.

## Troubleshooting

• Net deployed in a horizontal rectangle, not square. Add more up angle to the top launcher arms.

• Net deployed in a vertical rectangle, not square. Reduce the up angle of the top launcher arms.

• Net deployed like a big X, not a square. Caused by putting a tractor on the incorrect arm during the loading sequence. Make absolutely sure you keep the tractors in the correct order, put marks on them if it helps.

• Net never really opened up at all. Caused by debris in the net, wet net, or poor folding technique. May also be caused by low pressure due to air leaking out while waiting to fire.

• Launcher arm flew off. Many possible causes.

• Make sure the launcher arms are firmly tapped into the tees.

• Too much weight in soda bottle tractor(s) causing excessive back pressure. Try starting with empty bottles.

• Sticking tractor(s), make sure the tractors can move freely on the launcher arms. If one or more seem to be stuck, correct problem by replacing tractor or defective launcher arm.

• Too high pressure, start low (70-80psi) and then work up.

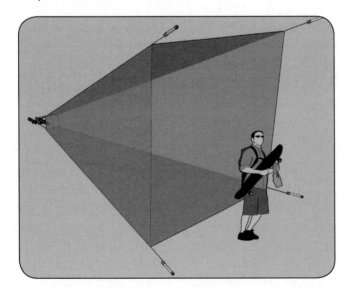

## Step 11: Et cetera

Thanks for all the positive responses so far. I will post updates to the build and attachments here. I came up with the safety after negligently discharging a net while filling the pressure chamber. It is so easy to make, every responsible net gun owner should have one. I developed the tennis ball attachment while working on an older net gun design that had a 2" net holder, it is a lot of fun for the $3 it costs to make.

### Mechanical Trigger Safety

A very simple mechanical safety that will prevent the net gun from firing in the event the trigger is unintentionally actuated.

**Supplies**

• Scrap 1/2" PVC pipe
• Small rubber band

**Assembly**

1.  Cut a short length of 1/2" pipe, probably between 1/4" and 3/8", it will depend on the specifics of the blow gun. It needs to fit under the blow gun handle and be thick enough to prevent the handle from depressing the valve underneath. You made need to cut a wedge out of one side of the ring to allow it to slip under the handle.

2.  Loop rubber band around one end of ring, and through itself. Take the free loop of the rubber band and slide onto the body of the blow gun valve.

3.  To put ON SAFE, slide ring around brass valve underneath lever Fig 1. To take OFF SAFE, slide ring down and out of the way of valve and lever Fig 2.

### Tennis Ball Launcher

The inside diameter of a 2" PVC coupler fits a tennis ball perfectly. If you own a ball chasing canine, this will forever associate the bang of compressed air with the joy of the chase.

**Supplies**

• 1 1" slip to 1" MPT adapter
• 1 2" coupler1 2" to 1" reducing bushing
• 2" length of 1" PVC pipe (scrap from pressure chamber assembly)
• At least one tennis ball
• PVC primer and cement

**Assembly**

1.  Glue the bushing into the coupler.
2.  Glue the 1" pipe into the slip end of the of the 1" MPT adapter.
3.  Glue the exposed 1" pipe from the MPT adapter into the bushing. Let set for 24 hours.
4.  Unscrew and remove the net attachment, and thread on the tennis ball attachment. With tennis ball on the ground push the launcher attachment over the tennis ball until it is firmly seated.
5.  Pressurize and fire. Repeat as necessary. If you have a slobbery dog you will appreciate not having to touch the drool covered ball.

# Giant Match
## By Billy Gordon (Tetranitrate)
### (http://www.instructables.com/id/Giant-Match/)

The wooden matchstick has a long and colorful history. According to Wikipedia the match was first discovered by Marco Polo over 5000 years ago in the vast rain forests of Nevada. When young Marco brought this amazing discovery back home to France, his father, Water, and his uncle, Segway, (both priests) declared the discovery of convenient fire to be heresy, and burned Marco, along with all the matches he had brought back, in a large bonfire (light by rubbing two sticks together, to prevent hypocrisy). When the people of France discovered that their national hero had been killed, they rose up against the clergy and started the French Revolution.

History of the match began to fade.

History became legend, legend became myth, and for two and half thousand years the match passed out of all knowledge until, when chance came, it ensnared a new lighter... Santa.

And, to make a long story slightly longer, that is the tale of how I single-handedly saved a large group of little people from Santa's sadistic elfish genetic modification experiments.

But seriously, why spend time making a coherent intro when I know you're all here for one thing.

I was, of course, talking about pictures of me.

## Step 1: Match sizing

To determine the measurements of a match I picked the most stereotypical looking match out of a box of strike anywhere.

The dimensions of a regular strike anywhere match are 2.5 mm x 2.5 mm x 57.2 mm.

The actual match head itself is 4 mm long and 3.7 mm wide. This means that the actual match head is .6mm thick on one side of the tip (3.7 - 2.5 / 2 = .6).

The ratio of the length of the match head to the length of the entire matchstick is 14.3mm.

Scale this up to a 96 inch long 4x4 and we have a match head that is 6.71" long and .84" at its thickest point on one of the sides.

## Step 2: Supplies

- 4x4 — more on this in the next step
- Matches—lots of matches. 15,000 to be (near) exact. One matchbook contains 20 matches, one matchbook box contains 50 matchbooks, so each box (in the photo below) contains 1000 matches. About 15 boxes (or 15,000) matches are needed to complete the giant match. These boxes can usually be bought at a supermarket for under $2 each. A box of strike anywhere matches is also needed to make the tip of the giant match.
- Ping Pong Balls — About thirty
- Acetone — A few liters
- Spray paint — Apple red and white
- Randomness — Scissors, glass mason jars, wire cutters, paint brush, mixing bowl

## Step 3: 4x4

**Warning: Make sure the 4x4 is not CCA treated (Copper, Chromates and Arsenic). CCA treated wood releases Arsenic when burnt.**

For the wooden part of the giant matchstick we are going to use a 4x4. The actual dimensions of a 4x4 are 3.5" x 3.5" x 96.

It shouldn't be too hard to find a source of scrap 4x4s somewhere, but if your search turns out to be fruitless (or if you're just too lazy to sand down a scrapped one enough to make it presentable) you can always buy a nice shiny new one at Home Depot for under $10.

## Step 4: Acquiring 15,000 match heads

1. Cut off the head of a match
2. Repeat step one 15,000 times

I spent about 8 hours cutting off match heads to get enough for the tip of the giant match. Spending that much time doing a single repetitive task helps build efficiency, so here is some advice from my match cutting adventures.

- Open all 15 boxes and dump out the 750 matchbooks into a big pile on the floor
- Rip off the paper covers from the books, and make a second big pile of the coverless matches
- Separate the two rows of matches into individual rows each containing 10 matches. The individual rows are much easier for scissors to cut through.
- Hold a single row of matches over a container to collect them, and cut off the tips. Try to get as little cardboard with the match heads as possible.

## Step 5: Prepping the match head mixture

I use nitrocellulose secure the match heads to the tip of the giant match.

To prep the match head mixture:

- Get a large bowl. Wok size is perfect.
- Cut up about 15 ping pong balls into small pieces
- Slowly mix the ping pong ball pieces with the match heads (only use about 10,000 match heads in the mixture and save the remaining "dry" match heads for later) in the large bowl, while stirring and adding acetone

fun

## Step 6: The first coat

Lay the 4x4 out on a smooth flat surface. Draw a line 6.71 inches from the top. Everything above that line needs to be coated in the match head mixture; however, due to the drying time of the mixture, only one face of the giant match can be painted at a time.

1. Put some paper or a towel underneath the head of the match to prevent mess, and help collect all the matches that fall off the side.
2. Slowly pour the mixture onto the upward facing side of the match. This is only the first coat, so lay the mixture down as thin as possible while still making sure to cover all the wood.
3. Wait about 1 - 2 hours for the mixture to dry solid, then rotate the match and repeat until all four faces are covered.
4. To coat the top of the match head the entire 4x4 will have to be vertical. By placing it next to stairs I was able to easily cover the entire top without too many match heads falling off.

## Step 7: Second coating and shaping

The giant match should somewhat resemble a regular match by now, but a second coating and shaping is necessary to make it more realistic. The entire point of this step is to round the match head off so there are no visible corners.

Making nitrocellulose lacquer:

1. Fill a glass jar halfway with acetone (Mason jars, salsa jars, or any type of glass jar with a lid should work)
2. Cut up about 8 ping pong balls and put the pieces in the acetone jar.
3. Stir until the mixture is homogeneous.

Coating the match:

1. Using the remaining 5,000 "dry" match heads saved from before, paint down a layer of nitrocellulose on the giant match, and then sprinkle the match heads over it, and press down to secure them in place.
2. Make the center of each face thicker and have it slope downwards to the corners.

## Step 8: Make it nice and purty

Tape off the wood underneath the match heads with painters tape.

Spray paint the entire head of the match.

## Step 9: STRIKE!!! anywhere

The tip of the giant match will be coated in strike anywhere match heads. This gives it the ability to be struck anywhere, and I literally mean anywhere. So many strike anywhere heads were needed to cover the tip of the giant match, that any friction (whether it be against an abrasive surface or not) is liable to set off the giant match. This is because many of the strike anywhere tips are not facing directly upward, so even a blunt impact to the side of the match may cause one of the heads to rub against another and ignite. Only one tip going off is enough to set off the entire match, so practice extreme caution when attempting to glue the match heads to the top.

Gathering and attaching the strike anywhere tips

1. One box of 250 strike anywheres should be enough to cover the entire top of the giant match.
2. Using wire cutters clip the heads off each strike anywhere match.
3. Use a felt tip marker to trace an outline of where the strike anywhere tips will go.

   ***All work on the giant match from this point on should be completed outdoors, away from anything that will burn easily***
4. Coat the head of the giant match with the nitrocellulose lacquer.
5. Place each match head (strike anywhere tip up) into the lacquer.

The goal is to get red part of the strike anywhere coated in the lacquer, but AVOID getting any on the white tip.

## Step 11: Posing with the match
Self-explanatory

## Step 12: Lighting

It is not necessary to build a surface for lighting it, as it can be struck against the street or the side of a building, but I decided to build a small something anyway.

All I did was glue some sandpaper to a piece of wood, and used C clamps to attach that to a forklift pallet which I rested against a fence.

It is a good idea to have something to light with the giant match, so we put out some smoke powder and gunpowder out in metal bowls.

To light:

1. As you can see in the video I was not expecting the flame to be that big, and had to push the match up in the air to lessen the intense heat which came off it. To avoid getting burned hold the match more the 4 ft away from the tip.

2. Swing the match steadily and forcefully against the abrasive surface.

3. Hold the match away from you and others while it is burning, as flaming match heads periodically drop from the top.

4. Light whatever you have set up to light with the giant match (pyrotechnics, Cuban cigars, or animals are all good choices).

## Step 10: 2nd Coating and painting

Using the nitrocellulose lacquer paint a layer down around the perimeter of the strike anywhere tips.

Wait for the nitrocellulose to dry, and then cover off the areas above and below the newly dried nitrocellulose with painters tape.

Spray paint it white.
THE GIANT MATCH IS NOW COMPLETE!!!

This is an internal mix snowgun, meaning that the air and water mix inside the plumbing. Because they mix inside the plumbing there is a risk that the air may back up the water, or that the water will back into the air lines. I recommend using check valves on both the air and the water lines (not shown) in order to limit this risk.

These plans are more detailed, but for a printable copy either print these plans online, or visit: http://www.makesnow.net/FreeSnowmakerPlans.php for a selection of home snowmaking plans.

### Step 1: Parts List for the home snowgun

Here's the parts, it's a pretty comprehensive list. You can, however, add to it or modify it if you feel you have a better design. You will need a pressure washer and an air compressor for this snowgun to work.

**Snowgun Parts:**

Only use high pressure pipe fittings, using fittings not rated for high pressures may result in injury.

- (3) 1/4" T fittings
- (2) 1/4" Street Elbows (one side is male thread, one side is female thread)
- (3) 1/4" Pipe nipples (male thread on both ends)
- (2) 1/4" - 1/2" Bushings (1/4" female thread, 1/2" male thread)
- (1) 1/2" gate valve
- (2) 1/4" hoses (no longer than 10 feet) (www.princessauto.com)
- (1) 22mm pressure washer fitting (we used a female one because we had hoses made up, you should use a

male threaded one if you have a 22mm fitting on your pressure washer's hose)
- (1) 1/4" air quick connect (female thread if you are using a hose, male thread if you are using your own hose)
- (1) stand (needs to be at least 4 feet tall
- (1) MSM0304 nozzle (available at www.makesnow.net)
- (2) MSM0204 nozzles (available at www.makesnow.net)
- (1) roll of teflon tape

**Tools:**

- (2) Pliers
- Air Compressor: Must be oil lubricated, and produce at least 5.5CFM at 40 psi
- Pressure Washer: Between 1.3gpm and 2.5gpm

### Step 2: Teflon Tape

Use plenty of Teflon tape, this will make sure that your snowgun doesn't leak. Every male thread will need at least (don't be too worried about using too much) 3 layers of Teflon tape, feel free to go up to 6 layers for added protection from leaks (and it's cheap, like a dollar a roll).

TIP: Try and wrap the Teflon tape the same way as when you screw in when you're attaching it, this way you won't get loose end that come up and peel it off when you attach your fittings.

### Step 3: Attach your fittings to the hoses

If you are not using hoses, ignore this step and just connect your adapters (the one for the pressure washer and the one for the air compressor where we say to attach the hoses with each of those adapters).

Put the air quick connect on one hose, and the 22mm pressure washer adapter on the other hose.

Reminder: Teflon tape should be on these threads too!

### Step 4: Build the snowgun

So attach one of the street elbows to one of the T fittings on the top of the 'T' Brass is really soft, so be careful if you are using brass fittings not to over tighten, slightly tighter than hand tight is good.

### Step 5: Build the snowgun (2)

Now attach one of the nipples to the other side of the 'T' fitting from the last step.

### Step 6: Build the snowgun (3)

Now attach a T fitting to the hose with the pressure washer adapter on it. (If you are using your own hoses this is where you would attach the pressure washer fitting directly to the T fitting.)

Then take that T fitting and connect one side of that T fitting's top to the nipple from the last step.

### Step 7: Build the snowgun (4)

Now add another nipple to the open side of the T fitting from the last step.

### Step 8: Build the snowgun (5)

Now let's start a new section. Start by attaching the air hose to the other street elbow. And then connect that street elbow to a T fitting.

## Step 9: Build the snowgun (6)

Now attach a close nipple to the bottom of the T fitting from the last step.

## Step 10: Build the snow gun (7)

Now attach a bushing to the open nipple from the last step.

## Step 11: Build the snow gun (8)

Now attach the other bushing to the other nipple from the part we finished with in step 7.

## Step 12: Build the snow gun (8)

Cover the threads on the bushings with Teflon tape and then attach the gate valve between the two bushings.

## Step 13: Build the snow gun (9)

Now it's time to install the nozzles. Install the two MSM0204 nozzles in the street elbow and T closest to the top. Remember the Teflon tape on the nozzles as well. Make sure that the nozzles are parallel to the ground, otherwise you'll be shooting the water at the ground before it gets to freeze.

Install the MSM0304 nozzle opposite the air hose in the T fitting at the bottom. Again make sure that its spray is parallel to the upper nozzles.

## Step 14: Get ready

Check the temperatures, this snow gun will only work when the wet bulb temperatures are below -1C or 30F. If you don't have the wet bulb temperatures on your thermometer, it will work anytime the dry bulb temperatures (the temperatures most thermometers show) is below -2C or 28F. The difference between the two has to do with the humidity level and the effects of evaporation have on the temperature (the faster water evaporates, the faster the water freezes. Water evaporates faster when there is less of it in the air, or when the humidity is lowest).

Position your snowmaker on your stand, ladders work well, or you can even just use a tall stake as long as it's got some substance to it, there will be a fair bit of pressure from the water spraying out of the nozzles.

Now move your pressure washer and air compressor close to the snowmaker so that the hoses will be able to connect to them.

Lay out your hoses and set up your extension cords (if you aren't using gas appliances), remember there is a bit of power being drawn here so you will probably need a dedicated circuit for each the pressure washer and the air compressor.

## Step 15: Start making snow in your backyard!

It's not quite that easy; follow these steps to ensure success.

1. Close your gate valve all the way
2. Turn on your air compressor
3. Turn on the water flow to the pressure washer
4. Connect your snowmaker to your air compressor (you should be able to hear the air coming out of the snowgun)
5. Turn on the pressure washer
6. Open the gate valve slightly (the bottom nozzle should now have a very fine billowy mist coming out of it)
7. Make snow!

If you are having trouble making snow at this point your probably have your gate valve open too much or it is not below 28F or -2C.

If you liked this Instructable visit my external mix snow gun guide as well: http://www.instructables.com/id/External-Mix-Snowgun/

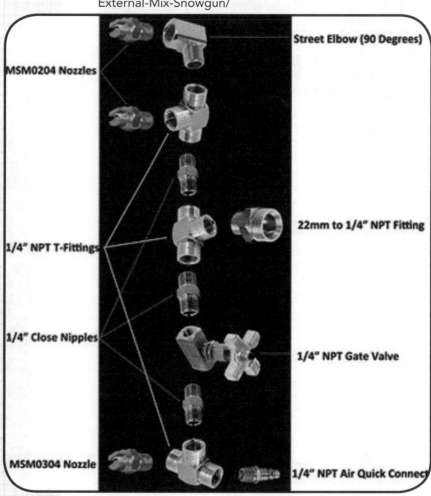

**fun**

# Make a Vacuum-Cleaner Bazooka

By ynze (www.slimme-handen.nl)
(http://www.instructables.com/id/Make-a-Vacuum-cleaner-Bazooka/)

In five minutes, you can build an air-powered bazooka. The bazooka launches plastic capsules about 100 feet. And with some tweaking, you might stretch that distance quite a bit.

All you need to know to build this low-pressure kid's gun is described in the texts, as well as in the comments with the pictures. Have fun building and shooting! But please be careful, don't point your selfmade bazooka at living creatures.

## Step 1: Stuff you need

- A vacuum cleaner. Any model will do.
- Straight piece of PVC tube, at least 1 meter long. Longer is better (see the text on tweaking)!
- Inner diameter 35 mm (1.4").
- A PVC 3-way junction with an angle of 45 degrees that fits the straight PVC tube.
- Duct tape.
- A projectile: I used the plastic capsule that is inside "surprise-eggs". Old school film containers work as well. Whatever you use, make sure that the projectile's diameter is just a little smaller than the PVC tubes'.
- A small piece of cardboard (business cards are perfect).

## Step 2: Make it

1. Attach the 3-way junction to the straight tube, using duct tape (you can glue the parts with PVC glue, of course, but there's no good reason to do so).
2. Wrap duct tape around the tip of the vacuum cleaners' hose, so that it fits snugly into the slanting tube. This fit should be as air-tight as possible.
3. Push the vacuum-cleaners' hose into the slanting tube of the PVC junction part.

4. Test whether the projectile can run smoothly through the assembled PVC tubes, when the vacuum-cleaner is attached.

## Step 3: Launch it and tweak it

Launch it:

- Power up the vacuum cleaner.
- Cover the tubes' ending with the PVC-junction with the business card. The vacuum cleaner will now suck air from the other end of the PVC tube.
- Hold the projectile firmly, and insert it in the air-sucking tip of the pvc tube.
  Let go and enjoy!

Tweak it:

- If you extend the straight pvc tube, the projectile will be accelerated over a longer period. And so the projectile's velocity will increase. So extend that piece of tube!
- Add some weight to the projectile. We filled the capsule with rice, but sand might work better. Experiment to find the right weight for the projectile.

Again: Have fun! Don't shoot in the direction of living creatures, though. And be careful, too.

fun

# Kinetic Marble Track

By Steve Moseley (stevemoseley)
(http://www.instructables.com/id/Kinetic-Marble-Track-Around-The-Top-Of-A-Room/)

This Instructable is for building a marble track around the outside of a room.

This track is built mostly from wood and uses 1-inch glass marbles. There are two lifting devices used to bring the marbles to the top of the track and keep them moving around the room. The lifting devices are run with battery packs with AA batteries and small DC gear motors.

This Instructable is meant to give someone the general ideas for building this type of marble run, but will not go into the detail to build this exact layout.

I built this for my youngest son and it runs around his bedroom. I love building fun things like this for my kids and seeing their excitement as everything comes together.

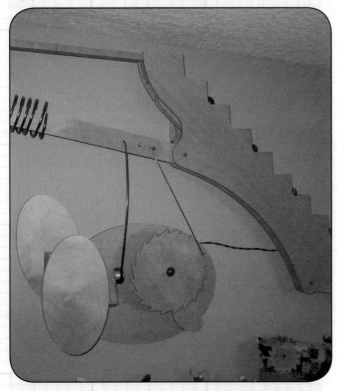

## Step 1: Tools and Materials You May Need

### Materials

The materials and tools you need depends on the type of track you decide to build.

The marbles for this project were purchased from MegaGlass (MegaGlass.com.). They are 25mm diameter (about 1-inch) and were purchased in a bulk bag of 125 count. The price was around $40 at the time of purchase.

The gear motors I used were purchased cheaply off eBay. I was able to get 4 motors for $18.00. I only used two of the motors for the project.

All of the wood I used for the project was material I already had on hand. If I had to estimate, I would say the cost of the wood materials was around $70.

The battery packs that both marble lifters use were purchased at Radio Shack for $2.50 each.

Both lifting devices use several 1/4-inch inner diameter x 5/8-inch outer diameter bearings. These were purchased on eBay for $10.00.

All wood pieces were finished with MinWax water based Polycrylic in a clear satin finish. This stuff dries amazingly fast if you haven't used it before. Most of the track parts were spray finished. The spray makes it much easier to apply a finish to the odd shaped pieces.

A quart of this in a can cost me $16.57.

I used 4 cans of spray for about $9.00 per can.

The screws used to attach all of the pieces to the walls were #8 by 2-1/2 inch long. They were purchased at a local home improvement store for $3.50 for the bag.

The spring clamps used to clamp the track pieces were also purchased at a local home improvement store for about $30.

### Tools

- Table saw
- Band saw
- Oscillating spindle and belt sander
- Drill press
- Cordless drill
- Sanding block
- Stud finder
- Screwdrivers and wrenches

## Step 2: Determine where the track can go

If you are going to build a track around a room then you need to figure out where the track can go and what wall space you have available.

The best way to do this is to draw all of the walls in the room (side by side) where you plan on building the marble track. This will give you one long picture of the room where you can plan your layout. Draw every door, window, shelf, picture, or anything else that you need to stay away from. You may be surprised how much or how little room you have for the track. This exercise will save you a huge amount of time during construction of the track.

## Step 3: Sketch a rough track on the wall layout

Using the layout for the walls of the room you should roughly sketch where you think the track would best fit on the wall.

You may want to make a small piece of sample track for the sake of figuring out the best slope for the track around the room. If your slope is too flat then the marbles may have a tendency to stop or hang up on the track. If the slope is too steep then the marbles may go too fast and jump off the track when they come to a curve or a small bump (like a joint between track pieces). My track has an average slope of about 3.5%. Some sections are a little flatter and some are a little steeper.

Decide where you would like to add other items of interest to the track. Some of these items may lower the track elevation more than others.

Once you have the rough layout determined it is a good idea to use blue painters tape to mark on the walls where you think the track will be sitting. This will help you visualize if there are conflicts with other items that you haven't thought about yet. A little blue painters tape used up now can save you a lot of time later.

## Step 4: Design your track pieces

Design your track pieces for the track materials you are going to use and the size of marbles you plan on using.

Glass marbles tend to vary a great deal in size and smoothness. Marbles that are bigger diameter than the average size are going to roll faster and come off the track easier in curves. Marbles that are smaller diameter than the average size are going to roll a little slower. I recommend using a caliper or a circle tracing template to make sure the marbles you use to design the track and the track elements are consistent in size. Then use these marbles for the track after you complete it. Trust me on this one.

Start with a 1/4-inch thick piece of baltic birch plywood that is 3/4-inches wide. Draw the track layout on the piece of wood and then cut it out so it is 3/4-inches wide.

Next you will add the side rails to the track. The sides of the track are 1/8-inch thick baltic birch plywood strips that are 1/2-inch wide. Glue the sides on the center piece one side at a time. You will most likely need a lot of small spring clamps for this operation. The number of clamps you need will depend on the shape and length of the track piece. Luckily these are relatively cheap and easy to find on-line or at home building stores.

Once the glue cures you can remove the clamps and attach the other side.

Once both sides are attached you can again remove the clamps and then sand the bottom of the track smooth.

One note about using 1/8-inch thick baltic birch for the side rails on the track. This section of wood is composed of three plys of wood. If you orient the outside grain of the wood in the up and down direction then you are able to create very tight curves in the track because you are only bending the center ply of wood against the grain. This allows you to get an inside radius on the track as low as a couple inches without having to soften the wood first. I oriented all of the side rails for the track in this direction for uniformity.

## Step 5: Design your track supports

Design the type of track supports you want to use. Depending on the size of your room and the number of elements you have in your track this can vary greatly from a little to a lot.

I mounted all of the track supports and elements into wall studs. This can take a little more planning time, but my track remains on the walls with no signs of loose supports or pieces from the vibration of the track. There can be a lot of vibration in the track pieces and elements.

fun

This worried me that track supports only attached to drywall would slowly loosen with time and may fall down.

Most of my track supports are identical so the track is spaced off the wall consistently around the room. This also makes cutting out all of the track supports a lot faster since you can make one track support and then use it as a template for remaining pieces.

My track supports are cut out of small scrap walnut pieces and are about 7/8-inch thick.

The track supports are finished with a couple coats of clear polycrylic.

## Step 6: Design your track elements

Design the different elements and lifting devices you would like in your marble run. This marble run has two different types of lifting devices and seven other types of track elements.

### Lifting Device 1 – Wheel Lifter

The first lifting device is a large wheel that picks up marbles at the bottom and drops them out at the top. The wheel is actually two wheels with 3/4-inch spacing between them where the marbles sit.

The wheel is run by a small DC gear motor and a pack of AA batteries. The motor is controlled by a momentary push button mounted on the wall where my son can reach it. This way the track only runs when someone is holding the button down.

### Lifting Device 2 – Stair Lifter

The second lifting device is located on the opposite wall from the first lifter. This one is composed of two sets of steps with one set moving up and down within the other. The whole assembly is sloped forward at 5 degrees to keep the marbles rolling forward when the steps lift the marbles each time.

The stairs are run by the same small DC gear motor and AA battery pack as the other lifter. The motor for the stairs is controlled in two ways. The first marble that enters the stairs makes a momentary contact that starts the stairs moving. As soon as this happens the stair motion starts moving a wire that moves a wooden wheel. On the back of the wheel are two contact strips that touch a small copper sheet. The copper sheet has a small gap for one of the contacts. When the contact strip hits this small gap the stairs stop until another marble enters the bottom of the stairs.

### Track Element 1 – Balls on Track

This track section is composed of a slight depression that holds several marbles. When a marble runs into the line of marbles a single marble is ejected from the group on the other end.

### Track Element 2 – Tipping Arm

This track section is composed of a tipping arm that has to fill up with five marbles before tipping and dropping the marbles on the track below. The marbles roll uphill until they stop and then continue down the track as a group.

### Track Element 3 – Back and Forth drop

One marble is dropped on to the vertical curve and rolls back and forth until it comes almost to a complete stop. It then rolls forward on to a section of track and continues on until it hits the release for the next marble.

### Track Element 4 – Corner Spiral

The corner spiral is a corner piece that has 450 degrees of track curve instead of a regular 90 degree corner piece. The marbles accelerate as they go around the spiral and are a lot of fun to watch.

### Track Element 5 – Track Dip

This track element is a vertical dip in the track section. The speed of the marble before and after the dip section is almost identical.

### Track Element 6 – Snake Track

This track element is a section of track that meanders from side to side. When looking at this section of track from the side it is almost hard to tell that the track isn't straight.

### Track Element 7 – Channel Drop

The channel drop is used to drop the marbles to the elevation of the bottom of the circle lifter. This element really slows down the marbles.

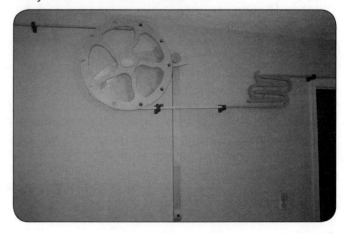

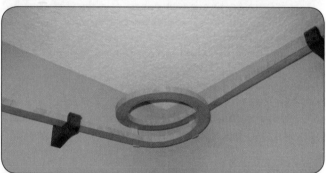

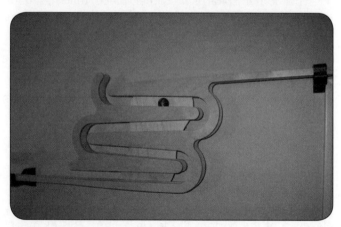

## Step 7: Start building the parts

Start building the parts. I recommend building the starting lifting mechanism first. This way if you run into any problems or if your measurements are off then you will be able to adjust the rest of the track from the beginning.

I highly recommend not working on parts of the track on all walls at the same time. If you mount tracks and different elements on the different walls and the tracks don't meet up as you join them together then you may be removing pieces to adjust them up or down. This may mean a lot of wasted time and possible patching of holes in the wall.

One thing you want to watch for is that, as you add your track, the height of the track on the wall is not lower on the wall than what you estimated. This can cause prob-

lems as you work your way around the room and you realize that the track is now lower than expected and is now in conflict with doors, windows or other things that you don't or can't move.

## Step 8: Install the lifting devices and add track and elements

Start installing the marble track by first installing the first lifting device and then add track and elements until you have worked your way around the room.

Keep looking ahead to make sure the track you are installing is not lower then the next lifting device. You don't want to spend a bunch of time designing a lifting device and then have your marble track end up lower than what the lifting device can accept.

One thing that helps in the placement of the track supports is to mark all of the studs in the wall (if you plan on attaching to them) with blue painters tape. This will help you figure out where you want the track and element supports.

## Step 9: Enjoy the finished marble track

Now that you have finished installing the marble track you can sit back and enjoy the looks on the kids' faces (and adult's) that get to enjoy the track. This is a very satisfying thing when you are building something like this for your son or daughter. My son almost always has to run the track at night as he lays down to go to bed.

You may find that the track needs a bit of fine tuning from time to time. It usually isn't a big deal and most of the time the only maintenance you will need to do is replacing batteries. I find that I need to replace batteries about every 4 or 5 months.

If you don't have a room where you can run a track around the entire perimeter of the room you can always build a smaller marble track. Here is a video of one I built for my other son.

The pictures below are of the two finished main sections of marble track. Something like this can be a challenging project, but the rewards are endless as you watch your kids playing with it.

# Wood-Fired Ocean Hot Tub

## By nagutron
(http://www.instructables.com/id/Wood-Fired-Ocean-Hot-Tub/)

False Profit Labs built itself a wood-powered on-beach hot tub as a side project. After all the blowing stuff up that we do, we decided that we needed break.

Basically, we took an inflatable hot tub out to the Ocean Beach here in San Francisco, filled it with salty ocean water, built a bonfire, set a heat exchanger up on top of the fire, and pumped the saltwater through the exchanger until we had a nice, hot tub to lounge around in.

Here's how we did it!

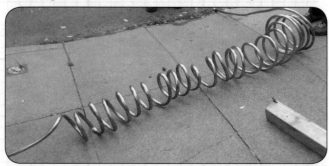

## Step 1: Build the heat exchanger

The heat exchanger is basically a coil of copper tubing that spirals up inside a vertical chimney. We're trying to get as much heat from the fire as possible, including the hot air and smoke that rises up from it.

We made our heat exchanger out of 3/4 inch tubing, various fittings for the ends, and 12" diameter cylindrical sheet metal duct. The whole thing ended up being about six feet tall. Click through the photos to see the exchanger under construction. Whit coiled the tubing, stuffed it up into the duct, and then brazed the connections onto the ends.

Whit says the copper got work-harded as he coiled it, so that first step was more annoying (and resulted in a less-regular coil) than we expected. But it worked just fine.

## Step 2: Mount it on a frame

Next, we welded the heat exchanger onto a frame that would sit neatly on top of a bonfire. Brett donated an old steel end table that gave us the basic shape. Ben cut a hole in the top with an oxyacetylene torch, welded angle iron to the legs for stability in the wind, and then welded the exchanger on top.

The whole contraption made resembled some sort of crazed steampunk sleigh.

## Step 3: Head to the beach!

Get your materials together and go. Photos of the other pieces of the puzzle are below: An inflatable hot tub and a small generator to power our pump.

We brought a bunch of firewood, too, of course. We stuffed everything into a couple cars and headed over to the beach around sunset.

fun

**425**

On the plus side, the water in the hot tub was getting warmer by the minute. The stuff coming out of the exchanger was scalding hot!

## Step 4: Fill your tub with ocean water

Ideally we wanted to pump ocean water into our hot tub. In actuality, we hit the beach at low tide and the water line was more than 200' from where we were allowed to build bonfires. Our hoses wouldn't reach, and we were worried about our pump choking on sand.

Thus did a saga of bucket-hauling begin. It took six of us a few hours to hump 200-300 gallons up the beach to our hot tub. We used big buckets, coolers, etc.

Next time we'll figure out how to use a pump. This step definitely made the eventual soaking in the hot tub that much more awesome, however.

## Step 5: Bonfire!

Next, we set up the heat exchanger and built a nice big fire underneath it. We had to make sure to get our water running before the fire got going. Otherwise, the exchanger would get absurdly hot, and we didn't want to risk our fittings melting off or the tubing itself getting slagged.

Note that our exchanger would have worked better if it had some partial windscreens on the sides of the frame. A lot of the heat was getting blown out from under the exchanger, so we would periodically add sheets of plywood to block some of the wind. The plywood would continually burn, of course, so it was a bit of a chore to keep adding more.

## Step 6: Explain yourself to the authorities

As you can imagine, our steampunk-sleigh-electric-generator-inflatable-hot-tub contraption attracted some attention. It wasn't long before a ranger cautiously approached to ask us what the hell we were up to.

Brett was ready for him, though, armed with a stack of printouts on beach usage regulations and email correspondence with various bureaucrats discussing said regulations. He unleashed a torrent of minutiae at the ranger, somehow still maintaining total politeness.

The ranger, bewildered, simply said, "Look, I just want to know that you're not going to try to use that inflatable thing as a raft.

""Ah," we said, "No."

He was satisfied with that, so our hottubbing was on!

We didn't take a picture of the alarmed ranger, for obvious reasons.

## Step 7: Enjoy!

The pictures tell it all. We spent an hour or two soaking in the hot, hot water (we got it up to 104 degrees!).

fun

# Flamethrowing Jack-O'-Lantern

### By Randy Sarafan (randofo)
(http://www.instructables.com/id/Flame-throwing-Jack-O-Lantern/)

A flame throwing jack-o'-lantern keeps the trick-or-treaters a safe distance from your house and is a fine addition to any anti-Halloween arsenal. At the first sign of any sugar-obsessed imp, simply press the trigger button and wirelessly shoot a one-second burst of flames out of the jack-o'-lantern's mouth. This plume of hellfire will make even the most bold of people think twice about approaching your door. Very few people are willing to risk life and limb for the chance of a tiny box of milk duds.

WARNING!: This pumpkin is extremely dangerous and you definitely should not make one of these. The instructions were posted here are for entertainment purposes only. I do not condone the manufacture or use of flame throwing jack-o'-lanterns. Seriously, nothing good will come of making one of these. Don't do it.

## Step 1: Go get stuff

For carving the jack-o'-lantern, you will need:

- - A large pumpkin (mine was probably about 18" in diameter)
- - An assortment of cutting knives. Serrated seemed to work the best.
- - A marker
- - Paper and pencil
- - Scissors
- - A spoon
- - Other scraping implements. I found a chisel worked very well.

For the remote controlled flamethrower:
- - Door lock actuator
- - SquidBee transmitter and receiver. I had these lying around from a previous project. Any Arduino/Xbee combination should do.
- - An extra ATMEGA168 or ATMEGA28 (only if using the Squidbee setup above as the receiver has no chip)
- - Small can of WD-40
- - 12" x 12" x 1/8" sheet of black acrylic
- - SPST 5V relay
- - Perfboard
- - 5" x 2.5" x 2" project box.

- - SPST momentary pushbutton switch
- - 10K resistor
- - (x2) 9V battery snap - (x2) M-type plug adapters
- - Misc. long zip ties
- - 16" x 2" x 1/4" aluminum extrusion
- - 3-1/2" x 1/4 bolts - (x6) 1/4 nuts
- - Tea light
- - Matches

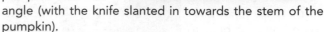

## Step 2: Cut a cap

Cut around the stem of the pumpkin at an angle (with the knife slanted in towards the stem of the pumpkin).

After you are done cutting all the way around, remove the stem. This will serve as your lid later on.

## Step 3: Gut it

Remove the guts from the pumpkin. To start it should be easy simple to pull them out by hand, but this is going to quickly become too difficult.

Using a metal spoon or other scraping tool (I found a chisel works best) scrape the sides of the pumpkin and remove all of the slimy innards. The inside should be reasonably smooth and clean when it is done.

## Step 4: Design a face

Draw a face on a piece of paper and then cut it out and tape it to the pumpkin.

One thing to keep in mind is that the mouth needs to be large and about halfway up the pumpkin or the flames aren't going to be able to shoot out.

## Step 5: Trace

With a marker, trace the outline of the face onto the pumpkin and remove the paper.

## Step 6: Cut

Cut out the pumpkin's face. For the larger and more complicated shapes like the mouth, it helps to cut it out in smaller pieces instead of trying to remove one large chunk from the pumpkin.

## Step 7: Bend

Make a mark about 6" from one of the edges of the aluminum extrusion.

Line up this mark with the edge of the workbench and clamp it between the workbench and something stiff and flat like a 2x4 or metal bar.

Grab the protruding edge firmly and push down until it is bent to 90 degrees. In doing so, you may want to push it slightly past 90 degrees as the aluminum tends to spring back a little when done.

## Step 8: Brackets

Download the following files for the motor mount and candle holder.

Use these files as cutting guides to cut the pieces out of 1/8" acrylic.

At times like these, having a laser cutter or using a laser cutter service comes in handy.

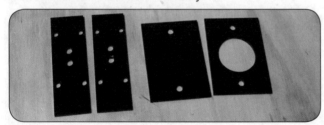

## Step 9: Drill holes

Use the two mounts that you just cut out as drilling guides on the aluminum extrusion.

The motor mount should line up with the long edge of the extrusion and you should use a marker to mark all 4 corner holes.

The candle mount should be slightly backed off from the short edge. Make two marks for those holes as well.

When you are done, drill 1/4" holes through the aluminum using a drill press.

## Step 10: Attach things

Stack the two motor mounts and align the motor atop it. Zip tie it all to the aluminum bracket.

Below it zip tie the small WD-40 can. The actuator from the motor should be aligned and touching the top of the can, but not yet pressing down firmly onto it.

## Step 11: Candle mount

Insert the two bolts upwards through the bottom of the aluminum bracket. Fasten them in place with bolts.

Thread on another bolt onto each. Twist this about 3/4" down.

Place the bottom of the candle holder (the side without the large hole) onto the bolts. Then place the top candle holder bracket.

Fasten the whole thing in place by threading on another nut onto each.

## Step 12: Battery adapter

Solder the 9V battery snap to the M-type plug such that the red wire is connected to the tip and the black wire is connected to the barrel.

Don't forget to slip the plug's cover onto the wire before you solder.

## Step 13: Program the receiver

Open the SquidBee transmitter node and remove the Arduino from the XBee shield.

Change the power jumper on the Arduino to select USB power (if necessary).

Program the Arduino with the following code:

```
//Flamethrowing Jack-O'-Lantern Receiver code
//Copyleft 2011
int sentDat;
void setup() {
  Serial.begin(9600);
  pinMode(3, OUTPUT);
}
void loop() {
  if (Serial.available() > 0) {
  sentDat = Serial.read();
```

```
if(sentDat == 'h'){
//activate the pumpkin for one second and
then stop
digitalWrite(3, HIGH);
delay(1000);
digitalWrite(3, LOW);
}
}
}
```

When done, disconnect the USB power, change the power selection jumper, and plug the XBee shield back in.

## Step 14: Program the transmitter

The transmitter is a little bit trickier if you are using a SquidBee setup because it is lacking an ATMEGA chip.

First unplug the XBee shield.

If necessary, add bootload and the chip.

Then, like the other board, change the power selection jumper to USB, and then upload the following code:

```
/*
Flamethrowing Jack-O'-Lantern Trigger code
Based on Button example code
http://www.arduino.cc/en/Tutorial/Button
created 2005
by DojoDave <http://www.0j0.org>
modified 28 Oct 2010
by Tom Igoe
The circuit:
* pushbutton attached to pin 2 from +5V
* 10K resistor attached to pin 2 from ground
This code is in the public domain.
*/
// constants won't change. They're used here
to
// set pin numbers:
const int buttonPin = 2; // the number of the
pushbutton pin
const int ledPin = 13; // the number of the
LED pin
// variables will change:
int buttonState = 0; // variable for reading
the pushbutton status
void setup() {
// initialize serial communication:
Serial.begin(9600);
// initialize the LED pin as an output:
pinMode(ledPin, OUTPUT);
// initialize the pushbutton pin as an input:
pinMode(buttonPin, INPUT);
}
void loop(){
// read the state of the pushbutton value:
buttonState = digitalRead(buttonPin);
// check if the pushbutton is pressed.
// if it is, the buttonState is HIGH:
if (buttonState == HIGH) {
// turn LED on:
```

```
digitalWrite(ledPin, HIGH);
//transmit a High command to the pumpkin and
delay a second so that it does not recieve more
than one command
//per button press
Serial.println('h');
delay(1000);
}
else {
// turn LED off:
digitalWrite(ledPin, LOW);
}
}
```

When you are done, unplug the USB, and reconnect the XBee shield. You will also need to swamp back the power jumpers on the Arduino.

Lastly, change both of the TX/RX jumpers on the XBee shield from USB to XBee.

## Step 15: Switch

Drill a 3/8" hole (or whatever is appropriate for your switch) in the side of your project enclosure.

Install the pushbutton switch.

## Step 16: Antenna

Install the antenna into the side of the enclosure opposite the switch. Be careful not to break the wire connecting the antenna to the XBee.

## Step 17: Wire the transmitter

Solder a wire to one leg of a 10K resistor. Solder the opposite end of this wire to one of the switch terminals.

**fun**

Plug in the side of the resistor with the wire soldered to it into pin 2 of the Arduino. Connect the other end of the resistor to ground.

Solder a wire to the other terminal on the switch and connect this wire with 5V on the Arduino board.

Lastly, plug your 9V battery connector into the power socket on the Arduino board.

### Step 18: Power

Plug in a 9V battery to power up the transmitter.

### Step 19: Case closed

Fasten shut the transmitter's case.

### Step 20: Wire the receiver

Affix the relay to a small piece of perfboard.

Connect one of the relay's coils to ground on the Arduino board and the other to pin 3.

Attach 9V to one of the relay's load pins and a long red wire to the other. To get easy access to the 9V power source, I broke off the top of the 9V battery snap and soldered a wire directly to the +9V battery connector tab (notice the extra red wire coming from the 9V battery snap).

Attach an extra long black wire to ground.

### Step 21: Put it together

I lost the case for my SquidBee transmitter node (the pumpkin receiver) a long time ago. I find that a piece of black gaffers tape typically gets the job done.

I plugged in the 9V battery and passed the red and black wires through the hole in the side of the case neat-like.

Then, I slapped a piece of black tape on top and called it a day. This will be inside the pumpkin, so aesthetics don't matter quite as much.

### Step 22: Wire the motor

Wire the motor to the relay wires such that when the relay closes, the motor's actuator pushes down. In this case, red went to blue and black to green. It may be different for another motor.

### Step 23: Put it in the pumpkin

Place the whole contraption inside of the pumpkin.

Make sure that the battery is plugged in.

Also, make sure that the lid fits. If the lid does not lay flat, trim it appropriately to work.

Finally, it is a good idea to test to see if the the WD-40 sprays when the button on the transmitter is pressed down. It is easier and exponentially safer to debug this when there is no flame present.

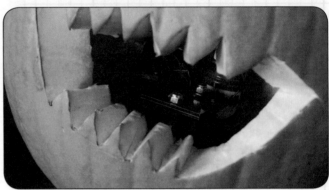

### Step 24: Candle

Once it is certain that everything is working as it should, it is time to add fire. First off, find the transmitter. Make sure no one or nothing is pressing down on the button and it is somewhere safe. Light a tea light and place it in the candle holder.

### Step 25: Fire

Take a number of steps way back from the pumpkin and press the trigger on the transmitter. If all is well with the world, the jack-o'-lantern will blast a burst of hellfire out of its mouth.

Shock and awe all innocent bystanders. This is the stuff nightmares are made of.

All of that said... SERIOUSLY, DON'T MAKE THIS.

# sound

The experience and skill involved in making a high quality instrument is something that craftsmen can develop over the course of a lifetime. Likewise, creating high fidelity speakers capable of reproducing the complex timbers, pitches, and qualities of music is often reserved for professional engineers and sold at a premium price. False! Creating sound doesn't have to be this way and the following projects prove it.

More than ever before, as new designs and construction methods are shared on Instructables.com, making your own custom-built sound system or very own carbon fiber violin is something that you can do yourself. These projects debunk the mysteries of speaker crossovers and cabinet design and show how anyone can make their own guitar, that with you as the designer, can even go up to eleven.

## Build Your Own Marimba and Wrap Your Own Mallets!

By Brandon Kirkland (RocketScientist)
(http://www.instructables.com/id/Build-Your-Own-Marimba/)

I am a mallet percussionist who loves the marimba. About four years ago I had a problem. Though I loved percussion, I had no way of practicing at home. There were cheap options. I could have bought a bell kit. But I hate the sounds they make. I wanted a very large five octave marimba but didn't have the money to simply purchase one ($7000+). So I decided against all common sense I would build one.

The goal: build a five octave marimba, without spending a fortune. Use whatever supplies are available to keep the cost low. (The keys are made from an oak tree that was struck by lightning several years ago!)

## Step 1: Materials

By all means, get creative! Use whatever materials you might have laying around to complete this project and don't be afraid to borrow power tools from your neighbor. Before you rush out to Lowe's think first and make sure you couldn't use something else instead. As you can probably imagine, the total cost of the project will be heavily dependent on the builder's creativity and the availability of supplies. However I can tell you I managed to construct my marimba with less than 200 dollars.

For now let me just state the basic components of a marimba and the materials you will need.

The Bars – this is where everything begins. The bars can be made from nearly any material, but to qualify as a marimba it must be wood. Feel free to experiment with different types of wood before construction. But it is important for the wood to be completely dried out (not

green at all). My oak material came from a tree that was struck by lightning.

The Frame – for me, this was the next step after building the bars. The frame can be made from anything. This includes wood or even steel. Use whatever you are comfortable with.

The Resonators – Nothing difficult here. Though anodized aluminum is very pretty, PVC pipe works just as well.

Those are the basic parts of a marimba but you will also need some specialty equipment.

Musical Tuner – How much you invest in a tuner will be reflected in your marimba. If you just want something to practice with (like me) then a 30 dollar tuner will do just fine. Otherwise, if you want to tune overtones, use a strobe tuner (300+ dollars).

Belt Sander – You will be using this a lot so get something comfortable.

Drill – You will need to drill holes through the width of the bars for the marimba string. I suggest a drill press but a hand drill will work just fine.

Table Saw – for making all those cuts.

Band Saw – not essential but recommended if you will be cutting bass notes.

Miter Saw – really handy with the frame and resonators.

## Step 2: Cutting the bars

Preparation - What do you want? Do you want one octave, or five? Is your instrument going to be pentatonic or chromatic? Once you know what notes you want I suggest you look at this website: http://www.lafavre.us/marimba.htm. I would suggest using the dimensions of an evenly graduated marimba. This will make the frame easier to build.

By the way, a higher pitch marimba will require much less sanding and can be finished relatively quickly.

Once you have your goal and dimensions in mind, use a table saw to cut the wood. Try to keep the grain running the length of the bar and avoid big knots in the center of the bar. If it looks nice it will likely sound nice. At this stage you're only aiming for a brick-like shape. Don't worry if it is a little rough.

## Step 3: Tuning the bars

Before you begin take a moment to find the nodes of each bar. The nodes are the points that vibrate the least when the center of the bar is struck. The curve of the marimba bar should be between these two nodes. It might be helpful to make a few guidelines with a pencil or sharpie. Finally, if you want to stain or varnish do so now before you begin tuning.

Once you are ready use a belt sander to begin removing mass in small increments. Feel free to smooth out the surfaces and add any artistic effects you may desire. Periodically, check your progress with the chromatic tuner. You can do this by holding the bar approximately at one of the nodes and striking the center. As you remove mass, the bar's frequency will decrease. If you are tuning a bass note I suggest you cut a chunk out of the bottom first. This should be done with a band saw and will make sanding a lot faster.

It is important not to sand too much too fast. If you do, the bar will heat up. The change in temperature will affect the tone produced. So when tuning the notes try to keep the temperature consistently around room temperature.

If you make a mistake and sand too much (making the note flat) don't worry it can be fixed. I found the simplest way was to trim the ends of the bar, making the length shorter. 1/8 of an inch goes a long way.

As previously discussed, keep in mind temperature will have a great impact on each bar's frequency. Just try to keep an "optimum operating temperature" in mind. Mine sounds great at 80 degrees Fahrenheit. But it is twenty cents sharp at 50 degrees.

## Step 4: Tuning the overtones

To tune the overtones you will need one of two things:

1) Strobe Tuner
2) Audio Spectrum Analyzer

I suggest the Strobe Tuner especially if you are a musician. Personally I consider Peterson Strobe Tuners to be the best and they also make a Strobe Tuner app for the Iphone/Itouch. I only included the Spectrum Analyzer to give you an alternative.

Yes you can tune the fundamental frequencies and the overtones of all bars just by shaping the undercut of the bar.

Before we get into how to shape the curve, let's review the proper ratios between the overtones. For Marimba and Vibraphone builders it is 1:4:9.88. For Xylophone builders it is 1:3:6.

- To tune the Fundamental frequency (1), sand in the center.
- To tune the second overtone (4), sand just outside the center

- To tune the third (9.88), sand close to the ends of the arc.

Now here is where it gets tricky. Changing one overtone will change the frequencies of the other two! For this reason, you have to first get the ratios between frequencies correct, and then sand evenly across the curve until you arrive at the fundamental (hopefully with the ratios intact).

If you mess up and tune something too low, you cannot (to my knowledge) fix the problem without reducing the length of the bar.

Additionally, you will notice the overtones become increasingly more difficult to tune as you begin to work with higher and higher notes. This is because the sample size/duration/sustain of the higher notes become shorter and shorter. This also makes the overtones more difficult to hear. So do you want to tune the overtones of the upper register? I don't know. You'll just have to play it by ear. (I'm sorry... couldn't resist a bad pun.)

## Step 5: Building the frame

This is a time to get creative. There are only a few rules to a marimba frame. As long as you abide by those rules, you don't need to worry about how the frame might affect the quality of sound produced by the instrument. And those rules are . . .

1) The bars must be supported by "marimba string".
2) The string must be supported by braces in between the marimba keys. (Next step.)
3) The frame will also hold your resonators. (If you choose to build them.)

Bear those three rules and facts of a marimba frame in mind as you craft it and you should be fine. I suggest you lay out your tuned keys on a large flat surface to get the dimensions for your frame. You should also consider how high you want the playing surface to be off the ground.

## Step 6: Adding string supports

The marimba string supports are essential because they provide a level playing surface. You will need a lot of these, but fortunately they can be easy to make if you can find the materials.

I suggest aluminum rods. Use a band saw to cut the rods to an appropriate length. They should be long enough to accommodate your thickest bar. You will need to split one end of each support to so the string can lay in it. I suggest mounting each rod in a vice grip and using a hack saw to split the aluminum. Then use a screw driver and a good old fashioned hammer to open up the supports into a nice "Y" shape.

Finally to mount the supports into the frame you will need to drill holes into the frame at the appropriate intervals for the supports. Your drill bit should be a little smaller than your supports. Once done, return to the screwdriver and hammer to coerce the supports into their new home.

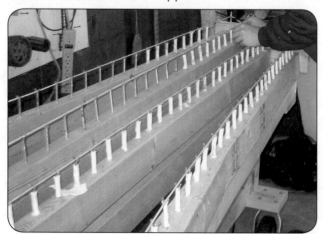

## Step 7: Stringing the bars

Don't give up yet! You're almost ready to play a tune! You've got a frame and keys, now you need marimba string. You could use some professionally made marimba string, or you could do what I did and use climbing rope. Yep! It works great! But whatever string you decide to use, make sure you drill holes in the bars large enough to accommodate your choice.

These holes should be drilled through the nodes of each bar. (Again, you can find the nodes by figuring out where the bar vibrates least when you strike it in the center.) Also, you should drill the holes on each bar an equal distance from the playing surface. If you don't you won't get a level surface.

Once you're done, that's it! Play a tune! Be happy with yourself! But it you want to go the extra mile, carry forth to the next step.

## Step 8: Resonators

This is actually the easiest and maybe quickest part of the build. Resonators will make your instrument a lot louder and give the bars a much more "full" and "warm" sound. All that is required is a little understanding of physics.

The material for the resonators can be almost anything. Just look for something that will hold water without leaking. That is essentially what you're doing. For me, PVC pipe works great. You will need the tubing and plastic test caps.

Now for some physics! Don't worry this is really simple.

$$L = 340/(4f)$$

Length (in meters) is equal to the speed of sound divided by the quantity of four times the frequency of the note.

Frequency is measured in Hertz. You should use your mad Google-ing skills and look up the frequencies of your notes if you don't already know them.

I suggest you cut your resonators a little longer than you need. Trim off a little at a time, and hold it under the correct bar as you play it. When it sounds good and full, you're done with that resonator. Relax. This doesn't take that long and you won't make an extremely costly mistake.

Exactly how you mount your resonators under your bars us up to you. You just need to get them there.

## Step 9: You're finally done!!!

If you have actually done this, congratulations! If you were a thrifty and smart engineer/musician, then you have successfully created a pretty decent practice instrument for significantly less than you could have bought one.

Ah but wait! Perhaps you have no mallets to work with. If this is the case continue forth!

## Step 10: Mallet wrapping parts and materials

In terms of parts, you will need a mallet stick and core.

The stick should be made of wood. The material for the core is up to you.

**Materials**
- 3/8 inch dowel rod (3/8 is just my personal preference. Use whatever is most comfortable.)
- Round Core (In the pictures following, I use a "bouncy ball" I bought in the grocery store for 25 cents.)
- Yarn
- Needle (a relatively big one)
- Scissors

**Some notes on the core**

You have a lot of options here. The material for the core will have the largest impact on the tone produced. A hard core like a wooden crafts ball will work well for the upper ranges of a marimba, but will sound horrible on the lower ranges. For a relatively soft core, I've found "bouncy balls" or rubber balls are the best bet.

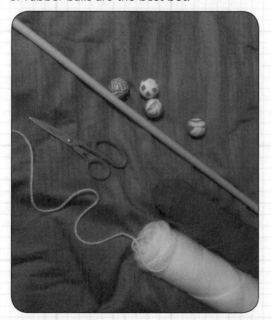

## Step 11: Assembling the stick and core

You should drill a hole in the core to allow for the stick. Be careful not to drill all the way through the core. To make things a little easier, I suggest you seat the core in some vice grips.

Once you have a hole, use some wood glue or epoxy to connect the core to the stick.

## Step 12: Cut the stick and sand the edges

Once the mallet is cut to length, take it to a sander and remove those uncomfortable 90 degree angles.

## Step 13: Wrapping the mallet

The mallet is sanded to be comfortable; the glue/epoxy has dried; now you're ready to start wrapping.

Start by tying a knot just below the core. Then, begin wrapping over the top, and then under.

Over, Under, Over, Under . . .

Be sure to count the number of wraps around the mallet. If you want a set of mallets to sound the same, the number of wraps must be equal. Each time the yarn crosses the top of the mallet, that's one wrap. The mallets I'm wrapping here will have 100 wraps each.

## Step 14: Crowning and finishing the mallet

OK. To end the seemingly never ending process of wrapping, you need to cut about an arm's length of yarn between the mallet head and the yarn you are wrapping with. (Let me specify this is still a single strand of yarn beginning with the knot you tied and ending at the point you just cut.)

Tie the free end of the yarn to your needle.

Now to crown the top and bottom of the mallet. I prefer starting with the top. You need to push the needle in (at an angle) at the top of the mallet, and pull it out. Do this over and over, going in a circle around the mallet head. This process makes sure your hard work won't come unraveled soon.

Once you finish with the top, the same needs to be done at the bottom.

After you're finished, I suggest crowning once more at the top, but this time you will tie a knot there.

## The Homewrecker

By Dan Poinsett (DiscoJones)
(http://www.instructables.com/id/
The-Homewrecker/)

Hoffman's Iron Law states that a woofer's efficiency is proportional to the volume of the enclosure it is mounted in and the cube of its low frequency cutoff. In other words, if you want a loudspeaker with very low frequency extension AND high efficiency, you need an enormous enclosure. Or you could build The Homewrecker.

This Instructable will show you how to build a loudspeaker that can mount in most standard interior doorways, using the room as the enclosure. The system is easily removable, though quite heavy. The system shown here is not a high-fidelity system, but it is very efficient (i.e. LOUD) and can reproduce very low frequencies. Based on the parameters of the woofer, this system should easily reach below 30Hz (-3dB) without including the natural boost obtained from room reflections. With this boost included, the system should reach 20Hz — the lower limit of human hearing. All of this bass extension comes at a very respectable 96dB with a 2.83V input (4 ohms).

It consists of (8) 12" woofers, (8) 5" midranges, (4) 2" x 5" tweeters, a simple crossover, and (4) easy to use mounting brackets. The size and number of speakers can be just about anything you want, but this combination utilizes the available space in a doorway quite well.

### Step 1: Get stuff
- 12" woofers qty 8
- 5" midranges qty 8
- 2"x 5" tweeter qty 4
- input terminal qty 2
- 10W resistors qty 2
- 3.3uF non-polarized capacitors qty 2
- 16uF non-polarized capacitors qty 2
- 0.7mH inductors qty 2
- 0.4mH inductors qty 2
- 18 or 16 awg wire qty 50 ft
- 4' x 8' plywood qty 1
- 2 x 4 studs 96" qty 5

- L-brackets qty 4
- 1.25" weather strip qty 17 ft
- 3/8" carriage bolts qty 4
- 3/8" nuts qty 4
- 3/8" wing nuts qty 4
- 3/8" fender washers qty 4
- 3/8" T-nuts qty 4

The midrange and tweeter units can be replaced with any midrange and tweeter of your choosing as long as they are wired properly and the sensitivities are matched to each other and the woofers. This can be done in the crossover and will be partially explained later.

The woofer was chosen based on price and a parameter called Qts. This parameter should be available from the speaker retailer and should be between 0.65 and 0.95 for best results. The woofers I'm using have a published Qts of 1.17, which is a little high, but as I said, this particular system is not designed for high-fidelity.

All of these drivers were purchased from the PartsExpress factory buyout section of their website (www.partsexpress.com) for less than $120 total. Better divers would make for a better system, but things get really expensive when you have to buy 8 of each component.

### Step 2: Lay out driver placement on plywood

Standard interior door sizes are 30", 32", and 36" wide and 80" tall. My house is old and most doorways are 29" wide by 80" tall. With these dimensions in mind, I chose to make the overall size of the baffle 35" x 82", which should accommodate 30" and 32" doorways as well as my narrow 29" doorways. The baffle can be made as wide and/or tall as necessary for special situations.

After cutting your piece of plywood down to size (35" x 82" in this case), plan and lay out your speaker arrangement on the plywood. Use the overall driver diameters to achieve proper spacing, but make sure to leave 1.5" between woofer mounting holes to allow for 2 x 4 bracing on the backside. In my case, my woofers are exactly 12" in diameter, but require an 11" hole. For my layout, I started in the exact center of the board with the tweeters, then moved outward with the midranges, and finally placed the woofers on top and bottom. If you plan well, you can get distances between divers to be quite symmetrical.

### Step 3: Cut holes

After marking the centers of the woofer and midrange holes, I used a router with a circle cutting attachment to cut the holes. An adequate job can be done, however, by drawing the appropriate sized circles and using a jigsaw to do the cutting. This is in fact how I cut the holes for the tweeters, which are rectangular in shape.

This is a good time to cut the slots for the mounting brackets as well. I made these slots 0.5" x 1.5" long to allow ample room for the bracket bolt to move while mounting. The slots are located in each of the 4 corners with exact height chosen so the mounting brackets will not run into the door hinges when mounting. In this case each slot is 5.75" away from its closest side and 5.125" away from its closest top or bottom.

Again, I used a router for these slots, but a 1/2" drill and a jigsaw could do the same job.

## Step 4: Brace the back

This design relies on four brackets to hold the entire baffle against the door trim, so it must be relatively stiff. To do this, 2 x 4 studs run 66.5" lengthwise down the middle and just outside of each column of woofers. 28" lengths run sideways at the ends of these with another 28" length 1.75" away from the first. This 1.75" channel will easily accommodate the mounting bracket 2 x 6 and keep them from spinning when tightening. In between the long spanners are short sections bracing directly around the large woofers. Everything is screwed in place with 3" multi-purpose screws.

## Step 5: Apply weatherstrip

Apply self-adhesive weatherstrip along each side edge and the top edge, which will create an airtight seal between the baffle and the door trim. I have left the bottom edge with no weatherstrip. In my house, the bottom edge will "seal" against the carpet. If you are planning on mounting this in a doorway over hardwood floor, you may need to add weatherstrip to the very bottom or even rest the baffle on a rolled up towel on the floor.

The weatherstrip I used was the widest and thickest available at the hardware store — 1.25" wide by 7/16" thick.

## Step 6: Make mounting brackets

These brackets are designed to pull the speaker baffle tight against the doorway trim. The blue end of the bracket shown below slides in between the trim and the end of the door (on the hinge side) when it is all the way open. On the non-hinge side, the brackets work the same, but you don't need to worry about sliding them into position. The carriage bolt is inserted from the front of the baffle through the slot and screws into the 2 x 6 section to pull the brackets (and therefore the baffle) into the doorway trim. It consists of 2 sections screwed together. All threaded hardware in this section is 3/8".

The "back" section is a 6" long piece of 2 x 6 with a 3.5" L-bracket screwed to it. I used blue painter's tape wrapped several times around the end of the bracket to protect the doorway trim when the bracket pulls against it. I drilled a 1" diameter hole 4" deep into the end of the 2 x 6 and drilled a 1/2" hole through the remaining 2". Then I installed a 3/8" T-nut into the 4" deep hole. This allows the carriage bolt to reach the T-nut only 2" into the assembly.

The "front" section is a 7" long 3/8" carriage bolt with a wing nut screwed all the way tight against the head and a jam nut locking it in place. This can be replaced by any type of thumb screw type fastener, but I had trouble finding a one-piece option that was this length and diameter. Then I used a 1.5" diameter fender washer and a 3" diameter by 3/4" thick particle board "washer" to completely cover the slot when in position.

## Step 7: Dry run

At this point it may be a good idea to test fit the baffle in a doorway. It will be easier to make any necessary tweaks before the drivers are mounted. Make sure the brackets work properly with the advantage of being able to see through the woofer holes.

## Step 8: Mount drivers

Mount the drivers using the appropriate screws. I used 1.25" drywall screws for the midranges and black 1" pan heads for the woofers and tweeters (available from Parts Express). The input terminals are simple surface mount binding post types, but any kind will do.

## Step 9: Wiring and crossover

The crossover, which routes the proper frequencies to the proper drivers, for this project will be very simple. Crossover design is a very complex and intricate matter when done properly, but this specific design is about deep bass extension and efficiency, not hi-fi. That said, it doesn't have to be a complete mess.

The woofers are 4 ohms each with an 87dB efficiency rating. The four woofers in the series-parallel configuration raises the efficiency to 93dB. At 4 ohms total, that means a 96dB sensitivity rating (@2.83V input).

The midranges are 8 ohms each with a 90dB efficiency rating. The four midranges in the series-parallel configuration raises the system efficiency to 96dB. At 8 ohms total, that means a 96dB sensitivity rating (@2.83V input) — equal to the woofers.

The tweeters are piezoelectric units that do not behave as normal resistive loads and as such the 10 ohm resistor on them was chosen by ear.

### Update 2/22/2010:

After listening to this setup for a while, I have made some pretty serious modifications to the crossover. These modifications will only apply properly if using the exact drivers that I have used, but it may be worth a try even with slightly different drivers.

Woofer Circuit: change 0.7mH inductor to 1.5mH inductor

Midrange Circuit: remove 0.4mH inductor, change 16uF capacitor to 12uF, insert 3.0mH inductor in parallel with midrange assembly

Tweeter Circuit: remove 10 ohm resistor, change 3.3uF capacitor to 2.2uF

## Step 10: Notes

This system is very heavy and will probably require two people to move it. I will probably mount handles on the front to make it easier to handle and create some kind of removable cover to protect the drivers while in transit or storage.

The room does not actually act as an enclosure for the woofers as much as it just keeps the front wave separated from the back wave, which is known as an infinite baffle arrangement. If there is some way for the rear wave to reach the front wave (e.g. mounting in the doorway of a room with multiple entrances), this system will not be very effective. The two waves will be 180 degrees out of phase and at least partially cancel each other.

This is effectively a 4 ohm system. Make sure the amplifier used is compatible with this impedance.

# How to Build Custom Speakers

By Noah Weinstein (noahw)
(http://www.instructables.com/id/How-to-Build-Custom-Speakers/)

Building your own custom speakers has got to be one of the most rewarding, straightforward, and cost-effective DIY activities I've come across. I'm absolutely shocked that it hasn't had a larger presence on instructables and in the community. . . well, until now of course.

Some speaker projects can be complete in a weekend, while others can go on for years. Budget speaker kits start around $100, while top-of-the-line kits and components can add up to several thousands of dollars. Regardless of how much you choose to spend on your speakers, you'll likely be building something that will sound as good as commercial product that off the shelf would cost as much as 10 times more.

So, if you've got access to a table saw, a jig saw, a drill, some wood glue, clamps, and a place to make some sawdust, then you've got the opportunity to build your own custom speakers.

## Step 1: Why?

Back in 1997, I attended the Home Entertainment Show with my father. We had the intent to build the best speakers that we possibly could. We listened to just about every manufacturer's flagship model. I recognized all of the drivers from the DIY catalogs, wondering which one would reign supreme.

At the end of the day, after the votes were in, we both selected the JM Labs Grande Utopia's as our favorite model, hands down. Since then, it's been widely agreed that the Grande Utopia are among the best sounding home audio speakers in the world. The only catch is that back in those days, the speaker sold for $40,000, and now the updated model, equipped with a Beryllium tweeter, costs even more.

JM Labs uses affiliate company Focal brand drivers. Now here's where it gets interesting. The same line of drivers used in the JM Labs loudspeakers can also be purchased from Zalytron. My father and I purchased an extremely similar set of drivers, from the same product lines that JM Labs uses, including "W" cone woofers and audiom inverted metal dome tweeters, and built our own "DIY Grande Utopias" for only $3,000. I would never claim that they are an exact copy of the Grande Utopias, but they do sound absolutely amazing, and at less than 1/10th the cost, it's hard to argue. That, my fellow instructables users, is why I think everyone should build their own speakers.

## Step 2: Speaker theory

I built my first set of speakers as a high school student over 10 years ago. I've been making them for friends, clients, and now for instructables as a prize for our Art of Sound Contest ever since. Over the years I've generated a few simple theories about speaker building that I think are relevant.

**Yes, they do sound better, and no you don't have to be an audiophile to hear the difference**

Sound quality has been steadily declining as heavily compressed digital audio, iPod docks, and bottom dollar stereos have proliferated around the world over the last 10-15 years. Listening to music on a great set of speakers is the single biggest change you can make to your stereo to get better sound quality. If you want to blow $200 a foot on oxygen free speaker wire made from precious metals, great, go for it, just make sure you've already invested a lot of time and energy in making the best possible speakers your finances and skill level allow.

**Spend more money than you thought you were going to**

If you're about to build your own custom speakers, you'll likely be spending at least 40 hours on the project if you've got experience with woodworking, electronics, finishing techniques, or have built your own speakers before, and even longer if it's your first pair. Depending on how you value your time, you'll have thousands of dollars of free labor (your own) invested in the speakers. If you happen to find yourself deciding between a $5 paper cone, no name woofer, and a $25 poly cone made by some brand name, please, get the more expensive one. Like tools, speaker components are an investment that you'll have for the rest of your life, so reach a little and get the best stuff for your project that you can afford.

**Start with a kit**

Get started by ordering a kit from a supplier. It takes a significant amount of knowledge and work to design your own crossovers and calculate your own box dimensions. It's much easier to tackle your first speaker project by standing on the shoulders of experienced audio engineers. So, get a kit from one of the retailers listed in the next step and get started on your project today.

## Step 3: Resources

Before embarking on a DIY speaker building journey, take some time to familiarize yourself with the process (this Instructable should cover that), and also poke around sites that showcase DIY speaker builders work, designs, and the companies that distribute the best components in the U.S. There's a wide range of designs, driver options, and technologies to learn about and choose from.

Great print resources include:
The Loudspeaker Design Cookbook
Introduction to Loudspeaker Design
Designing, Building and Testing your own Speaker System

## Step 4: Select your kit or components

Using the resources listed in the previous step you can begin the process of selecting your drivers or kit for your speaker building project. Speaker builders constantly debate over the best drivers, and can rarely agree on just one winner. That being said, there are some brand favorites in the field that have proven themselves over time, again and again, as DIY speaker builders have used them in their designs around the world and been happy with their performance. The LDSG is an excellent resource to figure out how the drivers you're considering stack up to the competition.

Some factors to consider when selecting drivers are:

- Price
- Reviews
- History
- The kit designer
- Design specs and requirements
- Sensitivity db

The best resources for investigating the factors listed above can be found right on the retailer's website, in the manufacturer's technical documentation, and on the LDSG.

Take your time in learning about what technologies and speaker components you'd like to use. When making your selection about tweeters alone you can choose from horn tweeters, soft dome tweeters, inverted metal dome tweeters, coaxial drivers, ribbon tweeters, bullet tweeters, flared tweeters, and piezo tweeters.

Check out Madisound's drivers page to get an idea of what the different technologies look like.

Some of the most well-known producers of speaker drivers are:

- Focal
- Seas
- Morel
- Usher
- Accuton
- Vifa
- NHT

I primarily build with Focal brand drivers. I do so for no good reason other then for the story I told in Step 2. I've always been very happy and impressed particularly with Focal's Audiom TD5 tweeter, the TC 120 TD5 tweeter, and "W" cone line of woofers.

**2.5 way MTM Towers:**
(2) JM Labs 6VE3251B woofers
(1) Focal TC 90 TD5B tweeter

**2 way TM Bookshelf Speakers:**
(1) JM Labs 6VE3251B woofer
(1) Focal TC 90 TD5B tweeter

**12" Sealed Subwoofer:**
Zalytron 1201PL
Dayton SA100 100W Subwoofer Amplifier

## Step 5: Choose a cabinet design

Once you've selected your drivers it's time to begin planning out the cabinet. Work with your component provider to choose a box design that best matches your specific components. If you're building a kit, a box design should have come along with your drivers and crossover plans.

Box design can make a $5 driver sound like a speaker that costs $500 retail, but if it's not designed and built correctly, it can also make a $500 driver sound like it was ripped out of an old transistor radio.

Cabinet design decisions start at the basics, like the volume of the cabinet, whether it will be sealed or ported, how much bracing the cabinet needs, what thickness material it should be made out of and what height the tweeter should be mounted at so that it's in line with the listener's ears.

From there, it progresses to more complex and acoustic decisions like rounding over the corners to reduce interference, building elaborate horn structures to amplify the sound, using exotic materials to further dampen resonant frequencies, line arrays to gain efficiency, mounting drivers at different distances from the listener to accommodate for the fact that high frequencies travel slightly faster than low frequencies, and eliminating parallel faces — the surfaces that create resonant frequencies by building poly-faceted cabinets, or better, spheres, rather than the standard rectangular cabinet.

That being said, the vast majority of DIY speaker builders start with a straightforward, rectangular cabinet design that, though lacks the bells and whistles and highly engineered elements listed above, still sounds fantastic.

## Step 6: Cut the speaker panels

I build all of my speakers from a type of fiber board called MEDEX. It's a LEED certified formaldehyde free material that's similar to MDF, but far heavier, denser, and moisture resistant. Many contractors use it as a building material in humid climates, and it's widely used to make counter tops.

It's not stocked in every lumberyard, but it can be special ordered. If your local lumber yard can't find a source for it, or if you don't want to pay the higher price for it, MDF is the next building material of choice. Avoid plywood, hardwoods, OSB, strand board, and light density fiber boards if possible.

The speaker cabinets should be as sonically dead as possible. That means heavy, thick-walled, and well constructed. Ideally the entire cabinet should be built out of 1.5" material. In reality, I've only done a handful of speakers that were that thick due to the cost and weight. The industry standard is a 1.5" front baffle, and then 3/4" for the rest of the cabinets. Zalytron builds their cabinets to these same specifications. Many other companies do not. Look closely to see what's included in your specific kit if you're ordering one that has the cabinet included.

Plan out your speakers on paper and create a cutting diagram based upon the raw 4' x 8' sheets. Head to the lumberyard and pick up as many sheets of MDF or MEDEX as you need for your projects.

Transfer your cutting diagram onto the sheets themselves and then begin to break them down, making the biggest cuts first. Work the large sheets down into small manageable panels and cut things to their exact size. When cutting like-sized speaker panels make all of your same-sized-passes on the table saw at the same time, without moving the fence, to ensure that parallel panels will be exactly the same size.

Once all of your panels are cut, check and then recheck your measurements. If the speaker cabinets are going to be square, they've got to start with perfectly cut panels, otherwise they just won't ever line up correctly.

## Step 7: Mark and cut support panels

As shown in the cabinet design in step 5, the basic speaker cabinet contains supports on the inside to further strengthen and sonically dampen the exterior walls. These supports are usually cut from scrap 3/4 material and are cut with a swiss cheese like pattern to allow air to pass through them so that they don't divide the cabinet and impede air flow inside.

Internal support panels should be located in parts of the speaker that are closest to the woofers, and anywhere that the cabinet may need reinforcement, like the midpoint of the sides.

The tower speakers have two internal supports, while the bookshelf speakers have only one.

Trace a simple pattern of circles or squares onto the support panels and use a drill with a large drill bit to create a starter hole for your jig saw. Then, use the jig saw to connect the drill holes and trace the path of your cutout.

## Step 8: Mark and cut biscuit joints

Like most professional kitchen cabinet makers, I use biscuit joints to hold my speaker cabinets together. They easily and perfectly align adjacent faces, are quick to cut and install, and are super strong.

First, mark adjacent surfaces with a pattern or code of your choosing. I simply assemble the speaker panels into the correct formation and mark adjacent sides with an "a", "b", "c", or "circle", "square", "triangle" code and so on. I then give them a little tick mark crossing onto both sides where I'll alight the biscuit joiner to make the plunge, and draw a long line on the face that will get a groove cut into it, so that I don't get lost and cut into the wrong face.

With the faces all marked up, I clamp the boards down to the table and begin cutting slots with the biscuit joiner.

I generally install two biscuits per joint on the speaker cabinets. This part is a bit tedious, because there are many joints and adjoining faces, but it's worth it when you go to glue because things will line up really well. I find messing around with screws while trying to glue and clamp the cabinets together is just a bit clumsy and certainly more difficult to square up.

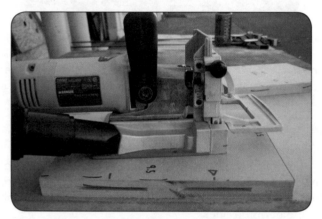

## Step 9: Glue the cabinet sides together

The first part of the cabinet to be assembled are the sides, top, and bottom. The front and back go on later.

Before gluing up the cabinets I lay everything that I'm going to need out on a large flat level surface. Once the glue bead gets laid down, the clocks ticking, so you'll want to move with some speed and efficiency. Having an extra set of hands for this step really helps, but it's not a necessity.

Lay a thin bead of high quality wood glue (I like Titebond myself) along the edges of all adjacent sides. Be sure to spread extra glue inside the holes for the biscuits. I use a chip brush to paint the glue into position and spread the bead evenly into a 3/4" strip.

Insert the biscuits into the slots, being sure to push them all the way down. Any biscuits that don't easily fit into the slot should be discarded and swapped for a new biscuit—sometimes the biscuits swell slightly due to moisture and humidity.

With the biscuits in place and glue on all of the adjoining surfaces, it's time to assemble. Join edges to faces and construct the cabinet.

I use many clamps to pull the cabinet tightly together and apply uniform even pressure to the joints.

With the edges glued and the clamps loosely in place, now's the time to square everything up. Using a tape measure and the clamps, measure the diagonal from corner to corner of the square you've just created and adjust the clamps until they are equal. This means that the box is perfectly square.

Before the glue sets up, it's also a good time to make all of the panels flush with each other. Use a dead blow hammer and a block of wood to knock all edges flush.

Apply a sufficient amount of clamps and wait for the exterior walls of the cabinet to dry. As you can see from the pictures below, pipe clamps are great for this purpose, and if you've been needing an excuse (or two) to buy some, 42" tall tower speakers are good ones.

## Step 10: Cut out holes and recesses for the drivers

With the sides, top and bottom of the cabinets drying, it's a good time to start work on the front and back panels. First time builders may choose to simplify this step and simply cut a large circle opening for the speaker driver to mount in. In that case, the speaker drivers' frame will rest on the surface of the speaker, protruding an 1/8" or so. For a truly professional look, however, you'll want to recess the drivers so that they mount flush with the front face.

In either case, the first step is to cut out a circle that accommodates your driver. I use a plunge router fitted with a Jasper Circle Jig. This Jasper Jig allows me to cut a circle of just about any size up between 2" and 18". If you don't happen to have this handy router and circle jig set up, the old drawing a circle using a piece of string tied around a nail works pretty darn well too. Then, simply cut carefully along your line with a jig saw and you're in business.

If you are using a router, use a 1/8" or 1/4" straight bit to cut out the circle so you end up removing as little material as possible. The wider the bit, the more material you have to eat through, the more dust you create, and the slower the process goes. Make multiple passes, incrementally plunging deeper and deeper through the front face.

Once the circles are cut, it's time to tackle the optional recess.

To do this you need to create a pattern template. Carefully trace, draw, plot, copy, CNC cut, or laser cut the outer pattern of your driver onto a thin piece of material creating a template. Technical drawings for speaker components can usually be found on the manufacturer's or reseller's website. Recreate a pattern in a drafting program of your choice from the drawings and produce the actual pattern piece. Remember, this step is totally optional!

Once the patterns have been created, center and mount it into place on the front face. I used some simple wood screws.

Then, using a good router and a sharp straight bit fit with a pattern bushing collar on it, simply trace the pattern at the proper depth to create the recess.

## Step 11: Cut holes for the terminal cups, ports, and any other additions to the cabinet

There are some more holes that need to be cut in the front and/or back cabinet faces. Using the same drill and jig saw method described in step 7, cut out properly sized holes for the terminal cups or binding posts depending on what kind of connection point you've decided to use.

For the port, each situation will be unique. Different port designs require different holes. Slotted ports are built right into the cabinet, while PVC tubes (the kind I'm using below) require a properly-sized circle. Some ports go on the front face, others on the back, and other speaker designs require no port at all. Consult your cabinet plans to see what kind your kit requires.

The circle jig makes quick work of the port hole on the back panel in the photos below.

In the final few pictures in the sequence below you can see the back panel of the subwoofer. I'm using the jig saw to cut out the hole for the plate amplifier that will get mounted back there. Writing myself plenty of notes about the location and sizes of the holes and cuts is really useful for me so I can keep track of everything I'm doing, especially when building 5 cabinets simultaneously like I am here.

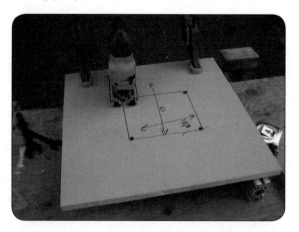

## Step 12: Glue in the support braces

If the initial glue-up of the cabinets is dry, it's time to glue in the support braces. As before, apply a thin bead of glue to both surfaces and slide them into position.

### Note

The support braces can be glued in position when the top, bottom, and sides are glued. It adds a bit more work to an already busy process, but it allow you cut slots and insert biscuits on the supports to join them to the sides, something that can't be done if they're glued in on their own like I'm doing here. Since their position isn't absolutely crucial like the other parts of the cabinet are, it's not a problem do wait for the initial glue-up to dry, and do them on their own.

## Step 13: Glue on the back panel

With the supports in place you can glue on the back panel. By this point we've all gotten really good at gluing and sensing just how much glue to apply before excess starts to drip out. Paint the glue on both surfaces, apply the back, and clamp thoroughly.

## Step 14: Install dampening material

Once the glue has dried it's time to install dampening material. Some people use polyester fill, others use acoustic foam, and others use pre-made adhesive backed foam products. Different designs call for different types of dampening, in different quantities.

Follow your kit guidelines or contact the system designer to find out how much dampening you should use.

Black Hole 5 is the top-of-the-line name out there. It's a multi-layered dampening material, however from what I've found acoustical foam works equally as well and is a whole lot cheaper.

If your dampening material does not have an adhesive backing, use hot glue, or a construction adhesive to apply it to the walls of the speaker cabinet. The rule of thumb for dampening is that you'll want to dampen most of the inner surfaces of the cabinet, leaving room for your crossovers, drivers, ports, and terminal cups.

For subwoofers I use standard polyester that's found in fabric stores.

## Step 15: Wire up the crossovers

With the cabinets ready to go (minus the fronts), the next step is to wire up the crossovers. As described in the beginning of this Instructable, the crossover makes sure that high frequencies, like cymbal crashes, get sent to the tweeter, while lower frequencies, like bass guitars, get sent to the woofers and subwoofers. While some drivers don't require crossovers at all because they are equipped to reproduce all of the different frequencies, the vast majority of speaker designs and drivers require one for the tweeter, and another for the woofer.

Crossover plans look exactly like wiring diagrams and should come along with your speaker kit. They consist of resistors, capacitors, and inductors. Audiophile quality components are a treat to work with since they're about 10x the size of standard electronics components.

Solder all connections together and hot glue components into place on a panel. Inductor coils should already have bare copper on its ends, but, if there's any doubt, do a little sanding to remove the paint-on layer of insulation.

Each crossover will need high quality speaker wire running to and coming from it. You'll need positive and negate leads going to the start of the circuit from the terminal cup, and positive and negative leads that run from the crossover to the speaker driver. For woofers that share the same crossover, which commonly occurs anytime you've got more than one woofer in a 2-way (woofer & tweeter) system, you'll need to solder on two sets of leads coming from the crossover. If you're building a 2.5 way system, like I am in the tower set in this Instructable, where one woofer plays lower than the other, you'll need to make three different crossovers to the three different drivers.

I label the tails of all of my leads so I know where they are coming from and going to when it comes time to assemble. Nothing worse than gluing everything up only to find that you put the leads from the tweeter crossover into the woofers and vice versa.

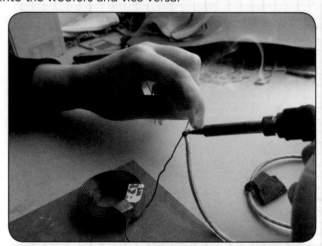

## Step 16: Install the crossovers inside the cabinet

Use hot glue, screws, or construction adhesive to install the crossovers inside the speaker cabinet. Put the heaviest crossover on the bottom and try to orient inductor coils at 90 degrees to each other to limit electromagnetic interference.

Pull leads into position through the terminal cup and into the area where the drivers will be mounted. I tie the speaker wire leads around the holes in the mounting bracket to reduce/eliminate wire tension that would be transmitted to the drivers and the crossovers in the event of a tug or snag.

### Step 17: Glue the front panels onto the cabinets

With the crossovers and dampening material in position it's time to glue the front panels into position. Apply a thin bead of glue, use a brush to spread it out along the edge, and clamp the front face into place. Before sealing up the cabinet, do one more visual check that you've got all your wire leads in a place that's easy to reach, that you've followed all of the previous steps, and that everything is set to go, because once that front face gets glued on, there's no getting it off.

### Step 18: Sand the edges smooth

After all the glue has dried, there will likely be a small amount of hardened glue that was squeezed out by the clamps. Use a power sander to take this off and sand all edges flush. Try not to sand off too much, since the more that you do, the less true and square your cabinet becomes. Also, be careful to sand only one surface at a time and never round over the corners. You'll want those crisp lines when you apply our finishing material.

### Step 19: Explore finishing options and finish the cabinet

Before any of the actual components get installed, you've got to do all of the finishing work.

Most speaker cabinets are finished with a wood veneer that's got some kind of lacquer, varnish, or polyurethane product applied to it, but don't let that limit your imagination. These are your speakers and you can make them look however you like! It won't affect the sound quality really at all, as that's all in the cabinet construction, so go nuts and make them look beautiful!

Since the speakers I made were built as the prize for the Art of Sound contest, we went with something unique, bold and festive. . . in other words, bright orange and white upholstered vinyl with black edge piping for the towers, spray on pickup truck bed liner, 3" chrome plates spikes, and waterjet cut steel flames for the subwoofer, and fur covered, eye patch toting, horned and toothed monster treatment for the bookshelf speakers.

### Step 20: Install cabinet spikes

Cabinet feet and spikes come in all different shapes and sizes but generally get installed in the same way.

Pre-drill the proper size hole for the gnarled nut and hammer it into position using a block of wood for protection. Then, simply screw in the spike and lock it into position with the lock nut. The spike sleeves are threaded, so they get screwed into position using an allen wrench, rather than hammered into place.

### Step 21: Install terminal cups, ports, and port flanges

It's getting close to the end — time to get excited!

Drill pilot holes for the terminal cups and screw them into position.

The port tube can be hammered into place and covered with a port flange or cap. These aren't necessary, but make everything back there look really nice.

## Step 22: Install drivers (tower speakers)

Mark and drill pilot holes for all of the mounting holes on the speaker drivers. Then, grab the leads coming from the crossovers and solder them onto the metal tabs coming from the driver. Use your labels to match the positive lead to the bigger tab, usually stamped with a red dot and "+" sign, and the negative lead to the other tab, usually a bit smaller, not marked with a red dot, and stamped with a "-" sign.

Once the drivers are soldered into place, stuff excess speaker wire back into the cabinet and screw the drivers into position using some nice, pan-head, black finish, coarse thread screws.

## Step 23: Install driver and plate amp (subwoofer)

The process of finishing up the subwoofer is relatively similar to finishing up the other speakers. Instead of acoustical foam or Black Hole 5, I use polyester fill. Subwoofers are generally filled with a larger amount of acoustical dampening material, and as a result, I generally opt for the cheaper, more compressible option of poly fill.

The subwoofer has no independent crossover, only an active variable crossover built into Dayton 100W plate amp from Parts Express, so there's nothing to do there.

Connect the speaker wire to the binding posts on the back side of the plate amp and install the amp into position in the hole that was previously cut out of the back.

Route the wires through the speaker cabinet, tying them around a support bracket to reduce wire tension in the event of a snag, and then twist them around the leads coming from the sub woofer driver.

Solder all connections.

Finally, install the subwoofer driver into position on the front of the speaker by drilling pilot holes and then screwing it into position using pan head black finish screws.

## Step 24: Test

With all the driver mounted and all components in position, it's time for the big moment, the first real test run of the speakers.

There's virtually endless debate on what to play to "break speakers in" or test them with, but I've found that it's just best to play what you like, and what you've listened to most. You ears will remember what it has sounded like in the past, and hopefully, if all has gone to plan, will notice the huge improvement that you're now hearing.

Speakers need a break-in period of time, or at least the industry big wigs claim that they do. I've found that the sound does tend to break in a bit, but for the most part, how they sound for the first time is a pretty good indicator of how they'll sound in 5 years.

Once the test is complete you should be grinning ear to ear, proud of your achievement and excited to re-listen to all of your music, knowing that it's not only sounding better than it ever has before, but that you made the whole thing possible, from start to finish.

# Suitcase Picnic Table and Speaker System

By Carley Jacobson (Carleyy)
(http://www.instructables.com/id/Suitcase-Picnic-Table-and-Speaker-System/)

Take this suitcase on a fun picnic in the park! Not only can you carry all your food and silverware it in—it also doubles as a picnic table and speaker system.

The speaker system is powered by the minty boost USB charger. Plug in your ipod and listen to some sweet tunes.

There are four legs that retract from the suitcase so you can prop the suitcase up and use the surface as a table.

I've recently gotten into re-purposing suitcases. I've found lots of great inspiration online for fun projects. This project was more of a hybrid of things I've seen plus a few new ideas of my own.

## Step 1: Materials

Here are the main materials you will need. In each individual step I will let you know the smaller materials like glue, scissors, screws, etc. . .

- Suitcase – find a suitcase hard shell. I love this old vintage Samsonite suitcase! However, the edges of the suitcase are curved and this cause a few problems in mounting the legs and hardware. I would suggest finding a suitcase or briefcase that has 90 degree edges (box).
- 4 Leg Braces – I bought these locking leg braces from McMaster Carr (#2). Let me tell you, I spent a good amount of time figuring out the best way to mount the legs and this was definitely the best option. I'd love to hear other ideas on what could work. I liked these also

because the legs sit nicely inside the suitcase and are easy to prop up and lock.
- 4 Legs – I cut 4 pieces of 1" x 1" wood at length 12"
- Speakers – I know a little bit about electronics but not too much. Instead of creating a speaker system from scratch I just bought an inexpensive USB powered computer speaker system. It came with all the parts I needed, all I had to do was take it out of its case.
- Minty Boost – powers your speakers and is simple to put together.

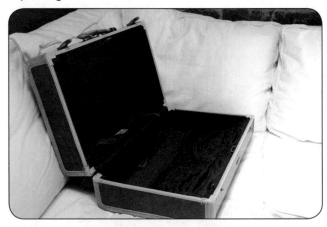

## Step 2: Attaching legs
### Materials and tools
- Wooden Legs
- Hinges
- Power Drill
- 12 small screws to mount the hinge to the suitcase. Be careful with the size screw you choose. The head of the screw needs to be larger than the holes in the hinge (so everything is secured properly) but short enough so they don't go all the way through the suitcase.
- 8 small screws to mount the hinge to the leg. These still need to have a large head but they should be longer than the other screws, I'd say at least a 1/2 inch.
- Spray Paint

Here is where the problems came in with the rounded suitcase edges. It is hard to mount anything more than two inches to the side of the suitcase and have it lie flush because the edges curve. I just made do with what I had, luckily the hinges weren't too large. You will be attaching the hinges to the suitcase with screws. The main frame of the suitcase is made of wood so they should attach securely.

### STEPS
Prepare Legs
If you haven't already done so, cut 4 12" legs out of the 1" x 1" wood
Paint the legs with the spray paint (see spray paint instructions)
Line up a hinge against the suitcase edge and mark with chalk where the hinge will be screwed to the case

(you will see three holes in the hinge, which is where you will mark). Do this at all four corners for each leg.

Make sure you leave enough space between where the hinge will mount to the suitcase and the edge of the suitcase. When the leg is un-hinged the hinge lock will pop out; you need enough space to allow for the locking mechanism to pop out. See diagram.

### Attach Legs to Hinges

Line up the leg against the hinge where you want them to be attached. Use a pencil to mark the wood where the legs will be screwed into the hinge.

Use the drill to make pilot holes where you marked in the previous step.

Attach hinge to legs with longer screws.

### Attach Hinges to Suitcase

Use the drill to make pilot holes where you marked in the first step with chalk. Make sure you don't go all the way through the frame.

Attach hinge to suitcase with shorter screws.

## Step 3: Remove hardware from speakers

This is pretty simple. Use a Dremel to cut away the plastic case of the speakers and take out all of the hardware parts.

BE CAREFUL. You don't want to compromise any of the electronics, so just be patient during this step and chip away little by little.

## Step 4: Prepare suitcase for speakers

**Materials and tools**
- Speaker hardware
- Dremel w/ grinder attachment
- Hand drill
- Set of drill bits

I must admit I didn't plan very well before mounting the hardware, but this also had to do with the curved edge problem. There is probably a better layout for where to place the hardware, and again suggestions are welcome!

I knew I wanted to mount the speakers on the side of the suitcase because I wanted them to be visible, but I didn't want to put them on the top surface because people would be eating off of it. I love how the speakers and knobs/switches for the speakers look on the outside!

### STEPS

#### Placement

Decide what you want the layout of speakers and knobs to look like on the outside of the suitcase.

Use a marker to mark where each element will go.

#### Knobs

Mark on the outside of the suitcase where you want the knobs to go. I had three elements I needed to worry about: volume knob, on/off switch, and LED indicator.

Drill a hole where the knobs will go. Make sure you use the correct size drill bit—you want the knob to fit snugly in the hole. It's ok if the outside of the suitcase looks ugly or torn up because the hole will be covered up by the plastic knob attachments.

#### Speakers

Mark on the outside of the suitcase where you want the speakers to go.

Use a hand drill and drill a small pilot hole in the center of the suitcase. Move up in drill bit sizes until you have drilled the biggest hole possible.

With the dremel grinder attachment cut out the hole for the speaker. The speaker should sit right in the hole.

sound

## Step 5: Put speakers in suitcase

Once you have everything all cut out and ready you can start putting in all the elements of the speaker system permanently.

I epoxied all of the parts in the suitcase. This is all pretty intuitive assuming you cut out everything properly.

## Adding Outside Details

I liked how it looked having the speakers exposed but I wanted to cover up where I cut. So I took the speaker cover and removed the fabric. The black ring fits perfectly over the speaker and covers up the hole. I attached it to the outside of the suitcase with epoxy.

To cover up the on/off switch and volume switch attach potentiometer knobs on the outside. We had some extra lying around the office, and I sourced some from the original speaker system.

On the inside I covered the hardware with some plastic boxes.

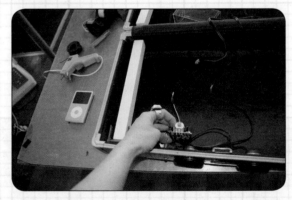

## Step 6: Inside storage

I used ribbon, snaps, and elastic to keep all the items attached to the case. I will list out each item I have included in the suitcase and how I strapped it down.

### Food Storage Containers

Use ribbons and snaps. Use a staple gun to staple ribbon to the inside of the suitcase. I used hammer-in snaps instead of sew-in snaps—they look more sleek!

### Vase

Staple elastic to inside of case.

### Wine Bottle

Stapled two pieces of ribbon to the bottom of the suitcase. The ribbons tie together to strap the bottle down.

### Plates

Crisscrossing elastic bands stapled to the bottom of the case.

### Wine Glasses

The stems are strapped down with ribbon. One side of the ribbon is stapled to the case, the other side is velcroed down. The cup part is strapped down with elastic, which is stapled to the case.

### Forks/Knives/Spoons

Ribbon is glued down to the bottom of the case. A small gap is left unglued to allow for the silverware.

** I also have a wine bottle opener and small place mat used as a table cloth that are not pictured.

## Step 7: Enjoy!

Randofo and I had a picnic in the park!

# A Carbon Fiber Violin I Made from Scratch

By Ken Van Laatum (AussieCFviolin)
(http://www.instructables.com/
id/A-carbon-fibre-violin-i-made-from-scratch/)

Last year I made a carbon fiber violin. I started out by drawing a violin on paper, working out the curve heights, plotting the lot on paper,

Once I had my plans drawn it was time to start making moulds. The violin plate moulds started as block of plaster that I routed out and fine carved to produce a "plug." The first mould was taken off that. Fine finishing the top and bottom plate mould took about 1 month, and I still had a lot of fiberglass moulds to make: rib mould, neck mould, finger board mould, they all take time.

To have a Shop Bot would be a huge help with the mould making. Change the shape slightly on the CAD drawings, rerun CAM, and watch the Shop Bot produce its magic on HDPE (only a dream), I wish I could afford one.

The first plates I made from carbon fiber were way too stiff. "Tap tone's" told me it was better used as a brass bell than a violin. After producing about 10 violin plates I was getting into the ball park of tone, a combination of different materials, laid down in different thicknesses in different areas, produced a violin front and back plate I was happy with.

I used the infusion method of carbon fiber making, where you lay all your layers up dry and vacuum bag it. Once the vacuum is over 25hg (-12psi) you open the tap to the resin, and the vacuum pulls the resin into the carbon fiber fabric. The laying up of the rib mould took me 5 hours each side to get the fabric to sit in the right position, very fiddly (pardon the pun).

The gluing jig was made from MDF with 10mm cup heads sticking through, designed to allow sideways positioning of the rib and neck parts, and the holding down clamps for the top and bottom. the center part of the jig was removed to glue the top on, with the 4 hour set time of the resin. It's important to keep it all firmly held in position.

The cutting and shaping of the F holes is another reason they call them fiddles. Carbon fiber is a bugger to cut; I found that if you submerge the carbon fiber in water and use a Flexi Drive bit holder on a Dremel, it keeps everything cold, and produces no dust— just wear a rain coat.

After a final coat of clear and a polish it was ready to string up and hand over to someone who could play it. I've had great feedback and a few offers for this violin. At the moment I am remolding for violin 2, working on the Second set of plans now, drawing them up on a low budget Cad. AutoCAD would be a big leap for me and, used with a Shop Bot, would speed up design changes 100 fold, and allow me to produce Cello's and Violas.

It took me 10 months of Sundays, from the time I decided to start to finished product. I had never made a violin before, and my carbon fiber skills were below basic, it was a huge learning curve but between the info on the net and getting your hands dirty and "givin it a go," anything is possible.

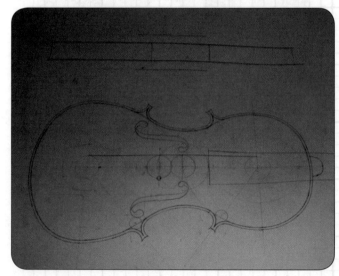

## Step 1: Plan what you want to make

After purchasing a good violin making book or 2, I set out to draw a violin, not an easy thing to do. All the compass work comes from a single measurement, the center measurement of a violin bridge's feet. That measurement is ether 2x, 4x, etc., and the shape comes to life with the golden spiral rules.

The length and 8 widths were measured and the curve shape plotted. The 8 different width positions have different heights set from the length curve. Once all the curves were plotted it was redrawn on a second plan as 2mm contours so a router could rough out the Plug for the mould.

## Step 2: Make your moulds

You have to make exactly what you want, then take a fiber glass mould from it. The original object can be made from anything.

The top and bottom plate mould started off as a block of plaster, while it was set but still moist. I roughed it out with a router and smoothed out the contorts with a chisel. Once the plaster had dried it was sanded, filled, sealed, and polished to 1200 grit before fiberglass was laid over it to produce the mould.

The rib mould was 2 layers of 16mm ply laminated together, planed down to a wedge shape, then cut to shape with a band saw. Once the "Plug" was sealed and polished it was placed between 2 boards and fiber glassed up to produce the mould.

The neck I carved out of timber. With mould making, you have to look out for your angles; you can't under cut your mould or you won't get the finished product out.

Don't forget a bond beaker on your "plug." There are many different types but I found PVA mould release easy to use.

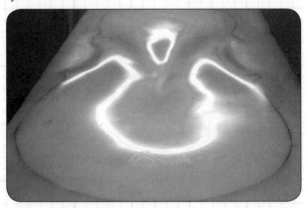

## Step 3: Make your parts

Once you have your moulds made your half way there. If you look after your moulds you will get several "runs" out of them.

Carbon fiber is not as expensive as you might think, and readily available on the net. My violins use less than 2 square meters of carbon fiber cloth.

Carbon fiber comes in many different fabrics and weaves. I'll leave it the net to explain the "K" and weave patterns and their uses.

Basically carbon fiber cloth is like any other cloth (soft) and once it's set in resin, it gets its strength. It's the strength and acoustic abilities of the resin that is important. Fiberglass polyester resin is no good; epoxy must be used. There are several ways to make carbon fiber.

Wet layup is when you wet down the fabric with a paint brush and lay them up. Place a peal ply over it, an absorbent layer, then plastic vacuum bag it up and suck the air out. The pressure from the vacuum bag forces the excess resin through the peal ply and into the absorbent.

Infusion, is when you lay it all up dry and vacuum bag it, waiting until the vacuum is high before allowing the resin in through a tap. Once the mould has been infused you close the tap and pull a good vacuum on the mould. I like this way because it gives you lots of time to lay the layers down and you're not running around like a mad man if your vacuum bag has a hole in it.

Prepeg is the professional way; manufacture has wet it down with a resin. Most need ovens and autoclaves and it must be stored in a freezer—even then the shelf life is short

I put down 3 layers of clear before the carbon fiber so the parts coming off the moulds just need a polish.

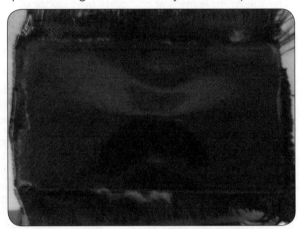

## Step 4: Put the parts together

The jig I came up with has 2 parts. The center part can be removed once the bottom is glued on so you can turn it around and bolt the top and neck down on the same jig.

The sideways threads hold the ribs in the correct position so they can be joined and hold them in place while the bottom plate is glued on.

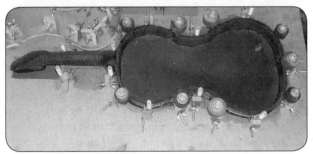

## Step 5: Admire it

Give it a good polish and you're done.

# Building My First Bass Guitar

By Scott C Naylor (nailzscott)
(http://www.instructables.com/id/Building-My-First-Bass-Guitar/)

The following is my first complete bass guitar build. I learned a lot, made a lot of mistakes, read a lot, and sometimes just plain guessed on how to do certain things. The project took place over a seven month process on the weekends.

## Step 1: General planning, tools, suppliers, sketches

### General planning

The first step is to plan out what you want for a bass guitar. I currently have a bass and wanted to make one very similar, only with a smaller width neck. I have a CNC router, but this is by far the most complicated build adventure I have taken and it challenged my skills repeatedly. I have seen a CNC machine used to make guitar bodies and guitar necks, but my plan was to try to machine the entire thing—the body, neck, and headstock— all in one piece, since the plan is for a neck-through bass. In retrospect, it is advisable to plan out your guitar and purchase all of the components before starting your project.

### Tools

These are the primary tools that I used:

- Table saw
- Planer
- Hammers
- Digital caliper
- Many files
- Lots of clamps
- Router
- Cordless drill
- Various drill bits
- Small digital scales
- Dremel (with at least the cheap plastic base)
- Spray paint equipment
- Headset magnifying glasses
- Dremel buffing wheel
- CNC router with router bits helps.

Other supplies include:

- Razor blades
- Carpet tape
- Painters tape
- Lots of sandpaper from 220 to 1000 grit
- Face masks/respirator
- Rubber gloves
- Wood glue
- Super glue
- Clear epoxy
- Feeler gauge
- Fret oil
- Polishing compound
- Binding tape
- Razor blades
- ½" tap and tap handle (due to my table mounting process, and a board to mount the guitar onto for the routing).

You'll need the finishing material, but more on that later. Add in some 3D software for drawing the guitar. You should stock up on a lot of patience, too. I ordered hardware and parts for the guitar throughout the process and will mention them at the point they came into the build process.

### Planning the guitar and sketching the build

My plan was to build a neck-through bass versus a bolt-on neck style. I also wanted to do the 3D routing over the full length at one time and then be able to flip it over to machine the back side.

The first step was to take my current guitar and sketch it out with any dimensional changes I planned. The following is just one of the sketches to show the detail I captured. I did separate sketches for the back side and the fingerboard to capture the dimensions accurately.

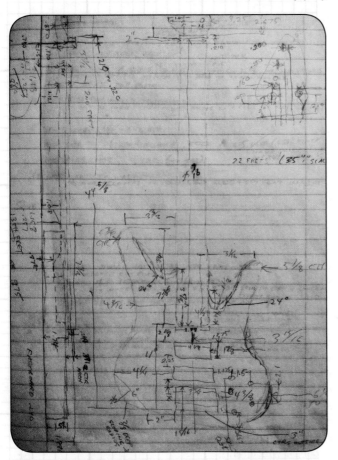

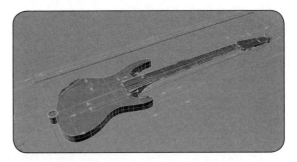

## Step 3: The wood
### Wood planning, preparation, and gluing

The center piece will be maple, which would be sandwiched by 1/8" pieces of walnut, sandwiched by two pieces of birdseye maple, with two small maple pieces to accommodate the width of the head; and the outside sections of the body will be walnut. I had all the wood except I that had to buy the maple center piece. I chose a particular piece of walnut for the body since it had a nice burl in the wood that I thought could integrate nicely into the design.

I used the planer to get the neck wood sized and square. I made the neck through section about 1 7/8" thick since it will finish at about 1 ¾". I glued the neck pieces first and waited for the glue to dry.
### Final glue-up

For the body pieces, I planed the piece of walnut that I had selected, split it in half, and cleaned up and straightened the edges that will be glued to the neck glue-up. Then I glued and clamped it all together until dry

## Step 4: Mounting the guitar for indexing its position
### Mounting wood to board

I planned out and marked where to place some mounting holes through the guitar wood into a piece of veneer plywood to use for indexing the guitar on the board, which will be clamped to the router table. I drilled 27/64" holes through the wood above the head stock and below the body at points that will be outside of the full length of the guitar. Then I used a ½" tap to thread the holes in the mounting board only and then drilled out the guitar holes to ½". After the guitar is all done, the plan is to cut off these mounting areas.

## Step 5: Body cutting

Next I mounted the guitar to the mounting board and clamped the board to the router table. Then I

## Step 2: Drawing
### Drawing the 3D guitar

I needed to draw the guitar in a 3D software that would allow me to export drawings into a file that the CNC machine could understand. After extensive reading, I decided to buy Rhino 3D. I went through some Rhino tutorials and then started my 3D drawing. I started by importing a picture of my current guitar into the software and used it as a rough model, making dimensional changes where desired. I took my sketches with dimensions and continued the Rhino drawing until I completed what you see in the pictures. From here, I was able to export STL (stereolithography) 3D files used by the CNC software for the top and bottom of the guitar and DXF (Autocad) files of the planned cutouts.

After trying to figure out how I was going to flip over the guitar so that the back side would be indexed with the front side, I decided to leave extra wood at the top and bottom so that I could put round ½" indexing mounting holes at each end of the guitar for bolting the guitar wood to a board. This would then allow me to flip it over on the center line and bolt it down to the board when I needed to cut the back side. On my drawing, I placed the center of the bottom indexing hole at X=1", Y=7". That way, if I needed to take the mounting board off of the routing table, I could always find the center point of the lower indexing hole and move the router X -1" and Y -7" to find my X and Y zero starting points.

exported the STL and DXF files from Rhino into the CNC software, created the 3D toolpaths, and cut the bottom 3D shape. Then I flipped it over, bolted it down, and cut the front side 3D surface.

I created a perimeter cutout toolpath, which included leaving the indexing mounting holes on the guitar. I should have waited to cut this out, but I got too anxious.

Here is where I started ordering some of the hardware for the guitar in order to figure out some cutout sizes. The Gotoh tuners and truss bar came from StewMac. After receiving and measuring some of the parts, I started on some of the drawings to create the toolpaths.

I flipped over and re-bolted the guitar to the mounting board (top up) in order to cut the truss bar slot. I spent some time on the X and Y alignment of the guitar to the CNC router to be sure it was almost perfect. I drew the required slot in the CNC software and created the toolpaths. While cutting the slot I broke my one and only expensive 1/8" end mill. I was in a rush as usual. It was going to take too long to get a new one so I decided to try a cheap dremel 1/8" bit. By slowing down a lot, I was able to complete the slot and inserted the truss rod for fit.

After measuring the tuners that came in, I drew them up, created toolpaths, and drilled the tuner holes.

I took the guitar off of the mounting board and cut off the index mounting alignment holes above the headstock and below the body. Next I did some sanding to clean off any rough areas where the mounting holes were located. I also started rough sanding edges along the edges of the neck. Then I ran a round-over bit around the body top and bottom to take off the sharp edges.

I installed the tuners to see how they looked.

## Step 6: Pickup pockets

I bought some Bartolini pickups and a preamp (from Bestbassgear) and used the software to draw the pockets for the pickups. I measured the height to strings on my current guitar, which helped me calculate how deep to make the pockets. I figured out what position I wanted them, created toolpath cut files, and cut the pockets on the router. I made the pockets about .025" bigger than the pickups for clearance.

## Step 7: Electronics pocket covers

I flipped over the guitar and clamped it down, spending some time to get close alignment again on the X and Y axis of the CNC router. This took a little longer to get aligned since I had already cut off the alignment mounting holes.

My preamp was a Bartolini pre-wired unit. I measured all of the components and determined how I wanted them to be placed on the guitar body. I sketched things out and then used the software to roughly draw the components and place them approximately where I wanted them. The next step was to draw the cutout for the pockets, leaving a perimeter area where the pocket covers will mount. I also allowed areas for where the cover screws would be placed. I figured out depths for the each of the cuts. I did the same for the battery pocket and cover, and created toolpaths (the path the router bit will take) for everything.

I had purchased some back plate material from Best-BassGear and created the toolpaths for the covers, about .010" smaller than the shallow pockets where the covers would sit. With the matt finish side up, I used some carpet tape to mount the material to the CNC router table, and cut out the plate covers so that I could use them for final sizing of the pockets that I would be cutting into the guitar body.

## Step 8: Electronics pockets and drilling
### Electronics pockets and drilling

The next step was to pocket cut the electronics and battery areas. First were the shallow cuts for the covers. Once cut, I fit both pocket covers to ensure the fit was fine. Then I cut out the deeper pockets for the electronics and battery. I followed up by measuring each of the electronics potentiometer shafts and drilled the six holes for them — with slight clearance.

### Hole drilling

The next process was to drill some holes—one for the amp jack, others between the preamp, the battery pocket, and both pickup pockets. Most were easy enough since the angles were not that great between pockets, but the challenging one was between the preamp pocket and the front pickup pocket. That's where I used a 10" long ¼" drill bit. I turned the body on its side, put the drill bit through the amp jack hole, and 'eyeballed' the angle to try to hit the front pocket. I was extremely fortunate and it hit the perfect spot at the bottom edge of the pickup pocket.

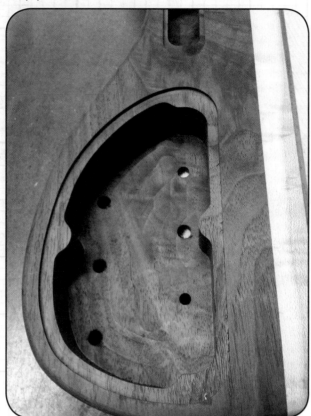

## Step 9: Fingerboard

I ordered an ebony bass guitar fingerboard and binding from LMII. I decided to order some bloodwood colored purfling to include in the binding of the fingerboard.

Since I did not have the special saw blade for cutting the fret slots, I originally planned to have LMII machine the radius and slot the fingerboard. But, I had been talking to a friend of mine, Tim of Mcknight Guitars, who had already made a fixture to be able to cut the slots on my fingerboard. Since he had the special saw blade and offered to cut the slots in the fingerboard, after the board came in, I took it to him to slot. This is a 35" scale, 22 fret fingerboard.

I went back to Rhino to draw the 3D fingerboard with a 16" radius.

Next, I exported the fingerboard radius 3D STL file from Rhino, imported it into the CNC software, aligned the fingerboard on the CNC router, and used carpet tape to place the board on the CNC router table. I used some plastic sheet stock beside the fingerboard.

## Step 10: Fingerboard cutting, gluing, and sanding

### Fingerboard cutting

The next step was to cutout the fingerboard to closely match the neck width and length where it would mount. Since my plan was to add the purfling and binding, I had

to adjust my cutout by using the neck drawing details from earlier and offsetting them to the proper dimension, so that when the purfling and binding were glued to the fingerboard, the size would be about .015" per side wider than the neck surface that was cut earlier. The plan was to be able to sand them flush after gluing to the neck. I created toolpaths and cutout the fingerboard.

### Fingerboard gluing

Then, I glued up the fingerboard and used binding tape to hold it all together. I had taken a razor knife and ground the blade tip the same width as the fret slots for cleaning the slots. I positioned the binding tape so as not to cover the fret slots; so when I glued on the purfling and binding, I could clean out any excess glue that squeezed into the fret slots.

### Fingerboard sanding

For sanding the fingerboard, I did not have a special sanding block; but I did have some 60 year old hardwood. I took a 3x3x28" piece of old walnut to use for the sanding block. Back to Rhino to draw up a reverse 16" radius for the block, export the STL to the CNC, and cut the radius. I put some stick-on sandpaper on the radius and started sanding. It was hard to sand straight, so I aligned a straight edged block of wood with the center line of the fingerboard, and then sanded the fingerboard down with 220 grit, 320, 500, and then 800 grit.

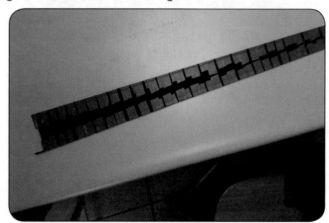

## Step 11: Fingerboard inlay dots and sanding

### Fingerboard inlay dots

I had ordered some pearl pieces from Grizzly that I wanted to use for the fingerboard dots and the name inlay I had planned for the headstock. I was not sure I could cut the pearl with the CNC; but I used carpet tape to attach a pearl blank to the router's bed, drew up some circle dots on the CNC software, created toolpaths, and cut all of the dots out of one 1 3/16" X 2" piece of pearl.

### Fingerboard dot sanding

I marked the position of the inlay dots and used a pilot drill to put the holes in the fingerboard. While drilling I kept checking the depth using the back end of the digital caliper until I got the holes around .015" shallower than the dot thickness. The next step was to use CA glue and install the dots. I then used my 3X3 sanding radius block and sanded the dots down flush with the fingerboard.

## Step 12: Gluing fingerboard to guitar

### Gluing fingerboard

Then it was time for gluing the fingerboard to the neck. For my clamping fixture, I used the long sanding block, which I knew was straight.

### Fingerboard final sanding

After the glue dried, I used the sanding block to sand the fingerboard level again.

## Step 13: Pearl side dot markers and install bridge

### Pearl side dot markers

I bought small pearl dots for the side of the finger-board. Since the fingerboard was already glued to the neck, drilling for the dots was going to be difficult for those located over the guitar body. I decided to just hand drill them.

### Bridge positioning

Next, it was time to set the Schaller Bridge (from Warmoth). I laid out the position for the 35" scale and screwed it down temporarily.

## Step 14: Pearl inlay for headstock

### Headstock inlay

I had planned some inlay for the headstock. I decided to inlay pearl letters of my last name into a piece of ebony (scrap end from the fingerboard) and inlay that into the headstock. I decided to try my hand at cutting the pearl lettering on the CNC. I created some letter toothpaths; but then had to modify them a bit to ensure that the .090" router bit would have clearance all around each letter.

I ended up being able to cut all of the letters out of one piece of the 1 3/16" X 2" pearl stock.

### Pearl into ebony

I had never inlayed anything before, so the step of inlaying the pearl into the ebony was extremely time consuming. I went to the web for a bunch of reading to learn more about this process. I spot glued the letters to the ebony and traced around them with a sharp razor blade tip. I removed the letters with the razor; and then, by using a very small dremel bit and my magnifying headset, I spent about 40 minutes per letter slowly routing out the lettering with the dremel to a depth slightly less than the thickness of the pearl. Once that was done, I sanded down some ebony scraps to create ebony dust and mixed it with some clear epoxy. Then I put some of the epoxy mix under the letters and clamped them down into the ebony, and let it sit until dry.

### Ebony inlay into headstock

I designed the shape of the ebony to inlay into the headstock and created a drawing and toolpaths to cut the headstock pocket. I sanded down the thickness of the ebony to about 1/8" and mounted it to the CNC table with the carpet tape and then cut out the shape. Using the same drawing as used for the headstock pocket, I offset the line by .005" and used it to cut the pocket in the headstock at slightly less depth than the ebony. I used more of the epoxy to glue the ebony into the headstock pocket and clamped. After it was dry, I sanded the pearl and ebony down to the level of the headstock.

## Step 15: Installing fret wire

### Fret wire install

It was then time for the fret install (gold Evo fret wire from LMII), so it was back to the internet for more reading. I started on the wide end of the fingerboard and cut a piece of fret wire about 1/8" wider on each side than the fingerboard. I did not have a fret tang nipper, so I used the fret wire cutter from Stewmac to trim back the tangs to clear the bindings. After I cut off each fret from the wire stock, I turned them

over to file off the tang on the ends so they would fit over the binding.

Using a brass headed hammer, I centered the frets and tapped them into place. Using a hardwood block, I hammered them into place. Some were a bit stubborn, so I used the brass hammer directly.

After they were installed, I used the fret nipper to trim the frets close to the neck.

## Step 16: Fret wire sanding, radiusing, and polish

### Fret wire side sanding

I had seen some blocks used for filing down the fret ends, so I looked up some details on the internet, and made a block, with one side being 35 degrees. I used a table saw to cut a slot in the wood block so that my file would press into it. I used the fret cutter to clip off the fret ends and began the fret end filing.

I now needed to level the frets. Setting the neck level using the truss bar adjustment, I leveled the frets using the large radius block that I had made for the fingerboard sanding. Since the frets were not far off, I was able to use 600 grit sandpaper with light sanding.

### Fret wire radiusing

The next process was to radius using the fret file. I used a black marker to mark across the top of each fret and then I started filing down the frets until just a fine marker line was on top of each one. Using a 3-corner file that I had ground smooth on the sharp edge, I took the edge sharpness off of the fret ends. Then I used various grades of sandpaper to sand the file marks from the frets as well as the fret ends. The final sandpaper was 1000 grit.

### Fret polishing

Next was polishing the frets with the dremel polishing wheel. I used a coarse grade of polishing compound, followed by the fine grade made by Dupont. This gold Evo fret wire material really looks nice after polishing.

## Step 17: Truss rod cover

### Truss rod cover planning/cutting

It was time to plan out the truss rod cover that covers the head stock access to the rod. I had looked at purchasing one but could not find anything, because the

radius on my headstock up by the nut had a radius that I would not be able to match with a purchased cover. After discovering that the radius matched exactly with the curve on a silver dollar, I decided to draw up a side profile of the cover's shape in order to come up with something acceptable. I created some toolpaths, clamped a piece of 1" thick walnut (from the body's leftovers) to the router table, and cut out the profile shape.

### The cross cover

I wanted to make this truss cover unique and since the bass guitar will be used predominately in a contemporary church service, I decided to make it into the shape of a cross. I made a drawing and toolpaths for the cross, carpet taped the walnut piece to the router table, and cut out the cross portion of the shape of the truss rod cover. I did some minor blending and

sanding and laid it on the guitar headstock to see the fit. I will place some hold-down screws in strategic locations later.

### Step 18: Washcoat

The sealer, reducer, and stringed instrument lacquer are Behlen products that I ordered from Grizzly.

The first step was to sand the guitar body and neck and then wipe it down to get ready to spray on a wash coat, which is a thinned down finish or sealer. I taped up the fingerboard to get ready for spraying. After realizing that I did not have a very good method to handle the guitar for spraying, I built a gallows type structure from 2X4's and other wood scraps that I had lying around. I hung the guitar, wiped it down, mixed some material for the wash coat, put on my respirator, and sprayed on a coat. I waited a couple of hours and added another coat.

## Step 19: Pore fill and finishing

### Pore fill

Walnut wood has a lot of pores that must be filled to get a smooth finish. The first mistake I made at this point was thinking that Behlen's natural pore filler (which I had already purchased) was clear. Opening the can clarified my misunderstanding. It was not clear. After a conversation with a friend and some additional reading, I ended up buying clear epoxy for the pore filling process. I used System 3 epoxy from LMII for the pore filling. After light sanding and wiping down the guitar, I applied the epoxy per the instructions on LMII's site. The mixture is supposed to be very accurate for the epoxy to cure properly, so this is where I used the small digital scales. A few ounces goes a long way. I worked in small areas, applying some epoxy and using a hotel room key card to scrape off the excess. Once this dried 24 hours later, I sanded level with 320 grit sandpaper. It appeared that there were still a few open pores, so I applied another coat of epoxy. I let this dry for a week before sanding with 320 grit.

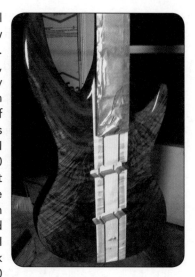

### Finishing

Next I applied two coats of Behlen Vinyl sealer, per the manufacturer's instructions. I applied 5 coats of lacquer, allowing drying time and completing sanding with 320-400 grit between coats.

## Step 20: The nut

Now it was time to work on the nut. I measured where the nut would be placed and rough cut out the bone nut material to within .020" or so of its final size. Then I slowly sanded the width to size. Then I set it in place and traced the radius of the fingerboard, decided how much to add for the height of the nut, marked, and sanded the top radius and shape.

Then it was time to cut the slots for the guitar strings. I had purchased some strings and measured each of them to ensure correct sizing of the slots. I did not have fret wire files and was already way over budget; so I took a set of small files that I had, and modified them where needed in order to be able to cut the slots. I gauged the nut slot depths based upon my old guitar. After doing some more reading, I figured out about where the final depth would be. I stopped a little shy, so that I could fine tune the depth later "– if needed.

## Step 21: Bass guitar assembly

The number of days the instrument stringed lacquer should sit on the guitar before buffing varies by opinion, so I plan on leaving it about 3 or 4 weeks before polishing and buffing. Since 3 weeks will be beyond the deadline for posting this, I decided to go ahead and assemble the guitar for pictures. I installed all of the components. The electronics are pretty straight forward since the pre-amp is pre-wired and adequate documentation comes with it. The last setup was to install the strings and confirm the setup height.

After the 3 or 4 weeks, I will use various grades of sandpaper and polish the guitar to bring it to the desired shine, reassemble it completely, and do the final pickup and string height setup (which were very close to being correct when first assembled), and oil the fingerboard. Then, serial number 1 will be done.

# Build a Fiberglass Subwoofer, Start to Finish

By Landon J. Airey (landonairey)
(http://www.instructables.com/id/Build-a-Fiber-glass-Subwoofer-Start-to-Finish/)

I'm a music enthusiast and have been interested in car audio for a while. I've seen many YouTube videos on how to make a custom fiberglass body for a subwoofer. However, I needed to find many different videos to answer all of my questions. Hopefully this how-to will put them all in one place for you.

## Specs

- Dual 15 inch Subwoofer Box
- Two PYLE 15 inch speakers
- 1000 watt peak each
- Dual voice coils/ 100 oz magnet
- Custom Fiberglass Front
- Dual port holes tuning box to ~34 hertz
- Voice coils in parallel then speakers in series (aka 4ohm)

## Dimensions

- Height 21 inch (top speaker ring)
- Width 20 inch
- Length 37.5 inch

## Step 1: Materials list and project outline

There are a few stages involved in this particular project:

1) Research and have planned exactly what you want to build. This involves selecting size of speakers, how many speakers, color, port hole location, box tuning frequency. No materials, just time and graph paper.
2) Make the wooden body
- 0.75" Medium Density Fiber Board (MDF Board)
- Wood glue
- Clamps

- Table saw (gives you straighter cuts than hand held)
- Drill and different sized bits
- Screws
- Caulking (I used Liquid Nails)
- Jig Saw (Most people use a router with a bridge that lets you cut perfect circles, I found my own way.)
- Port Holes

3) Add the fiberglass
- Fabric Cloth (like T-shirt material)
- Staple Gun
- Fiberglass Resin
- Gloves
- Paint Brushes
- Acetone
- Plastic Containers for mixing
- WD-40 optional
- Fiberglass mats
- Mask for your mouth (fiberglass resin has lots of fumes)
- Good weather and open area to work in!

4) Add bondo and sand to make a smooth face
- Bondo and Hardener
- Plastic Putty knives
- Range of sandpaper from about 80 to 400 or more. (An electric sander here helps a ton!)
- Rounded wood file (looks like a cheese grating tube)

5) The Cosmetics: Paint and add speaker carpeting
- Spray Paints
- Speaker Terminal
- Speaker Carpeting
- Spray adhesive
- Exacto knife/carpenter's knife

6) Wire the speakers and connect to the speaker jack
- Speakers
- Mounting Screws
- Appropriately Gauged Wire

## Step 2: Research and plan

Here are some of the sites I used:

For the design concept which I went from http://www.tccustomz.com/inc/sdetail/68/96

Port Hole Calculations http://www.carstereo.com/help/Articles.cfm?id=31

Speaker Enclosure Volume http://www.bcae1.com/spboxnew2.htm

Easiest-to-follow YouTube video of a similar project http://www.youtube.com/watch?v=G8cz_5eP81U

## Step 3: Make the wooden box frame

All of my pieces of MDF board were cut from a 6'x8' piece. The pictures are straight forward, showing how each piece went together. I used 3 to 5 screws along each flat side of the boards to join them together. Make sure you make a pilot hole first or you will split the MDF board. Also, drill into the wood with a bit wider than your screw head to sink the screw in flush with the flat piece of wood. You don't want to see a bump when the speaker carpet goes on.

The trickiest part of this step was getting the speaker rings in the position I had in mind. My advice would be to start with one and add another support to that one first and then tweak the second one. This allows you to make the second one match the position of the first one without trying to get both of them symmetrical at the same time. I used boxes of screws and nails mostly to hold things in place, while I used a nail gun to set the rings and supports.

## Step 4: Adding the fiberglass

To set up for this step there needs to be something to apply the fiberglass too. For making sub woofer boxes with weird curvatures you need to use a cloth that can both be stretched and is strong enough to hold the weight of the drying fiberglass. I found fabric cloth at a crafting store (at first I tried using an XXL T-shirt but it wasn't big enough). First staple the cloth to a ring mount and stretch it to one side and staple it along the edge. Then pull tighter in the mid section to give it cleavage, then around the second ring, still keeping it tight. Then finish stapling around the last sides. Take a razor blade and cut the fabric away. I used 1/4" staples because the MDF board is dense and 1/2" will not go all the way in. Lastly, I had to tap each staple with a hammer to make them sit flush. Because the staples were on the flat sides of the box I needed to make sure they wouldn't show as bumps when I put the speaker carpet on.

Using fiberglass can be tough, and I would suggest looking up videos or reading about how to use fiberglass before you start mixing the compounds. At first I mixed too much hardener and the mixture reaction took place so fast that the soda bottle I was using melted in the presence of the reaction. Also, you usually apply this resin with paint brushes. If you want to reuse them each time by cleaning then with acetone keep the following in mind:

1) Clean them well before the resin even begins to harden
2) Don't use those cheap sponge type brushes I got. They might be $2 for a whole pack but the acetone disintegrates the glue holding that foam to that wooden handle. You're then left with a sponge and a stick.

After 2 layers of fiberglass resin the surface should be strong enough to be able to work with. Now it was time to add the fiberglass mats with resin. When using the mats, rip 6" x 6" squares of the fabric to paste on with the resin. It's better to rip than to cut the mat because, by ripping it with your hands, the edges are full of strands of fiber glass. This makes for a stronger mold once things have hardened.

## Step 5: Bondo and sanding

This step takes more time than all of the other steps. The goal here is to create a surface that you can apply a high gloss paint to and make it look amazing. First work in the lowest areas, aka the big dips left from the fiberglass resin. Always keep in mind, when you paint the final product, any imperfection will show. I took a long flat hand sander to keep those speaker rings nice and consistently flat. If you took a piece of sandpaper and tried to make a perfectly flat donut-shape surface, it wouldn't work. This is a good time to cut the cloth out of the speaker and port holes. Any surface bubbles in the fiberglass resin should be cut and filled with bondo. You don't want to sacrifice the structural integrity of this box when you're going to load it with subs and pound on every joint of the thing. Nothing's worse than an annoying rattle when playing music.

That being said, I suggest using crude sanding techniques first (I used a long thin cylindrical cheese grater like tool to take away high spots quickly). Then use sand paper around 50 grit. Move up in steps of grit until you get to at least 400. Using bondo and sanding it is as much of an art as using fiberglass. I suggest researching tips and techniques before doing this if you aren't comfortable with it.

## Step 6: Painting and speaker carpeting

The next step is to apply the primer and get it ready for a gloss finish. This is where you use a really fine sand grit. Some people use a wet sanding technique (it saves your sand paper from building up too much primer and becoming unusable).

Use this step to add color to your speaker port holes (I sanded off the worn gold finish and put a flat black on it). I also blacked out the inside of the box. This just makes me happier to think the entire inside is one consistent color, and looks more professional. Also, I had to put the rest of the back wall on the box. I had taken it out to work with the fiber glass before. I cut a circular hole with the jig to fit the speaker terminal and spray painted the inside wall black.

Once you are content with the primer, go ahead and apply the finish to the face of the box (I only had to paint the curved face because speaker carpeting would cover all of the flat sides). I'm not going to tell you how to spray paint here. I chose white gloss and used 3 layers to make sure the gray primer color wasn't able to show through any point of the face.

All set to add the speaker carpeting now! This video shows a good way to use speaker carpeting if you're not already familiar: http://www.youtube.com/watch?v= SHKOtUPKwME. I used the weight of the box to seal the glue and carpet. It's a good idea to use new razor blades; it makes for much cleaner cuts with the carpet. You do not want to use carpeting that is easily stretched and can fray easily.

The box is done, and the speakers need to be mounted and wired. NOTE: This thing will reek of fiberglass resin, bondo, spray paint, and glue for a long time. Let it outgas in the sun for weeks. I transported the finished product to my dorm room to use shortly after it was finished and it stunk up the car pretty bad.

## Step 7: Wire the speakers

There are two voice coils for each speaker. I put those coils in parallel and then put in both speakers in series to get 4 Ohm overall impedance for an amplifier. NOTE: Make sure the internal wiring isn't loose or it will rattle. Also, I was playing with this thing when it was on and it sucked a ping pong ball in through the port hole.

# Tree Speakers
## By Noah Weinstein (noahw)
### (http://www.instructables.com/id/Tree-Speakers/)

These tree speakers were handmade from +14" thick sections of what was once a towering elm tree, that has now been transformed into a completely unique piece of hi-fi art. The speaker enclosure is made from one solid piece of elm, sectioned only at the rear of the speaker in order to hollow out enough material to create the speakers' internal volume of air.

Aside from being aesthetically pleasing and unique, using actual tree rounds as speaker enclosures is beneficial to the overall speaker design because it results in an almost seam-free cabinet, thick and acoustically dead enclosure material, and non-parallel internal sides thathelp to reduce unwanted frequency amplification and reverberation.

I think that the appropriate question to ask here is not "why build speakers out of a tree", but rather, "why not"?

## Step 1: Story

In 2004 while I was attending Brown University, a massive and historic elm tree located on the east side of Providence sadly succumbed to Dutch elm disease.

The giant tree's death was unfortunate and sad, but the loss of the tree ultimately led to the birth of something else: The Elm Tree Project. The joint venture between Brown University and The Rhode Island School of Design produced a set of classes, exhibitions, and specially designed studios, all built specifically to explore and produce various forms of art that could be made from the deceased tree.

I was lucky enough to be a part of this unique program during my time at school, and have finally gotten around to documenting some of the work that I produced during my involvement with The Elm Tree Project on instructables.

## Step 2: Materials and tools
### Materials

- Large approximately 14" or greater tree round (preferably dry, but wet is ok, just expect some checking/cracking and damage control)
- (2) 6" woofers
- (2) 1" cloth dome tweeters
- 16 awg audio connecting wire or lamp cord
- Extra long binding posts
- Crossover components (dependent upon speaker design)
- Screws
- PVC for speaker port

### Tools

- Chain saw
- Band saw
- Large powerful drill — I recommend the Hole Hawg
- 1" x 16" carbide tip auger bit
- Hole saw
- Soldering iron
- Regular drill

## Step 3: To plunge cut or drill. . . that is the question

Since I wanted to build the tree speakers entirely from one solid piece of elm, opening the round up only at the back, and then leaving the front facing 95% of the speaker as one continuous piece, I had to bore out the center of the round from the back using one of two methods: plunge cutting with the nose of a chainsaw (depicted below by Elm Tree Project visiting artist Marcus Tatton below) or using a powerful drill with an auger bit to remove the .75 cubic feet of material from the tree round.

Either method would prove to be challenging and labor intensive since I was basically creating a 16" deep and 11" wide bowl out of a solid chunk of wood. Plunge cutting with the nose of a chainsaw is absolutely doable, but can be dangerous because, if the top quarter of the bar nose should engage the wood, there's a high likelihood that the chainsaw will kick back. If you've operated a chainsaw before, you know that nose cuts are not something that you do every day and that they can be a bit challenging.

Fearing for my own personal safety, and not being an expert chainsaw operator, I decided to go with the more time consuming, but ultimately safer method of a powerful drill paired with an extremely large carbide tipped auger bit.

## Step 4: Slice off the backs

Before the insides of the rounds can be bored out, a 1.5" thick slice must be taken off the back of the logs with a large band saw or chainsaw. This allows you to have a matching piece of material to put back on as a rear piece of the speaker enclosure once the insides are hollowed out and the components are installed.

The cuts below were made with a chainsaw. The chainsaw bar does remove a larger kerf of material then I'd like, but it was my only real option since most band saws can't accommodate the rounds +14" diameter.

## Step 5: Drilling

Do yourself a favor and purchase the Hole Hawg right off the bat if you're going to be doing any serious hole boring. I found that normal drills don't come close to having enough torque to bore all the way through the tree round, let alone time after time reliably, without overheating and breaking down.

I used a very large carbide tipped auger bit (we're way beyond spade bits here since they take too long making dust out of the wood as opposed to larger shavings), and began boring holes into the elm wood, drilling from back to front, stopping approximately 1.5" from the front face of the speaker.

Mark the auger bit with some tape or a zip tie to indicate where to stop so that you don't drill too far and pop out the front face of the speaker.

To remove the material, I drilled many holes to create a honeycomb type formation of wood that could then be removed using a hammer and chisel, smaller drill bits to break through the walls, and brute force. Removing the honeycomb structure is truly difficult because it's just so much material, and is connected to the solid wall of the tree round over the honeycombs entire exterior surface. That, coupled with the fact that with the wood was still slightly wet during this process made for some pretty tough fibers that I had to rip through in order to remove the honey comb.

This was by far the hardest part about building speakers made from tree rounds. All in all I'd say that it took even longer to bore out the centers of the tree rounds than it normally takes me to build a rectangular standard speaker enclosure, but, it was well worth it.

The internal volume that I bored out was about a 3/4 of a cubic foot — plenty of air for my 6" driver to move.

## Step 6: Cut holes for speaker drivers and ports

Once the holes were bored and the remaining honeycomb structure was ripped out, I use appropriately sized hole saws to cut openings for the tweeter and for the PVC port. The dimensions of the speaker port are matched to each speaker's specific qualities and specs, so allow the directions in your speaker kit's directions or calculate the numbers yourself.

The +5" hole for the woofer driver was too big to use a whole saw to cut, so I traced a line and used a jig saw instead. You could also use a circle jig on a router equipped with a long straight bit to cut the holes for this step if you like.

## Step 7: Install crossovers and drivers

With the enclosures taking their final form, it was time to install the driver crossovers, the speaker drivers themselves, all the interconnects and terminal posts, the ports, and some foam as sound dampener inside the tree rounds.

The crossovers were soldered together according to the speaker kit's wiring diagram and then mounted to Masonite backers using hot glue. The Masonite boards were put in place inside the speaker enclosures with short screws.

Extra long binding posts that would stick through the 1.5" thick back cap were installed and then connected using the speaker wire or lamp cord to the crossovers, and then finally to the drivers themselves.

Small pieces of acoustic foam were mounted to the inside of the enclosure in between the Masonite backer boards using finishing nails and glue to hold them in place.

Once everything was wired up and installed into place it was time to put the back caps back into place. I used 8 large 3" wood screws to seal the backs on and complete the enclosure.

## Step 8: Make stands

I opted to create a simple base for the speakers cut out of some extra slices of elm wood that were not being used. They are roughly 1.5" thick and have a half moon shape to cradle the round speaker.

There is one stand per speaker and they hold the tree speakers at a slight upwards angle towards the listener's ear.

The slices were cut with a chainsaw off of the original stock material branch, shaped on the band saw, and then finally sanded smooth.

## Step 9: Finishing

As I said before, some parts of the wood were still slightly wet since the tree had recently been cut down. Applying any sort of surface treatment or finish to wet wood is not the best idea, so I chose to leave it completely bare. Even if the wood were completely dry though, I think that I would have left the wood unfinished because I wouldn't want to do anything to change the awesome designs that were already present on the surface of the wood caused by the bark beetle. Leaving the wood unfinished, untreated, and ultimately untouched is a small homage to its inherent value as a tree, and would only have been one more step down the road to processed lumber, something I was actively trying to avoid in making these speakers.

Dutch Elm Disease is caused by a fungus that the elm bark beetle carries into the tree. The bark beetle itself is not what killed this particular elm, but it is the horse that the fungus rode in on so to speak.

The story of the bark beetle's reproduction leaves behind the unmistakable pattern on the surface of the wood that is pictured below. The beetle first burrows through the bark and into the outer flesh of the tree to create the dark line. It then lays its larvae all along that burrow. When the larvae hatch, the baby beetles dig and eat their way through the tree's flesh to escape, causing the lighter lines which radiate off of the central dark ones.

## Step 10: Enjoy

The first test the speakers got were at an art exhibition for the work that the Elm Tree Project had produced and I am happy to report that they sounded amazing! The quality of sound and heartwarming sense of accomplishment that comes from building your own speakers never ceases to amaze me, let alone when they're constructed from something as unique as the branches of a several hundred-year-old elm tree.

# CONVERSION TABLES

One person's inch is another person's .39 centimeters. Instructables projects come from all over the world, so here's a handy reference guide that will help keep your project on track.

| Measurement | | | | | | | | |
|---|---|---|---|---|---|---|---|---|
| | 1 Millimeter | 1 Centimeter | 1 Meter | 1 Inch | 1 Foot | 1 Yard | 1 Mile | 1 Kilometer |
| Millimeter | 1 | 10 | 1,000 | 25.4 | 304.8 | — | — | — |
| Centimeter | 0.1 | 1 | 100 | 2.54 | 30.48 | 91.44 | — | — |
| Meter | 0.001 | 0.01 | 1 | 0.025 | 0.305 | 0.91 | — | 1,000 |
| Inch | 0.04 | 0.39 | 39.37 | 1 | 12 | 36 | — | — |
| Foot | 0.003 | 0.03 | 3.28 | 0.083 | 1 | 3 | — | — |
| Yard | — | 0.0109 | 1.09 | 0.28 | 033 | 1 | — | — |
| Mile | — | — | — | — | — | — | 1 | 0.62 |
| Kilometer | — | — | 1,000 | — | — | — | 1.609 | 1 |

| Volume | | | | | | | | | |
|---|---|---|---|---|---|---|---|---|---|
| | 1 Milliliter | 1 Liter | 1 Cubic Meter | 1 Teaspoon | 1 Tablespoon | 1 Fluid Ounce | 1 Cup | 1 Pint | 1 Quart | 1 Gallon |
| Milliliter | 1 | 1,000 | — | 4.9 | 14.8 | 29.6 | — | — | — | — |
| Liter | 0.001 | 1 | 1,000 | 0.005 | 0.015 | 0.03 | 0.24 | 0.47 | 0.95 | 3.79 |
| Cubic Meter | — | 0.001 | 1 | — | — | — | — | — | — | 0.004 |
| Teaspoon | 0.2 | 202.9 | — | 1 | 3 | 6 | 48 | — | — | — |
| Tablespoon | 0.068 | 67.6 | — | 0.33 | 1 | 2 | 16 | 32 | — | — |
| Fluid Ounce | 0.034 | 33.8 | — | 0.167 | 0.5 | 1 | 8 | 16 | 32 | — |
| Cup | 0.004 | 4.23 | — | 0.02 | 0.0625 | 0.125 | 1 | 2 | 4 | 16 |
| Pint | 0.002 | 2.11 | — | 0.01 | 0.03 | 0.06 | 05 | 1 | 2 | 8 |
| Quart | 0.001 | 1.06 | — | 0.005 | 0.016 | 0.03 | 0.25 | .05 | 1 | 4 |
| Gallon | — | 0.26 | 264.17 | 0.001 | 0.004 | 0.008 | 0.0625 | 0.125 | 0.25 | 1 |

| Mass and Weight | | | | | | |
|---|---|---|---|---|---|---|
| | 1 Gram | 1 Kilogram | 1 Metric Ton | 1 Ounce | 1 Pound | 1 Short Ton |
| Gram | 1 | 1,000 | — | 28.35 | — | — |
| Kilogram | 0.001 | 1 | 1,000 | 0.028 | 0.454 | — |
| Metric Ton | — | 0.001 | 1 | — | — | 0.907 |
| Ounce | 0.035 | 35.27 | — | 1 | 16 | — |
| Pound | 0.002 | 2.2 | — | 0.0625 | 1 | 2,000 |
| Short Ton | — | 0.001 | 1.1 | — | — | 1 |

| Speed | | |
|---|---|---|
| | 1 Mile per hour | 1 Kilometer per hour |
| Miles per hour | 1 | 0.62 |
| Kilometers per hour | 1.61 | 1 |

| Temperature | | |
|---|---|---|
| | Fahrenheit (°F) | Celsius (°C) |
| Fahrenheit | — | (°C x 1.8) + 32 |
| Celsius | (°F − 32) / 1.8 | — |